KING GEORGE V

Kenneth Rose

KING GEORGE V

M

MACMILLAN

First published in Great Britain in hardcover 1983 by
George Weidenfeld & Nicolson Limited

First published in Great Britain in paperback 1984 by
PAPERMAC
a division of Macmillan Publishers Limited
4 Little Essex Street London WC2R 3LF
and Basingstoke

Associated companies in Auckland, Dallas, Delhi, Dublin,
Hong Kong, Johannesburg, Lagos, Manzini, Melbourne,
Nairobi, New York, Singapore, Tokyo, Washington
and Zaria

ISBN 0 333 37224 7

Printed in Hong Kong

To
Edward Duke of Kent
grandson of King George V

CONTENTS

ILLUSTRATIONS

Grateful acknowledgement is made for permission to reproduce the following photographs: Nos 2, 3, 7, 9, 14, 15, 20, 21, 22, 23, 26, by gracious permission of Her Majesty the Queen; No. 16, the Earl Lloyd George; No. 1, the Mansell Collection; Nos 4, 6, 8, 13, the National Portrait Gallery; No. 5, the National Maritime Museum; Nos 11, 12, the Imperial War Museum; No. 10, the British Library; Nos 18, 19, 25, the BBC Hulton Picture Library; No. 24, *Times* Newspapers Ltd.

The Family of King George V

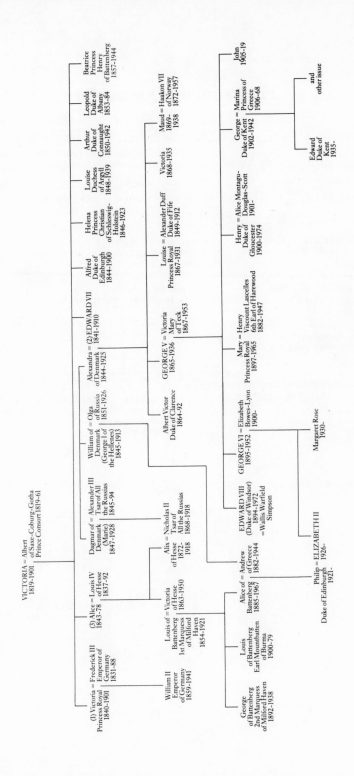

VICTORIA = Albert
1819-1901 of Saxe–Coburg-Gotha
Prince Consort 1819-61

(1) Victoria = Frederick III
Princess Royal Emperor of
1840-1901 Germany
1831-88

William II
Emperor
of Germany
1859-1941†

(3) Alice = Louis IV
1843-78 of Hesse
1837-92

Louis of = Victoria
Battenberg of Hesse
1st Marquess 1863-1950
of Milford
Haven
1854-1921

Alice = Nicholas II
of Hesse Tsar of
1872- All the Russias
1918 1868-1918

George Louis
of Battenberg of Battenberg
2nd Marquess Earl Mountbatten
of Milford Haven of Burma
1892-1938 1900-79

Alice of = Andrew
Battenberg of Greece
1885-1967 1882-1944

Philip = ELIZABETH II
1921- 1926-
Duke of Edinburgh

Dagmar of = Alexander III
Denmark Tsar of All
(Marie) the Russias
1847-1928 1845-94

William of = Olga
Denmark of Russia
(George I of 1851-1926
the Hellenes)
1845-1913

Alexandra = (2) EDWARD VII
of Denmark 1841-1910
1844-1925

Albert Victor
Duke of Clarence
1864-92

GEORGE V = Victoria
1865-1936 Mary
of Teck
1867-1953

EDWARD VIII
(Duke of Windsor)
1894-1972
=Wallis Warfield
Simpson

GEORGE VI = Elizabeth
1895-1952 Bowes-Lyon
1900-

Margaret Rose
1930-

Mary = Henry
Princess Royal Viscount Lascelles
1897-1965 6th Earl of Harewood
1882-1947

Henry = Alice Montagu-
Duke of Douglas-Scott
Gloucester 1901-
1900-1974

George = Marina
Duke of Kent Princess of
1902-1942 Greece
1906-68

Edward and
Duke of other issue
Kent
1935-

John
1905-19

Alfred
Duke of
Edinburgh
1844-1900

Louise = Alexander Duff
Princess Royal Duke of Fife
1867-1931 1849-1912

Victoria
1868-1935

Maud = Haakon VII
1869- of Norway
1938 1872-1957

Helena
Princess
Christian
of Schleswig-
Holstein
1846-1923

Louise
Duchess
of Argyll
1848-1939

Arthur
Duke of
Connaught
1850-1942

Leopold
Duke of
Albany
1853-84

Beatrice
Princess
Henry
of Battenberg
1857-1944

The Family of Queen Mary

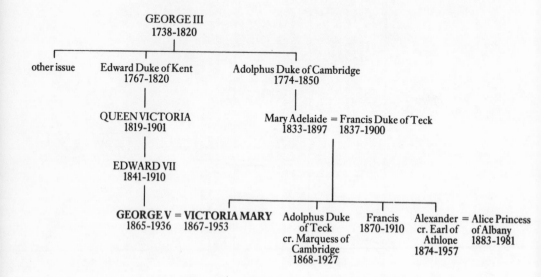

GEORGE III
1738-1820

other issue

Edward Duke of Kent
1767-1820

Adolphus Duke of Cambridge
1774-1850

QUEEN VICTORIA
1819-1901

Mary Adelaide = Francis Duke of Teck
1833-1897   1837-1900

EDWARD VII
1841-1910

GEORGE V = VICTORIA MARY
1865-1936   1867-1953

Adolphus Duke
of Teck
cr. Marquess of
Cambridge
1868-1927

Francis
1870-1910

Alexander = Alice Princess
cr. Earl of   of Albany
Athlone   1883-1981
1874-1957

PROLOGUE

KING GEORGE V spanned the centuries. At his christening in 1865 the minister in attendance on his grandmother, Queen Victoria, was Lord Palmerston. Shortly before his death in 1936 he handed the seals of office to a new Foreign Secretary, Anthony Eden. Yet the wonder lies not in the King's longevity but in the speed with which the world could change during a lifetime of only seventy years.

His reign, from 1910 to 1936, was of unparalleled restlessness. He lived through the ordeal of one world war and died under the approaching shadow of another. He saw the downfall of the great empires of Russia, Germany and Austro-Hungary. He was embroiled in demands for Irish Home Rule and for Indian self-government: claims that presaged the dissolution of the British Empire itself. He mourned the increasing impotence of his country in the face of the dictators, and the shift of sea power westwards across the Atlantic.

The scene at home was equally mercurial. The King was obliged to preside over the decline of the House of Lords and the rise of the Labour Party; to take a watchful and sometimes active interest in those bitter disputes which culminated in the General Strike of 1926; to curb the trade in honours no less than the flight from the pound.

Like all hereditary institutions, monarchy is something of a lottery; and the student of affairs who read of Edward VII's death in May 1910 might have concluded that the nation's luck had at last run out. The new King, born out of direct line of succession to the throne and with only the limited education of a nineteenth-century naval officer, was further handicapped by an ingrained conservatism. It betrayed itself as much in the changeless cut of his clothes as in the immutable routine of his daily life. On the eve of his forty-fifth birthday, his horizons did not stretch beyond the duties and pastimes of a Norfolk squire. He was indifferent to science and politics, to history and the arts; he spoke scarcely a word of any foreign language. Public ceremonial affected his nerves and entertainment his digestion. Few could regard his accession with enthusiasm, or even confidence.

King George V confounded every doubt. Under the tutelage of two experienced private secretaries, Knollys and Stamfordham, he set about learning the trade of a constitutional monarch. To each of the problems which relentlessly crowded in on him, day after day for a quarter of a century, he brought an inspired common sense and kindliness. By temperament a man of peace, he showed himself the most robust of wartime patriots. His welcome to the first Labour Government in 1924 was considerate, uncondescending, almost paternal. He was without prejudices of class, colour or race. If he did have a preference, it was for his poorer subjects, on whose behalf he would plead with his ministers to show generosity and compassion. Always within the limits of a constitutional monarchy, he similarly took the initiative in seeking an Irish settlement in 1914 and again in 1921; and in restoring Britain's credit abroad by insisting that Ramsay MacDonald should form the all-party 'National' Government of 1931.

No longer did he look on public engagements as a penance. That familiar bearded face, those impeccable frock coats and tall hats, dignity tempered by gruff quarterdeck humour: the nation responded with loyalty and affection. Although mistrustful of all modern inventions except the telephone, he was persuaded late in life to deliver an annual Christmas broadcast. He proved a master of the art, and year after year would reach out into the hearts of his people.

The King's married life was idyllic. For more than forty years Queen Mary protected and sustained him in his lonely task. It was a devotion for which she paid a price, subordinating her own independence of mind and sophisticated tastes to her husband's every wish and whim. Neither in the upbringing of their children nor even in her choice of clothes was she permitted the discretion that any other wife would have taken for granted. The people knew nothing of her sacrifice. They saw only a partnership, a little stiff and old-fashioned perhaps, yet perfect in its trust and understanding. Together the King and Queen had come to symbolize both national pride and domestic virtue; together they shared the unsought apotheosis of the Silver Jubilee.

Within a year the King was dead. 'In the end,' wrote Violet Markham, 'it is character not cleverness that counts; goodness and simplicity, not analytical subtlety and the power to spin verbal webs.'

ONE

SAILOR PRINCE

'AT half-past three in the morning,' Queen Victoria wrote in her journal on 3 June 1865, 'was quite startled by being brought two telegrams which they said I *must* have. They were from Bertie, announcing that dear Alix had been taken ill and then had been safely delivered of a boy at half-past one this morning.'

It was thus that the second son of the Prince and Princess of Wales, later King Edward VII and Queen Alexandra, was born at Marlborough House, London, a month before his time. Such improvidence was out of character. The rest of his long life was to be governed by precedent and punctuality.

'As to the names of the young gentleman,' the Prince of Wales wrote to the Queen a few days after his wife's confinement, 'we had both for some time settled that, if we had another boy, he should be called *George*, as we like the name and it is an English one.' He proposed that his son should also bear the name Frederick, much used by his wife's ancestors, the Kings of Denmark.

The Queen, still haunted by memories of her disreputable uncles, King George IV and Frederick, Duke of York, replied:

I fear I cannot admire the names you propose to give the Baby. I had hoped for some fine old name. Frederick is, however, the best of the two, and I hope you will *call* him so. *George* only came in with the Hanoverian family. However, if the dear child grows up good and wise, I shall not mind what his name is. Of course you will add *Albert* at the end, like your brothers, as you know we settled *long ago* that *all* dearest Papa's male descendants should bear *that* name, to mark *our line*, just as I wish all the girls to have Victoria after theirs.

Since the marriage two years earlier of Albert Edward, Prince of Wales, to Princess Alexandra of Denmark, Queen Victoria had exercised more than the usual prerogatives of a grandmother. Soon after the birth in 1864 of their first son, whom the parents dutifully called Prince Albert Victor, she had written: 'Bertie should understand what a strong right I have to interfere in the management of the child or children.' This time the young father proved more stubborn. 'We are sorry to hear that you don't like the

names that we propose to give our little boy,' he told the Queen, 'but they
are names that we like and have decided on for some time.' He was dutiful
enough, however, to add the name Albert to those of his own choice. On
7 July 1865, in St George's Chapel, Windsor, the child was christened
George Frederick Ernest Albert.

Growing up in the sombre middle years of his grandmother's reign, he
could count himself fortunate in his parents. At the time of Prince George's
birth, his father was twenty-three, his mother not yet twenty-one. The
Prince of Wales, recalling the harsh discipline imposed on him by that
archetypal Victorian papa the Prince Consort, proved a genial and indulgent
father. He declined to endorse the educational methods of his own youth:
a system that stretched young minds beyond their natural capacity, equated
bewilderment with disobedience, clouded the bright horizons of childhood
with a mist of tears. The more relaxed regime favoured by the Prince of
Wales ensured a deeply affectionate and high-spirited family circle such as
he himself had hardly ever experienced as a boy. For the first time in a
century or more, the dynastic tensions that traditionally separated one
generation of the royal house from another gave way to love and respect.

Historians have been reluctant to acknowledge virtue in the Prince of
Wales. They concede that he was punctilious in correspondence, stylish in
his public duties, eager to bear a heavier burden of statecraft than the
Queen would entrust to him. Yet they qualify these merits with disparagement. His pleasures and his extravagances are recorded with scandalized
delight; sport, gambling and gluttony by day, creaking floorboards in
country houses by night. His angry resentment at slovenly standards of
ceremonial or dress is contrasted with the tolerance he brought to the moral
and intellectual failings of friends. 'He does not get on with me, nor indeed
much with any but chatty, fast people,' the strait-laced Lady Frederick
Cavendish wrote of him. Queen Victoria herself also expressed alarm at the
exposure of her grandchildren to what she called 'fashionable society'.

The children themselves would have been mystified by such reproaches.
Their father's bellowing rage might ring down the corridors of Marlborough House at some lapse of protocol or sudden check to his plans, but
never at the peccadilloes of nursery or schoolroom. Throughout a life that
was sometimes selfish and always restless, he loved to have his family about
him, cared for their happiness, protected their interests. When Henry
Labouchere, MP, opposed increases in grants to the royal family, the Prince
of Wales indignantly asked whether he was expected to drown his children
like puppy dogs as soon as they were born. 'No, Sir,' Labouchere replied,
'but Your Royal Highness should live within your income.' Weighed against
the Prince's paternal concern, the radical voice of reason fails to convince.

'I was brought up in an age of beautiful women,' King George v liked to tell his family, 'and the two most beautiful of all were the Empress Elisabeth of Austria and my own mother.' The uncritical admiration which the Princess of Wales inspired in her adopted country never wavered through six decades. Tennyson greeted her betrothal in 1863 with the celebrated lines:

> Sea-King's daughter from over the sea,
> Alexandra!
> Saxon and Norman and Dane are we,
> But all of us Danes in our welcome of thee,
> Alexandra!

She died in 1925 as Queen Mother, more fragile but hardly less captivating than in the radiance of her youth. Eyes luminous in their darkness; a nose too delicate to be merely pretty; lips never far from laughter; a bewitching chin that in displeasure could become not so much determined as positively imperious: such were the features set in a perfect oval of a face and crowned by hair whose lustre survived even the coquettish ringlets of a Victorian toilette. Princess Alexandra carried herself gracefully and wore both clothes and jewels with stylish confidence. Yet she was no slave to fashion. Shortly before her coronation as Queen she wrote to an officious courtier: 'I know better than all the milliners and antiquaries. I shall wear exactly what I like and so shall my ladies. *Basta!*' Nor can she be identified with the unnamed 'very great lady' who once assured the diarist Augustus Hare: 'The consciousness of being well dressed gives me an inward peace which religion could never bestow.'

In 1867, when Prince George was not yet two years old, the Princess of Wales gave birth to her third child, Louise. The confinement was complicated by rheumatic fever, which left her with a slight but permanent limp. She looked on it as no more than a mild misfortune: indeed, some considered it a becoming attribute in so beautiful a woman. It was the prelude, however, to a more tragic consequence: a progressive and ultimately total deafness.

The Princess bore her affliction with courage, refusing to curtail her charitable and other public duties. Year by year, however, she was increasingly obliged to withdraw from that demanding social world of which she and her husband were the acknowledged leaders. Opera and the theatre became mere spectacles; the conversational delights of wit and allusion, of epigram and repartee were lost to her for ever. Although she was skilful in disguising how little she heard, the time came when only a few familiar voices could penetrate her prison of silence.

A husband endowed with imagination and patience might have done more to sustain his wife through her ordeal; but the Prince of Wales, although affectionate by nature, could not bring himself to modify, much less abandon, his pursuit of pleasure. The Princess found consolation less in his company than in home and family, in flowers and animals and the tranquillity of country life. Yet one sure refuge of the deaf was denied her. She had never acquired the habit of reading. Nor in truth had her husband. 'The melancholy thing', Lady Frederick Cavendish confided to her diary, 'is that neither he nor the darling Princess ever care to open a book.' But whereas the Prince could learn the ways of the world in conversation – and thus in time acquire a shrewdness of judgement from those about him – his wife could not. She radiated every generous instinct, she bubbled with humour and fantasy, she won every heart; her mind, however, remained that of an adolescent.

Long after her children had embarked upon lives of their own, she clung to the endearments of the cradle. She would write to Prince George: 'With a great big kiss for your lovely little face.' Her son was then a bearded naval officer of twenty-five in command of a gunboat. It caused him no embarrassment. Well into manhood he would begin his own letters to her, 'My own darling sweet little beloved Motherdear', and end them, 'Your loving little Georgy'.

The Princess's mawkish style did not exclude common sense. Even Queen Victoria recognized her insistence upon 'great simplicity and an absence of all pride' in the upbringing of her children. They also acquired from her an uncomplicated Christianity and habits of devotion that sustained them throughout life. The Princess was less well equipped to expand their minds, to rouse their curiosity, to unveil the joys of literature and the arts. Their intellectual progress was slow and reluctant. 'I am not a professor like my grandfather,' Prince George admitted in middle age. It was hardly a boast; nor was it exactly a confession of failure.

By 1869 the family of the Prince and Princess of Wales was complete. It consisted of two boys and three girls, all born between January 1864 and November 1869. (A sixth child, born in 1871, survived for only a few hours.) The eldest, christened Albert Victor but known as Eddy, was created Duke of Clarence and Avondale in 1890, less than two years before his premature death. Then came George (1865–1936). Of the three daughters, Louise (1867–1931) was married to the first Duke of Fife, a Scottish landowner; Victoria (1868–1935) remained a spinster; Maud (1869–1938), whom the family called Harry, became the wife of Prince Charles of Denmark, elected in 1905 to the throne of Norway as King Haakon VII.

The formal education of the two young princes began in 1871 with the appointment of the Revd John Neale Dalton as their tutor. He was then a bachelor of thirty-two. Son of the vicar of Milton Keynes in Buckinghamshire, he had taken first-class honours in Theology at Cambridge, followed by Holy Orders. It was as curate to Canon Prothero, rector of Whippingham, near Osborne, that he had attracted the notice of that observant parishioner, Queen Victoria; without her express approval he would never have been chosen to supervise the schooling of her grandsons. His qualifications were in every sense Victorian. He was a kind but firm disciplinarian, well-informed and industrious, with a high regard for neatness and order. If he also resembled the pedagogue of fiction, it was in the resonant and rarely silent voice which he bequeathed to his own son, Chancellor of the Exchequer in the Labour Government of 1945.

Throughout his fourteen years with Prince Eddy and Prince George, Dalton displayed character as much as intellect. He did not flinch from the scrutiny of a sovereign who was sometimes less than enchanted with his pupils. 'They are such ill-bred, ill-trained children,' she complained in 1872, 'I can't fancy them at all.' Nor did he willingly allow his timetable of lessons to be interrupted by an indulgent father and a doting, impulsive, incurably unpunctual mother. Only when the Prince and Princess of Wales left Dalton alone with his pupils in the country could he be certain of his planned programme. In 1874 the royal parents travelled to Russia for a family wedding. From Sandringham, the Prince of Wales's estate in Norfolk, Dalton reported to the ever-watchful Queen Victoria:

The two little Princes ride on ponies for an hour each alternate morning in the week, and take a walk the other three days, in the afternoon also their Royal Highnesses take exercise on foot. As regards the studies, the writing, reading and arithmetic are all progressing favourably; the music, spelling, English history, Latin, geography, and French all occupy a due share of their Royal Highnesses' attention.

To do Dalton justice, there were rowdier moments in that seemingly severe regime. Many years later, when King George v was walking in the grounds of Sandringham, which he loved more than any other place on earth, he would pause at a certain point and recall: 'It was here that Dalton used to teach us to shoot with bow and arrow, and down there that he ran when he allowed us to shoot at him as the running deer.' Not until Prince George was twelve did he receive a more lethal weapon, the first of many dedicated to a lifelong pursuit of game. Meanwhile there were happy hours of swimming and skating, cricket and lawn tennis and croquet.

One problem clouded the plans of the parents and tutor. The Wales children were a sickly brood. 'Most wretched,' Queen Victoria wrote of them, 'excepting Georgie, who is always merry and rosy.' A sturdy, handsome, lively boy, though small for his age, he showed to particular advantage against his taller but lethargic elder brother. Their mother, worried by the disparity, would again and again warn George against irritating or quarrelling with Eddy, sixteen months his senior and in direct line of succession to the throne. George's character was no more perfect than that of any other boy of eleven; 'fretfulness of temper' and 'self-approbation' were among the faults ponderously recorded by Dalton in a big bound volume. But he did take his mother's admonition to heart. Throughout years of shared education it was the younger brother who watched over the elder with protective affection.

As the second son of the Heir Apparent, Prince George had always been destined for a career in the Royal Navy. The Queen and his parents therefore agreed that in the autumn of 1877 he should join the training ship *Britannia* as a naval cadet. The backwardness of Prince Albert Victor, however, and his dependence on Prince George, complicated the decision. It would be undesirable for Eddy to continue his education alone in the seclusion of Sandringham, relieved only by short periods in London and occasional visits to his grandmother in Scotland and the Isle of Wight. Rather must he rub shoulders with boys of his own age and acquire something of that social ease which is required of royal personages.

The Queen favoured Wellington College, the public school founded in 1859 to commemorate England's greatest soldier and much commended by the Prince Consort. At this point in the discussion Dalton intervened. In a tactful memorandum he reminded the Queen of the relationship between the two brothers:

Prince Albert Victor, requires the stimulus of Prince George's company to induce him to work at all ... The mutual influence of their characters on one another (totally different as they are in many ways) is very beneficial ... Difficult as the education of Prince Albert Victor is now, it would be doubly or trebly so if Prince George were to leave him. Prince George's lively presence is his mainstay and chief incentive to exertion; and to Prince George again, the presence of his elder brother is most wholesome as a check against that tendency to self-conceit which is apt at times to show itself in him. Away from his brother, there would be a great risk of his being made too much of and treated as a general favourite.

Dalton concluded that the best course would be for the elder brother to join the younger in *Britannia*. It would, he asserted, help Prince Albert Victor to develop 'those habits of promptitude and method, of manliness and self-reliance, in which he is now somewhat deficient'.

The mind of Queen Victoria never ceases to astonish. Far in advance of her aristocratic Court, she held views unknown to those who have pursued her memory with braying laughter. She detested the heartlessness of bureaucracy; she defied the prejudices held by so many of her subjects against humble origins, a dark skin or an unfamiliar creed. Her reaction to Dalton's plea was no less startling. Although the very focus and epitome of patriotism, she responded in terms which would have captivated the League of Nations Union half a century later:

Will a nautical education not engender and encourage national prejudices and make them think that their own Country is superior to any other? With the greatest love for and pride of one's own Country, a Prince, and especially one who is some day to be its Ruler, should not be imbued with the prejudices and peculiarities of his own Country, as George III and William IV were.

The Queen nevertheless allowed herself to be persuaded that the two boys should join *Britannia* in September 1877 'as an experiment'. They were accompanied by Mr Dalton in the role of resident tutor. The training ship was a comfortless vessel that had survived from Nelson's day and now lay anchored in the river Dart, in Devon. The only privilege which the royal cadets enjoyed was to sling their hammocks in a private cabin. Prince George was at first known to his shipmates as Sprat, a diminutive of W(h)ales, later by the more respectful sobriquet of P.G. He rapidly acquired a seamanlike skill in handling and sailing boats, and found advanced mathematics no obstacle.

In November 1877, Dalton was writing confidently to the Queen: 'It is impossible that two lads could be in more robust health or happier than the two Princes are.' Prince George's own account of life in *Britannia* was less rhapsodic. In old age he told his librarian, Sir Owen Morshead:

It never did me any good to be a Prince, I can tell you, and many was the time I wished I hadn't been. It was a pretty tough place and, so far from making any allowances for our disadvantages, the other boys made a point of taking it out of us on the grounds that they'd never be able to do it later on. There was a lot of fighting among the cadets and the rule was that if challenged you had to accept. So they used to make me go up and challenge the bigger boys – I was awfully small then – and I'd get a hiding time and again. But one day I was landed a blow on the nose which made my nose bleed badly. It was the best blow I ever took for the Doctor forbade my fighting any more.

Then we had a sort of tuck-shop on land, up the steep hill; only we weren't allowed to bring any eatables into the ship, and they used to search you as you came aboard. Well, the big boys used to fag me to bring them back a whole lot of stuff – and I was always found out and got into trouble in addition to having the stuff confiscated. And the worst of it was, it was always *my* money; they never paid me back – I suppose they thought there was plenty more where that came from, but in point of fact we were only given a shilling a week pocket money, so it meant a lot to me, I can tell you.

There were times, too, of acute homesickness, as when he wrote to his mother in red ink from HMS *Britannia:* 'Please give Victoria my very best love and many kisses, and mind you kiss her properly, like I would if I was there because I am sure that when I send kisses to people in your letter you never kiss them.'

The Princess of Wales replied in a letter that combined affectionate greetings on his fourteenth birthday with an inimitable touch of tactlessness: 'Victoria says "so old and so small"!!! Oh, my! You will have to make haste to grow, or I shall have that sad disgrace of being the mother of a dwarf!!! But let me wish you many happy returns of that dear day, which we ought to spend together always.'

As the training of the two Princes in *Britannia* drew to a close, their further education continued to agitate grandmother, parents and tutor. Prince George, it was agreed, would spend the next two or three years cruising round the world, an essential stage of his naval career. Whether his elder brother ought again to accompany him was less clear. The past two years had not noticeably improved Prince Eddy's vitality. 'It is to physical causes', Dalton told the Prince of Wales in April 1879, 'that one must look for an explanation of the abnormally dormant condition of his mental powers.' Perhaps a further period of naval routine, with the added stimulus of sea air and foreign landscapes, would awaken that torpid personality. Prince George's lively company was once more thought to be an essential part of the treatment. Yet what if the ship in which they sailed were overwhelmed by sudden disaster? The simultaneous deaths of the two boys would be both a family tragedy and a needless hazard in the lottery of hereditary rule. Should they not go to sea in separate ships after all?

The initial suggestion that the Princes should embark together in HMS *Bacchante*, a corvette of 4,000 tons, fully rigged but with auxiliary engines, precipitated one of those distinctive royal disturbances which punctuate the Victorian Age. It involved the Queen, the Prince of Wales, their respective private secretaries (Henry Ponsonby and Francis Knollys), the Prime Minister (Lord Beaconsfield), the First Lord of the Admiralty (Mr W. H. Smith) and the Captain of the *Bacchante* (Lord Charles Scott). Ponsonby, master of the pithy memorandum, noted its course:

1 Plan proposed to the Queen who did not at all like it.
2 Dalton sent by the Prince of Wales to urge it. Queen's objections not pressed.
3 Unanimous condemnation by the Cabinet of the plan.
4 Indignation of the Queen and Prince at their interference.
5 Cabinet said they didn't. Plan adopted.
6 Controversies on the selection of the officers. The Queen supporting what she believed to be the Prince of Wales' choice. Sometimes it appeared He wished for others. Final agreement on the officers.
7 The *Bacchante* announced to be the ship. Who chose her, when and where I don't know.
8 Chorus of approbation.

9 Strong whispers against her. No stability. The Queen doubtful. The Prince of Wales doubtful. Dalton very doubtful – prefers *Newcastle*.

10 Smith furious, outwardly calm. Offers to turn over crew to *Newcastle* – an old ship full of bilge water. Sends report in favour of *Bacchante*.

11 Scott ordered to cruise in search of a storm so as to see if she will capsize.

12 Scott returns, says she didn't. Dalton not satisfied. Wants to separate Princes.

13 Queen says this is what she first thought of but Dalton said it was impossible. Let him consult Prince and Princess of Wales.

14 Queen mentions doubts to Lord Beaconsfield.

15 B. observes he has been already snubbed – but if his advice is wanted, he will give it.

16 Knollys says Dalton is wrong.

The Queen ultimately decided that her grandsons should sail together in *Bacchante*, whatever the supposed risks. Dalton, unnerved by weeks of wrangling and an apparent loss of royal confidence, offered his resignation. He was persuaded to withdraw it only just in time to join the two naval cadets on their maiden voyage. The warship he so mistrusted, justly as it turned out, left Spithead for the Mediterranean on 17 September 1879.

For the next three years, the *Bacchante* was the princes' home. The three voyages they made in her took them round the world. The first lasted from September 1879 to May 1880: Spithead – Gibraltar – the Balearic Islands – Palermo – Gibraltar – Madeira – Barbados – Granada – Martinique – Jamaica – Bermuda – Spithead. In the course of it the princes were promoted to the rank of midshipman. The second voyage was a short cruise to Spain and Ireland in the summer of 1880. The third was with Admiral Lord Clanwilliam's Detached Squadron, from September 1880 to August 1882: Spithead – Madeira – Montevideo – Buenos Aires – Falkland Islands – Cape of Good Hope – Australia – New Zealand – Fiji – Japan – China – Hong Kong – Singapore – Ceylon – Egypt – Palestine – Greece – Italy – Spain – Gibraltar – and so back to England.

Three years in a warship was an exacting education for any boy between the ages of fourteen and seventeen, yet not unprecedented even among princes. Exactly a century earlier the future King William IV had gone to sea in HMS *Royal George* accompanied by the Rev. Henry Majendie, the Mr Dalton of his day. It was perhaps with some prompting from his tutor that the fourteen-year-old Prince William wrote to his father, King George III, in November 1779: 'I hope I am in the way of proving an honour to my country and a comfort to my parents; that my moral conduct is not infected by the great deal of vice I have seen, nor my manners more impolite by the roughness peculiar to most seamen.'

Dalton was similarly anxious to protect his charges from the moral perils of the deep. He had insisted that the officers of the *Bacchante* should be

chosen as much for their steadiness of character as for qualities of seamanship. The list appears decidedly aristocratic. The Captain was Lord Charles
Scott, a son of the Duke of Buccleuch; the Commander, George Hill,
a kinsman of the Viscount Hill who had succeeded Wellington as
Commander-in-Chief of the Army. Among the lieutenants was Assheton
Curzon-Howe, son of Earl Howe and bearer of a name renowned in British
naval history. The midshipmen included William Peel, a great-nephew of
the Prime Minister, and John Scott, nephew of Lord Charles Scott and
himself a future Duke of Buccleuch. The cadets could claim a son of the
Duke of Leeds; a son of Viscount Hardinge, one of the Queen's aides-de-
camp; and Rosslyn Wemyss, the future Admiral of the Fleet, who was a
great-grandson of King William IV by his mistress Mrs Jordan. The quality
of these officers was reflected in a contented lower deck. In Australia the
squadron of five ships lost 108 of its 1,700 men by desertion. Only one
belonged to *Bacchante*.

Prince George and his brother enjoyed few privileges. They shared a
cabin; they could call on the services of Charles Fuller, the Sandringham
footman promoted to be their personal attendant; they were excused boat
duty in stormy weather. Those meagre concessions, however, were outweighed by the demands of their conscientious tutor. 'In the afternoon',
runs a typical extract from Prince George's diary, 'we had the bar up for
gymnastics as usual, and afterwards in the evening went on reading about
Free Trade and Protection.'

That journal was not the least of his tasks. After a false start in 1878
which lasted less than two weeks, he began again on 3 May 1880 and
continued a sparse but unbroken record until three days before his death.
Written in a clear schoolboy hand that hardly changed in half a century, it
reveals the methodical pattern which governed his leisure as well as his
work. He breathed little life and no colour into his discreet daily chronicle.
The perspectives of history failed to move him; he was enthralled less by
events than by their anniversaries, which he noted again and again. Thus
on 6 August 1935: 'We joined *Bacchante* 56 years ago today.' Each morning,
whether on land or at sea, he recorded the direction of the wind and other
meteorological detail. It is idle for his biographer to sigh for the richer fare
of a Pepys or a Creevey. Prince George belonged to a generation of sailors
who depended upon the weather for their lives.

By the age of fifteen he had faced both danger and death. Between South
Africa and Australia, the *Bacchante* ran into a severe gale. Her sails in
ribbons, her rudder almost torn off at the shaft, she drifted helplessly, out
of touch with the other ships of the squadron and four hundred miles from
the nearest port. For three days and nights the senior officers had no sleep,
until makeshift repairs allowed the corvette to limp on her way. Prince

George's account of the storm is that of a seasoned professional, untinged by emotion. Earlier, however, on two successive days in the South Atlantic, a seaman had fallen to his death: one from the fore topsail yard of *Bacchante*, the other overboard from the flagship *Inconstant*. The Prince was deeply moved by the loss of a shipmate and drew a neat black border round his diary for that day. These were not the only tragedies of the voyage. Here Dalton describes an eerie episode as *Bacchante* cruised between Melbourne and Sydney:

At 4 a.m. the *Flying Dutchman* crossed our bows. A strange red light as of a phantom ship all aglow, in the midst of which light the masts, spars, and sails of a brig 200 yards distant stood out in strong relief as she came up on the port bow. The look-out man on the forecastle reported her as close on the port bow, where also the officer of the watch from the bridge clearly saw her, as did also the quarterdeck midshipman, who was sent forward at once to the forecastle; but on arriving there was no vestige nor any sign whatever of any material ship was to be seen either near or right away to the horizon, the night being clear and the sea calm. Thirteen persons altogether saw her ... At 10.45 a.m. the ordinary seaman who had this morning reported the *Flying Dutchman* fell from the foretopmast crosstrees on to the topgallant forecastle and was smashed to atoms.

Almost at the end of the cruise, as *Bacchante* made her way home through the Mediterranean, Prince George's friend John Scott 'fell from under the maintop, nearly forty feet, but was providentially brought up by the leg within a few feet of the deck by a couple of crossed side ropes, or he must have been killed'.

The Prince did not allow such memories to haunt him. A fellow midshipman later recalled:

I was shipmates for five years with our late King, when we were both youngsters. The companionship in one of Her Majesty's gunrooms in those days was of necessity a very close and intimate one. Weeks and weeks at sea, sometimes very monotonous weeks, living on food that was more than monotonous, and also exceedingly nasty. Mostly salt pork and ship's biscuit.

Remember, there were no comforts in those days. No such thing as electrical freezing plant. So fresh vegetables, fruit and fresh provisions lasted a very, very short time after leaving harbour. Also, one got rather bored at always seeing the same old faces round the same old table, and tempers at times were apt to get a little frayed and irritable. Yet in all those years I never remember Prince George losing his temper. I certainly never had even a cross word with him. Unselfish, kindly, good tempered, he was an ideal shipmate.

Long after Prince George had retired from active service he liked to look back, as sailors do, on the hardships of those early days: cold, wet hours on watch, chairs lashed to table legs, hardly a piece of crockery remaining unsmashed. With artful absent-mindedness he would, as he talked over his port, dislodge an imaginary weevil or two from his biscuit by tapping it on the polished mahogany of Sandringham or Windsor. The diaries, however, disclose an almost sybaritic diet whenever the *Bacchante* put into port: shellfish and turtle, pineapple and avocado pears, known as 'midshipman's butter'. In any case, boys are not gourmets. At a State banquet in Japan, Prince George enjoyed best of all 'some plain boiled rice, which was very nice'.

It was not easy for Lord Charles Scott and Dalton to decide when the princes should be treated as grandsons of the Queen and when as humble midshipmen. Sometimes the change from one status to another could be abrupt. At the end of a ceremonial call in Alexandria the boys were returned to *Bacchante* in 'two tremendous state barges, in one of which there was a great blue velvet and gold sofa, beneath a heavy silk canopy, in thoroughly oriental style'. The diary entry for the next day begins: 'Got up at 5 a.m., had the morning watch.' Nor were they allowed to acquire their father's extravagant habits. When in later years Prince George was shown an album of Trinidad stamps collected by a midshipman, he observed that the young man must have had a great deal more pocket money than he ever had in the same station.

Whenever the ship put into port, Dalton was ready with his relentless programme of sightseeing. But the princes were also allowed to enjoy the traditional hospitality offered to all naval officers ashore: bathing and cricket, riding and dancing, picnics and expeditions inland. After an evening of rowdy games on the Nile, the composer Arthur Sullivan wrote that Prince George 'knocked me about a good deal'. The pastimes on board *Bacchante* were even less decorous. Between Fiji and Japan, sharks were lured to their death by floating tins filled with gun cotton and baited with pork. As the fish approached, a ship's battery fired the charge which blew off the shark's head. The most bizarre sport was practised between South Africa and Australia:

After breakfast we went to the 'chief' who had his hook and line overboard fishing for albatross, of which there were a great many flying round the ship. We were not long before we hooked one, and hauled him upon the glacis, and took him under the poop, where we skinned him: he was a beauty, measuring ten feet from tip to tip of his wings.

Coleridge's *Ancient Mariner* obviously found no place in the otherwise exhaustive reading list which Dalton prepared for his pupils.

Neither on board *Bacchante* nor in later years did Prince George feel that a love of birds and animals need preclude their pursuit and death in the name of sport. The same boy who revelled in the pointless destruction of sharks and albatross showed a tender concern for any little bird which landed exhausted on the deck; he would chop up raw mutton in strips to look like worms. He also kept a tame baby kangaroo to take back to Sandringham for his sisters. It would make the rounds of the various messes to be fed until one day it fell unnoticed into the Pacific.

Dalton's role in *Bacchante* cannot have been enviable. As a chaplain and a royal tutor he was treated with respect, lodged in comfort, invited to mess with the Captain. The officers of the wardroom, however, did not care to have this opinionated parson thrust on them. They thought him too zealous in supervising the leisure of his charges: a prig, a killjoy, a sneak, even a man who would not scruple to listen at keyholes. Dalton must have sensed such resentment and suffered accordingly.

To add to his burden, there were occasional misunderstandings with the Prince and Princess of Wales. During the cruise to the West Indies, a newspaper reported that the two boys had been tattooed on the nose while ashore in Barbados. 'How could you have your impudent snout tattooed?' the Princess of Wales wrote to Prince George. 'What an *object* you must look, and won't everybody stare at the ridiculous boy with an anchor on his nose! Why on earth not have it put somewhere else?' The Prince of Wales, who in youth had acquired extensive tattoos on more conventional parts of his body, held the tutor responsible. Dalton hastened to assure him that neither of his sons had been tattooed on the nose or anywhere else. After sniffing some lilies in the botanical gardens at Barbados they had emerged with pollen on their noses; it was this which had misled a local journalist. With the measured emphasis of an ill-used man, Dalton concluded his letter: 'The Princes' noses are without any fleck, mark, scratch or spot of any kind whatever. The skin is as white as the day they left home.'

By the time the Princes had been delivered back to their parents more than two years later, they could boast a whole range of seamanlike tattoos. In Tokyo each spent three hours under the needle acquiring elaborate dragons of red and blue on their arms. Further designs were added in Kyoto and in Jerusalem. George Burchett, the doyen of British tattooists, was many years later able to inspect the ornaments which Prince George continued to carry for the rest of his life. 'I was honoured', he wrote demurely in his memoirs, 'to be called upon to make certain improvements to them which the King instituted on Queen Mary's suggestion.'

Whatever the strains endured by Dalton afloat and ashore, he had his rewards: not least in the lifelong affection which he inspired in the two young princes. Soon after returning with them to England he was appointed a Companion of the Order of St Michael and St George, a chaplain to Queen Victoria and a canon of St George's Chapel, Windsor. A friendship at sea also brought him a wife: Catharine Evan-Thomas, the sister of a shipmate in *Bacchante*. In 1886 he acquired literary fame, too, by a gigantic but well-meaning deception.

Aristotle left no record of his years as tutor to Alexander the Great.
Dalton compressed his own experiences into a two-volume work of nearly
1,500 pages and three-quarters of a million words. It was entitled *The
Cruise of HMS Bacchante, 1879-1882* and dedicated to the Queen by her
grandsons Prince Albert Victor and Prince George. There the responsibility
of its two putative authors ended and that of its editor began. Dalton
explained in his preface that the book was based upon the diaries and letters
written by his young charges during the voyage; and that he had resisted
the temptation to improve upon the spontaneous vigour of the original text.
Only the first of these claims was true.

A simple test will warn the reader to be on his guard. During the weeks
that the *Bacchante* lay off Cape Town, the princes were taken to see an
ostrich farm. The ultimate fruits of that visit were four closely-printed
pages on the genus *Struthio*. They embraced the finances of artificially
incubating their eggs; the census of birds which in 1879 produced a return
of 32,247; their diet and aggressive habits; the price of their feathers on the
open market. Prince George's diary for 2 March 1881, which finds no place
in the book, is less informative. 'We then passed an ostridge farm', he wrote,
'and saw a good many ostridges.'

It is improbable that any midshipman would have described St Vincent
in these words: 'Groups of negro bearers were found in every stage of
drunkenness, maudlin or defiant, but all alike parts of one repulsive pandemonium.' The most ardent monarchist may doubt whether either of the
princes, as he sailed between St Lucia and Martinique, murmured to
himself: 'Was it for this that these islands were taken and retaken, till every
gully and every foot of the ocean bed holds the skeleton of an Englishman?'

Boys like bangs, but the princes are made to deplore that as much as
£70,000 a year is spent on firing naval salutes at Hong Kong alone. And
although King George V was known to care much for the well-being of his
subjects, he is unlikely to have soliloquized in youth: 'If some of the
Chinamen's houses seem squalid to herd in, they are at any rate better than
the dens which some English and Irish landlords think good enough for
their Christian brothers.'

Dalton's two polymathic princes are never at a loss for the telling
quotation. By page six, with *Bacchante* not yet at Gibraltar, they flourish
Psalm 103 from the Vulgate, swiftly followed by Browning's *Home-Thoughts
from the Sea* and Green's *History of the English People. The Tempest* blows
in Bermuda and the clarion call from *Henry V* on St Crispin's Day. In an
Athens café, 'there was much to remind us of Aristophanes'. But Dalton
does not sail under royal colours throughout the entire two volumes. Certain
long passages he surrounds with square brackets to indicate that they are his

own observations, not those of his pupils. No church, monastery, mosque
or temple eludes his eye; no creed or heresy goes unrecorded. The reader
may learn from him how to farm sheep in Uruguay or to tame elephants in
Ceylon; to prepare tapioca, to refine cane sugar or to make tallow candles.
He touches as lightly on the manufacture of umbrella handles from the
pepper tree as on the life cycle of the banana; he is as sagacious on the
economics of West Indian slavery as on the servicing of the Egyptian
National Debt.

Through 1,500 pages of vaunted knowledge and pretentious style, the
authentic voice of Midshipman HRH Prince George of Wales is only occasionally heard. 'The stinks', he wrote of China, 'are something awful.'

By grotesquely exaggerating the princes' attainments, Dalton concealed
both their shortcomings as pupils and his own as an instructor. They
disembarked from HMS *Bacchante* less well educated than their public-
school contemporaries. That was perhaps inevitable in the congenitally
listless Prince Eddy, but Prince George, too, an alert and cheerful boy who
had readily absorbed the practical lessons of seamanship, was deficient in
even the most elementary subjects. His spelling remained permanently
insecure. Well into manhood he called our greatest poet 'Sheakspeare',
described his having 'wrung up' somebody on the telephone, and wrote one
of the most cherished words in the royal vocabulary as 'perrogative'.
Perhaps it was a family failing. Although the Prince of Wales would
sometimes remonstrate with his son, he himself was not the most reliable
of mentors. From Ceylon he complained of the jungle leeches which
'climb up your legs and bight you'. And during the Tranby Croft
scandal he resented 'the spiteful way in which the Sollicitor General attacked
me'.

Prince George's grammar and syntax were likewise uneasy, although
they improved with the years. What remained exceptional in a member of
a European royal house was his lifelong inability to speak either French or
German with any degree of fluency. Queen Victoria, whose own girlhood
diaries are sprinkled with quotations from both these languages, not to
mention Italian, blamed his parents. 'You and your sisters', she reminded
the Prince of Wales in 1880, 'spoke German and French when you were
five or six.' It was a theme to which she returned again and again, alarmed
by the prospect of a tongue-tied successor. Immediately after the cruise of
the *Bacchante*, Prince George and his brother were sent to Lausanne to
learn French under the supervision of Dalton and Monsieur Hua, who later
taught the language at Eton. During six months in Switzerland their
progress was negligible. Ten years later Prince George made a last morose
attempt to master what his Danish mother unhelpfully called 'that old
Sauerkraut the German language'. He wrote from Heidelberg to a friend:

'Well, I am working away here very hard with old Professor Ihne at this rotten language which I find very difficult and it certainly is beastly dull ... I really can't remain here much longer than two months and miss all my shooting and hunting in England.'

The reluctant linguist hardly ever tried to speak German again. When in 1890 his father took him to see Bismarck in Berlin, the Chancellor asked Prince George whether he spoke the language. The Prince of Wales answered for him: 'My son is not fluent.' Bismarck then continued the conversation in excellent English. Prince George received no such helping hand when as King he attended the wedding of the German Emperor's only daughter in 1913. 'It is really hardly credible', the British consul-general in Berlin wrote to his wife, 'that Royal George cannot speak a solitary word of German, and his French is atrocious.'

What the young Prince lacked in intellect he gained in character; a distaste for languages and letters was balanced by the robust virtues of a naval education. But his development was slow. 'Prince George's old enemy', Dalton noted towards the end of the cruise in *Bacchante*, 'is that nervously excitable temperament which still sometimes leads him to fret at difficulties instead of facing them.' Increasingly, however, his superior officers noted an indifference to hardship or danger, obedience tempered by initiative, a willingness to assume responsibility without fear of the consequences. There is every reason to suppose that in the normal course of events Prince George would have risen on his merits to high rank, as did his uncle Prince Alfred, Duke of Edinburgh, and his cousin Prince Louis of Battenberg. Instead, the early death of his brother obliged him to abandon his chosen career for the role of an heir apparent, then of a constitutional sovereign. The qualities that served him well in an Atlantic gale or when training for battle carried less of a premium in Marlborough House or Buckingham Palace. It was then that the narrowness of a naval upbringing became apparent: its mental indigence, its impatience with qualifications, distinctions and subtleties, its mistrust of imagination and intuition. He had never before encountered the ambiguities of politics and the deviousness of politicians. He found himself at a disadvantage. 'These sailors go round and round the world,' one of his soldierly courtiers used to remark, 'but they never seem to get into it.'

Prince George had hardly returned from Lausanne in 1883 when he was posted to the corvette HMS *Canada* on the North America and West Indies station. For the first time in his naval career he would be separated not only from his parents and sisters but also from his elder brother and his tutor. The parting was hardly bearable. He found some comfort in Christian faith. His mother assured him with moving simplicity a few days after his eighteenth birthday:

Remember darling that when all others are far away God is always there – and He will never forsake you – but bring you safe back to all of us who love you so. ...

Remain just as you are – but strive to get on in all that is good – and keep out of temptation as much as you can – don't let anyone lead you astray – Remember to take the Sacrament about every quarter which will give you fresh strength to do what is right – and also never forget either your morning or your evening Prayer.

His old tutor and friend was scarcely less heartbroken than the Princess of Wales. Immured with Prince Eddy at Sandringham, later at Cambridge, he wrote to the younger brother: 'I thought much of my darling little Georgie receiving the Holy Communion last Sunday.' He signed his letters: 'Now dearest boy with much love, ever your affectionate J. N. Dalton.' His correspondence fortunately did not consist entirely of such endearments. Dalton also kept the Prince supplied with cigarettes. Having acquired the habit of smoking, his pupil carried it to the grave.

So Prince George climbed the ladder of his profession. While with the North America squadron he was promoted to sub-lieutenant, then posted back to England for further training at the Royal Naval College, Greenwich. The subjects included Algebra, Geometry, Trigonometry, Mechanics, Physics, Steam Engines, Winds and Currents, Practical Navigation, Nautical Astronomy, Nautical Surveying and Instruments. He did best in Practical Navigation, with 165 marks out of 200, and worst in Mechanics, with a mere 9 out of 125. He also completed a course in HMS *Excellent*, the shore-based school at Portsmouth, with a first class in Gunnery, Torpedo Work and Seamanship, and a very near miss in Pilotage. The commandant was Captain J. A. Fisher, the future Admiral of the Fleet, who in later years became an embittered enemy of King George V. On this occasion, however, he wrote to the Queen of her grandson's tact and good judgement, his pleasant and unassuming manner.

The Prince of Wales never ceased to take a close and even technical interest in the career of his younger son. He was therefore delighted when the Admiralty agreed to his suggestion that Prince George should next serve in the battleship *Thunderer*, forming part of the Mediterranean fleet and commanded by his old friend Captain Henry Stephenson. The Prince of Wales wrote to him in July 1886:

I feel that in entrusting my son to your care I cannot place him in safer hands only don't *spoil* him *please*! Let him be treated like any other officer in the Ship and I hope he will become one of your smartest and most efficient Lieutenants. He is sharp and quick and I think likes the Service, but he *must* be kept up to his work, as *all* young men of the present day are inclined to be lazy.

That was only the first of several such admonitions; for although the Prince of Wales was not noted for his own abstemiousness, he encouraged it in others: 'The dear boy ought to "put the muzzle on" in hot climates or else he will be seedy. Too much meat is best avoided and I hope he doesn't smoke too much.' Nor did the most convivial of princes approve of Maltese social life: 'It is a waste of time, and there is nothing but gossip and tittle-tattle and what I call "coffee-housing"!'

Prince George enjoyed little luxury during his Mediterranean years. 'That brute Charles Cust', he wrote genially of a brother officer, 'is sitting on the deck of my cabin behind me, because I have not got another chair, abusing me and my cabin.' Throughout his career at sea he spurned any suggestion of privilege at the expense of others. While serving in the battleship *Northumberland* he was transferred at his father's request to the royal yacht *Osborne* for a short cruise. Prince George was mortified to discover that his name remained on the books of the *Northumberland*, obliging his old shipmates to carry out his watch-keeping duties in addition to their own. 'These sort of mistakes only make me very unpopular in the Service,' he complained.

The Prince received his first independent command in July 1889. She was HMS Torpedo Boat No. 79, a vessel of only 75 tons that did nothing either to comfort or to cure her young captain's habitual seasickness. During her short commission he distinguished himself by the skill and nerve with which he rescued a sister ship whose engines had failed in heavy seas off the rocky coast of Northern Ireland. His grandmother asked for a report of the episode and minuted on it: 'The Queen cannot help feeling anxious about her dear Grandson, for torpedo boats are dangerous.'

In 1890 he was given a bigger ship, the first-class gunboat HMS *Thrush*. A generation later, when as King he congratulated Lord Louis Mountbatten on receiving his first command, he reminded his young cousin how much naval life had changed since his own days at sea:

I suppose you will now have an office and a typewriting machine and a man to work it? When I took over the *Thrush* I had nothing of the sort: just an enormous sackful of official papers and correspondence. I fished out the ship's log and one or two other things. All the rest I threw overboard. I knew it would take the Admiralty three months to discover the loss, and I didn't expect the *Thrush* to have a long commission.

Old sailors are not on oath; but there is contemporary evidence of Prince George's robustness during his first voyage in the *Thrush*, a hazardous journey from Plymouth to Gibraltar with a torpedo boat in tow. He wrote to Stephenson on reaching harbour:

We went on gaily until Monday night at 9.30 when we were in the middle of the Bay, when suddenly without any warning our engines brought up all standing; we then discovered that the slide and eccentric rods were both bent nearly double, lucky to say it was a dead calm at the time and I made the T. boat get up steam and remain by us all night, we were quite helpless, we proceeded at once to put the spare rods in, and with the whole engine room staff working all night we were ready in exactly 12 hours, when we went on again. It then came on to blow hard from S.W. with a heavy sea and the poor boat was having a very bad time of it, so I decided to go in to Ferrol, where we arrived the following day at noon, we knocked about a good deal all night and needless to say I was seasick, but this ship is an excellent sea boat and we took very little water in. We stopped at Ferrol two days and had lovely weather there, arriving here on afternoon of 9th.

After repairs in Gibraltar, he sailed the *Thrush* across the Atlantic to rejoin the North America and West Indies station. He took his duties seriously. 'I am always on board on Sundays for divisions,' he told Stephenson nearly a year later. 'I have not missed a single Sunday since we have been in commission.' It was also characteristic of him to make seamanlike amendments to the Prayer Book. 'We have done those things that we ought to have done,' he would declaim to the ship's company each Sunday morning, 'and we have left undone those things which we ought not to have done.'

Something, however, eluded him: he had few naval friends and no intimates of his own age. Partly it was the result of Dalton's protective concern in *Bacchante*. For although the Princes' fellow midshipmen had been selected with care, there was always the danger of an undesirable relationship that might haunt their later years. Among their young shipmates, therefore, the boys were discouraged from any exchange of confidences beyond the boisterous camaraderie of the gunroom. The possessive, almost conspiratorial spell which the Princess of Wales cast over her children also helped to isolate them from their contemporaries. Soon after Prince George's twenty-first birthday, the smile disappears from his much-photographed face, to be replaced by the familiar bearded stare that scarcely changed for the next half century. Yet in the same year he writes of his distress at missing a Sandringham reunion with his mother: 'How I wish I was going to be there too, it almost makes me cry when I think of it. I wonder who will have that sweet little room of mine, you must go and see it sometimes and imagine that your little Georgie dear is living in it.' Few stranger letters can ever have emerged from a ship called the *Dreadnought*: and on the anniversary of Trafalgar, too.

The Princess not only made herself the focus of her son's emotions, but also seems to have inspired in him a severe self-discipline. She wrote:

I must say it is good of you to have resisted all temptations so far, and it is the greatest proof you could possibly give of how much you wish to please me that you should have done it for my sake and the promise you gave me of your own accord a few nights before you left. No words can express how grateful I feel to God for having given me such a good son in every way.

Not until two years later does the Prince's diary reveal that he kept a girl with whom he used to sleep at Southsea and another, whom he shared with his brother, in St John's Wood. 'She is a ripper,' he wrote. Meanwhile the austerity of Prince George's life was relieved by his chaste love for Miss Julie Stonor. The granddaughter of a Prime Minister, Sir Robert Peel, and orphaned daughter of a lady-in-waiting to the Princess of Wales, she was almost a part of the Sandringham family circle. Yet 'my own darling little Julie', as she appears in Prince George's diary, could never become his bride. She was doubly disqualified for such a role. For the Prince to marry a commoner would have been unusual, even unacceptable in the grandson of the sovereign; for him to choose a Roman Catholic would, by the Act of Settlement of 1701, have denied him the right of succession to the throne. 'There it is,' the Princess of Wales wrote to her son, 'and, alas, rather a sad case I think for you both, my two poor children. I only wish you could marry and be happy, but, alas, I fear that cannot be.' In 1891 Miss Stonor was married to the Marquis d'Hautpoul. She remained a much-loved friend of her would-be suitor, and the only commoner permitted to address him as George. At his funeral in 1936, a wreath of blazing red flowers bore the last greeting: 'From your broken-hearted Julie.'

A more conventional match with his cousin, Princess Marie of Edinburgh, also foundered. Having become the wife of King Ferdinand of Rumania, she too retained a place in her heart for the young sailor whom she called 'a beloved chum'.

Throughout 1891 these affairs of the heart were eclipsed by other worries. The Princess of Wales, humiliated by the open attachment of her husband to Lady Brooke, the future Countess of Warwick, went abroad on a protracted round of family visits. The Prince of Wales, for his part, was obliged to give evidence in the libel action brought by Sir William Gordon Cumming, a member of his circle accused of having cheated at cards during a house party at Tranby Croft, in Yorkshire. The presence of the heir to the throne in such company evoked sanctimonious reproaches from prelates but characteristic loyalty from his second son. 'This Baccarat scandel [sic] seems to have caused great excitement,' he wrote, 'what a lot of rot the papers say about it.'

In November, on leave at Sandringham after being promoted to the rank of commander, Prince George fell ill with typhoid fever. It was the disease which had carried off the Prince Consort in 1861 and almost claimed the Prince of Wales ten years later. The course of Prince George's malady was followed with profound concern, for more was at stake than the life of an

able young naval officer. In 1891 the Queen was seventy-two. Next in line
of succession came the Prince of Wales, followed by his two sons, both
unmarried. Had Prince George died in that year, his reversion to the crown
would have passed to his eldest sister, Princess Louise; only the life of the
effete Prince Eddy would then have stood between her and eventual accession to the throne. Queen Victoria's majestic strength of character and
conduct of State business had put beyond all doubt the fitness of a woman
to reign, or even to rule. Princess Louise, however, shy and ill at ease except
in the seclusion of the country, was not cast for such a role. Nor would her
husband have inspired confidence as a consort. The sixth Earl of Fife,
created a duke on his marriage in 1889, was eighteen years her senior, a
banker and a coxcomb. It was with more than conventional sympathy that
the hopes of the nation centred on Prince George's sick-room.

In the event he survived the bout of typhoid fever, although unable to
leave his bed for six weeks and reduced to little more than nine stone in
weight. Yet he had hardly begun his convalescence when a new and
calamitous blow fell on the royal family: the sudden death of Prince Albert
Victor.

Since the cruise of the *Bacchante*, Prince Eddy had failed to match the
progress of his younger brother. Dalton, assisted by a team of tutors, could
instil into him neither the application nor the manliness of Prince George.
'I do not think he can possibly derive much benefit from attending lectures
at Cambridge,' one of his mentors reported. 'He hardly knows the meaning
of the words *to read*.' The university of Milton, Newton and Darwin
nevertheless saluted him with an honorary Doctorate of Law. Soon after
the Prince's twenty-first birthday, the Prime Minister, Mr Gladstone,
loyally asked permission to publish the reply he had received to his letter of
congratulation. Gladstone's secretary wrote in his diary: 'On reading it over
again this afternoon, I found part of it admitted of no possible grammatical
construction; so I took it to Marlborough House and got the Prince of
Wales to agree to my suggested alterations and then sent copies of it round
to the papers.' In conversation, too, Prince Eddy was listless and vacant.
Incipient deafness may have been partly responsible. But the Queen's
private secretary, Sir Henry Ponsonby, noted that his sentences trailed off,
as though he had forgotten what he was going to say.

On being commissioned into the Tenth Hussars, the Prince showed
animation only in matters of uniform and accoutrements: an obsession, it
must be admitted, that was shared both by his own father and by a
celebrated brother officer of a previous generation, Beau Brummell. The
Duke of Cambridge, Commander-in-Chief of the Army, thought his cousin
'charming' and 'as nice a youth as could be', but also 'an inveterate and
incurable dawdler, never ready, never there'. He mastered neither the

theory nor the practice of arms and shocked the veteran Field-Marshal by knowing nothing of the Crimean campaign and being unable to perform elementary drill movements on the parade ground.

Yet he was a quiet, modest and well-mannered young man, popular in the regiment and adored by his family. In 1890 his grandmother created him Duke of Clarence and Avondale. Her reluctance to do so was founded not on any mistrust of his character but on a quite different and inimitable Victorian conception:

I am very sorry Eddie should be lowered to a Duke like any one of the nobility which a Prince can never be. Nothing is so fine and grand as a Royal Prince – but it is very good he should be a Peer. I don't think Georgie will ever be made a Duke in my life time.

In the following year rumours of the new Duke's dissipated private life caused his father increasing vexation. 'Collars and Cuffs', as the Prince of Wales chaffingly called his elegant elder son, was more often than not up to the neck in trouble (although allegations that he used to visit the notorious homosexual brothel in Cleveland Street rest on unconvincing evidence). As a short-term solution, the Prince considered sending him on a tour of the colonies: an infallible nineteenth-century panacea for moral delinquency. He told the Queen:

His remaining in the Army is simply waste of time ... His education and future have been a matter of some considerable anxiety to us, and the difficulty of rousing him is very great. A good sensible wife with some considerable character is what he needs most, but where is she to be found?

There had already been several unsuccessful raids on the royal marriage market. One possible candidate for Prince Eddy's hand was his cousin Princess Alexandra of Hesse. She turned him down in favour of the future Tsar Nicholas II, with whom she died at the hands of the Bolsheviks in 1918. Princess Margaret of Prussia, a sister of the Emperor William II, was another possible fiancée, but Prince Eddy's heart lay elsewhere. His own choice was the doubly unsuitable Princess Hélène d'Orléans, daughter of the claimant to the French throne and a Roman Catholic; when her father refused to allow her to change her religion, the Prince had to abandon his suit.

It was then that the Queen, with the connivance of the Prince and Princess of Wales, decided on an arranged marriage. The bride was to be Princess May of Teck, a girl of exemplary repute and intelligence, whose mother was the Queen's first cousin. The preliminary negotiations were entrusted to senior courtiers. On 19 August 1891, exactly two weeks after the Prince of Wales had noted his son's need of 'a good sensible wife with some considerable character', his private secretary wrote to Sir Henry Ponsonby: 'Do you suppose Princess May will make any resistance? I do not anticipate any real opposition on Prince Eddy's part if he is properly managed and is told he *must* do it – that it is for the good of the country, etc., etc.'

In November the Queen summoned Princess May to Balmoral for a visit that lasted ten days. Neither her parents nor her intended fiancé were invited. At the beginning of December, while staying with the Danish minister and his wife at Luton Hoo, Princess May wrote in her diary: 'To my great surprise Eddy proposed to me in Mme. de Falbe's boudoir – Of course I said yes – We are both very happy.' Although cousins, the betrothed pair hardly knew each other.

The Prince and Princess of Wales were taking no chances with their wayward son; the wedding was arranged for February. Princess May and her parents meanwhile arrived at Sandringham in time to celebrate Prince Eddy's twenty-eighth birthday on 8 January. He returned from shooting on 7 January feeling unwell, and retired early to bed. Next morning, suffering from influenza, he could barely struggle downstairs to look at his presents. On 9 January he developed inflammation of the lungs. Five days later he was dead.

In the Royal Archives for that tragic month, the arrangements under discussion for the Duke of Clarence's marriage change with hardly a break in sequence to those for his funeral. It took place in St George's Chapel, Windsor. On the coffin lay Princess May's unworn bridal wreath of orange blossom.

❧

TWO

MARRIAGE

Betrothed — Princess May — Domestic harmony —
Shotgun and stamps

WEAK from typhoid and desolate with grief, Prince George found himself at the age of twenty-six in direct line of succession to the throne. It was a daunting role for which he felt himself ill-equipped both by temperament and training. Certain changes in his daily life, however, helped to restore self-confidence. He was given quarters of his own: part of St James's Palace in London and the Bachelors' Cottage, a few hundred yards from Sandringham House. He also acquired a small staff to organize his growing but far from onerous programme of public engagements; it included his shipmate Charles Cust, who as equerry, candid friend and court jester remained with him for almost forty years. Financially, too, he was free from care. In 1889 the Prince of Wales, after exhaustive negotiations and parliamentary debate, had secured an annual grant of £36,000 from the Consolidated Fund to be divided among his children as he thought fit. On the death of Prince Eddy, the greater part of this sum devolved on Prince George. It proved more than enough to support his sober tastes.

In the summer of 1892 the Queen ensured that her grandson should enjoy the same status as his late brother by creating him a duke. She conferred the dignity with reluctance, repeating her belief that 'a Prince *no one* else can be, whereas a Duke any nobleman can be, and many are!' She disliked the proposed title Duke of York, the last holder of which, her uncle, had been disgraced as Commander-in-Chief of the Army by his mistress's illicit sale of commissions. It was for that reason that the Queen had made her own second son not Duke of York but Duke of Edinburgh. For her grandson she would have preferred the title Duke of London, but did not press the point. Prince George was introduced into the House of Lords by his new title in June 1892. 'Fancy my Georgie boy doing that,' the Princess of Wales wrote playfully to him, 'and now being a Grand Old Duke of York.'

The Queen was no more successful in another matter of nomenclature. By calling her eldest son Albert Edward and prompting him to have his own heir christened Albert Victor (though known in the family as Eddy), she had apparently ensured that the next two British sovereigns at least would bear her husband's name. Now that Albert Victor was no more, she wished George to use his own last and hitherto concealed name of Albert. He respectfully refused. After the fashion of a royal duke, whose signature is not his title but his chosen christian name, he continued to sign George; and it was as King George V that he had himself proclaimed on ascending the throne in 1910. Like his father before him and his second son after him, he well knew the importance of not being Albert.

The new Duke of York had to resign himself to the virtual end of his career at sea. For a few weeks, however, he was allowed to command the cruiser *Melampus*, named after the soothsayer and physician of Argos who understood the language of birds and beasts. No such magic marked the fleet's summer exercises off the Irish coast. The captain who remained on the bridge for six days and nights wrote in his diary: 'The flagship made any number of mistakes and we all got anyhow. I hope I shall not be in any other manœuvres ... Hate the whole thing.'

It was followed by a no less disagreeable duty: his final but profitless struggle to master the German language in the house of a professor at Heidelberg. While in Germany he represented the Queen at the golden wedding of the Grand Duke of Saxe-Weimar. The Prince of Wales, an incomparable master of haberdashery, warned his son to take out his '*whole* German uniform, with boots' and '*all*' his German orders. This equipage the Duke of York had received in 1890, when given honorary command of a Prussian regiment. It evoked a characteristic tirade from his mother: 'And so my Georgie boy has become a real live filthy bluecoated *Pickelhaube* German soldier!!! Well, I never thought to have lived to see *that*! But never mind; as you say, it could not have been helped – it was your misfortune and not your fault.'

Furnished with a dukedom, an income, two houses and a household, Prince George still lacked the ultimate requirements of his hereditary role: he had neither wife nor children. Within weeks of Prince Eddy's death, family and nation were determined that he should marry his brother's fiancée. It was Queen Victoria who, as always, reflected the common sense of her subjects. In the spring of 1892 she was at Hyères, near Toulon, enjoying (if such a word may ever be used of that perennial tragedienne) a Mediterranean holiday. She wrote cryptically to her grandson: 'Have you seen May and have you thought more about the *possibility* or *found out* what her feelings might be?' By chance both the Wales and the Teck families had also sought to assuage their grief on the French Riviera. Prince George and his parents were at Cap Martin, Princess May and her parents a few miles along the coast at Cannes. Not until nearly a month after his arrival did he address this diffident letter to the Princess:

Papa and I are coming over to Cannes towards the end of the week for a few days (incog.) and so I hope I shall see you then, we hope one day you will give us a little dinner, we are going to stay at a quiet hotel, only don't say anything about it. The others will remain here ... Goodbye dear 'Miss May' ... ever your very loving old cousin Georgie.

So began Princess May's second courtship. Her parents, the Duke and Duchess of Teck, having been so cruelly cheated of their daughter's happiness and of a dazzling alliance with the British Crown, were enchanted. Impoverished and, in the eyes of other German royal houses, diminished by the taint of morganatic blood, they could scarcely have dared to hope for such a revival of good fortune.

The attitude of the Prince and Princess of Wales was more ambivalent. Naturally they felt the utmost pity for the bereaved fiancée. 'It is hard', the Prince wrote to the Queen, 'that poor little May should virtually become a widow before she is a wife.' On what should have been her wedding day they gave her a *rivière* of diamonds, their own intended present, together with the dressing-case which Prince Eddy had ordered for his bride. If, during that sad reunion, they were reminded of how much they had lost both in a son and a daughter-in-law, they must also have recognized that Princess May would make a steady and amiable wife for their surviving son. Such speculation, however, was tempered by doubt. Were May to marry George, might not a cynical world assume that she had never truly loved Eddy? For the Princess of Wales in particular, the suggested betrothal presented an acutely painful dilemma. Having already lost one son by death, that most possessive of mothers would not readily allow the other to be parted from her by matrimony. She wrote to Prince George: 'There is a bond of love between us, that of mother and child, which nobody can ever diminish or render less binding – and nobody can, or ever shall, come between me and my darling Georgie boy.'

In contrast to that devouring maternal affection, Prince George's own letters to Princess May were hesitant, almost dejected. One of them, he hoped, 'Won't bore you too much, when you are stop and throw it away.' The reproachful shade of his dead brother seems often to have hovered over his wooing. Gradually his confidence returned. There were exchanges of little presents, family visits, private assignations. On 3 May 1893 Prince George, Duke of York, proposed to Princess May of Teck and was accepted.

The nation rejoiced at what in retrospect seemed to have been the inevitable solution to both private grief and dynastic need. Not without irony, the betrothal took place in the garden of Sheen Lodge, Richmond Park, the home of Princess Louise, Duchess of Fife. It was to remove the eldest and most withdrawn of Prince George's sisters from direct line of succession to the throne that the Queen had encouraged her grandson's match.

Neither of the young pair could immediately surmount a sense of restraint. Princess May wrote to her fiancé:

I am very sorry that I am still so shy with you, I tried not to be so the other day, but alas failed, I was angry with myself! It is so stupid to be so stiff together and really there is nothing I would not tell you, except that I *love* you more than anybody in the world, and this I cannot tell you myself so I write it to relieve my feelings.

Prince George replied the same day:

Thank God we both understand each other, and I think it really unnecessary for me to tell you how deep my love for you my darling is and I feel it growing stronger and stronger every time I see you; although I may appear shy and cold. But this worry and busy time is most annoying and when we do meet it is only [to] talk business.

The betrothed couple also had to endure an undercurrent of spiteful comment from those who lacked the vision and understanding of the old Queen. Lady Geraldine Somerset, lady-in-waiting to the Duchess of Cambridge, Princess May's maternal grandmother, noted unamiably in her diary: 'It is clear that there is not even any pretence at love-making. May is radiant at her position and abundantly satisfied, but placid and cold as always, the Duke of York apparently nonchalant and indifferent.'

Both were fortunately too preoccupied with the arrangements for the wedding to brood on malicious whispers. The presents numbered 1,500 and were valued at £300,000: several million pounds in the currency of almost a century later. For Princess May, brought up frugally by the standards of other royal families, there was the delight of choosing a trousseau. Paid for by a generous uncle and aunt, the Grand Duke and Grand Duchess of Mecklenburg-Strelitz, it included forty outdoor suits, fifteen ball gowns and innumerable bonnets, shoes and gloves. Princess May was about to become the third lady in the land, exposed to relentless public gaze.

The wedding took place on 6 July 1893 in the Chapel Royal, St James's Palace. By some rare error of ceremonial, the Queen arrived not last of the royal family, as protocol demands, but first; unusually tolerant of the mistake, she enjoyed for once seeing the guests assemble. The Duke of York wore the uniform of a captain in the Royal Navy, the rank to which he had been promoted earlier that year. Princess May was in white silk with a train of silver and white brocade. Lady Geraldine Somerset alone resisted the charm of the scene: 'Instead of coming in the exquisite, ideal way the Princess of Wales did at her wedding with her eyes cast down – too prettily – May looked right and left and slightly bowed to her acquaintances! a great mistake.'

Nor did it turn out to be an entirely flawless celebration for the Queen. At a garden party in Marlborough House the day before the ceremony, she acknowledged the presence of Mr Gladstone with a stiff bow rather than with the handshake which would have greeted Mr Disraeli. Her octogenarian Prime Minister nevertheless passed behind her and sat down uninvited in the royal preserve. 'Does he perhaps think this is a public tent?' the Queen indignantly observed.

Otherwise all was sunshine as the newly married couple took leave of the Queen and drove through cheering crowds to catch the train for Sandringham.

Princess May's early life has sometimes been depicted as that of a Cinderella: a tale of rags to riches with not one but two princes as her prize, and ultimately what the Empress Frederick called 'the first position in Europe, one may say in the world'. It is a fable which requires many qualifications.

Her father was Francis, Prince of Teck, the son of Duke Alexander of Württemberg. The Duke's descendants would eventually have succeeded to the throne of that small German kingdom had he not contracted a morganatic marriage with Claudine, Countess Rhedey; a Hungarian of ancient family, she lacked the immediate royal blood that alone would have made the alliance acceptable to a nineteenth-century reigning house. The son of that marriage, Francis, was consoled with the style of Serene Highness and the title Prince of Teck, a subsidiary name of the royal house of Württemberg. A man of striking good looks but volatile temperament, he served in the Austrian Army and took part in the Battle of Solferino. It was in Vienna that he caught the eye of his near contemporary the Prince of Wales, who invited him to England as a possible suitor for the hand of Princess Mary Adelaide of Cambridge.

The Princess was a daughter of Adolphus, Duke of Cambridge, the youngest son of King George III. She was thus a sister of George, Duke of Cambridge, Commander-in-Chief of the British Army for almost forty years, and a first cousin of Queen Victoria. By the pedantic standards of the German monarchies, Prince Francis of Teck was not *ebenbürtig*, or of equal birth, for such a match. The Queen took a more robust view of dynastic niceties. 'I have always thought it and do think it very wrong and very absurd,' she wrote, 'that because his Mother was not a Princess he is not to succeed in Württemberg.' Prince Francis did, however, suffer from a more practical handicap. He had no money.

If he was not the ideal suitor for a Royal Highness and Princess of Great Britain and Ireland, she too displayed certain defects. In 1866, when the Prince of Teck arrived in England, she was thirty-two, four years older than her prospective suitor, and long resigned to being 'a jolly old maid'. One reason for her prolonged spinsterhood was an excessive stoutness. 'Alas,' Lord Clarendon wrote ungallantly in 1860, 'no German prince will venture on *so vast an undertaking*.' (The Whig Foreign Secretary was proud of his wit and boasted that he never told his best jokes to the royal family, since pretending to pinch his finger in the door amused them more.) The Princess did little to curb her corpulence. She enjoyed life, not least a well-furnished table. Travelling by train to Sandringham with the Prince of Wales in the days before restaurant cars, she noted with relish 'a capital *hot* lunch of chicken and rice and beefsteaks and fried potatoes'. A lady-in-waiting described her in middle age as very handsome but rather like a large purple plush pincushion.

After a brief courtship, Princess Mary Adelaide was married to Prince Francis of Teck on 12 June 1866 in Kew Church, near the home of the bride's mother. The Queen set her seal of approval on the match by allowing the couple to live in the same spacious apartments of Kensington Palace where she herself had been born and spent her childhood. It was there that Princess May was born on 26 May 1867, two years after the Princess of Wales had given birth to Prince George. The infant's first name was originally to have been Agnes, after her maternal great-grandmother; at her baptism, however, with the Queen as a godparent, she was christened Victoria Mary Augusta Louise Olga Pauline Claudine Agnes. Princess Mary Adelaide would refer to her as 'my May-flower', and it was as Princess May that she was everywhere known until her husband ascended the throne in 1910. She then assumed the more majestic style of Queen Mary.

'A very fine child,' the Queen wrote on 22 June 1867, 'with quantities of hair – brushed up into a curl on the top of its head! – and very pretty features and a dark skin.' In the following year, 'a dear, merry, healthy child, but not as handsome as she ought to be'. Princess May never achieved beauty. She held herself with a dignity that seemed to add inches to her medium height, and she had fine observant blue eyes; but a firm jaw, full mouth and turned-up nose denied her the flawless radiance of the Princess of Wales.

Brought up in Kensington Palace, the great-granddaughter of King George III and goddaughter of Queen Victoria was never allowed to think of herself as anything but English. The first letter she wrote in French to her grandmother, the Duchess of Cambridge, includes the words: 'Je puis vous dire aussi le "bon jour", et beaucoup d'autres mots en français, mais je serai toujours une vraie petite Anglaise.' The author of that sturdy sentiment was then aged nine. May was joined in the nursery by three brothers: Adolphus in 1868, Francis in 1870 and Alexander in 1874. All were educated at British public schools, two at Wellington and the youngest at Eton.

The limited influence of Prince Francis of Teck on the children reflected his anomalous role; he was regarded in his adopted country as not only foreign but also, in a sense, stateless. Exclusion from the line of succession in his native Württemberg and his subsequent military career in the service of Austria implanted in Princess May a romantic affection for Vienna and a corresponding distaste for the stiff little courts of Germany. But the Prince's repeated efforts to raise his place in the table of royal precedence, to be recognized as *ebenbürtig* in spite of his father's morganatic marriage, left him frustrated and irritable. In 1871 he persuaded his cousin the King of Württemberg to create him Duke of Teck. Again and again, however, Queen Victoria rejected his plea for the British style of Royal Highness.

The Duke of Teck might have borne such setbacks more equably had he found some useful employment other than gardening and rearranging the furniture of his wife's boudoir. During the Egyptian expedition of 1882 he served briefly on the staff of Lord Wolseley; but poor eyesight and a melancholy temperament diminished his chances of military glory. From being gazetted Honorary Colonel of the Post Office Volunteers he was advanced to the rank of colonel in the Army. Even that had its disappointments. On the first occasion he appeared in his new uniform, the Prince of Wales observed with pity: 'Francis has got the wrong buttons.'

Nor did the Queen smile on Disraeli's suggestion that the Tecks should represent her in Ireland as Viceroy and Vicereine. The obstacle to that appointment is likely to have been the character of Princess Mary Adelaide; good-natured, philanthropic and popular, she nevertheless lacked the royal virtues of discretion and punctuality. In any case, neither she nor her husband had the means to support the dignity of proconsular life in Dublin Castle. A later suggestion that the Duke should become the ruler of Bulgaria was similarly rejected because of his poverty. That argument did not convince Lord Rosebery, who replied with scorn: 'Then put Vanderbilt on the throne of Bulgaria.'

The financial distress of the Duke and Duchess of Teck, which cast fitful shadows over Princess May's youth, was largely self-inflicted. Prince Francis had brought nothing more to the marriage than a fine profile and a shapely figure. Princess Mary Adelaide, however, received an annual parliamentary grant of £5,000 and a similar sum each year from her mother. In an age of plentiful servants and low wages, that should have sufficed to live comfortably and to raise a family. The Duchess of Teck, however, had generous instincts of hospitality; and her proud, touchy husband feared that any apparent economy in his establishment would detract from his already uneasy status. Not only were there lavish entertainments at Kensington Palace. In 1870 the Tecks also persuaded the Queen to let them have the additional use of White Lodge, Richmond Park, ten miles from Kensington. This substantial house belonging to the crown doubled their household expenses.

The Tecks were soon grievously in debt and looked about them not for means of economizing but for a rescuing hand. The Queen, who felt she had done enough for her improvident cousin, refused all help. The Duchess of Cambridge gave generously within her limited means. Baroness Burdett-Coutts added her royal friends to the long list of charitable causes on which she spent her immense banking fortune; she lent them £50,000, with scant hope of ever seeing it again. But the more the Duchess of Teck received, the more she spent. At a time when tradesmen were pressing her for the payment of bills amounting to almost £20,000, she was invited to open a new church hall in Kensington, to which John Barker the grocer had contributed handsomely. 'And now,' she told her amused audience, 'I must propose a special vote of thanks to Mr Barker, to whom we all owe so much.' When it became apparent that even the most patient and loyal of creditors were about to issue writs, the Tecks took the traditional course of those who, to use their daughter's own evocative phrase, were in Short Street. They went abroad.

Between 1883 and 1885, Princess May shared her parents' temporary exile in Florence, living first at an hotel and later in a villa lent by friends. Whatever the failings of the Tecks as practical economists, they ensured a far better education for their daughter than ever the Wales children received. Already well-grounded in English, French and German, she now studied Italian and the history of art, took lessons in singing and painting, learned to name the wild flowers of Tuscany. Princess May did not at first care for the cultural riches so fortuitously put at her disposal. 'We think Florence rather a dull place,' she told her eldest brother, 'but of course much of our time is spent in seeing churches.' Florentine houses, she added, 'seem so uncomfortably arranged and so dirty, and the people always smell of garlic'. Only sixteen at the time, she soon outgrew her insularity.

The Teck family returned to England in the spring of 1885, settling permanently at White Lodge. Princess May continued her education with a new governess. Madame Hélène Bricka, a French Alsatian, displayed all the intellectual curiosity of a Dalton, but with a lighter and more penetrating touch. She introduced her pupil to the perspectives of history and to the problems of a rapidly expanding industrial society; she instilled habits of concentration and order in a world of royal dawdlers. From her mother May acquired a lifelong interest in philanthropy that was not confined to committee work. Dutifully, but without enjoyment, she became accustomed to visiting the poor, the sick and the distressed in the institutions devoted to their care; no dripping tap or recalcitrant lavatory chain ever escaped those watchful blue eyes. One recurring duty was helping the Duchess to collect second-hand clothes that were sold in aid of charities. The Prince of Wales always gave generously from his wardrobe, adding a jocular message that he hoped the Duke of Teck 'would not take the best clothes for himself this time'.

Princess May could hardly have been expected to spend the rest of her life in ragged schools and asylums. Yet when the desires of this attractive, well-educated and serious-minded girl turned to marriage, she found herself almost an outcast. The reason was neither her parents' insolvency nor her own shyness; both could have been accommodated in an age of arranged matches. What made her an apparently unsuitable consort for even the smallest reigning houses of Europe was her morganatic blood. Her only remaining hope, marriage to a British commoner, seemed equally elusive. Neither her consciously royal mother nor her querulous semi-royal father would have encouraged Princess May's necessary descent in rank. Nor would an English or Scots suitor of ancient line relish being treated with condescension. The most recent example was discouraging. In 1871 the Queen's fourth daughter, Princess Louise, had been married to the Marquess of Lorne. It proved an unhappy, childless match. The heir to the dukedom of Argyll and to a score of other splendid titles had to accustom himself to an inferior place in the royal family circle. As James Pope-Hennessy wrote in his incomparable biography, *Queen Mary*: 'Princess May thus had the worst of both worlds: she was too Royal to marry an ordinary English gentleman, and not Royal enough to marry a Royalty. Or so, in the late eighteen-eighties, it seemed.'

She was rescued from her dilemma by the one person in Europe who possessed both the will and the means. Queen Victoria did not share the antipathy of her continental cousins to morganatic blood. Sweeping aside their stiff, traditionalist arguments, she determined that Princess May would make an admirable wife for first one and then another of her own grandsons. So it came about that a young woman without a fortune, seemingly condemned to spinsterhood by a flawed pedigree, found herself destined to be Queen Consort of Great Britain. In that sense Princess May

was indeed a Cinderella and Queen Victoria a godmother of unbounded
benevolence.

'The young people go to Sandringham to the Cottage after the Wedding,'
the Queen wrote to her eldest daughter, the Empress Frederick, 'which I
regret and think rather *unlucky* and sad.' The honeymoon cottage, which
remained their home for the next thirty-three years, was but a short walk
across the park from Sandringham House itself. It was there, only eighteen
months before, that Princess May had witnessed the deathbed agony of her
first fiancé. 'All is left just as it was,' the Empress noted, 'his dressing table
with his watch, his brushes and combs and everything. His bed covered
with a Union Jack in silk, and his photos and trifles and clothes, etc. in a
glass cupboard.' That was not a welcoming prospect. Nor can Princess May
have been pleased to discover that her husband, in a well-meaning attempt
to spare her trouble, had himself chosen new carpets, curtains and wallpaper
for York Cottage and filled its rooms with modern furniture from the
emporium of his father's friend, Sir Blundell Maple. The newly-married
couple also had to endure the invasion of their Petit Trianon by the
occupants of the big house; the Princess of Wales and her boisterous
daughters were forever dropping in unannounced, even at breakfast time.
That was more of a penance for May than for her husband. She later wrote
to him:

I sometimes think that just after we were married we were not left alone enough
and had not the opportunity of learning to understand each other as quickly as we
might otherwise have done, and this led to so many little rubs which might have
been avoided. You see we are both terribly sensitive and the slightest sharp word
said by one to the other immediately gave offence and I fear that neither you nor
I forget those things in a hurry.

Prince George loved his wife dearly, but found difficulty in telling her so
except on paper. When he did pick up his pen, his words glowed with
ardour, as in this letter written during the first year of marriage:

I know I am, at least I am vain enough to think that I am capable of loving anybody
(who returns my love) with all my heart and soul, and I am sure I have found that
person in my sweet little May. You know by this time that I never do anything by
halves, when I asked you to marry me, I was very fond of you, but not very much
in love with you, but I saw in *you* the person I was capable of loving most deeply,
if you only returned that love ... I have tried to understand you and to know you,
and with the happy result that I know now that I do *love* you darling girl with all

my *heart*, and am simply *devoted* to you ... *I adore you sweet May*, I can't say more than that.

For all his tenderness of heart, he at first failed to support and encourage his wife in her new role or to protect her from the hostility that lurked behind the banter and endearments of his own family. The Prince of Wales, generous by nature, was guilty of no more than occasional impatience with his fastidious daughter-in-law; it was nevertheless noticed in later years that the thickets of *memorabilia* with which Queen Mary surrounded herself – her writing-desk alone bore ninety objects – included no likeness of her father-in-law. The Princess of Wales, torn between pleasure at her son's happiness and the loss of his undivided devotion, could scarcely conceal her jealousy of the intruder. Her three daughters were even more resentful of their new sister-in-law. Envious of her superior talents and mistaking her shyness for arrogance, they waged a campaign of sly disparagement. Princess Victoria, the most spiteful of all, once warned a guest at Windsor: 'Now do try to talk to May at dinner, though one knows she is deadly dull.' And Princess Louise, contemptuous of the Duchess of York's morganatic lineage, would remark: 'Poor May! poor May! with her Württemberg hands.'

Those early years of marriage undermined her confidence. Starved of reassurance even by her loving but inhibited husband, aware of feline glances that did not need to be translated into words, she felt as if she were on permanent probation. Her oldest friend, Mabell Countess of Airlie, once wrote after an emotional reunion:

As a girl she had been shy and reserved, but now her shyness had so crystallized that only in such moments of intimacy could she be herself. The hard crust of inhibition which gradually closed over her, hiding the warmth and tenderness of her own personality, was already starting to form.

The Empress Frederick noted 'something very cold and stiff – and distant in her manner: each time one sees her again one has to break the ice afresh'. The Empress, Queen Victoria's eldest daughter, could not forget that a Teck princess had been preferred to her own more eligible daughters as the bride first for Prince Eddy and then for Prince George. But May was thought to be lacking in social ease even by the well-disposed. Sir Henry Ponsonby, after sitting next to her at dinner on three successive nights in 1894, told his wife: 'She is pretty and what you would call voluptuous, but decidedly dull.' A lady-in-waiting added: 'She is a clever woman with great ideas of her own, and if only she could break down that stiff manner she could become a powerful factor for good in society. As it is, people say she gives herself airs.'

Almost alone of the royal family, the old Queen showed affection and appreciation. 'Each time I see you,' she told May, 'I love and respect you

more and am so truly thankful that Georgie has such a partner – to help
and encourage him in his difficult position.' Yet her kindly but unnerving
flow of questions and advice left its mark on Princess May for life. In 1934
Queen Mary was invited to visit an exhibition of historic clothes in a
London house. Placed in a corner by itself was a plain black dress of silk
once worn by Queen Victoria. As Queen Mary entered the room and
suddenly caught sight of that alarming dumpy shape, she started and
exclaimed: 'How on earth did they get that?' For a fleeting moment she was
once more a frightened young woman facing her formidable grand-
mother-in-law.

The Duke of York was spared such anguish in the years immediately
following his marriage; but he did have to go back to school. The task of
initiating a naval officer of twenty-eight into the nuances of constitutional
history was entrusted to J. R. Tanner, a Fellow of St John's College,
Cambridge. He instructed his fretful pupil to make a digest of that classic
work *The English Constitution*, by Walter Bagehot. The Queen, however,
was displeased to hear that the essays of so volatile, so irreverent a com-
mentator had been chosen for her grandson's enlightenment. In a confiding
letter to Princess May she also returned yet again to a favourite theme: 'I
hope that you will brush up and practise Georgie's French and German,
for you *must both* be able to speak it with foreigners – and with so many
relatives ... You should *not* speak English to them when they come here as
I observe you do.'

That failing, which the Duke never overcame, helps to explain his
growing dislike of foreign travel, a rare prejudice in a sailor. There were
other causes. In 1894, accompanying his father to Russia for the funeral of
the Tsar Alexander III, he wrote to his wife from St Petersburg: 'I really
believe I should get ill if I had to be away from you for a long time.' A
courtier added another reason for his homesickness: 'I think the Duke of
York is rather bored here and pining to get back to shoot.' Prince George
seldom neglected his duty; but the twin lodestars of those serene years were
family and sport.

He was in fact required to make few public appearances, a fraction of
those undertaken by members of the royal family a century later. During
the forty years spent by the Queen in near seclusion, the Prince and Princess
of Wales assumed almost all the ceremonial and social functions of the
monarchy. In the eyes of the world, however, the sovereign was sovereign,
her heir a stylish substitute and the rest mere reflections of a distant
effulgence. That was well understood by the Shah of Persia during his visit
to England. Invited to Waddesdon, the home of Baron Lionel de Rothschild, he was chagrined to discover that the Prince of Wales had deputed
his son to represent him at the entertainment. Nasr-ed-Din sulkily with-

drew to his bedroom, from which he was at length lured only by the prospect of a hired conjuror.

Although the Duke's programme was hardly exacting, he resisted any attempt to extend it. In April 1896, Lord Salisbury, Prime Minister and Chancellor of Oxford, invited him to make a formal visit to the university. From Coburg, where he was attending a family wedding, the Duke wrote to ask that it be postponed to another year 'owing to the number of my engagements already arranged for on my return to England after more than a month's absence'. The Duke's diaries for the rest of that summer, however, reveal a sparse calendar of duties. In June he joined his father and his uncle the Duke of Connaught in voting for a measure in the House of Lords that permitted a man to marry his deceased wife's sister. The bishops, scandalized by the royal intervention, were presumably mollified later that year by the Duke's presence at the funeral of the Archbishop of Canterbury, Edward Benson. Between those two events he watched his father's horse Persimmon win the Derby; he attended the wedding of his sister Maud to Prince Charles of Denmark; and at Marlborough House he marvelled at a new invention called the cinematoscope. Then the shooting season opened and the Duke could lay down his burden.

He was essentially a countryman. The Duke of Cambridge, after watching his nephew by marriage and godson open a new footbridge and automatic lock at Richmond, admired his bearing, his clear enunciation and his technical grasp of machinery. But he was disturbed that the eventual heir to the throne 'can't bear London and going out, and hates society'. One of the advantages of York Cottage which most satisfied its owner was that the rooms were too small for entertainment. Unable to offer the same excuse when occupying the spacious apartments of York House, St James's Palace, he nevertheless remained as reluctant a host in London as in the country. When the Duke and Duchess of York did entertain, however, they followed the liberal standards of the age. At York House (which, as at Sandringham, the Duke had furnished without consulting his wife) their first dinner party took place on 4 March 1894. The guests, all members of the family, consumed oysters, thick soup and clear soup, soles and turbot, some fussy little French entrées, mutton, chicken, quails, asparagus, a soufflé, apricot tart and ices. A few days later there was a more formal party for the new Prime Minister, Lord Rosebery, at which his predecessor, Mr Gladstone, was also present.

The Duke of York had yet to acquire a knowledge of politics. It was perhaps to mask his insecurity that he fell into the lifelong habit of voicing his opinions at length and in trumpet tones. A lady-in-waiting noted in her diary after dining at Windsor: 'The Duke of York spoke loud and abused the German Emperor, not caring what he said, but the Queen was silent.'

Half a century later Queen Mary recalled that trait of her late husband: 'He never liked going round and round.' And as she spoke, she made a circular movement with her fingers.

He showed the same spirited independence after the birth of his eldest child, which took place at White Lodge, Richmond Park, on 23 June 1894. Three days later the Queen reached for her pen and with practised piety asked that the first name of her first great-grandson should be Albert. Once more she was to be disappointed. In a long letter of reverent affection, the Duke conceded that Albert would be one of the infant's names. But as he explained to the Queen: 'Long before our dear child was born, both May and I settled that if it was a boy we should call him Edward after darling *Eddy. This is the dearest wish of our hearts*, dearest Grandmama, for Edward is indeed a *sacred* name to us.'

The Queen was obliged to accept the decision of the Duke and Duchess of York, although her reply contained just a touch of crossness and a lesson in logic: 'Of course if you wish Edward to be the first name I shall not object, only I think you write as if *Edward* was the *real* name of dear Eddy, while it was *Albert Victor*.'

The infant Prince was baptized Edward Albert Christian George Andrew Patrick David. The family called him David, the name of the patron saint of Wales. With the birth at Sandringham of a second son on 14 December 1895, the thirty-fourth anniversary of the death of the Prince Consort, the Yorks were at last able to gratify the Queen's wishes. He was christened Albert Frederick Arthur George and known in the family, like his grandfather, as Bertie. Four more children were born to the Duke and Duchess of York, all at Sandringham: Princess Mary (1897), Prince Henry (1900), Prince George (1902) and Prince John (1905). Some of them were to cause their father much anguish in adolescence, and they in turn were to fear him as a stern and unreasonable parent. For the present, however, all was content. The Duke of York would boast of the deftness with which he had learned to bath a lively baby, then settle down to read the Greville memoirs to his wife.

The only shadow to fall across the domestic harmony of York Cottage came not from his own family but from the Tecks. All three of Princess May's brothers served with gallantry in the British Army, two of them winning the Distinguished Service Order. The eldest, Prince Adolphus, known as Dolly, and the youngest, Prince Alexander, known as Alge, were as circumspect and reliable as their sister. The middle brother, Prince Francis, known as Frank, was not. From his mother, the Duchess of Teck, he inherited both an endearing extravagance and an optimistic temperament. Stationed with his regiment in Dublin, he found himself in debt to the tune of £1,000. He determined to extricate himself by a single daring coup. On 27 June 1895, the racecard at The Curragh included the Stewards' Plate for two-year-olds, run over five furlongs. Of the four horses entered for the event, Bellevin was considered so vastly superior to his three rivals that he started at the excessively cramped odds of 10 to 1 on: in other words a gambler would have had to risk £10,000 to win £1,000. Although Prince Francis was almost penniless, it did not prevent him from striking precisely that bet with the bookmakers. Bellevin was beaten by an unconsidered horse called Winkfield's Pride and his unfortunate backer left owing a total of £11,000. To avoid a family disgrace, the Duke of York agreed to help pay his brother-in-law's debts. The rash gambler was packed off to serve with the Army in India, but remained cheerfully unrepentant. He wrote to his mother in the following year: 'I was much amused at Master and Mistress York going to Newmarket. I think I must write and warn her simple soul against the evils of the race – I shall send her a betting book as Xmas present.'

Prince Francis remained the black sheep of the family. Having retired early from the Army, he drifted on his insouciant way, an engaging idler and spendthrift. He never married. After the Duchess of Teck's death in 1897, Princess May was outraged to learn that he had made off with their mother's emeralds and bestowed them on his ageing paramour. Brother and sister were reconciled not long before he died in 1910 from the effects of a minor operation. For almost the only time in her life she wept publicly at his funeral. She also took steps to recover the errant emeralds.

The expense and pain of helping to rescue Prince Francis from the Dublin bookmakers did not permanently deflect the Duke of York from a knowledgeable interest in horseracing. Indeed, he was at Ascot in 1897 to see his father's Persimmon inflict a family revenge on Winkfield's Pride by beating him eight lengths in the Gold Cup. But he never paid the same fervent allegiance to the so-called sport of kings as he brought to shooting.

John Gore, whose personal memoir of King George V is a masterpiece of tactful illumination, wrote of his subject when Duke of York: 'For months of the year on end he lived the life of the squire to whom money was no object, and business duties but an interlude of no grievous length.' He was a squire, moreover, with all the privileges of a great estate but few of the responsibilities. It was his father who had bought Sandringham in 1862 at the hugely inflated price of £220,000, rebuilt the house, laid out the gardens, extended its boundaries, made it one of the most prolific sporting properties in the country; during his tenure of half a century, about one million head of game were shot there. The Empress Frederick, staying with her brother at Sandringham in 1894, wrote to a daughter: 'It is impossible to find an estate in finer order than Uncle Bertie's, plantations, fields, roads, fences and walls, cottages and churches and all, so trim and so well cared for.' Disraeli, who saw English country life through the eyes of a romantic cosmopolitan, left a more picturesque description of those bleak Norfolk horizons: 'I fancied I was paying a visit to some of the dukes and princes of the Baltic: a vigorous marine air, stunted fir forests but sufficiently extensive ... and the splendour of Scandinavian sunsets.' The Prince of Wales, denied even the most remote participation in affairs of State as long as his mother lived, found a solace in managing Sandringham that he was not prepared to share even with his son and eventual successor.

The Duke of York proved an unambitious tenant. He remained content with a house just large enough to contain his family and the enjoyment of the shooting as an ever-welcome guest. After leasing a shoot of his own and buying a share in that of his father's neighbour, Lord Farquhar, he had 30,000 acres over which to pursue pheasants and partridges, woodcock and duck. Nor did that include the shoots to which he was invited again and again by the richest landowners in the kingdom.

As early as 1881, on shore leave in Australia, Dalton had noted his pupil's confidence in bringing down high-flying duck. But for the next ten years Prince George could not rely on that regular practice which so swiftly improves the performance of even the born shot. Season after season, his only sport was to sigh over the daily game cards which the Prince of Wales used to send his sailor son. Marriage brought him the leisure of a country gentleman and freedom to live according to the shooting calendar. Except for a few weeks as Captain of the cruiser *Crescent* in 1898, he never again held executive command in the Royal Navy. Seasick, homesick and denied the sport which had become almost a passion, he noted the end of his professional career without a word of sorrow or even of regret. In later life, on those few occasions when he failed to do himself justice with a gun, he would explain: 'I can't hit a feather. But I've been at sea for a good many years and one doesn't see many pheasants there.'

The Duke of York shot with incomparably more skill than any other member of his family. The Duke of Connaught, Queen Victoria's third son, while aiming at a pheasant in December 1891, had inadvertently put out the eye of his brother-in-law, Prince Christian of Schleswig-Holstein. There was something suspect, too, about the game bag of the Prince of Wales. It included mounds of bewildered, half-tame pheasants; twenty-eight flamingos potted on the banks of the Nile; a sleepy old bull of the Chillingham wild herd killed as the royal marksman lay concealed in its hay cart; the tail of an Indian elephant (the elephant itself escaped). His son showed no distaste for slaughtering huge numbers of driven pheasants and partridges, but was as happy shooting the more elusive woodcock. One of his most memorable days at Sandringham was in 1893 when for the first time in his life a right and left fell to his new 12-bore Purdey, one of a pair given to him by the people of nearby King's Lynn as a wedding present; he had the brace of woodcock preserved in a glass case. The Duke of York also disliked an excessive competitiveness and persuaded Lord Leicester, his neighbour at Holkham, not to put up in the smoking-room each evening the names of the guns with the individual score of each. He himself had nothing to fear; within a few years of leaving the navy he ranked with such accomplished shots as Lord Ripon and Harry Stonor, the brother of his early love Julie. But he realized that the custom provoked anguish and mockery, and that even the most competent sportsman might have had few birds over him that day.

Year after year, as the old century neared its end, the Duke's life continued its placid course: a sedate procession of events reflected more in his game book than in the Court Circular. After each day's shooting he would punctiliously record the bag in his diary. When the season came to an end he was content with the vague entry: 'Busy arranging my things.' Discouraged from too close an interest in current politics or from displaying any but domestic virtues, he scarcely ever mentioned national or international affairs. The only reference to the blackest week of the South African War, when British troops suffered humiliating defeats at the hands of the Boers, occurs on 16 December 1899: 'Got bad news about the war. It makes one very anxious.' The shooting season was under way at Sandringham, too. That winter they killed 12,109 pheasants.

It was to a fellow sailor that the Duke of York owed his other lifelong pastime: collecting postage stamps. Prince Alfred, Duke of Edinburgh, the second of Queen Victoria's four sons, joined the Royal Navy at the age of fourteen and by his own exertions rose to command the Mediterranean Fleet. Prince George served as a junior officer in his uncle's flagship, enjoyed his hospitality in Malta, admired his stamp collection and was encouraged to form one of his own. When the Duke of Edinburgh opened the first London Philatelic Exhibition in 1890, he mentioned that his nephew was about to cross the Atlantic in HMS *Thrush*, and hoped he would 'return with a goodly number of additions from North America and the West Indies'. The library at Buckingham Palace today contains the Prince's copy of the Stanley Gibbons catalogue for 1891, specially bound in morocco, with all the stamps in his collection ticked in red. News of his interest spread; among his wedding presents in 1893 were 1,500 additional varieties. The following year he invited his uncle to be a godfather to his first child.

Few others, however, shared his affection for the Duke of Edinburgh. He was said to drink too much, to make mischief in the family, to behave boorishly to his Russian wife, the daughter of the Tsar Alexander II. In the smoking-room at Balmoral (an amenity conceded by the Queen with much reluctance) he would talk about himself by the hour until his brother-in-law, Prince Henry of Battenberg, was driven to give up his nightly cigar. Another of the Duke's disturbing relaxations was the violin, which he played with more enthusiasm than skill. 'Fiddle out of tune and noise abominable,' Sir Henry Ponsonby wrote of the royal recital that followed a dinner party given by the Prince of Wales. Even that most indulgent of hosts once or twice broke out with, 'I don't think you're quite right.' And when the virtuoso Joachim was asked whether the Duke could have made his living as a professional violinist, he replied: 'Yes, on the sands.'

In 1893 the Duke of Edinburgh inherited from his uncle Ernest, the Prince Consort's brother, both the Duchy of Saxe-Coburg-Gotha and the debts of its late ruler. (The Prince of Wales escaped the double burden by having earlier renounced his right to the succession.) As he nevertheless insisted on retaining a London residence, Clarence House, he was soon in financial difficulty himself. To appease his English creditors, the Duke of Edinburgh offered to reduce his expenditure on shooting by £2,750 a year and on theatres by £1,250, only a fraction of what he continued to spend on those pleasures. He did, however, make one substantial sacrifice. Shortly before his death in 1900 he sold his collection of stamps to his brother the Prince of Wales, who in turn gave it to the Duke of York.

On that foundation the Duke of York built up the most comprehensive collection in the world devoted to the stamps of Great Britain and her Empire. He enjoyed every advantage, particularly the rich harvest of his own imperial tours. Courtiers were also pressed into service. 'The King is delighted to hear that you are endeavouring to pinch as many stamps for him as you can during your travels,' one wrote to another in 1920. Colonial Governors and High Commissioners watched on his behalf for the appearance of new issues. Only once did they fail him. A British diplomatist in the Middle East, hearing of a suspected case of smallpox in the local printing works, feared that the royal tongue might be contaminated; so he assiduously boiled his entire offering of 400 stamps in a saucepan before despatching them to Buckingham Palace.

Although the Duke of York liked a bargain, marking the price of each new purchase in code under its hinge, he soon acquired the means to pay exceptionally high prices for rarities. From 1901 his annual income as heir to the throne was £100,000: £60,000 from the revenues of the Duchy of Cornwall and a parliamentary grant of £40,000. 'Did Your Royal Highness hear that some damned fool has just paid £1,450 for a single stamp?' a courtier jocularly asked him one morning. 'I was the damned fool,' he replied.

Such prices have sometimes exposed collectors to the sneers of the sophisticated. 'There are people in the world', an eminent man of letters once declared, 'who are prepared to pay for these scraps of paper a sum which would endow a respectable scholarship or purchase a fine Sickert for the National Art-Collections Fund.' And he went on to express his horror and contempt for those who 'become excited by objects which are totally unworthy of man's unconquerable mind'. The author of those wounding words was Harold Nicolson. He wrote them, however, before he had agreed to undertake the official biography of King George v. His references to philately in that majestic work are brief but urbane.

The Duke of York's collection, which at his death in 1936 consisted of 250,000 stamps in 325 large volumes, has in monetary terms proved an investment of almost incalculable value. Although much of it was purchased with his private funds, it is today regarded as inalienable. Like the royal library and picture collections, it cannot be sold for the private benefit of the monarch or the royal family but has become part of the national heritage. That is as its begetter would surely have wished.

THREE

HEIR TO THE THRONE

Empire tour—Fathers and sons—Passage to India—
Public duties

As the year 1900 drew to a close, the Duke of York prepared for a long abstinence from stamps and shotgun. Accompanied by his wife, he was to represent the Queen at the opening of the first Parliament of the Commonwealth of Australia. He resented any interruption to his busy, undemanding routine yet never failed to answer the call of duty. Earlier that year, when required to be in Berlin for the Crown Prince's coming-of-age, he had written: 'I hate going of course, but am always ready to do what the Queen wishes or anything that may in any way benefit my country.' On being asked to undertake his mission to Melbourne, he even enlisted the Prime Minister's help in extending the journey: 'Please ask the Queen whether we can visit Canada on our way home from Australia. She is averse to it owing to our long absence from England. But we think it would cause great disappointment and perhaps jealousy. Use your influence.'

Lord Salisbury did persuade the Queen to extend her grandson's itinerary. But on 22 January 1901 she died. The Duke, reflecting what lay in the hearts of almost all her subjects, wrote in his diary: 'Our beloved Queen and Grandmama, one of the greatest women that ever lived, passed peacefully away.' Although present at her deathbed, he was mortified not to be able to attend her funeral, having been struck down a few days earlier by German measles. It was not illness, however, which threatened the cancellation of his tour little more than a month before the proposed date of departure. The newly proclaimed King Edward VII declared that he and Queen Alexandra could not bear to be separated from their only surviving son for the best part of a year. The Government recognized both the strength of family unity that had prompted the King's protest and the burden of ceremonial duties that would fall on him in his son's absence. The Cabinet nevertheless decided that for political reasons the visit to Australia must continue. Arthur Balfour, soon to succeed his uncle as Prime

Minister, was deputed to explain to his sovereign the realities of modern imperialism:

The King is no longer merely King of Great Britain and Ireland and of a few dependencies whose whole value consisted in ministering to the wealth and security of Great Britain and Ireland. He is now the greatest constitutional bond uniting together in a single Empire communities of free men separated by half the circumference of the Globe. All the patriotic sentiment which makes such an Empire possible centres in him or centres chiefly in him; and everything which emphasises his personality to our kinsmen across the seas must be a gain to the Monarchy and the Empire.

Now the present opportunity of furthering the policy thus suggested is unique. It can in the nature of things never be repeated. A great commonwealth is to be brought into existence, after infinite trouble and with the fairest prospects of success. Its citizens know little and care little for British Ministries and British party politics. But they know, and care for, the Empire of which they are members and for the Sovereign who rules it. Surely it is in the highest interests of the State that he should visually, and so to speak corporeally, associate his family with the final act which brings the new community into being; so that in the eyes of all who see it the chief actor in the ceremony, its central figure, should be the King's heir, and that in the history of this great event the Monarchy of Britain and the Commonwealth of Australia should be inseparably united.

Overwhelmed but not entirely convinced by Balfour's eloquence, the King withdrew his objections to the tour. He caused surprise, however, by not immediately conferring on his son and heir the traditional title of Prince of Wales. It was as Duke of Cornwall and York that Prince George embarked for Australia in March 1901. The Dukedom of Cornwall, with its comfortable income from Duchy properties, is the perquisite of the sovereign's eldest son, inherited by him either at birth or on the sovereign's accession to the throne; the more ancient and familiar title of Prince of Wales requires to be specifically conferred. In withholding it until November 1901, the King was thought to have behaved with an uncharacteristic lack of generosity to a model son now in his thirty-sixth year. The probable explanation of the delay is that the King and Queen wished to avoid confusion in the minds of their subjects. The King had been Prince of Wales for sixty years, his wife Princess of Wales for nearly forty. By accustoming the public to their own regal styles before the advent of a new Prince and Princess of Wales, they hoped to retain the separate identities of each generation.

Of the King's affection for Prince George there can be no doubt. 'I have always tried to look upon you far more as a brother than a son,' he told him in August 1900, 'though I have never had occasion to blame you for any want of filial duty!' The Duke of Cornwall more than reciprocated such loving sentiments. From Gibraltar, the first port of call on the voyage to Australia, he told his parents how distressing he had found their last farewells at Portsmouth. 'May and I came down to our cabins,' he wrote, 'and had a good cry and tried to comfort each other.'

That affecting scene took place on board the *Ophir*, an Orient Line steamship of 6,900 tons chartered by the Admiralty. Her cruise was in its way no less rigorous than that of the *Bacchante* twenty years earlier. It is true that in 1901 the royal passengers travelled in luxury and that their shipmate Canon Dalton found fewer opportunities for imparting knowledge in his role of domestic chaplain. But the Duke, who preferred statistics to picturesque description, noted that he and his wife were separated from home and children for 231 days; and that during those eight months they covered 45,000 miles, laid 21 foundation stones, received 544 addresses, presented 4,329 medals, reviewed 62,000 troops and shook hands with 24,855 people at official receptions alone. He wrote to Queen Alexandra from New Zealand:

It is all very well for you and Papa to say we mustn't do too much but it is impossible to help it. Our stay at each place is so short that everything has to be crammed into it, otherwise people would be offended and our great object is to please as many people as possible.

That gruelling programme set the pattern for all future royal tours of Empire and Commonwealth. The monarchy was becoming not only peripatetic in habit but mercantile of mind. On 1 November 1901 the travellers returned to England amid many congratulations. The Duke, who was created Prince of Wales on his father's sixtieth birthday eight days later, accepted an invitation in the following month to address the City of London at Guildhall. He concluded his speech with a twofold call to the nation:

I appeal to my fellow countrymen at home to prove the strength of the attachment of the Motherland to her children by sending to them of her best . . .

To the distinguished representatives of the commercial interests of the Empire whom I have the pleasure of meeting here today, I venture to allude to the impression which seemed generally to prevail among their brethren across the seas, that the Old Country must wake up if she intends to maintain her old position of pre-eminence in her Colonial trade against foreign competitors.

In striking that mercantile note, he showed more awareness of Great Britain's economic needs than did his father. The King had earlier that year told the Duke of some unsolicited advice received from Lord Charles Beresford: 'The pith of his letter was that you should associate yourself, in each place you visit, with Trade and Commerce (!) by personal interviews with Chambers of Commerce.' Although the King added that the subject was 'doubtless a most important one with regard to the Mother Country, our Colonies and India', that exclamation mark is no tribute to his vision. Within half a century, the pursuit of trade had become an essential and often paramount factor in all royal tours overseas.

'Wake up, England!', the label which the press affixed to the Duke's Guildhall speech, exaggerated both his devotion to travel and his relish for the role of ambassador. He had done his duty and more. His true feelings, however, were revealed in a letter to Queen Alexandra from Canada: 'Of course our tour is most interesting, but it is very tiring and there is no place like dear old England for me.'

A few years later, when seemingly punitive taxes imposed by the Liberal Government were causing apprehension among landowners, Lord Esher made a bold suggestion to the recently crowned King George V:

In view of possible fiscal and social legislation in the future, based upon prin- ciples even more hostile to holders of real or personal property in Great Britain, it is worthy of careful examination whether prudence does not require that any savings effected by Your Majesty or by the Trustees of the Duke of Cornwall, might not be invested in real estate in the Dominion of Canada. Apart from the financial advantages of such a policy, which might possibly be very great hereafter, there are other considerations – popular and political – that might commend it to Your Majesty.

King George rejected the advice of his father's confidant. And when in 1925 his own eldest son bought a ranch in Canada, he thought it 'a mistake'.

The success of that first tour strengthened the confidence of the Duke and Duchess alike. Warmed by the nation's approval, the Duke felt able to express to his wife a sense of gratitude which shyness had so often kept locked in his heart. He wrote to her soon after their return:

Somehow I can't tell you, so I take the first opportunity of writing to say how deeply I am indebted to you darling for the splendid way in which you supported and helped me during our long Tour. It was you who made it a success ... If you had not come with me, it would not have been at all a success ...

Although I have often told it you before, I repeat it once more, that I love you darling child, with my whole heart and soul, and thank God every day that I have such a wife as you, who is such a great help and support to me and I believe loves me too.

The Duke delighted to share his pride with others. The Revd W.A. Spooner, Warden of New College, Oxford, met him at a dinner in Lincoln's Inn in April 1904. Referring to him by his old style of Duke of York, the warden afterwards wrote: 'He was very easy to get on with and told me a good deal about his Colonial Tour ... I liked the way in which he kept the Duchess to the front and made me understand that she was associated in everything with him; it gave me a pleasant impression of a thoroughly happy and virtuous life.'

Throughout the long cruise of the *Ophir*, the Duke of Cornwall was not alone in pining for England. 'It is exactly 20 weeks since we came on board this good ship,' a fellow passenger noted, 'please God in 13 weeks more we shall be at home again.' The writer was Sir Arthur Bigge, whom the King had recently appointed to be his son's private secretary. Most courtiers of the Victorian Age came of aristocratic family: Grey and Ponsonby, Phipps and Knollys. Bigge was the son of a Northumbrian parson. As a young officer in the Royal Artillery he formed a close friendship with the Prince Imperial, son of the deposed Emperor Napoleon III, who after joining the British Army had been posted to Bigge's battery. Although in hospital with fever when the Prince was ambushed and killed during the Zulu War of 1879, Bigge was later chosen to accompany the Empress Eugénie to the scene of the tragedy. That in turn brought him to the notice of Queen Victoria, who in 1880 appointed him to be an assistant private secretary. On the death of Sir Henry Ponsonby in 1895, Bigge succeeded to his post, displaying tact, wisdom and ingenuity during the last, increasingly difficult years of the Queen's reign.

On her death in 1901 he might reasonably have expected to become private secretary to the new sovereign. King Edward, however, wished to retain Sir Francis Knollys, his private secretary for the past thirty years. Bigge was instead offered the post of private secretary to the Duke of Cornwall, who as heir to the throne stood in need of an experienced counsellor. In a strictly hierarchical sense his appointment was a demotion. That, however, was of no importance to a man of such modesty. As it turned out, he remained with his new master until his own death in 1931, serving him successively as Duke of Cornwall, Prince of Wales and King. Although Bigge's judgement during the constitutional crisis of 1910-11 may be questioned, his contribution to the strength and stability of the monarchy during those thirty years can scarcely be exaggerated.

Bigge's tribute to Ponsonby defines his own ideal of a private secretary:

The longer I live and the more I look back, the more remarkable man he seems to me. One of, if not the greatest gentlemen I have known: the entire effacement of *self*: the absolute non-existence of conceit, side or pose: the charming courtesy to strangers old, young, high, low, rich, poor. His extraordinary wit and sense of the ridiculous, his enormous powers of work - too much - it killed him, but I never heard him say he was hard-worked or had too much to do, nor did I ever hear him say 'Oh, don't bother! Come back in five minutes; I am writing an important letter to the Queen or Prime Minister or Archbishop of Canterbury, Cardinal Manning,

Mrs. Langtry etc.' The letter was put down and he listened patiently and considered whether the Crown Equerry or the Equerry-in-Waiting should ride on the right of the Queen or whether next Sunday's preacher should refer to this or that.

Bigge served the Queen, and from 1901 her grandson, with the same selfless fidelity. Certain habits acquired during those Victorian years persisted to the end of his long life. One was to conduct an immense official correspondence almost entirely by hand, sometimes making his own copies of letters for future reference. The Queen not only preferred to transact business in writing rather than in conversation, even with ministers staying under her own roof; she also frowned on modern aids to communication. The typewriter, introduced into government offices in the late eighteen-eighties, prompted Lord Rosebery, Foreign Secretary in Mr Gladstone's last Cabinet of 1892-94, to address this appeal to Ponsonby:

The Queen dislikes our typewriting. We swarm with typewriters, here, and in every embassy, legation and consulate – or most of them. These ingenious machines are paralysed by the Queen's displeasure. We have consequently set ourselves to mend our ways, and I now send you for submission to Her Majesty a specimen which, to my admiring eye, is rather the print of a family Bible than the faint scratch of the typewriter. Will she deign to smile on it, and so liberate a fettered industry?

Rosebery's plea was rejected; by the Queen's command, ministers and officials continued to submit all business in manuscript. The first typewritten letter to emerge from the private secretary's office is dated 30 June 1897; but the use of the typewriter was a practice of which Bigge took little advantage and the Queen none at all.

The royal holograph tradition died hard. Even on official topics, King Edward VII was almost as prodigious a correspondent as his mother; nor did he grudge the labour of making copies of his own letters. His son, as Prince of Wales, was equally assiduous, in spite of writing with exceptional slowness. He told Bigge on 2 January 1908: 'What a blessing for you to have received no letters. Xmas and the New Year for me is an awful time, I have written nearly 40 in the last week and have not finished them yet.' On succeeding to the throne in 1910 he instructed Lord Hardinge, Viceroy of India, to write to him in his own hand. Eight years later, however, Bigge (by now Lord Stamfordham) told the Lord Lieutenant of Ireland: 'The King appreciates your adhering to the good old custom of writing to the Sovereign in your own handwriting. But in these days of strain, he hopes you will have recourse to the typewriter, which he knows means considerable saving of time and trouble.' When the King visited the British Industries Fair in 1926, he was enraged to learn that the typewriters used in government offices were American. 'It is scandalous,' he cried. That, however, was more a criticism of all things transatlantic than a commendation of the typewriter.

Bigge's sustained faith in pen and ink added several hours to each day's toil yet was not unwelcome to his correspondents. To relieve the strain on Queen Victoria's failing eyesight he had changed his handwriting to a bolder script and used ink as thick and black as pitch; before submission to the Queen, each completed sheet was then dried on a heated tray of his own invention. That fine clear hand lasted him through life. His letters lacked Ponsonby's humour; but he was well-read enough to quote *Vivian Grey* to a Conservative statesman and *Soapey Sponge* to a sporting courtier.

Slight of build and unassuming in manner, Bigge displayed courage from the moment he began to serve the Duke of Cornwall in 1901. He expressed disapproval of King Edward's decision not to create the heir to the throne Prince of Wales until after the return of the *Ophir*: as much a slur on the overseas dominions, he felt, as on the Duke himself. Nor was Bigge deterred from tendering unpalatable advice when he thought his master in need of it. He pleaded with him firmly but in vain to abandon York Cottage in favour of a more spacious country house where he could entertain and so broaden his social and political horizons. The Prince of Wales (as he must now be called) wrote to his private secretary on New Year's Day 1902: 'I feel that I can always rely on you to tell me the truth however disagreeable and that you are certainly in my confidence. To a person in my position it is of enormous help to me.'

In a letter written from Sandringham on Christmas Day 1907, the Prince paid an even more remarkable tribute to his mentor:

Fancy, how quickly time flies, it is nearly seven years already since you came to me. You have nothing to thank us for, it is all the other way and we have indeed much to thank you for. As for myself during these seven years you have made my life comparatively an easy one, by your kind help and assistance and entire devotion to work connected with me. What would have happened to me if you had not been there to prepare and help me with my speeches, I can hardly write a letter of any importance without your assistance. I fear sometimes I have lost my temper with you and often been very rude, but I am sure you know me well enough by now to know that I did not mean it ...

I offer you my thanks from the bottom of my heart. I am a bad hand at saying what I feel, but I thank God that I have a friend like you, in whom I have the fullest confidence and from whom I know on all occasions I shall get the best and soundest advice whenever I seek it.

The Prince of Wales ended his letter with a piece of family news: 'My two eldest sons enjoyed their first day's shooting, the eldest got 12 rabbits and the second got 3.'

With an annual income of £100,000, the Prince of Wales was a rich man;
an agricultural labourer at the turn of the century could expect to earn
rather less than £40 a year, a domestic servant half that amount. He
nevertheless took good care of his money, and disappointed his father by
refusing to occupy Osborne, Queen Victoria's large Italianate house on the
Isle of Wight. He could well afford it, the King urged, having few social
obligations and no other country house to maintain, 'as I can hardly look on
the Cottage as a country house'. The Prince, however, disliked large houses
and the hospitality required of their owners. So Osborne was handed over
to the nation. The state rooms, except for Queen Victoria's own apartments,
were opened to the public and the rest turned into a convalescent home for
officers. The stables became the nucleus of a new junior naval college,
successor to the old *Britannia* in which Prince George had received his first
lessons in seamanship.

The Prince of Wales was equally stubborn in declining to leave York
Cottage, Sandringham, for a more spacious house in Norfolk. The King,
who knew precisely the style in which an heir to the throne should live,
thought he had found just the thing for his son. Lord Esher described the
expedition:

I have been driving with the King most of today. We went to Houghton, Chol-
mondeley's place, a splendid house built by Walpole but frightfully neglected
owing to poverty. A sleepy hollow of a park. Possibly the Duke of York may rent
it. . . . We drove 8 miles in 19 minutes in the King's motor – really very pleasant –
only you have to wear spectacles.

King Edward's expedition was in vain. The Wales family remained in
the cramped little rooms of York Cottage for the next twenty-five years.

They were grateful, however, to be lent one of the most delectable and
least known of royal residences for their occasional use during the summer.
Frogmore House, scarcely a mile from Windsor Castle, was built in the
reign of William and Mary, purchased a century later by Queen Charlotte
and refaced by Wyatt in the Georgian style. A handsome colonnaded building
of cream-coloured stucco, it lies in a secluded corner of the Home Park.
Rooms of manageable size overlook a pleasing prospect of lawn, lake and
trees that conceals two mausoleums. One, of classical elegance, contains the
tomb of the Duchess of Kent, Queen Victoria's mother and a resident of
Frogmore House; the other, a cheerless structure of granite and Portland
stone, was built by the Queen to unite her own remains with those of the
Prince Consort.

It was to Frogmore that the Prince and Princess of Wales would come
each year for Ascot races. Princess May also liked to escape from the bustle
of the London season to spend an afternoon writing letters under the lime

trees while her children fed the ducks or played hide-and-seek in the
shrubberies. 'It is too divine here and everything is looking lovely,' she told
her husband, 'the house charming and fresh and the garden and grounds a
dream.' In widowhood she arranged some of the rooms as a museum of
family history: a harvest of presents and souvenirs from George III to
Elizabeth II. There are china animals from the nursery and exercise books
from the schoolroom, Princess Christian's wedding wreath and a tiny loaf
baked on the day of Queen Victoria's Golden Jubilee.

In London, the Prince of Wales was obliged to exchange his unpretentious corner of St James's Palace for the Wren grandeur of Marlborough
House, where his father and mother had lived for the past forty years. This
time he dispensed with the prosaic tastes of Sir Blundell Maple and allowed
his wife a free hand. To her surprise, the King expressed annoyance that
she should want to redecorate the house, though he had himself just spent
a fortune on renovating Buckingham Palace before taking up residence
there. 'Surely he must know we really cannot go into a filthy dirty house,'
she wrote to her husband with unusual asperity, 'not even to oblige him.'
To restore the eighteenth-century rooms to their original proportions, the
Princess removed the Victorian accretions introduced by her father-in-law.
Then she had the ceilings, cornices and panelling stripped of their once
fashionable pinks and greens; these features she ordered to be painted
white, with a touch of gilt for relief.

It is not known how much the King and Queen resented the changes to
their old home, but two or three years later Princess May was wounded at
being omitted from the list of those to whom the King gave the recently
published volumes of Queen Victoria's letters. Nor was Queen Alexandra
the most considerate or understanding of mothers-in-law. She would
address letters not to 'Her Royal Highness the Princess of Wales' but to
'Her Royal Highness Victoria Mary, Princess of Wales': a subtly incorrect
designation that implied the existence of a whole host of variously named
Princesses of Wales.

Sometimes the Queen's disparagement of Princess May was more overt.
Suffering from a cold the day before a Court, she asked King Edward to
cancel it. This he refused to do at such short notice. Instead he invited the
Princess of Wales to take his wife's place. The Queen was furious, and
allowed neither her Mistress of the Robes nor her other ladies to be present
in attendance on the usurper. Even less amiably, she failed to conceal her
jealousy of the woman who had won her son's love. While the Princess was
preparing for the Indian tour of 1905-6, the Queen wrote to the Prince of
Wales: 'So my poor Georgie has lost his May, who has fled to London to
look in her glass!! What a bore and a nuisance, but I cannot understand
why she should have gone so soon, as dresses for India cannot take quite

such a long time to do or try on either.'

In fairness to Queen Alexandra, it must be remembered that she was a creature of moods, her perception distorted by deafness. At heart she appreciated the affectionate nature of her daughter-in-law, and occasionally brought herself to say so: 'You my sweet May are always so dear and nice to me – and whenever I am not quite "au fait" on account of my beastly ears you always by a word or even by a turn towards me make me understand – for which I am most grateful as nobody can know what I often have to go through.'

It is perhaps remarkable that there were not more collisions of will between Queen Alexandra and Princess May, and none at all between King Edward and Prince George. The values of one generation rarely appeal to the next; the House of Hanover in particular has sustained a long history of strife between the sovereign and his heir. Living within a few hundred yards of each other for so much of the year, the two families had additional opportunities for misunderstanding, even estrangement.

Their migratory routes overlapped again and again. Both families spent Christmas and the New Year at Sandringham, returning to London in February. The Court moved to Windsor in April, with the Prince of Wales a frequent guest; then back to the capital until the call of Ascot in June. The Prince would accompany his father both to Goodwood races in July and to Cowes in August, where he sailed the King's yacht *Britannia*. They separated for the early days of the grouse-shooting season but were soon reunited in Scotland, the King at Balmoral, the Prince at the nearby castle of Abergeldie. Sandringham beckoned both father and son for the partridges in October. During the rest of the year they met again and again on State occasions in London, welcoming foreign monarchs to Windsor, shooting pheasants at any of a dozen hospitable houses.

Yet the sybaritic, cosmopolitan father and his self-disciplined, insular son never grated on each other. The King could scarcely bear to be parted from him for more than a week or two at a time, suffered each separation as if it were the last and rejoiced in each homecoming with exuberant happiness. Whenever he spoke of Prince George, a friend noted, it was with a softening of the voice and a look, half smile and half pathos, which he reserved for those he loved. Bruised by his own exclusion from affairs of State until he ascended the throne in his sixtieth year, the King determined that his heir should be better equipped to succeed him. So the Prince received the more important Cabinet papers; and whenever he stayed at Windsor he was given a writing-table next to that of his father. Both those privileges would have been inconceivable in the previous reign.

Prince George's devotion to his father was no less firm. Certain tremors in the King's private life must have disturbed his own domestic quietude.

Yet only once is he known to have ventured a word of protest: on learning that the bowling alley at Sandringham had been turned into, of all things, a library. Nor would he tolerate censure of his father's conduct by others. The future Archbishop Lang once expressed regret to the Prince that the King had attended a Roman Catholic requiem mass for the assassinated King Carlos of Portugal, adding that to find a precedent it would be necessary to go back to James II. Although no champion of the ecumenical movement, the Prince retorted: 'And a very good precedent, too.' Lang, whose silver tongue never learned the virtue of silence, primly reminded the Prince of James II's fate.

The Prince of Wales displayed not only the understandable loyalty of a son to his father, but also the awe of a subject for his sovereign. That one king at least could do no wrong was for him not so much a constitutional dictum as a literal truth. He took a hierarchical view of humanity: the rich king in his castle, the rich prince at his gate. While his father lived, this subservience robbed their intimacy of spontaneity and vigour; and once Prince George had himself succeeded to the throne, it inhibited his own relationship with both wife and children.

A hurtful legend has pursued the memory of the Prince and Princess of Wales: that he was an unkind father, she an unfeeling mother. There is no contemporary evidence to support such a myth, much to disprove it. The children were as happy as any of their generation. Admiral Fisher wrote to his wife from Balmoral in the autumn of 1903: 'The two little Princes are splendid little boys and chattered away the whole of their lunch-time, not the faintest shyness.' David, the future King Edward VIII, was then aged nine; Bertie, the future King George VI, was seven.

Nearly half a century later, in exile as Duke of Windsor, the eldest child wrote a volume of memoirs entitled *A King's Story*. In it he dwelt with irony on the supposed shortcomings of his parents. He admitted, however, that whatever frustrations he recalled in retrospect, the years immediately before and after his father's succession to the throne had been far from miserable. 'Sandringham', he wrote, 'possessed most of the ingredients for a boyhood idyll.' And a little later: 'I find today that my diary during that period at Windsor was actually full of sunny and intimate details.' There were long hours exploring the royal estates on bicycles, boisterous games of golf, lavish presents on birthdays and at Christmas. The Prince of Wales taught his sons to shoot when they were thirteen, allowing them to roam the coverts at the end of the season in search of stray cock pheasants. 'He laughed and joked,' the Duke of Windsor recalled, 'and those "small days" at Sandringham provided some of my happiest memories of him.'

Like the children of most royal families, they worked and played alone, denied the stimulus of classroom and football field, but they were a high-spirited band of brothers, abetted and sometimes dominated in their schemes by a single sister. Affecting to believe that their French tutor, Monsieur Hua, yearned for his native diet of frogs, they tricked him into eating a dish of tadpoles on toast. Professor Oswald, who laboured to teach them German, was given an even rougher passage. 'It isn't only that Prince Albert is inattentive,' he complained, 'but when I scold him he just pulls my beard.' The boys played pranks even on their supposed ogre of a father. One day they watched in ecstasy as the spoon with which he was stirring his tea dissolved in the cup; it came from a joke-shop and was made of an alloy with a low melting point. That does not sound like an oppressive father and his dejected children.

How then did the legend originate? Mabell, Countess of Airlie, Princess May's girlhood friend and subsequently her lifelong companion and lady-in-waiting, wrote in old age:

King George v and Queen Mary have often been depicted as stern unloving parents, but this they most certainly were not. Remembering them in my early days at Sandringham before their family was even complete, I believe that they were more conscientious and more truly devoted to their children than the majority of parents in that era. The tragedy was that neither had any understanding of a child's mind.

The Victorian upper classes were accustomed to rear their children behind green baize doors, employing a whole hierarchy of nannies and nursery maids, governesses and tutors, to relieve themselves of day-to-day cares. The Prince and Princess of Wales, choosing to spend much of the year in the cramped quarters of York Cottage, saw more of their children than did their contemporaries in spacious country houses. Yet there were constraints in the relationship, some avoidable, others inseparable from a royal heritage. 'While affection was certainly not lacking in my upbringing,' the Duke of Windsor wrote, 'the mere circumstances of my father's position interposed an impalpable barrier that inhibited the closer continuing intimacy of conventional family life.'

Awed by his approaching succession to the throne and apprehensive of his fitness for the task, the Prince of Wales imposed a rigid pattern of conduct both on himself and on his sons. He loved his children, was proud of their good looks, gave praise where it was due. 'I must compliment you on your manners and general behaviour,' he wrote to David in 1907. 'Everyone was very pleased with you at Cowes.' Yet even by the stern standards of the age he was a watchful and exacting father who let nothing go by default. His early years in the navy had trained him to instant submission and he saw no reason why his own sons should not benefit from the same discipline. 'Now that you are five years old,' he told Bertie, 'I hope you will always try and be obedient and do at once what you are told, as you will find it will come much easier to you the sooner you begin.' Not many children can ever have received so daunting a birthday letter.

The Prince of Wales had a quick temper which did not spare even the trusted Bigge, much less his own sons. Children, however, accept sudden gusts of adult rage as among the natural phenomena of a capricious world, like thunderstorms and pallid puddings and bedtime. They find it harder to bear the embarrassing chaff with which parents as well as schoolmasters sometimes express good humour. The Prince of Wales, like his father, was a lifelong exponent of the art, practising it relentlessly on family and friends. During an inspection of the fleet he caused agonies of shame to the future Lord Mountbatten by loudly inquiring about a rag doll which the young midshipman had dearly loved in childhood. Archbishop Lang, on resuming his duties after an illness that cost him his hair and made him look twenty years older, was greeted by his sovereign 'with characteristic guffaws'. And on one of the very last evenings that King George v dined among friends at Sandringham, he asked a guest: 'How many woodcock did you shoot today?' followed instantly by the question: 'And how many did you miss?'

Archbishops and skilled shots could look after themselves; the young lacked protection against such sustained banter. Some of the jokes to which they were exposed may well have left an emotional scar. King Edward vii, taking his little grandchildren down to Portsmouth for the return of the *Ophir* from her eight-month cruise, warned them that their parents' faces would have turned quite black from exposure to tropical sun. In the same jovial vein, the Prince of Wales wrote on the birth of his fourth son Prince Henry, known as Harry: 'David of course asked some very funny questions. I told him that baby had flown in at the window during the night, and he at once asked where his wings were and I said they had been cut off.' The Victorians brought up their offspring unaided by psychologists.

Both as heir to the throne and as king, the Prince of Wales appeared to treat other people's children with a genial indulgence which he denied to his own. On shooting mornings it was his habit at 11 o'clock to eat a sandwich carried for him by his loader in a little silver box. One day, as he had not asked for it by 12, the loader gave it to the young son of a Norfolk neighbour who was following the guns. A few minutes later the King demanded his rations, but in vain. He was hugely amused by the culprit's inadvertent *lèse-majesté*, and ever afterwards would address him as The Boy Who Ate My Sandwiches. He also liked to call on the daughter of another Sandringham neighbour whose father was serving abroad as Governor-General of the Sudan. 'What have you got in your larder today, Penelope?' he would inquire, 'I am sure you are a very bad housekeeper.' The girl, wishing she could boast of sucking pig and quails in aspic, had to admit to nothing more luxurious than cottage pie. 'Well,' the King replied, 'you must not starve while your parents are away'; then, to the keeper: 'See that Miss Maffey is sent a brace of pheasants and a hare.'

His own children could never depend on the good humour of those occasional encounters. But then his own children were destined for a royal role which, he believed, could be learned only under a quarterdeck discipline tempered by the equally alarming badinage of the gunroom.

The Prince of Wales might have established an easier relationship with his family had he been able to commit to paper the affection which he felt in his heart but found so difficult to express. He was, however, a laborious correspondent. Letters to his children might begin with reflections on the weather and end, particularly in later years, with a damn and blast at the Government of the day, but their bulk consisted largely of what his children had already told him in their own letters, perhaps embroidered with a few paternal words of encouragement or rebuke. Among the more lively is this exchange between Bertie, then a midshipman in HMS *Collingwood*, and his father:

On Friday night after I was turned in, I fell out of my hammock, with the help of someone else, and hit my left eye on my chest. It swelled up very much and yesterday it was bandaged up. I did not cut it, or actually hurt the eye-ball but it was very sore all round. It is much better to-day but I expect I shall have a black eye for a few days.

His father replied: 'Sorry that with the help of someone else you fell out of your hammock and hit your eye on your chest, it must have hurt a good deal, but glad it didn't damage your eye permanently. I should do the same to the other fellow if I got a chance.'

And here is the future King Edward VIII, then an Oxford undergraduate, giving his father a circumspect account of a Bullingdon Club dinner: 'Most of them got rather, if not to say very, excited and I came back early. There was a good deal of champagne drunk and that accounted for it. It is interesting for me to see the various forms of amusement that undergraduates indulge in.' David's letter evoked this reply: 'I was amused with your description of your dinner at the Bullingdon Club, it appears that a good many of the young men drank more champagne than was good for them and became very noisy and excited, different people have different ways of enjoying themselves.'

Although the Prince of Wales ensured that his children grew up with impeccable manners and an entire lack of that high-born arrogance which characterized so many other royal houses of Europe, his reputation as a father has been much disparaged in print. Even Harold Nicolson, in his tactful and urbane official life of King George v, felt impelled to write: 'In seeking to instill into his children his own ideals of duty and obedience, he was frequently pragmatic and sometimes harsh.' Nicolson gave renewed currency to that disobliging view with an anecdote he omitted from his own book but later made available to Randolph Churchill for use in a biography of the seventeenth Earl of Derby. Since the story has been widely quoted to illustrate the King's unsympathetic character, it should be examined with a more critical eye than either Nicolson or Churchill brought to bear. Here then, in Nicolson's words, is the tale which he claimed to have heard from Lord Derby and subsequently told to Randolph Churchill, who published it verbatim in 1959. It thus appeared in print for the first time nearly half a century after the episode it purported to record:

Derby was distressed by the way King George bullied his children, and he ventured one day at Knowsley, when they were walking up and down the terrace, to raise the subject, justifying his remarks on the ground that he was the King's oldest friend. He said what delightful companions his own children had become for him when they grew up, and begged the King to realise that the royal children were on the verge of manhood and that he was missing very much in life by frightening them and continuing to treat them as if they were naughty schoolboys. Lord Derby told me that the King remained silent for some four minutes after this and then said: 'My father was frightened of his mother; I was frightened of my father, and I am damned well going to see to it that my children are frightened of me.'

An anecdote almost half a century old is likely to have suffered many vicissitudes. Derby, Nicolson and Churchill were all truthful men, but Derby was not the most accurate of chroniclers; Nicolson's sensibility sometimes prompted him to improve the rough-hewn material of lesser stylists; and Churchill was a biographer who inherited his father's relish for the drama of history. To put the matter bluntly, there is hardly a detail of the story which resists scrutiny or can be confirmed from independent sources.

Although born in the same year as the future King George v, Derby was neither his oldest nor his most intimate friend; the Duke of Buccleuch and Sir Charles Cust, to mention only two, had longer and far stronger claims on the King's affection. Nor would Derby have risked royal displeasure by so bold a display of candour; genial but irresolute, he was all things to all men. It is equally unlikely that the hot-tempered and outspoken King would have paused for four whole minutes while digesting Derby's admonition. Least convincing of all is the King's supposed retort. There is scarcely any reliable evidence that the future King Edward VII was frightened of Queen Victoria, none that the future King George v was frightened of King Edward. Each, in common with his generation, was brought up to respect his parents; on the steps of the throne, respect turned to awe. It is that numinous quality which throughout history has separated a prince from a president and a sovereign from his subjects – even when they happened to be his own children. Some may find it anachronistic in an age of parliamentary democracy, yet cannot deny its continuing potency. The Duke of Windsor well recognized the subtlety of the relationship when he wrote in his memoirs: 'Kings and Queens are only secondarily fathers and mothers.'

If Prince George was an anxious and overbearing father, Princess May was an uncommonly detached mother. That social conscience which she had inherited from the Duchess of Teck embraced the welfare of children in general rather than her own brood. It prompted her in 1904 to question the Prime Minister about the adequacy of classrooms and meals in State schools. ('When I went to Eton more than forty years ago,' Mr Balfour replied unhelpfully, 'few parents or masters thought it necessary either that our schoolroom should be properly warmed, or that we should have anything to eat before early school!') Yet she hated the routine of child-bearing and took no interest in babies. Like all affluent parents of the day she delegated the upbringing of her children to others; there was nothing unusual or heartless in that. But even in York Cottage, a house no larger than a vicarage, she failed to discover that a nurse was physically ill-treating one of her sons and ruining the digestion of another for life.

As the children grew up, Princess May's shyness dissolved into warmth and gaiety. In contrast to the admonition and reproof which they associated with their father's library, their mother's sitting-room came to represent a sanctuary. She did her best to protect the adolescent princes from the rebukes of a man whose ingrained conservatism could not tolerate changing standards of behaviour and dress. Yet her influence was limited. She believed that her first duty was to a husband invested with both the lonely burden and the mystique of monarchy. 'I always have to remember', she once said of her sons, 'that their father is also their King.'

Whatever the failings of Princess May as a parent, she herself failed to recognize them. In 1908 Lord Esher sent her a copy of Edmund Gosse's recently published *Father and Son*, that classic work on the upbringing of a sensitive child. 'This book', the author explained, 'is the record of a struggle between two temperaments, two consciences and almost two epochs. It ended, as was inevitable, in disruption.' The Princess thanked Esher warmly for his present: 'I am delighted with "Father and Son", quite admirably written as you say, and one thoroughly enters into the narrow-minded surroundings of the child's life and feels it is all so true and real.' 'How misguided some people are', she ended her letter, 'without realising it.'

Even while the two eldest sons of the Prince of Wales were in the nursery, their father decided that they should one day follow him into the Royal Navy. In the spring of 1902 he appointed Mr Henry Hansell to be their tutor. The son of a Norfolk squire, Hansell had taken Second Class Honours in History at Oxford, taught at both public and preparatory schools, and ensured that Prince Arthur of Connaught passed into Eton. 'Absolutely straight but very broad-minded,' Lord Derby wrote of him, 'I can imagine no man better able to guide rather than drive a boy.' The Prince agreed: 'I always think his judgement is good.' Hansell, however, shared Dalton's humourless solemnity without Dalton's intellectual appetite. He sent this report to the Prince of Wales when Bertie was eight: 'I am very sorry to say that Prince Albert has caused two painful scenes in his bedroom this week. On the second occasion I understand that he narrowly escaped giving his brother a very severe kick, it being absolutely unprovoked.'

Although conscientious, Hansell was qualified for his task more by muscle than by mind. In youth he had excelled at cricket and football; as an introspective bachelor of forty had spent his leisure at the helm of a sailing boat or striding over the golf links. He lacked the inspiration of the born teacher. The Duke of Windsor later wrote of him:

I do not wish to be critical of Mr Hansell: but, on looking back over those five curiously ineffectual years under him, I am appalled to discover how little I really learned. He could scarcely be said to have possessed a positive personality. If he harboured strong views about anything, he was careful to conceal them. Although I was in his care on and off for more than twelve years I am to-day unable to recall anything brilliant or original that he ever said.

It is to Hansell's credit that he recognized the inadequacy both of his own talents and of any attempt to educate a future sovereign by private tuition alone. He repeatedly warned the Prince of Wales that if the boys were to hold their own at Naval College they ought to exchange the seclusion of Sandringham for a well-managed preparatory school. There, he urged, they would benefit not only from a specialized curriculum but also from the friendship and rivalries of communal life. The Prince would have none of it. 'My brother and I never went to a preparatory school,' he told Hansell. 'The Navy will teach David all that he needs to know.'

The Prince of Wales also harboured Daltonian doubts about the wholesomeness of boarding schools. Thirty years earlier, Queen Victoria had insisted that if Prince Eddy and Prince George were to be sent to Wellington College, they must live not in the school but in a nearby, quite separate house. 'I have a great fear', she wrote, 'of young and carefully brought up Boys mixing with older Boys and indeed with any Boys in general, for the mischief done by bad Boys and the things they may hear and learn from them cannot be overrated.' Her grandson, now grown to manhood, similarly feared the perils of a fashionable preparatory school. He would keep his children at home until they were old enough to join a well-supervised and morally aseptic naval establishment.

One shortcoming of Hansell's methods came to light when the Prince of Wales discovered that his own eldest son, in his eleventh year, could not calculate the average weight of the stags shot by his father at Balmoral during the previous stalking season. So he engaged a special tutor who taught the boys enough mathematics for each in turn to pass into the Naval College at Osborne. Their progress was not maintained. Prince Edward emerged from his first term 'not far from the bottom'; Prince Albert's place was sixty-eighth out of sixty-eight.

Princess May, who had no high opinion of Hansell, recognized the bleakness of his regime. She tried to modify it by introducing the children to her own cultural interests, yet dared not challenge her husband's stubborn will. She had told Lord Esher, one of her very few confidants:

See how George has suffered from not knowing French and German. The other day in Paris *I* enjoyed everything. But *he* was not really amused. He knows nothing about pictures or history. He is told something about Francis I, and it conveys nothing to him. He could not follow the plays easily, and it is a great pity.

Her eldest son, she continued, ought to learn history and languages, even if he had to follow a different curriculum from the other cadets at Osborne; but her husband disagreed. She added, with prophetic insight: 'Albert ought to be educated also. Look at William IV – he was a long way from the throne, yet he succeeded.'

Not until the Prince of Wales had ascended the throne in 1910 and come to realize the inadequacy of his own education did he concede that Prince Edward's plans should be modified: the boy was to abandon his career in the navy, to study in France and Germany, to enter Magdalen College, Oxford, as an undergraduate. The new King made another concession during the early years of his reign. He sent his third and fourth sons, Prince Henry (later Duke of Gloucester) and Prince George (later Duke of Kent) to St Peter's Court, a preparatory school at Broadstairs, on the south coast. Although they undoubtedly enjoyed mixing with boys of their own age, Hansell may have exaggerated the academic galvanism of such institutions. The twelve-year-old Prince Henry was told sharply by his mother: 'Do for goodness sake wake up and work harder and use the brains God has given you.... All you write about is your everlasting football of which I am heartily sick.' And Prince George, in spite of being the only one of Princess May's children to inherit her aesthetic tastes and collector's eye, fared no better than his brothers in the naval classroom. Prince Albert wrote of him:

'He has kept up the best traditions of my family by passing out of Dartmouth one from bottom, the same place as I did.'

Reluctantly abandoning both children and pheasants, the Prince and Princess of Wales left Sandringham in October 1905 for their first visit to India. They landed at Bombay from the battleship *Renown* on 9 November and sailed for Europe on 19 March 1906. During those eighteen weeks they covered 9,000 miles by train and several hundred more by carriage and motor car. It was a journey that carried them to Jaipur and Lahore, Delhi and Agra, Gwalior and Lucknow, and so on to Calcutta, Rangoon and Mandalay; then by sea across the Bay of Bengal to Madras; on to Mysore and then North to Hyderabad; through the Central Provinces to the north-west frontier; down to Karachi and the voyage home.

The cold print of that itinerary conceals an exhilarating and at times almost mystical experience which the Prince and Princess of Wales never forgot. More than seventy years later it is not easy to recapture the near unanimous satisfaction and pride with which Great Britain gazed upon her Indian Empire: more a sacred trust than an administrative or commercial union, a partnership in which the balance of advantage was held to lie less with the governors than with the governed. Lord Curzon, one of whose last duties after nearly seven years as Viceroy was to welcome the royal visitors to India, embroidered the theme with rare eloquence:

For where else in the world has a race gone forth and subdued, not a country or a kingdom, but a continent, and that continent peopled, not by savage tribes, but by races with traditions and a civilization older than our own, with a history not inferior to ours in dignity or romance; subduing them not to the law of the sword, but to the rule of justice, bringing peace and order and good government to nearly one-fifth of the entire human race, and holding them with so mild a restraint that the rulers are the merest handful amongst the ruled, a tiny speck of white foam upon a dark and thunderous ocean?

The Prince and Princess of Wales shared those beliefs. Curzon himself, however, left an unfavourable impression on his guests. Three months before their arrival, having scarcely begun his second term of office as Viceroy, he had been provoked to resign. It was the culmination of his bitter quarrel with both Lord Kitchener, Commander-in-Chief of the Army in India, and the Cabinet in London: a formidable pair of adversaries. Ostensibly the dispute was between two conflicting views of military administration, but those issues were blurred by personal enmity. Balfour's Government, obliged to sacrifice one or other of the Indian antagonists, decided that Curzon was the more expendable. To succeed him as Viceroy they appointed the Earl of Minto, a less brilliant but energetic proconsul who had five times ridden in the Grand National and survived a broken neck.

Curzon, having spent many months planning the tour of the Prince and Princess of Wales, begged that he might remain in India long enough to entertain them in Calcutta, the then capital and seat of government. Balfour and his colleagues were in no mood to make the slightest concession to so disobedient and openly contemptuous a viceroy. At the suggestion of the King, however, they accepted a compromise. Minto's arrival in India was to be postponed for a week so that Curzon might have the honour of receiving the Prince and Princess as they disembarked from HMS *Renown* at Bombay. The royal tour would then begin. A week later Curzon would return to Bombay to greet his successor and to hand over the office of viceroy with traditional formality; next day he would sail for Europe. Curzon did not keep his side of the bargain. He welcomed the royal party as they set foot for the first time on Indian soil; but a week later he cancelled the compliments that should have been paid to the new Viceroy at the quayside, failed to receive him as custom demanded on the steps of Government House, and after an embarrassing pause appeared in a shooting coat, and slippers. For his own departure on the following day, however, Curzon drove down to the dock with a full viceregal escort of two cavalry regiments and a battery of the Royal Horse Artillery. The Superior Person, as he was known in Oxford days, had lived up to his name.

The Prince and Princess of Wales had already left Bombay before Minto's arrival. But on reaching Calcutta at the end of December to stay with the new Viceroy and Lady Minto, they not only heard of Curzon's outrageous behaviour, they had a saga of their own to tell. Curzon, it seemed, had neglected to supervise the arrangements for their own arrival in Bombay. Their rooms at Government House had been occupied by others until the very last moment, so that they almost found the servants changing the sheets on the beds; and because Curzon had insisted on using the viceregal train until only four days before the royal party began their tour in it, neither carriages nor locomotive had been properly cleaned or overhauled.

In a more relaxed age, such lapses may appear trivial. In the unyielding social structure of British India, any breach of protocol that affected the sovereign or his representative was profoundly shocking. The King, replying to the Prince of Wales's account of events at Bombay, wrote: 'It is simply inconceivable that Lord Curzon should have shown such bad manners. Let us hope that his state of health had much to do with it, as his mind before leaving India was simply unhinged.' The clubs, officers' messes and drawing-rooms, which thrived on tales of social solecism and Curzonian arrogance, were less charitable. They believed that Curzon's discourtesy had been deliberate. 'Imagine sending to succeed *me*', he was alleged to have said, 'a gentleman who only jumps hedges.' The royal party heard many such stories during their tour and did not forget them.

Talks with Kitchener also hardened the mind of the Prince of Wales against Curzon. He wrote to his father in January: 'I have gained a lot of most interesting information since I have been in Calcutta with regard to the controversy between Lord C. and Lord K. I fear the latter has been grossly misrepresented.' The Prince and his staff, particularly Sir Arthur Bigge, returned to England with an ingrained prejudice against Curzon that persisted for many years.

Nothing was wanting in the hospitality of the new Viceroy and his wife. Lady Minto wrote in her journal:

During our absence at Barrackpore 700 men have been employed in painting, cleaning and in preparing the house for the Royal visit ... The grounds in front of the house have fifty large tents to accommodate the staff and servants – not our English idea of tents which one sees at Aldershot, but great rooms with a brick floor covered with mats and carpets; each person has a bed-room, sitting room and bath-room, and even the valets have two arm chairs apiece. . . .

By luncheon time bullock waggons by the score piled with Royal luggage were to be seen at the back premises stretching as far as the eye could see. Five hundred coolies have been engaged to handle the luggage.

The only hitch occurred at a levée. Lady Minto's record of it is imperturbable:

A rumour was circulated that the Prince did not intend remaining beyond a certain hour, upon which a free fight ensued ... Men fainted and were nearly trampled on, their coats were torn, the plaster was broken off the pillars, the barriers were thrown down. The maimed and bleeding of course had to return home, but the remaining 2,123 were disposed of in one hour and three quarters.

The Prince's courtly manners were much appreciated. Whenever he and the Viceroy appeared together in public, he insisted that the King-Emperor's representative should take precedence. Here Lady Minto describes a dinner party in Government House, Calcutta:

Shortly before the ladies left the room the Prince said to me: 'I hope the Viceroy realizes that I shall join him after dessert; he must on no account come round to me.' I told him how much Minto felt the difficulty of the position. His answer was: 'Surely I am the first person to show consideration to my father's representative?' He then took up the menu, on which he wrote: 'You must remain in your place. I will come and sit beside you when the ladies leave the dining-room.'

Lady Minto enjoyed her guest's mild indiscretions. The Prince described a recent dinner at Buckingham Palace enlivened by Margot Asquith, wife of the future Prime Minister. Seeing Queen Alexandra and the rotund Lord Halsbury in conversation, Mrs Asquith had exclaimed: 'Look at beauty and the beast.' The Prince continued: 'As this was said in the hearing of Lady Halsbury, there was rather a scene and Lady Halsbury refused to accept her apology.'

His high spirits could be deceptive. Sir James Dunlop Smith, the Viceroy's private secretary, wrote in his diary:

After Church the Prince sent for me and I had a talk with him for $1\frac{1}{2}$ hours. My impression of him in Calcutta was that he was a very cheery talkative young sailor and just a little bit too outspoken. But at Barrackpore I found that he has distinct ability, great shrewdness and a wonderful memory. He talked to me about Native States, the Indian Army, Irrigation, Railways and Sport.

Throughout the tour, the Prince owed much to the guidance of Sir Walter Lawrence, temporarily appointed to be his chief of staff. One of the ablest members of the Indian Civil Service, he had recently retired after five years as private secretary to Lord Curzon; his knowledge of the subcontinent was therefore exceptionally wide. The Prince and Lawrence acquired a respect for each other that survived occasional differences. The Prince would object to the Curzonian eloquence of the speeches which Lawrence wrote for him. 'Too high-faluting,' he complained, 'everyone will know those are not my words.' And he hated to be shadowed by the detectives whom Lawrence had summoned for his protection. The chief of staff also laid down conditions: that the Prince should break with custom by accepting no presents from the Indian Princes, who otherwise would have competed with each other in extravagance.

The notes on India which the Prince of Wales prepared for the King bear every mark of his own character: observant, kindly and cautious. What particularly strikes the reader nearly eighty years later is an entire absence of that colour prejudice which permeated every level of society in the Edwardian Age. There is a well-known story of how Sir Charles Cust, in attendance on the Prince at a shooting party in England, rebuked a woman guest who had shown undue familiarity towards his master: 'I have grown up on the steps of the throne and I can tell you that there are three kinds of people in the world: blacks, whites and Royalties.' The Prince himself drew no such distinction between British subjects of different colour. It was a family virtue which Queen Victoria had constantly displayed, not least in employing an Indian, the Munshi Abdul Karim, as a confidential secretary. In her eightieth year she wrote to the Prime Minister, Lord Salisbury:

The future Vice Roy must really shake himself more and more free from his red-tapist narrow-minded Council and Entourage. He must be *more independent*, *must hear for himself* what the *feelings* of the Natives really are, and do what he thinks right and not be guided by the *snobbish* and vulgar, over-bearing and offensive behaviour of our Civil and Political Agents, if we are to go on peaceably and happily in India, and to be liked and beloved by high and low – as well as respected as we ought to be – and not trying to trample on the people and continually reminding them and making them feel that they are a conquered people.

King Edward VII, touring India as Prince of Wales, had similarly written: 'Because a man has a black face and a different religion from our own, there is no reason why he should be treated as a brute.' And having ascended the throne, he complained of 'the disgraceful habit of officers in the King's service speaking of the inhabitants in India, many of them sprung from the great races, as "niggers"'.

His son noted in 1906 that although instances of ill treatment were rare, disdainful attitudes could be hardly less wounding:

I could not help being struck by the way in which all salutations by the Natives were disregarded by the persons to whom they were given. Evidently we are too much inclined to look upon them as a conquered and down-trodden race and the Native, who is becoming more and more educated, realizes this. I could not help noticing that the general bearing of the European towards the Native was to say the least unsympathetic. In fact not the same as that of superiors to inferiors at home.

He was astonished to learn that no Indian, whatever his birth or education, could be a member of the clubs frequented by Europeans; and he remained unconvinced by Sir Walter Lawrence's explanation that the clubs would otherwise become too crowded and that the British required an evening of unfettered conversation after a long day's work among Indians. The ruling chiefs, he continued, 'ought to be treated with greater tact and sympathy, more as equals than inferiors. They should no longer be treated as schoolboys but even consulted by the Government on matters which concern their States individually and as a whole.' Indeed, he wondered whether the term 'Native States' was not in itself outmoded and offensive.

With a characteristic attention to detail, the Prince of Wales also noted some puzzling anomalies. Why was the King-Emperor's birthday celebrated in India on 23 June, the hottest time of the year, instead of on his actual birthday, 9 November? Why were civil servants not allowed white uniforms? Why were the Governors of Bombay and Madras not greeted on official occasions by the National Anthem? Why did not all British officers in Native regiments wear the same uniform as Native officers?

The remarkable aspect of the Prince's views is not that he wished to see his father's Indian subjects treated with justice and respect – by 1906 those

sentiments were widely shared – but that he did not accept the permanence
of British tutelage as inevitable. He wrote to Lord Esher in the year after
his Indian tour:

Personally I think we have now come to the parting of the ways, we cannot let
things rest as they are. We must either trust the Natives more and give them a
greater share in the Government or anyhow allow them to express their views; or
else we must double our Civil Service, the latter have now got out of touch with
the villages on account of the great increase in their work, it is now all office work,
where formerly they went amongst the Natives every day, who learned to know
them and trust them.

In recognizing the possibility – to put it no higher – that the people of
India must be encouraged to mould their own political destiny, the ill-
educated heir to the throne revealed more vision than the most intellectually
brilliant of viceroys, Lord Curzon. During his seven years in India, Curzon
had worked unsparingly to ensure the prosperity of her 300 million people,
to preserve their customs and monuments, to maintain the highest standards
in every branch of the administration. Kitchener and his staff had impressed
the Prince with tales of Curzon's hostility to the army. What they failed to
tell the visitor was its main cause: the severity with which the Viceroy had
punished the mindless brutality committed by private soldiers and con-
doned by their officers. 'I will not be a party to any of the scandalous
hushing-up of bad cases,' Curzon wrote to the King, 'or to the theory that
a white man may kick or batter a black man to death with impunity because
he is only a "damned nigger".' It was admirable but it was not enough.
Curzon would do anything for the Indian except trust him. When a friend
in the Cabinet wrote from England to ask why he did not educate Indians
for senior government posts, he replied: 'We cannot take the Natives up
into the administration. They are crooked-minded and corrupt. We have
got therefore to go on ruling them and we can only do it with success
by being both kindly and virtuous. I daresay I am talking rather like a
schoolmaster; but after all, the millions I have to manage are less than
schoolchildren.'

The Prince, by contrast, saw that some measure of self-government was
the only alternative to an increasingly ponderous and alienated British
administration. He liked neither solution; but at least his practical mind
recognized the existence of both. The Prince did, however, share with
Curzon a sense of grievance that his country's well-meaning mission should
evoke only hatred from the Indian National Congress. 'It is becoming a
power for evil,' he told the King, 'it misrepresents every action of the
Government and holds us up to the ignorant masses as monsters and
tyrants.' When in the course of his tour he met Mr Gopal Gokhale,

1 The Prince and Princess of Wales, later King Edward VII and Queen Alexandra, with their two sons in about 1868. Prince George sits on his mother's knee; his elder brother, Prince Albert Victor, stands by his father. The Prince of Wales, recalling the harsh discipline of his own childhood, was a kind and indulgent father. The Princess and her children doted on each other. Well into manhood, Prince George would begin a letter to her: 'My own sweet little beloved Motherdear.'

2 Prince George: a study by
J. Sant, R.A., 1872.

3 A family group, 1873. The three sisters are, from left to right, Princess Louise, who was
to marry the Duke of Fife; Princess Maud, later Queen of Norway; and Princess Victoria,
who never married. They were not a healthy brood. 'Most wretched,' Queen Victoria
wrote, 'excepting Georgie, who is always merry and rosy.'

4 Prince George as a naval cadet. He was a sturdy, handsome and lively boy who showed to advantage against his taller but lethargic elder brother. Their tutor, however, the Rev. J. N. Dalton, would ponderously note in a big bound book such faults of George's as 'fretfulness of temper' and 'self-approbation'.

5 HMS *Bacchante*, a fully-rigged corvette of 4,000 tons with auxiliary engines, in which the two brothers sailed round the world. Dalton, who accompanied them, had from the beginning mistrusted her seaworthiness. He was proved right in the Indian Ocean when the *Bacchante* was disabled by a storm, drifting helplessly for three days and nights.

6 Princess May of Teck. She was first betrothed to Prince Albert Victor, Duke of Clarence, who died of influenza in 1892, six weeks before the wedding. In the following year she was married to his younger brother Prince George, now in direct line of succession to the throne and created Duke of York. Her new sisters-in-law were jealous of her superior education, mistook her shyness for arrogance and despised the morganatic blood of the Tecks. 'Poor May,' Princess Louise would remark spitefully, 'with her Württemberg hands.'

President of the Congress Party, he asked: 'Would the people of India be happier if you ran the country?' Gokhale replied: 'No, Sir, I do not say they would be happier, but they would have more self-respect.' 'That may be,' said the Prince, 'but I cannot see how there can be real self-respect while the Indians treat their women as they do now.' 'Yes,' said Gokhale, 'that is the great blot.' The Congress leader later reproached Sir Walter Lawrence for having put that retort into the Prince's mouth, but Lawrence denied it.

The Prince of Wales mistrusted the motives of the nationalist leaders, confident that India's needs were best served by a just paternalism. As heir to the throne he shared his father's anxiety at the constitutional reforms inspired by the Liberal Government. As King-Emperor he watched India's troubled advance to independence with concern and sometimes anger. Yet he was no die-hard partisan. Rather did he see that his role transcended the conflict of politics; that his duty lay in the healing of discord and the protection of the inarticulate. On returning to London, in a speech which required weeks of preparation and days of rehearsal, he called for 'a better understanding and a closer union of hearts between the Mother Country and her Indian Empire'.

Princess May, too, acquired a lifelong love of India during that winter tour. Before leaving England she had read several substantial works on the history and religion of the sub-continent. 'She knows more about the country', Dunlop Smith wrote in his diary, 'than a good many ladies I know out here who have been years in India.' She and her husband were alike moved to see the Union Jack floating over the fortress of Jamrud and stirred by the splendour of mediaeval pageantry which greeted them at Benares. But her curiosity and imagination opened up horizons that lay hidden from the Prince. 'We went on the bridge,' she wrote as the *Renown* began the long voyage home, 'and watched dear beautiful India vanish from our sight.' Those romantic memories never faded. Nearly fifty years later, on the night before she died, she had a book about India read aloud to her.

The Prince and Princess of Wales were soon on their travels again. Within a few weeks of returning from the East, they witnessed two of the traditional hazards of European monarchy: attempted assassination in Spain and democracy in Norway. The first took place at the wedding in Madrid of Princess Ena of Battenberg to the reigning sovereign, Alfonso XIII. The bride, a daughter of Princess Beatrice, Queen Victoria's youngest child, was obliged to abandon the Anglican faith of her upbringing before marrying into the most tenaciously Roman Catholic of all royal houses. The Prince of Wales, her first cousin, did not attempt to hide his disapproval. Two months before the wedding, Dunlop Smith noted in his Indian diary: 'The Prince and the King are *very* angry about Ena Battenberg marrying the King of Spain and turning Roman Catholic. The Prince's language wasn't even Parliamentary and the Princess had to say "George!!!" more than once.'

That outburst at Princess Ena's conversion sprang less from religious bigotry than from a respect for established custom. It took unlikely forms. Stern disapproval had recently fallen on Sir Walter Lawrence, who was lunching one Sunday with the Wales family. When he declined the roast beef, the Prince said: 'You call yourself an Englishman and do not eat roast beef on Sunday? You cannot be an Englishman.' The reluctant carnivore saw all the little eyes of the children on him, as though he were a renegade.

On the way to Madrid for the wedding, the Prince and Princess of Wales spent a day in Paris. 'We went to the Salon', he wrote, 'and saw some ghastly pictures.' Worse was to come. Here is the Prince's own account of what followed the marriage ceremony:

Just before our carriage reached the Palace, we heard a loud report and thought it was the first gun of a salute. We soon learned however that when about 200 yards from the Palace in a narrow street, the Calle Mayor, close to the Italian Embassy, a bomb was thrown from an upper window at the King and Queen's carriage. It burst between the wheel horses and the front of the carriage, killing about 20 people and wounding about 50 or 60, mostly officers and soldiers. Thank God! Alfonso and Ena were not touched although covered with glass from the broken windows. . . .

Of course the bomb was thrown by an anarchist, supposed to be a Spaniard and of course they let him escape. I believe the Spanish police and detectives are about the worst in the world. No precautions whatever had been taken, they are most happy go lucky people here. Naturally, on their return, both Alfonso and Ena broke down, no wonder after such an awful experience. Eventually we had lunch about 3. I proposed their healths, not easy after the emotions caused by this terrible affair. . . .

It is one of the ironies of royal life that the first gun of a salute and an anarchist's bomb make precisely the same sound.

A week or two later, the Prince and Princess of Wales sailed across the North Sea in the royal yacht *Victoria and Albert* to attend the coronation at Trondheim of the King and Queen of Norway. For nearly a century Norway had been unhappily united to Sweden. After the dissolution of the union in 1905, Prince Charles of Denmark had ascended the throne of Norway as King Haakon VII. He was, however, a king with a difference. He reigned not by hereditary right but by invitation, not by the Grace of God but by the majority vote of a plebiscite. King Leopold II of the Belgians spoke for all his brother sovereigns in refusing to equate Vox Populi with

Vox Dei. A leader of the Socialist Party, by profession a doctor, once ingratiatingly observed that if ever Belgium became a republic, the King would be chosen as its first president. Leopold replied: 'I suppose, my dear doctor, that you would be flattered if someone told you what an excellent veterinary surgeon you would make.'

There was a sparse attendance of European royalty at the coronation festivities in Trondheim; it is doubtful whether King Edward would have sent his heir to represent him had not the new Queen been his own daughter Maud and the new King a nephew by marriage. Princess May's aunt, the Grand Duchess of Mecklenburg-Strelitz, broke out into a rash of italics: 'A *revolutionary* Coronation! such a *farce*, *I* don't like your being there ... makes me sick and I should say *you too*!' Her niece replied: 'The whole thing seems curious, but we live in *very* modern days.' The Prince of Wales consoled himself with catching a 28-pound salmon, his wife with shopping for furs, china and enamels.

Queen Maud, shy and plagued by neuralgia, never wholly adjusted herself to Norwegian life. Her subjects thought her remote and disobliging; she thought them ungrateful and insatiable. A prolonged legal squabble over the interpretation of her marriage contract cast another shadow over those years of exile. She sought relief in laying out an English garden at the royal residence of Bygdö Kongsgaard and in returning to spend each summer at her house near Sandringham.

Her brother, too, was thankful to be home again. Under Bigge's guidance he settled down to a programme of public engagements that in its essentials differed little from year to year. Lady Monkswell, wife of the chairman of the London County Council, described in her diary the opening of a new Westminster tramway: 'The poor Prince, who has not too much hair, had to hold his hat three inches above his head nearly the whole way to Tooting and back. These kind, good Royalties took such trouble to do everything as well as possible.'

He also broadened his political knowledge by reading Cabinet and Foreign Office papers made available to him by the King's command; attending debates in the House of Lords; sitting on a Royal Commission to consider food and imports in time of war; and dining with the leading statesmen of the day. After one such meeting, Balfour told Esher: 'Except the German Emperor, he is the only royal prince to whom I find I can talk as man to man.' The author of *A Defence of Philosophic Doubt* added: 'He is really clever.' There is no reason to dispute the sincerity of Balfour's first remark; his second was surely a piece of flattery which, knowing his man, he could expect Esher to pass on to the Prince.

For all his growing dedication to duty, the Prince of Wales did not take easily to public life. He was troubled by a succession of minor ailments, including chronic dyspepsia, that was almost certainly due to frayed nerves. When the Prince visited Holy Island in 1908, the architect Edwin Lutyens noted: 'He was terribly alarmed at the gangway up and wanted a wall built. . . . He was awfully anxious to get away when he found the tide was rising; for a sailor I thought him over-nervous.' That year he attended the annual dinner of the Royal Academy of Arts, but absolutely refused to make a speech. Esher wrote: 'However much H.R.H. may dislike it he will have to give way, or the monarchy will be doomed!'

One appointment in particular provoked him to ill temper: that of Lord Warden of the Cinque Ports. The holder of that ancient office had originally been responsible for the defence of the Channel coast by sea and land. In the eighteenth century, however, it had become a well-paid sinecure for a royal favourite such as William Pitt. By the reign of Queen Victoria, the post had not only been stripped of its emoluments; it also required the Lord Warden to pay for the upkeep of his official residence, Walmer Castle. The Duke of Wellington was well content to occupy it on those terms, and died there in 1852. Later Lords Warden included Palmerston, Granville, W.H. Smith, Salisbury and Curzon. The last of these held the appointment for barely four months, resigning in 1904 after his wife had almost died of an illness which he attributed to the faulty drains of the castle. 'That charnel-house,' he called it, 'unfit for human habitation.'

The Prince was not exactly flattered when Balfour, as Prime Minister, invited him to succeed Curzon as Lord Warden. He accepted, but on certain conditions. He would neither occupy nor maintain so inconvenient and insanitary a residence as Walmer Castle; he would dispense with the elaborate installation ceremony; and while proud to bear the title of Lord Warden, he would undertake none of its parochial duties. Almost at once he began to receive requests to perform just those local functions which he had asked to relinquish. He was urged to convene the Court of Shipway, to attend to the business of the Dover Harbour Board, to nominate the magistrates of the Cinque Ports. 'I deeply regret', he told Bigge on 15 August 1905, 'that I ever accepted the position. I was against it from the beginning.' Bigge agreed. The Cinque Ports, he observed, seemed to regard the Prince as their own property. After two years of grumbling, the Brotherhood and Guestlings of the Cinque Ports publicly declared that the Prince's refusal either to be installed as Lord Warden or to fulfil the duties of the office was 'detrimental to the best interests of the Ports and would imperil one of the most ancient Institutions of the Kingdom'. The Prince had had enough of those disrespectful burghers. 'No nonsense this time,' he told Bigge in September 1907, 'I shall stick to my guns and resign.' He was succeeded by Lord Brassey, whose ample fortune derived from railway contracting enabled him to make many improvements to Walmer Castle.

Brassey resigned as Lord Warden in 1913. 'More was expected of me', he wrote, 'than I was able to do.'

Only in name did the Prince of Wales belong to the Silent Service. In contrast with his wife, whose strongest expression of disapproval was, 'Not very wise', he would damn and blast with the best. Lord Esher called him a *garçon éternel*. Perhaps it was the brisk intemperance of youth which continued to release in him a flow of outspoken and sometimes indiscreet talk; or perhaps his chatter masked an insecurity which neither Princess May nor Bigge could relieve. He returned from India in 1906 using what John Morley, the Secretary of State, called 'most unmeasured language' against Curzon; and complained to Charles Hardinge, the future Viceroy, that Curzon had not done a single thing right in India – an opinion which Hardinge instantly challenged.

The Prince found much to disparage in the Liberal Government which was swept to power by the general election of 1906. After dinner at Windsor one night in 1908, he discussed with Winston Churchill who was likely to succeed the ailing Campbell-Bannerman as Prime Minister. When Churchill said it would be Asquith, the Prince replied in a loud voice that although he trusted Asquith, he thought him 'not quite a gentleman'. This remark was overheard by Knollys, who in some alarm went up to Princess Victoria and asked her to break up the conversation. Recalling the episode in 1914, the Prince of Wales, by now King, admitted that Asquith had later shown his dislike, and that he could not blame him: 'I ought not to have said it, and it was a damned stupid thing to say; but Winston repeated it to Asquith, which was a monstrous thing to do, and made great mischief.' At another dinner party the Prince leaned across the table towards Sir George Murray, Permanent Secretary of the Treasury, and bellowed: 'I can't think, Sir George, how you can go on serving that damned fellow Lloyd George.'

Admiral Sir John Fisher was another powerful man whom the Prince's indiscretions turned into a lifelong enemy. They had known each other since 1882 when one was a midshipman in *Bacchante* and the other in command of the *Inflexible*. For many years they maintained a confidential correspondence. In 1903, as Second Sea Lord, Fisher noted: 'He is most cordial and friendly and has helped me immensely with all these new arrangements we have been introducing.' Those changes included improvements in naval entry and education, the recognition of engineering as an essential subject of study and better conditions on the lower deck. In the following year Fisher became First Sea Lord and embarked on a series of even more radical reforms. He strengthened the Home Fleet at the expense of less vulnerable stations; he conserved manpower by scrapping large numbers of small and obsolete ships; he put 'nucleus crews' on board reserve ships to keep them in a state of permanent efficiency; he initiated a construction programme of fast battleships and cruisers with big guns. Fisher also demonstrated his faith in the submarine by taking the Prince to sea in one of them off Portsmouth. Princess May, who remained on the quay, was heard to murmur: 'I shall be very disappointed if George doesn't come up again.'

In 1908 the Prince sailed to Canada and back in HMS *Indomitable*, a new battle cruiser that owed as much to Fisher's vision as to the builders' yard. Her armament was not in doubt – she mounted eight 12-inch guns – nor, by the end of the voyage, was her speed. During the return journey her average was a fraction below 25 knots, almost equalling the record for an Atlantic crossing of 25.08 knots, set by the liner *Lusitania*. Both the Prince and Bigge took their turn in the stokehole, emerging black with coal dust. 'She is indeed a grand ship,' the Prince told Fisher, 'and the finest steamer I have ever seen.'

Those friendly congratulations masked the Prince's growing mistrust of the First Sea Lord. It was not so much that he disagreed with Fisher's naval policy, although he did regret the reduction of Britain's traditional naval strength in the Mediterranean; what provoked him to outspoken hostility was the ruthlessness of Fisher's methods. 'I don't believe in the Sermon on the Mount for managing the Fleet,' the First Sea Lord liked to boast. Or, borrowing both the language and sentiments of the Old Testament, he would swear that of those officers who attempted to thwart him, 'their wives should be widows, their children fatherless, their homes a dunghill'. The price which the nation paid for a powerful navy was a professional feud which embittered personal relationships for almost a generation.

Fisher's principal antagonist was Admiral Lord Charles Beresford, Commander-in-Chief of the Channel Fleet. He was less intellectual, less shrewd, less visionary than Fisher, but wanting neither in patriotism nor courage and adored by his men. Vain and volatile in temperament, he allowed patrician attitudes to affect his judgement; the brother of the fifth Marquess of Waterford scorned Fisher's middle-class parentage and supposed Asiatic blood. The two admirals fought each other with every weapon that came to hand, and both had powerful allies in Parliament, Press and Court. It was a measure of the Prince of Wales's involvement that he should have sought the downfall of one of his father's closest friends and confided in one of his father's most troublesome enemies. For King Edward VII, although sometimes exasperated by Fisher's boisterous manners, was captivated by his prophetic genius and rejuvenated by his salty wit.

Beresford, by contrast, had been in disfavour with the King since a quarrel in the eighteen-nineties. Both men in their time enjoyed the favours of Lady Brooke, who later became that celebrated Socialist, the Countess of Warwick. Indeed, the Prince of Wales (as he then was) would end his letters to her with the unusual endearment: 'Goodnight and God keep you, my own adored little Daisy wife, for ever yours, your only Love.' Beresford was less constant in his affection, breaking off the liaison in 1889 in order to be reconciled to his own wife. Lady Brooke not only reproached her late lover with 'infidelity'; she also appealed to her royal protector, who unwisely had Lady Charles Beresford banished from Court during her husband's absence at sea. On his return to London, Beresford was reported to have struck his future sovereign in the course of an angry encounter at Marlborough House; certainly he cut him dead in the royal enclosure at Ascot. Although apologies were eventually exchanged, their friendship had lost its pristine bloom.

Prince George was a stranger to that world of domestic disorder. He nevertheless gave loud and unqualified support to Beresford in the battle of the Tritons. Any lingering regard which the Prince might have felt for Fisher vanished when he learned that the First Sea Lord had encouraged one of Beresford's subordinate officers, Captain Reginald Bacon, to send him private reports on the conduct of his own commander-in-chief. Beresford wrote to a friend in October 1909: 'I saw the Prince of Wales yesterday at Newmarket. He was really quite violent against the Mulatto. . . . He said . . . that he must go, or the Navy would be ruined. I told him that the Navy was nearly ruined now.'

Fisher was not only aware of the Prince's hostility but also suspected that there had been a spy in his own camp, too. He asked Lord Esher:

Do you think the Prince of Wales at all realizes what would happen if the Public (*and especially the Radical Party*) knew he was actively taking Beresford's side and saying I must go (as he is now doing and openly said at Royal Yacht dinner last Saturday), and that his bosom friend Captain Campbell had been doing 'Judas'! perpetually at my house, and selling me all the time to Beresford!

There was justice in Fisher's complaint. It was imprudent of the Prince to allow himself the same luxury of expression as a private person. The feud between him and Fisher continued to smoulder throughout the next decade.

FOUR

EARLY REIGN

End of an era—Hat, stick and gloves—Poison pens—
Esher and Mensdorff—Royal residences—
Crowned and anointed

ON 6 May 1910, the Prince of Wales entered upon his proud but dreaded heritage. He wrote in his diary:

At 11.45 beloved Papa passed peacefully away and I have lost my best friend and the best of fathers. I never had a word with him in my life. I am heartbroken and overwhelmed with grief but God will help me in my responsibilities and darling May will be my comfort as she has always been. May God give me strength and guidance in the heavy task which has fallen upon me.

King Edward's last days mirrored the restless energy of his life. He had returned to London from a holiday in Biarritz on the evening of Wednesday, 27 April. Although troubled by bronchitis and tired by the Channel crossing, he was at Covent Garden two hours later to hear Tetrazzini sing in *Rigoletto*. The next morning he resumed his daily programme of State business and audiences, attended the private view of the Royal Academy and dined out with Miss Agnes Keyser, founder of the London hospital which bears his name; Queen Alexandra was staying at Corfu with her brother, the King of the Hellenes, and did not reach London until the day before her husband's death. King Edward was again at the opera house on Friday to hear *Siegfried*. He spent the weekend at Sandringham, stumping the estate in wind and rain to inspect improvements to his property. By the time he arrived back at Buckingham Palace on Monday afternoon his heart had begun to fail and he could breathe only with difficulty. Throughout that last week he nevertheless refused to cancel a single engagement. 'I shall not give in,' he replied to a visitor who remonstrated with him. 'I shall work to the end.' On the morning of Friday, 6 May, he struggled to smoke a cigar, insisted on donning a frock coat to receive his closest friend Sir Ernest Cassel. Soon after midday he collapsed but resisted attempts to put him to bed. As the flame flickered, he was able to take in the news that his horse

Witch of Air had won the 4.15 race at Kempton Park. When the Prince of Wales repeated the message, his father replied: 'Yes, I have heard of it. I am very glad.' They were the King's last coherent words. He died just before midnight.

Early on the following morning King George v, as he had now become, was told by his eldest son that the Royal Standard was flying at half-mast over Buckingham Palace, where the late King lay dead. He at once gave orders that it was instead to float in full majesty over his own residence, Marlborough House. Just such an incident had marked the accession of Edward vii nine years earlier, when the new King noticed that the Royal Standard flying on the yacht which bore his mother's remains across the Solent from Osborne was at half-mast. On being asked for an explanation, the captain of the yacht said: 'Sir, the Queen is dead.' Edward vii replied: 'The King lives.'

After attending to the small but significant matter of the Royal Standard, King George v spent the first morning of his reign at a full meeting of the Privy Council, whose members he addressed with simple sincerity. Two days later he watched the ancient ceremony at which Garter King of Arms proclaimed his accession:

WHEREAS IT HAS PLEASED ALMIGHTY GOD TO CALL TO HIS MERCY OUR LATE SOVEREIGN LORD KING EDWARD THE SEVENTH OF BLESSED AND GLORIOUS MEMORY, BY WHOSE DECEASE THE IMPERIAL CROWN OF THE UNITED KINGDOM OF GREAT BRITAIN AND IRELAND IS SOLELY AND RIGHTFULLY COME TO THE HIGH AND MIGHTY PRINCE GEORGE FREDERICK ERNEST ALBERT:

WE, THEREFORE, THE LORDS SPIRITUAL AND TEMPORAL OF THIS REALM, BEING HERE ASSISTED WITH THESE OF HIS LATE MAJESTY'S PRIVY COUNCIL, WITH NUMBERS OF OTHER PRINCIPAL GENTLEMEN OF QUALITY, WITH THE LORD MAYOR, ALDERMEN AND CITIZENS OF LONDON, DO NOW HEREBY WITH ONE VOICE AND CONSENT OF TONGUE AND HEART, PUBLISH AND PROCLAIM:

THAT THE HIGH AND MIGHTY PRINCE GEORGE FREDERICK ERNEST ALBERT IS NOW, BY THE DEATH OF OUR LATE SOVEREIGN OF HAPPY MEMORY, BECOME OUR ONLY LAWFUL AND RIGHTFUL LIEGE LORD GEORGE THE FIFTH, BY THE GRACE OF GOD, KING OF THE UNITED KINGDOM OF GREAT BRITAIN AND IRELAND, AND OF THE BRITISH DOMINIONS BEYOND THE SEAS, DEFENDER OF THE FAITH, EMPEROR OF INDIA; TO WHOM WE DO ACKNOWLEDGE ALL FAITH AND CONSTANT OBEDIENCE, WITH ALL HEARTY AND HUMBLE AFFECTION; BESEECHING GOD, BY WHOM KINGS AND QUEENS DO REIGN, TO BLESS THE ROYAL PRINCE GEORGE THE FIFTH, WITH LONG AND HAPPY YEARS TO REIGN OVER US.

GOD SAVE THE KING!

Less resoundingly, his wife also changed her name and style. Until 1910 she had been known as May, using her first two names, Victoria Mary, for her official signature. She wrote to an aunt a few days after her accession: 'I hope you approve of my new name Mary. George dislikes double names and I could not be Victoria, but it strikes me as curious to be rechristened at the age of 43.' Queen Mary added: 'I regret the quieter, easier time we had, everything will be more difficult now and more ceremonious.'

A pressing duty of the new sovereign was to receive the members of his Government. As the Prime Minister, Mr Asquith, had not yet returned from a visit to the Mediterranean, the first Minister to be summoned to Buckingham Palace was the Chancellor of the Exchequer. 'The King exceedingly nice,' Mr Lloyd George wrote. 'Talked a good deal about his father of whom he was evidently very fond. His eyes suffused with tears.'

Grief at King Edward's death took many forms, some of them bizarre. One hostess of the late monarch threaded black ribbons through her daughter's underclothes; another tied a large black bow of crepe round a tree which he had planted in her garden five years before. A grocer in Jermyn Street saluted the passing of a dedicated trencherman by filling his window with black Bradenham hams. Sir Arthur Herbert, who as British Minister to Norway had allowed dancing in his Legation on what turned out to be the evening of the King's death, was reprimanded by the Foreign Office and retired prematurely in the following year.

A silent crowd of 250,000 subjects filed past the catafalque in Westminster Hall during three days of laying-in-state. Sir Schomberg McDonnell, Secretary to His Majesty's Office of Works, noted that they were led by 'three women of the seamstress class: very poorly dressed and very reverent'. Their sense of decorum, he added, was in sharp contrast to that of more exalted mourners: 'The Prime Minister was there with Miss Asquith leaning against one of the lamp standards and watching the people pass. I thought his attitude and general demeanour rather offensive. I fear he had dined well and he seemed to regard the occasion as a mere show.'

The behaviour of the Home Secretary, Winston Churchill, was even more insensitive. At 10.40 one evening, after the hall had been closed for the night, he and his family descended on Westminster in a procession of four motor cars to view King Edward's coffin. On being refused admission, he argued and abused an outraged custodian before withdrawing his party. That was characteristic of Churchill's early years in office. A few days earlier, during a formal audience with the new King, he had at once asserted that a great change was necessary in the constitution. The sovereign, hurt by Churchill's lack of sympathy, contented himself with replying that he was against all violent change.

Eight kings and an emperor attended the funeral at Windsor; the bills for feeding them and other official mourners came to no less than £4,644. King Edward's pet terrier, called Caesar, was given a place in the procession immediately behind the coffin; the German Emperor observed that he had done many things in his life, but had never before been obliged to yield precedence to a dog. Lord Kinnoull's little daughter, an awed witness of the funeral, refused to say her prayers that night. 'It won't be any use,' she explained, 'God will be too busy unpacking King Edward.'

Even in the midst of his grief, the new King was plagued by those trivialities of protocol which at court so often jostle problems of more lasting moment. Thus the Household Cavalry protested that they, not the Grenadier Guards, ought to have been entrusted with the protection of Edward VII's body before its removal from Buckingham Palace to Westminster Hall. The Grenadiers, they conceded, had in 1901 guarded the remains of Queen Victoria at Osborne; but that was a private residence, not a royal palace. The question was referred to the Lord Chancellor, who sensibly decided that the sovereign could not be bound by precedent in selecting his servants for any particular duty.

Another annoyance was the administrative incompetence of the Duke of Norfolk, who as hereditary Earl Marshal of England bore responsibility for organizing the funeral in St George's Chapel, Windsor. On the very day before the service, the ceremonial published by the Earl Marshal proved to be full of mistakes; a senior courtier and four clerks shut themselves up for several hours rewriting it correctly. 'I love the Duke,' King George told Schomberg McDonnell, 'he is a charming, honourable, straight-forward little gentleman, no better in the world. But as a man of business he is absolutely impossible. I ask you, Pom, is it not hard on me?'

The most disturbing influence during those first days of the new reign was Queen Alexandra's strong-willed and possessive sister, Marie Feodorovna. The Dowager Empress of Russia prompted King Edward's widow to claim precedence over the wife of the reigning sovereign: a custom followed in St Petersburg but unknown to the Court of St James's. With characteristic restraint, neither King George nor Queen Mary was willing to challenge Queen Alexandra's pretensions at such a moment, and the Dowager Empress had her way. At the funeral, therefore, Queen Alexandra stood at the foot of her husband's coffin, accompanied only by her sister, while Queen Mary was relegated to an inferior place.

Some of the special diplomatic missions proved equally troublesome. Monsieur Pichon, the French Foreign Minister, was scandalized to observe that Orleanist princes had been given precedence over him in the funeral procession and complained to the Foreign Secretary, Sir Edward Grey. Sharing a carriage with ex-President Theodore Roosevelt of the United States, he also grumbled at the discourtesy shown to the representatives of republics. Their coachman, he pointed out, was dressed in black, whereas the coachmen of the preceding royal carriages wore scarlet liveries. Roosevelt replied that he had not noticed and would have been equally content with a coachman clad in yellow and green. That crushing retort, delivered in imperfect French, was lost on Pichon, who understood Roosevelt to be demanding a coachman dressed in just those colours.

Nor did the special envoys always accept the ruling that they should take the precedence of their respective embassies and legations in London. Shortly before the King was to receive each in turn at a stated time, one of them wrote to the Master of the Ceremonies, Lord Ormathwaite. He would be much obliged, he said, if the King would receive him and his compatriots first of all, as they had an important engagement that day in Manchester. Ormathwaite, tempted to reject the request out of hand, felt it his duty to submit it to the King. That evening he received a reply. There was no outburst of rage, simply five pencilled words and the King's initials: 'I will receive them last.'

The other problems of the new reign were not to be solved so imperiously.

King George V was within a few weeks of his forty-fifth birthday at the time of his accession. Although hardly less tall than his father, he lacked the majestic presence of the late King. Throughout life he remained slight of build and scorned the raised heels with which Edward VII added to his height. When Lady Minto entertained the then Prince of Wales at Government House, Calcutta, in 1906 she noted that the Weighing Book, in which even the most eminent guests were required to register, had been inaugurated by the future King Edward VII on 3 January 1876: 'Albert Edward,' he wrote jocularly, '14 st. 9¾ lbs., *in heavy military uniform.*' On the same date exactly thirty years later, his son signed his name: 'George P: 10 st. 7 lbs.' During the next quarter of a century, his weight crept up little more than seven pounds. Then illness robbed him of his usual exercise, and in 1930 he wrote in his diary: 'Saw tailors about my uniforms which are too tight alas!'

Not even the most skilled tailor could disguise one defect in his appearance of which he remained unhappily aware: he had knock-knees. To cure this congenital malformation in his children he obliged them to sleep in leg splints designed by Sir Francis Laking, his physician-in-ordinary. Once it was reported to him that Frederick Finch, the children's personal attendant, had given in to young Prince Albert's plea that they should be removed. The King sent for his kind-hearted but misguided retainer. Drawing his trousers tightly against his legs to display his own knock-knees, he said sternly: 'Look at me. If that boy grows up to look like this, it will be your fault.' The treatment was resumed and proved successful.

During a royal tour of South Yorkshire in the early years of the reign, Archbishop Lang overheard this conversation between two coalminers:

'Na then, which is t' King?'
'It's t' little chap i' the front wi' a billycock hat.'
'Nay, he ain't seech a fine man as Teddy.'
'Well anyway, he's gotten him a fine oopstanding wife.'

Saloon-bar wits spoke of King George the Fifth and Queen Mary the Four-Fifths. The French were similarly impressed by Queen Mary's stature and called her '*Soutien-Georges*', literally 'George's Support', but also a pun on *soutien-gorge*, meaning a brassière.

Although she appeared to be a tall, imposing woman who towered over her husband, that was an illusion. Her back was as stiff as a ramrod, and both hats and heels played a part in enhancing her stately deportment. She was in fact exactly the same size as the King: five feet, six inches. Shyness also made her seem more formidable than she was. Lord Lincolnshire, created a marquess in 1912, wrote in his diary: 'The King and Queen both very gracious; congratulated me warmly; and both gave me their hands: a rare occurrence with the present Queen.' Another courtier noted 'that shy nod which offends so much'. And Mr Asquith claimed that he was more exhausted after dining next to her than at the end of a debate in the Commons.

Endowed with neither inches nor a commanding presence, the King made the most of his modest attributes. His hair was always brushed with care, his beard neatly trimmed and anointed with lavender water, his manicured hands protected by gloves when shooting. Almost at death's door in 1928, he insisted on sending for a looking glass. He liked to have his family round him as he completed the ritual of dressing for dinner: the winding of the watch, the touch of scent on the handkerchief, the last adjustment to white tie and Garter star. It was as if the centuries had rolled away and the Sun King reigned once more at Versailles.

Like his father, King George was obsessively concerned with what he wore. He grew up in an age that cared for such things. At the turn of the century not even the poorest of his grandmother's subjects would venture out of doors without a hat: the rich changed their clothes several times a day. Sartorial decrees made no concessions to either climate or comfort. Arthur Lee, the Member of Parliament who presented Chequers to the nation as a country residence for the Prime Minister, resigned from the fashionable Hurlingham Club in 1908 after his first visit; the flannel suit and panama hat he thought appropriate for that hot summer afternoon had attracted unfriendly glances from his top-hatted and tail-coated fellow members. It was unusual for a man not to wear full evening dress in the stalls of a theatre or when dining in his London club. What distinguished the King from his contemporaries was a lifelong obedience to Edwardian custom: an unobtrusive elegance of style that concealed nature's deficiencies.

On formal occasions he remained faithful to the frock coat and tall hat, their sombre glow relieved by a protrusion of starched cuff, a white slip under the waistcoat and perhaps a gardenia. For Ascot and other summer events, the entire ensemble might be grey. At a race meeting or at some such *rus in urbe* as the Chelsea Flower Show, the King wore a no less impeccably cut suit of the finest brown or grey cloth – he had seen enough of blue in the Navy – crowned by a hard, high, curly-brimmed bowler hat of black, brown or grey. His trousers were creased down the side, his overcoats generally long, his gloves ribbed in black. He pulled his ties through a ring rather than knot them, and kept them in place by a jewelled pin. He preferred boots to shoes and invariably carried a stick. On shooting days his valet laid out tweeds of a surprisingly bright check, eight-button spats that came almost up to his knees, and a Homburg hat. When sailing his yacht, the King wore a white flannel suit and flat cap without a peak. Scotland received the compliment of kilt, Inverness cape and feathered bonnet. It was as much a liturgy as a wardrobe.

The King not only revered what had been fashionable in his early manhood, but expected his family and household to share the same conservatism of taste. The refusal of his adventurous eldest son to accept such restrictions strained an already uneasy relationship between the King and his heir: a theme which belongs to a later chapter. Queen Mary, however, submitted to the King's almost oriental requirements with the meekness she brought to every aspect of their marriage. Her husband, she never forgot, was also her sovereign; and in response to his dictates she continued for the rest of her life to wear only such styles and colours as he decreed. Little pleased him in women's fashions later than the bustle: a taste that may perhaps be traced to his perennial attachment to Motherdear. Lady Airlie believed that Queen Mary secretly yearned to escape from those long dresses and toque hats which will be forever associated with her. In the event she permitted herself only one tiny flash of defiance. She refused to abandon those long ear-rings which, the King complained, distorted her ears. Jewelled and gowned for some great ceremonial occasion or evening party, she epitomized the traditional splendour of monarchy. By day her appearance could evoke affectionate satire. 'The Queen had a wonderful success,' a courtier wrote of a State visit to France in 1914. 'The Paris mob went mad about her, and it was rumoured that her out-of-date hats and early Victorian gowns would become next year's fashions!'

It was with no sense of elation that King George V embarked on his reign. 'He told me that he cannot sleep', Lord Esher wrote in his diary ten days after the accession. 'He wakes about five and finds himself making notes of things which lie before him in his day's work.' The King also suffered from indigestion and toothache, maladies on which he brooded with nervous melancholy. He was less superstitious than his father, who would never allow his mattress to be turned on a Friday or willingly sit down thirteen to dinner. King George was nevertheless haunted by a mid-nineteenth-century prophecy of obscure origin, told to him as Prince of Wales by some tactless well-wisher. It was that Queen Victoria would have the longest and most memorable reign of all English sovereigns; that she would be succeeded in turn by two kings with short reigns; then by a third called David, whose reign would be as glorious as hers. George was too considerate a son to mention the prophecy to his father; but in May 1910, with the death of King Edward VII after only nine years on the throne, he had cause to reconcile himself to an equally short reign. And even if it were to be prolonged, the prospect of a burden which could be laid down only at the grave was scarcely more encouraging. 'The King of England is always King,' Lord Chancellor Eldon had observed during the reign of an earlier George, 'King in the helplessness of infancy, King in the decrepitude of age.'

George V was also the despairing victim of two virulent slanders. One labelled him a drunkard, the other a bigamist.

The myth of the King's addiction to alcohol had pursued him for several years. Lady Minto wrote in her diary at the time of his visit to India as Prince of Wales:

I heard from England the other day that the night of the Calcutta illuminations the Prince dined with Lord Kitchener; this is quite true, as I sat next to him. The story went on that both the Prince and Lord Kitchener were so drunk that they couldn't appear after dinner. I drove with the Prince for an hour after dinner myself, and Lord Kitchener was in the next carriage. The Prince knows about these reports and spoke to me about them; he said I suppose they think the same thing in India because over one of the triumphal arches was written 'God help the Prince' ... I think it is cruel, especially as he hardly touches any wine, no Champagne or liqueur, only a light Moselle.

Soon after the King's accession five years later, Count Mensdorff, the Austrian ambassador, mentioned the rumours in a despatch to Vienna:

His Majesty hears all sorts of remarks about his alleged alcoholism made by crowds in the streets. At pious meetings in the East End of London, prayers are said for Queen Mary and the royal children, begging the protection of Heaven on their unhappy drunkard's home. The Archbishop of Canterbury and the clergy, as well as those whose charitable works bring them into touch with the lower classes, are now trying to fight this risible legend of the drinker King, but it will take a long time to eradicate.

Except for a red face and a loud voice, the King betrayed none of the symptoms associated with intemperance. He was in fact an abstemious man, although he did like a glass of port after dinner. This he would fill to the brim, then lift to his lips with the same steadiness of hand and eye that had made him so commanding a shot. By continuing to excel at the sport he loved best, the King shamed some of his detractors into silence. The rest grew weary of the joke, and eventually the sniggers ceased.

The other rumour to cast a slur over the King's middle years had reached him in the week before he proposed to Princess May of Teck. On 25 April 1893, at the end of a Mediterranean holiday, he wrote to his father's private secretary from the British Embassy in Rome: 'The story of my being already married to an American is really very amusing. Cust has heard the same thing from England only he heard that my wife lived at Plymouth, why there I wonder?' On 3 May, the very day of his betrothal, the *Star* newspaper in London published a more circumstantial account: that the Duke of York had lately contracted a secret marriage in Malta with the daughter of a British naval officer.

At first he took it lightly. 'I say, May,' he told his fiancée one day, 'we can't get married after all. I hear I have got a wife and three children.' In the following year, however, the radical Member of Parliament, Keir Hardie, scandalized the Commons during a debate on a motion to congratulate the Duke and Duchess of York on the birth of their first child. He said of the infant Prince Edward: 'In due course, following the precedent which has already been set, he will be sent on a tour round the world, and probably rumours of a morganatic alliance will follow, and the end of it all will be the country will be called upon to pay the bill.'

Whispers of alleged bigamy continued to disturb Prince George throughout his years as Duke of York and as Prince of Wales. 'He is particularly depressed at being powerless to deal with them,' Mensdorff wrote in March 1910. 'He lacks the happy insouciance of King Edward.' With his accession to the throne in May the rumours revived, in spite of formal denials by the Dean of Norwich in July and by Bigge three months later. Towards the end of the year, however, there came an opportunity to destroy the lie once and for all. A republican paper called the *Liberator*, published in Paris but sent free to every British Member of Parliament, printed an article by E. F. Mylius entitled 'Sanctified Bigamy'. It asserted that in 1890 the future King George V had contracted a lawful marriage in Malta with a daughter of Admiral Sir Michael Culme-Seymour; that children had been born of the union; and that three years later the bridegroom, having by his brother's death found himself in direct line of succession to the throne, 'foully abandoned his true wife and entered into a sham and shameful marriage with a daughter of the Duke of Teck'. The article continued:

The Anglican Church, with its crew of emasculated, canting priests, presents little more resemblance to Christianity than if it were some idol-fetish of a tribe of South Sea Cannibals. . . .

Our very Christian King and Defender of the Faith has a plurality of wives just like any Mohammedan Sultan, and they are sanctified by the Anglican Church.

The next issue of the *Liberator* returned to the theme: 'The *Daily News* of London tells us that the King plans to visit India with his wife. Would the newspaper kindly tell us which wife?' Already, however, the Law Officers of the Crown had decided that Mylius should be prosecuted for criminal libel. The Attorney-General was Sir Rufus Isaacs, later Lord Reading, the future Lord Chief Justice and Viceroy of India; the Solicitor-General was Sir John Simon, the future Foreign Secretary and Lord Chancellor. In a joint opinion dated 23 November 1910, those two astute and formidable lawyers doubted the wisdom of giving world-wide publicity to an article in an obscure paper with a small circulation. They nevertheless recognized that all the principal witnesses to the falsehood of the story were still alive: the eldest, Admiral Culme-Seymour, being in his seventy-fifth year. That tipped the scales in favour of prosecution. Winston Churchill, the Home Secretary, had preferred such a course from the beginning. He wrote to the King on 18 December 1910: 'The libel is only an obscure undercurrent circulating among the credulous and base. Still it is sufficiently widespread to be a source of vexation to Your Majesty.' Mylius was arrested on 26 December.

The Government, determined to deny the prisoner every opportunity of appealing for public sympathy before his trial, appeared to strain the spirit of the law. Mylius was allowed bail, but as Churchill told the King, 'The amount, £10,000 and two sureties of £5,000 each, was prohibitive.' Nor was there a preliminary hearing of the charge before a magistrate. 'Thus it is probable', the Home Secretary reported to his sovereign, 'that the attention of the public will not be directed to the matter at all until the whole case will be put before them with the Attorney-General's carefully considered statement, the full evidence of the falsity of the libel and, it is to be expected, the sentence of the court.'

A bold move on the part of Mylius to have a subpoena served on the King as a witness was also frustrated. The application was heard privately in the chambers of the Lord Chief Justice, Lord Alverstone, and rejected. That claim by Mylius was in fact contrary to constitutional law. As the source of justice, the sovereign himself cannot give evidence (although King

Edward VII did so as Prince of Wales on two occasions; once during the Mordaunt divorce case and again in the action for slander brought by Sir William Gordon Cumming against his fellow guests at Tranby Croft). In any case, Churchill assured Bigge, 'in the absence of the slightest shadow or vestige of evidence to justify the libel, the claim of the defendant that the King should appear is a mere piece of impudent buffoonery and should be brushed away with the contempt it deserves.'

The case came before the Lord Chief Justice and a jury on 1 February 1911. Admiral Sir Michael Culme-Seymour gave evidence that he had assumed command of the Mediterranean Fleet in 1893; that his wife and two daughters who joined him in Malta in the same year had never before been on the island; that his younger daughter Laura Grace had died unmarried in 1895 without ever having spoken to the King; and that his elder daughter May had not met the King between 1879, when she was eight years old, and 1898. May, who in 1899 had married the future Vice-Admiral Sir Trevylyan Napier, gave supporting testimony, as did her three brothers. It was also proved that the King had not been in Malta between 1888 and 1901, and that there was no record of his alleged marriage in the registers of the island, which the jury were invited to inspect. Mylius, who chose to be unrepresented by counsel, did not attempt to refute the evidence, but clung to his claim that the King should be summoned as a witness. When that renewed plea was again rejected, he offered no further defence. The jury returned a verdict of guilty, and the Lord Chief Justice sentenced Mylius to twelve months' imprisonment, the maximum if his various publications were not to be treated as separate libels.

After sentence had been passed, the Attorney-General read a statement signed by the King. It declared that he had never been married except to the Queen nor gone through any ceremony of marriage except with her; and that he would have given such evidence in person had not the Law Officers advised him that it was unconstitutional for the sovereign to appear in the witness-box.

That in fact was the real purpose of the prosecution: less to punish Mylius than to vindicate the King's honour. Within the existing framework of the law it had not been easy to achieve. Simon, the Solicitor-General, wrote in his diary:

We were very lucky to bring the Mylius case to so satisfactory an end. If Mylius, instead of justifying, had pleaded guilty and explained that he was only repeating what thousands of reputable people had said for years without being prosecuted for it, we could never have established the falsity of the lie so effectually.

A few hours after hearing the verdict, the King wrote in his own hand to Churchill, thanking him for his help in proving 'to the world at large the baseness of this cruel and abominable libel'. He marked his indebtedness to Isaacs and Simon by appointing each to the Royal Victorian Order, a distinction founded by his grandmother to reward personal service to the royal family.

Over the years the King continued to demonstrate his gratitude to the two Law Officers. An opportunity occurred in 1913 when, on the retirement of Lord Alverstone, the Prime Minister nominated Sir Rufus Isaacs to succeed him as Lord Chief Justice of England. The Attorney-General had a prescriptive right to the office, and Isaacs was acknowledged to be at the summit of his profession. A few months earlier, however, a division in the House of Commons along party lines had endorsed by only 346 votes to 268 the probity of his stock-exchange dealings in Marconi shares. Isaacs had behaved imprudently by investing in the Marconi Company of America as a result of confidential information given to him by his brother, managing director of English Marconi – itself a company engaged in negotiating an important contract with the British Government that would need to be ratified by Parliament; and in purporting to explain his speculation to the Commons, the Attorney-General had displayed a deplorable lack of candour. It was therefore understandable that his swift elevation to be Lord Chief Justice should arouse both spiteful comment and genuine dismay.

As a constitutional monarch, the King was required to do no more than give his formal approval to the appointment. He nevertheless sent Isaacs a message of warm congratulation. The new Lord Chief Justice wrote to Lord Stamfordham (as Bigge had become in 1911): 'Please tell the King that he has given me the loftiest encouragement to serve him and the State and that I shall ever treasure and remember his words.'

The King similarly showed more cordiality to Sir John Simon than did the Solicitor-General's political colleagues, who thought him able but devious and insincere. On being made a Privy Counsellor in 1913, Simon wrote to thank his sovereign for the honour. The King noted: 'A charming letter from a very nice man.'

Nearly twenty years of sly persecution had left too deep a wound in the King for him to show magnanimity to his tormentor Mylius. Two weeks after the trial, Stamfordham wrote to Edward Marsh, Churchill's private secretary, expressing the hope that the prisoner would not be released before his sentence had expired. 'Any leniency', he added, 'will produce no gratitude in him or his friends and might lead the public to think that the trial was a "put-up" affair.' Stamfordham later telephoned Marsh to confirm 'that this represents the King's wish'.

That hint to the Home Secretary, although vindictive, was justified. On his release from prison, Mylius returned to the attack in a pamphlet entitled *The Morganatic Marriage of George V*, published in New York. In it he not only rehearsed all the arguments which had been refuted at his trial; he also produced what he claimed to be new evidence to support his allegations of bigamy. May Culme-Seymour, he wrote, had been mistaken in swearing that she had never met the King between 1879 and 1898. Having combed the files of the *Hampshire Telegraph and Sussex Chronicle*, he discovered that the Admiral's daughter had opened the dancing with the Duke of York at a ball in Portsmouth Town Hall on 21 August 1891. That slip of memory on the part of Miss Culme-Seymour about an event that had taken place twenty years before was utterly irrelevant to the accusation of bigamy; not even Mylius was prepared to assert that the supposed marriage had been either consecrated or consummated in Portsmouth Town Hall.

The pamphlet made a more plausible point when it turned to the whereabouts of the future King during the year he was alleged to have secretly married May Culme-Seymour:

Crown witnesses testified that King George had not been officially in Malta in the year 1890. Investigations made subsequent to my trial showed that in the year 1890 Prince George was appointed commander of the gunboat *Thrush* which arrived in Gibraltar on June 9th, 1890 on its way to the North American station, and left on the 25th of the same month after an interval of sixteen days. Malta is only five days trip from Gibraltar....

What was Prince George doing between June 9th and June 25th, 1890? There is no record of his stay in Gibraltar during those days or of his having attended any social functions in that city.... And why should George go 4,000 miles out of his course on his way to the North American station?

Readers of this work will know exactly why Prince George went 4,000 miles out of his course on the way to North America: HMS *Thrush* was required to tow a torpedo boat to Gibraltar before crossing the Atlantic. As for those supposedly missing sixteen days, the Prince's own letters and diaries provide a full and exact chronicle of how he spent them while awaiting the completion of repairs to his ship's engines. Like any other young naval officer, he played polo and tennis, billiards and whist; he went on picnics and watched the apes; he dined in the messes of hospitable regiments such as the Black Watch. That left no time for a clandestine return voyage to Malta and a secret marriage. The reputations of King George and of Miss May Culme-Seymour emerge unsullied from Mylius's deceitful postscript.

The trial of 1911 evoked a widespread public sympathy for the King. It was reflected in the changing attitude to the monarchy of the novelist Henry James who, although remaining a United States citizen until 1915, took a fervent interest in British institutions. On the death of Queen Victoria in 1901, James had written 'The Prince of Wales is an arch-vulgarian ... the wretched little Yorks are less than nothing ... I am very pessimistic.' Ten years later he discovered that his nephew Edward Holton James had been associated with Mylius in producing the *Liberator*, and he cut him out of his will.

❧

The King's respect for his father's memory did not extend to those rich, restless cosmopolitans who epitomized the Edwardian era. Soon after the accession, Max Beerbohm drew a cartoon of Lord Burnham, Sir Ernest Cassel, Alfred and Leopold de Rothschild and Arthur Sassoon walking apprehensively along a corridor of Buckingham Palace to meet their new sovereign. It is entitled: 'Are we as welcome as ever?'

In all King George's letters, diaries and reported conversations there is not a trace of the mild, mindless anti-semitism to be found throughout his reign in every class of society: nothing of that contempt with which one of his own private secretaries would refer to 'Lyons the Jew restaurant keeper'. It was simply that his father's fast friends, whether Jew or Gentile, were not to his taste. 'Dull perhaps,' the King would say of his Court, 'but certainly respectable.' Even when he condescended to shoot Lord Burnham's pheasants at Hall Barn, sustained by a luncheon of turtle soup, snipe pudding and truffled turkey, he felt uneasy at the prodigality of the slaughter. After 4,000 birds had fallen in a short December day, 1,000 to his own gun, the King remarked to his eldest son on the way home: 'Perhaps we went a little far today, David.'

A very few of King Edward's old cronies continued to find favour at court. Among them were Lord Esher and Count Albert Mensdorff, who have already appeared in these pages playing Boswell to the King's Dr Johnson. Indeed, what has ensured them a place in the life and times of King George V is less their excursions into statecraft than their industry as diarists.

Reginald Brett, second Viscount Esher, was born in 1852, thirteen years before the King. His father, an ambitious middle-class lawyer who rose to be Master of the Rolls and a peer, sent him to Eton. There the boy was fortunate in becoming a pupil of William Cory, poet, historian and romantic. Among Cory's other pupils was the young Lord Rosebery, of whom the tutor wrote: 'He is one of those who like the palm without the dust.' Rosebery did nevertheless win the palm, only to reject it for its very dustiness; he was Prime Minister for fifteen months in 1894-95, after which he never again held or sought to hold office. Esher, even more fastidious, disdained to enter the race.

His ability is to be measured not by the offices he held but by those he refused. Salisbury urged him to govern Cape Colony; Balfour invited him to be Secretary of State for War; Campbell-Bannerman proposed that he should succeed Minto as Viceroy of India. He spurned them all, preferring

the freedom of obscurity or, as he called it, 'the guarded life'. The world at
large knew him as no more than a transient Member of Parliament and the
holder of minor places in the public service and the royal household.

Esher's career owed much to Rosebery, one of whose last acts as Prime
Minister was to appoint his fellow Etonian and friend secretary to the
Office of Works; the vulgarities of competitive examination had scarcely
begun to sully the silver age of patronage. Responsibility for the royal
palaces brought him to the notice of Queen Victoria and her family. A
deferential manner and an attention to detail did the rest. King Edward
VII, impressed by his mastery of ceremonial and historical precedent, made
him Deputy Constable and Lieutenant Governor of Windsor Castle. There
he rescued Queen Victoria's archives from forty years of neglect and
published an illuminating edition of her letters. He lived to enjoy the trust
of three successive sovereigns.

Gradually Esher began to exert a political influence unknown to established constitutional practice. As a member of the Royal Commission
appointed to inquire into the military preparations and conduct of the
South African War and as chairman of the War Office Reconstruction
Committee he revealed the day-to-day deliberations of both bodies to King
Edward VII. St John Brodrick, Secretary of State for War from 1900 to
1903, wrote with some bitterness:

By the time any decision had come to the point when the Cabinet could lay it
before the Sovereign, the issue had been largely prejudged, on the incomplete
premises of an observer who had no official status. In other words Esher, whether
intentionally or not, had constituted himself the unofficial adviser of the Crown.

Courtiers and civil servants were similarly dismayed by Esher's influence
on King Edward, whatever Government happened to be in power. 'He
certainly is an extraordinary man, and has a wonderful footing in Buckingham Palace,' a Liberal minister noted. 'He seems to be able to run about
it as he likes and must be a considerable nuisance to the Household.'
Stamfordham, ever imperturbable, merely observed: 'He has a curious love
of acquiring knowledge, and generally succeeds!' But when Esher telegraphed to the Foreign Office asking on behalf of the King for a certain
memorandum, he was sharply told, on the authority of Sir Edward Grey,
that it could be supplied only if demanded by the King's private secretary.

To play the part of *éminence grise* in the floodlit arena of twentieth-century
politics required a peculiar combination of qualities: experience, perception,
wisdom, tact, humour, self-effacement. Perhaps there was something alien
in both the detachment with which Esher analysed the motives of his
political contemporaries and the romantic affection which he brought
to King Edward's person. He wrote of an audience at Buckingham

Palace: 'On parting the King said to me, "Although you are not exactly a public servant, yet I always think you are the most valuable public servant I have," and then I kissed his hand, as I sometimes do.'

After the death of King Edward, his ingratiating ways appealed more to Queen Mary than to her husband. 'If you were not Queen and came into a room,' Esher told her, 'everyone would ask who you were.' Queen Mary replied complacently that her mother used to say the same. It is unlikely that King George ever allowed Esher to kiss his hand; but during the politically troubled years of the early reign he would call on Esher's knowledge of constitutional precedents to reinforce his own faded memories of Bagehot. And so Esher retained his deceptively unimportant office at court; less powerful than in the days of King Edward, yet continuing to exert an influence far beyond the drains and foundations of Windsor Castle.

Albert Mensdorff, the Austrian ambassador, was another relic of the Edwardian Age who survived into the next reign; in contrast to Esher, he established a far closer intimacy with George V than with Edward VII. He had spent much of his diplomatic career in London before being appointed ambassador in 1904; he was then forty-two, the youngest of his rank in the Austrian service. Although he did not neglect work, he preferred pleasure. He could scarcely hide his dismay at the change of Government in 1905, when the splendours of the Foreign Secretary's hospitality at Lansdowne House gave way to Sir Edward Grey's simple fare served by parlourmaids. King Edward complained that the ambassador spent too much time at house parties and race meetings, although 'he does not know a horse from a cow'. And Robert Vansittart, a future Permanent Under-Secretary at the Foreign Office, called him 'a flabby tabby, anglophil but impotent'.

Mensdorff was even less esteemed in Vienna. The Minister for Foreign Affairs, Baron von Aehrenthal, believed that the ambassador had so fallen in love with England as to be incapable of pursuing Austrian interests. Again and again it was rumoured that he would be withdrawn from his post. How then did he survive in London from 1904 until the outbreak of war in 1914? His privileged position at the Court of St James's outweighed any professional shortcomings. Count Mensdorff-Pouilly-Dietrichstein, to give him his full style, was a cousin of the British royal house twice over. His grandmother was a sister both of the Duchess of Kent, Queen Victoria's mother, and of Ernest I, Duke of Saxe-Coburg-Gotha, the Prince Consort's father.

In Vienna his colleagues called him Royal Albert; but they envied and respected his intimacy with successive British sovereigns. Queen Victoria invited the young secretary to Windsor, where he played the part of Charles II in an elaborate Van Dyck tableau. He was also a guest at Sandringham for the Duke of Clarence's ill-fated birthday party in 1892; Mensdorff too caught influenza but survived. In later years, it is true, King Edward would vent his rage on Mensdorff when displeased by the anti-British tone of Austrian newspapers; a fellow guest described him after one such encounter as looking 'like a whipped hound'. Yet it was the King who saved his career by warning Vienna that Mensdorff's premature recall would damage Anglo-Austrian relations. With the accession of King George, Mensdorff could do no wrong. The new sovereign addressed his letters, 'My dear Albert', and ended them, 'Your affectionate friend and cousin.' He allowed him to wear the 'Windsor uniform' designed by King George III, a blue evening coat with gold buttons and collar and cuffs of red: a privilege usually confined to members of the royal family and a few favoured Prime Ministers. He assured Mensdorff that Austrians enjoyed a special place in the hearts of Englishmen. He talked freely of personal problems: of health and money, of family tensions and slanderous whispers. Mensdorff enjoyed basking in the favour of his illustrious kinsman, whose confidences he would diligently betray to his masters in Vienna.

Both Esher and Mensdorff were busy with their diaries during the first summer of the new reign. As a guest at Balmoral, the King's Scottish retreat, Esher noted how things had changed:

It is altogether different here from former years. There is no longer the old atmosphere about the house – that curious electric element which pervaded the surroundings of King Edward. Yet everything is very charming and wholesome and sweet. The house is a home for children – six of them at luncheon – the youngest running round the table all the while. The Queen knits of an evening. Not a sign of 'bridge'. The King sat on the sofa talking with me until bed-time ... We go to bed early, which I like, and breakfast at nine ... Last night the French governess sat on the King's right hand at dinner. Imagine the courtiers of Berlin or Vienna if they could have seen.

Mensdorff painted a similar picture of domestic tranquillity:

Here I am, staying at Balmoral with the third generation of the family in succession. How times change. A small party. Very peaceful life, enormously punctual in contrast to former years. Everything very orderly, which I appreciate after my cure. Not even bridge, so that the evenings are rather tedious. Fortunately we all go to our rooms soon after 11. The King and Queen very gracious. He was most forthcoming about politics and his own beliefs. His opinions are wholesome and straightforward. The children very nice and well brought up.

Towards the end of his visit, Mr Asquith joined the party, and a table of bridge was arranged as a concession to the Prime Minister.

Yet Balmoral was not in itself a welcoming house. Bought and rebuilt by Prince Albert in the baronial style of tower and turret, it looked handsome enough from a distance: a castle of sparkling white granite rising from the banks of the River Dee and enclosed but not menaced by the Cairngorm mountains. Within it was dark and draughty, a penance to all except the old Queen herself. There must have been heating of a sort, for Princess Alice, the last surviving grandchild of Queen Victoria, recalled the distinctive smell of Balmoral: wood fires, stags' heads, rugs and leather. But one of the ladies-in-waiting confided to her husband that she was never really warm except in bed. Whatever the temperature, etiquette demanded that women should dine *décolletées*: men fared better, permitted to wear trousers instead of the knee-breeches and silk stockings prescribed for Buckingham Palace and Windsor. Lord Salisbury nevertheless had such painful memories of a previous visit to Balmoral that when the Queen summoned him there in 1896 his private secretary implored Bigge to see that the Prime Minister did not freeze. 'A cold room', he wrote, 'is really dangerous to him.' Not even Queen Mary was spared the caprice of a Balmoral summer. 'The weather has again been too awful,' she wrote one September during the early part of the reign, 'and I am in consequence suffering tortures from neuritis which makes me rather grumpy.' She never resigned herself to what she called 'sitting on a mountain'.

The tartan-drenched décor of the castle affronted Queen Mary's aesthetic sense. Lord Rosebery thought that the drawing-room at Osborne was the ugliest in the world – until he saw Balmoral. Queen Mary tried to relieve its gloom by having the dark panelling stripped and lightened; but any drastic alteration, like an abrupt change in the style of her clothes, would have distressed the King. He was happy enough to wake to the wail of pipes, to shoot grouse and stalk stags, to play the laird, to take pride in the trickle of Stuart blood that still coursed through essentially Hanoverian veins. It was a romantic family trait. Queen Victoria would even assume a Scots accent when north of the Border. 'I always give her five poond,' she explained to Lady Lytton during a visit to an old cottager. King Edward was no less diplomatic. As Prince of Wales he warned his son not to offend the Scots by using the word 'English' when 'British' would be more correct. And in later years, as the royal yacht approached the coast of Scotland, he instructed a Swiss valet: 'Un costume un peu écossais demain.' His sartorial progress from one kingdom to another demanded subtlety: a simple tartan waistcoat, perhaps, heralding the full exuberance of kilt, sporran and skean-dhu.

King George and Queen Mary were unadventurous in their choice of guests. Balmoral house parties usually included Esher, Mensdorff, Canon Dalton, Archbishop Lang, and an occasional soldier or proconsul such as Kitchener or Curzon (although not together). Sister Agnes, King Edward's old friend, cut a more incongruous figure, striding over the heather wearing bright mauve and an orange wig. The King followed the custom of his grandmother and father by summoning a succession of Ministers in Attendance to deal with the State business that pursues a monarch even to the Scottish Highlands: as if to emphasize that their presence was more a duty than a pleasure, wives were not invited.

One of the first ministers to arrive at Balmoral was Lloyd George, Asquith's Chancellor of the Exchequer, whose budget of 1909 had provoked a constitutional crisis between the two Houses of Parliament. Although taxes on land did not commend themselves to the squire of Sandringham, the King proved a genial host. Lloyd George wrote to his wife: 'The King is a very jolly chap but thank God there's not much in his head. They're simple, very, very ordinary people, and perhaps on the whole that's how it should be.'

Two days later the Chancellor described an interlude that further disproves the legend of a tyrannical father and cowed children:

Sat between the Queen and the Prince of Wales at lunch. Quite a nice little fellow. After lunch when the cigars came on the Queen remained to smoke a cigarette, the boys began the game of blowing out the cigar lights – then little Princess Mary wanted to join in and got very excited over it – then the Queen and the rest of us all joined in and the noise was deafening until the little Princess set her lamp on fire. We thought then it was time to stop.

On being told of Lloyd George's success with the royal family, one of his most radical Cabinet colleagues, John Burns, said: 'Yes, and he's had housemaid's knee ever since.' A year later, however, after a second visit to Balmoral, Lloyd George's mood had turned to snarling resentment:

I shall be so glad to find myself in the car starting. I am not cut out for Court life. I can see some of them revel in it. I detest it. The whole atmosphere reeks with Toryism. I can breathe it and it depresses and sickens me. Everybody very civil to me as they would be to a dangerous wild animal whom they fear and perhaps just a little admire for its suppleness and strength. The King is hostile to the bone to all who are working to lift the workmen out of the mire. So is the Queen. They talk exactly as the late King and the Kaiser talked to me if you remember about the old Railway strike. 'What do they want striking?' 'They are very well paid', etc.

Another member of Asquith's Government recorded his impressions of Balmoral in the summer of 1910. He was Sir Charles Hobhouse, Financial Secretary to the Treasury, a conceited yet unremarkable minister. He noted in patronizing tones:

The wit was poor, but not unnatural, and the King laughed continually and loudly. I had some talk with the Queen after dinner, in which he also joined. She speaks with a noticeable German utterance but not unpleasantly so, and was anxious to be at ease, which she soon showed she was. Clearly they liked leading the simple and healthy life of a country gentleman.

Winston Churchill, a more appreciative guest, told his wife of an energetic morning on the hill:

Quite the best day's sport I have had in this country – four good stags and home early. Three were running and one of these a really difficult shot – downhill, half covered, and running fast. Not a bad performance for I have not fired a shot since last year. I hope they won't think I shot too many: but the King complained to me bitterly about the few they have killed this year and the bad effect on the forest of so many being left; and the stalker urged me to go on – so I did – and redressed the balance a little. Shooting three in quick succession I could have shot more – but refrained not wishing to become a butcher.

Years later, after he had taken up painting, Churchill would pack palette and brushes when staying with the King at Balmoral. 'I am very glad that he did not disapprove of my using the Ministerial room as a studio,' Churchill wrote to Stamfordham. 'I took particular care to leave no spots on the Victorian tartans.'

King George and Queen Mary were not able to move into Buckingham Palace, the sovereign's London residence, until December 1910; even then they had to make do with temporary quarters for a further two months while the private apartments were redecorated. With determined indecision, Queen Alexandra had lingered on, immobilized in a sargasso sea of possessions. Her dilatory character was only one cause of the delay. Mensdorff reported the increasing influence of her strong-willed sister, the Empress Marie Feodorovna, who had arrived in England soon after the King's death for a visit lasting three months.

There were smouldering discussions about the ownership of certain jewels, including King Edward's insignia of the Garter and the diamond circlet or crown worn by the Queen at the opening of Parliament. Another dispute concerned the standard to be flown by Queen Alexandra. The Royal Standard, bearing the arms of the United Kingdom, may be flown only by the sovereign; a widowed Queen Consort who flies a standard must impale the royal arms with those she has borne before marriage. Queen Alexandra nevertheless continued to fly the Royal Standard itself over Buckingham Palace. So trivial an infringement of precedent, it may be thought, was scarcely worthy of notice. Yet the mystique of monarchy has long rested on symbolism, and Queen Alexandra's flouting of tradition evoked dismay. When writing to her son, she similarly refused to address the envelopes in the expected style, 'The King'. Regarding him as hardly more than the surrogate of her late husband, she would instead write, 'King George'.

That dutiful son did not attempt to hasten Motherdear's departure from either Buckingham Palace or Windsor Castle. At last, in her own time, she went, taking possession once more of Marlborough House where as Princess of Wales she had lived for forty years. She also retained Sandringham, bequeathed to her by King Edward for her lifetime, together with a legacy of £200,000. One delicate matter had still to be adjusted. While Queen Alexandra was preparing to move house, the King learned that with impulsive generosity she had begun to distribute royal heirlooms among deserving institutions and friends. Esher, despatched to retrieve them, accomplished his mission with inimitable tact.

'Buckingham Palace is not so *gemütlich* as Marlborough House,' Queen Mary wrote in December 1910 to her sixteen-year-old eldest son, by now proclaimed Prince of Wales. Cosiness it certainly lacks, yet little else. It is the Janus of London houses. The eastern façade of the palace, built by Edward Blore for Queen Victoria and refaced by Aston Webb for Edward VII, frowns stonily down the Mall, sombre, respectable, dull. The western or garden front, built by Nash for George IV a century earlier, is of captivating elegance with its great central bow, its pillars and friezes, its urns and balustrades. The interior of Buckingham Palace is no less capricious: a labyrinth that could as conveniently house the kings and queens of Alice's Wonderland as the crowned heads of more substantial dynasties. 'Doors open where we least expect them,' an art historian has written, 'and they lead from rooms which can hold two hundred people quite comfortably into the kind of fastidious crevice which might have been designed for one particularly spruce young bachelor.'

For almost a year after King Edward's death, court mourning laid a pall of silence over the palace. Drawing-rooms slept under dustsheets, ballroom and throne room admitted only ghosts. Queen Mary used this respite from ceremonial to rearrange some of the less awesome apartments: here an oasis of Chinese Chippendale, there a more discreet reflection of the Regency. Shrinking from the ostentation of the previous reign, from what she called 'this surfeit of gold plate and orchids', she sought comfort but not luxury, beauty elevated by restraint. In every sense the Edwardian Age was at an end.

The King was proud of his wife's eye for interior decoration, a talent inherited from her father the Duke of Teck, but he always looked on Buckingham Palace as an official residence rather than a home. The grandiose was not to his taste. During a royal visit to Chatsworth, the Duke of Devonshire's seat in Derbyshire, a courtier noted the King's misery at being lodged in a huge panelled room with Gobelin tapestries and Grinling

Gibbons carving. As the new tenant for life of Buckingham Palace, the King told Esher that he would gladly pull it down, sell off its forty-acre garden as a public park, and use the money to rebuild Kensington Palace to his own modest taste. It was one of his rare flights of fancy.

In the heart of London, the King established the clockwork routine of a ship's captain. First thing in the morning and last thing at night he consulted the barometer; between those two fixed points his daily progress was as predictable as the course of a planet. By the time he sat down to breakfast on the stroke of nine he had been up for two hours: working on his boxes of State papers, writing up his diary, reading *The Times* newspaper. The rest of the morning was devoted to his secretaries and other officials, to receiving ministers and ambassadors, perhaps to an investiture or similar ceremony. Before lunching with the Queen at half past one he took a sharp walk round the garden: a mechanical, somewhat joyless exercise over a measured mile. At the end of luncheon he would sleep in an armchair for exactly fifteen minutes, waking, his eldest son observed, as if an alarm clock had gone off in his head. In the afternoon there might be engagements outside the palace, a game of tennis with his household or an hour with his stamp collection. The day's flow of red despatch boxes would claim his early evening. Once court mourning was at an end, he would sometimes dine out with the Queen at one of the remaining patrician houses in London or watch a not too demanding play. But he preferred to dine quietly with his family, albeit in white tie and Garter star. The equerry-in-waiting could safely set his watch at 11.10 when he heard the King making his way to bed.

The same placid timetable governed life at Windsor. An ancient fortress transformed by George IV into the loveliest of palaces, the castle looms majestically above the River Thames, offering all the delights of park and forest scarcely twenty miles from London. The royal family would spend short periods there throughout the year. It was a sign of the King's peace of mind at Windsor that he allowed the household to wear short jackets instead of the obligatory frock coat worn in London. He rode in the early morning, played golf, took the children out in a brake drawn by four greys and during the whole of one April afternoon picked primroses for his mother. The Queen was happy, too. She went to work in the library, tracing forgotten treasures, cataloguing and arranging. Her husband's contribution to such pursuits was entirely negative. He ordered Esher to destroy all the letters of Georgiana, Duchess of Devonshire to George IV. For once, however, that faithful servant seems to have disobeyed a command. The indiscreet letters passed into his own library, and nearly half a century later were sent to the saleroom by his descendants.

'Nothing can be quieter or more domestic,' Esher wrote in the spring of

1911. 'We have reverted to the ways of Queen Victoria. Dinner in the Oak Room, sitting in the Corridor till tea, when all go to their avocations – the King to his work and early to bed.' He told Admiral Fisher that it was like staying in a quiet vicarage. Not all the guests appreciated the change. Lord Crewe, the Liberal minister, invited to Windsor for Ascot week, missed King Edward's 'intense and commanding personality'. And Mensdorff noted crossly: 'The evenings were tedious. No bridge, so we just stood about, which makes me incredibly bored and weary.'

Max Beerbohm echoed the discontent of the fashionable world in a slight piecè entitled *Ballade Tragique à Double Refrain*. Here are two stanzas from this imaginary exchange between a lord-in-waiting and a lady-in-waiting:

HE:

Last evening
I found him with a rural dean
Talking of District Visiting....
The King is duller than the Queen.

SHE:

At any rate he doesn't sew;
You don't see him embellishing
Yard after yard of calico....
The Queen is duller than the King.

At dinner one night, Lady Leicester, wife of the King's neighbour in Norfolk, complained in similar vein to Lord Lincolnshire, the Lord Great Chamberlain. But that Liberal landowner had no sympathy with the whims of society ladies. He wrote in his diary:

When the King came to the throne they all said, 'At last we have got a strong man': and he has shown his strength in a very unexpected way. He used to talk very freely as Prince of Wales and they all thought he was a strong Tory; and that the aristocracy would be able to do what they liked with him. They have discovered that he is a man of strong will, and not as yet in any way susceptible to female influence: and so in their disappointment the society people lose no opportunity of 'crabbing' him.

The King's opinion of the smart set was emphatic. 'We have seen enough of the intrigue and meddling of certain ladies,' he told Mensdorff. 'I'm not interested in any wife except my own.'

That, however, did not protect him from paying the penalty of his father's less austere habits. Hardly had the Mylius case subsided when the blameless King was exposed to another seamy scandal. The Countess of Warwick, in desperate need of money to satisfy her creditors, let it be known that she was prepared to sell the letters written to her by King Edward VII when Prince of Wales. Her price approached £100,000. King

Edward was no Voltaire; but that was the sum she claimed to have spent entertaining her royal lover in the style he demanded of his friends. Told of her blackmailing intentions, Arthur du Cros, Conservative Member of Parliament and founder of the Dunlop Rubber Company, felt obliged to act as an honourable though increasingly reluctant intermediary between Lady Warwick and the royal household. In Lord Stamfordham, however, she had met her match. He persuaded du Cros to keep the financial negotiations on the boil until the King's solicitor was ready to make a sudden and stealthy application to the High Court. The judiciary declared that it would be illegal to publish the compromising letters, at least in Great Britain; and to ensure that Lady Warwick should not be tempted to sell them to an American publisher, du Cros generously paid £64,000 of her debts. For these and other services he was in 1916 created a baronet.

An immeasurable gulf separated the private lives of King George and Queen Mary from that imbroglio of adultery, improvidence and blackmail. They were not unworldly. As occasion demanded, the King and Queen appeared in public, gave banquets and balls, progressed from one palace to another; that was their duty. Virtue, however, was to be sought in seclusion, in a modest house which for more than thirty years they regarded as their only home.

York Cottage, Sandringham, has won no prizes for architectural merit. Harold Nicolson's description strikes a note of well-bred disdain:

It was, and remains, a glum little villa, encompassed by thickets of laurel and rhododendron, shadowed by huge Wellingtonias and separated by an abrupt rim of lawn from a pond, at the edge of which a leaden pelican gazes in dejection upon the water lilies and bamboos. The local brown stone in which the house was constructed is concealed by rough-cast which in its turn is enlivened by very imitation Tudor beams. The rooms inside, with their fumed oak surrounds, their white overmantels framing oval mirrors, their Doulton tiles and stained glass fanlights, are indistinguishable from those of any Surbiton or Upper Norwood home.

That aesthetic shudder would have seemed not so much impertinent as incomprehensible to those who lived in York Cottage. It was compact; it was comfortable; it was home. The Empress Frederick, considered by the family to have inherited the artistic taste of her father the Prince Consort, wrote to her daughter, the Queen of the Hellenes: 'York Cottage is very small, but most charmingly arranged, it would quite delight you, and you might take many a hint for your own house.' The future Archbishop Lang was equally enchanted: 'It might have been a curate and his wife in their new home.'

Later generations, however, may wonder at a monarch who owned some of the most splendid collections in the world yet bought his furniture in the Tottenham Court Road and hung his walls with reproductions from the Royal Academy. The King was not indifferent to his surroundings. Throughout his career as a naval officer he had endlessly fussed over the paintwork and fittings of his ship's cabin; but having made a decision, he hated change. What had pleased the young Duke of York on his honeymoon continued to satisfy the sovereign. One touch was entirely his own. He lined his study walls with the scarlet cloth used for making the trousers of the French Army. Today York Cottage is the Sandringham estate office and the study houses a telephone switchboard; although faded by time, the red of the Republic still glows with warmth.

If Queen Mary found the cottage ugly, she held her peace. In any case, her appreciation of pictures was guided more by family sentiment than by recognized canons of taste. She would be less captivated by a Rembrandt or a Rubens than by a framed princeling in bobtail wig and Garter ribbon. The limit of her criticism was to observe ruefully as she looked at some patterns for curtains: 'One should really have in mind a doll's house.'

York Cottage was undeniably small. The regular arrival of children, all of whom except the eldest were born there, required continual extensions, including those essential amenities of Edwardian country life, a schoolroom and a billiard-room. By the beginning of the new reign, forty people could crowd into a maze of twisting passages, narrow stairs and bedrooms the size of a housemaid's cupboard; a Cambridge vicar, Canon Edward Woods, invited to preach in 1924, noted that the drawing-room was smaller than his own. A perpetual smell of cooking implied the presence of that host of servants indispensable to even a Petit Trianon. But there was nowhere for them to sleep on the premises and the King said he supposed they roosted in the trees. The resident private secretary had to grapple with the sovereign's business in his bedroom; he could telephone only from the schoolroom or the passage, and visitors were accommodated with a chair outside his door.

Sir Charles Cust, the King's lifelong equerry and candid friend, once ventured to say that it was absurd for a large house like Sandringham to be inhabited by an old lady and her unmarried daughter while York Cottage had to house a married man, his wife and six children, especially when that man happened to be King. Although allowed more licence than any other courtier, he was on this occasion told very sharply to mind his own business. There was a compelling reason why the King could not ask his widowed mother to exchange Sandringham for a smaller, more suitable house: King Edward had specifically bequeathed it to her for her lifetime. Only after Queen Alexandra's death in 1925 did her son at last abandon York Cottage, albeit with some regret, and move to Sandringham House.

Yet at any time during those fifteen years he could have taken a lease on some equally large Norfolk property, as his father had wished. Landowners were still feeling the pinch of the late nineteenth-century agricultural depression and would have been only too willing to welcome the King as a tenant. That, however, would have required him to lead the life of a county magnate, to accept and dispense hospitality. He preferred his cottage. In just such a mood, Mr Gladstone had turned down a plan to move his official residence from No. 10 Downing Street to the far more magnificent Dover House. 'It would', he explained, 'oblige the Prime Minister to receive.'

Although immured in the cramped and sunless confines of York Cottage, the King and Queen did not live like slovens. The Duke of Windsor wrote of his father:

Everything about him was always of the best – his clothes, his fine hammer guns by Purdey, his food, his stationery, his cigarette cases by Fabergé, the presents he gave to his friends.

My father's life was a masterpiece in the art of well-ordered, unostentatious, elegant living. No matter the place, no matter the occasion, perfection pervaded every detail.

Those 12-bores made by Purdey were among the King's most cherished possessions. As in dress, so in sport, he resisted the tide of fashion, clinging to a hammer mechanism long after other shots of his stature had ceased to use it. His guns were a delight both to the touch and to the eye, beautifully balanced and of incomparable workmanship. They had to be: he required them to fire as many as 30,000 cartridges a year.

Throughout the season the King and his friends would tramp those Norfolk coverts where the cry of a cock pheasant falls as music on the ear. He loved best to match his skill against the wily flight of the woodcock; partridges, too, he enjoyed. He shot with elegant ease, left arm very straight, hands gloved; an appreciative female audience improved his performance. It has sometimes been said that he despised those *battues* of hand-reared pheasants which among rich Edwardians passed for sport. That is untrue. He did not encourage such competitive carnage; but neither did he spurn it, particularly if the birds flew high and fast. 'I watched the King and kept count,' Lord Burnham's agent reported of a shoot at Hall Barn. 'He brought down thirty-nine birds with thirty-nine consecutive cartridges and only with the fortieth did he miss.'

On home ground, too, he would blaze away until he stood on a carpet of spent cartridges, each bearing a tiny red crown. Behind the King and his loaders, a detective clicked up each addition to the bag on a pocket instrument that could record a four-figure total. Even his entourage sometimes flinched. Lord Lincolnshire wrote: 'Seven guns in four days at Sandringham killed 10,000 head. The King one day fired 1,700 cartridges and killed 1,000 pheasants. Can this terrific slaughter possibly last much longer?' Lord Stamfordham wrote of the same shoot in December 1912: 'They have been slaughtering thousands here all this week. De Grey, Stonor and co. say the pheasants are ridiculous in their slow flight. Pity.' The King would have been shocked had anyone questioned his love for the animal kingdom. A niece, walking with him at Windsor, noticed that when they came on a dead garden bird his eyes filled with tears.

Sandringham at first cost the King £50,000 a year. It was a prodigious sum in the currency of the day, although he could well afford it. His civil list, the money voted by Parliament, was £470,000 a year, with another £50,000 or so from the estates of the Duchy of Lancaster. Much of the cost of Sandringham went in wages and pensions and donations to local charities; in keeping farms and cottages in good repair; in rearing many thousands of pheasants and protecting them from poachers and vermin. Huge quantities of game were given away to tenants and hospitals, to stationmasters and postmen. Domestic servants, who knew their rights in such matters, would, however, become restive if subjected to a surfeit of game in place of their traditional beef and mutton.

Extravagance, too, swelled the bills for Sandringham. Although the King himself scarcely entertained at York Cottage, he grudged his mother nothing. Acres of glass ensured an abundance of exotic fruit and flowers for the big house, where Queen Alexandra's hospitality remained reassuringly Edwardian. Mensdorff, a perennial guest, found it too much of a lotus land. 'Actually very tired after ten days at Sandringham,' he wrote. 'The dawdling finishes me off.'

The King had been allowed to play no part in the management of Sandringham during the seventeen years he spent at York Cottage between marriage and accession; it was his father's house and hobby. He thus inherited the estate in 1910 knowing little of its economics or of the conditions in which the farm labourers lived and worked. According to Lord Lincolnshire, President of the Board of Agriculture from 1905 to 1911 and himself the owner of 25,000 acres, the low wages at Sandringham were well known and often discussed in Norfolk. He noted in his diary that although the estate was run wastefully, 'some of the labourers on the Royal Farm only get (including harvest money) 16s. a week: and as they pay 1s.8d. for a cottage, it brings the total cash wages down to 14s. a week. There will be a terrific scandal if this comes out.'

Lincolnshire was fortunately well placed to secure a remedy: not as Lord Great Chamberlain, an hereditary office which brought him control of the Palace of Westminster, but as the brother of Sir William Carington, the King's Keeper of the Privy Purse, or treasurer. In spite of opposition from the agent at Sandringham, responsible for day-to-day administration, Lincolnshire persuaded his brother that a labourer's weekly wage should at once be raised to 19s. and that there should also be a Saturday half-holiday. 'The King never hesitated,' Carington reported. In the same open-handed way, the King gave orders to the Chancellor of the Duchy of Lancaster: 'Everything to be fair and more than fair; wages, cottages, everything.' It was not long before a standard minimum wage of £1 a week, high for those days, had been introduced on all the royal estates.

The King's Norfolk neighbours had no such scruples and resented a generosity that could not fail to squeeze their own, often less well-lined pockets. It was therefore with satisfaction that they heard of a strike at Sandringham only a few weeks after wages had been raised; the men were protesting against the summer custom of working from six in the morning to six in the evening, with a two-hour break in the middle of the day. Farmers said that the King's bounty had served only to unsettle the labourers and to make them greedy; Lincolnshire replied that it showed how the Sandringham reforms had been carried out only just in time.

That considerable landowner the Earl of Leicester was among those who had felt obliged to follow his lead in raising wages. Soon afterwards his wife said to him: 'It is rather a long time since the King and Queen have been to Holkham. Should I ask them to luncheon?' Lord Leicester replied: 'No, Alice, don't encourage them.'

A country gentleman of orderly habits sometimes found the demands of monarchy unsettling. 'The most terrible ordeal I have ever gone through,' was how he described the events of 6 February 1911. In retrospect his anguish seems excessive. The King was referring not to catastrophe or bereavement but to the State opening of a new Parliament; to his presence at the Palace of Westminster, where he addressed the assembled Lords and Commons. It could have imposed no strain of literary composition. The purpose of the Speech from the Throne was, and remains, to announce the future legislative programme of the Government. Every word had thus been written by Mr Asquith and his Cabinet colleagues. No more was required of the King than a clear enunciation; yet the nervous strain it imposed on him was acute and prolonged. The Queen shared her husband's distress. 'It was a terrible ordeal for us yesterday,' she told Esher, 'as you will readily understand, but the sympathetic attitude of the crowds and of everybody helped us greatly and gave us confidence.'

The King never quite came to terms with this annual duty. Exactly seventeen years later he wrote in his diary: 'May's cough is still rather troublesome, so she was unable to accompany me to Westminster when I opened Parliament; therefore I felt more nervous; luckily the speech was a short one.' Stamfordham tried to protect his master by begging the Prime Minister of the day not to burden him with speeches of 'inordinate length'. And the King, unable to control a shaking hand, had them printed in large type on thick paper that did not rustle. He did, however, enjoy the humour of this letter from an equally oppressed subject:

Dear King,
Please will you not put quite such hard words in your speeches, because at my school we have them for dictation. Your speeches are very interesting but there are hard words in them.
                                    Yours respectivly,
                                    Enid Prichard.

Stamfordham took a mildly malicious pleasure in sending the letter to the real author of the speech. 'It is impossible', he told the Prime Minister, 'to please everyone.'

A generation earlier, during Queen Victoria's visit to Coburg, Sir Henry Ponsonby had written: 'So what with uniform and not uniform, one is all day dressing or bothering.' Neither of those royal functions troubled the King; indeed, they were the only ceremonial duties which he found more or less tolerable. An exacting patron of civil and military tailors, he wore his clothes and accoutrements with pride; even his stars of the orders of chivalry were made slightly smaller than regulation size to form a pleasing pattern on the breast. Occasionally he allowed himself a private grumble. 'Very tired,' he wrote when obliged to wear German uniform during a visit to Berlin. 'I had my long boots on from 3.45 to 10.30 and they were new and patent leather.' He demanded the same dedication from others. At the opening of Parliament he was not too nervous to detect that Lord Morley was wearing plain clothes instead of the uniform of a Privy Counsellor, although the old statesman had tried to avoid that gimlet eye by wrapping himself up in his peer's robes. A peeress who inadvertently attended the ceremony in a hat instead of a tiara received a severe rebuke. 'I made her write a humble apology,' the Lord Great Chamberlain noted, 'which was accepted.'

Four months after opening Parliament for the first time, the King underwent a sterner test. On 22 June 1911, he and the Queen drove to Westminster Abbey for their coronation. The sacred ceremony, enriched by the most sumptuous pageantry of Church and State, embodies a thousand years of history. For a few hours the monarch is required to assume the symbolic role of a more heroic age. He is presented to his people for recognition; swears to uphold their laws and religion; is anointed with

consecrated oil and invested with ancient regalia; crowned and enthroned, he receives the homage of the Lords Spiritual and Temporal. In a hardly less majestic ceremony, the Queen Consort is similarly revered.

One of the most perceptive commentaries on George v's coronation was written by a Liberal minister: Alexander Murray, Master of Elibank, the courtesy title he bore as the eldest son of a Scottish peer. 'The King', he noted, 'behaved throughout as those who knew him expected him to act: evidently profoundly impressed with the importance and sacredness of the occasion, but with the calmness and quiet dignity of a perfect English gentleman.'

The same restraint marks the King's own account, as detached as an extract from a ship's log. 'Overcast and cloudy,' it begins, 'with some showers and a strongish cool breeze, but better for the people than great heat.' Only when he mentions his eldest son and his wife does his record glow with emotion: 'I nearly broke down when dear David came to do homage to me, as it reminded me so much of when I did the same thing to beloved Papa, he did it so well.'

As if time had stood still for centuries, the golden-haired boy prince removed his coronet, knelt at the King's feet and spoke these words: 'I, Prince of Wales, do become your liege man of life and limb, and of earthly worship; and faith and truth I will bear unto you, to live and die, against all manner of folks. So help me God.'

The Prince rose, touched the crown upon the King's head and kissed him on the left cheek. So much was required by custom. But the boy's sovereign was also his father. The King drew his son gently towards him and kissed him on the right cheek.

King, Queen and Prince all suffered from nerves that day. Here is another passage from the Master of Elibank's long letter to his wife:

The Queen looked pale and strained. You felt she was a great lady, but *not* a Queen. She was almost shrinking as she walked up the aisle giving the impression that she would have liked to have made her way to her seat by some back entrance: the contrast on her 'return' - crowned - was magnetic, as if she had undergone some marvellous transformation. Instead of the shy creature for whom one had felt pity, one saw her emerge from the ceremony with a bearing and dignity, and a quiet confidence, signifying that she really felt that she was Queen of this great Empire, and that she derived strength and legitimate pride from the knowledge of it.

In his own account of the coronation, the King's tribute to his wife was brief but heartfelt. 'Darling May looked lovely, and it was indeed a comfort to me to have her by my side, as she has been ever to me during these last eighteen years.' As an imaginative gesture to the Queen, he proposed that her eldest brother, the Duke of Teck, should receive the style of Royal

Highness which their father had coveted in vain. When 'Dolly' Teck modestly declined the honour, the King offered both him and his only surviving brother, Prince Alexander, the Grand Cross of the Order of the Bath; this they accepted.

Other ceremonial details of the coronation were settled less easily. Again and again, the King had to interrupt his spiritual preparation to pronounce upon such trivia as the length and colour of princesses' trains or the distribution of decorations to foreign guests. Mensdorff, an authority on stars and ribbons, was asked 'whether it would quite do to give the same order to an archduke as to a Bulgarian general or Swedish admiral as members of a suite'.

Mr Asquith's proposed place in the Abbey also provoked an appeal to the King. 'It had been intended to conceal him amongst the Colonials,' Elibank wrote, 'but I made a row with the Earl Marshal's people ... After all, he is Prime Minister of Great Britain, and on the point of precedence arranged by King Edward he goes before Dukes.' Eventually Asquith was accommodated with a seat at the very heart of the ceremony. Two other statesmen appeared to be well satisfied with their respective roles. Balfour slept peacefully throughout the preliminaries of the service. And Curzon, in the words of Elibank, 'processed as if the whole proceedings were in his honour: the aisle was just wide enough for him'. Not all the coronation guests seem to have behaved so decorously. A young gold staff officer, or usher, reported at the end of the day that he had picked up three ropes of pearls, three-quarters of a diamond necklace, twenty brooches, six or seven bracelets and nearly twenty balls knocked off coronets. He estimated his haul of debris to be worth £20,000; and there were about 200 such officials on duty.

'Uneasy lies the head that wears a crown,' the lament which Shakespeare put into the mouth of King Henry IV, has in a very literal sense been echoed by succeeding sovereigns. St Edward's crown, worn only at the coronation, weighs five pounds, and becomes oppressively painful in the course of a long ceremonial service. 'The Crown hurt me a great deal,' Queen Victoria wrote after her coronation in 1838. Even the Imperial State crown weighs three and a half pounds, and she soon ceased to wear it at the opening of Parliament. Edward VII followed her example, wearing instead the cocked hat of a Field-Marshal. But George V cherished the crown as a symbol of the duties to which he had dedicated his life. In 1913 he therefore sought the advice of his Government. Sir Charles Hobhouse superciliously noted: 'Cabinet this morning. The King is much exercised as to what he ought to wear on his head at the opening of Parliament ... As we none of us cared what he wears, we agreed to the Crown.' Four days later the King himself

wrote in his diary: 'I wore my Crown as many people wished it and had not been worn for opening of Parliament for over 60 years.'

It proved an increasing burden. In 1924 the King confessed to Lord Lincolnshire that the crown had given him so bad a headache, he could not have gone on five minutes longer. In 1935, at the age of seventy, he asked the Prime Minister whether it was necessary for him to continue wearing it. MacDonald replied that there was no such need. As it turned out, the King never again opened Parliament. That year the ceremony he had so dreaded was cancelled on the death of Princess Victoria; and within a few weeks the crown lay on his own coffin.

FIVE

CONSTITUTIONAL MONARCH

Red boxes — Lords v. Commons — Delhi Durbar —
Irish Home Rule — Naval rearmament — The Kaiser

'MY Ministers come and go and are relieved of their duties,' the King told a friend, 'but I am here always.' Balfour, summoned to Osborne where Queen Victoria lay dying, was astounded by the relentless flow of despatch boxes demanding her attention; and he had been in high office almost continuously since 1885. Her grandson was no less a prisoner for life. Even at Sandringham, free from ceremonial cares, he had to spend between three and four hours a day reading and annotating State papers. In the last year of his reign, his doctors ordered him to prepare for his Silver Jubilee celebrations by taking a short holiday by the sea. Sir Samuel Hoare nevertheless found him at work each morning from 8 to 9.30, when he joined the Queen for breakfast. What power lay concealed in those increasingly battered red boxes?

Unfettered by a written constitution, the theoretical responsibilities inherited by the sovereign were boundless. Bagehot fancifully claimed that the monarch, without parliamentary restraint, could declare war on France for the conquest of Brittany and conclude peace by the sacrifice of Cornwall; make every man and woman in the kingdom a peer and every village a university; disband the army and the navy, dismiss the civil service and pardon all prisoners.

The obsequious language in which it was – and remains – customary to address the sovereign lends apparent substance to the fantasy. Winston Churchill, who could be an exceptionally wilful Minister, wrote to the King on exchanging the Home Office for the Admiralty in October 1911:

The very gracious words which your Majesty used to me yesterday will ever be remembered in my heart with a deep sense of pleasure and gratitude. It has been a high honour to me to have stood so near to your Majesty during the moving and memorable events of the first year of a happily and brilliantly inaugurated reign.

Even that, however, seems almost disrespectful when compared with the inimitable fulsomeness of another royal intimate:

Lord Esher presents his humble duty to Your Majesty and with great deference begs to recur to the question of whether the *Selection from Queen Victoria's Correspondence* should be in the form of three or four volumes. . . .

Viscount Esher hopes that Your Majesty will forgive him for venturing to offer these observations. . . .

Viscount Esher begs humbly to be allowed to wish Your Majesty the happiest and most prosperous New Year. . . .

Professor Harold Laski later expressed his wonder that a man of Esher's obvious capacity could live for some forty years in a state of constant genuflexion.

These picturesque relics of absolutism conceal a constitutional revolution. Throughout the past three hundred years, the authority of kingship has been transferred to an abstraction called the Crown; to a succession of governments which act in the sovereign's name but are themselves dependent upon parliamentary elections. Charles Masterman, a minister in Asquith's Cabinet, wrote drolly of the contrast between the architecture of the House of Commons and its radical members:

Everywhere the eye is greeted by sumptuous panelling and a multiplicity of those rigid lines in which the Tudors delighted. What we are seeing today is Mr. Keir Hardie in the environment of Henry VIII – that is the splendid and characteristic contradiction which lends such piquant meaning to the new democracy. Here in the style of pure royalism . . . you expect to meet Queen Elizabeth, and lo! it is John Burns.

Bagehot put it more concisely: 'A Republic has insinuated itself beneath the folds of a Monarchy.'

Paradoxically, this erosion of royal power rests upon the doctrine that the King can do no wrong: a charter, it may be thought, of majestic misbehaviour. That is not its meaning. Rather does it imply that the King is infallible only because his acts are not his own; that as head of State he can perform scarcely any constitutional functions except on the advice of his ministers, who accept responsibility for them. The King can do no wrong; but his ministers can.

Although increasingly impotent, the sovereign remains an essential instrument of government. Without royal assent, parliament may not be summoned or its measures become law; taxes may not be levied; no minister, judge, magistrate, bishop, ambassador or officer of the armed forces can take office, no honour or pardon or promotion in the public service is valid.

In theory, therefore, the sovereign could swiftly bring the machinery of government to a stop by a wholesale rejection of ministerial advice. In practice it is a course which he dare not contemplate except to preserve the peace and safety of the realm.

If for example a Government attempted to perpetuate itself in office, the sovereign would be justified in reviving his dormant power; by threatening to dismiss the factious ministers, he would oblige them either to abandon their assault on the constitution or to seek the approval of the electorate. On any issue less grave, the sovereign would be wise to act with caution. For if his thwarted advisers should seek and win a general election fought on the emotive theme of monarch versus people, the fate of monarchy itself would be at risk.

Thus far the constitutional sovereign seems to have many duties but little initiative. His role, however, need be neither so insipid nor so frustrating. In his relations with ministers he may claim three prerogatives: the right to be consulted, the right to encourage and the right to warn. These can enable a determined monarch to modify government policy without changing its ultimate direction, to restrain though not to obstruct. It is an influence most effective when used sparingly. A perpetual state of tension, a nagging challenge to this aspect of policy or that, will provoke only a bland unconcern. Nor dare an aspiring sovereign be less well-informed than his ministers. Here is Bagehot's illuminating advice:

The characteristic advantage of a constitutional king is the permanence of his place. This gives him the opportunity of acquiring a consecutive knowledge of complex transactions, but it gives only an opportunity. The king must use it. There is no royal road to political affairs: their detail is vast, disagreeable, complicated and miscellaneous. A king, to be the equal of his ministers in discussion, must work as they work; he must be a man of business as they are men of business.

Queen Victoria set an example to all succeeding monarchs. Her industry was so prodigious as sometimes almost to overwhelm her ministers. In 1846 Sir Robert Peel warned Gladstone what was expected of a Victorian Prime Minister:

There is the whole correspondence with the Queen, several times a day, and all requiring to be in my own hand, and to be carefully done; the whole correspondence with peers and members of parliament, in my own hand, as well as other persons of consequence; the sitting seven or eight hours a day to listen to such trash in the House of Commons.

Nearly half a century later, Lord Salisbury uttered a similar *cri de cœur*: 'I could do very well with two Departments, in fact I have four – the Prime

Ministership, the Foreign Office, the Queen and Randolph Churchill; and the burden increases in that order.'

The Queen was particularly vigilant in diplomatic and military affairs. During negotiations for the treaty with Russia after the Crimean War, every draft and despatch had to be discussed with her line by line. Nor could any promotion, appointment or reward be gazetted for any officer above the rank of colonel without a long written explanation to the Queen in the minister's own hand. Again and again she put her own distinctive interpretation on constitutional practice. In 1881 she refused to approve the Speech from the Throne prepared by Gladstone's Cabinet until it had been amended to meet her wishes. With wicked irresponsibility, Disraeli stiffened her resolve in a letter beginning: 'Madam, and most beloved Sovereign, The principle ... that the Speech of the Sovereign is only the Speech of the Ministers is a principle not known to the British Constitution. It is only a piece of Parliamentary gossip.' With the same cavalier disregard for precedent, she also demanded a decisive voice in ecclesiastical appointments.

King Edward was equally conscious of his traditional rights, but failed to exert the influence of his mother. One reason was the increasing range and pace of government business which led his ministers to resent too close a scrutiny of departmental policy. Another was the King's supposed inexperience. Having been starved of responsibility during his long years as Heir Apparent, he had no obvious claim on their respect. Balfour would punctiliously report Cabinet conclusions to him, but declined to elaborate on the discussions and differences which lay behind them. His Liberal successor as Prime Minister, Campbell-Bannerman, was almost insultingly casual in keeping the King informed.

The accession of George v seemed to herald a further erosion of the royal prerogative. Lacking both a political education and the urbane self-assurance of his father, the new King was thought unlikely to be the match of his radical ministers. He proved unexpectedly tenacious in defending his rights. As Prince of Wales he had been encouraged by King Edward to read Cabinet papers and Foreign Office telegrams, to follow the debates in both Houses of Parliament, to discuss the issues of the day with politicians and civil servants. 'I am not a clever man,' he said, 'but if I had not picked up something from all the brains I've met, I would be an idiot.'

What led his contemporaries to underestimate him was a nervous loquacity, a torrent of not always well-chosen words which inhibited discussion. A Colonial Governor who was summoned to Buckingham Palace described the occasion as an audience in its absolute sense: 'I listened and the King did all the talking.' Asquith wrote to Churchill one summer: 'I understand that it is your turn to go to Balmoral next week: so I send a word of friendly warning. You will find the Royal mind obsessed and the Royal tongue exceptionally fluid and voluble.'

When Morley grumbled about this habit of the King, the faithful Lincolnshire defended his sovereign in the idiom of Newmarket: 'I pointed out that the Almighty was a very good handicapper, and no one was chucked into the race of life at 6 stone 10.' It was a venial fault. All who did business with the King soon came to realize how thoroughly his deliberative mind mastered the topics of the day.

In what the King called 'my responsible and rather lonely position', he was well served by his immediate entourage. Soon after his accession he appointed Lord Knollys to be his joint private secretary with Lord Stamfordham. Knollys came of a long line of courtiers stretching back to Sir Francis Knollys, Treasurer of the Household to Queen Elizabeth I. He himself worked in the office of his father, Sir William Knollys, Treasurer of the Household to Edward VII when Prince of Wales. In 1870 he became private secretary to the Prince, remaining with him until his death as King forty years later. All King Edward's children had loved 'Fooks' from their days in the nursery, and George V would often refer to him as 'my oldest friend'. He had every quality required of a private secretary except a respect for orders and decorations, which he acquired in profusion but affected to despise. A convivial man suspected in youth of rakishness, he displayed a sense of humour that contrasted with Stamfordham's awesome austerity. When arranging King Edward's visit to Lord Rosebery at Mentmore, Knollys told the host: 'He would like either sparkling moselle or champagne. I should prefer *both*!'

Behind the *bonhomie*, however, lay resolve. The two private secretaries, who between them could boast seventy years in the highest royal service, had no intention of letting their master's prerogatives go by default. Few ministers escaped their plaintive or admonitory letters. Sometimes these were justified, as when the King first learned of government intentions from the newspapers. Here, for example, is the pained rebuke which Knollys wrote to Asquith in November 1911:

He feels sure you have never any wish to treat him but with the utmost attention and propriety, but he still cannot help feeling surprised that you made no reference to the Manhood Franchise Bill when you had so good an opportunity on Monday. ... The King feels very strongly that he should have been formally informed of what was proposed, and that he should not have been left to hear what was contemplated through the Press.

Other missives from Buckingham Palace were of the utmost triviality. A minister might be reproved for wearing the wrong sort of hat or for a chance phrase in an unimportant speech or letter. It was an exegesis which kept the Government on its toes, but at a needless cost of time and trouble.

The most bizarre conflict of the early reign concerned Winston Churchill. It had long been customary for either the Prime Minister or a member of his Cabinet to write a nightly letter to the sovereign describing the parliamentary proceedings of the past twenty-four hours. Since these accounts were designed to supplement rather than duplicate the verbatim reports of *Hansard*, they reflected the personality of the author; and Churchill was not a man to conceal his opinions. On 10 February 1911 he sent the King an account of a Commons debate on the relief of unemployment. It included this passage: 'As for tramps and wastrels there ought to be proper Labour Colonies where they could be sent for considerable periods and made to realise their duty to the State. . . . It must not however be forgotten that there are idlers and wastrels at both ends of the social scale.'

Knollys was at once instructed to protest to the Prime Minister. He wrote:

The King thinks that Mr. Churchill's views, as contained in the enclosed, are very socialistic. What he advocates is nothing more than workshops which have been tried in France and have turned out a complete failure. In 1849 Louis Blanc introduced them in Paris and we all know what was the result: they were in reality the forerunner of the street fighting in June of that year when so many thousands lost their lives.

HM considers it quite superfluous for Churchill in a letter of the description he was writing to him, to bring in about 'idlers and wastrels at both ends of the social ladder.'

Churchill reacted angrily to this message of royal displeasure. He denied that his views were, or could fairly be interpreted, as socialistic; and in deferential language which nevertheless hinted at mockery, he invited the King to find a less contentious correspondent:

Mr. Churchill will also feel a serious difficulty in writing these letters in the future after what has occurred, for fear that in a moment of inadvertence or fatigue some phrase or expression may escape him which will produce an unfavourable impression on Your Majesty. He therefore would earnestly desire that Your Majesty would give commands that the duty should be transferred to some other Minister who would be able to write with the feelings of confidence in Your Majesty's gracious and indulgent favour, which Mr. Churchill deeply regrets to have lost.

Knollys was annoyed by that defiant reply. 'I don't think the tone of the letter is quite a proper one,' he noted, 'nor has he taken the matter in the right way.' He told Churchill that the King would have preferred the Home Secretary to suppress his remark about idlers and wastrels, 'to which moreover an obvious answer might be offered that the cost of support in one case falls on the State and does not do so in the other'. Knollys ended on a more conciliatory note: 'The King directs me to add that your letters are always instructive and interesting and he would be sorry if he were to receive no further ones from you in the future.' After further exchanges, that in all ran to several thousand words, a barely mollified Churchill agreed to continue his task.

With more experience, the King might have hesitated before reproving his Home Secretary for a personal opinion which did not represent government policy; with more self-confidence he would certainly not have felt obliged to defend a handful of society wastrels from Churchill's contempt. As it was, the most constitutionally correct and industrious of monarchs appeared to identify himself with Conservative prejudices and aristocratic excess. His wise grandmother, by contrast, wrote in 1868:

Danger lies *not* in the power given to the Lower Orders, who are daily becoming more well-informed and more intelligent, and who will *deservedly* work themselves up to the top by their own merits, labour and good conduct, but in the conduct of the *Higher Classes* and of the *Aristocracy*.

The King's error of judgement was provoked less by Churchill's sentiments than by his character. Only a few days earlier he had written to thank the Home Secretary for his deft handling of the Mylius affair. Yet he remained mistrustful of Churchill's ebullient personality and political opportunism. 'Almost more of a cad in office than he was in opposition,' had been King Edward's verdict, and his son agreed. Knollys, too, showed a lack of proportion in encouraging his master to rebuke Churchill; it is unlikely that his rejoinder on Louis Blanc's workshops came from the King's own slender store of French history. Trifling in itself, the episode cast doubts on the political impartiality of the Sovereign and the sagacity of his joint private secretary. In the protracted constitutional crisis of 1910–11, the King could not afford to incur either suspicion.

The quarrel between Lords and Commons which embittered the first year of the reign had been smouldering for almost a century. Again and again, an hereditary House of Lords had exercised its right to amend or reject the legislation of an elected House of Commons. Conservative administrations had nothing to fear; they could depend upon a permanent majority of Conservative peers to endorse their policies. The Liberals, by contrast, lived in the shadow of the veto; holding office by the expressed will of the people, they governed only by the consent of a few hundred Tory landowners.

In the House of Lords, Conservative ascendency was further strengthened by a mass defection of Liberal peers. Unable to stomach Gladstone's pursuit of Home Rule for Ireland and other radical measures, the Liberal Unionists became Conservative in all but name. In 1893 the new alliance ensured the defeat of Home Rule in the Lords by 419 votes to 41.

Divided and crushed, the Liberal Party could do no more than huff and puff at the affront to parliamentary democracy. In the 1906 general election, however, they swept back into power with one of the largest majorities of any House of Commons: 377 Liberals, buttressed by 83 Irish Nationalists and 53 Labour members. That made a combined strength of 513, compared with 132 Conservatives and 25 Liberal Unionists. Would the House of Lords dare to continue using its Conservative majority of almost 400 to thwart so decisive a verdict of the electorate? The answer came from Arthur Balfour himself, who lost not only the election but also his own seat. That master of ambiguity, speaking for once with absolute clarity, claimed that 'the great Unionist party should still control, whether in power or whether in Opposition, the destinies of this great nation'.

Campbell-Bannerman's new Government, pledged to an ambitious programme of social reform, could make little progress against a hostile House of Lords. Some measures were sent back to the Commons amended to the point of emasculation: among them the Education Bill of 1906, designed to abolish the financing of religious instruction in Church schools out of local rates. Others were rejected outright, such as the Licensing Bill of 1908 which sought to limit the number of public houses yet offered scant compensation to dispossessed owners. Lloyd George spoke for all frustrated Liberals when he declared that the House of Lords, far from being the watchdog of the constitution, was Mr Balfour's poodle: 'It fetches and carries for him. It barks for him. It bites anybody that he sets it on to.' King Edward disliked such invective from a Cabinet Minister, but as he told his son, 'You cannot make a silk purse out of a sow's ear.'

It was not until 1909, the year after Asquith had succeeded Campbell-Bannerman as Prime Minister, that the conflict between Lords and Commons moved towards a crisis. The Budget introduced by Lloyd George, the new Chancellor of the Exchequer, was primarily designed to raise additional revenue for old-age pensions and naval rearmament; but it also heartened his fellow radicals by imposing a whole series of new taxes on the rich. In addition to a surtax of $2\frac{1}{2}$ per cent on the amount by which all incomes of £5,000 or more exceeded £3,000, there were four separate taxes on land: on future unearned increment of land values, on undeveloped land, on the realization of leases and on mineral rights.

The Conservatives determined to fight the proposals clause by clause, line by line. Not until November 1909, after 544 divisions and several all-

night sittings, could the Government complete the passage of the Finance
Bill through the Commons. The measure was then sent to the Lords to be
formally approved – not since the seventeenth century had the Upper
House refused to pass a money Bill. This time the peers rejected it out of
hand by 350 votes to 75. They were not acting wholly from self-interest;
however vindictive in intent, the Budget was far from extortionate in
practice. What outraged them more was the unprecedented use of financial
legislation as a weapon of class vengeance. On the highest constitutional
grounds they could also argue that the Chancellor had provoked their own
breach of custom by including in his Finance Bill an extraneous measure
for the compulsory registration of land. Lord Salisbury, son of the Conservative Prime Minister and himself a leading intransigent, declared during
the Budget debate that such a stratagem would enable a government to
reverse any previous legislation merely by inserting a clause to that effect in
a Finance Bill; the country could thus be reduced to single-chamber rule.

Since the State cannot function without money, the rejection of the
Budget forced an immediate general election. It was fought not only on the
issue of whether the Commons should retain absolute control over national
finance, but also on the broader theme of how far the Lords could be
permitted to amend or veto any other measure passed by the elected
chamber. Both major parties, as is their custom, claimed to be acting on
behalf of the people; one appealed to the authority of the ballot box,
reflected in the huge parliamentary majority of 1906, the other to the role
of an Upper House in curbing democratic tyranny.

The result of the general election in January 1910 satisfied neither party.
The Conservatives won back 100 seats. Yet the Liberals retained, with the
support of Labour and the Irish Nationalists, a majority large enough to
persuade the peers that it was now their duty to pass the previously rejected
Finance Bill. The House of Lords duly gave their assent to it without a
division.

In the Commons, Asquith had meanwhile tabled three resolutions which,
when embodied into an Act of Parliament, would permanently restrict the
powers of the Upper House. First, the Lords could neither amend nor
reject a money Bill, each such measure to be certified by the Speaker of the
Commons according to stringent rules. Secondly, the Lords could not delay
other legislation for more than two years and one month. Thirdly, the life
of any Parliament would be reduced from seven years to five, as a balance
to the increased authority of the Commons.

The Prime Minister embarked on his punitive programme with caution.
By winning the recent general election, he had ensured that the Lords
would now pass the Budget; but the loss of 100 Liberal seats to the
Unionists was scarcely a mandate for drastic constitutional reform. He

foresaw that to curb the veto of the Upper House by Act of Parliament would require a second general election, not to mention the assent of the intended victim; that if the Lords proved disobliging, he would have to ask the King to create enough Liberal peers to swamp the Conservative majority; that the King would regard such a wholesale creation as an affront to his dignity and an abuse of the royal prerogative; that there would be little enthusiasm outside Westminster for so unseemly a pantomime.

Yet Asquith was the prisoner of his reduced majority in the Commons; without the support of Labour and Irish Nationalist MPs, his Liberal followers numbered no more than the Unionist Opposition. Each of those uncertain allies demanded the same price: the abolition of the Lords' veto. Labour detested the Upper House and all its works on principle; John Redmond's Irish Nationalists saw the veto as the only obstacle to Home Rule. Throughout the spring of 1910, the Prime Minister trod a dialectical tightrope between those impatient suitors and an apprehensive Sovereign. On 6 May, the sudden death of King Edward VII left the problem unresolved. Thus from the very moment that King George V came to the throne he found himself at the centre of a constitutional crisis. For the next year and more it cast a fitful shadow over his life.

'I gave an audience to the Prime Minister,' the King wrote in his diary on 18 May 1910. 'We had a long talk. He said he would endeavour to come to some understanding with the Opposition to prevent a general election and he would not pay attention to what Redmond said.' Asquith had not abandoned his intention to curb the powers of the House of Lords, if need be by persuading the King to create enough new Liberal peers to overcome Unionist resistance. But out of consideration for a bereaved and inexperienced monarch, he would first try to resolve the problem in private talks with the Opposition. Balfour readily agreed to this sensible plan.

The Prime Minister had his own reasons for seeking a negotiated settlement: it would avoid the need for a second general election and allow the Government to resume its legislative programme. Yet it was the King who stood to gain most from the conference, whatever its outcome: a respite from constitutional turmoil at a time of anxiety and grief. His gratitude was not apparent. Only ten days after the comforting audience of 18 May, he told the Prime Minister not to make the usual recommendations for new peerages in the Birthday Honours, 'as during the transitional state of the House of Lords he would be reluctant to agree to them'. When Asquith protested at this breach of custom, Knollys sent an ungracious reply. 'The King', he wrote, 'yields reluctantly and hopes that only a limited number of names, carefully selected, will be submitted to him.' Asquith, he implied, could not logically continue to use the Upper House as an instrument of political patronage while seeking to diminish its role. It was a needless pinprick to inflict on a Prime Minister who had so far shown the utmost consideration.

Asquith and Balfour, each accompanied by three henchmen, began their constitutional talks on 17 June 1910. The following day the Prime Minister received one of Knollys's more constructive messages: 'The King hopes that the question of Life Peers may if possible be brought before the conference. He is strongly in favour of them as I believe are most sensible people.' That prescient suggestion had to wait more than half a century for fulfilment. The discussions which began in an atmosphere of goodwill soon felt the strain of political differences. A call by Lloyd George for a Coalition Government found some favour with Balfour, none with his party. By November the conference had foundered on an unacceptable Conservative proposal that any Bill for Irish Home Rule which was twice rejected by the Lords should be submitted to a national referendum.

The breakdown of the talks exposed both Prime Minister and Sovereign to the realities of political life. After six months of fruitless delay, Asquith's discontented parliamentary allies demanded retribution against the Lords and a swift advance to Irish Home Rule. The Prime Minister could no longer postpone an appeal to the country on the crucial issue of the veto. Yet without an assurance or guarantee of the King's willingness to create Liberal peers by the hundred there could be no prospect of surrender by the Lords. King Edward's last months had been made miserable by the dilemma; the burden of decision had now passed to his son.

On 11 November 1910, the Prime Minister travelled down to York Cottage, Sandringham. The King was relieved to hear how formal a role Asquith expected him to play: merely the granting of a dissolution of Parliament as a necessary preliminary to the general election. The King wrote in his diary for that day: 'At 6.30 the Prime Minister arrived. Had two long talks with him. He reported that the Conference had failed and he proposed to dissolve and have a general election and get it over before Xmas. He asked me for *no guaraniees*.' Sir Arthur Bigge – he did not become Lord Stamfordham until the following year – also kept a record of the conversation with Asquith: 'He did not ask for anything from the King: *no promises, no guarantees during this Parliament.*'

The joy expressed by those italics was short-lived. Three days later, Knollys was called to No. 10 Downing Street, where he learnt that the Prime Minister had apparently changed his mind. 'What he *now* advocates,' Knollys wrote to the King, 'is that you should give guarantees *at once* for the next Parliament.' Asquith justified this abrupt reversal by pleading that the object of his visit to Sandringham had not been 'to tender any definite advice, but to survey the new situation created by the failure of the Conference'. From a misleading delicacy of approach, it seemed, he had failed to warn the King that he was merely expounding in general terms the constitutional role of the monarch, and that the unpalatable advice was yet to come. A more probable explanation is that between the audience at Sandringham and the interview with Knollys three days later, Asquith succumbed to considerable pressure from his more radical colleagues.

Shocked by the Prime Minister's *volte-face*, the King instructed Bigge, who had remained with him at Sandringham, to send this telegram to Downing Street: 'His Majesty regrets that it would be impossible for him to give contingent guarantees and he reminds Mr. Asquith of his promise not to seek for any during the present Parliament.'

Even before Bigge's telegram reached Downing Street, the Prime Minister and his colleagues had drafted a minute that left the King in no doubt of their intentions:

The Cabinet has very carefully considered the situation created by the failure of the Conference, in view of the declaration of policy made on their behalf by the Prime Minister in the House of Commons on the 14th of April, 1910.

The advice which they feel it their duty to tender to His Majesty is as follows:

An immediate dissolution of Parliament, as soon as the necessary parts of the Budget, the provision of Old Age Pensions to paupers, and one or two other matters have been disposed of . . .

His Majesty's Ministers cannot, however, take the responsibility of advising a dissolution, unless they may understand that, in the event of the policy of the Government being approved by an adequate majority in the new House of Commons, His Majesty will be ready to exercise his constitutional powers (which may involve the Prerogative of creating Peers), if needed, to secure that effect should be given to the decision of the country.

His Majesty's Ministers are fully alive to the importance of keeping the name of the King out of the sphere of party and electoral controversy. They take upon themselves, as is their duty, the entire and exclusive responsibility for the policy which they will place before the electorate.

His Majesty will doubtless agree that it would be undesirable, in the interests of the State, that any communication of the intentions of the Crown should be made public, unless and until the actual occasion should arise.

The King read the document with suspicion and alarm, for it seemed to make demands on him which were unknown to the constitution. As recently as February 1910, while Edward VII still reigned, Asquith had professed a more orthodox doctrine in the Commons:

To ask in advance for a blank authority for an indefinite exercise of the Royal Prerogative in regard to a measure which had never been submitted to, or approved by, the House of Commons, is a request which, in my judgement, no constitutional statesman can properly make and it is a concession which the Sovereign cannot be expected to grant.

In the intervening nine months, nothing had happened to justify the Prime Minister's abandonment of that principle. The Parliament Bill to curb the Lords' veto had received only a formal first reading in the Commons; the Upper House had not yet had an opportunity of considering, much less of rejecting it. The one new factor was political not constitutional. In the course of a Commons debate on the veto in April, Asquith had made a rash promise in order to placate both his radical backbenchers and his Irish and Socialist allies. Speaking of the need for a second general election before the introduction of the Parliament Bill, he said: 'In no case shall we recommend Dissolution, except under such conditions as will secure that in the new Parliament the judgement of the People, as expressed in the Election, will be carried into law.'

So that Asquith might keep faith with his reckless pronouncement, the King was being asked to promise that he would if necessary create an un-limited number of Liberal peers in ill-defined circumstances. The Cabinet minute of 15 November was riddled with ambiguity. What was meant by 'the policy of the Government', the Parliament Bill itself or the general principles on which it was based? How many seats made 'an adequate majority'? To what did 'the actual occasion' refer? Would the King's pledge still be binding if amendments were made to the Parliament Bill? It is difficult to surmise how the author of so enigmatic a State paper could have earned his reputation, both in the Commons and at the Bar, for a precise mind.

For a Government to require the sovereign to create peers was not in itself unprecedented. Had the House of Lords declined to pass the Reform Bill of 1832, King William IV would have ensured the necessary majority. King Edward VII was similarly prepared to create enough peers to pass the Parliament Bill, but only after a second general election had tested public opinion. What he would not do was to give contingent guarantees, a refusal which Asquith had recognized in his speech of February 1910. Now the Cabinet was insisting, even before a second general election, that his son should *promise* to create peers. King George V, it seemed, could not be trusted to do his duty.

Asquith's principal reason for demanding such an assurance was to redeem, if challenged, the pledge he had given to the Commons in April. But he and his colleagues may also have doubted whether they could depend upon a King who as Prince of Wales had scarcely bothered to conceal his dislike of Liberals and Liberalism. After an encounter at Lord Londonderry's house, Edmund Gosse described the Prince as 'an overgrown schoolboy, loud and stupid, losing no opportunity of abusing the Government'. A stentorian voice trumpeted his careless disparagement of Lloyd George and Churchill, even of Asquith, throughout the official world. Mensdorff regularly reported his Conservative sentiments to Vienna. And while awaiting the first general election of 1910, the Prince made known his dread of a renewed Liberal victory.

From the moment he came to the throne, however, the King strove to maintain the traditional impartiality of the sovereign. In this he had the guidance of two experienced private secretaries, Knollys and Bigge. What nobody had foreseen is that at the most testing crisis of his reign they would fail to agree on the course their master should take. Although each had unrestrained access to the King, Knollys possessed an initial advantage over Bigge. In their division of duties, Knollys was responsible for corresponding on the King's behalf with all government departments except the War Office, which remained Bigge's province. He could thus exercise a general control over the Sovereign's relationship with the Prime Minister, and he did not hesitate to use it. When the tendentious Cabinet minute of 15 November 1910 reached the King at Sandringham, it was accompanied by a letter from Knollys:

I have just finished a conversation with the P.M. and Crewe and they have shown me the Cabinet Minute, which I think is couched in studiously moderate terms. I feel certain that you can safely and constitutionally accept what the Cabinet propose and I venture to urge you strongly to do so. What is now recommended is altogether different in every way from any request to be allowed publicity to announce that you have consented to give guarantees. It is a great compromise on the part of the Cabinet, made entirely to fall in as far as possible with your wishes and to enable you to act conscientiously.

Should you not approve of the proposal, it may be that the matter has not been sufficiently explained to you, and in that case, of course, I should be quite ready, should you desire it, to go to Sandringham tomorrow. Or, and what would be better, if you disagree, perhaps you might think it right to come to London to see the P.M. and Crewe.

Not satisfied with commending the Cabinet minute to the King in such fulsome terms, Knollys also enclosed a letter he had received that morning from the Master of Elibank, who as Liberal Chief Whip was responsible for the discipline of the parliamentary party in the Commons. It included this passage:

I am sure you will recognise that the Prime Minister has come through a year of unexpected difficulty and that in arranging and entering the Conference, he strained the loyalty of his party to a very strong degree. If there is a feeling in the country that he is in any way flinching from his duty now that the crisis is upon us again, it would only serve as help and encouragement to the Socialist and extreme forces in the country. A spirit of unrest pervades the working classes at this moment, and I am particularly anxious that nothing should occur to drag the King into the vortex of our political controversies.

Elibank ended by hoping that some way would be found of defining 'His Majesty's attitude as correct and constitutional, while at the same time safeguarding the Prime Minister'. Neither the letter from Knollys nor that from Elibank persuaded the King that he should agree to the demands of the Cabinet. He arranged to travel to London on the following day for further talks with Asquith at Buckingham Palace. Meanwhile he asked Bigge˙ to prepare a memorandum on the correspondence. It was at this point that the contrary views of the two private secretaries became apparent. Knollys had told the King: 'I feel certain that you can safely and constitutionally accept what the Cabinet propose and I venture to urge you strongly to do so.' Bigge urged him no less vigorously to reject the Cabinet minute:

The King's position is: he cannot give contingent guarantees. For by so doing he becomes a Partisan and is placing a powerful weapon in the hands of the Irish and Socialists who, assured of the abolition of the veto of the House of Lords, would hold before their electors the certainty of ultimate Home Rule and the carrying out of their Socialist programme. The Unionists would declare His Majesty was favouring the Government and placing them (the Unionists) at a disadvantage before their constituencies. Indeed, it is questionable whether His Majesty would be acting constitutionally. It is not His Majesty's duty to save the Prime Minister from the mistake of his incautious words on the 14th of April.

Bigge also replied sharply to Elibank's plea that it would be in the King's interest 'to safeguard the Prime Minister':

The King's position must also be considered. His Majesty fully recognises what must be the ultimate solution of the political situation if a dissolution takes place and if the Government are returned by an adequate majority. But why is he to make any promises now? Why should he be asked to deviate by an inch from the strictly constitutional path? You reply 'to safeguard the Prime Minister' and to avoid the King's name being dragged into the vortex of the political controversies and to prevent a handle being given to the Socialists to attack the King. But surely, so long as His Majesty adheres to what is constitutional, he can be indifferent to whether the Socialists 'so furiously rage together and imagine a vain thing' or not. . . .
I repeat, the King will do what is right.

The Cabinet, however, would not budge. At Buckingham Palace on the afternoon of 16 November, the King was overwhelmed by the menacing arguments of Mr Asquith and Lord Crewe, leader of the House of Lords. That night he wrote in his diary:

After a long talk I agreed most reluctantly to give the Cabinet a secret understanding that in the event of the Government being returned with a majority at the
General Election, I should use my Prerogative to make Peers if asked for. I disliked
having to do this very much, but agreed that this was the only alternative to the
Cabinet resigning, which at this moment would be disastrous.

Francis [Lord Knollys] strongly urged me to take this course and I think his
advice is generally very sound. I only trust and pray he is right this time.

It was a humiliating occasion. Here is what his friend Lord Derby noted
after talking to the King during a shooting party nine months later.

The King afterwards went to London and here saw Asquith and Crewe. When
they asked him for guarantees he complained that this was putting a pistol to his
head and asked Asquith what he (A) would do if he refused. The answer was: 'I
should immediately resign and at the next election should make the cry "The King
and the Peers against the people."' He then appealed to Crewe, who said that he
supported Asquith and that the whole Cabinet was united on the subject. He
further urged that they were asking the King to do nothing unconstitutional. He
begged to be allowed to see Arthur Balfour and Lansdowne but this was peremp-
torily refused. They bullied him for an hour and a half and he then told them that
he would give guarantees if they got a majority and asked to be allowed to make
this public. He said: 'I have been forced into this and I should like the country to
know it.' They declined and said that this was a confidential pledge and must be
kept so. In fact they bullied him and in his own language 'behaved disgracefully to
me'.

Bigge, having lost the battle for the King's will, could scarcely contain
his rage. He found relief in a scathing memorandum on his colleague's
conduct:

In less than 48 hours, Lord Knollys' mind has been entirely changed, as he was
adamant as to any assurance being given; today he strongly urges the King to come
to a secret understanding and tells me that by advocating resignation rather than
agree to any understanding I am exposing the King and the Monarchy to the
gravest dangers. He told the King he would have advised King Edward as he had
advised King George and that he was convinced his late Majesty would have
followed his advice. This quoting what a dead person would do is to me most
unfair, if not improper, especially to the King, who has such a high opinion of his
father's judgment. But might I not equally have urged that I was perfectly certain
Queen Victoria would have done what I advised? ... I solemnly believe that a great
mistake has been made resulting from a dread, which to say the least has been
much exaggerated, of danger to the Crown; whereas the real danger is to the
position of the P.M. In the conversation of the 16th even the instability of Foreign
Thrones was dragged in to intensify this Bogey!

His Majesty has given way! How could he do otherwise, with the P.M., the
leader of the House of Lords and Lord Knollys assuring him he was doing what
was right and constitutional? Please God they are right and that we may not regret

the step taken and find before long that fresh demands will be made entailing, either further concessions, or resistance resulting in more danger to the Throne than that which might have been incurred by a bold, fearless and open line of action in the present crisis.

Bigge's bravado paid tribute more to his heart than to his head. A constitutional monarch rejects ministerial advice at his peril, however unreasonable or distasteful it seems to him. He may use all the arts of argument in trying to dissuade the Government from its purpose. But having failed, there remain only two courses open to him. He must accept the Prime Minister's advice or he must find a new Prime Minister capable of commanding a majority in the House of Commons. Had the King defied Asquith's request for contingent guarantees, the Prime Minister would have resigned: not because he had lost the confidence of the Commons but because he had lost the confidence of the sovereign. From that moment the King would have been drawn into a conflict from which neither he nor the monarchy could have emerged with credit.

The resignation of Asquith and his colleagues would have required the King to seek a new Prime Minister. The only possible candidate was Balfour, the leader of the Opposition. If Balfour had declined the commission, the King would have been obliged to recall Asquith and, with diminished reputation, to surrender on such terms as the Liberal leader demanded. Even if Balfour had agreed to form a Government, the new Prime Minister's lack of a majority in the Commons would have led him to ask the King for a dissolution of Parliament. The ensuing general election would have been fought not only on the veto but also on the King's conduct. The Liberals would have claimed that he was in unholy alliance with the peers against the people; the Conservatives that he was defending the constitution against a revolutionary intrigue. Whatever the outcome of the poll, the King would have been the loser. A Liberal victory would have delivered him once more into Asquith's hands, chastened and defenceless; a Conservative victory would in retrospect have justified his resistance to Asquith, but at the cost of alienating, perhaps permanently, Liberal respect and goodwill.

Such were the hazards to which Bigge would have exposed the King and from which Knollys saved him. Both private secretaries, in seeking how best to serve their master, behaved out of character. Bigge, whose habitual caution later earned him the sobriquet Better-not, displayed a rashness that has no parallel in the rest of his career. Knollys, for forty years the candid friend and counsellor of Edward VII, seems to have felt unable to convince the new King without resorting to deception. There is evidence, not conclusive, that the letter from Elibank which he hoped would reinforce Asquith's advice, had been written at his own prompting. Even more reprehensible was Knollys's failure to tell the King that, should Asquith resign, Balfour would – or at least might – be prepared to form a Government. Earlier that year, exactly a week before King Edward's death, the Archbishop of Canterbury, Dr Randall Davidson, had tried to solve the constitutional problem at a private meeting with Knollys, Balfour and Esher. The record of it prepared by Knollys for King Edward included these words:

Mr. Balfour made it quite clear that he would be prepared to form a Government to prevent the King being put in the position contemplated by the demand for the creation of Peers.

Seven months later, in November 1910, Knollys neither showed nor mentioned that document to the King, thus leading him to believe that there was no alternative to accepting Asquith's advice. Balfour's reported conversation of April 1910 was not brought to the King's attention until after Knollys had retired from his service three years later. The King then had this minute attached to the record in the Royal Archives:

It was not until late in the year 1913 that the foregoing letters and memoranda came into my possession. The knowledge of their contents would, undoubtedly have had an important bearing and influence with regard to Mr. Asquith's request for guarantees on November 16, 1910.

> George R.I. January 7, 1914

The discovery of the documents was a double mortification for the King. Three years too late, he concluded that he might after all have been able to thwart Asquith by sending for Balfour; and that the faithful Knollys had so little trusted his master's judgement as to suppress essential information.

Thirty years after Harold Nicolson first revealed these facts in his official life of the King, it is possible to put a more honourable construction on Knollys's conduct. A memorandum written by Balfour in October 1910, only one month before the King's confrontation with Asquith, has recently come to light in the Royal Archives. It reveals that the Leader of the Opposition may have changed his mind since the previous April and no longer felt able to form an alternative Government in the event of Asquith's resignation. Apparently written at Esher's prompting, it bears a note in the handwriting of that industrious busybody to say that he had sent it to Knollys.

Balfour declared in his memorandum that, 'as at present advised', he would not be justified in accepting office should Asquith resign. On the face of it, that would seem to supersede his earlier judgement. But there was a profound difference of form as well as of content between the two conflicting opinions. In April, Balfour was giving his considered reply to an inquiry put to him by the sovereign's private secretary; in October he was doing no more than allow his thoughts to play over the problem. The October memorandum includes not only Balfour's doubts on whether he could take office, but other speculative musings about a possible caretaker Government headed by a 'neutral' elder statesman or one manned by civil servants.

Knollys can have attached little importance to it; otherwise why did he not produce it in the following month to reinforce his advice that the King had no alternative but to submit to Asquith? Again, when Balfour later complained that Knollys had misrepresented his views to the King, why did the angry private secretary not confront Balfour with his October memorandum? Perhaps he had failed to read it; or perhaps he had read it only to decide that it was too opaque a document to be taken seriously. The discovery of the October memorandum allows a new and more charitable interpretation to be put on Knollys's conduct: that he concealed from the King the opinion Balfour had given in April only because he was aware of Balfour's apparent change of mind in October. But there is scant evidence to support such a hypothesis.

Whether or not Knollys consciously deceived his master, he emerges in retrospect with more wisdom, more caution than does either the King or Sir Arthur Bigge. As the omniscient Esher wrote in his diary three days after the King had given Asquith a secret and reluctant pledge to create peers: 'There was only one possible and prudent course for a young Monarch i.e. to abide strictly within the Constitution and to take the official advice of his responsible Ministers.' Esher could with justice have added, 'even when that official advice was unprecedented, ambiguous and designed to protect his Ministers from the consequences of a reckless promise'.

The episode of contingent guarantees left the King with a lifelong grievance. He resented not so much the supposed strain put on the constitution by the Cabinet's demands; that was a matter for interpretation on which two such experienced public servants as Knollys and Bigge could take contrary views. What rankled in the King's mind was the indignity of having been browbeaten and bullied, of not having been trusted to do his duty when the time came. Above all, he was shocked by Asquith's insistence that his pledge should remain secret. He told Esher: 'I have never in my life done anything I was ashamed to confess. And I have never been accustomed to conceal things.' Bigge expressed himself more vehemently: 'Is this straight? Is it English? Is it not moreover childish?'

There is a more honourable interpretation of Asquith's demand for secrecy. He hoped that if a second election returned his Government to power, the House of Lords would agree to pass the Parliament Bill and so avert the need for a mass creation of Liberal peers. In that event there would be no disclosure of the King's pledge and thus no public controversy on the use of the royal prerogative. As Roy Jenkins, Asquith's biographer and apologist, has written: 'This part of the arrangement, of course, was inserted against the convenience of the Liberal Cabinet in an attempt to ease the position of the King.' Others continue to believe that Asquith did not wish to reveal how shamefully he had imposed upon an inexperienced monarch for political ends.

The King forgave, but he did not forget. Twenty-one years later, in November 1931, Lord Crewe had an audience at Buckingham Palace on resigning as Secretary of State for War in MacDonald's National Government. The King soon reverted to old times, telling Crewe that the forcing of his hand in 1910 was 'the dirtiest thing ever done'. He continued:

What right had Asquith to bring you with him to browbeat me? I remember that after talking to him I walked over to the fireplace and I heard Asquith say to you, 'I can do nothing with him. You have a go.' A dirty, low-down trick.

I wish that I had then had all the experience I have now. I ought to have said: 'All right, Asquith. Put everything on paper and I will give you my answer by 12 noon tomorrow.'

In his chaffing way, the King brought that uncomfortable audience of 1931 to an end by saying that it had all been a plot between Asquith, Crewe and Knollys. Crewe agreed that they had not treated the King very well.

'The King is hoarse from talking,' Esher noted on 4 February 1911. He had cause for agitation. Two months earlier, having secured both the King's secret pledge and a dissolution of Parliament, Asquith had appealed to the country on the specific issue of the Lords' veto. The Liberals had emerged from the election with a slightly increased majority of 126 seats, more than enough to justify the reintroduction of a Bill to curb the powers of the Upper House. The way was now clear for a graceful retreat on the part of the Unionist peers. Yet their leader, Lord Lansdowne, had just told the King that he and his colleagues might nevertheless continue to resist the Parliament Bill. Knowing nothing of the King's promise to Asquith, Lansdowne indicated that a mass creation of Liberal peers 'was a step which I felt sure H.M. would be reluctant to take, and his Ministers not less reluctant to advise'.

The prospect of Unionist intransigence haunted the King. He knew that if the Lords either rejected or emasculated the veto measure, Asquith would not hesitate to demand a mass creation of Liberal peers. The King would then be unable to withhold his consent: not only because he had pledged his word, but also because the result of the recent election had left him without an alternative Government.

His fears were not immediately realized. The Parliament Bill was re-introduced into the Commons on 21 February and by 15 May had passed through all its stages there. Two weeks later it was given a second reading in the Lords. That did not signal a surrender on the part of the Unionist peers. They might still choose either to amend the Bill out of all recognition at the committee stage or reject it outright on third reading.

At this point there was a political truce for the coronation and its elaborate programme of celebrations. Even that was not entirely lacking in political controversy. When Asquith submitted names for the Coronation Honours, the King instructed Knollys to reply:

His own strong impression is that to create Peers under existing circumstances and until the crisis is over would be a mistake and a mockery, especially in view of the possible or probable creation of 500 Peers. . . .

The King says he does not pretend to understand the logic of those people who while vilifying the House of Lords on every convenient occasion are yet apparently anxious to become members of that Body.

Having made his protest, the King accepted the Prime Minister's list, as he had done in the previous year. It included a barony for one of Asquith's brothers-in-law, Edward Tennant; a viscounty for the Master of Elibank's father; and a marquessate for the Earl of Crewe. The King also bestowed a barony on Bigge, who became Lord Stamfordham, and promoted Knollys to be a viscount.

Eight days after the coronation ceremony, the King and Queen dined with Mr and Mrs Asquith at No. 10 Downing Street. The evening concluded with a theatrical entertainment: Act III of *John Bull's Other Island* by George Bernard Shaw, and *The Twelve Pound Look*, by James Barrie. Neither was designed to divert the royal mind from the problems of the day. Shaw's piece is on the vexed theme of Irish unrest; Barrie's about a new knight, ambitious and self-satisfied, who as the curtain rises is insisting that his wife should play the part of the sovereign and bestow the accolade in a drawing-room rehearsal.

The battle between Lords and Commons was resumed at the end of June. Within six days the Unionist peers had so amended the Parliament Bill as to frustrate every Liberal intention. They even revived the proposal on which the conference of the previous year had broken down: that important constitutional changes such as Home Rule should be submitted to a national referendum. In the face of continuing Unionist defiance, the Cabinet decided to make known its secret understanding with the King. If that alone did not prompt the Unionists to end their resistance, then the King would be asked to create enough Liberal peers to ensure the enactment of the Parliament Bill in its original form.

An extraordinary circumstance of the King's promise of 16 November 1910 was that it did in fact remain secret for the following eight months. Sir

Algernon West, Mr Gladstone's private secretary, used to say that a secret is no longer a secret when known to more than three persons. In the Cabinet alone there were as many as twenty who knew of the understanding between Sovereign and Prime Minister. Liberal ministers, moreover, were notoriously indiscreet. A few years later, when Lord Kitchener was asked why he was so reluctant to discuss military operations in Cabinet, he replied: 'Because they all tell their wives, except Asquith, who tells other people's wives.' Knollys was well aware of those loose tongues when urging the King to accept the Government's advice on contingent guarantees. He felt impelled to add that 'the whole Cabinet (including Lloyd George and W. Churchill) will keep the confidential agreement inviolably secret'. That parenthesis hardly inspired trust. Yet Balfour, an inveterate diner-out, did not learn of the King's pledge until the beginning of July 1911, only a few days before the Government told him of it officially. It had been one of the best kept secrets of the reign.

From the moment the King's pledge was made known, the struggle for the Parliament Bill lay not so much between Liberals and Unionists as between two factions of the Unionist Party. The Government was assured of its measure. Either the Unionist peers would abstain from opposing its final passage through the House of Lords or a mass creation of Liberal peers would overwhelm them in the division lobbies. All that remained in doubt was which school of thought would prevail within the Unionist Party. The majority, who by now included Lord Lansdowne, echoed the view of Balfour that further resistance to the Parliament Bill would be 'essentially theatrical'. The minority, whose readiness to die in the last ditch earned them the name of die-hards or ditchers, remained inflexible, whatever humiliating consequences might await King, Parliament and nation.

Although the King was prepared to redeem his promise, he dreaded the task of creating several hundred new and largely unknown peers. How could any self-respecting sovereign be expected to relish such a pantomime? He therefore set himself, within the limits of constitutional monarchy, to dissuade the die-hards from their heedless course. At once he scored an important tactical success. On 22 July the Government reacted to the wrecking amendments of the Unionists by requiring the King to authorize a wholesale creation of Liberal peers in two days' time. The King pleaded for delay. He instructed Knollys that he could not accept the Cabinet's advice until the Lords had been given another chance to change their minds. He therefore proposed that the Lords' amendments should first be debated by the Commons, then sent back to the Upper House for consideration. Only if the Lords insisted on clinging to their provocative amendments would he then authorize a creation of peers. He also hoped that the Commons would not reject the Lords' amendments *en bloc*, but

would instead make such concessions as they felt able. Knollys's letter to
Asquith included this trenchant passage:

He has been fully under the impression that the peers would as far as possible
be conciliated by every reasonable attention and civility being shown to them; and
it is repugnant to his feelings that they should be treated with a want of consideration or harshly, or cavalierly. To do so, moreover, will probably have the effect of
increasing the number of those who intend to vote.

The Prime Minister at once deferred to his Sovereign's wishes. It was a
generous gesture. Had he ignored the King's plea and insisted on an
immediate creation of Liberal peers, the Government would have secured
the Parliament Bill within days and Irish Home Rule in the following
session. Any other course was bound to delay the Government's legislative
programme. If the Lords ultimately surrendered, then the Parliament Bill
would pass; but under its provisions, Irish Home Rule could be blocked for
more than two years. If the Lords remained defiant, not even the creation
of new peers could avoid the postponement of the Parliament Bill to the
following session.

The Unionist die-hards were neither mollified by concessions nor intim-
idated by threats. To the very end they doubted whether the Government
would create enough new peers to ensure a permanent Liberal majority in
the House of Lords. At worst, they believed, the King would authorize only
enough creations to ensure the passage of the Parliament Bill; since most
Unionist peers intended to abstain, that meant fewer than a hundred.

Those die-hards deluded themselves. Asquith had already prepared a list
of 245 men whom he would invite to become peers on the understanding
that they accepted the Liberal whip. They were apparently only his first
choices; it would not have proved impossible to produce as many names
again, less distinguished than the original selection but not inferior to those
who sat by hereditary right on the Unionist back benches.

More than half of them were established men of substance: Privy Counsellors, Members of Parliament, baronets and knights. Some were heirs to
peerages, including Esher's son, Oliver Brett. Others were eminent in their
profession or in industry. They included the composer Sir Charles Parry;
the jurist Sir Frederick Pollock; the surgeon Sir Victor Horsley; the engineer
Sir William Garstin; the chemist Sir Henry Roscoe; the financiers Sir Abe
Bailey, Sir Edgar Speyer and Sir Edgar Vincent; the soldiers Sir Ian
Hamilton and Sir Robert Baden-Powell; the solicitor Sir George Lewis
who, as his biographer delicately put it, held 'the practical monopoly of
those cases where the seamy side of society is unveiled and where the sins
and follies of the wealthy classes threaten exposure and disaster'.

Literature and learning were represented by Thomas Hardy, Bertrand

Russell, Gilbert Murray, James Barrie, Anthony Hope, G.P. Gooch, J.A. Spender and Sir George Otto Trevelyan, biographer of his uncle Lord Macaulay and father of G.M. Trevelyan. Perhaps Sir George Riddell, chairman of the company that owned the *News of the World*, could also be claimed by the fraternity of letters. (Ten years later he became the first divorced person to receive a peerage, an honour approved by the King with the utmost reluctance.) Sir Jeremiah Colman, Sir Thomas Lipton and Joseph Rowntree were in every sense household names. Family loyalty was reflected in the choice of H.J. Tennant, another of the Prime Minister's brothers-in-law, and of John Churchill and W.S. Haldane, the brothers of the Home Secretary and the Secretary for War.

There was one name, however, which the King warned Asquith he would absolutely refuse to consider for a peerage: that of the Baron de Forest, newly elected to the House of Commons as a Liberal. An adopted son and heir of Baron Hirsch, the Austrian financier and friend of King Edward, Baron de Forest had been educated at Eton and Christ Church, Oxford. In 1900 he became a naturalized British subject, but continued to use his Austrian title by virtue of a royal licence. A fortune of several million pounds allied to extreme radicalism did not commend itself to the King, and de Forest never became a British peer. In 1932 he transferred his allegiance to the Principality of Liechtenstein, which honoured her newest citizen by proclaiming him a Councillor of State.

All Asquith's potential peers, it must be admitted, would have been equally obnoxious to the sovereign. They were eclipsed in royal disfavour, however, by the die-hard Unionists. Lord Crewe wrote: 'The King, whom I saw for a long time yesterday, was greatly vexed at these hot-headed people, and keenly anxious for their defeat, in order to be saved from the very unpalatable necessity which would have been forced on him and us.'

He was no less mortified to hear that those same Unionist peers were defaming him for having consented in November to a creation of Liberal peers, an accusation of betrayal repeated in a spate of anonymous letters to Buckingham Palace. The King would have been wise to ignore such hurtful slanders. Instead, stung by a reflection on his honour, he asked the Government to make clear that he had given his promise to Asquith 'with natural and legitimate reluctance'. Crewe met the King's wishes in the course of repelling a vote of censure on the Government, itself a prelude to the final vote that would decide the fate of the Parliament Bill.

That royal admission had an unfortunate effect. It led the die-hards to believe that they might yet depend upon the King to refuse a creation of peers should the Bill be defeated; at the very least it reinforced their hope that he would create only enough peers to ensure that the Bill passed. To dispel such credulity, the King again requested the Government to make a statement: this time lending his full support to ministerial policy. It was in these unambiguous words that Lord Morley, Lord President of the Council, addressed the Upper House:

If the Bill should be defeated tonight, His Majesty would assent – I say this on my full responsibility as the spokesman of the Government – to a creation of Peers sufficient to guard against any possible combination of the different Parties in Opposition by which the Parliament Bill might again be exposed a second time to defeat.

The occasion for that momentous announcement was the second and final day of the Lords debate on whether the Commons amendments, restoring the Bill to its original potent form, should be accepted or rejected. It left no room for doubt. If the Unionists remained defiant, they would be overwhelmed by a large and permanent creation of Liberal peers. Yet such was the tension, not to say hysteria, that even Morley's warning failed to convince the die-hards. It chanced to be one of the hottest summers ever known in London. The debate had opened on 9 August with the temperature at the Greenwich observatory that day touching an unprecedented 100 degrees Fahrenheit. The atmosphere in the Lords' chamber was not conducive to cool thought; and although 300 Unionist peers had decided to abstain, another 100 led by the 87-year-old Lord Halsbury were still determined to vote against the Government. Since the Liberal peers numbered scarcely more than 80, the die-hards seemed set to destroy the Parliament Bill.

Then unexpected allies appeared. The Archbishop of Canterbury persuaded twelve of his brethren on the episcopal bench to vote for the Government, although two insisted on supporting the die-hards. And Lord Rosebery, who since the end of his premiership in 1895 had become increasingly disenchanted with his Liberal colleagues, returned to the fold. Even that access of strength, however, was likely to leave the Government in a minority. There remained only one way in which the Parliament Bill could be saved: by the courageous decision of certain Unionists to vote with the Liberals and so prevent a mass creation of peers that would bring ridicule upon both sovereign and nation.

The debate dragged on throughout the sultry evening of 10 August from one repetitious speech to the next, and it was not until 10.40 that the last peer cast his vote. The King wrote in his diary:

At 11.0 Bigge returned from the House of Lords with the good news that the Parliament Bill had passed with a majority of 17, 131 to 114. So the Halsburyites were thank God beaten. It is indeed a great relief to me and I am spared any further humiliation by a creation of peers. Rosebery saved the situation by voting for the Government and 20 eminent Unionist peers joined him. Bed at 12.

That entry in the King's diary was the truth but not the whole truth. The faithful Bigge, who had been created Lord Stamfordham only a few weeks earlier, denied himself the exciting scene inside the chamber in order to remain near the telephone room of the House of Lords. The moment the result was known, he telephoned it to Buckingham Palace. But the King was the last to hear the most eagerly awaited message of the reign. The figures were passed in a desultory way from footman to footman, and so to the equerry on duty, Commander Bryan Godfrey-Faussett. He assumed that they had already been given to his master, and went on working in his room. Godfrey-Faussett's diary continues:

When I had finished my letters, I went up to ask the King if I could carry on early next morning about arrangements for his journey to Ripon the same day, and as I entered the room I said, 'I *am* so thankful, Sir.' He said, 'What for?' and I told him. He had never been told anything and I was the first to bring the news. The Queen jumped off the sofa and the King made a few just remarks about why he had not been told. However thank goodness it had nothing to do with me. I told him all I knew. The King's relief was immense. While we were talking, Lord Stamfordham (old Bigge) rushed in, having hurried up from the House of Lords in a taxi; he was astonished and furious when he heard the King had not been told sooner, as he had arranged it so carefully. It was some footman's mistake, no doubt.

The King, whose belated bedtime is itself a measure of the importance he attached to the events of that evening, was mistaken in thinking that Rosebery had 'saved the situation'. The former Prime Minister's vote helped to secure the passage of the Bill but attracted no others in its train. Those Unionists who threw in their lot with the Government (37, as it happened, not 20, as the King wrote) were moved to do so by consideration for their sovereign rather than out of respect for an aloof and isolated elder statesman. The man most deserving of praise was Lord Curzon, who almost single-handed had engaged and routed Lord Halsbury's cohorts. His quixotic conduct in 1911 did something to erase the unfavourable impression he had made on the King in India six years earlier. Stamfordham wrote to Curzon on 11 August:

What a relief that all is well! The King is quite another man – and, if I may say so, is deeply grateful to you for the very valuable service which you have rendered to save the situation.

That day the King left joyfully for Yorkshire to shoot grouse.

Almost from the moment the King ascended the throne he determined to revisit India. The sovereign who literally trembled when required to open Parliament before five hundred well-disposed English gentlemen yearned to present himself, robed and crowned, to the untold millions of the sub-continent. In the winter of 1911-12 the vision became reality. Accompanied by Queen Mary, he set sail once more for Bombay, the first King-Emperor to receive the homage of his Indian subjects on their native soil. 'It was', he noted with pride, 'entirely my own idea.'

The Cabinet did not share his enthusiasm. A whole year before his departure he discussed the plan with Esher, who left this record of their conversation:

He said that the Government had raised all sorts of objections and difficulties – making out that there was no precedent for so long an absence from England of the Sovereign. I ventured to suggest that there was no precedent for the British Empire. The King sees that and understands the shrinkage of the world, owing to steam and electricity. His home-staying Ministers do not.

They agreed to the King's visit with surly reluctance, refusing out of hand to authorize the largesse which traditionally marked great events in the imperial calendar. The King insisted, however, that he could not appear empty-handed at his Indian Durbar; state ceremonial must be buttressed by some memorable pronouncement. The Prime Minister and Lord Crewe, the Secretary for India, showed more imagination than had their Cabinet colleagues. In collusion with the Viceroy, Lord Hardinge, they decided that the King should announce two momentous administrative changes: the transfer of the Indian capital from Calcutta to Delhi and the annulment of the partition of Bengal, the least popular measure of Curzon's recent viceroyalty. To forestall controversy, the proposed changes were to remain secret until they had been proclaimed by the King himself. Scarcely a dozen officials in London and as many in India knew what was afoot; not even the Queen was told until she reached Bombay. Charles Hobhouse, Chancellor of the Duchy of Lancaster, was among the overwhelming majority of ministers who resented the *fait accompli* sprung on them by Crewe only three days before the King's departure. 'The Cabinet was very uneasy about it,' he wrote. 'I trust we may not suffer – as I think we ought.'

As if deliberately to provoke those sobersides, George v suggested a spectacular culmination to the Delhi Durbar: he would crown himself Emperor of India in the sight of his people. The Archbishop of Canterbury led the opposition to that unexpectedly Napoleonic flourish. He argued that coronation implied consecration; and that in a land of Moslems and Hindus, any such act of Christian worship would be misplaced. It was therefore agreed that the King should arrive at the Durbar with the crown already on his head. But which crown? 'I really do think,' the Viceroy wrote in April 1911, 'that before the question of a Crown had been settled upon, it should have been considered where the Crown was to come from.' The Imperial

State Crown, weighing less than three pounds, would have been the least oppressive to wear under the hot Delhi sun; but neither that nor the far heavier Crown of St Edward could lawfully leave the shores of England. So Garrard, the Crown Jeweller, was ordered to make a new one at a cost of £60,000. Much of this sum, it was hoped in London, would be met by gifts of precious stones from the ruling princes of India; but the Viceroy vetoed the scheme as politically undesirable. The Government's next proposal was both parsimonious and lacking in dignity. Garrard would make the crown, hire it out for the Durbar at a fee of £4,400, then break it up on its return to England. That unworthy plan was abandoned in case it should become known that the sacred symbol of the King-Emperor had been desecrated for a handful of rupees. Ultimately it was the people of India who paid the full cost of the new crown; but they were denied the privilege of retaining it as part of their national heritage. If so venerated an object remained in Delhi, the Government feared, it would become a perpetual temptation to any would-be usurper or dissident. Briefly displayed at the Durbar, the Indian Crown has since been preserved in the jewel house of the Tower of London.

Students of the viceregal correspondence which passed between Calcutta and London throughout 1911 might suppose that the British Raj depended less on justice and good administration than on precedence, honours and minute distinctions of dress. Even the Queen showed a spirited interest in such *esoterica*. She refused an entourage of ladies bearing mere courtesy titles; her progress through India demanded none but the higher ranks of the peerage. Eventually her choice fell on the Duchess of Devonshire and the Countess of Shaftesbury – 'my woman Shaftesbury', as she imperiously continued to call her.

The King also suffered an initial disappointment when Lord Rosebery declined to accompany the royal party to India as Lord High Steward, or titular head of the household. 'I am not fitted by experience or manners or appearance for court functions,' the former Prime Minister explained. His place was taken by Lord Durham, a horseracing peer and Knight of the Garter untroubled by self-doubt. Other specially attached members of the suite included Lord Crewe, forgiven for his part in the constitutional imbroglio of November 1910 and one of the few Liberal ministers whom the King always found congenial; John Fortescue, royal librarian and historian of the British Army; a Windsor cowman and three cows. On 11 November 1911 all embarked in the new P & O ship *Medina* for the three-week voyage to Bombay. After a few days of storm and seasickness, the waters grew calm and the sun shone. The King listened to the band of the Marine Artillery playing his favourite piece, *In the Shadows*; the Queen read the works of Rudyard Kipling and A. E. W. Mason.

A cloud no bigger than a Viceroy's vanity alone marred their arrival in India. The royal suite apparently thought Lord Hardinge of little account when he came on board *Medina* to welcome the King-Emperor, and failed to pay him the traditional compliments. It is true that he had ceased to be Viceroy the moment the King reached Bombay; but he remained Governor-General, the first subject in the sub-continent, and in no uncertain terms he let this be known. (Crewe, by contrast, was so self-effacing that before submitting the Viceroy's Honours List to the King, he struck out his own name.) Hardinge, however, had inherited not only Curzon's pomposity but also his relentless industry. Under his supervision, 40,000 tents arose on the outskirts of the new capital: not so much a camp as a canvas city of 300,000 inhabitants. To add to their comfort, the Viceroy boasted, 90,000 rats had been killed in a single month. The King was delighted at the prospect of roughing it in a tent; the Queen, perhaps not entirely reassured by those ratcatching statistics, would have preferred a good stout roof over her head. In the event, the silk-lined and carpeted apartments of the royal party were of incomparable splendour. Fire remained the only danger. One outbreak destroyed the fireworks intended for the King-Emperor's garden party, another obliged the Duchess of Devonshire to flee her tent in dressing-gown and pigtail.

Despite months of careful preparation, the State entry into Delhi lacked grandeur. The Indian princes had advised the use of elephants, for centuries identified with imperial rule. Their suggestion was set aside for reasons both of economy and security. Instead the King-Emperor rode a horse. He was not, however, a skilled equestrian and rejected the Viceroy's charger, a coal-black thoroughbred standing seventeen hands, in favour of a small dark-brown horse of docile temperament but poor appearance. Wearing Field-Marshal's uniform and a white sun-helmet that hid much of his face, the King could scarcely be picked out from the attendant military staff. 'A good many did not recognise him,' an equerry wrote, 'and one saw their eager faces peering about.' Too late it was realized that the King-Emperor ought to have ridden apart from his suite, preceded by a Royal Standard.

If disappointment lingered, it was not for long. Five days later, Delhi witnessed the most splendid spectacle in Indian history. *The Times*, with its fine amplifying style, was worthy of the occasion:

The great Coronation Durbar, which has occupied the thoughts of India for more than a year, has involved the most elaborate preparation, and has brought a quarter of a million people together from every part of the Indian Empire, was held to-day on the vast plains beyond Delhi. Enthroned on high beneath a golden dome, looking outwards to the far north whence they came, their Majesties the King-Emperor and Queen-Empress were acclaimed by over 100,000 of their subjects. The ceremony at its culminating point exactly typified the Oriental conception of the ultimate repositories of Imperial power. The Monarchs sat alone, remote but beneficent, raised far above the multitude, but visible to all, clad in rich vestments, flanked by radiant emblems of authority, guarded by a glittering array of troops, the cynosure of the proudest Princes of India, the central figures in what was surely the most majestic assemblage ever seen in the East.

It was a sight which will remain indelibly engraved upon the memory. Not a soul who witnessed it, not even the poorest coolie who stood fascinated and awed upon the outskirts of the throng, can have been unresponsive to its profound significance. There can be only one verdict upon it. The Durbar has been far more than a mere success. It has been a triumphant vindication of the wise prescience which conceived and planned it. The King-Emperor's mission to his Indian peoples has been fulfilled with a completeness which places it beyond the reach of criticism.

Even the King himself, who shunned hyperbole, described the Durbar as 'the most beautiful and wonderful sight I ever saw'. The rest of his account is inimitably homespun. It ends:

Reached the Camp at 3.0. Rather tired after wearing the Crown for $3\frac{1}{2}$ hours, it hurt my head, as it is pretty heavy. . . .

Afterwards we held a reception in the large tent, about 5,000 people came, the heat was simply awful. Bed at 11.0 & quite tired.

The day's demonstration of loyalty was marred by a single uncouth incident. The Gaekwar of Baroda appeared at the Durbar, like his fellow maharajas, wearing a festive display of jewels. These he removed shortly before the arrival of the King-Emperor. When it came to his turn to pay homage, he sauntered towards his Sovereign in the everyday dress of a Mahratta, a walking-stick in hand. After a perfunctory obeisance, he turned abruptly and walked back to his seat. Baroda later denied that he had shown intentional disrespect and offered an apology. This the King accepted; but he remained unconvinced of the Gaekwar's good faith.

The King had done his duty. Now he claimed his reward: almost a fortnight in pursuit of tiger, rhinoceros and bear. Throughout the year, he had given almost as much thought to his Nepalese expedition as to the Durbar itself. He told the Viceroy: 'As probably this will be the last and only time in my life when I shall get big game shooting of this kind, I naturally want to have as many days in Nepal as possible.' Crewe would have preferred the time to be spent on an official tour of Madras. He wrote mournfully to Hardinge: 'It is a misfortune for a public personage to have any taste so strongly developed as the craze for shooting is in our beloved Ruler. . . . His perspective of what is proper is almost destroyed.' Both Secretary of State and Viceroy were nevertheless obliged to meet the King-Emperor's wishes, thankful that at least he had relinquished a plan to shoot duck; for a semi-divinity to be seen wallowing through a swamp in waders could not have been borne.

The Maharajah Chandra Shamshere Jung of Nepal excelled himself as host. Six hundred elephants and more than 14,000 beaters and other retainers were engaged in providing suitable sport. The total bag was thirty-nine tigers, eighteen rhino and four bears, of which the King shot twenty-one tigers, eight rhino and one bear. 'A record,' he noted, 'and I think will be hard to beat.' The *battue* failed to impress Lord Durham, who wrote to Lord Rosebery that the tigers had been slaughtered without any chance of escape. That was not the King's wish. As deadly with his rifle as with his shotgun, he would have welcomed a more searching test of skill.

During the King's shooting holiday, the Queen went sightseeing in Agra (where seventy years later some of the shops she visited still proclaim her patronage), then on a tour of Rajputana. Whether outshining the Indian princes with the magnificence of her recently retrieved family emeralds or going for a drive in a bullock-cart, she was equally imposing, equally imperturbable. The Queen showed to particular advantage in Calcutta, where she rejoined the King for their last week in India. The mercantile community felt betrayed by the transfer of the capital from their own city to Delhi, a natural resentment which the royal visitors did their best to appease. An equerry noted the Queen's painstaking success with 'the big commercial people here who are rather neglected generally'.

The King was overcome with emotion during his farewell speech in Bombay; he knew he had little hope of seeing India again. But as he was about to embark with the Queen for the journey home, he could not resist chaffing Hardinge: 'You seem very pleased, Charlie, to be getting rid of us!' If the Viceroy appeared content, it was not at parting from two such grateful and considerate guests, but at the unbroken success of their visit. In 1912 India had already begun her chequered progress towards self-government. Yet paternalism and pageantry, it seemed, still retained their place in her national life: at best ties of affinity between one civilization and another, at worst the bread and circuses with which an earlier empire had stilled disaffection. A few months after the King's return to England, the Viceroy wrote to him:

When I look upon the past year, I cannot help feeling profoundly satisfied with the peace, contentment and prosperity that prevail throughout your Majesty's Indian Empire.

Six days later, as Hardinge made his first State entry into the new capital, a bomb was thrown at his elephant, seriously wounding the Viceroy and killing his personal attendant.

The King was glad to be back in London again. 'Went for a solitary walk in the garden,' he wrote in his diary, 'with my umbrella as a companion.' The passing of the Parliament Bill had enabled him to tour India free from political anxiety; but the respite was short-lived. From the spring of 1912 until the outbreak of war more than two years later he was embroiled in the constitutional problems of Home Rule for Ireland.

The Parliament Bill, it will be recalled, was designed to protect the programme of a Liberal Government from the hereditary hostility of the House of Lords. It ensured that the peers could neither amend nor reject any money measure approved by the Commons; and that their power to delay all other legislation should be limited to two years. The Liberals had won their victory only with the support of John Redmond and his fellow Irish members. In April 1912 the Government prepared to repay its debt by introducing a Bill for Irish Home Rule. It was not a bold or radical measure. The powers of the proposed Irish Parliament in Dublin resembled those of a county council rather than of a national legislature. Taxation, defence, foreign policy, external trade, even the design of postage stamps, would all remain the responsibility of the British Government and the Imperial Parliament. The Home Rule Bill nevertheless aroused deep emotion on both sides of the Irish Sea. The prospect of a national assembly dominated by Roman Catholics evoked a fierce response from the Protestants of Ulster, whose threat to establish an independent administration in Belfast won general sympathy from the Unionists at Westminster.

The likelihood of civil war seemed scarcely to perturb Mr Asquith and his colleagues. Brushing aside all suggestions that the Protestant counties be excluded from the operation of the Home Rule Bill, they completed its progress through the Commons on 16 January 1913. Two weeks later the measure was rejected by the Lords. That defeat did nothing to lessen the Government's determination. 'The Prime Minister came,' the King wrote in his diary on 7 February. 'He seemed very optimistic about everything as usual.' Under the terms of the Parliament Act, the Home Rule Bill need only be reintroduced and approved by the Commons in two more successive sessions for it to elude the reach of a hostile Upper House. By the summer of 1914, the Liberals exulted, it would be presented to the King for the formality of the Royal Assent.

Yet there were those who maintained that the Royal Assent was no mere formality; that the sovereign's power of veto, although dormant for the past two centuries, could be revived at will; and that King George v should withhold his endorsement from so contentious a measure as the Home Rule Bill until the Government had submitted it to the test of a general election. To justify that abrupt change of constitutional practice, its advocates invoked an ingenious argument. They pleaded that the Parliament Act of

1911, by failing to fulfil one of its declared purposes, had created a constitutional void which only the sovereign could fill. The preamble to that measure had declared that 'it is intended to substitute for the House of Lords as it at present exists a Second Chamber constituted on a popular instead of a hereditary basis'. Once the Bill had been enacted, however, the Government found it convenient to forget that promise. In radical eyes, an unwieldy, hereditary and much abused Second Chamber with limited powers was preferable to a compact, elected and respected Second Chamber whose virtues entitled it to powers scarcely inferior to those of the Commons. Conservatives, by contrast, declared that until the promised reform of the House of Lords had been completed, its pre-1911 right of veto devolved upon the sovereign.

The most strident advocate of that dubious constitutional doctrine was Andrew Bonar Law, the Glasgow industrialist who in the autumn of 1911 had succeeded a weary and irresolute Arthur Balfour as leader of the Unionists. Dining at Buckingham Palace in May 1912, he addressed his host and sovereign with unamiable crudity:

I think, Sir, that the situation is a grave one not only for the House but also for the throne. Our desire has been to keep the Crown out of our struggles, but the Government have brought it in. Your only chance is that they should resign within two years. If they don't you must either accept the Home Rule Bill or dismiss your Ministers and choose others who will support you in vetoing it – and in either case half your subjects will think you have acted against them.

The King turned red at those blunt words, and Bonar Law asked: 'Have you never considered that, Sir?' The King replied: 'No, it is the first time it has been suggested to me.' Law continued: 'They may say that your assent is a purely formal act and the prerogative of veto is dead. That was true as long as there was a buffer between you and the House of Commons, but they have destroyed that buffer and it is true no longer.'

Describing the conversation to a colleague, Bonar Law said: 'I think I have given the King the worst five minutes that he has had for a long time.' That attempt to use the King as an instrument of Unionist ambition must be accounted one of the most unscrupulous of modern politics. Even those followers of Bonar Law who did not share his detestation of Home Rule were willing enough to see the Government exposed to an untimely general election and the prospect of defeat at the polls. That such a manœuvre would involve the King in either dismissing ministers who commanded a majority in the Commons or exercising the long dormant prerogative of veto weighed little with the party that professed a near monopoly of patriotism. As Esher put it: 'Those who hate Home Rule sufficiently should be ready to risk their skins, but they should not skulk behind the Throne.'

The King was not in principle opposed to Home Rule. In any case, his personal opinion on such a political issue was irrelevant to his constitutional duty. What caused him literally sleepless nights was the predicament so artfully laid bare by Bonar Law. He confided his anxieties to a handwritten memorandum that has hitherto remained unpublished. It includes this poignant passage:

In May 1914 the Bill will automatically come before me for my assent.... I shall then be face to face with a serious dilemma. If I assent, half the people of this country will rightly or wrongly consider that I have not been faithful to my trust, while the people of Ulster will declare that I have deserted them. On the other hand, if I withhold my assent, my Government would resign, the other half of the people would condemn my action and the whole of Ireland except Ulster would be indignant against me.... In either case I should not be able to put my foot in Ireland again, a position of affairs which would be intolerable and one to which no Sovereign has ever been exposed.

Some members of the Government, the King discovered, were as coldly unsympathetic as their Unionist counterparts. When at Balmoral he complained to Lewis Harcourt that if he signed the Home Rule Bill he would be hissed in the streets of Belfast, the Minister in Attendance replied that if he didn't sign the Bill he would be hissed in the streets of London. 'Damned impertinent', was the King's comment on his outspoken guest. Harcourt incurred more disfavour two months later when, in a public speech at Bradford, he warned that any unconstitutional action on the King's part 'would reduce the throne to a hopeless ruin which no one would attempt to rebuild'. Stamfordham reproved him for having, as a Cabinet Minister, entered upon such delicate ground. 'The terms in which you did so,' he continued, 'appeared to His Majesty somewhat trenchant and monitory.'

Other Ministers were more understanding. Haldane, who had recently become Lord Chancellor after five energetic years at the War Office, wrote to his mother:

I have in these days come to greatly admire the King. He has shown himself to have far more of his father's qualities of tact and judgement than I supposed. He is being bombarded by the Tory extremists with all sorts of suggestions. He is to dismiss the Government and appeal to the people, refuse assent to the Home Rule Bill and other wild ideas are thrust upon him. He remains quite calm, is sure of his constitutional position and is being of real service in seeking a way out.

The most memorable solution to be pressed upon the King was that of Lord Rosebery. Looking at the Windsor collection of miniatures, he came to one of Oliver Cromwell and said to his host:

'That is the man we want now.'

'To cut my head off?'

'No, but to turn out the Parliament.'

Esher also invoked the shade of Cromwell, although his counsel was as comfortless as Rosebery's. The King, he declared, may exert all the arts of interrogation and persuasion on his Ministers; but having failed to deter them from their chosen course, he must accept their advice, however damaging to the welfare of the State. Esher continued austerely:

In the last resort the King has no option. If the constitutional doctrines of ministerial responsibility mean anything at all, the King would have to sign his own death-warrant, if it was presented to him for signature by a Minister commanding a majority in Parliament. If there is any tampering with this fundamental principle, the end of the monarchy is in sight.

The King could well have replied that the execution of the monarch, particularly if it were to become an established constitutional practice, might destroy the monarchy even more swiftly. As it was, he kept his head in every sense: striving to save Ireland from civil war while simultaneously preserving his political impartiality.

In the spring of 1913, as the Home Rule Bill began the second of its three required parliamentary circuits, there was an important change in the royal household. Lord Knollys retired, leaving Lord Stamfordham as the sovereign's sole private secretary. It seemed a natural enough transition. Knollys was seventy-six, fourteen years Stamfordham's senior, and had agreed to remain at Buckingham Palace after King Edward's death only at the pressing invitation of the new sovereign. The Court Circular placed on record the King's gratitude to him for more than half a century of devoted service. In private audience Knollys received a more personal expression of thanks and a commemorative silver inkstand. Behind those civilities lay a less happy saga. The King wrote in his diary on 13 February 1913:

Saw Francis and told him that I feared my having two private secretaries was not satisfactory and that perhaps he might consider whether it was not best for him to resign. He took it quite quietly and said that he thought I was perfectly right. Very disagreeable for me to have to say this to such an old friend as Francis, but I am sure it is for the best.

Three days later, Knollys gave Asquith his own account of the parting:

I think I ought to let you know that I am leaving the King's service and that in fact I have practically left it.

Quite between ourselves, my position had become almost an impossible one, and it was made worse by the strong divergence of opinions which existed between the King and his surroundings (*not the Queen*) on one side and myself on the other, on nearly every question of a public nature . . .

The gulf that had separated the two private secretaries since their struggle for the King's mind in November 1910 was largely political. Each cherished his master's interests; but Knollys was at heart a Liberal, Stamfordham a Tory. Knollys believed that the throne could best be preserved by prudent submission to ministerial advice; Stamfordham feared that each successive erosion of the royal prerogative heralded the ultimate destruction of both the monarchy and a stable society. They were united only in the zeal with which they rebuked an unfortunate phrase in a minister's speech or a failure to inform the King of a departmental decision. On the deeper issues of policy, such as that of contingent guarantees, they were poles apart.

Stamfordham's sharpness of pen and tongue accentuated the clash of political creeds. He wrote on 15 November 1912:

Two years ago tomorrow Asquith commenced his policy of intimidation and dragooning: he put a pistol to the King's head: and during that short time he has treated the House of Lords and House of Commons very much in the same manner. . . . He is going to reap his own reward.

Not even the Prime Minister himself was spared Stamfordham's admonishments. 'I received from him yesterday', Asquith complained in the same year, 'a letter which both in tone and substance is quite unexampled in my communications with the Crown.' After a chance meeting at Buckingham Palace, Lord Lincolnshire wrote of Stamfordham: 'He is a very strong Tory and does not hesitate to show his colours. He seems to me to be developing into a public danger. It is the mercy of God that Francis Knollys kept on.' And when eventually Knollys retired, Hobhouse recorded its depressing effect on the Cabinet: 'Everyone lamented the loss of Knollys and the influence of Stamfordham, whose wings the P.M. earnestly desired should be clipped.' Such was the impression that the most correct, cautious and politically impartial private secretary of the nineteen-twenties left on the previous decade.

Knollys, too, had his detractors. The Unionists saw him as the ally, perhaps even the agent, of the Liberal Party. They treated him, he complained, 'with studied coldness'. Balfour, once his friend, conceived so strong an antipathy to the man and his methods that by the autumn of 1911 he would no longer meet him socially; and of all politicians, Balfour was the least quarrelsome.

The cause of the breach lay in the constitutional crisis of November 1910. Knollys, determined to avoid a conflict between Crown and Cabinet, had told the King that if Asquith were either dismissed or provoked into resigning, Balfour would decline to form an alternative Government. The King had therefore felt obliged to submit to Asquith's demand for a secret pledge to create unlimited peers. That was Knollys's first alleged misrepresentation of Balfour. The second came two months later. The King had continued to brood over whether or not he should have resisted Asquith's threats of resignation and, in spite of Knollys's advice, have sent for Balfour. Accordingly, with the King's knowledge, Knollys asked Balfour at a private dinner in January if he would in fact have been prepared to form a Government in November. Balfour replied that in the interests of his party he might have been forced to take office; but that it would have been imprudent of the King to dismiss his ministers and send for the Leader of the Opposition. Knollys had the answer he was seeking; retrospectively it seemed to justify what he had told the King. It was, however, an answer extracted under false pretences. In January 1911, Balfour believed that the issue between Sovereign and Prime Minister two months earlier had been the King's reluctance to grant Asquith a dissolution of Parliament – and thus a general election – for the second time within a year. Knollys omitted to reveal that far more had then been at stake. As Balfour wrote in August 1911, after the King's secret pledge of November 1910 had been made known:

Had I been asked to form a Government in order to protect His Majesty from giving a promise, not merely that a Parliament Bill should be passed over the heads of the Lords, but that it should be passed in a form which by implication carried Home Rule with it, I should not only have formed a Government, but I should have had great hopes of carrying the country with me.

In a further letter to Stamfordham a week later, Balfour turned from his lost opportunity of thwarting Asquith to Knollys's want of candour on the night of their dinner:

Do you think it fair that I should be asked to discuss public affairs, under circumstances which imply freedom and confidence, with an ambassador by whom I was deliberately kept in ignorance of the most essential features of the situation? Both Lord Knollys and the Prime Minister were, from the very nature of the case, intimately acquainted with all that had taken place with regard to the pledges in November. I had not an inkling that in November anything of importance on this subject had been arranged between the King and his Ministers. Lord Knollys seems, therefore, to have endeavoured to extract from me general statements of policy to be used as the occasion arose, while studiously concealing the most important elements and the actual concrete problem that had to be solved.

Knollys, to whom Stamfordham showed Balfour's letter, as its author doubtless intended, had no possible defence against the imputation of deceit. With less justification, however, Balfour also alleged that Knollys had repeated their dinner table conversation to Asquith. A sinner accused of the wrong sin, Knollys reacted with outraged virtue. He stormed down to the House of Commons to confront Balfour, but found only his secretary, Sandars. 'I told him', Knollys wrote, 'that in the days of duelling I should have called Balfour out; that the whole thing was a lie and that I demanded an apology and a retraction from Balfour of the vile and calumnious charge he had brought against me.'

Balfour, a notoriously slothful correspondent, allowed three weeks to pass before sending a reply. It did not satisfy his assailant. 'We shall for the future', Knollys wrote, 'meet as strangers.' Although a formal reconciliation eventually took place, it failed to heal the breach. When Lady Desborough asked Balfour whom he would like as fellow guests at a house party, he replied: 'My dear Ettie, I should enjoy meeting any man in England, except Lord Knollys; him I will not meet.'

Did the King know of these discords and their cause? Although it was not until the end of 1913, several months after Knollys had retired, that he learned of the misleading advice given him in November 1910, he was almost certainly told of the quarrel between Knollys and Balfour soon after it occurred. Nor can he have been unaware of the political differences which continued to fray the tempers of his two private secretaries and in turn add to his own burden.

Both Knollys and Stamfordham were men of high personal honour. If one acted with too much discretion, the other with too little, it was only in order to serve what they believed to be the best interests of the monarchy. Yet each had become a focus of political discontent within an institution dependent upon political impartiality. The uneasy partnership must be broken.

Knollys accepted his retirement with good grace; he was, after all, in his seventy-seventh year and could not have been expected to retain his post indefinitely. The King took untold pains to soften the blow. He asked that master of English prose Lord Rosebery to compose a sympathetic announcement for the Court Circular, anxiously inquired a few days later whether Knollys harboured any bitterness, wrote him this letter of heartfelt consolation:

My dear Francis,

I wish to send you these few lines, as I could not tell you *all* I felt when I saw you this morning. I have known you ever since I can remember anyone or anything. You are my oldest friend and the one whose advice I have so often sought and never in vain. When you were with my dear Father, you never failed to give me help and assistance, however often I asked. Your 47 years with my Father was one long faithful service of devotion, and no-one knows better than I do the trust and reliance he placed in you and how much it was justified.

Since you have been with me – I never forget that you remained on with me because I asked you to do so for a time, when perhaps the shock to you of my dear Father's death may have made you wish to retire – you have done all that you could, to help me with your knowledge and experience. I am very grateful to you, my dear Francis, grateful for your lifelong help and for the advice and assistance you have always been so ready to give, and for the support on which I relied.

It is a real pain to part with a friend and I can assure you that I felt it most keenly today, especially when the friend is one's oldest, but I hope the parting is only in an official sense, and that the friendship which has lasted so long between us, may continue till the end.

I remain my dear Francis

Your very affectionate and grateful old friend

George R.I.

Knollys's retirement barely disturbed the rhythm of the King's well-ordered life. Stamfordham took charge of all important duties and many that were not. The rest were distributed between the two assistant private secretaries, Lieutenant-Colonel Sir Frederick Ponsonby and Major Clive Wigram. The Prime Minister, smarting from the loss of Knollys, told Stamfordham how much he wished that the King would include an able civilian among his secretaries, 'instead of always drawing them from more or less (mostly less) instructed soldiers'. Asquith's jibe was unfair to all three.

Wigram, like Stamfordham, had been commissioned into the Royal Artillery, later transferring to the Indian Cavalry. As an aide-de-camp to Lord Curzon, he had caught the eye of Sir Walter Lawrence, who recruited him to help organize the King's first Indian tour as Prince of Wales. The King in turn appointed him a part-time equerry, and in 1910 invited him to join the permanent household as an assistant private secretary. Although approaching forty, Wigram embarked on his new career with humility. Finding his lack of languages a handicap, he gave up his lunch hour to have French lessons. His English was vigorous but idiosyncratic. Having been an outstanding games player at Winchester College, he acquired a lifelong habit of peppering even his official correspondence with sporting metaphors. Thus he would write to a proconsul: 'The King never had such a good set of Ministers and it is wonderful how we can put a strong team into the field whenever required. . . . Even our second eleven would defeat most other countries.'

When Stamfordham was ill for a few weeks in 1912, Wigram more than held his own. 'He has done quite splendidly,' the King noted, 'never made a mistake and is simply a glutton for work, besides being a charming fellow. I am indeed lucky in having found a man like him.' Stamfordham, too, thought highly of him, writing to Wigram's mother in the same year: 'His natural power of looking ahead, his accurate mind and common sense, his charming and patient temper, his untiring energy and industry have enabled him to achieve successfully what would have baffled not one man but several.'

Sir Frederick Ponsonby saw fewer virtues in his fellow private secretary. He told Lord Hardinge:

He is a very nice fellow and very hard-working and business-like, but his horizon is limited and he does not seem to be able to take a broad-minded view of the many perplexing questions that come here. He has the true British contempt for all foreigners which is now rather out of date, and his political views are those of the ordinary officer at Aldershot.

That cool assessment of a colleague throws as much light on its author as it does on Wigram. 'Fritz' Ponsonby, a son of Queen Victoria's private secretary, had been at court since 1895. He shared his father's reverence for the institution of monarchy, but lacked both the tact and the adroitness with which Sir Henry overcame the foibles of an obstinate old lady. The Ponsonby family, it must be admitted, was censorious by nature. Queen Victoria once felt obliged to call on Lady Ponsonby with a request that she should tell her husband not to say, 'It is absurd', when the Queen made a remark. Lady Ponsonby, too, could be sharp of tongue, as when she referred to a lady-in-waiting 'foolishly cringing to all the little miseries of etiquette'. Their son inherited the same independence of mind, but also displayed an obstinacy which could cause resentment.

At the very outset of his career at court he unwittingly caused deep offence to the Queen. One reason why she had appointed him an equerry was to please his father; another was in the hope that his months as aide-de-camp to Lord Elgin, Curzon's predecessor as Viceroy, would have equipped him to manage her Indian attendants. The Queen's favourite among them was Abdul Karim, whom she made first her Munshi, or teacher, then her Indian Secretary. The rest of her household deplored the promotion, partly from racial prejudice, partly from a genuinely held belief that the Munshi was in correspondence with Indian dissidents; they took their revenge by disparaging his social origins. The Queen thereupon telegraphed to Fritz Ponsonby, who was about to leave India on appointment as her equerry, instructing him to call on the Munshi's father, supposedly a medical practitioner or even a surgeon-general of the Indian Army. On obeying her command, Ponsonby found that the man was neither, but the apothecary of the jail in Agra. The Queen was displeased by the report and told Ponsonby that he must have seen the wrong person. Instead of conceding so sensitive a point, he insisted that he was right. Throughout the whole of his first year at court, the Queen barely spoke to him and not once did she ask him to dine. As for the irrepressible Munshi, his pride was soothed by the Queen's insistence that he should become a Companion of the Order of the Indian Empire.

Even when taken back into royal favour, Ponsonby sinned again by getting married, albeit after waiting three years to suit the Queen's convenience. Like Lord Kitchener, she feared that no wife could keep a husband's secrets.

Ponsonby endured occasional storms during his nine years as assistant private secretary to Edward VII, but always survived. The King appreciated his eye for correct ceremonial, his cosmopolitan outlook, his easy command of French. Unlike his father, who once shocked the King by appearing at dinner with two identical Jubilee medals on his chest, Fritz won his sovereign's respect with a prodigious knowledge of orders and decorations; in the course of the reign he personally received almost a score of them. It was equally characteristic of Ponsonby to teach himself shorthand so that he could conduct the King's business with more despatch.

On the accession of King George V, Ponsonby continued in the role of assistant private secretary, the repository of court custom and etiquette. His skill as a raconteur and his nose for fine claret ensured a convivial social life. It was a strain, however, to support a wife and two children on little more than £1,000 a year. In 1912 he had hopes of being appointed Governor of Bombay; but when Asquith learned that the King would not welcome Ponsonby's departure, the tentative offer was withdrawn. His thoughts often turned to ways of increasing his income, some of them improbable: writing film scripts, for instance, or planning to recover King John's treasure from the Wash.

'Kings never like opposition or remonstrance,' Esher used to say, 'even the best of them.' Ponsonby recognized that truth, but did not allow it to interfere with a lifelong habit of outspokenness. In later years he wrote:

King George V hated all insincerity and flattery, but after a time he got so accustomed to people agreeing with him that he resented the candid friend business. At one time he took a dislike to me as he thought I invariably disagreed with any views he happened to express, but after a time he regarded me as an unavoidable critic.

There is contemporary evidence to support that somewhat ungracious confession. During the first years of the reign, the King used often to play royal, or indoor, tennis with members of his household. Here is an account of one such contest in 1913, written by Ponsonby to his wife:

We played tennis. The King, Derek Keppel, Harry Verney and me and a pretty rotten game we had. It appears that Wigram and Willy Cadogan were accustomed to send easy ones over to the King. So when we played the usual game the King sulked and refused to try after the first set, he told us we didn't understand the game and we ought to send easy ones. I was furious as pat ball is such rot. So I proceeded to exaggerate this and lopt slow easy ones in a babyish way over the net. This annoyed the King who saw how absurd it must look and we had an altercation at the net.... After some heat the King said all right play any way you like. So I then proceeded to smash them at him and he sulked and wouldn't move. Then an awkward pause after Derek and I won two sets. Then I asked him to try my way of cutting down properly and proposed he and I should play Harry Verney and Derek and give them 15. I really knew we could give them 30. So we started and had a capital game, the King cutting them down beautifully, they never had a look in as we were much the best. H.M. made some really beautiful strokes and it was a different game so all ended happily but I mean to tell Wigram he must not kowtow to the King in this way.

A middle-aged monarch seeking relaxation from the problems of Home Rule might have wished so insolent a tutor elsewhere. In Sir Charles Cust he already had one candid courtier; two could be depressing. The King nevertheless saw beyond Ponsonby's provocative qualities, promoted him to be Keeper of the Privy Purse and Treasurer, heaped him with honours. Created Lord Sysonby in June 1935, he died in the King's service.

The retirement of Knollys in March 1913 left Stamfordham as the King's closest confidant and principal channel of communication with the Government. It was not, however, until August of that year, a month after the Home Rule Bill had for the second time been approved by the Commons and rejected by the Lords, that his powers of persuasion and draftsmanship were put to the test. Throughout the summer, men of all parties and none had burdened an increasingly worried sovereign with their views on Home Rule. The Prime Minister alone, trusting in his impregnable parliamentary majority, remained supine and silent. On 11 August he was summoned to an audience at Buckingham Palace. He cannot have much enjoyed it.

In reply to the King's complaint that the Prime Minister had not mentioned the Irish problem to him for several months, Asquith said that he had not felt it was proper for him to ask for an audience; that he now welcomed an opportunity of discussing Home Rule; that he had served three sovereigns, two of them as Prime Minister, and wished to take the King entirely into his confidence. When the King expressed concern at the role which he himself might be called upon to play, Asquith reminded him that the sovereign was unassailable as long as he continued to act only on the advice of his ministers and refrained from exercising a veto that had lain dormant since the reign of Queen Anne. Should the King think that the actions of his ministers were detrimental to the country or to the throne, Asquith continued, it was his duty to warn them in writing of his misgivings.

At that moment, perhaps to Asquith's surprise, the King handed him a long memorandum on Home Rule. A few days earlier he had interrupted a sailing holiday at Cowes to confer with Stamfordham aboard the royal yacht *Victoria and Albert*. Between them they had composed a formidable document, reproachful yet constructive. It reminded the Prime Minister of the rising tide of rebellion in Ulster; of the pressures on the sovereign to avert civil war by some personal initiative; of the likelihood that whatever he did would alienate half his Irish subjects. 'I cannot help feeling', the King wrote, 'that the Government is drifting and taking me with it.' He therefore suggested a conference between all the parties to consider such possible solutions as the exclusion of Ulster from the Home Rule Bill and the extension of devolution to other parts of the United Kingdom. The Prime Minister promised to prepare a detailed reply to all those points. On the following day the King went north to shoot grouse.

Asquith was disturbed by the King's initiative. He wrote to Churchill, the Minister in Attendance at Balmoral: 'You probably find yourself in a rather "fuliginous" atmosphere. Between ourselves, I have already sent the first part, and tomorrow or next day hope to send the second, of a Memorandum which I have drawn up for the Royal Eye on the whole situation.'

Balmoral turned out to be less oppressive than the Prime Minister had supposed. The King, Churchill reported, was 'extremely cordial and intimate'; and Stamfordham, freed from the irritant of Knollys's contrary influence, was 'friendly and moderate'. It was with a stiffening resolve, however, that sovereign and private secretary read Asquith's promised apologia on Home Rule. The first part of the document, which dealt with the constitutional issues, reflected the Prime Minister's mind at its most pellucid:

We have now a well-established tradition of 200 years that, in the last resort, the occupant of the Throne accepts and acts upon the advice of his Ministers. The Sovereign may have lost something of his personal power and authority, but the Crown has thereby been removed from the storms and vicissitudes of party politics. ... Its impersonal status is an invaluable safeguard for the continuity of our national life.

The Parliament Act, Asquith continued, was not intended to affect, nor had it affected, the constitutional role of the sovereign; it concerned only the relations between the two Houses of Parliament. If the King refused to give his assent to one Bill, he would be expected to refuse it to others: 'Every Act of Parliament of the first order of importance, and only passed after acute controversy, would be regarded as bearing the personal *imprimatur* of the Sovereign ... the Crown would become the football of contending factions.'

That forcefully phrased essay was worthy to be pasted into the notebook on Bagehot which the King had compiled twenty years earlier. Yet it did nothing to allay his anxiety. Was he expected to shelter behind the Prime Minister's polished prose while his Irish subjects tore themselves to pieces? To that question, too, Asquith offered a supposedly reassuring answer in the second part of his memorandum. When the Home Rule Bill became law, he explained, there was 'the certainty of tumult and riot, and more than the possibility of bloodshed'; but to call it civil war would be 'a misuse of terms'. If, however, the Bill failed to become law, 'it is not too much to say that Ireland would become ungovernable'. Nor would the Prime Minister agree to a general election in order to test public opinion. Such a course would thwart the purpose of the Parliament Act, yet achieve no practical result in the pacification of Ireland. Finally, although not opposed to some compromise on Home Rule, Asquith saw little hope of a settlement by negotiation as long as the antagonists were separated by an 'unbridgeable chasm of principle'.

The King was not a man to share the Prime Minister's complacent immobility. In a letter of more than 2,000 words, he subjected Asquith's memorandum to an exegesis that not even his grandmother could have improved upon. Rightly or wrongly, he protested, his people would associate him with the policy adopted by his advisers. He repeated his conviction that the virtual emasculation of the House of Lords had cast an additional burden of responsibility on the sovereign. He asked whether there was any precedent for not submitting to the electorate a Bill 'opposed by practically the whole of the House of Lords, by one third of the House of Commons, by half the population of England': a Bill, moreover, 'forced through the House of Commons, pages of it never having been discussed'.

Turning to the Prime Minister's almost insouciant forecast of tumult and bloodshed, the King came to the heart of the matter:

Do you propose to employ the Army to suppress such disorders?

This is, to my mind, one of the most serious questions which the Government will have to decide.

In doing so you will, I am sure, bear in mind that ours is a voluntary Army; our Soldiers are none the less Citizens; by birth, religion and environment they may have strong feelings on the Irish question. . . .

Will it be wise, will it be fair to the Sovereign as head of the Army, to subject the discipline, and indeed the loyalty of his troops, to such a strain?

The King ended his letter on a less contentious note:

I rejoice to know that you are ready and anxious to enter into a Conference if a definite basis can be found upon which to confer.

For my part, I will gladly do everything in my power to induce the Opposition to meet you in a reasonable and conciliatory spirit.

For it behoves us all to withhold no efforts to avert those threatening events which would inevitably outrage humanity and lower the British name in the mind of the whole civilised world.

As the Prime Minister was shortly to be the King's guest at Balmoral, Asquith replied to that formidable letter with brevity and restraint. But he could not resist a flash of resentment on the use of the army: 'There is, in my opinion, no sufficient ground for the fears – or hopes – expressed in some quarters, that the troops would fail to do their duty.' Like much else in the King's admonition, Asquith thought the royal view hardly distinguishable from a manifesto of Unionist policy. The Prime Minister's newfound willingness to seek a compromise on Home Rule nevertheless sprang directly from the King's initiative.

Once at Balmoral, Asquith was exposed to further royal argument; and it was from there that he wrote to Bonar Law on 8 October, suggesting that they should hold informal and secret talks 'as a first step towards the possible avoidance of danger to the State'. Prime Minister and Leader of the Opposition met on 14 October, then at intervals during the next three months. Asquith proposed that Ulster should accept Home Rule in principle but be entitled to veto any act of the new Irish Parliament which infringed her autonomy; Bonar Law replied with a demand for Ulster's total exclusion from Home Rule for an indefinite period. Each side rejected the contention of the other out of hand.

Throughout the negotiations, Bonar Law no less than Asquith was subjected to Palace pressure. Stamfordham wrote to Bonar Law: 'His Majesty still clings to the belief in British common sense and trusts that by "give and take" by *all* parties concerned, an amicable solution may yet be found.' Bonar Law's reply was discouraging:

I am sorry to say that I do not share the hopeful view your letter expresses ... I now despair of any agreement between the parties ... In our belief there are now only two courses open to the Government: They must either submit their Bill to the judgment of the people, or prepare to face the consequences of civil war.

Brazenly attempting to extract a political advantage from his own intransigence, he went on to suggest that the King should write to his ministers, telling them it was their duty to hold a general election before Home Rule became law: a course the King had imprudently mentioned to the Leader of the Opposition a few months earlier. Stamfordham reacted frostily to Bonar Law's impertinence: 'As to any special communications to his Ministers, His Majesty's action will be guided by time and circumstances.'

The King had not abandoned his desire to see Home Rule put to the test of a general election, even if that required so hazardous a measure as the dismissal of the Government or the withholding of the Royal Assent. Yet in his heart of hearts he was unwilling to change his advisers, least of all at the prompting of Bonar Law. He admitted to Esher that he liked Asquith, 'with whom he was upon the frankest and most friendly terms'. For the dour and abrasive Leader of the Opposition he felt no such regard. The King was even more reluctant to see the departure of Sir Edward Grey from the Foreign Office, considering him to be 'the most respected figure in the European diplomatic world and impossible to replace'.

The Prime Minister did not reciprocate his sovereign's confidence. To his face, Asquith expressed gratitude for the King's tactful mediation; behind his back, he was less than respectful. At the end of a Cabinet meeting, when Harcourt mentioned that he was going to have a tooth extracted, the Prime Minister said he was in a similar plight: he was going to see the King. He told Venetia Stanley that he had received 'a letter (of rather a neurotic kind) from the highest quarters'. And he later wrote: 'I found the main preoccupation of the Other Party to my interview at the Palace was with his own position, and the "terrible cross-fire" to which he conceives himself to be exposed.'

The wry humour with which Asquith referred to his sovereign was unkind but not undeserved. In his considered utterances, the King could match the statesmanship of any minister. In the drawing-room, however, his artless comments on men and manners worried even Queen Mary. 'He was sometimes too outspoken,' she admitted in the last year of her life. 'I remember that I once had a lady-in-waiting who was a fool and used to ask indiscreet questions of my husband in the motor-car. He always answered exactly what he thought. I had to get rid of the woman.' Curzon, a member of a royal house party at Chatsworth in the winter of 1913, told Bonar Law:

The King was less temperate in language and more excited in manner than at Balmoral. He is of course greatly keen on a settlement.

Forgetting, I think, that Lady Crewe was the wife of an eminent Cabinet Minister he poured into her astonished ear terrific denunciations of Lloyd George on the subject of pheasants and mangold-worzels.

It would have been asking too much of the squire of Sandringham to remain silent. A few weeks earlier, Lloyd George had renewed his attacks on landowners by alleging that their pheasants devoured whole fields of mangold-worzels, an absurd complaint, as any countryman could have told him. The King's indignation at Lloyd George's howler seems less tactless than Curzon's choice of Bonar Law as his confidant. Perhaps Curzon had not yet heard how his Glaswegian colleague, staying at one of the great houses of England, was startled during his morning walk by a cock pheasant which rose suddenly from under his feet. The recently elected leader of the country gentlemen's party inquired of his host: 'Pray what bird might that be?'

Lloyd George was not the only target of the King's displeasure during that shooting party at Chatsworth. Among the other guests of the Duke and Duchess of Devonshire were the Abercorns and the Crewes, two families that had long been close friends. Inflamed, however, by the spectre of civil war in Ireland, the Duchess of Abercorn refused to dine next to even so mild a member of the Government as Lord Crewe, and the table had to be swiftly rearranged. The King was annoyed by that insult to a minister in his own presence. At the end of the visit he invited the Crewes, but not the Abercorns, to travel back to London with him in the royal train.

The King and his cousin Mensdorff shook their heads over the growing intrusion of political bitterness into social life. 'Nowadays one can hardly invite Government and Opposition,' the ambassador wrote in his diary. 'Women are more passionate than men, as usual, and do their best to make matters worse.' The Londonderrys, as fervently Unionist as their fellow Irish landowners the Abercorns, refused an invitation to Windsor for Ascot races; they would not be seen in the same carriage with Liberals such as the Chesterfields or the Granards. And at an evening party given by the Duchess of Sutherland, Lord Londonderry turned on his heel and left the house just as he was about to be received by his hostess; he had noticed Lord and Lady Lincolnshire in the crowd.

To a monarch who valued an established social order, such tantrums were disagreeable but overshadowed by the darker prospect of civil war. Undaunted by the failure of the private talks between Asquith and Bonar Law, the King maintained a relentless pressure on both. 'I shall certainly ask the P.M. to come here to see me for one night,' he wrote from Sandringham in the New Year of 1914. 'I shall keep on bothering him as much as possible.'

Inadequate concessions, the King insisted, were worse than none. At his prompting, the Cabinet abandoned its proposal for what was known as the 'veiled exclusion' of the Protestant counties from Home Rule. 'I have always given you as my opinion,' the King told Asquith, 'that Ulster will never agree to send representatives to an Irish Parliament in Dublin, no matter what safeguards or guarantees you may provide.' He again demurred when the Cabinet produced a new plan, completely excluding Ulster from the provisions of Home Rule, but for a period of only three years; so short a reprieve, he warned, would not be acceptable to Sir Edward Carson, leader of the militant Ulster Unionists.

By sheer persistence, the King had his way. In March 1914 the Prime Minister made a concession that at any time during the previous two years would have been thought inconceivable. Introducing the Home Rule Bill for the third and last of its required parliamentary circuits, Asquith proposed that Ulster should be excluded not for three years but for six; by the time that period had elapsed, two British general elections would have tested the nation's opinion of Home Rule. Even before the Prime Minister had spoken, the King privately begged both Bonar Law and Carson to examine the Government's forthcoming declaration with a generous eye. He asked in vain. Carson demanded Ulster's absolute and indefinite exclusion from Home Rule. He told the Commons: 'We do not want sentence of death with a stay of execution for six years.' Redmond had reluctantly agreed to the delay of six years only under severe pressure from his Liberal allies; he could go no further without betraying his fellow Irish Nationalists. The deadlock was once more complete.

Relations between the two parties were further inflamed by Winston Churchill, who in a public speech at Bradford revealed a seeming determination to impose Home Rule on Ulster by force. He accused Carson of 'a treasonable conspiracy', proclaimed that there were 'worse things than bloodshed even on an extended scale' and invited his audience to join him in putting 'these grave matters to the proof'.

The King was both alarmed and bitter at the approach of civil war and begged Asquith to submit the Home Rule issue to a national referendum. His present Government, he said, would in due course disappear and be forgotten, but he himself would remain and his action be remembered. Yet even as the King pleaded with the Prime Minister at Buckingham Palace on 19 March, what he most dreaded had apparently come to pass: a mutinous refusal by officers of the British Army to take part in operations against Ulster. He wrote in anguish two days later: 'I am grieved beyond words at this disastrous and irreparable catastrophe which has befallen my Army, which whatever may now happen will tarnish its long and glorious history.'

Throughout the Home Rule controversy, the King had repeatedly warned Asquith against the use of the army to coerce Ulster; and the Prime Minister had as frequently brushed aside his sovereign's apprehension. The Government, he assured the King, had no intention of employing troops for political purposes. 'Whom are they going to fight?' he inquired blandly. In any case, Asquith added, the King was no more head of the army than he was head of every other public department; any order given to the troops would be on the responsibility of ministers, not of the monarch. That lecture on constitutional practice failed to impress the King. He saw himself, if not quite as Henry v, at least entitled to a more positive role in military matters than in the affairs of the Treasury or the Post Office. His belief was shared by the armed forces themselves, who claimed a personal allegiance to their Sovereign unknown among Whitehall clerks or postmen.

It was therefore with a sense of both national and personal humiliation that on the morning of 21 March the King read reports of unrest among his troops at the Curragh, near Dublin. That he first learned of it from the newspapers, without a warning word from the Government, added to his astonishment and anger.

The truth, it emerged, was less calamitous: a tale not so much of ministerial deceit and military disaffection as of hysteria and muddle, of ambiguous orders and poor leadership.

A few days earlier, the Cabinet committee that watched over Irish affairs had summoned Sir Arthur Paget, the General Officer Commanding troops in Ireland, to a conference in London. There he received certain orders, but since they were given to him orally, it is not known precisely what they were. The ministerial committee, which included such experienced rhetoricians as John Seely, the Secretary for War, and Winston Churchill, the First Lord of the Admiralty, later insisted that it had done no more than instruct Paget to safeguard the military installations of Northern Ireland against expected attacks from Carson's Ulster Volunteers. For such purposes he would have at his disposal substantial military and naval reinforcements. When Paget expressed anxiety about the possible conduct of his officers, most of whom sympathized with Ulster, the Secretary for War laid down two guiding principles. Officers required to suppress disorder in support of the civil power should not be permitted to resign their commissions but must, if they refused to obey orders, be dismissed from the army; officers domiciled in Ulster, however, could be excused such duties. (It may be noted in passing that the consciences of the non-commissioned officers and other ranks serving in Ireland received no such consideration.)

Having returned to Ireland, Paget summoned the senior officers of his command. The orders which he gave to them, when not incoherent, were very different from those he had received in London. With a theatrical self-importance that on any less momentous occasion would have been merely comic, he predicted that 'active operations were about to commence against Ulster', that Ireland would shortly 'be in a blaze', that officers must decide where their duty lay within a matter of hours. At no time did the excitable General Paget say that the impending troop movements were precautionary or that subsequent operations would be confined to the maintenance of law and order in support of the civil power. When he was asked, somewhat naively, whether his orders came from the King, he replied that they did. 'Don't think, officers,' he added on the following day, 'that I take orders from those swines of politicians! No – I only take orders from the Sovereign.'

Paget's muddled grasp of his War Office instructions and inflammatory language had an immediate and deplorable effect on the officers under his command. Led by the hot-headed but popular Brigadier-General Hubert Gough, fifty-eight cavalry officers prepared to sacrifice their careers (although it is often forgotten that 280 officers from less glamorous regiments declined to do so). They would fight the King's enemies but not the King's loyal subjects of Ulster. At no time, however, did any of the fifty-eight refuse to obey orders. Paget had offered them the alternative course of instant dismissal, and they took it. Without that abrupt ultimatum – which the historian of the episode rightly calls unnecessary, injudicious and improper – every officer would have done his duty and the so-called Curragh mutiny would never have taken place.

Asquith shared the King's dismay at the news from Ireland and acted with resolution. He was soon able to assure the King that Paget's provocative orders lacked the authority of the Government and that the recalcitrant officers would at once resume their duties. 'In the view of the Cabinet,' he wrote, 'it was wrong to demand from the officers any assurance as to what their conduct might be in a contingency which might never arise.' The King forbore to reply that the Prime Minister had shown no such scruple in November 1910, when extracting an assurance from his sovereign in equally opaque circumstances.

In spite of Government protestations that the troop movements had been purely defensive, the belief persisted that General Paget was the instrument of a larger but unauthorized design by Seely and Churchill to overwhelm Ulster's resistance to Home Rule. Only with the surmise of such a plan do certain events became intelligible: Seely's failure to give Paget written orders, the general's whirling words to his officers, the appointment of a military governor of Belfast, Churchill's secret despatch of eight battleships and attendant vessels to nearby waters.

Whether Machiavellian or merely inept, Seely was fortunate to escape dismissal from office; but the Arch-Colonel, as Asquith called him, did not long survive the consequences of his folly. The cause of his downfall was Gough's attempt to blackmail an already embarrassed Government. Gough refused to return to Ireland without a written declaration that the army would never be used to crush political opposition to Home Rule. Fearing a further display of military disaffection, the Secretary for War weakly agreed to Gough's terms but was disowned by the Cabinet. If it was wrong for General Paget to demand on behalf of the Government an assurance of future conduct from his officers, it was equally wrong for General Gough to demand a similar assurance from the Government. Asquith, a new-found man of steel, called for Seely's resignation and assumed the duties of Secretary for War in addition to his own. The crisis was at an end.

Lacking the resilience of his minister, the King remained deeply distressed by the Curragh imbroglio. However cosmetic the military role to which constitutional purists might limit him, he felt the near disgrace of his army as a personal mortification. He was vexed, too, that his political neutrality should be questioned, his name dragged into the arena of party strife. As Stamfordham wrote: 'The chief complaint of the Army is against the King. They say he ought to have asserted himself and prevented all this trouble.... On the other hand the Radicals are denouncing "Buckingham Palace" and its evil influences.'

That disparaging use of the euphemism 'Buckingham Palace' was an additional irritant. 'What do they mean by saying that Buckingham Palace is not me?' the King would exclaim. 'Who else is there, I should like to know? Do they mean the footmen?'

Even members of the royal household tactlessly tried to enlist him on one side or other of the Home Rule controversy. Queen Alexandra's comptroller, General Sir Dighton Probyn, who had won the Victoria Cross in the Indian Mutiny of 1857, once more scented the smoke of battle and assured the King: 'We don't care a rap for the Government, but we are all ready and will begin shooting as soon as Your Majesty tells us to.' The King replied with restraint: 'Oh, I see you mean to drag me in and make me responsible.'

There was only one ultimate relief from malicious enemies and embarrassing friends: the settlement of the Ulster problem by compromise. 'You appreciate, I know,' the King told Asquith in April, 'the terrible position in which I shall be placed if that solution is not found.' Asquith, writing to Venetia Stanley, dismissed his Sovereign's plea as 'a rather hysterical letter from G.R.'. But even the imperturbable Prime Minister realized that time was running out. Only weeks remained before the Home Rule Bill would pass the Commons for the third time, immune from amendment or rejection by the Lords. Both the Protestants in the North and the Roman Catholics in the South were meanwhile smuggling in rifles by the ten thousand, cartridges by the million.

It was not, however, until July, after another round of private talks between Government and Opposition had failed, that the Prime Minister agreed to repeated suggestions from the King: that Asquith and Bonar Law, Redmond and Carson, each accompanied by a single supporter, should attend a round-table conference under the chairmanship of the Speaker in what the monarch modestly called 'my house'.

The conclave, which began on 21 July, assembled in one of the more chaste apartments of Buckingham Palace: the 1844 Room, so called after the year in which the Russian Emperor Nicholas I had lodged there. Queen Victoria's insight into his character may serve as an epitaph on the Home Rule conference of 1914:

Politics and military concerns are the only things he takes great interest in; the arts and all softer occupations he is insensible to, but he is sincere, I am certain, *sincere* even in his most despotic acts.

In the course of the preceding negotiations, the Government had come to accept the principle of Ulster's exclusion from Home Rule; what remained to be decided were the boundaries of the excluded territory. That, in practice, meant the future of Tyrone. On the eve of the Buckingham Palace conference, Stamfordham had written to its chairman, Mr Speaker Lowther: 'It is obvious that Civil War cannot be permitted on the subject of the delimitation of a county. The King is sure you will not allow the Conference to break off without finding a solution.' Within three days, both sovereign and private secretary were undeceived. Again, it was Miss Stanley who first heard the news from the Prime Minister:

We sat again this morning for an hour and a half, discussing maps and figures, and always getting back to that most damnable creation of the perverted ingenuity of man – the County of Tyrone. The extraordinary feature of the discussion was the complete agreement (in principle) of Redmond and Carson. Each said 'I must have the whole of Tyrone, or die; but I quite understand why you say the same.' The Speaker, who incarnates bluff unimaginative English sense, of course cut in: 'When each of two people say they must have the whole, why not cut it in half?' They would neither of them look at such a suggestion.

That, in effect, marked the collapse of the conference. 'At the end,' Asquith noted, 'the King came in, rather *émotionné*, and said in two sentences (thank God! there was not another speech) farewell, I am sorry, and I thank you. He then very wisely had the different members brought to him privately, and saw each in turn. Redmond was a good deal impressed by his interview, especially as the King told him that he was convinced of the necessity of Home Rule.'

The King's initiative seems in retrospect to have been ill-advised. It offered little hope of success, yet involved a constitutional sovereign in the most contentious of all political issues. Even before its failure, Charles Trevelyan, MP, epitomized the hostility of his fellow Radicals:

If Asquith didn't supervise it, it is grossly unconstitutional and partisan. If he did, he is responsible for allowing the King to justify the conduct of the disloyalists. The only advantage is that it will lead to outspoken protests by the Labour and Radical sections and a turning of the politics of working men towards republicanism.

And when the conference proved fruitless, Trevelyan exulted: 'So much for the King's interference. Larn him to be a toad.'

The victim of such spite had every reason to be aggrieved. 'Thanks for your kind letter and sympathy,' the King replied to a friend's condolence.

'I want sympathy in these days and I can't help thinking I am being badly treated.' The ordeal of the sovereign and his subjects had in fact hardly begun. Two days after the end of the conference, the King took the almost unprecedented step of cancelling a sporting engagement. He wrote to the Duke of Richmond:

I very much regret to say that I find it is quite impossible for me to leave London tomorrow to pay you my promised visit at Goodwood which I had been so much looking forward to. The political crisis is so acute with regard to the Irish question and now the probability of a general European war necessitates my remaining in London for the present. . . . I hope you will have fine weather and that the racing will be good.

Scarcely more than a week later Great Britain was at war with Germany and the conflict over Irish Home Rule postponed, indefinitely.

The fleet that assembled off Portsmouth for the coronation review of 1911 included thirty-two battleships, thirty-four cruisers and sixty-seven destroyers. Britannia ruled the waves, and her sovereign determined that she should continue to do so. He was as much a professional sailor as a constitutional monarch, with a confident grasp of detail that could disconcert his ministers. Here is Esher's description of Asquith at an audience with the King in 1912:

The Prime Minister gave him an account of the plans proposed for the Mediterranean, and spoke rather vaguely about cruisers, etc., which they proposed to send there and the strength of the cruiser squadron. Also the two fourteen-inch guns they proposed to mount at Malta.

The King showed far more accurate knowledge than Asquith possessed about the ships, and floored him!

Successive First Lords of the Admiralty could always rely on royal support in maintaining a wide margin of naval superiority over Germany. Yet the King retained the prejudices as well as the patriotism of a serving officer, notwithstanding this passage from Harold Nicolson's official life:

He deeply regretted, and remained aloof from, the internecine quarrel which arose between Admiral Lord Charles Beresford and Sir John Fisher. He strove to approach the problem, with all the technical controversies which it aroused, in an impartial spirit.

There is evidence to suggest that Nicolson was mistaken; and that the intense dislike of Fisher which the King had conceived as Prince of Wales did not abate after his succession to the throne. By then both admirals had ceased to hold active commands, but their enmity continued. In October 1910, Fisher wrote to a friend: 'Heaven and earth is moving to make

Beresford an Admiral of the Fleet ... and the King's name freely imported. Kings like herrings are cheap today!' The report was true; the King had indeed asked the Prime Minister for Beresford's promotion, albeit in retirement, to the highest naval rank of all. The First Lord, however, Reginald McKenna, turned down the request. Other and more deserving admirals, he told Asquith, 'would justly feel aggrieved at a promotion which they could not fail to regard as being due to some other influence than to spontaneous recognition of merit by the Board of Admiralty'.

According to Fisher, McKenna's robust refusal so displeased the King that he took a mean revenge. Trinity House, Fisher claimed, the ancient authority for lighthouses and pilotage, nominated McKenna to be an Elder Brother, a much-valued honour often bestowed on First Lords of the Admiralty. But when the recommendation was shown to the King, he scratched out McKenna's name and substituted that of another Liberal minister, Lord Crewe. Although the archives of Trinity House do reveal that Crewe became an Elder Brother, there is no evidence that McKenna was ever considered for the honour. What makes Fisher's allegation seem improbable is that the appointment of a new Elder Brother does not require the sovereign's approval. Nor would so spiteful an act accord with the King's generosity of mind.

Fisher made the most of the tale. And when Esher attempted to heal the breach between admiral and sovereign, Fisher replied sarcastically: 'It is *more than gratifying* what you say to me about the King having kind words and thoughts for me, for it is so diligently circulated about that the state of his mind is the exact contrary!'

Thereafter he would refer to those surrounding the King as 'the Royal Pimps'.

Fisher's allegations against King and Court may have been exaggerated; his barometer of personal esteem swung wildly between radiant affection and black hate. What seems certain, however, is that McKenna would rather offend his sovereign than make an enemy of Fisher. Even in retirement, the former First Sea Lord remained the dynamic and imaginative ally of any politician who had the defence of his country at heart.

When, therefore, in October 1911 Winston Churchill succeeded McKenna as First Lord of the Admiralty, Fisher resumed his campaign of conversion. As President of the Board of Trade and as Home Secretary, Churchill had grudged the money demanded for naval expansion, preferring that it should be used for social services. But from the moment he arrived at the Admiralty he was Fisher's man, sharing his dedication to a fleet of dreadnought battleships and submarines, to the virtues of oil over coal, to wider channels of promotion from the lower deck.

The King approved of Churchill's new-found zeal for naval rearmament and determination to maintain a margin of sixty per cent over Germany's growing strength in capital ships. He disagreed, however, with the First Lord's plan to withdraw battleships from the Mediterranean in order to safeguard British waters. The King had a sailor's sentimental regard for the Mediterranean as well as an awareness of its importance in preserving links with India. He did not hesitate to make his views known. Churchill resented that royal lesson in strategy. 'The King talked more stupidly about the Navy than I have ever heard him before,' Churchill wrote to his wife on 12 May 1912. 'Really it is disheartening to hear this cheap and silly drivel with which .he lets himself be filled up.' He was particularly vexed that his predecessor as First Lord, McKenna, should as Home Secretary have submitted a memorandum to the King criticizing the paucity of British naval strength in the Mediterranean. Throughout this dispute Churchill could at least rely on the professional support of Prince Louis of Battenberg, the Second Sea Lord, who wrote to him: 'It is sad to think that our Sailor King stands on McK's level as a naval strategist!' For his part, the King found Churchill an able but awkward minister.

It was typical of Churchill's tactlessness that in submitting names to the King for newly constructed battleships of the 1911-12 programme he should have included the regicide Oliver Cromwell. The King replied that His Majesty's Ship *Oliver Cromwell* could have no place in the Royal Navy. A year later, Churchill again submitted that offensive oxymoron; once more the King refused to accept it. Churchill was incapable of leaving ill alone. Fortified by some notes on the Lord Protector prepared by his Cabinet colleague John Morley, he wrote to Stamfordham:

Oliver Cromwell was one of the founders of the Navy, and scarcely any man did so much for it. I am quite sure that nothing in history will justify the view that the adoption of such a name would constitute any reflection, however vague, upon His Majesty's Royal House. On the contrary, the great movement in politics and in religion of which Cromwell was the instrument, was intimately connected with all of those forces which, through a long succession of Princes, have brought His Majesty to the Throne of a Constitutional and a Protestant country. The bitterness of the rebellions and tyrannies of the past has long ceased to stir men's minds; but the achievements of the country and of its greatest men endure.

Those were ill-timed sentiments to express on the eve of the Irish Home Rule crisis, and Stamfordham must have enjoyed dispelling Churchill's rhetoric:

The arguments you adduce do not alter the King's views on the subject. You express your conviction that the name would be extremely well received; but may I remind you that when the Government of the day in 1895 proposed to erect out of public funds a Statue of Oliver Cromwell they were rigorously opposed by the Irish and the Opposition and defeated by a majority of 137 . . .

If the idea of a Statue aroused so much animosity it is reasonable to expect no less opposition to the association of Cromwell with a Warship costing millions of public money.

Whatever His Majesty's own personal feelings may be with regard to Cromwell he is satisfied that your proposal would revive similar feelings of antagonism and religious bitterness to those of 17 years ago, and especially now at a time when there are alas, and especially in Ireland, signs that 'the bitterness of the rebellions and tyrannies of the past' have by no means 'ceased to stir men's minds.'

Even then Churchill would have prolonged the struggle had he not received this daunting note from Prince Louis of Battenberg, about to be promoted to First Sea Lord:

You told me the other day that on your second application to the King re *Oliver Cromwell* he had again raised objections.

All my experience at the Admiralty and close intercourse with three sovereigns leads me to this: from all times the Sovereign's decision as to names for HM Ships has been accepted as final by all First Lords.

I am inclined to think the Service as a whole would go against you in this choice.

Nothing more was heard of an HMS *Oliver Cromwell*. But in 1913 Churchill fought another unsuccessful engagement against Buckingham Palace. This time he asked that one of the new battleships should be called HMS *Pitt*, after the two statesmen of that name. It had, he added, been suggested by Mr Asquith as particularly appropriate.

The King, however, knew better than his Prime Minister what would be considered appropriate by wardroom and lower deck. He instructed Ponsonby to write: 'His Majesty is inclined to think that the name *Pitt* is neither euphonious nor dignified, although Battleships have formerly been so named. There is moreover always the danger of the men giving the Ship nicknames of ill-conditioned words rhyming with it.'

When Churchill persisted, Stamfordham discharged the final salvoes of the contest. In reply to the First Lord's contention that *Pitt* evoked 'historical associations of the greatest moment', he wrote:

His Majesty noticed from the records you sent that the two last vessels called *Pitt* were used as Coal Depots: two previous ships of that name being respectively a captured French Privateer, and a vessel brought from the East India Company and changed from *Pitt* to *Doris* ...

The King quite recognises the interest and trouble which you have taken in this matter, and indeed in everything connected with the great Service over which you preside. But at the same time his Majesty yields to no one in his concern for all that affects the daily life of the Sailor, with which the name of the Ship, wherein he lives, and wherein he may have to fight, must always be closely associated.

Insensitive as Churchill could be, it is impossible not to applaud his single-minded attachment to the navy. 'You have become a water creature,'

Lloyd George told him. 'You think we all live in the sea, and all your thoughts are devoted to sea-life, fishes and other aquatic creatures. You forget that most of us live on land.' In the three years 1911–14, he spent eight months afloat in the Admiralty yacht *Enchantress*, visiting every naval establishment in the British Isles and Mediterranean, every important ship. The Prime Minister was his guest on one such cruise in May 1914. Miss Violet Asquith wrote of Churchill in her diary:

As we leaned side by side against the taffrail, gliding past the lovely, smiling coast-line of the Adriatic, bathed in sun, and I remarked, 'How perfect!' he startled me by his reply: 'Yes – range perfect – visibility perfect – If we had got some six-inch guns on board how easily we could bombard ...'

Another two months, and the nation was grateful for such dedication to the arts of war.

The power of a constitutional monarch to influence international affairs has long been disputed. Even the exertions of that restless cosmopolitan King Edward VII are suspect. Did the visit which he made to Paris in 1903 on his own initiative inspire the Anglo-French *entente*? Was his outspoken resentment of the German Emperor a cause of Anglo-German antagonism and naval rivalry? Or were those factors incidental to the broader themes of geography and economics which hastened the outbreak of war in 1914?

The Kaiser himself doubted neither the malignity nor the power of his uncle. On 30 July 1914, when war seemed inevitable, he wrote:

So the celebrated encirclement of Germany has finally become an established fact, and the purely anti-German policy which England has been pursuing all over the world has won the most spectacular victory ... Even after his death Edward VII is stronger than I, although I am still alive!

Arthur Balfour, by contrast, Prime Minister at the time of the *entente*, denied King Edward any enduring influence whatsoever. He told Lansdowne, the former Foreign Secretary: 'During the years when you and I were his Ministers, he never made an important suggestion of any sort on the larger questions of policy.'

No such conflict of evidence clouds the story of King George v's attachment to foreign affairs. Unlike his father, who crossed the Channel six times during the last year of his life, he came increasingly to detest the continent of Europe. He found no stimulus in the sights and sounds of travel, displayed no curiosity about the history, literature and arts of other lands. The Empire alone continued to touch a romantic chord in that heart of oak. For the rest, as Mensdorff wrote, he was 'through and through an English-

7 The Duke and Duchess of York at home in York House, St. James's Palace after two years of marriage. Arriving there from the honeymoon, the Duchess found to her dismay that her husband, with a misplaced desire to spare her trouble, had engaged Maples to decorate and furnish the entire house.

8 The Duke of York and some of his children at Sandringham. From left to right: Prince Albert, Princess Mary, Prince Edward (known as David) and Prince Henry. The legend has persisted that they spent a miserable childhood. Certainly their father epitomized the Victorian papa. Yet even the Duke of Windsor admitted in his memoirs that whatever frustrations he recalled in retrospect, 'Sandringham possessed most of the ingredients of a boyhood idyll.'

9 The Prince of Wales (on the right) with his cousin the Emperor Nicholas II of Russia, at Cowes in 1909. Their friendship was as close as their resemblance. But when in March 1917 the Emperor was forced to abdicate, King George V, in the most questionable intervention of his reign, persuaded the Lloyd George Government to withdraw its offer of asylum to his cousin. The imprisonment of the Emperor and his family thereafter became increasingly rigorous, and in 1918 they were murdered by the Bolsheviks.

10 Robed and crowned as Emperor of India, King George V, with Queen Mary, receives the homage of his subjects at the Delhi Durbar of 1911. This triumphant visit to the sub-continent was entirely his own idea, achieved in the face of reluctance on the part of the Liberal Government.

11 The Prince of Wales as a young staff officer, with the King, behind the lines on the Western Front. He desperately wanted to go into battle with his regiment, the Grenadier Guards, but the Government would not allow it. 'I feel such a swine having a soft comfortable time out here,' he wrote, 'while the Guards Division is up at Ypres.'

12 The King surveys the devastation of war, 1917. It was while inspecting troops in France two years earlier that he was thrown from his horse and badly injured: an accident that for the rest of his life left him stiff of limb and sometimes in pain.

13 The King encourages a young war worker in Sunderland. It was often noted how much more at ease he was with other people's children than with his own.

14 At work with his devoted private secretary, Lord Stamfordham, in the garden of Buckingham Palace.

Stamfordham.

man, with all the prejudices and insular limitations of the typical John Bull'.

That preference for hearth and home, for the solace of stamp album and shotgun, was not entirely irrational. The King never overcame a shy distaste for public occasions or a dyspeptic aversion to rough seas and rich food. Above all, he remained a lamentable linguist, reluctant to expose his weakness before others. The ultimate blame for this deficiency in a royal education must rest with his parents who, in spite of Queen Victoria's prompting, failed to ensure that their children were taught fluent French and German at an impressionable age. The Tecks, for all their improvidence, made no such mistake with the future Queen Mary; in later years, when listening to a broadcast by Hitler, what struck her most was his abominable German.

Incorrigibly insular, the King was not tempted to follow his father's example in pursuing a foreign policy independent of his ministers. Yet he was neither ignorant of international affairs nor timid in expressing his views. He interrogated ambassadors, annotated diplomatic despatches, read the newspapers; and when required by the Government to make State visits abroad, he ultimately complied if convinced that they were in the national interest.

King George's growing distaste for foreign travel did not extend to the Empire overseas, in whose welfare he took a paternal pride. Although it was the one sphere of statecraft for which he was uniquely qualified both by birth and experience, his Liberal ministers lacked the imagination to harness their sovereign's enthusiasm. They had tried in vain to discourage him from holding the Delhi Durbar of 1911, and in the following year would not let him accept an invitation from General Botha to visit South Africa. Charles Hobhouse was present when the Cabinet discussed the proposal, and wrote nastily: 'We decided he had much better stay at home, and not teach people how easily the machine worked without a King.'

There were further differences between King and Cabinet about State visits to the capitals of Europe. The King recognized that he had a constitutional duty to make such visits, whatever personal inconvenience they caused him. But the order in which they should take place brought him into conflict with his political advisers. The Foreign Secretary, intent on preserving the Anglo-French *entente*, insisted that Paris should come before Vienna, Berlin and St Petersburg. The King replied that France, 'being only a republic', must yield pride of place to the three continental monarchies. Intimacy with Mensdorff and the advanced age of the Emperor Franz Josef led him to put Austria at the top of the list. Stamfordham supported his master. He told Sir Francis Bertie, the British ambassador in Paris, that in such revolutionary times sovereigns should stand together. 'We make too much of the French,' he added. Stamfordham's coolness towards France and desire for an understanding with Germany further sharpened his antipathy to Knollys, who shared Edward VII's affection for the French and belief that 'all public men in Germany, from the Emperor downwards, are liars'.

Before these differences could be resolved, the coal strike of 1912 and persistent industrial unrest had caused the postponement of all State visits. In the following year the King and Queen travelled privately to Germany for the marriage of the Emperor's daughter; but their presence in Berlin lacked the political weight of a State visit and gave scant comfort to their host. Not until the spring of 1914 did the King make the first European State visit of the reign. It was to Paris, undertaken on the advice of the Foreign Secretary but without the least enthusiasm of the sovereign.

The occasion proved less of an ordeal than the King had feared. The warmth of a Parisian welcome restored his self-confidence, and even his hesitant command of French attracted sympathy. President Poincaré, noting his guest's 'slight British accent', continued: 'He seeks for the right word, but in the end he finds it, and finally expresses his thoughts with perfect lucidity.' Certainly the King's knowledge of the language was good enough for him to recall how the republicans in the crowd preserved both their principles and their manners by shouting not 'Vive le roi!' but 'Vive la reine!' The Foreign Secretary, as Minister in Attendance, also found the gift of tongues. Paul Cambon, France's ambassador to the Court of St James's, observing him in conversation with Poincaré, exclaimed: 'The Holy Ghost has descended on Sir Edward Grey and he now talks French!'

The goodwill engendered by the King's visit could hardly have been more timely. Within weeks of his return to London, the outbreak of war had welded the fragile understanding with France into an armed alliance strong enough to withstand four gruelling years of German attrition. Too much must not be claimed for the efficacy of State visits. Yet if it is conceded that Edward VII's inspired opportunism and genial charm laid the foundation of Anglo-French amity, his son's more stolid, dependable qualities cannot be denied their place in consolidating the *entente*.

In the volatile field of Anglo-German relations, King George's patience and restraint showed to particular advantage. He had been brought up by his parents to see little merit in Germany, much less in the young Emperor, his cousin William. Queen Alexandra, who never forgot or forgave Prussian aggression against her native Denmark, wrote of him to Prince George in 1888: 'Oh he is mad and a conceited ass – who also says that Papa and Grandmama don't treat him with proper respect as the *Emperor* of old and mighty Germany. But my hope is that pride will have a fall some day and won't we rejoice then!'

The Prince dutifully echoed his mother's disparaging tone: 'I see William the Fidgety has just been to Copenhagen, what the devil does he want to go there for, he must always be racing about somewhere interfering in other people's business which does not concern him.'

King Edward encouraged the feud. Stung by the cruel contempt with which the Emperor treated his mother, the King's sister, he could never resist pricking the pretensions of his bombastic and sometimes insolent nephew.

With the years, however, the future King George v declined to pursue the family vendetta. Lacking his father's sensitivity, he took William's mercurial behaviour in his stride. He also admired the courage and dexterity with which the Emperor overcame the handicap of a withered arm when shooting at Sandringham. In 1900, as Duke of York, he asked him to be godfather to his third son, Prince Henry, later Duke of Gloucester.

The death of Edward VII seemed at first to herald a permanent improvement in Anglo-German relations. During the lying-in-state in Westminster Hall, spectators were moved by the sight of the new sovereign and his cousin clasping hands at the head of the late King's coffin, and Mensdorff contrasted the Emperor's sympathetic self-effacement with the noisy merriment of the Greek family mourners. In 1911 the Kaiser returned to London for the unveiling of the memorial to his grandmother, Queen Victoria, outside Buckingham Palace. Again he proved an agreeable guest, even though the King turned down his bizarre request that the German Crown Prince, a recent visitor to India, should be appointed Honorary Colonel of the Khyber Rifles.

Behind the Emperor's affability, however, lay a deep and unreasonable suspicion of British foreign policy. The King, regretting that he should so often 'rattle the sabre', told Mensdorff:

The Germans suspect that there are English spies everywhere. Yet we have no secret service funds, or at least they are much smaller than those of any other State, and our spies are the worst and clumsiest in the world. German espionage, on the other hand, is magnificently organized and lavishly financed. In Portsmouth and Southampton there is always a certain number of German spies. We have no protection against them, and so far as I am concerned German officers can examine all our ships.

The Kaiser gave particular offence on the eve of his departure from Portsmouth in 1911 by uttering 'threats and curses against England' to Prince Louis of Battenberg, one of the most senior of serving British admirals and a cousin of the King. That was not the only awkward moment of what the King had intended to be a purely family occasion. In casual conversation at Buckingham Palace, the Emperor had expressed his country's resentment at France's colonial presence in Morocco and the intention of Germany to seek compensation elsewhere in Africa. Two months later, when the British Government reacted with fury to the despatch of a German gunboat to the Moroccan port of Agadir, the Emperor claimed that he had warned the King of the proposed demonstration of strength, and that the King had raised no objection to it.

The episode, which brought Europe to the brink of war, illustrates the dangers of informal discussions between constitutional sovereigns. For whereas the Emperor possessed the power to initiate and guide his country's policy, his British cousin did not. The King never forgot how in 1890 his father had taken him to see Bismarck only three days after the seemingly impregnable Chancellor had been dismissed by a young and inexperienced Emperor. Bismarck told his visitors:

I always said it would be a matter of three years. The first year the Emperor would be an infant. The second year he would be in leading strings. The third year he would be guided by me, and at the end of that year he would walk away by himself. I have been wrong by one year in my calculations.

King George v had achieved no such independence by the third year of his own reign. The prisoner of a parliamentary democracy, he could neither dismiss his ministers nor even expound policy without their leave. In seeking a personal solution to the Irish problem he was already exceeding the accepted limits of his constitutional role; international diplomacy he must leave to others. It was therefore with misgiving that in 1913 he agreed to attend the wedding in Berlin of the Emperor's only daughter to the Duke of Brunswick: a private family reunion, yet a potential source of misunderstanding and mischief.

The simultaneous presence of King George and of the Tsar Nicholas II of Russia both gratified and disturbed the Kaiser. He was proud to entertain his cousins, each the head of an ancient dynasty, yet alarmed at what he neurotically imagined them to be plotting behind his back. The King would later recall how William was almost childish in his jealousy of the intimate friendship between his British and Russian kinsmen, forever trying to ensure that they should never be alone. When they did manage a private talk, the King suspected that 'William's ear was glued to the keyhole.'

The German Emperor was the most garrulous of potentates. He would even inflict sermons on the crew of the imperial yacht *Hohenzollern*, omitting, he tactfully assured the Archbishop of Canterbury, 'all dogmatic trash'. At his daughter's wedding he spared cousin George, but not the King's private secretary, a jobation on international affairs. Fritz Ponsonby noted:

The Emperor kept off any delicate political questions with the King, but when he sat next to Bigge at the luncheon given by the officers, he let drive freely. He said that it hurt him very much to find we had agreed to send a hundred thousand men to help the French against him. 'I don't care a fig for your hundred thousand. There you are making alliances with a decadent nation like France and a semi-barbarous nation like Russia and opposing us, the true upholders of progress and liberty. . . .

On the whole the visit was a great success, but whether any real good is done, I have my doubts. The feeling in the two countries is too strong for a visit of this sort to alter.

That was the heart of the matter. The Emperor's outbursts reflected not only an excitable temperament but also national frustration and discontent, fears and frictions beyond the control of monarchs. No ruler, however autocratic, could have averted the ultimate collision of powers in August 1914. The genesis of the Great War is a momentous theme of history, but a tragedy of which King George V was no more than an anguished and impotent spectator.

It began, as the world has never since forgotten, with the assassination at Sarajevo of the Archduke Franz Ferdinand, heir to the throne of Austria, and his morganatic wife. 'Terrible shock for the dear old Emperor', the King wrote in his diary on 28 June 1914. Twice in recent years he had entertained the Austrian couple; once at Buckingham Palace, where he found them 'charming', and again at Windsor, where the Archduke brought down a gratifying number of royal pheasants. It was thus with a genuine sense of loss that the King reacted to the murder of his friends, defying protocol to make an unannounced visit of condolence to Mensdorff at the Austrian Embassy. Neither he nor his ministers, however, realized as yet the wider implications of the outrage.

Vienna saw it both as a blow to imperial pride and the culmination of a terrorist campaign by Slav nationalists that could no longer be endured; 'as if', H.A.L. Fisher wrote, 'at a moment of acute political tension, the Prince of Wales had been murdered in Ireland'. Austria determined that her unfriendly neighbour Serbia, the instigator of the crime and protector of Slav dissidents, should be humbled before all Europe. The ultimatum she despatched to Serbia on 23 July 1914 was so humiliating, so burdensome in its terms, that no self-respecting nation could have accepted it. Serbia nevertheless agreed to all its demands except one, the least onerous. That last flash of defiance plunged the world into war.

The King, already harassed by the failure of the round-table conference on Irish Home Rule, mentioned the impending disaster in his diary for the first time on 25 July. Next day he cancelled his annual visit to Goodwood races. On 28 July, Austria declared war on Serbia, which prompted Russia to mobilize against the Austrian Empire. That in turn drew Germany into the conflict. 'Foreign telegrams coming in all day,' the King wrote on 30

July, 'we are doing all we can for peace and to prevent a European War but things look very black.' In the early hours of 1 August he was awoken by Asquith to approve a telegram the Prime Minister wished to send in his name, urging restraint on the Russian Emperor. It was in vain. That evening Germany and Russia were at war. France hurried to the defence of her ally Russia, thus provoking a declaration of war by Germany.

Even then, Great Britain, bound to France only by sentiment, could perhaps have held aloof. 'Whether we shall be dragged into it God only knows,' the King wrote. 'France is begging us to come to their assistance. At this moment public opinion here is dead against our joining in the War but I think it will be impossible to keep out of it as we cannot allow France to be smashed.' The King's instinct rarely played him false. By 2 August, the mood of the country had changed and singing crowds flocked to Buckingham Palace, to cheer the royal family. On the following day, patriotic euphoria grew as the Government made known its intention of upholding Belgian neutrality, guaranteed by a treaty of 1830. It was in effect a promise that Great Britain would stand by France in the face of an invasion by Germany. Three times that evening the King and Queen were recalled to the palace balcony amid a tumult of cheers. 'Now everyone is for war and our helping our friends,' the King recorded with satisfaction.

The entry in his diary for 4 August 1914 made no concession to the emotions of the hour:

Warm, showers and windy. At work all day ... I held a Council at 10.45 to declare War with Germany, it is a terrible catastrophe but it is not our fault. An enormous crowd collected outside the Palace; we went on the balcony both before and after dinner. When they heard that War had been declared, the excitement increased and May and I with David went on to the balcony; the cheering was terrific.

The King's last thoughts that evening were for his second son, the future George VI, serving as a midshipman in HMS *Collingwood*. 'Please God it may soon be over,' he wrote, 'and that He will protect dear Bertie's life.'

SIX

THE GREAT WAR

House of Windsor — Austerity — With the troops —
Business as usual — Fisher overboard — Haig v. French
— Lloyd George v. Asquith — Defending the generals —
Tsar Nicholas abandoned — Princes under fire — Victory

THE dedication to duty which had sustained the King through four uneasy
years of peace sufficed to meet the heavier strains of war. He asked nothing
for himself; popular acclaim he left to his ministers, glory to the fighting
men. His own role was unobtrusive: to carry on the business of a constitutional monarch. He must know all yet relinquish ultimate responsibility,
ease the path of his Government while safeguarding those prerogatives
which in the stress of war could so easily be lost forever.

He was also required to exhort the nation to victory, and to place himself
at the head of the armed forces who waged war in his name. He donned the
mantle of King Henry v with diffidence; he would always do his best, but
he was not a born leader. The cheers outside the palace saluted the symbol
rather than the man. He embodied his people's pride but had still to win
their affection. Like his father, he cherished the hieratic trappings of
monarchy: crowns and sceptres, robes and regalia, ceremonial and precedence. Yet he could not radiate that warmth with which King Edward
reached out into the hearts of his subjects. In vain Stamfordham begged
him to display in public some of the geniality which delighted guests at his
own table. 'We sailors', the King replied, 'never smile on duty.'

The effect was dispiriting. Raymond Asquith, the Prime Minister's eldest
son, wrote from France where he was serving with the Grenadier Guards:
'The King came to see us this morning, looking as glum and dyspeptic as
ever.' It was not the kind of criticism which the King minded. He would
rather be thought a dull dog than 'an advertising sort of fellow': a phrase
which ranked high in his vocabulary of contempt. The young Prince of
Wales once referred enthusiastically to something the King had done as

'good propaganda'. His father rebuked him: 'I do things because they are my duty, not as propaganda.'

For all these self-imposed handicaps, the King eventually – and much to his own surprise – achieved popularity. A kindliness and common sense hitherto known only to a circle of intimates became public knowledge. What still remained concealed from all but a handful of ministers and officials was his moral courage: a conviction that civilized values must not be sacrificed to the clamour of patriotism. In war as in peace he struggled to preserve the decencies.

The King's determination to love his enemies, even though they must ultimately be defeated, began with Albert Mensdorff. For eight days after the outbreak of hostilities between Britain and Germany, the ambassador remained at his post in London, hoping against hope that the conflict between Austria and Russia would not provoke a declaration of war from Russia's allies, Britain and France. During that period of suspense, Mensdorff could have expected correctness, perhaps courtesy, yet hardly cordiality. On 9 August, however, he was summoned to Buckingham Palace for tea. Entering through a side gate to avoid journalists and photographers, he found his royal cousin 'as friendly and good natured as one could possibly be'. Mensdorff reported to Vienna:

The King expressed the hope that it would not come to a state of war between England and Austro-Hungary ... He said that England had gone to war about the neutrality of Belgium and the protection of French frontiers, not about Serbia and the Balkan question.

It was not to be. The respite lasted only as long as it took France to bring back her troops from North Africa, safe from interception by Austria's Mediterranean Fleet. On 12 August, a day that in happier times marked the beginning of the King's annual grouse shooting holiday in Yorkshire, Britain and France declared war on Austria. Mensdorff wrote in his diary:

An hour later I received a letter from King George speaking of our old friendship and lifelong intimacy and expressing the hope of later 'welcoming you back to London', etc. Really touching. It must indeed be without precedent in history that at the same time as the declaration of war the Sovereign writes such a letter to the ambassador beginning 'My dear Albert' and ending 'ever your devoted friends and cousins George and Mary.'

The King was not alone in his tenderness for Austria. Although it was Austria's deliberately harsh ultimatum to Serbia which had set Europe alight, she remained almost guiltless in English eyes. Lord Harewood, the Yorkshire landowner whose son was later to marry the King's only daughter, wrote to Mensdorff on 14 August: 'It is lamentable that your nation and ours should be at war, for we owe you no grudge except for having put the match to the fire.'

The British people showed no such indulgence to Germany. As confidence in an Allied victory before Christmas gave way to the enemy's advance on Paris and the retreat of the British Expeditionary Force, derision turned to a near hysterical hatred of all things German. Men and women bearing Teutonic names, for all their long residence and unblemished character, were reviled as traitors, arrested and imprisoned without trial. Spies were reported from every corner of the realm. Lord Kitchener, newly appointed Secretary of State for War, had solemnly to assure the Cabinet that lights seen flashing over Sandringham during a German air sortie were caused by the car of the rector returning home after dinner. It became as unpatriotic to consume German wine as to keep a dachshund, although John Morley would have none of that nonsense. Rebuked for drinking hock, he replied: 'I am interning it.'

The King, too, kept a sense of proportion. He was disturbed by the campaign of vilification waged against two dedicated public servants because of their supposed German sympathies: Admiral Prince Louis of Battenberg and Lord Haldane. Prince Louis, a member of the Hesse family, had indeed been born a German; but at the age of fourteen he became a naturalized British subject and joined the Royal Navy as a cadet. Marriage to a granddaughter of Queen Victoria was no obstacle to his promotion. After nearly half a century of service he reached the pinnacle of his profession as First Sea Lord. What he lacked in imagination was more than balanced by industry and attention to detail. In the last days of July 1914, when it fell to him to mobilize the fleet, the operation was carried out with prompt efficiency. Even that, however, was not enough to protect a man of German name and accent from public insult. His younger son, the future Earl Mountbatten of Burma, then a naval cadet, wrote to his mother from Osborne:

What d'you think the latest rumour that has got in here from outside is? That Papa has turned out to be a German spy and has been discreetly marched off to the Tower, where he is guarded by Beefeaters ... I got rather a rotten time of it for about three days.

The First Sea Lord's fate was scarcely less humiliating. After two months of vicious attacks by the popular press, Asquith wrote to Miss Stanley: 'Our poor blue-eyed German will have to go.' On the following day Prince Louis resigned, 'driven to the painful conclusion that at this juncture my birth and parentage have the effect of impairing in some respects my usefulness on the Board of Admiralty'. Honourable and patriotic to the end, he disappeared into private life, consoled by the empty distinction of a Privy Counsellorship. 'I feel for him deeply,' the King wrote in his diary, 'there is no more loyal man in the country.'

It took a few months longer to eject Lord Haldane from the Woolsack. As a vigorous and far-sighted Secretary for War from 1906 to 1912, he had forged three essential weapons: an Expeditionary Force, a Territorial Army and a General Staff. Those achievements counted for nothing when set against the chance remark, dropped at dinner one night in 1912 and later made public by his host, that Germany was his 'spiritual home'. It was useless for him to explain that he had been referring to his studies in philosophy at Göttingen University forty years earlier. At the height of the disparaging campaign against him, the Lord Chancellor received 2,600 abusive letters in a single day. Asquith, overwhelmed by the pressures of war and politics, felt unable to protect his old friend, whom he excluded from the reconstructed Government of 1915. 'I make no complaint,' Haldane observed. 'In time of war it is only natural.'

The King had a high regard for his ill-used minister. Unlike Edward VII, who would refer to Haldane as a 'damned radical lawyer and a German professor', he was put off neither by Haldane's excursions into Hegelian metaphysics nor by his ponderous manner – what Admiral Fisher called 'his elephantine sinuosities'. In 1912, when Haldane exchanged the War Office for the Woolsack, the King suggested to him that he could well combine not only those two offices, but also that of ambassador to Berlin. Repeating the compliment in a letter to his mother, Haldane felt it necessary to explain: 'This was his joke.' Three years later, the King could not save him from what at the time seemed to be political extinction. But to demonstrate to the world his own continuing confidence in Haldane, he conferred on him the Order of Merit: a distinction that lay within the sovereign's personal gift. At the end of the war, when the King held a victory parade of London Territorials, he insisted that Haldane should stand by his side on the dais.

It was not only on behalf of those fallen Titans that the King demonstrated his compassion. He also secured the release of two unhappy members of Gottlieb's German Band, whose pre-war popularity in London had failed to protect them from internment. At a time when few were prepared to defend the rights of conscientious objectors, he tried to prevent their internment in Dartmoor, the bleakest of criminal prisons. And when Prince Henry wrote from Eton to ask whether he could go and look at a camp for German prisoners of war, the boy received a stern rebuke: 'I think it is in very bad taste, I don't wish you to go there at all ... How would you like it if you were a prisoner for people to come and stare at you as if you were a wild beast.'

The King reacted with contemptuous anger to the enemy's methods of warfare. The sinking of unarmed merchant vessels provoked the comment: 'It is simply disgusting that Naval Officers could do such things.' And the haphazard bombing of civilian targets by Zeppelin airships he condemned as 'simple murder'. Yet he disdained any suggestion that the Germans should be repaid in kind. Stamfordham wrote on his behalf to the Prime Minister:

The King yields to no one in abominating the general conduct of the Germans throughout this war; but none the less he deprecates the idea of reprisals and retaliation; he has always hoped that at the end of the war we shall as a Nation stand before the world as having conducted it as far as possible with humanity and like gentlemen.

Those were courageous sentiments to express in April 1915. The King similarly disapproved of an Admiralty order that British merchant ships should fly the flag of the United States, who had not yet entered the war, in order to deceive German submarines. He said he would rather be sunk under his own flag.

It may be that the King carried his quixotry too far. His resistance to the erosion of civilized standards was not confined to the sinking of merchant ships, the bombing of civilians and the ill-treatment of prisoners of war. He also objected to proposals that the Kaiser and his family should be deprived of their honorary commands of British regiments; that their Garter banners should be removed from St George's Chapel, Windsor; that they and all other enemies should be stripped of their honorary appointments to British orders of chivalry. For him, those pre-war exchanges of uniforms and ribands were part of history and should be left undisturbed. Queen Alexandra, in a letter to her son, echoed the widespread resentment of his subjects: 'Although as a rule I never interfere, I think the time has come when I must speak out ... It is but right and proper for you to have down those hateful German banners in our sacred Church, St. George's at Windsor.'

With reluctance, the King yielded, and the banners were removed. 'Otherwise', he told a friend, 'the people would have stormed the Chapel.' Trivial in themselves, such episodes did the King harm; they seemed to indicate the survival of a royal trade union that cut across national loyalties. Even Asquith looked askance when the King explained to him that his cousin, Prince Albert of Schleswig-Holstein, was 'not really fighting on the side of the Germans', but had only been 'put in charge of a camp of English prisoners', near Berlin. 'A nice distinction,' the Prime Minister observed satirically to Venetia Stanley. Lloyd George was more brutal. On receiving a summons to the palace in January 1915, he remarked to his secretary: 'I wonder what my little German friend has got to say to me.'

In spite of an ancestry that for centuries had thrived on infusions of German blood, the King considered himself to be wholly and impregnably British. When H.G. Wells spoke of 'an alien and uninspiring Court', the King retorted: 'I may be uninspiring, but I'll be damned if I'm an alien.' Habits, opinions, pastimes, devotions, dress: all were indistinguishable from those of any other old-fashioned English country gentleman. The Queen, too, would refer to herself as 'English from top to toe'. She was the first Consort for four hundred years to speak the language as her mother tongue, albeit with a slight guttural accent from which her husband was entirely free.

Both, therefore, were mortified by whispers that doubted their whole-hearted support for the Allied cause. Such rumours were confined to a tiny minority: the malicious, the republican, the simple-minded. But as the casualties of battle mounted year by year, they were joined by embittered victims of suffering or grief. The wartime conduct of the King and Queen, austere in private, tireless in public, should in itself have been enough to refute such slanders. Yet in 1917, with what seems to have been a momen-tary loss of nerve, the King determined to restore confidence by means of a theatrical gesture. He would rid the royal family of its Germanic taint by proclaiming his dynasty the House of Windsor.

If a change had to be made, Lord Stamfordham's suggestion of Windsor was inspired, recalling as it did the best known and most beautiful of English silhouettes outside the capital: ancient, sturdy, benevolent. Yet what did the new name replace? Guelf was the historic patronymic of the House of Hanover, Wettin that of the Prince Consort; neither of those names, however, was used or even known outside the field of genealogy. Lord Rosebery, who as the most historically minded of living Prime Min-isters was consulted at every stage, warned Stamfordham that 'the enemy to be feared on such a question is ridicule'. In Britain, the proclamation was received with a renewal of patriotic fervour. Germany was less respect-ful. The Kaiser let it be known that he would be delighted to attend a performance of that well-known opera, 'The Merry Wives of Saxe-Coburg-Gotha'. The ultimate judgement on the creation of the House of Windsor came from a Bavarian nobleman, Count Albrecht von Montgelas: 'The true royal tradition died on that day in 1917 when, for a mere war, King George v changed his name.'

A more practical and timely measure accompanied the proclamation of the House of Windsor. Members of the royal family were enjoined to relinquish all 'German degrees, styles, dignities, titles, honours and appel-lations'. Sir Frederick Ponsonby, an authority on such matters, explained the edict to his wife with his usual drollery:

The King came to the conclusion that something must be done about the names of the Royal Family. Here we are breeding innumerable Battenbergs & Tecks and are they for ever to remain Princes of Battenberg & Dukes & Princes of Teck? He accordingly sent for Prince Louis whose whole attitude was splendid. He said of course it is absurd that I should be a Prince of Battenberg, but when the war broke out I did not want to be like Schmidt who became Smith. I have been educated in England and have been in England all my life. I am absolutely English and if you wish me to become now Sir Louis Battenberg I will do so. The King explained that he did not wish that but would like to make him a Peer.

His Serene Highness Prince Louis of Battenberg accordingly relinquished his German style and title, assumed the anglicized surname of Mountbatten and was created Marquess of Milford Haven. His elder son, Prince George of Battenberg, acquired the courtesy title of Earl of Medina; his younger son, Prince Louis of Battenberg, that of Lord Louis Mountbatten, the style he bore until created Viscount Mountbatten of Burma in 1946 and Earl Mountbatten of Burma a year later. Another member of the Battenberg family, Prince Alexander, a captain in the Grenadier Guards, was created Marquess of Carisbrooke. The Queen's two surviving brothers, both senior officers in the British Army, assumed the surname of Cambridge, after their maternal grandmother's family, and each was created a peer. The Duke of Teck became Marquess of Cambridge; he asked for a dukedom, but the King decided to reserve the highest rank in the peerage for his own sons. His younger brother, Prince Alexander of Teck, became Earl of Athlone. The King also made regulations to define and restrict the use of such princely styles and titles as survived, lest they proliferate like those of continental royalty. He deplored having had to sweep away so much of the past, yet was not ashamed of his handiwork. Carisbrooke and Cambridge, Milford Haven and Athlone: Shakespeare himself could not have composed a more resonant or patriotic call to arms.

The war seemed scarcely to touch the home life of the nation. Families mourned their dead; otherwise it was both business and pleasure as usual. When in December 1915 General Sir Douglas Haig was promoted to be Commander-in-Chief of the British Forces in France, he asked the War Office who was to succeed him in command of the First Army. He received the reply that both the Prime Minister and the Secretary for War, Lord Kitchener, had left London for the weekend and that nothing could be settled until Monday. A few months later he was ordered to cancel all army leave between 18 and 25 April 1916, because the home railways would be too busy dealing with the Easter traffic. 'I wonder what the future historian will write about Great Britain, whose inhabitants in a period of crisis insist that these holiday makers should be given preference in travelling to soldiers from the seat of war.'

The profusion of domestic servants on which all but the poorest classes of society depended was only slowly depleted. By the second month of the war, sixty-one of the male staff at Buckingham Palace had volunteered for the armed forces, but many remained. Not until the introduction of military conscription in 1916 did large numbers of women begin to replace men in the munitions industry and other male preserves. Fritz Ponsonby's wife, working for much of 1915 in a soldiers' canteen in France, received a War Office travelling pass made out for 'Lady Ponsonby and maid'.

Lord Bertie, the British ambassador to France, dined at the Carlton Hotel while on leave in London that autumn.

I found the restaurant cram-full. No signs of war within, except for some few men in khaki and a few limping. All the rest in piping times of peace, low gowns (very low), nearly all the men in evening swallow-tail coats and most of them wearing white waistcoats.

He was even more scandalized by the failure of politicians and senior officials to set an example of restraint.

During a journey on the Continent – less than 48 hours – a British Minister and five companions with three servants consumed, or are charged as having drunk, 27 bottles of wine at prices ranging from 2 francs to 12 francs per bottle, 39 glasses of liqueur, and 19 bottles of beer. Who on a journey on *private* account would drink, in a railway car, claret at 12 francs a bottle? It is discreditable that this should be at the public expense.

As late in the war as January 1918, Bonar Law's private secretary, dining in Paris with a fellow Treasury official, Maynard Keynes, complained that he 'could not find champagne dry enough but Napoleon brandy was excellent'. And a few days later, at Maxim's: 'Dinner consisted of oysters, trout, chicken, spring peas, fruit, coffee, claret – red and white – liqueur brandy ... We then went to the Folies Bergère.' The secretariat of the Committee of Imperial Defence celebrated Maurice Hankey's knighthood with a dinner of eight courses at the Army and Navy Club; the invitations parodied the style of an official minute and were printed on the pale green paper always used by that department.

The King and Queen, by contrast, imposed an austere restraint on their public and private pleasures alike. 'I cannot share your hardships,' the King told his troops, 'but my heart is with you every hour of the day.' While preserving the essentials of monarchy, he saw to it that no immeasurable gulf should separate his own life from that of any other soldier or sailor on active service. He gave away most of his civilian wardrobe, and ordered no new clothes except uniforms of khaki and navy blue. As long as the war lasted he rarely dined out and never went to the theatre. His only relaxation in London was to spend an hour or two each week with his stamp collection. Balmoral was closed, the gardens at Frogmore turned over to potatoes planted during afternoons of strenuous digging. And although he continued to shoot during brief holidays at Sandringham, that too could be regarded as a patriotic contribution to the nation's larder. General Smuts, the South African representative in the Imperial War Cabinet, wrote from the Savoy Hotel in October 1917 to thank the King for a brace of pheasants, six partridges and a hare, 'most welcome and cheering in these days of short rations and Food Control'.

Always the most thrifty of housekeepers, Queen Mary rooted out extravagance with virtuous enthusiasm. Balfour's private secretary noted that the courtier returning to duty at Buckingham Palace dreads 'the change from the ample luxury and service of his own table to the Spartan regime of the Royal household'. An equerry who came late to breakfast, having been delayed by a telephone call, found that there was nothing left to eat, so rang the bell for a boiled egg. 'If he had ordered a dozen turkeys he could not have made a bigger stir,' Ponsonby wrote. 'The King accused him of being a slave to his inside, of unpatriotic behaviour, and even went so far as to hint that we should lose the war on account of his gluttony.' Poussins and lamb were banished from the royal kitchens, to be replaced by fowls and mutton, though neither in profusion. No longer was each member of the family given a clean table napkin at every meal, but made use of that economical device the napkin ring. On a fine summer day, the King and Queen ordered tea at Adelaide Cottage, in Windsor Park; it was prepared by a single servant using a very dirty kettle instead of the usual silver urn.

Guests were unanimous in recording the simplicity of the fare, at least by peacetime standards. 'It was a very plain little dinner, I remember,' wrote Mrs Fortescue, wife of the King's librarian. 'Mulligatawny soup; turbot, shrimp sauce; vegetable cutlets, green peas, new potatoes; asparagus; cold baked custard in china cups; dessert.' The future Prime Minister, Neville Chamberlain, recorded a menu of 'soup, salmon trout, chicken and a nasty sort of pink mould for a sweet'. Even the traditional Derby Day dinner for thirty-two at Buckingham Palace consisted in 1917 of soup, fish, chicken and macaroni, without either meat or wine. It may be contrasted with a dinner given in the same year by the President of the French Republic: caviar, turbot, saddle of lamb, roast partridge and roast pheasant, salad, neapolitan ice, strawberries, gâteaux, grapes, peaches and pears.

Not until the last year of the war did the British Government declare a Public Meals Order of any severity. It imposed two meatless days in each week and the rationing of fats, bread and certain other foods. Although applying principally to hotels and restaurants, the restrictions placed an additional burden on private households, even the richest of them. But it cannot have made much difference to the elevated frugality already enforced at Buckingham Palace and Windsor. Elsewhere the shock was considerable. A guest of the Asquiths complained in her diary: 'I had a minute snipe – wished they were served like whitebait.'

A zealous minister once assured the King that if Buckingham Palace were to be bombed by German aircraft it would have a stimulating effect on the people. He received the brisk reply: 'Yes, but rather a depressing effect on me.' Lloyd George risked precisely that answer when in the spring of 1915 he raised an equally unpalatable topic. He urged the King to set an example to the nation by abstaining from alcohol for the duration of the war. What might otherwise have been thought an impertinence on the Chancellor's part sprang from his alarm at the disruptive effect of heavy drinking by factory workers, particularly in the armament and shipbuilding industries. 'Drink is doing more damage in this war', Lloyd George told a meeting of fellow Welshmen, 'than all the German submarines put together.'

Although a man of temperate habits, the King was accustomed to drink a little wine with his meals and a glass of port after dinner. He nevertheless responded instantly to the call of patriotism. On 30 March 1915, Stamfordham wrote to Lloyd George: 'If it be deemed advisable His Majesty will be prepared to set an example by giving up all alcoholic liquor himself and throughout his household, so that no difference shall be made so far as he is concerned between the treatment of rich and poor.'

Privately the King allowed himself a quiet grumble. 'It is a great bore,' he told his uncle, the Duke of Connaught. He expressed the same sentiment to Lord Hardinge in more stately language: 'I confess that total abstention is not agreeable to me.'

His self-denial evoked ribaldry rather than respect. By a happy mischance the Court Circular announcing the edict from Windsor was followed by the words: 'The Earl of Rosebery and the Rt. Hon. A. J. Balfour, M.P., have left the Castle.' Writing that day to thank the King for his hospitality, Rosebery added: 'I shall never forget the wistful carnival of Monday, when a last farewell to alcohol was said with marked sadness, or the deluge of the waters on Tuesday.'

It was reported that Rosebery got such a hiccough after drinking one glass of unaccustomed ginger beer that he could not continue talking to the Queen. And Ettie Desborough, a lady-in-waiting, told a friend:

I hear a sad account of Windsor Castle on the wagon. Tempers were but little improved by temperance and a crepe wreath was fastened to the cellar door and

Charlie Cust fainted the first night after dinner; the only cheerful person being Margot, who took copious swigs out of a medicine bottle and talked a great deal, but no one else spoke except to contradict her.

The King's visits to the fleet and to his troops in France ceased to be convivial. 'The teetotal business is a severe trial,' Admiral Beatty noted. 'The old boys don't get communicative without drink of some form or other ... We have struggled along supported by Barley Water!!' Nor did Haig ever forget General Joffre's look of abhorrence when, invited to a lunch for the King at British GHQ, he was offered the choice of lemonade or ginger beer. The sybaritic Haldane was more fortunate. On being replaced as Lord Chancellor, he found consolation in abandoning the pledge he had taken as Keeper of the King's Conscience. 'So we enjoyed his dry champagne and his super-excellent liqueurs,' wrote Beatrice Webb in the summer of 1915.

Perhaps the rules of abstinence at Buckingham Palace and Windsor were not as rigid as some supposed. Cider, certainly, was deemed to be non-alcoholic. There is also the mischievous testimony of the Prince of Wales, who claimed that his father would withdraw after dinner 'to attend to a small matter of business'. This was assumed to be a small glass of port. That dutiful son also alleged that his mother's fruit cup was sometimes fortified with champagne.

Both the King and Queen would have borne their self-imposed asceticism without complaint had it achieved its purpose and encouraged others to follow the royal example. Their gesture, however, was generally ignored and sometimes derided. The King did not hide his belief that Lloyd George had made him look foolish. And the Queen, who liked to flourish an occasional colloquialism, confided to a sympathetic Mr Asquith: 'We have been carted.'

Uncomforted by wine or spirits, the King resumed his treadmill routine. He rose from a writing-table piled high with red boxes only to embark upon yet another mission of encouragement. In four years of war he undertook 450 visits to troops, 300 to hospitals, almost as many to munitions factories and shipyards. With his own hands he conferred 50,000 awards for gallantry. It was a programme to tax even the most robust of men; and by his fiftieth year the King had begun to lose resilience.

He could scarcely ever inspect a battleship without being seasick or a regiment without catching cold: unheroic ailments in themselves, yet a penance for any man so constantly in the public eye. The suffering of others preyed on his nerves and would haunt him for days; but that did not deter him from expressing gruff sympathy with the wounded or hastening to comfort air raid victims still drenched in blood. 'The weather has gone mad,' he confided to his diary, 'so has the world.' And on being taken to see some captured German trenches: 'All very pathetic, such is war.'

As the King's car passed slowly through the lines of an infantry regiment on the Western Front, a young officer described him as looking like a big, rather worn penny. That mournful countenance could be deceptive. Among fighting men he concealed his melancholy and drew strength from those about him. 'I saw several hundred thousands of them from all parts of the Empire,' he told his uncle, the Duke of Connaught. 'I did indeed feel proud that I was an Englishman.' He was particularly concerned for the welfare of his Indian troops, whom he found uncomplaining but obviously suffering from a northern winter. 'The accommodation did not seem to me at all suitable,' he wrote to the Viceroy. 'I spoke to Lord Kitchener about it, and he has appointed Sir Walter Lawrence a special Commissioner to look after the Indian wounded.' He was moved to find a member of the Botha family serving on the Western Front, and chaffingly asked him how a former enemy in the Boer War had now come to take up arms as a friend. The young South African replied with engaging frankness: 'Then you were wrong. Now you are right.' At British GHQ the King was no less pleased to meet two liaison officers whose names recalled even remoter foes: the Duc d'Elchingen and Prince Murat, each descended from one of Napoleon's Marshals.

Bumping over *pavé* roads and shell-holed tracks for anything up to a hundred miles a day, the King knew exactly what his troops expected of him. Here Oliver Lyttelton describes an inspection of the Guards division immediately before an attack on the enemy lines:

We expected and feared a battle speech, but the King talked to us in the most down-to-earth way: an example of timely tact. He asked Sherard Godman of the Scots Guards, the senior commanding officer present, what sort of food we carried into the attack. 'Cold chicken?' he suggested, and when Sherard Godman replied 'Mostly bully beef, Sir,' he rightly looked a little incredulous, and repeated, 'Cold chicken, I expect.'

The King was well aware that even in battle his regiments of Foot Guards never accepted discomfort as a necessary ingredient of excellence. The pages of Lyttelton's wartime letters from the trenches record that he and his fellow Grenadiers enjoyed plovers' eggs, foie gras, roast woodcock, cold partridge and Port-Salut cheese: though not all on the same day.

It was while inspecting troops in France on 28 October 1915 that the King suffered one of the cruellest misfortunes of his life. Having arrived at Hesdigneul by motor car, he mounted a chestnut mare provided by General Haig and rode towards a detachment of the Royal Flying Corps. For the past two weeks the charger had been specially schooled for the task of carrying the sovereign. A senior officer later wrote:

It would rest its head happily all day long against the big drum of a band playing *God Save the King*. Gunfire did not make it even twitch an ear, I think it would have sat in an aeroplane doing stunts. But what had not been foreseen was the extraordinary noise emitted by 20 flying men trying to cheer. The wretched animal reared up like a rocket and came over backwards.

The King was at once picked up and driven back to the country house where he had spent the previous night. He was in agony but far from unconscious. When told that the Commander-in-Chief thought it unsafe for him to remain in the château as the Germans might bomb it, he retorted: 'You can tell him from me to go to hell and stay there. I don't intend to move for any bombs.' It was also characteristic of the King to send a message to Haig hoping that the mare was none the worse and assuring him that he was not to feel perturbed at what had happened.

The medical men called to examine the King either failed to detect the extent of his injuries or, as one of them later claimed, felt obliged to conceal the truth. Misled by their too-optimistic reports, Haig made light of the episode. Here are his previously unpublished diary entries for three days following the accident:

The King had a good night and is only bruised. Few bruises have had so much attention! The bulletin last night was signed by 5 surgeons and Drs.

The King was anxious about himself and so was X-rayed today. This showed nothing was broken. He is going on well.

His Majesty said that at first he thought his bladder was burst and his pelvis broken! Needless to say there was nothing so serious. His temperature only went up half a degree and his pulse was also normal!! Sir Anthony Bowlby travelled in the train to Boulogne and said to me His Majesty was really well, and had had a splendid night's sleep.

That levity was misplaced. The King had in fact received severe injuries, including a fractured pelvis, and suffered intense pain and shock. Before leaving for England in the hospital train he nevertheless insisted on sending for Sergeant Oliver Brooks, of the Coldstream Guards, and decorating him with the Victoria Cross: a ceremony which would have taken place publicly had the accident not intervened. Seasickness added to the misery of the journey back to London, where convalescence was slow and burdensome. At the end of November the King wrote to the Duke of Connaught:

I was extremely lucky that I was not killed or otherwise seriously damaged, as it was I cracked three ribs & was terribly bruised about the back and legs and all my muscles were torn & wrenched. I am glad to say I am making an excellent recovery & can walk in my room with the aid of a stick, but now nearly 5 weeks since it occurred I am still very stiff & have a good many aches which are getting less every day. I am able now to do my work & see a few people. For the first fortnight I never remember having suffered so much pain.

Lord Dawson of Penn, the royal doctor, noted twenty years later that irregular bony nodules which had formed at the sites of the injury permanently limited the King's freedom of movement. To the end of his life he had to endure stiffness and sometimes pain.

There is a happier footnote to the story of the King's accident. Henceforth, his medical advisers decreed, he should be released from his pledge of total abstinence and for the sake of his health 'take a little stimulant daily during his convalescence'.

So concerned was the Queen about her husband that when in the following year he resumed his tours of the Western Front she asked Wigram to send her a nightly telegram saying how each day had gone. In 1917 she insisted on accompanying the King to France. 'This is the first lady to have a meal at my headquarters since War began!' Haig noted without enthusiasm. The Queen found it an exciting change from inspecting the rhubarb mould and rice pudding of workers' canteens. She even managed some sightseeing. Escorted by her eldest son, serving on the staff of an army corps, she walked the fields of Agincourt and Crécy. 'It was probably the first time that a Prince of Wales had visited the scene,' she wrote, 'since Edward the Black Prince was there at the time of the battle.' The current holder of the title was less impressed. 'Very *historical*!!!' was his irreverent response.

From every public engagement, the King returned to an accumulation of papers that demanded immediate attention: sometimes merely his signature, more often decision or comment. It was a duty which he never shirked. However wistfully his thoughts might stray to stamp collection or gunroom, he would first clear his red boxes.

Yet the more he toiled, the less his efforts were appreciated. Even in time of peace, the Cabinet had sometimes reacted with impatience to the claims of the royal prerogative: the right to be consulted, to encourage and to warn. Under the stress of war, harassed and overworked ministers came to dread that peevish royal inquisition, those shapeless harangues which the sovereign would inflict on his advisers.

With Stamfordham at his elbow, the King could be both formidable and cogent on paper; in conversation he could neither marshal his thoughts nor master his tongue. Asquith, more tolerant than some of his colleagues, told Venetia Stanley: 'I am going to see the King at 6 when I suppose we shall have the usual all-round-the-place talk about things in general.' Lloyd

George found him 'much more interested in petty personal details than in the turning out of hundreds of guns and millions of shells'. Neville Chamberlain, summoned to dine at Windsor, was put out by the King's apparent lack of interest in his work as Director-General of National Service. 'He hardly mentioned it and talked about anything else that came into his mind, forestry, drink, food control, race horses, etc.' The King met his match only in the strong but far from silent Kitchener; throughout a long motor journey from Winchester to London, the King complained, he had been unable to get a word in edgeways.

Soldiers and diplomats on home leave had the same tale to tell. 'The King explained to me exactly how I had fought my battles,' General Byng confided to a friend. 'He never asked me a single question.' And Robert Bruce Lockhart, invited to describe an exciting mission to Russia, afterwards wrote: 'He did most of the talking and during the forty minutes I was with him I didn't really get much in.'

Asquith nevertheless valued the King's talk as an accurate reflection of popular opinion. A generation earlier, Lord Salisbury had similarly confessed: 'I have always felt that when I knew what the Queen thought, I knew pretty certainly what view her subjects would take, and especially the middle class of her subjects.' That is no negligible role for a constitutional monarch.

In the first weeks of the war he told the Prime Minister that the country was unlikely to accept a pension of only 5s for a widow whose husband had been killed in action. 'Mr. Bernard Shaw', he continued, 'is "out for" £1 a week and 35s a week pay for every soldier.' Rarely again were sovereign and playwright to be allies in the same cause. The King was no less concerned about food shortages. He instructed Stamfordham to write to Downing Street: 'This morning Their Majesties in going to and from Deptford saw instances of these queues and it brings home to the King and Queen the hardship experienced by the poor, while the richer portion of the community do not suffer in this respect.' A few months later it was the struggling middle class who won his sympathy. He noted that the proposed increase in Income Tax from 5s to 6s in the pound 'will hit very hardly the man with an income just over £500 a year with children to educate and the price of living just double what it is in peace'.

Before the introduction of conscription, the King also urged the Government to employ more women in factories, thereby releasing large numbers of men for military service; and to impose a poll tax on all male employees in shops where the work could equally be carried out by women. But he frowned on other aspects of female emancipation. On being told that the Asquith girls and the Duchess of Sutherland had visited an army headquarters, he ordered Stamfordham to write to Kitchener that the King was 'surprised and not agreeably so' to hear of these 'female excursions'.

None could object to so reasonable, so unobstructive an exercise of the royal prerogative. Yet in other ways the Court failed to adapt itself to the needs of the hour. Lord Esher wrote in February 1918:

At five I went to Buckingham Palace. It was a Rip Van Winkle appearance upon the scene. Either the world has stopped still, or Buckingham Palace remains unchanged. The same routine. A life made up of nothings – yet a busy scene. Constant telephone messages about trivialities.

Esher, it must be added, was a jaundiced witness. As early in the reign as October 1911 a fellow member of the royal household noted that Esher was out of favour. He retained his minor offices of Deputy Constable and Lieutenant Governor of Windsor Castle; but the King, less receptive than his father to Esher's ingratiating manner, ceased to use him as confidential adviser and emissary. He had to be content with little errands entrusted to him by the Queen: bidding for ancestral letters, binding up her own correspondence, matching the exact shade of silk for the walls of a picture gallery, seeking an elegant coal scuttle. Nor, after Knollys's retirement, did Esher manage to establish anything approaching the same degree of intimacy with the more cautious Stamfordham. Throughout the war he continued to flit busily between politicians and generals; Buckingham Palace, however, became an increasingly rare port of call, and his lifelong regard for its imperturbable traditions turned to scorn.

There was some justice in Esher's mockery. It was not so much that the King and his entourage confined their energies to the minutiae of courtly custom as that they seemed unable to distinguish between what mattered and what did not. None followed the fortunes of war with greater concern or worked more unselfishly for ultimate victory. Yet throughout those years of carnage and misery, no breach of peacetime etiquette was allowed to go by default.

In September 1914, as the German armies fell back from their all but successful lunge on Paris, the First Lord of the Admiralty heartened an audience of 15,000 by threatening that if the enemy fleet did not come out and fight, 'they would be dug out like rats in a hole'. Stamfordham at once wrote to the Prime Minister: 'His Majesty did not quite like the tone of Winston Churchill's speech especially the reference to "Rats in a Hole"! ... The King feels it was hardly dignified for a Cabinet Minister.'

A year later, on the eve of the Battle of Loos, Stamfordham rebuked Downing Street for failing to tell the King of the appointment of a new Dean of Ripon. He added: 'I quite realize that you are thinking of and working at bigger questions than that of procedure in filling up Church appointments! But I felt it better to allude to the matter, feeling that it was only one of oversight.'

His apologetic tone signified no relaxation of palace standards. In the summer of 1917, as Haig began planning the Battle of Passchendaele, Wigram wrestled with the problem of whether women workers at a munitions factory about to be visited by the Queen should or should not remove their gloves to shake hands.

Clothing was a perennial theme of discussion and dispute. Auckland Geddes, Neville Chamberlain's successor as Director-General of National Service, came to be sworn of the Privy Council in a cutaway morning coat instead of the prescribed frock coat; he was reproachfully fitted out with one belonging to a groom-in-waiting. The King, although 'in despair' at the news of the Tsar's dethronement less than forty-eight hours earlier, summoned the Lord Chamberlain three times in a single day to settle the ceremonial of the Duchess of Connaught's funeral. In the same year, 1917, there was a spacious three-cornered correspondence between Stamford-ham, Curzon and Crewe on whether peers should be required to wear robes at the opening of Parliament.

Stamfordham was not the man to curb such mistimed zeal. Nearly forty years of obedience to royal whims had dulled his ability to distinguish the trivial from the momentous; to each and every command he applied himself with selfless devotion. As private secretary to Queen Victoria he had once spent eighteen months persuading a reluctant War Office to grant the honorary rank of second-lieutenant to Mr Ladislao Zavertal, Bandmaster of the Royal Artillery. Coinciding with the Boer War, Stamfordham's campaign was ultimately as successful, but no less gruelling. It must have been with a comforting sense of continuity that a whole war later he took up his pen to challenge the granting of an honorary rank to Sam Hughes, Canadian Minister of Militia and Defence.

Unlike Stamfordham, Sir Frederick Ponsonby brought a sardonic humour to the almost sacred subject of honours. Soon after the outbreak of war, he entertained his friend Lord Rosebery with an account of how an elderly Knight of the Garter and member of the royal household, Lord Lincolnshire, had conceived a fanciful ambition: 'Wishing to disguise himself as a soldier in order to inspect some regiment, he asked why he should not put a bit of blue Garter ribbon on his khaki uniform with the Jubilee and Coronation medal ribbons.' Ponsonby explained that it was because Knights of the Garter were supposed always to wear their full insignia according to the earlier practice, and so could never wear merely a strip of ribbon. Lincolnshire then proposed wearing the star and broad riband of the Garter on his khaki uniform. No, Ponsonby replied patiently, for that would be a breach of military regulations. Still unsatisfied, Lincolnshire demanded that his request be submitted to the judgement of Garter King of Arms, whence it disappeared into deserved oblivion.

Further friction was caused by the King's affection for his old tutor, Canon Dalton, whom he appointed to be a Knight Commander of the Royal Victorian Order. As the clergy could not receive the accolade, his wife remained Mrs Dalton. This, Ponsonby wrote, had raised hideous and perplexing problems:

The question whether Mrs. Dalton, wife of Canon Dalton, K.C.V.O., should take precedence of Lady Parratt, wife of Sir Walter Parratt, Knight Bachelor, had shaken Windsor to its foundations, but as it had never been officially settled even the strongest refrained from inviting these two ladies to meet at dinner.... In order to appreciate the subtleties of this question, it is necessary to wade in depths of vulgarity which have rarely been plumbed before.

Such persistent mummery in time of war prompted Ponsonby to seek the comparative sanity of the trenches. Although in his forty-eighth year, he managed to rejoin the Grenadier Guards as a junior officer, remaining at the Front long enough to be mentioned in despatches. He was then recalled to London as Keeper of the Privy Purse and later played a notable part in designing the ribbon of the newly instituted Military Cross.

The King's preoccupation with dress and deaneries might amuse or irritate his ministers but provoked no constitutional friction. Yet there was another, more troublesome field of royal activity which added to Asquith's burden:

By an odd convention all our Sovereigns (I have now had to deal with *three*) believe that in Army and Navy appointments they have a special responsibility and a sort of 'divine right of Kings' prerogative. Anyhow they have to be humoured and brought in.

As early in the war as October 1914, King and Prime Minister were in conflict over a successor to Prince Louis of Battenberg at the Admiralty. Churchill, supported by Asquith, wanted to recall the 74-year-old Lord Fisher from retirement to resume his old post of First Sea Lord; the King, still consumed with loathing for the man and his methods, instead suggested what Asquith called 'nonsense people like Hedworth Meux and Sir Henry Jackson, whom Winston will not have at any price'. Effectively the appointment rested with Churchill, who as the political head of the Admiralty would be responsible for defending it in the Commons. But the King was constitutionally entitled, not to overrule his ministers in such matters, but to warn them of what he considered their unwise choice. This right he pressed to the utmost, declaring that he felt it his duty to record a protest. Asquith rejoined: 'Perhaps a less severe term – "misgivings" – might be used by Your Majesty.' A few hours later the King signed the appointment, but simultaneously registered his dismay in a letter to the Prime Minister:

Following our conversation this afternoon, I should like to note that, while approving the proposed appointment of Lord Fisher as First Sea Lord, I do so with some reluctance and misgivings. I readily acknowledge his great ability and administrative powers, but at the same time I cannot help feeling that his presence at the Admiralty will not inspire the Navy with that confidence which ought to exist, especially when we are engaged in so momentous a war. I hope that my fears may prove groundless.

Fisher knew nothing of these astringent exchanges between Downing Street and the palace. On 26 October 1914 he told a friend that he intended to winter in Italy, which had not yet joined the Allied cause: 'I don't see any use my being in England with the dead set at me by the King and the Prime Minister kow-towing to him.' Three days later he was called out of retirement. Installed once more in the Admiralty, he must soon have learned from Churchill of the King's opposition to his appointment and returned that royal enmity salvo for salvo. He even blamed his sovereign for the destruction of Admiral Cradock's ships at Coronel: 'The person chiefly responsible is the present King, who blazed away against my policy to all and every person who came near him.' The credit for the Battle of the Falkland Islands, when Admiral Sturdee more than avenged the loss of Cradock's squadron, Fisher kept for himself. A few weeks later he told Churchill: 'I spent a maudlin hour yesterday with the King. He is quite mischievous. He told French that I had said 150,000 Germans would invade us! What I did say was that if 150,000 Germans did come they would never go back! I won't go any more. *I'll be sick.*' The King, for his part, found no pleasure in Fisher's company, maintaining what Stamfordham called 'an unconquerable aversion' to the First Sea Lord.

Yet as the months went by, it seemed that the King had judged him too harshly. Working in tandem round the clock, Churchill and Fisher generated an energy and enthusiasm that made the Admiralty hum with confidence. They planned daring operations and amassed the men and ships to sustain them. A building programme of almost 600 new vessels evoked a boast from Fisher that not even Churchill's rhetoric could have surpassed:

Such an Armada - *a veritable Armada it is* - has never in the memory of man or the annals of the world been devised and constructed in so short a time ... every one of them new in type and revolutionary in design and all worked out for a specific strategic idea.

The bold partnership lasted barely six months; the Admiralty was not large enough to contain two such impulsive autocrats, each the prisoner of his own pride. Fisher, although careless of the feelings of others, displayed an acute sensitivity to Churchill's methods of business. He found himself frequently ignored or overruled on those professional matters, such as the movement of ships, that traditionally lay within the First Sea Lord's competence. His final breach with Churchill was provoked by Churchill's imaginative but luckless plan to force a naval passage through the Dardanelles, capture Constantinople and so relieve the pressure exerted on Russia by Germany's Turkish ally.

Fisher opposed such a strategy from its inception. The decisive theatre of the naval war, he insisted, was the North Sea. He was nevertheless prepared to accept the Dardanelles operation, though with reluctance, as long as it employed only ships which could be spared from home waters. But in April 1915, after several failures to subdue the Turkish forts by naval bombardment, British troops were put ashore on the Gallipoli peninsula; and there they remained, gallant but impotent, until their evacuation at the end of the year. What Fisher feared had come to pass. The soldiers could not be abandoned to their precarious hold; yet to ensure their protection required naval reinforcements that were vital to British supremacy in the North Sea.

In reply to Fisher's strongly worded protest, Churchill wrote on 11 May:

You are absolutely committed ... A great army hanging on by its eyelids to a rocky beach, and confronted with the armed power of the Turkish Empire under German military guidance: the whole *surplus* fleet of Britain – every scrap that can be spared – bound to that army and its fortunes as long as the struggle may drag out.

Fisher was by now immune to such appeals, knowing that each concession he made to the First Lord would provoke further demands. In the early morning of 15 May he wrote a brief letter of resignation to Churchill. 'I am off to Scotland at once', it concluded, 'so as to avoid all questionings.' In fact he went to ground in the Charing Cross Hotel, only a few hundred yards from the Admiralty. It was there that this note reached him from a scandalized Prime Minister: 'In the King's name I order you to remain at your post.' Fisher postponed his departure for Scotland but refused to return to the Admiralty. His conflict with Churchill coincided with – indeed, helped to precipitate – a crisis in the Liberal Government. Attacked by the Opposition for failing to ensure an adequate supply of high-explosive shells on the Western Front, Asquith decided to broaden his administration by inviting the Conservatives to fill a substantial number of Cabinet places. Fisher believed that the Conservatives, rather than allow him to resign, would support any demands he cared to make. As opportunist as any professional politician, he therefore confronted Asquith with the conditions on which he would resume his duties. The document included such fantasies as these:

That Mr. Winston Churchill is not in the Cabinet to be always circumventing me, nor will I serve under Mr. Balfour ...

That there shall be an entire new Board of Admiralty, as regards the Sea Lords and the Financial Secretary (who is utterly useless).

That I shall have complete professional charge of the war at sea, together with the absolute sole disposition of the Fleet and the appointment of all officers of all ranks whatsoever, and absolutely untrammelled sole command of all the sea forces whatsoever ...

No Government could submit to such terms and retain its independence, or even its self-respect. The Prime Minister rejected Fisher's conditions out of hand and allowed him to resign without further argument.

Asquith conceded that the King's misgivings about Fisher at the time of his recall to the Admiralty had been justified. Fisher's ultimatum, he told the King, 'indicated signs of mental aberration'. For years afterwards the King would go red with anger in speaking of Fisher's irresponsible conduct at a moment when the German Fleet had been thought likely to put to sea. 'If I had been in London when Fisher was found,' he said, 'I should have told him that he should have been hanged at the yardarm for desertion of his post in the face of the enemy.' But it was not in the King's nature to humiliate a fallen enemy. When in June 1915 Fisher sent the King an apologia that included a list of all the ships built at his instigation, the King replied: 'It is indeed an Armada, and will be a testimony of your zeal, foresight and knowledge with regard to our naval requirements in order to bring this terrible war to a victorious conclusion.'

Fisher lacked the generous instincts of his sovereign, never ceasing to defame him with whatever weapons came to hand. Thus in December 1916 he wrote this characteristic letter to C.P. Scott, editor of the *Manchester Guardian*:

I hear amongst the proletariat is a deep feeling that both Buckingham Palace and Sandringham should long ago have been given up for our wounded and sick heroes when every other crowned head has done so, and all our dukes and others have given up their homes for the purpose. Kings will be cheap soon!

Not even Queen Mary was spared his venomous pen. He would refer to the King and Queen as 'Futile and Fertile'. He was not a lovable man.

Churchill survived Fisher at the Admiralty by less than a week, and the King was equally relieved by his departure. 'I am glad the Prime Minister is going to have a National Government,' he told the Queen while on tour in the North of England. 'Only by that means can we get rid of Churchill from Admiralty ... He is the real danger.' Three days later he wrote in his diary: 'I hope Balfour will be 1st Lord of the Admiralty in place of Churchill, who has become impossible.' The King's wish was granted. If the Prime Minister's new-found Conservative colleagues had had their way, Churchill, like Haldane, would have been excluded from the Coalition Government. In the event, he was fortunate to retain a seat in the Cabinet, although in the lesser office of Chancellor of the Duchy of Lancaster.

The King's dislike of Churchill was largely personal. He could not abide that flamboyant personality, so combative in argument, so interfering in the concerns of others, so restless even in repose. Professionally, too, he mistrusted the First Lord. Like most naval officers of his generation, he believed that British sea power in wartime should be concentrated overwhelmingly in home waters, not dissipated on such precarious ventures as the Dardanelles; in this, as it happened, he was of the same mind as Fisher. With Balfour newly installed in the Admiralty, the King awaited the decisive battle against the German Fleet in a renewed spirit of confidence. Meanwhile the Royal Navy was well placed to guard the sea routes on which both survival and victory ultimately depended.

If Churchill knew of the King's satisfaction at his removal from the Admiralty, he showed none of Fisher's rancour. Fifteen years after the end of the war, he inscribed these words in a presentation copy of his life of the great Duke of Marlborough:

This is the story of how a wise Princess and Queen gave her trust and friendship to an invincible commander, and thereby raised the power and fame of England to a height never before known, and never since lost; and is submitted in loyal duty to a Sovereign under whom our country has come through perils even more grievous with no less honour.

Fisher also put pen to paper after the war, producing two self-congratulatory volumes of memoirs. Although he wrote fulsomely of his patron, King Edward VII, the name of King George V is nowhere mentioned.

The King was as conventional a strategist on land as at sea. He wrote in December 1915:

I consider that this war will be lost or won in the main theatres of the war, – I mean in France, in Russia and in Italy, – and the British Empire must make haste and concentrate all our strength and all our energy to produce as strong an army as possible to take the offensive in France in the spring and the Allies must deliver their attacks simultaneously and by then the Central Powers I am sure will not be able to stand the strain.

It was a view shared almost unanimously by the British and French general staffs. With the repulse of the German advance on Paris in the autumn of 1914, the war on the Western Front had frozen into stalemate.

Two entrenched armies faced each other along a line that stretched from the English Channel to the Alps. Each side in turn tried to break the deadlock by launching a succession of massive attacks against the enemy's front: assaults which did no more than gain a strip of ravaged battlefield at an almost unendurable price. From time to time the balance of advantage would be tilted by a new tactical weapon such as poison gas or the tank. Yet throughout four long years of attrition, neither Germany nor the Allies believed that the war could be won elsewhere.

The King put no faith in those men of inventive mind who, like Churchill, sought an alternative strategy. As early in the war as December 1914 he regretted that troops were being deployed against Germany's colonies in the comparatively unimportant theatre of East Africa. The subsequent failure of other 'sideshows' strengthened the King's prejudice. After the humiliating reversals of Gallipoli and Mesopotamia, he entreated his ministers not to embark on the Salonika campaign, 'which is little likely to be attended with more success than those unfortunate enterprises'.

Although wholly committed to a Western Front strategy, the King sometimes doubted the ability of the generals entrusted with its operation. Foremost of them was Field-Marshal Sir John French, Commander-in-Chief of the British forces in France from August 1914 until his unwilling retirement sixteen months later. French, like so many senior generals of his day, was a cavalryman. That was not necessarily a handicap, even when fighting a campaign that depended almost entirely on infantry and artillery. But he also lacked that nimbleness of mind and phlegmatic temperament which sustain great commanders throughout the hazards of battle. Nearly sixty-three years of age on the outbreak of war, he was obstinate, obstructive and choleric; disloyal to Kitchener, suspicious of his Allies and jealous of his subordinates. During the first operations of the war, a sullen determination to act independently of the French armies put the whole Allied front in danger; and when the German advance on Paris faltered, his lack of determination lost the British Expeditionary Force its chance of mauling a retreating enemy. In September 1915 his conduct of the unsuccessful Battle of Loos convinced both King and Prime Minister that he must be replaced. He not only withheld vital reserves from his senior army commander, Douglas Haig, but later doctored his despatch on the battle to make it seem as if the blame lay elsewhere.

In his mistrust of French, the King did not of course possess any of that professional knowledge and experience which he could bring to bear on naval matters. But he maintained a close friendship and correspondence with one of the ablest generals of the day: none other than Douglas Haig, to whom he gave his complete trust and support. Haig's intimacy with the King owed much to family connections. His sister, married to a rich whisky distiller, was a friend of King Edward VII, who appointed Haig to be an aide-de-camp. By 1904, after making his reputation as an exceptionally competent staff officer in the South African War, he found himself at forty-three Inspector-General of Cavalry in India, with the rank of major-general.

On home leave in the following year, Haig was invited to spend Ascot week at Windsor. It was here that the future King George V, then Prince of Wales, unwittingly drew him even closer into the royal circle. The Prince had asked Haig to play golf on the private course of the castle, but was prevented from keeping the appointment. So a foursome was arranged: Haig and Miss Dorothy Vivian, a maid of honour to Queen Alexandra, against the Duke of Devonshire and another member of the house party. As the Duke kept finding himself in a bunker, Haig and his partner found plenty of time to talk. Two days later the shy soldier with the reputation of a misogynist proposed to Miss Vivian and was accepted. Crowned heads are notoriously averse to losing members of their entourage through marriage. Queen Alexandra, however, always moved by affairs of the heart, encouraged the match; and knowing that by Edwardian standards Haig was a poor man – he held no shares in the family whisky business and had been left only £500 by his father – she insisted that the marriage ceremony and wedding breakfast should take place at Buckingham Palace.

Haig's friendship with the royal family continued into the new reign. A week after the outbreak of war, the King asked for his opinion of Field-Marshal French. 'In my heart', Haig wrote in his diary, 'I know that French is quite unfit for this great command at a time of crisis in our Nation's history. But I thought it sufficient to tell the King that I had "doubts" about the selection.' French's inept performance as Commander-in-Chief on the Western Front soon provoked both the King and Haig to speak more frankly to each other. The King, however, was embarrassed at asking Haig to send him private reports on a senior officer: just the sort of underhand conduct that he had condemned in Admiral Fisher. He confessed to Kitchener what he had done, adding that a boy who told tales out of school would be called a sneak. The Secretary for War, who shared his sovereign's misgivings about French, replied that they were no longer schoolboys. Haig, too, felt uneasy at conspiring behind the back of both his Commander-in-Chief and a friend who had done much to further the younger man's career. But he overcame his scruples. After entertaining the King at his headquarters in France, he wrote an account of their talk. It concluded:

French's handling of the reserves in the last battle, his obstinacy and conceit, showed his incapacity, and it seemed to me impossible for anyone to prevent him doing the same things again. I therefore thought strongly that, for the sake of the Empire, French ought to be removed.

Other generals whom the King consulted during that tour of the British lines in October 1915 echoed Haig's judgement and convinced him that French must go. A few days later, while continuing his inspection of troops, the King suffered that crashing fall from a horse which was to affect his health for the rest of his life. Although in severe pain, he pressed the Prime Minister from his sick bed to replace French; and when the Field-Marshal appeared reluctant to go even on generous terms – a peerage, the promise of a monetary grant at the end of the war and immediate command of the Home Forces – the King insisted that Asquith should act without delay. On 4 December 1915, French was at last prised from his command of the British armies on the Western Front. It was a notable victory for the King, who did not readily forgive the newly created Lord French his obstinacy.

By contrast, French's successor as Commander-in-Chief received the warmest of royal welcomes. The King wrote to Haig on 17 December 1915:

Remember that it will always be a pleasure to me to help you in any way I can, to carry out your heavy task and important responsibilities.

I hope that you will from time to time write to me quite freely and tell me how matters are progressing. Naturally I shall consider your letters in the strictest confidence.

Throughout the next three years, often to the annoyance of his ministers, the King kept faith with his friend.

'For three weeks no one has thought of the enemy,' Churchill told his wife on the day French agreed to resign his command. Asquith must bear much of the blame for so scandalous a delay in removing the Field-Marshal. It was but one example of his increasing failure as a war leader. That precise, reflective mind which had served him well enough in the tactics of parliamentary manœuvre was ill-suited to meet the crises of Armageddon. Nor had the inclusion of certain Conservative statesmen in the reconstructed Government of May 1915 proved reassuring. Kitchener gave Esher a chilling account of a Cabinet discussion on conscription:

After a long debate, at half-past two, the Prime Minister said to the Cabinet: 'Please remember that in an hour's time I have to tell the House of Commons what the Cabinet have decided.' There was a silence for a minute or two, and then A.J.B. said: 'You had better tell them that the Cabinet has decided it is quite incapable of conducting the business of the country and of carrying on the war.' No one having made any observation upon this, the Prime Minister asked:

'Am I to say that to the House of Commons?' Upon which A.J.B. observed: 'Well! If you do, you will at any rate be telling them the truth!'

The Cabinet broke up without a decision.

During Asquith's occasional absence from No. 10, the conduct of business was even more undisciplined. Here, from Haig's diary, is a vignette of a Cabinet meeting presided over by Lord Crewe:

Everyone seemed desirous to speak at the same moment. One would say, 'Please allow me to finish what I am saying.' Another would interrupt, and a third would shout from the far end of the table that he meant to have his say on the matter too. Poor Lord Crewe feebly rapped the table, and said 'Order please,' in a disconsolate way! This sort of thing really makes one tremble for the Empire!

That master of invective, General Sir Henry Wilson, called the Coalition Cabinet 'a miserable pack of Hesitations and Hiccoughs'. His friend Leo Amery, the Tory MP, described it as 'Twenty-two gabblers round a table with an old procrastinator in the chair'. As if a dilatory Prime Minister were not alarming enough, there was an element of self-indulgence in Asquith which further eroded confidence. He seemed to have as much leisure in war as he had enjoyed in peace. No day was complete without a budget of indiscretion written to Miss Stanley at the Cabinet table itself (though his son Raymond did not receive a single line from him throughout ten months at the Front); an hour or two of reading each evening in the library of the Athenaeum Club; a cosy dinner party followed by several rubbers of bridge. And at the end of each exhausting week there would be two or three recuperative days in the country. It was a regime in sharp contrast to that of his sovereign.

Asquith was also said to be addicted to drink. Certainly he did not volunteer to share the King's pledge of abstinence; and there were occasions in the Commons, as at the lying-in-state of Edward VII, when he appeared to have dined well. The historian should treat such rumours with reserve. The Prime Minister could be a wiser man fuddled than many of his contemporaries sober. Haig wrote of a visit by Asquith to France:

The P.M. seemed to like our old brandy. He had a couple of glasses (big sherry glass size) before I left the table at 9.30, and apparently he had several more before I saw him again. By that time his legs were unsteady, but his head was quite clear, and he was able to read a map and discuss the situation with me.

Such fortitude was magnificent but it did not win the war. Throughout Asquith's premiership, the country endured an almost unbroken succession of reverses and humiliations. Haig succeeded French but casualties on the Western Front continued to mount by the hundred thousand and still the enemy lines held firm: among the dead were John Bigge, Stamfordham's only son, and Raymond Asquith. There was rebellion in Ireland, treachery in the Balkans, disease and defeat in Mesopotamia. German U-boats took their toll of Allied shipping, so that food became scarce and unpalatable; German aircraft bombed London and other cities, affecting both industrial production and morale. The Battle of Jutland revealed faults in British naval construction, signalling and gunnery, although the King could at least rejoice that his second son, serving in HMS *Collingwood*, had survived his baptism of fire.

These events caused dismay yet did nothing to arrest the palsied drift of the Government. It was the death of Kitchener, drowned at sea in June 1916 while on his way to put new heart into Russia, that set in train Asquith's downfall six months later. The nation mourned a leader of reassuring stature and the King broke with protocol by attending a memorial service to a subject. Lloyd George was also stirred by the death of his Cabinet colleague; he was to have sailed with Kitchener to Russia, but had remained behind to deal with the Easter Rebellion in Ireland. At the very height of his confidence, no man had less wish to share Kitchener's noble epitaph: 'Coffined in a man of war, he passed to the great beyond.' The place for Lloyd George was at the heart of events, and neither sorrow nor decorum deterred him from laying siege to the vacant War Office. Until the matter was settled, Asquith acted as Secretary of State for War. He told Stamfordham: 'All this canvassing and wire-pulling about the succession, while poor K's body is still tossing about in the North Sea, seems to me to be in the highest degree indecent.'

Springing from patriotism and ambition alike, Lloyd George's claims could scarcely be denied. As Minister of Munitions for the past year he had infused the industry with energy and imagination, appealing to the nation with a Celtic eloquence that made toil a duty and sacrifice a joy. Yet there was considerable opposition to his appointment. The King, while admiring the dynamo, mistrusted the demagogue. Maurice Hankey, secretary of the Cabinet War Committee, wrote after an audience at the palace on 10 June: 'The King ... went into a most violent diatribe against Lloyd George, as I thought he would. I kept trying to stand up for Lloyd George and reminded the King of all he had done and how useful he is on the War Committee ... but the King would hardly listen.' The King's own choice would have been the decent and reliable Austen Chamberlain, Secretary of State for India and Neville Chamberlain's half-brother; failing that, he wanted Asquith himself to continue indefinitely as both Prime Minister and Secretary of State for War, with the malleable Lord Derby as his deputy. At such a time of political stress, however, the King's preferences carried little weight.

Whether or not Lloyd George won the coveted post turned not on royal disfavour but on the support or enmity of Cabinet colleagues. Most of the

Conservatives in the Coalition were against him, impressed by almost unanimous opposition to Lloyd George from the War Office staff. Even the support of his fellow Liberals was not always what it seemed. Edwin Montagu (who in the previous year had married the Prime Minister's confidante, Venetia Stanley) wrote to Asquith: 'It would also be clearly advantageous to have L.G. at the War Office during the announcement of heavy casualties and a possibly unfruitful offensive.' The Prime Minister tried to solve the impasse by dangling the War Office before Bonar Law; but the Conservative leader had already made common cause with Lloyd George and declined to move from the Colonial Office. That set the seal on Lloyd George's appointment. Although he appeared to lose a last tussle about the division of powers between a civilian Secretary of State and a professional military staff, it was a concession he could afford to make. Few doubted that he would remain at the War Office only long enough to seize the highest place of all. On the day his new post was announced, Margot Asquith wrote in her diary: 'We are out: it can only be a question of time now when we shall have to leave Downing Street.'

Lloyd George took exactly five months to displace Asquith as Prime Minister: five frustrating months during which not even an imaginative Secretary for War could arrest Britain's declining fortunes. At the very outset he inherited ministerial responsibility for the disastrous Battle of the Somme, which on the first day alone claimed 57,000 British casualties. He tried to wean the generals from their obsessive strategy, what he called 'the unintelligent hammering against the impenetrable barrier'; but the Chief of the Imperial General Staff, Sir William Robertson, resisted every attempt by the War Minister to influence military operations. Hankey warned Lloyd George that he could not hope to prevail against the most conservative and powerful trades union in the world. Thwarted by such consecrated obstruction, he could achieve no more than the appointment of Sir Eric Geddes, an experienced railway manager, to reorganize the transport system in France. Nor could he rouse his colleagues to lend him their support. The fate of the nation depended upon an incoherent Cabinet of twenty that deliberated without agenda, secretary or minutes. Only a small and resolute body could win the war, and this Lloyd George was determined to create.

The King noted in his diary on 4 December 1916: 'The Prime Minister came and told me about the Cabinet crisis, started by Lloyd George who wants to run the War Committee. The Government will have to be reconstructed. I told the Prime Minister that I had the fullest confidence in him.' It was the climax to weeks of feverish talks between members of the Coalition: a series of conclaves and cabals inspired by Sir Max Aitken, Conservative MP and newspaper owner, soon to be created Lord Beaverbrook. Lloyd George's ultimatum to Asquith demanded the creation of a small War Committee with executive powers. It also implied, without naming either antagonist, that the Prime Minister would be merely its titular head. Asquith was to remain at No. 10 but Lloyd George was to rule the roost. The Prime Minister replied the same day. He accepted the need for an authoritative War Committee but insisted that the Prime Minister must be its chairman. At the same time he suggested that there should be a vice-chairman: a conciliatory hint that he might be prepared to leave its day-to-day decisions to Lloyd George. Pleased with his draftsmanship, Asquith departed for a quiet weekend by the sea. Less than twenty-four hours later he was back in London fighting for his ministerial life. Bonar Law had been persuaded to support Lloyd George's demands. Rather than risk their resignations and the collapse of his Coalition, Asquith agreed to a War Committee with Lloyd George as chairman. To save his face it was to be announced that the Prime Minister should have 'supreme and effective control of war policy' as well as the right to attend meetings of the War Committee. The Government would be reconstructed accordingly. The crisis, it seemed, was over.

On the following morning, however, the Prime Minister changed his mind. A leading article in *The Times* described the compromise as a humiliating surrender imposed upon an ineffective war leader. Believing that it could have been inspired only by Lloyd George, the Prime Minister insisted that their compact should be cancelled. He wrote to Lloyd George: 'Unless the impression is at once corrected that I am being relegated to the position of an irresponsible spectator of the War, I cannot possibly go on.' In a second letter to Lloyd George that day, Asquith's attitude stiffened further. He rejected Lloyd George's demand that Carson should replace Balfour as First Lord of the Admiralty. There could be but one reply to the Prime Minister's intransigence. 'As all delay is fatal in war,' Lloyd George wrote, 'I place my office without further parley at your disposal.' His letter ended on a note of barely disguised menace:

As I am fully conscious of the importance of preserving national unity, I propose to give your Government complete support in the vigorous prosecution of the war; but unity without action is nothing but futile carnage, and I cannot be responsible for that. Vigour and vision are the supreme need at this hour.

The King was infuriated by the conduct of Lloyd George, 'a blackmailer, whom it is better to tackle and have done with'. But Asquith was in no position to survive Lloyd George's resignation. Learning in the course of the day that almost every leading Conservative had also deserted him, he too resigned that evening. The King much regretted the loss of his Prime Minister: 'I fear that it will cause a panic in the City and in America and do harm to the Allies. It is a great blow to me and will I fear buck up the Germans.'

Following constitutional custom, the King then sent for the leader of the next largest party in the Commons, Bonar Law, and asked him to form a Government. It was an acrid encounter. The King had not forgotten Law's near-treasonable sentiments and disrespectful homily during the Home Rule controversy. Four years later the two men argued with a rancour that permeates even Stamfordham's dispassionate record. They clashed on the relative merits of Asquith and Lloyd George (the King denied that Asquith had mismanaged the war); on the relations between ministers and the military (the King said that politicians should leave the conduct of the war to experts); on Law's request for the promise of a dissolution of Parliament as a condition of undertaking to form a Government (the King, anxious to avoid an unsettling general election in wartime, was constitutionally correct in refusing such a pledge to a supplicant who had not yet become Prime Minister). Law nevertheless said that he would try to form a Government.

His hope of success hinged on whether he could persuade the fallen Prime Minister to join his administration in a subordinate office. But when he called at Downing Street after his audience with the King, he was rebuffed. Asquith did, however, agree to attend a conference at the palace summoned by the King for the following day. It was attended by Asquith, Lloyd George, Law, Balfour and Arthur Henderson, who represented the Labour Party. Each participant in turn pleaded with Asquith to serve under Law on patriotic grounds and so maintain an appearance of national unity. Asquith refused. In a long apologia tinged with bitterness, he observed that throughout his alleged mismanagement of the war he could not recall any issue on which a decision had been reached without the concurrence of Lloyd George; that he had been subjected to vindictive and merciless attacks by the press; that he was grateful to His Majesty for the trust placed in him; but that he had awoken that morning thankful to feel he was now a free man. At this point the King, with his habitual common sense, reminded the politicians that they had discussed the matter fully but had not yet come to a decision. The meeting thereupon agreed that Asquith should further consider whether or not he was prepared to serve under Law; and that if he still felt unable to do so, Lloyd George rather than Bonar Law should try to form a Government.

The conference broke up at 4.30. Asquith immediately consulted his Liberal colleagues. Then, fortified by their almost unanimous approval, he delivered his final answer to Law. Rather than join any administration of which he was not the head, he would lead 'a sober and responsible Opposition, steadily supporting the Government in the conduct of the War'. Lloyd George now remained the sole contender for the premiership. At 7.30 he was entrusted by the King with the formation of a new Ministry. Twenty-four hours later, his Cabinet complete, he kissed hands as Prime Minister.

On Lloyd George's death in 1945, it fell to the Prime Minister of the day, Winston Churchill, to pronounce the traditional eulogy in the House of Commons. He was heard in approving silence until he touched on the events of December 1916.

CHURCHILL: Presently Lloyd George seized the main power in the State and the headship of the Government.
HON. MEMBERS: Seized?
CHURCHILL: Seized. I think it was Carlyle who said of Oliver Cromwell: 'He coveted the place. Perhaps the place was his.'

The King did not welcome the change. Since his early collisions with Asquith over the Parliament Bill and Home Rule he had come to depend on the Prime Minister's calm judgement and reassuring manner. Lloyd George, by contrast, suffered from what Esher called an over-elasticity of mind. The Chancellor of the Exchequer who had jolted the Treasury by using figures like adjectives brought the same restless imagination to the problems of war. 'It is amusing to see him among our stolid officers,' wrote Esher. 'It is like a fire burning away in the midst of a frozen world.' Such ebullience was not to the King's taste.

The new premiership nevertheless began on an unexpectedly fulsome note. In answer to some advice from the King on how a parliamentary question might best be answered, Lloyd George wrote: 'I am profoundly impressed by the wisdom of the course suggested by Your Majesty.' The complications of reconstructing the Government found Lloyd George no less anxious to please. He deferred to the King's view that Carson would make a more effective First Lord of the Admiralty than Lord Milner, the former African proconsul; Milner instead joined Lloyd George, Curzon, Bonar Law and Henderson as minister without portfolio in the newly-fashioned War Cabinet. Nor was the King dissatisfied with the allocation of the other senior posts. He regretted losing Grey as Foreign Secretary and Crewe as Lord President of the Council; but their successors, Balfour and Curzon, were tried and trusted administrators.

Derby took Lloyd George's place at the War Office, hardly an inspiring choice for the new belligerency. Haig was to write of him in a celebrated epigram: 'A very weak-minded fellow, I am afraid, and, like the feather pillow, bears the marks of the last person who has sat on him!' But the King had faith in Derby's judgement and knowledge of the army; and at least he could be relied upon not to ruffle the plumes of the generals. Another measure of the limitations imposed on Lloyd George by his Conservative allies was the exclusion from office of Winston Churchill. That, too, the

King welcomed in the interests of harmony. Demoted by Asquith after the failure of the Dardanelles, Churchill had remained Chancellor of the Duchy of Lancaster for only five muted months before resigning to command an infantry battalion in France. Not until 1917 did Lloyd George feel secure enough to defy public opinion by recalling him to be Minister of Munitions.

Among the names submitted by the Prime Minister for the lesser offices of his Government, the King objected only to Sir Alfred Mond, the son of a German-Jewish immigrant, as First Commissioner of Works; he wondered whether Mond's marked guttural accent might not be a handicap in wartime. The Prime Minister assured the King that the future founder of Imperial Chemical Industries spoke 'perfect English'.

Their new-found cordiality was broken by one of Lloyd George's first reforms. He insisted that an efficient Cabinet must be served by a secretariat responsible for daily agenda and minutes. Before his premiership, astonishing though it may seem, no such records were kept, although the Prime Minister did send a summary of each day's Cabinet's business to the sovereign. With the appointment of Maurice Hankey to be the first Secretary of the Cabinet and the circulation of printed minutes both to its members and to the King, the Prime Minister's letters were discontinued. Not only were they now unnecessary, but Lloyd George detested putting pen to paper; even when the King and Queen celebrated their silver wedding, he sent them a dictated, typewritten letter of congratulation, to which the King punctiliously replied in his own hand. In vain Hankey observed: 'I hate time-honoured customs that waste time.' The King yearned for the personal flavour of Asquith's letters and was aggrieved at Lloyd George's neglect.

As long as the printed Cabinet minutes continued to reach the palace regularly, the King had no constitutional grounds for complaint. Increasingly, however, the minutes arrived late or not at all. 'His Majesty is deeply pained', Stamfordham complained in April 1917, 'at what he regards as not only a want of respect, but as ignoring his very existence.' Such official carelessness could perhaps be attributed to the weightier matters which occupy the mind of a wartime Prime Minister; or to the inexperience of Lloyd George's staff, few of whom were drawn from the civil service. Even Asquith had sometimes earned a royal reprimand by failing to meet the King's exacting standards of consultation. But whereas Asquith recognized the need to humour a monarch who could be needlessly loquacious and interfering, Lloyd George displayed a nonchalance not far removed from contempt. Over the years the King had not troubled to conceal his dislike of Lloyd George; now the Prime Minister seemed to be taking a spiteful revenge. He left letters unanswered, ignored a summons to a Privy Council without explanation or apology, gleefully admitted to his secretary that he had treated the King 'abominably' and claimed that Balfour had once asked him, 'Whatever would you do if you had a ruler with brains?'

An acute difference of opinion on the conduct of the war inflamed their mutual dislike. Lloyd George was determined to curb Haig's costly and ineffective assaults on the Western Front; to hit the enemy at his weakest points, not his strongest. The King, convinced that military operations must be left to professional soldiers, deplored such political influence. In 1915, it is true, he had played a part in replacing French by Haig. That, however, was the result of his having lost confidence in an incompetent commander, not in the Western strategy of the general staff. Like his father and grandmother before him, the King did not doubt that he was the Head of the Armed Forces in more than name: the guardian of military sentiment and tradition, the protector of senior officers from a too meddlesome ministerial control.

Lloyd George would have none of it. He had seized power to win the war yet found himself as impotent as Asquith. Before he could defeat the Germans he must first subdue the British Army. 'I had to contend,' he wrote, 'not with a profession but with a priesthood, devoted to its chosen idol.' The antagonists seemed ill-matched. Lloyd George's Eastern heresy was shared only by the rump of the divided Liberal Party. The military high command, Westerners almost to a man, could depend on the support of Conservative Party, Cabinet and King. For the Conservatives, Lloyd George had a wary respect; by combining with the Asquithian Liberals they could bring down his Coalition whenever they chose. The War Cabinet he would charm into reluctant acquiescence. His duty to the King he discharged only when it suited him. A myopic radicalism blinded him to the virtues of an hereditary sovereign whose views he found obstructive. In spite of his attachment to the mystical traditions of Wales (though he had, as it happened, been born in Manchester) he found no merit in the most romantic of all English institutions. Other men were proud to serve and die by the hundred thousand in the name of the King. Lloyd George demanded their allegiance to five frock-coated politicians round a table in Downing Street.

The King put little faith in democracy, least of all when its self-proclaimed champion had become Prime Minister by intrigue. Yet in defending those generals who clung to a wholly Western strategy, he was not consciously defying constitutional practice. He may nevertheless have been encouraged to do so by Stamfordham, the private secretary who six years earlier had rashly advised his master to reject Asquith's demands for contingent guarantees. In December 1916, Stamfordham asked Hankey whether he thought that the King ought to take 'a more active share in the government of the country'. Hankey prudently replied that with so doubtful a financial and economic outlook, the King ought on no account to extend his role.

Throughout the first of his bitter confrontations with Lloyd George, it was the Prime Minister who acted unconstitutionally by withholding an important decision of the War Cabinet from the King until it was too late for him to make known his views. Lloyd George had every cause for deceit. Not yet strong enough to challenge the general staff on the wisdom of their Western Front strategy, he would try to curb the reckless expenditure of British lives by placing Haig and his armies under the orders of the new and supposedly less obtuse French Commander-in-Chief, General Nivelle. On 24 February, at a War Cabinet to which neither Derby nor Robertson had been summoned, the Prime Minister persuaded his colleagues to endorse the plan. Two days later, at an inter-Allied conference in Calais, ostensibly arranged to discuss railway transport, he reached rapid agreement with the French on unity of command during the forthcoming offensive; indeed, he was suspected of having already acted in collusion with them behind the backs of his own countrymen. Not until two more days had passed did the King receive the minutes of that crucial War Cabinet of 24 February, a *fait accompli* that denied him any voice in so controversial a decision.

Furious that the largest British army ever raised should be placed under foreign command, Haig was able to secure some slight modification of his humiliating sentence: 'a free hand to choose the means and methods of utilising the British troops in that sector of operations allotted by the French Commander-in-Chief'. He nevertheless resented the lack of trust shown him by Lloyd George, and feared for the future. But he was not without friends. On Haig's appointment as British Commander-in-Chief, the King had assured him of his constant support and urged him to write freely but secretly whenever he wished. Immediately after the Calais conference, the disgruntled Field-Marshal sent him a long account of Lloyd George's deception. Hinting at his own resignation, he ended his letter: 'I leave myself in Your Majesty's hands to decide what is best for me to do at this juncture.'

The King was alarmed. Through Stamfordham, he urged Haig on no account to resign: 'Such a step would never have His Majesty's consent, nor does he believe that it is one entertained for a moment by his Government.... I am to say from His Majesty that you are not to worry: you may be certain that he will do his utmost to protect your interests.' When Haig arrived in London on leave a few days later, it became clear just how little the King could do on Haig's behalf. For neither King nor Field-Marshal could hope to prevail against Lloyd George's popularity as a war leader. Haig described the audience in his diary:

The King was most pleased to see me and stated that he would 'support me through thick and thin,' but I must be careful not to resign, because Lloyd George would then appeal to the country for support and would probably come back with a great majority, as LG was at present very popular it seems. The King's position would then be very difficult. He would be blamed for causing a General Election which would cost the country a million and stop munition work, etc. We went over the whole Calais conference ... He was furious with Lloyd George, and said he was to see him tomorrow.

Lloyd George was duly summoned to the palace. 'On the whole,' an assistant private secretary noted, 'His Majesty did not consider the interview satisfactory.' The King had two complaints. He observed 'with surprise and pain' that Lloyd George had omitted to send him the minutes of the War Cabinet meeting that preceded the Calais conference; and that the arrangement entered into with the French was offensive to national sentiment:

The King told the Prime Minister that if he were an officer serving in the British Army and realized that he was under the command of a foreign general, he would most strongly resent it and so would the whole Army. If this fact too were known in the country it would be equally condemned.

The Prime Minister said that in the event of any such public expression of feeling, he would go to the country and would explain matters and very soon have the whole country on his side.

In warning Haig not to resign, the King had foreseen that Lloyd George would not hesitate to fight a general election on the issue, employing all the arts of the demagogue to discredit his critics. It was a threat that left the King defenceless. In the circumstances of 1917 Lloyd George was unassailable.

As it turned out, his shabby intrigue with the French had been in vain. Nivelle's offensive, to which Lloyd George had sacrificed British military pride, was as disastrous a failure as any. By now, however, the Western policy had acquired a momentum of its own, immune to the protests even of the Prime Minister. At the end of July, Haig launched the most heartbreaking of all campaigns, to which history has given the name Passchendaele. By mid-November it had claimed 240,000 British casualties without either breaking the enemy front or liberating the Belgian ports from which German submarines continued to win the war at sea. Far from moving Haig to reconsider his belief in frontal assault, Passchendaele goaded him to try yet again. He found no fault with his plan, only with the inadequacy of the forces at his disposal. As the British Army drowned in the Flanders mud he wrote to the Chief of the Imperial General Staff:

One more indispensable condition of decisive success on the Western Front is that

the War Cabinet should have a firm faith in the possibility and resolve finally
and unreservedly to concentrate our resources on seeking it, and to do so at once
... We have need of every man, gun and aeroplane that can be provided.

It was a familiar refrain. Month after month Lloyd George had pleaded
for an alternative strategy, for the cancellation of Passchendaele in favour
of an Italian offensive against Austria; but Robertson and Haig rejected
such 'sideshows' out of hand. The Prime Minister longed to replace them
by more imaginative advisers, yet dared not dismiss two soldiers whose
renown seemed to thrive on failure. Instead he devised an ingenious variant
on the Calais theme. In November 1917 he proposed the establishment at
Versailles of a Supreme War Council to co-ordinate Allied policy, including
that of the United States, which had declared war on Germany in April. Sir
Henry Wilson, a less enthusiastic Westerner than his fellow generals, was
appointed Britain's military representative. Two months later, Lloyd
George went a stage further. He persuaded the French Government that
there should be an executive committee of the Supreme War Council
having at its disposal an Allied reserve of thirty divisions, together with the
power, at least in theory, to instruct both the British and French
Commanders-in-Chief on its deployment. That was Lloyd George's first
purpose: to deny Haig the use of British reserves unless sanctioned by
Versailles. The second was equally astute. He would rid himself of Robertson by sending him to Versailles, simultaneously recalling Wilson to London as Chief of the Imperial General Staff. If, however, Robertson refused
the Versailles post, he would be allowed to remain as CIGS, although with
reduced powers. Lord Beaverbrook, who knew as much of conspiracy as
any man alive, wrote admiringly of Lloyd George's design:

What a dilemma for Robertson! What a desperate confusion of all his hopes and
aspirations. Either way he was done.

For it was apparent that if he stayed on at the War Office, military power would
be vested with Sir Henry Wilson at Versailles by reason of his authority over the
Reserve. If he accepted the Versailles appointment, London would become the
centre of military authority where Sir Henry Wilson would fill the role of Military
Adviser to the Cabinet. The Prime Minister would, of course, throw his support
behind whichever post Robertson rejected.

Robertson, as was to be expected, refused both alternatives. He wished
to remain at the War Office with undiminished control of military operations; otherwise he would retire. It was at this point that the King came to
his defence. Robertson was all that he admired, Wilson all that he detested.
Robertson had risen from the ranks to be Chief of the Imperial General
Staff in a profession where birth and wealth still counted for much.
Although he never commanded troops in the field, he became an able

Quartermaster-General of the British Expeditionary Force, a competent administrator and a sound but unimaginative strategist. 'He was an impressive personality,' Lloyd George wrote of him, 'with that slowness of speech and positiveness of statement which gives confidence to the uninitiated.' His infrequent utterances had retained the vigour of the barrack room, and that too added to his reputation for sagacity. Leo Amery, however, serving with the Cabinet secretariat, noted in November 1917 that he could not recall a single occasion during the past year on which the CIGS had ventured to forecast either the enemy's plans or our own. Although he harboured a suspicion of foreigners that fell with impartial malevolence on French and German alike, his knowledge of the French language was no worse than the King's. At inter-Allied conferences he would speak it correctly but with an English accent. His discouraging response to the brainwaves of French politicians earned him the nickname of Général Non Non.

Wilson was the very antithesis of Robertson; mercurial of mind and lucid in exposition. But the insinuating charm and whimsical humour that captivated his French colleagues at Versailles found no welcome among his brother officers; and even Lloyd George, who preferred to cross-examine his advisers rather than wade through their memoranda, condemned Wilson's 'facetious and droll frivolity'. It took such forms as referring to politicians as Frocks (after their frock coats) and to the Commander-in-Chief as Sir Haig. The King, who had mistrusted Wilson ever since his collusion with Bonar Law at the time of the Curragh unrest, was infuriated by his flippancy, as when he reported on a sudden advance by the enemy: 'Sir, the Boche has been very naughty, very naughty indeed, Sir; we must give him a whipping.' That was not how the sovereign expected to be addressed; better Robertson's costive grunts than Wilson's unseemly badinage.

'I am much worried as the PM is trying to get rid of Robertson,' the King wrote in his diary on 13 February 1918. As so frequently happened, Lloyd George had failed to warn the King of the change of CIGS. When reproached by Stamfordham, he replied that he had left the task to Derby, who had apparently forgotten. The removal of Robertson in favour of Wilson provoked another sharp tussle between the King and Lloyd George. Stamfordham, ordered to remonstrate with the Prime Minister, wrote of their interview:

I told him that the King strongly deprecated the idea of Robertson being removed from the office of CIGS, that his loss in that capacity would be an incalculable one to the Army, would be resented in the country, rejoiced in by the enemy, and I thought would damage the Government, and the King considered that Sir William Robertson had enjoyed the absolute confidence of the Army –

Officers and Men. The Prime Minister said that he did not share the King's extremely favourable opinion of Sir William Robertson, who had never fought at the Front, had hardly ever visited the trenches and was not known by the rank and file. . . .

The Prime Minister said that Robertson had been offered either Paris or to remain as CIGS, he declined either and wished to dictate to everyone, whereas the Prime Minister repeated what he said on the 22 January, that Robertson had displayed no capacity as a strategist, and asked where anyone could put their finger on the map and say that this or that is due to Robertson's advice. In fact his forecasts had generally been wrong.

Impressed by the Prime Minister's refusal to moderate the terms on which Robertson could continue to be CIGS, Stamfordham spent the next three days trying to persuade the stubborn soldier to accept them, 'for the sake of the King, the Army and the Country'. Lloyd George misinterpreted Stamfordham's activity. Before an audience with the King on 16 February he delivered as stern a warning as lay in the power of any Prime Minister. Stamfordham wrote of the confrontation:

The King saw the Prime Minister. Before doing so Mr. Lloyd George told me that the question of Sir William Robertson had now reached a point that if His Majesty insisted upon his (Sir W. R.) remaining in office on the terms he laid down the Government could not carry on, and the King would have to find other Ministers. The Government must govern, whereas this was practically military dictation.

I assured the Prime Minister that His Majesty had no idea of making any such insistence. That since I saw him (Mr. Lloyd George) on the 13 February, I had by the King's instructions done all in my power to induce Sir William Robertson to remain as CIGS even though he might consider that the Government's scheme was so dangerous as even risking our loss of the War. But Sir William Robertson said he could not do so, therefore the King regarded the matter as settled, and considered that Sir William Robertson had practically ceased to be CIGS.

It was indeed the end of Robertson's reign. Deserted by both Derby and Haig, he resigned as CIGS and was appointed to an inferior command of home troops. Wilson succeeded him at the War Office.

At one moment during the dispute, the King wrote of Lloyd George: 'If he doesn't look out, his Government will fall. It is in deep water now.' That was a mistaken appreciation. The King had either to accept Robertson's demotion or find a new Prime Minister able to command a majority in the Commons; and in February 1918 no such candidate existed. Asquith was too dilatory, Balfour too detached, Carson too identified with Northern Ireland to unite the nation. Churchill was discredited by the Dardanelles, Chamberlain by Mesopotamia. Curzon and Milner both lacked popular appeal, and in any case were immured in the House of Lords. Bonar Law would have been the only acceptable substitute, and he refused to desert the Prime Minister. Lloyd George was as secure as at any time during his six-year premiership.

Throughout the remaining months of the war, the King suffered one rebuff after another. He had earlier resisted Lloyd George's recommendation of a peerage for Sir Max Aitken, refusing to accept that his public services 'called for such special recognition'. Only under the strongest pressure from both the Prime Minister and Bonar Law did the King eventually give his consent. Now Lloyd George, in appointing the recently created Lord Beaverbrook to be Minister of Information, insisted that he should also hold the Cabinet office of Chancellor of the Duchy of Lancaster. As Stamfordham pointed out, the Duchy 'is the personal property of the Sovereign, entailing closer relations between the King and its Chancellor than with many of his Ministers'. Lloyd George replied that Beaverbrook 'is a first-rate business man and will administer the Duchy well'. The King was thus obliged to accept the Canadian adventurer in one of the most historic of Crown offices. Within a few weeks, Beaverbrook's *Daily Express* was blaming the King for a visit by the Prince of Wales to the Pope. The King had in fact opposed the visit, but the Foreign Secretary had overruled him. To be attacked so unfairly, and by a newspaper belonging to a member of the Government, was a double humiliation – and one without redress.

On 16 April 1918, Stamfordham was instructed to make two quite separate protests to Lloyd George. The first was against the removal of General Sir Hugh Trenchard, the virtual creator of the Royal Air Force, from the post of Chief of Air Staff; the second against the replacement of Lord Bertie, British ambassador in Paris, by Lord Derby. In neither instance had the Prime Minister followed the customary practice of consulting the King, who learned of Trenchard's dismissal from the newspapers and of Bertie's fate by telephone, shortly before the news was made public. A Downing Street secretary apologized for the discourtesy, explaining that the Prime Minister had been working a twenty-one-hour day at the time. It was a plausible excuse. The changes in London and Paris had coincided with a last desperate attempt by Germany to breach the Allied lines on the Western Front: an assault so nearly successful as to evoke Haig's famous order of the day: 'With our backs to the wall, and believing in the justice of our cause, each one of us must fight to the end.' Stamfordham had not chosen the best of moments for his pained protest.

Lloyd George was impenitent about the changes themselves. He told Hankey that he had 'got very angry and sent Stamfordham away with a flea in his ear, telling him that the King was encouraging mutiny by taking up the cause of these officers, Trenchard and Robertson, whom the Government had decided to get rid of'.

Nor was the King able to prevent the enforced retirement of Bertie or his replacement by Derby, whom Lloyd George wanted to remove from the War Office. Although Derby was an old friend, the King doubted (wrongly, as it happened) whether he possessed the necessary skills for so sensitive a diplomatic post as Paris. Bertie, by contrast, had built up an impregnable reputation during his thirteen years there. Robert Vansittart, who served under him as a young man, wrote:

Once or twice a week he would tug his white moustache, cock his high hat – immensely high with a narrow ribbon at the base – and strut into the Quai d'Orsay, where he would speak his mind to the transient Minister in a fashion no longer heard. He made one feel that the finest thing in the world was to be His Britannic Majesty's Ambassador in Paris.

Although Bertie spoke French fluently, it was with an English accent. When asked why, he would reply: 'C'ay pour montray que j'ai la flotte Anglayse derrière moi.' His descents on the chancery of his own embassy were also memorable. One morning he greeted a particularly mild peer with the inquiry, 'Well, my lord, did you leave her half dead?'; and asked another member of his staff who was suffering from a cold whether he had slept with a damp woman. The King's pre-war misgivings about a diplomatist so wedded to the Republican French gave way to admiration. In 1917, prompted by Jules Cambon, the equally remarkable French ambassador in London, he successfully urged the Government not to replace the robust, experienced and well-informed Bertie by a more politically minded envoy. A year later, however, Bertie was abruptly superseded by Derby. The King could neither save him nor soften the blow by creating him an earl; Lloyd George insisted that Bertie's services deserved no more than a single step in the peerage, from baron to viscount. Even on such a trivial issue the King could not prevail over his graceless Prime Minister.

Only once throughout four years of war did the King persuade Lloyd George to change course on an important matter of policy. It proved in retrospect to be the most perplexing act of his reign: the abandonment of a loyal ally and much-loved cousin to degradation and death.

'Exactly like a skinny Duke of York – the image of him,' one of Queen Victoria's ladies wrote of the Tsar Nicholas II when he visited Balmoral in 1896. More than a physical resemblance united the future King George V and his Russian cousin, the son of Queen Alexandra's sister. Although they met only fitfully, when the dynasties of Europe gathered to celebrate or to mourn, their affection for each other was genuine enough. From St Petersburg, where in 1894 the Duke of York was attending the marriage of

Nicholas to another of his cousins, Princess Alix of Hesse, he wrote to
Queen Victoria: 'Nicky has been kindness itself to me, he is the same dear
boy he has always been to me and talks to me quite openly on every subject.'
The young Tsar's goodwill survived even his visit to Balmoral, where in
freezing rain he shot not a single stag and only one brace of grouse yet left
a *pourboire* of £1,000 to be divided among the Queen's servants. Throughout the diplomatic friction caused by Russia's designs on Persia and
Afghanistan, the friendship of King and Tsar never faltered. They talked
for the last time in 1913, when both were guests of the Kaiser in Berlin,
but for the next four years continued to exchange messages of trust and
encouragement. It was therefore with acute anxiety that on 13 March 1917
the King wrote in his diary:

Bad news from Russia, practically a Revolution has broken out in Petrograd [the
name by which St Petersburg had been known since 1914] and some of the Guards
Regiments have mutinied and killed their officers. This rising is against the
Government not against the Tsar.

Two days later he heard from Sir George Buchanan, the British ambassador in Petrograd, that Nicholas had been forced to sign his abdication.
'I am in despair,' wrote his cousin. The causes of his downfall do not belong
to this story. Lloyd George's epitome will suffice:

A virtuous and well-meaning Sovereign became directly responsible for a regime
drenched in corruption, indolence, debauchery, favouritism, jealousy, sycophancy,
idolatry, incompetence and treachery – an accumulation of all those vices that make
for utter misgovernment and inevitably end in anarchy.

Both the King and the Prime Minister reacted impulsively to news of
the Tsar's abdication. The King despatched this sympathetic telegram:
'Events of last week have deeply distressed me. My thoughts are constantly
with you and I shall always remain your true and devoted friend, as you
know I have been in the past.'
Nicholas was in fact denied his cousin's consolation. The Provisional
Government, which at that time was anxious to protect the ex-Tsar's life,
withheld the message lest it should provoke revolutionary violence against
him.
Lloyd George's sympathies were more for the new regime than for its
principal victim. He addressed a fulsome telegram to Prince Lvov, head of
the Provisional Government in Russia, declaring that

the Revolution whereby the Russian people have placed their destinies on the sure
foundation of freedom is the greatest service which they have yet made to the cause
for which the Allied peoples have been fighting since August, 1914. It reveals

the fundamental truth that this war is at bottom a struggle for Popular Government as well as for liberty.

The King was displeased by the tone of the message, which he found 'a little strong'. Stamfordham complained to Lloyd George that the word revolution had a disagreeable sound coming from a monarchical Government. But as usual the Prime Minister had the last word. He good humouredly replied that the present British monarchy was founded upon a revolution, which Stamfordham could not deny.

In the contrasting attitudes of King and Prime Minister lay the seeds of a persistent myth: that it was the King who strove to rescue his cousin from the perils of the Russian revolution, only to be thwarted by a heartless and opportunist Lloyd George. The late Lord Mountbatten, with all the authority of close kinship and apparent omniscience, gave currency to the legend. As a nephew of the Tsar – his mother and the Russian Empress were sisters – he continued to proclaim almost to the end of his life that Lloyd George's hands were stained with the blood of the Imperial family. Correspondence between the King and his ministers in March and April 1917 reveals a different chain of events leading to the murder of the Tsar and his family fifteen months later. It shows that the British Government would willingly have offered them asylum but for the fears expressed by Buckingham Palace; and that at the most critical moment in their fortunes they were deserted not by a radical Prime Minister seeking to appease his supporters, but by their ever affectionate Cousin Georgie.

The first suggestion that the Imperial family should come to England was made by Pavel Milyukov, the Foreign Minister of the Provisional Government, on 19 March 1917. Sir George Buchanan at once reported it to the Foreign Office in London. Even before there had been time to consider it, a second telegram arrived from Petrograd; Milyukov's inquiry about asylum for the Tsar now took the form of a request. To this the Foreign Office sent a guarded reply. The British Government would be glad to see the Tsar leave Russia, but wondered whether Denmark or Switzerland would not be a more suitable place of residence. This in turn provoked a more urgent message from Petrograd. Buchanan reported to London that Milyukov was 'most anxious to get the Emperor out of Russia as soon as possible, the extremists having excited opinion against His Majesty'. The ambassador concluded: 'I earnestly trust that, in spite of the obvious objections, I may be authorized without delay to offer His Majesty asylum in England and at the same time assure the Russian Government that he will remain there during the war.'

On 22 March, Lloyd George invited Stamfordham to Downing Street to discuss the Tsar's future; there they were joined by Bonar Law and

Hardinge, who on ceasing to be Viceroy of India had become Permanent Under-Secretary at the Foreign Office. 'It was generally agreed', Stamfordham wrote in his minute of the meeting, 'that the proposal that we should receive the Emperor in this country (having come from the Russian Government which we are endeavouring with all our powers to support) could not be refused.' The King's private secretary then raised a more practical problem. How would the Tsar and his family support themselves in exile? When the Prime Minister suggested that the King should place a house at their disposal, Stamfordham replied that only Balmoral was available, 'which would certainly not be a suitable residence at this time of the year'. The meeting concluded that Buchanan, in formally offering asylum to the Tsar, should ask the Russian Government to provide enough funds for him to live in suitable dignity.

Buchanan's message that Britain was prepared to receive the Imperial family evoked no immediate response from the Russian Government. Although anxious to be rid of the Tsar, they dreaded the anger of the extremists if any attempt were made to remove him to safety. Milyukov did not reject the British offer for which he had so urgently pleaded only two days earlier, yet made no effort to accept it. The delay proved fatal. It allowed those Russians who sought revenge on the fallen Tsar to consolidate their strength; and it prompted the King to have second thoughts about his cousin's future.

The change of mind was reflected in a letter from Stamfordham to Balfour, the Foreign Secretary, on 30 March, eight days after the meeting at Downing Street:

The King has been thinking much about the Government's proposal that the Emperor Nicholas and his family should come to England. As you are doubtless aware, the King has a strong personal friendship for the Emperor and therefore would be glad to do anything to help him in this crisis. But His Majesty cannot help doubting not only on account of the dangers of the voyage, but on general grounds of expediency, whether it is advisable that the Imperial Family should take up their residence in this country. The King would be glad if you would consult the Prime Minister, as His Majesty understands that no definite decision has yet been come to on the subject by the Russian Government.

Balfour replied on 2 April. After patiently recounting the exchange of telegrams with Petrograd that had led to the Government's decision, he ended:

His Majesty's Ministers quite realize the difficulties to which you refer in your letter, but they do not think, unless the position changes, that it is now possible to withdraw the invitation which has been sent, and they therefore trust that the King will consent to adhere to the original invitation, which was sent on the advice of His Majesty's Ministers.

The Foreign Secretary's rebuff drew a frosty acknowledgement from Stamfordham. 'His Majesty must regard the matter as settled,' he wrote, 'unless the Russian Government should come to any fresh decision on the subject.' Stamfordham's acquiescence lasted no more than forty-eight hours. On 5 April the King's daily box of Foreign Office papers included a telegram from Buchanan, seeking permission for two cousins of the Tsar to come to London. Stamfordham thereupon wrote to Sir Eric Drummond, Balfour's private secretary:

As entirely my own personal view I *do* trust the whole question of the Emperor and Empress of Russia's coming to England and also that of the proposal now made that the Grand Dukes George and Michael should do the same will be reconsidered. It will be very hard on the King and arouse much public comment if not resentment.

Twenty-four hours later, this warning shot was followed by a heavy salvo directed at the Foreign Secretary himself. With all the authority of the sovereign, Stamfordham wrote to Balfour:

Every day, the King is becoming more concerned about the question of the Emperor and Empress coming to this country.

His Majesty receives letters from people in all classes of life, known or unknown to him, saying how much the matter is being discussed, not only in clubs, but by working men, and that Labour Members in the House of Commons are expressing adverse opinions to the proposal.

As you know, from the first the King has thought the presence of the Imperial Family (especially of the Empress) in this country would raise all sorts of difficulties, and I feel sure that you appreciate how awkward it will be for our Royal Family who are closely connected both with the Emperor and the Empress.

You probably also are aware that the subject has become more or less public property, and that people are either assuming that it has been initiated by the King, or deprecating the very unfair position in which His Majesty will be placed if the arrangement is carried out.

The King desires me to ask you whether after consulting the Prime Minister, Sir George Buchanan should not be communicated with, with a view to approaching the Russian Government to make some other plan for the future residence of their Imperial Majesties?

The King must have felt that the letter lacked emphasis. For that same evening Stamfordham was instructed to write again to Balfour in more peremptory terms:

He must beg you to represent to the Prime Minister that from all he hears and reads in the press, the residence in this country of the ex-Emperor and Empress would be strongly resented by the public, and would undoubtedly compromise the position of the King and Queen. . . .

Buchanan ought to be instructed to tell Milyukov that the opposition to the

Emperor and Empress coming here is so strong that we must be allowed to withdraw from the consent previously given to the Russian government's proposal.

Under such sustained bombardment, the Foreign Secretary's resolution faltered. That night he sent a minute to the Prime Minister:

I think the King *is* placed in an awkward position.

If the Czar is to come here we are bound publicly to state that *we* (the Government) have invited him – and to add (for our own protection) that we did so on the initiative of the Russian Government (who will not like it).

I still think that we may have to suggest Spain or the South of France as a more suitable residence than England for the Czar.

Stamfordham followed up his successful assault on the Foreign Office with a descent on Downing Street four days later. He told the Prime Minister of the protests received by the King, both anonymous and from friends, against the proposed arrival in London of the Tsar and his family; and he reminded Lloyd George of the similar abuse to which the King had been exposed after receiving members of the supposedly pro-German Greek royal family. He continued that even if the Government accepted responsibility, the people would reply that this was done to screen the King. To illustrate the point, Stamfordham flourished a copy of the radical paper *Justice*, containing an article by the Socialist H. M. Hyndman on the disastrous consequences of the Tsar's presence in England. The Prime Minister admitted the force of these arguments and promised to consult the French Government in the hope that the Tsar might be invited to make his home in France.

The King's campaign to deny asylum to his cousin was going well, but Stamfordham had not yet finished with Balfour. Having read in the telegrams from Petrograd that Milyukov still expected the Tsar to travel to England after certain obstacles had been cleared, he spoke firmly to the Foreign Secretary. He told Balfour that after what the King had written to him, His Majesty expected that Buchanan would by now have been informed that the previous agreement to admit the Tsar could no longer be held as binding. Balfour meekly promised to draft a telegram to Petrograd that very afternoon.

By now the prospect of the Tsar's residence in London had become no less embarrassing to the British Government than to the King, although for different reasons. The King feared for his popularity, even for his throne; the Government wished for a close understanding with Russia's new rulers and their continuance as military allies. Neither spared much thought for the deposed Tsar and his family. Both arguments were set out in the Foreign Secretary's telegram to Buchanan, which concluded by instructing him to say nothing further to Miliukov on the subject unless the Russians themselves raised the question.

Forty years later, the ambassador's daughter, Miss Meriel Buchanan, was at pains to refute accusations that her father had made no effort to save the Imperial family and that he must bear a share of the blame for their ultimate fate. The ambassador's reply to Balfour's telegram of 13 April does nothing to support her case. 'I entirely share your view', he began, 'that, if there is any danger of anti-monarchist movement, it would be far better that the ex-Emperor should not come to England.' He was confirmed in this, the telegram to London continued, after talking to the Labour MP, Will Thorne, a member of a fraternal delegation to Petrograd. Buchanan attached less importance to Balfour's contention that the Tsar's presence in England would damage relations between the British and Russian Governments. He agreed, however, that the extreme Left in Russia, as well as German agents, would be sure to stir up public opinion against Britain. Buchanan's telegram ends with this disingenuous sentiment:

If only the French Government would consent, it would be far better from our point of view that the Emperor should go to France. Perhaps it would be well to sound them on the subject and, in the event of their consenting, I might tell the Minister for Foreign Affairs that the Revolution, which had been welcomed with such enthusiasm in England, had so indisposed the British public against the old Régime that the presence of the Emperor in England might provoke demonstrations that would cause serious embarrassment.

The King's *volte-face* was complete. With the concurrence of his ministers he had ensured that whatever else might happen to his Russian cousins, they should not set foot in England. The original offer of asylum to which both sovereign and Prime Minister had subscribed was a dead letter.

For their part, the Russian Government still hoped to be rid of the Tsar, although under increasing pressure from extremists not to allow him his freedom. But as the weeks slipped by, their tentative inquiries about British plans for the journey were met by a bland immobility. In July, Kerensky replaced Prince Lvov as a liberal-minded but powerless Prime Minister soon to be overthrown by the Bolsheviks, Lenin and Trotsky. The Imperial family had meanwhile been moved from the palace of Tsarskoe Selo, near Petrograd, to Tobolsk, in distant Siberia. In April 1918, the Tsar, his wife and his children were taken to the even more inaccessible town of Ekaterinburg, in the Ural Mountains. There, three months later, they were done to death.

How far was the King responsible for their ultimate fate? Had he at once urged the Prime Minister to send a British cruiser to the Baltic, the Provisional Government might have seized the chance to bundle the Imperial family on board and be well rid of them. Against this, it may be argued that Milyukov and Kerensky, for all their humane intentions, lacked the strength to defy those extremists who sought revenge. In any case, the Tsar's children were suffering from measles and their parents might well have pleaded for delay. What does remain certain is that the King, by persuading his Government to withdraw their original offer of asylum, deprived the Imperial family of their best, perhaps their only, means of escape.

In retrospect, the King's refusal to help his Russian cousins seems wholly out of character; it becomes intelligible only in the context of an England burdened by war-weariness and discontent. The first principle of an hereditary monarchy is to survive; and never was King George v obliged to tread the path of self-preservation more cautiously than in 1917. He felt himself doubly menaced: by a whispering campaign that doubted his patriotism, and by an upsurge of republicanism. At just such a time of insecurity, his Government urged him to endorse their offer of sanctuary to the Imperial family, a gesture that would have identified him with Tsarist autocracy and imperilled his own repute as a constitutional monarch. Kings are more sensitive to the spectre of revolution at home than abroad; and if in March 1917 George v failed to foresee the descent of Russia into Bolshevik barbarism, he was not more obtuse than his Prime Minister.

The King particularly feared the consequences of inviting the Tsar's wife to England, holding her 'largely responsible for the present state of chaos that exists in Russia'. Lord Bertie, asked by Hardinge whether the French Government might accept the Imperial family, put it more harshly:

I do not think that the ex-Emperor and his family would be welcome in France. The Empress is not only a Boche by birth but in sentiment. She did all she could to bring about an understanding with Germany. She is regarded as a criminal or a criminal lunatic and the ex-Emperor as a criminal from his weakness and submission to her promptings.

Whatever regrets the King may have felt at abandoning Cousin Nicky during those first weeks of revolution, his compassion did not extend to that discredited consort.

Stamfordham's part in these events can scarcely be exaggerated. He determined that whoever else might suffer, it should not be his master: that was the single end which he pursued with relentless vigour and ultimate success. Nor did his efforts to protect the King from any damaging taint of Russian Imperialism cease with the murder of the Tsar and his family at Ekaterinburg sixteen months later. When the first reports reached London, the Grand Duchess George organized a memorial service. Stamfordham told the Foreign Secretary that in normal circumstances the King would either attend or be represented. He continued:

On the other hand public opinion is in a hyper-sensitive condition and might misconstrue anything done by the King into sympathy with the counter-revolution in Russia. Meanwhile it seems to me we could decline to join in the G. Duchess George's service on the grounds that the Government have no official news of the Emperor's death.

The King spurned such deception. On 25 July 1918 he wrote in his diary:

May and I attended a service at the Russian church in Welbeck Street in memory of dear Nicky, who I fear was shot last month by the Bolshevists. We can get no details. It was a foul murder. I was devoted to Nicky, who was the kindest of men and a thorough gentleman: loved his country and people.

A month later he wrote:

I hear from Russia that there is every probability that Alicky and four daughters and little boy were murdered at the same time as Nicky. It's too horrible and shows what fiends these Bolshevists are. For poor Alicky, perhaps it was best so. But those poor innocent children!

The King mourned his cousin and abused their murderers; yet there is no record of his having expressed sorrow, much less contrition, at his own role in the tragedy. It was as if those agitated letters to Balfour had never been written, those appeals to Lloyd George never been made. There is a possible explanation of this apparent insensitivity. On 4 June 1917, two months before the Tsar was removed to Tobolsk, the King wrote to his retired private secretary, Knollys: 'I own that I feel very anxious for the safety of the Emperor . . . If he once gets inside the walls of the prison of St. Peter and St. Paul, I doubt he will ever come out alive.' Having belatedly realized the danger to which his cousins were now exposed, he may have instigated or at least encouraged the British Secret Service to rescue them by bribery or force. The planning of such a scheme, although in the end it came to nothing, would have taken the will for the deed, stilled the King's uneasy conscience and enabled him to recall his conduct towards the Tsar without guilt.

All this is mere conjecture. No evidence exists to link the King with those abortive plans known to have been made by Russian refugees for the rescue of their ex-ruler. Yet it is significant that the Royal Archives at Windsor contain hardly any documents dealing with the imprisonment of the Imperial family between April 1917 and May 1918, precisely those months during which rescue must have been considered if not planned. The absence of such papers points less to the abandonment of the Tsar by the King than to an exceptional need for secrecy. For until March 1918, when Russia made peace with Germany at the Treaty of Brest-Litovsk, the British Government hoped to retain Russia as a military ally; hence the need to conceal from her any British interest in releasing the Tsar from revolutionary control. It is a tenuous theory, yet not implausible.

Stamfordham's amnesia remained as complete as the King's; he felt no responsibility for the fate of the Romanovs. In July 1918, three days after suggesting that it might be imprudent for the King to attend a public memorial service to his cousin, he wrote to congratulate Esher on a newspaper tribute to the dead Tsar:

Was there ever a crueller murder and has this country ever before displayed such callous indifference to a tragedy of this magnitude: What does it all mean? I am so thankful that the King and Queen attended the memorial service. I have not yet discovered that the P.M. or the S. of S. for F.A. were even represented. Where is our national sympathy, gratitude, common decency gone to? . . .

What were the sufferings of that poor unfortunate Emperor during the past year? . . . Why didn't the German Emperor make the release of the Czar and family a condition of the Brest-Litovsk Peace?

The irony of Esher's reply cannot have been intentional:

If this country had been led by the Duke of Wellington or Lord Beaconsfield, the unfortunate Royal Family would have been in safety at Claremont.

You ask why the German Emperor did not make the release of the Czar a condition of the Brest-Litovsk treaty! I should suppose for the same reason that prevented our Government from obtaining the Czar's release from Miliukoff. Moral cowardice. Fear of insinuation, of criticism, of abuse.

Stamfordham did not trouble to correct Esher's distorted version of events. By now, it may be presumed, he had himself come to believe in the myth.

The secret of the King's involvement in the negotiations of 1917 was well kept. Lloyd George honourably refused to justify his apparent abandonment of the Tsar by revealing the pressures which the King's private secretary had brought to bear on the Government. In 1934, however, three years after Stamfordham's death, it became known that Lloyd George was writing his *War Memoirs*. According to custom, the Government of the day asked the Cabinet Secretary, Maurice Hankey, to decide how far the former Prime Minister could quote from official documents. Hankey recommended that the chapter on the future residence of the deposed Tsar should be suppressed altogether. Lloyd George's secretary wrote of Hankey in his diary:

Some parts of it made him feel that it would be premature to publish – for instance the reference to the anti-monarchical movement that was developing in England at the time. Hankey thought that the King would object to this and to the extract from the Cabinet minutes on the subject.

Lloyd George did not welcome Hankey's criticism and complained that 'the Court were very jumpy and nervy'. Two months later he changed his mind, scrapped the original chapter and wrote a new one containing no reference to either the King or Stamfordham. Here is its crucial passage:

An agitation had also started in this country, which indicated that there was a strong feeling in extensive working-class circles, hostile to the Czar coming to Great Britain. However, the invitation was not withdrawn. The ultimate issue in the matter was decided by the action of the Russian Government, which continued to place obstacles in the way of the Czar's departure.

That is not a strictly true account of events, but it did save the King's honour.

The King and Queen shared the wartime anxieties of all parents. Their eldest son, who was twenty in August 1914, at once joined the Grenadier Guards and began training as an infantry officer. Prince Albert was already serving as a midshipman in the battleship *Collingwood*, part of the Home Fleet guarding the North Sea approaches. Of the other three brothers, Prince Henry was still at Eton, Prince George at St Peter's, Broadstairs, and Prince John, subject to fits of epilepsy, living happily but in seclusion at Sandringham.

It was only after a stubborn struggle with authority that the Prince of Wales received permission to serve on the Western Front. Opposition to his wishes came not so much from the King as from the Government. 'If I were sure you would be killed,' Kitchener told him, 'I do not know if I should be right to restrain you. But I cannot take the chance, which always exists until we have a settled line, of the enemy taking you prisoner.' By November 1914 the Secretary of State for War had relented, and the Prince departed for France. Even then, however, it was a lasting blow to his pride that he should be denied service in the trenches with his regiment.

Beginning his tour of duty on the staff of the Commander-in-Chief, thirty miles behind the lines, he contrived to have himself transferred to a divisional headquarters only five miles from the fighting; but whenever an attack was imminent, he was at once whisked away from the remotest chance of shellfire. He wrote bitterly to his father: 'I shall have to remember the war by the various towns and places far back which were headquarters of generals I was attached to, of meals, etc.!!' The King was proud of his son's spirit but neither willing nor indeed able to overrule his advisers. The

Prince found a more sympathetic audience in Lady Coke, the first of those married women whose friendships were to punctuate his life. He told her in March 1915: 'The Grenadiers have had 35 officers killed; isn't it too ghastly to think of ... But of course I never went near the fighting; kept right away as usual!!' Although he did not achieve his ambition of leading men into battle, he found some consolation and a measure of physical danger on the staff of Lord Cavan, the general commanding the Guards Division. Occasionally he came under fire and returned from one inspection of the trenches with Cavan to find that the driver of his car had been killed by a burst of shrapnel. Such forays, however, were not enough to still his discontent. He minded even more when sent on an unnecessary mission to Egypt for six weeks: 'I feel such a swine having a soft comfortable time out here while the Guards Division is up at Ypres.' Lord Edward Cecil, Financial Adviser to the Egyptian Government and a former Grenadier, wrote sardonically of the twenty-one-year-old Prince's shyness in Cairo:

He is a nice boy of fifteen, rather immature for that age. He cannot get in or out of a room except sideways and he has the nervous smile of one accustomed to float ... He adores the Regiment and would talk all day about it, but beyond love of all military matters and outspoken hatred of politicians and a very fine English accent when he speaks French, he has no apparent special characteristics. I think one day he will fall in love and then he will suddenly grow up.

On his return to France, the Prince rejoined Cavan, now promoted to command XIV Army Corps. He wrote in his misery to Marion Coke during the Passchendaele offensive: 'I do so resent being kept back, tho' really I loathe going forward and am terrified far more than anyone else could be; but I have the devil of a big conscience, that's the trouble, and do feel such a soft rotter!!!'

The Prince's emotional turmoil was reflected in a growing disobedience to his father. He continued to write dutiful, affectionate letters about the campaign which the King would proudly read out to the family or show to ministers and officials. Yet there were perennial irritants in their relationship, such as the Prince's addiction to violent exercise and a sparse diet. He had acquired those habits as an Oxford undergraduate in order to shine at sport. Now he pursued them with morose ferocity as a form of self-punishment, even after Cavan had warned him that he would have no strength left for battle. He also offended the King, for whom orders and decorations were part of the fabric of society, by refusing to wear the ribbon of the French Legion of Honour on his tunic and by resenting the award to him of the recently instituted Military Cross. 'I don't feel I deserve it *in the least*,' he wrote, 'having never served in the trenches. Besides there are *so* many gallant yet undecorated officers who should have M.C.s long before me, who has never been out of an office.'

He showed the same resentment when required to spend his home leave in the family circle. The sombre austerity of a royal residence in wartime could scarcely appeal to any young soldier anxious to erase his memories of the Western Front. 'It is *too* nice of you to suggest a little dancing for me tomorrow night,' he wrote to Lady Coke from Buckingham Palace. 'It will be my only chance of getting out at all in the evening from this *most* depressing of places!' A few months later, when his parents asked him to spend a fortnight's leave with them at Sandringham, he told her: 'This little boy somehow says NO; he might possibly spend two or three days there, but not more, not for nobody.' The gulf between father and son, as much of temperament as of age, had begun to widen.

Prince Albert was proving a more tractable son; and, in the face of continual and mishandled illness, a courageous one too. Throughout the war his naval service was again and again interrupted by a succession of gastric illnesses which two surgical operations and prolonged diet failed to relieve. He nevertheless rose from a sickbed to resume his duties in a gun turret of HMS *Collingwood* during the Battle of Jutland and was mentioned in despatches. It was characteristic of this shy, thoughtful boy that even while under treatment in a nursing home and fretting at his own inglorious fate, he should have written to his father: 'You must be very tired after all this very trying time with so much work to do, and so many people to see, and never getting a rest.'

The King and Queen were spared anxiety about the health and safety of their third son, Prince Henry. Fourteen at the outbreak of war, he had in 1913 been sent to Eton, just across the river Thames from Windsor, where he remained for the next five years. He was a modest, kind, good-mannered boy, but without intellectual or athletic gifts and often rebuked for inatten-tion. The King, who wisely insisted that Harry should concentrate on modern languages at the expense of the school's traditional diet of Latin verses, was disappointed by his son's progress. He was also indignant at the way in which Etonians failed to remove their hats when he and the Queen drove by, merely touching their brims with a languid forefinger. Prince Henry, destined for the Regular Army, showed little early promise for soldiering; joining the school Officers' Training Corps in 1914, he was not promoted lance-corporal until four years later, when on the point of leaving for the Royal Military College, Sandhurst. He did, however, surprise his parents by passing the entrance examination half-way up the list. Basking in a rare message of paternal congratulation, he wrote to his old tutor, Henry Hansell: 'Mama and Papa are delighted. They think rather more of Eton than they did before.'

Prince George, nearly three years his junior, was still at St Peter's before joining the navy as a cadet. A cheerful, alert and well-balanced boy, he encountered fewer problems than his brothers, whom he outshone in the classroom. Alone of Queen Mary's children, he shared her love of furniture and paintings, books and bibelots. Prince Henry, by contrast, was to leave Cambridge after a year as an officer-undergraduate without once having set foot inside that treasure house of museums, the Fitzwilliam.

Although the King and Queen were able to celebrate both their Silver Wedding and the coming of peace untouched by personal bereavement, their relief and thanksgiving soon gave way to sorrow. In January 1919, Prince John died suddenly at Sandringham after an epileptic attack. The Queen wrote to a friend: 'For him it is a great release ... I cannot say how grateful we feel to God for having taken him in such a peaceful way, he just slept quietly into his heavenly home, no pain, no struggle, just peace for the poor little troubled spirit.'

Outwardly stoical, she mourned in her heart the loss of her youngest child and the first break in the family circle.

'Very often I feel in despair,' the King told his wife, 'and if it wasn't for you I should break down.' In the fourth year of war, the strain began to show. Curzon noticed that 'the little man's stumpy beard is getting quite white at the point'. Wigram wrote to a fellow private secretary from Windsor:

The atmosphere here has been decidedly low, and I have been endeavouring to assure the King that it is the last battle that wins the war.... It is unfortunate that the Royal Family do not go to public schools and learn to play a losing game on the cricket and football fields.

It was both naive and patronizing of Wigram to suppose that the King's training as a naval officer had been a less gruelling test of character than his own conquests on the playing fields of Winchester. The King's fitful depression was a matter of temperament, not of upbringing. He displayed every quality required of a constitutional monarch except optimism; but even a more euphoric sovereign who had reigned for eight such troubled years might have wondered whether the clouds would ever lift.

The King was sickened by a carnage that continued to take its monthly toll by the hundred thousand yet seemed to bring victory no nearer. His thoughts echoed those despairing lines from Thomas Hardy:

> I have beheld the agonies of war
> Through many a weary season; seen enough
> To make me hold that scarcely any goal
> Is worth the reaching by so red a road.

Changes in the Allied High Command failed to break the deadlock on the Western Front. Indeed, it was the Germans who in March 1918 launched an offensive that smashed the British Fifth Army, threatened the Channel ports and drove back the French from the Aisne to the Marne. Adoption of the convoy system reduced the losses to British shipping from U-boat attacks; but the decisive battle that was to sweep the German Fleet from the North Sea eluded both Admiral Jellicoe and his more enterprising successor, Admiral Beatty. Russia was lost to the Allied cause, although the entry of the United States offered a gleam of hope from the West. (It was the King, more understanding than his Prime Minister, who pointed out that a message of welcome to American troops should omit a reference to their not being 'seasoned'.)

Reverses on land and sea, continual friction between Buckingham Palace and Downing Street, anxiety about his own sons and his Russian cousins: these worries were aggravated by the growth of republicanism and a revival of xenophobic hysteria which the proclamation of the House of Windsor had done little to avert. It was disheartening for the King to practise virtue yet be identified with tyranny; to live austerely, hand over savings of £100,000 to the Treasury and drive himself to the limit of endurance with State papers and public appearances, yet be reminded by Ramsay Mac-Donald that 'it is the Red Flag which now floats over the Imperial Palace in Petrograd'. As for the renewed hounding of those with foreign blood, Leo Amery noted in July 1918:

The poor King is very annoyed and indignant over the alien hunt: the latest proposals if applied all round would presumably involve his submitting himself to Justice Bankes's Committee to justify his functioning as King, and would certainly involve his having to drop the name of Windsor again for the original German name, whatever it is. Poor Mountbatten would also have to lose not only his name but his seat on the Privy Council.

Then suddenly the tide of battle turned. The German offensive faltered and the Allied armies under Marshal Foch struck back. Throughout August and September the enemy were on the run, leaving no fewer than 350,000 of their men as prisoners. The King's dejection gave way to contemptuous anger: 'Max of Baden has now become Chancellor and wants to start negotiating for peace. At the same time the Germans continue to burn the houses in towns and villages in France as they retreat. Curious ideas of peace!' Turkey surrendered on 30 October, Austria on 4 November, Germany a week later. 'Today,' the King wrote on 11 November, 'has indeed been a wonderful day, the greatest in the history of the Country.'

As on 4 August 1914, the population of London streamed down the Mall to salute the man who so modestly embodied the nation's pride. Night after night, he and the Queen were called to the palace balcony to receive their homage. By day they drove through the capital in an open carriage to cheers that had acquired a note of affection as well as of deliverance and joy. 'This has repaid us for much hard work and many moments of keen and bitter anxiety,' the Queen wrote to one of her children. There was a more intimate celebration, too. The King went to the theatre for the first time in five years; his unlikely choice was 'The Bing Boys of Broadway'.

In the midst of his triumph, the King did not forget the general whose Western Front strategy had survived both the armed might of Germany and the subtler attentions of the British Prime Minister. He telegraphed to Haig: 'It is through your military knowledge and ability, combined with patient resolve, that you have led the British Armies to victory.' The country was denied knowledge of his tribute; Stamfordham decided against its publication in case Lloyd George should object. Beatty, too, received a memorable mark of royal favour. The monarch who has sometimes gone down in history as the Sailor King declined to accept the surrender of the German Fleet in person lest it eclipse his old shipmate's hour of glory.

For the common man, for the civilian in uniform, the King showed the same humble admiration; and for those of them who had suffered in body or mind, a shy but paternal concern. Soon after the Armistice he reviewed more than 30,000 disabled soldiers and sailors in Hyde Park. In their enthusiasm they broke ranks and almost pulled the King from his horse. Each later received a copy of his speech. 'I am glad to have met you today,' it began, 'and to have looked into the faces of those who for the defence of Home and Empire were ready to give up their all, and have sacrificed limbs, sight, hearing and health.'

This was no fleeting sentiment, to be uttered and as soon forgotten. In the following year the King watched the first post-war running of the Derby at Epsom. Gazing down from the royal box, he saw that the crowd had suddenly parted to let through a long line of disabled men in hospital blue, walking slowly and painfully. The King jerked his hand towards them. 'They have paid the price for us,' he said in his gruff voice. 'Without them there would be no Derby today.'

SEVEN

RESTLESS DECADE

Changing monarchy — Peace of a sort — Irish settlement —
Money — Honours for sale — Honours not for sale —
Upheavals at No. 10 — My dear Horace

Two weeks before the Armistice, Asquith remarked to the King that the war had brought a slump in Emperors which neither of them could have foreseen four years earlier: Russia murdered, Austria a fugitive and Germany on the verge of abdication. The King agreed that they were not good days for monarchies. All the minor German rulers had lost both place and power (a fate which Princess May of Teck would have shared had those stiff-necked princelings not disdained her taint of morganatic blood). Within little more than a decade, the thrones of Greece and Spain were to disappear, albeit temporarily; there would remain in Europe only those of Britain, Belgium, Holland, Italy, the Scandinavian countries and the unpromising Balkans.

Not even the future of the British monarchy could be taken for granted during the aftermath of war. In 1922, looking back on the first twelve years of his reign, the King drew comfort from having come through so many ordeals with only two Prime Ministers. 'That shows how sound this country is,' he wrote, 'no other country in the world has got a record like that.' Yet the republicanism which had so unnerved him during the war continued to flourish. At a meeting in the Albert Hall organized by the Communists to celebrate the third anniversary of the Soviet Socialist Republics, the name of the King evoked a wave of hissing. Stamfordham wrote to the Prime Minister a year later:

The King is daily growing more anxious about the question of unemployment during the coming winter. . . .

The people grow discontented and agitators seize their opportunities; marches are organised; the police interfere; resistance ensues; troops are called out and riot begets revolt and possibly revolution.

King George v's ability to withstand such assaults could not be taken for granted. Now well into middle age, with impaired health and a shyness that continued to make every public appearance a trial, he seemed ill cast as the symbol, much less the saviour, of his country. The euphoria that had engulfed the King and Queen in the moment of victory gave way to the embittered introspection of a bereaved, impoverished and restless nation.

It was daring but not inappropriate of Asquith, when publicly congratulating the King on his wartime courage and endurance, to quote some lines from the seventeenth-century poet James Shirley:

> The glories of our blood and state
> Are shadows, not substantial things;
> There is no armour against fate;
> Death lays his icy hand on kings.

His purpose, he later explained, was to qualify them with a couplet from the same poem which he saw to be the secret and safeguard of the monarchy in testing times:

> Only the actions of the just
> Smell sweet, and blossom in their dust.

But could an unblemished family life and an unobtrusive dedication to duty alone repel the tide of republicanism? Might not a more positive effort be required to project the virtues of monarchy? The King himself regarded any striving for popularity with repugnance, and would refer to the Press as 'these filthy rags of newspapers'. Nor were his private secretaries experienced in such artifice. They lived by habit rather than design, by precedent rather than compromise. They were men of conservative tastes, set in their ways. Stamfordham, listening to a post-war debate on India in the House of Lords, heard his contemporary, Lord Parmoor, inadvertently refer to Her Majesty's Government. This, he confessed, had touched him, 'as I fancied his mind was, like mine, often wandering back to the much despised Victorian period'. In a sense, Stamfordham's mind had never left it. The principles that had guided him in the old Queen's reign would as well serve her grandson, not least in defending the royal prerogative against the growing pretensions of parliamentary democracy.

In any case, courts are by nature resistant to change. Lord Esher, entrusted with editing the girlhood diaries of Queen Victoria, printed this extract from 1838:

Lady Lyttelton asked leave to put on spectacles for working; and Lord M. said, her asking leave showed she understood *etiquette*, for he said formerly nobody was allowed to come to Court in spectacles, or use glasses; that Mr. Burke, when he was first presented at Court, was told he must take off his spectacles; and that Lord M. said he remembered as long as anything, that no one (man) was allowed to wear gloves at Court.

At the foot of the page, Esher added an editorial note: 'These customs have never been abandoned, and still obtain.' When he wrote those words in 1912, King George v had already been on the throne for two years.

Through peace and war, the Court continued to be hedged round with quaint practices and traditions, though no more so than in any other closed society such as a public school, a cathedral chapter or a regiment of Foot Guards. There was, for example, its excessive discretion, which at Windsor one day provoked Sir Philip Hunloke, the King's sailing master, to confide to his colleagues: 'There is a blackbird on the lawn. But for God's sake don't quote me.'

Every royal pronouncement had to be cast in a distinctive language, the last purpose of which was clarity. If Counsellors of State were required, the sovereign appointed them 'of Our most special grace, certain knowledge and mere motion'. During royal tours, municipalities were addressed with a vapid spaciousness exactly caught in Arthur Benson's parody: 'This is a larger town than I expected to see, and a more important town than I had anticipated. It seems indeed so flourishing a place that in the future when I hear the word Progress mentioned I shall think of Dewsbury.'

The royal vocabulary was rich in well-upholstered words such as *gratified*, *distressed* and *heartfelt*, and there was a special usage for announcing an imminent royal marriage. A journalist who inquired whether it was true that Princess Margaret of Connaught was engaged to the Crown Prince of Sweden received this majestic rebuke: 'Young man, I regret to find that you are ignorant of the very alphabet of your calling. Members of royal houses are *not* engaged. They are betrothed. In similar manner we speak of the conjunction of elephants and the copulation of mice.'

There was one private secretary at Buckingham Palace who took a broader view of newspapers and their purpose. Clive Wigram wrote to a friend in 1917:

I think that in the past there has been a tendency to despise and ignore, if not insult, the Press, which is a powerful weapon in the twentieth century. I have been working very hard to try to get Their Majesties a good press, and have been to the Press Bureau and other places. I hope you may have noticed that the movements of the King have been better chronicled lately.

Wigram was by no means a radical at heart. He looked on conscientious objectors as 'absolute cowards', labelled wartime trades union officials 'shirkers and traitors', and hoped that neither politicians nor other civilians would become 'sentimental about casualties'. But he did see that one necessary way of disarming republicanism was to present the public with a full and accurate picture of the monarchy at work. 'His Majesty must get out of the habit of hiding his light under a bushel,' he told Haig. To encourage the co-operation of newspapers, he wanted 'a well-paid Press representative, with an office at Buckingham Palace, and sufficient sums for propaganda purposes should be forthcoming'. A full-time, salaried Press Secretary was in fact appointed in 1918; but the office was discontinued in 1931, when press matters were transferred to the assistant private secretary, and not revived until 1944.

Through lack of foresight, Wigram believed, several imaginative gestures had gone unnoticed. He thought it tragic that the King's wartime gift of £100,000 to the Treasury had not been allocated to a scheme for the benefit of the working classes; and he was disappointed at the tepid response to a proposal that convalescent officers and their families could use the gardens of Buckingham Palace. In future, he wrote, there should be well-publicized royal visits to industrial areas and closer links with Labour and its representatives. More cynically, he suggested that the clergy should be invited to the palace in greater strength: 'Preachers propagate better than most people the gospel of devotion to the throne.'

Wigram shrewdly enlisted Archbishop Lang, one of the King's most intimate friends, as a fellow conspirator, writing this letter to him in January 1919:

I am very keen that all the old Court and State functions should be revised and opened up to more classes of the community. People of all classes should have an opportunity of coming into Buckingham Palace and its garden. I should like to see something started on the lines of the White House receptions – school teachers, civil servants etc. should all have the entrée. I go as far as saying that trains and feathers at Court should be abolished.

We have to look ahead, and it is quite on the cards that the next Government will be a Labour Government. I feel that there is no place now for any duds about the Court – everyone must pull his or her weight. It is ridiculous to think that at present there is no retiring age for Court officials. There are many well over 70 who have no business to be there. The organisation and inner workings of some of the Departments are puerile and pre-Victorian. ...

Opposed to the reforming party are the Palace Troglodytes, who shudder when any changes are proposed, and consider any modification of the present Court functions as lowering to the dignity and status of the Sovereign. They are hard nuts to deal with, as from their long years of attendance they carry a good deal of influence. We are up against them, but the barriers have to be broken down if the Monarchy is to live.

The path of the reforming royalist is unusually delicate. Let there be too little change, and the monarchy succumbs to republicanism; too much, and the monarchy becomes an hereditary republic, a mere constitutional device shorn of awe and romance and colour. Ponsonby had that danger in mind when in 1919 he told the Prince of Wales: 'I think there is risk in your making yourself too accessible. ... The Monarchy must always retain an element of mystery. A Prince should not show himself too much. The Monarchy must remain on a pedestal.'

Sixty years later, Wigram's bold proposals are no more than platitudes. At the time, however, it seemed to him almost revolutionary to suggest that young ladies presented at court should abandon the trains on their shoulders and the feathers in their hair. Those adornments, as it happened, survived until 1939. So did much else of the Victorian monarchy. Lord M. would have felt quite at home in the Court of King George v between the wars.

Anxious letters passed between Ottawa and London on whether the Governor-General of Canada could emboss a red crown on his stationery, the device of Buckingham Palace, instead of the gubernatorial blue. A Lady of the Bedchamber was allowed a two-horse carriage from the Royal Mews to take her to and from her duties at the palace; a Woman of the Bedchamber warranted only a one-horse brougham. An equerry was reproved for addressing an envelope 'His Majesty The King'; the correct style was simply 'The King', although Queen Mary was to be addressed as 'Her Majesty The Queen'. The twin daughters of Major-General Lord Ruthven were denied admission to the royal enclosure at Ascot because they were actresses; their father showed his resentment by refusing the KCVO traditionally conferred on the General Officer Commanding London District. Lady Astor, invited to a State banquet at Buckingham Palace for the King and Queen of Rumania, created scarcely less of a scandal by going up to the dais after dinner and sitting in one of the four royal chairs for a gossip with the visiting Queen.

And always there were disputes about precedence. The Lord Chamberlain, the Lord Steward and the Master of the Horse argued interminably about their places at court. Staying at Windsor, Winifred, Duchess of Portland, insisted on going ahead of the Duchess of Roxburghe, whose rightful place it was, claiming that a former Mistress of the Robes took precedence of all other duchesses for the rest of her life. When the Allied Prime Ministers came to London in 1918, should the Duke of Connaught go in front of Lloyd George or Orlando behind Clemenceau? 'The German war', Hankey wrote, 'was a trifle compared with this.'

The monarchy nevertheless survived its burden of archaic practices; and with scarcely any of those artificial aids essential to totalitarian regimes it continued to gather strength and confidence to the very end of the King's reign. Wigram, to do him justice, had misjudged neither the menace of republicanism nor the inertia of the Court. He had, however, underestimated the nation's ability to recognize virtue in a humble heart.

This grudging yet perceptive tribute to George v was written by Professor Harold Laski, the very apostle of republicanism, soon after the King's death:

He was identified with the spirit of hard work and personal sacrifice that had won the war; he established a friendly and considerate relationship with the first British Labour Government; his family life epitomised middle-class virtues and avoided overt ostentation; he, the Queen and the princes were identified with a concern, albeit superficial, for the problems of social and industrial welfare.

The Monarchy, to put it bluntly, has been sold to the democracy as the symbol of itself; and so nearly universal has been the chorus of eulogy which has accompanied the process of sale that the rare voices of dissent have hardly been heard. It is not without significance that the official daily newspaper of the Trades Union Congress devotes more space, of news and pictures, to the royal family than does any of its rivals.

Stripped of Laski's understandable sourness, those are the themes which illuminate the way ahead as we rejoin King George V in the closing days of the Great War.

'How are the mighty fallen,' wrote the King on hearing that the Kaiser had abdicated. His diary continues:

He has been Emperor just over 30 years, he did great things for his country but his ambition was so great that he wished to dominate the world and created his military machine for that object. No man can dominate the world, it has been tried before, and now he has utterly ruined his Country and himself. I look upon him as the greatest criminal known for having plunged the world into this ghastly war which has lasted over 4 years and 3 months with all its misery.

The magnanimity which the King had tried to preserve throughout the war gave way at last to a revulsion from all things German. 'In all my life', he told Franklin D. Roosevelt, the future President of the United States, 'I have never seen a German gentleman.' A few weeks after the Armistice, his son Prince Albert, by now serving with the Royal Air Force in Germany, met the Kaiser's sister, Princess Victoria. He wrote to his father: 'She asked after you and the family, and hoped that we should be friends again. I told her politely I did not think it was possible for a great many years!!!' The King replied: 'Your answer to Cousin Vicky (who of course I have known all my life) was quite correct. The sooner she knows the real feeling of bitterness which exists here against her country the better.' In October 1920, when obliged to receive the first post-war ambassador from Germany, he noted that it was more than six years since he had shaken hands with a German. Not until 1935 could he write to a German cousin, the Grand Duke of Hesse: 'That horrible and unnecessary war has made no difference to my feelings for you.'

Sir Ernest Cassel, King Edward VII's intimate friend and financial adviser, was among those to experience a chill of disfavour that lasted until his death in 1921. Although he had emigrated from Germany at an early age and displayed what in 1916 Mrs Winston Churchill called his 'red-hot patriotism', neither he nor even his money was acceptable to war-scarred English society. When the Marlborough Club ran heavily into debt, Cassel offered to meet the entire deficit, but its members refused to be rescued by a one-time alien. Instead they turned to King George V, son of the club's founder, who produced the necessary £7,000. Whether from pride or insensitivity, Cassel courted further humiliation in 1919 by attending a service for the Order of St Michael and St George, of which he had been appointed a Knight Grand Cross fourteen years earlier. Another old friend of King Edward's, the Marquis de Soveral, was angry at having to walk with Cassel in the procession; and Lord Lincolnshire turned his back on him. Cassel died only a few months before an event that would surely have erased the bitter memory of such slights: the marriage of his granddaughter Edwina to Lord Louis Mountbatten.

Even Albert Mensdorff, the King's cousin and former Austrian ambassador, did not feel able to return to England until 1924, ten years after his reluctant departure for Vienna. During the war he was rumoured to have spoken insultingly about Britain; but being an Austrian, not a German, was given the benefit of every doubt. Lord Crewe, asked what he would do if he chanced to meet Mensdorff again, replied: 'First I would shake hands with him, because he is an old friend. Then I might ask him about an unpleasant report that had appeared in the newspapers, and about which he could no doubt offer some satisfactory explanation.' The King was more cautious in his welcome. On Mensdorff's first reappearance, he was invited to tea at the palace, but the occasion was not recorded in the Court Circular. In 1925 it was announced that the former ambassador had been to lunch. In 1926 Mensdorff again had tea with the King and Queen, but noted in his diary: 'There is nevertheless a certain carefulness. For example I was not asked to come to Sandringham ... which they would previously have done.' In 1927 he returned to Sandringham for the first time since before the war, and was told by the King to wear once more his Royal Victorian Order. Thereafter the visit became an annual event in Mensdorff's calendar. His lot may be contrasted with that of Count Metternich, German ambassador in London until two years before the war. In 1923 he lunched with Asquith, who wrote:

He is a tragic figure: everything he had he invested here under Sir E. Cassel's advice, and the utmost that so far he has been able to recover from the wreckage is £200. When I asked him after lunch whether I should call a taxi, he replied No – that he always went now by bus.

Another of the King's cousins waited in vain for a friendly word from Buckingham Palace. The Kaiser, who before the war had been much criticized for the Englishness of his ideas, his habits, even his clothes, resented this silence. Yet the King's stern condemnation of November 1918 was tempered by pity; he was not a man to kick a fallen enemy. It infuriated the King to hear that the wife of the British minister to Holland had jeered at the Kaiser as he arrived from Germany to begin his exile; a few months later her husband was prematurely retired from the Diplomatic Service. Lloyd George's proposal to have the Kaiser extradited from Holland and put on trial for war crimes also incensed the King, particularly as he first learnt of it through the newspapers. It moved him, Hankey noted, to 'a violent tirade ... on and off for half an hour'. The King warned the Prime Minister that to parade the Kaiser through the streets of London would provoke disorder. Lloyd George's response seemed to recall an earlier age of justice: the State prisoner would be lodged at Syon, the Duke of Northumberland's house on the Thames, and brought down the river each day to stand trial in Westminster Hall. An alternative plan was to try the Kaiser in the ancient royal palace of Hampton Court on the outskirts of London; but that would have meant evicting all the courtiers' widows and other old ladies from the apartments which they occupied by the grace and favour of successive sovereigns.

To the King's relief, the Dutch Government refused all requests for extradition. The ex-Kaiser settled down at Doorn as an industrious, enterprising, rather vain country gentleman, his long exile consoled by the novels of P. G. Wodehouse and cups of properly brewed English tea. The King never again met or corresponded with his cousin, who was hurt at receiving no word of condolence from England on the death of his first wife in 1921. Yet an ultimate reconciliation did take place. In January 1936, hearing that King George V lay dying at Sandringham, the former Emperor telegraphed his sympathy to the Queen. She responded with a grateful message accompanied by a present. It was not quite their last exchange. In October 1938 the Kaiser wrote to the widowed Queen Mary for the first time since 1914, congratulating her on the Munich agreement, which both supposed would avert a second World War. He signed his letter, 'Your affectionate cousin, William.' Queen Mary, much moved by the restoration of a family link at such a time of emotion, sent it to her son, King George VI, to be preserved in the Royal Archives.

Lloyd George's failure to consult the King about the proposed trial of the Kaiser was perhaps the most wounding but not the most momentous of their post-war clashes. That began six days before the Armistice, when peace was already assured. The Prime Minister demanded an early general election, from which the King tried to dissuade him. The arguments for and against such a course were nicely balanced. The King cited the precedent of the so-called khaki election of 1900, which had renewed the Unionists' lease of power for five years, but had then provoked such a reaction as to keep them out of office ever since. That was a long-term risk which Lloyd George was prepared to take. He told the King that in 1900, Parliament had been in session for only five years of its seven-year span; whereas in November 1918, emergency legislation had already extended by three years its statutory life, limited to five years since the Parliament Act of 1911. Fortified by this apparent concern for the restoration of democracy, Lloyd George had his way. He appealed to the country to allow the Coalition Government which had won the war to safeguard the peace. The country responded by giving him 526 of the 707 seats in the Commons, at the same time almost extinguishing the Independent Liberals led by Asquith, who was himself defeated in the Scottish constituency he had held for thirty-two years.

Even before the new Parliament met in February 1919, the King and his Prime Minister had once more begun to spar. In December 1918, the Government invited President Wilson to pay a State visit to England that was to begin on the day after Christmas. Stamfordham protested that the King was 'surprised and hurt' at not being consulted about the arrangements, and that the proposed plan would interfere with his much-needed and well-earned holiday at Sandringham. Lloyd George brusquely replied that the King's objections had been put to the Imperial War Cabinet, and that 'the Imperial War Cabinet had overruled the King'. So the sovereign dutifully remained at Buckingham Palace to greet the President and to hold a State banquet in his honour. Wilson made a deplorable impression. In reply to the toast of his health, he omitted any reference to the part played or the sacrifices endured by the British Empire in their joint struggle. 'Not a word of appreciation, let alone gratitude, came from his lips,' Lloyd George wrote. The King was equally disenchanted. 'I could not bear him,' he told a friend, 'an entirely cold academical professor – an odious man.' Only the Sandringham pheasants rejoiced.

The reconstruction of the Coalition Government after the election brought few surprises to a King who disliked change. Of its seventy-seven members, all but ten had served in the previous administration. Balfour remained for a few months at the Foreign Office before handing over to Curzon and in turn replacing him as Lord President of the Council. At the Treasury, Austen Chamberlain succeeded Bonar Law, who was content to combine the Leadership of the Commons with the sinecure office of Lord Privy Seal; Lloyd George's dependence on his support and counsel needed no outward display of power. Churchill became Secretary of State for both War and Air. There was one appointment, however, which the King at first resisted: the promotion of Sir Frederick Smith, the Attorney-General, to be Lord Chancellor and, in ancient parlance, Keeper of the King's Conscience. Stamfordham wrote to the Prime Minister assuring him that the King appreciated the difficulties of forming a Government and did not want to add to them. The letter continues:

But taking into consideration Sir Frederick's age, 47, and that he has only been Attorney General for between three and four years, His Majesty fears the appointment will come as somewhat of a surprise to the legal profession. The King knows that his career both at the bar and in Parliament has been very successful: but His Majesty does not feel sure that Sir Frederick has established such a reputation in men's minds as to ensure that the country will welcome him to the second highest post which can be occupied by a subject of the Crown. His Majesty however only hopes that he may be wrong in this forecast.

Lloyd George replied that many distinguished Lord Chancellors had attained the office between the ages of thirty and forty. The King gave way and 'F.E.', as Smith was known to the world of politics, took his seat on the Woolsack as Lord Birkenhead. Both Stamfordham and the Prime Minister, as it happens, had gone astray in their arithmetic. Smith was not forty-seven but forty-six; and only the notorious Judge Jeffreys, appointed Lord Chancellor in 1685 when thirty-seven, had been younger than Smith at the time of his elevation.

Birkenhead proved more than worthy of his office. Both as Speaker of the House of Lords and as head of the judiciary he embodied wisdom, learning and energy in a dignified presence. He abhorred the tempering of justice with levity, and when sitting as a Lord of Appeal prided himself that no observation of his was ever followed by the reporter's phrase, 'laughter in court'. But when he put aside the trappings of State, conviviality re-asserted itself. Owen Morshead, the King's librarian, liked to recall an evening at Sandringham when the King beckoned Birkenhead to sit on one side of him, Lord Hailsham on the other. 'I wished it would never end,' he wrote, 'and began to think it never would.' There was a less decorous occasion on board the royal yacht *Britannia* at Cowes, when Birkenhead, having dined well, puffed a huge cigar in the Queen's face until a courtier tactfully persuaded him to go up on deck to see the stars. The pastime bored him, so he made his way below again, went into one of the ladies' cabins and said: 'Hallo, my little birdie, what a pretty little nest you have got.'

The Lord Chancellor could also display an ill temper which did not spare even his sovereign: as when the King, outraged by a newspaper photograph of Birkenhead at No. 10 Downing Street in an old grey suit and slouch hat, told Stamfordham to rebuke such informality. The culprit replied:

I almost invariably wear a silk hat though very many of my colleagues, who have not received remonstrances, never do. On the morning in question I came up from the country where I had no silk hat and my train did not arrive in time to enable me to go home before the Conference. It will not, I think, be suggested that it would have been proper to arrive late at the Conference in order to make good the defect in my equipment.

The measure of my shortcoming therefore is that I did not remember to take a silk hat with me when I left London three days earlier.

Inasmuch as this circumstance has caused annoyance to the King I regret it and in deference to his expressed views frequently wear a style of hat which I have the misfortune to detest. We must hope that I shall be able to avoid such lapses in the future.

And after all in days far more formal than ours it was never the custom to appraise the adequacy or dignity of Lord Chancellors in terms of head-gear.

'I consider this a very rude letter,' wrote the King; and it was left to Stamfordham to patch up the peace.

There was a similar exchange a few years later when Stamfordham suggested that Birkenhead ought to ask the King's permission before going abroad:

His Majesty has noticed of late that his Ministers leave the Country without asking for leave to do so. It is a good old custom which the King hopes will be adhered to – of course H.M. does not expect to be asked when Ministers go over to Paris for a few days. . . .

Instead of humouring the King, Birkenhead bombarded Stamfordham with constitutional precedents for coming and going as he pleased; and in petulant vein he concluded: 'You will assure the King, with my deep respect, that if he would wish to be consulted as to my brief absences (after seven months arduous and unbroken labour) I should of course consider it my duty to take His Majesty's pleasure.'

The King had known outspoken extroverts in the navy or at shooting parties; and his occasional collisions with Birkenhead, whose merits as Lord Chancellor he soon came to appreciate, left no bad blood. The Prime Minister was a more persistent cause of pain and worry, generally through thoughtlessness and neglect rather than a determination to be unpleasant. He knew, for instance, how annoyed the King had been at having Lord Beaverbrook thrust on him as Chancellor of the Duchy of Lancaster, a minister responsible in part for the sovereign's private finances. Yet during the post-war Government, Lloyd George repeated his blunder by appointing Sir William Sutherland to the post. Stamfordham gave the King's formal approval, but added that 'His Majesty would have hardly thought him suitable for the office in question.' Few had a good word for him. 'My travelling companion in the car was an odious fellow called Sutherland,' Hankey had written during the war, 'some sort of political parasite of L.G.'s.' He was known to fix the Press on his master's behalf, and reputed to 'hawk baronetcies at the clubs'. Both the King and his Duchy deserved a less compromised Chancellor.

Even at Buckingham Palace, the King was sometimes no better informed than any other newspaper reader about government business; at Balmoral he felt 'isolated ... more or less cut off from official sources'. Partly it was his own fault. On resuming his annual Scottish holiday in 1919, he at first dispensed with a Minister in Attendance. The ostensible reason was to relieve members of an overworked Cabinet from additional duty. But it is also likely that he did not trust Lloyd George to send him congenial colleagues who could fit easily into the family circle. In the absence of the traditional link between Balmoral and Whitehall, it fell to the Prime Minister's staff to keep the King abreast of current problems; and this they failed to do. Bonar Law's private secretary, touring the Highlands with his wife one summer, telephoned Balmoral to ask whether there was any news of the railway strike which for several days had paralysed the country. 'Not a word,' Stamfordham replied. 'I have sent telegram after telegram from the King, and I have not had a single reply.'

It may be wondered why Stamfordham had not simply lifted the telephone and asked for a call to be connected to No. 10 Downing Street. The reason lay not in any lack of equipment, but in the reluctance of King and Court to use it. As early as 1883, a telephone line was installed between Balmoral and the post office at Ballater so that telegrams could be sent and received with speed; in 1908, the castle acquired a complete telephone service linked to the Aberdeen exchange, and so to London. By 1896, Windsor could speak to Buckingham Palace and Marlborough House; and to this day, Buckingham Palace retains its original subscriber's number of 4832, although the name of its exchange, Victoria, has become an impersonal 930. Sandringham, too, acquired an early telephone. But a letter written from there in 1906 by Sir Dighton Probyn reveals impatience at its intrusion: 'Let me take my "stylo" and write quickly for the next quarter of an hour – as I have that time before the post goes, if not interrupted – Bother it – the telephone went and has delayed me 5 minutes.'

The King, it is true, liked the telephone as a means of gossip. He would delight in telling the by now celebrated story of how each morning at 9.30 he would ring up his sister, Princess Victoria, for a chat. 'Of course,' he would explain, 'we're not always too polite. One day her telephone bell rang at the usual time and she took up the receiver and said, "Hallo, you old fool." And the voice of the operator broke in, "Beg pardon, Your Royal Highness, His Majesty is not yet on the line." ' But the King avoided the instrument for serious business, and the Lord Chamberlain was so astonished at receiving a call from him one morning that he noted it in his diary.

Ministers shared his mistrust of the telephone: largely because every call in those days had to be connected by an operator who might overhear their secrets. Not even Downing Street manned its telephones day and night. Lloyd George, dining at Haldane's house in 1919, found he had forgotten a paper he wanted to discuss, so asked the butler to telephone No. 10 for it. There was no reply. And Clement Attlee has recorded how, until the advent of Churchill in 1940, there was no private line between Downing Street and Chequers, the Prime Minister's country house, just a single telephone in the butler's pantry. Even Geoffrey Dawson, editor of *The Times* from 1912 to 1919 and again from 1923 to 1941, had no telephone in his house in Yorkshire throughout the first term and for the first twelve years of the second; when he wanted to speak to his office in London, he would walk a mile to the nearest post office. It was scarcely surprising that in 1919 Balmoral relied upon telegrams from the Prime Minister rather than resort to the telephone.

Lloyd George's neglect wounded the King's pride and provoked Stamfordham to anger. Miss Stevenson, Lloyd George's confidante, urged him to be more considerate. 'I told him that he does not pay the King very much attention,' she wrote in her diary, 'he gets out of going to the Palace if he can, and has constantly refused invitations to Windsor. He cannot be surprised if the King is a little hurt.' The Prime Minister's discourtesy infected his staff, particularly Sutherland and J. T. Davies, who did not trouble to rise to their feet when the King's private secretary entered their room. A less churlish official was shocked one day to discover Stamfordham sitting patiently in the hall of No. 10 on a wooden chair, as if in a railway waiting-room. Stamfordham, who even among his colleagues at the palace could be 'peppery, alarming and critical', took his revenge by letting no lapse on the part of Downing Street pass unnoticed or unrebuked. He spoke bitterly to Hankey of the Prime Minister's absence from the Commons when a message from the King was being read. Hankey explained that he had been ill. Stamfordham replied: 'Well, I suppose one suspects Lloyd George of things which one would not suspect in another man.'

The King displayed a more forgiving disposition. While staying with Lord Derby at Knowsley in 1921, he heard that Lloyd George was in low spirits after Bonar Law had been obliged by ill health to retire from the Government. He at once wrote a letter of friendly encouragement, addressed to Stamfordham in London but really for the eyes of the despondent Prime Minister. It included these warming sentiments:

I firmly believe that L.G. is now more necessary to his country than he ever was and that the vast majority of the people are behind him. ... You can tell the P.M. that I have complete confidence in him and will do everything in my power to help him. ...

There really ought to be two P.M.'s! No man can do the work L.G. has to do now. I quite understand his feeling lonely and almost lost without B.L. who did so much for him. . . . .

I was talking to two Labour M.P.s here today and they were loud in singing the P.M.'s praises and both said he is the strongest man we have had since Pitt.

There were attentive little courtesies, too. The King, as Colonel-in-Chief of the Welsh Guards, refused even to consider their abolition as a post-war economy until he knew Lloyd George's opinion. The regiment was reprieved.

Lloyd George was slow to recognize magnanimity or indeed to find any virtue in his sovereign until long after he had ceased to be Prime Minister. In 1937, however, laughing heartily, he told this story to his secretary:

One day during the peace conference Clemenceau came in late, in a towering rage, because he had been summoned to see Poincaré (the President), who was evidently bothering the old man a great deal. Clemenceau whispered in L.G.'s ear: 'Can't you lend me George V for a short time?'

The King was more generous in recognizing the achievements of Lloyd George. On 29 June 1919, after months of arduous negotiation in Paris, the Prime Minister returned from signing the Treaty of Versailles. Abandoning protocol, the King met him at Victoria Station. On the drive back to Buckingham Palace, the crowds threw flowers into the carriage and a laurel wreath fell on the King's knees. 'This is for you,' he said, and handed it to the peacemaker.

Peace with Ireland took longer. The postponement of Home Rule for the duration of the war was accepted by John Redmond. Others seized on the decision as a breach of faith that invited retaliation by violence. The failure of the Easter Rising of 1916, the execution of Sir Roger Casement and the imposition of military conscription infected those volatile minds with bitterness and illusions of betrayal. Conciliatory attempts to resolve the differences between North and South by an all-party Convention failed as decisively as had the Buckingham Palace conference three years earlier. At the general election of 1918, Eamon de Valera's Sinn Fein party won 73 of the 105 Irish seats at Westminster, declared Ireland an independent Republic, and embarked on a campaign of terrorism and murder against British rule.

To reinforce a hard-pressed army and police force, the Government sent over a body of ex-servicemen whose methods of reprisal were no more honourable or humane than those of their opponents. Dubbed the 'Black and Tans', from their distinctive uniform, they were loathed in Ireland and looked on with mistrust from Westminster. The King, who increasingly came to see himself as the father of all his people, agonized over the bloodshed and the cruelty, some of it self-inflicted. He found no comfort in his Prime Minister, who thought that the King was taking an altogether too detached view of the struggle. During the prolonged and eventually fatal hunger strike of Terence McSwiney, Lord Mayor of Cork, Lloyd George wrote unpleasantly: 'The King is an old coward. He is frightened to death and is anxious to make it clear that he has nothing to do with it.' A more accurate reflection of the King's opinion can be found in a letter written by Stamfordham only five days earlier:

The King feels that the probable results arising from McSwiney's death will be far more serious and far-reaching than if he were taken out of prison and moved into a private house where his wife could be with him, but kept under strict surveillance so that he could not escape and return to Ireland.

Abused behind his back by Lloyd George for timidity, the King was reproached to his face by Ponsonby for callousness. 'The King and I had a fierce argument on Ireland which ended in a yelling match,' that insubordinate royal servant told his wife. 'I supported Asquith, Grey and Robert Cecil, he the P.M.'

In 1920 Lloyd George took a new initiative. The Government of Ireland Bill established two Irish parliaments with limited powers, one in Dublin, the other in Belfast. Although repudiated by the South, the measure was welcomed by the leaders of the Protestant North, who invited the King to open their new Parliament in June 1921. Others warned him that his presence in Belfast would antagonize Dublin, and even expose him to physical danger. Those fears he dismissed; he would turn a ceremonial duty into a mission for peace. It has since been said that the King was in effect challenging his intransigent ministers. That is a mistaken interpretation. The speech with which he opened the new Parliament of Northern Ireland, like those he delivered over the years at Westminster, had been prepared in Downing Street and approved by the Cabinet. His only departure from custom lay in persuading the Government to cast his speech in the form of a personal appeal for reconciliation in Ireland. General Smuts, who happened to be in London for the Imperial Conference, may be credited with implanting that visionary plan in the King's mind and producing an early draft of the speech. But the text from which the King spoke was the work of Sir Edward Grigg, later Lord Altrincham, one of the Prime Minister's private secretaries. Originally a journalist on *The Times*, and affectionately dubbed 'The Scribe' during his wartime years in the Grenadier Guards, he now brought exceptional gifts of insight and sympathy to his composition.

On 22 June 1921, with the Queen at his side, the King pronounced this striking peroration:

The eyes of the whole Empire are on Ireland today – that Empire in which so many nations and races have come together in spite of the ancient feuds, and in which new nations have come to birth within the lifetime of the youngest in this hall. I am emboldened by that thought to look beyond the sorrow and anxiety which have clouded of late my vision of Irish affairs. I speak from a full heart when I pray that my coming to Ireland today may prove to be the first step towards the end of strife amongst her people, whatever their race or creed.

In that hope I appeal to all Irishmen to pause, to stretch out the hand of forbearance and conciliation, to forgive and forget, and to join in making for the land they love a new era of peace, contentment and goodwill.

It is my earnest desire that in Southern Ireland, too, there may, ere long, take place a parallel to what is now passing in this hall; that there a similar occasion may present itself, and a similar ceremony be performed. For this the Parliament of the United Kingdom has in the fullest measure provided the powers. For this the Parliament of Ulster is pointing the way.

The future lies in the hands of my Irish people themselves. May this historic gathering be the prelude of the day in which the Irish people, north and south, under one Parliament or two, as those Parliaments may themselves decide, shall work together in common love for Ireland upon the sure foundation of mutual justice and respect.

'I think my speech was appreciated,' the King wrote. 'I never heard anything like the cheering.' The Prime Minister came to welcome him home at Euston Station and was unusually effusive in his congratulations. That did not deter the King from sending Stamfordham to No 10 two days later with both a warning and a complaint. The private secretary urged Lloyd George to take immediate advantage of the improved atmosphere in Ireland. The moment was a very fleeting one, he continued, 'especially when dealing with a quick-witted, volatile and sentimental people'. Lloyd George agreed, assuring him that the Cabinet was about to invite de Valera and Sir James Craig, the Prime Minister of Northern Ireland, to meet in London. Stamfordham went on to deplore the minatory tone of Birkenhead's speech on Ireland in the House of Lords on the very eve of the Belfast ceremony, as well as Churchill's unhelpful statement in the Commons promising military reinforcements. Lloyd George replied that the line taken by the Lord Chancellor would emphasize that what the King had done was His Majesty's action, independent of the Government and thus carrying its own popular appeal: an artful response from the Prime Minister that concealed by flattery what he knew to be constitutionally untrue.

After much prevarication, de Valera accepted Lloyd George's invitation to talks in London, and on 10 July a formal truce was signed by the British forces in 'Ireland and the Irish Republican Army. The terms offered to de Valera for a permanent settlement were more generous than could have been envisaged at any time during the previous decade: what amounted to full Dominion status but qualified by a provision that the existence and rights of the Government of Northern Ireland must be both recognized and respected. This de Valera rejected on 21 July, although leaving the truce intact and the door open for further discussion.

Throughout the weeks of negotiations between London, Dublin and Belfast, the Prime Minister kept the King fully informed and in turn received wholehearted encouragement. Then came a check. At the end of July, the British press reprinted an interview supposedly given to an American newspaper by Lord Northcliffe, proprietor of both *The Times* and the *Daily Mail*, who in failing health had just begun a world tour. It purported to reveal a sharp division of opinion between the King and his Prime Minister on Irish policy. Here are its most sensitive passages:

It is not generally known that under the constitutional form of government the King has still a good deal of power when he chooses to use it. In this case he has done so with good effect. At the last meeting he had with Lloyd George before leaving for Ireland, the King asked him, 'Are you going to shoot all the people in Ireland?' 'No, your Majesty,' the Premier replied. 'Well, then,' said the King, 'you must come to some agreement with them. This thing cannot go on. I cannot have my people killed in this manner' . . .

When King George sailed for Ireland, the Cabinet tried to spike his efforts by making speeches in the Lords and Commons three hours afterwards which were intended to irritate the Irish people. This annoyed the English people very much and when the King returned he had the biggest reception outside of Buckingham Palace he had ever received since the war began in August 1914.

The authenticity of the interview was at once repudiated by both North-cliffe and his travelling companion, Wickham Steed, editor of *The Times*. Fatigued by the hot weather, Northcliffe had authorized Steed to give interviews in his name; it was Steed, not Northcliffe, who had in fact spoken to the man from the *New York Times*. In a public disclaimer, Steed made it plain that since he could not have possessed any knowledge of what passed between the King and the Prime Minister, he could not have quoted their conversation. As to the conduct of the reporter from the *New York Times*: 'It was not a question of violation of confidence, which would have been bad enough. I never said it at all.'

Lloyd George, too, made a statement in the Commons on behalf of both himself and the King. He denied that any such reported conversation between them had taken place; and he confirmed that the King, in his

Belfast speech, had followed the invariable constitutional practice relating to Speeches from the Throne at Westminster.

Destroyed by that chorus of denials, the supposedly fake interview faded from contemporary interest. We, however, may pursue it a little longer. For in 1952 the authorized *History of The Times* revealed that part at least of that interview had been based on a conversation between Steed and the reporter about the King's desire for peace in Ireland and his solicitude for all his people: a talk which Steed regarded as private and 'off the record', but which the American journalist felt at liberty to print. What the King was alleged to have said about bloodshed in Ireland, moreover, carries a ring of truth and conforms to similar reproaches which we now know he addressed to his ministers. Even his supposed choice of words – 'I cannot have my people killed' – foreshadowed a celebrated rebuke ten years later: 'Remember, Mr Gandhi, I won't have any attacks on my Empire.' Steed's alleged reference to the King's resentment at disobliging ministerial speeches on the eve of his visit to Belfast was, as we have seen, equally well founded. If not from Steed, where did the *New York Times* reporter gain so accurate an insight into the King's relationship with his ministers? And if indeed it was Steed who had talked so freely, what was his own authoritative source?

The probable answer to the first question is that the American journalist, far from reporting Steed inaccurately, had reported him with embarrassing fidelity, private confidences as well as public platitudes. The probable answer to the second question is to be found in the diary of Lloyd George's secretary, Frances Stevenson, who always referred to him as D. (for David):

He then sent for Lord Stamfordham and found out in the course of discussion that Lord S. had seen Wickham Steed and had obviously been talking to him in such a way as to give him the impression that the King and D. had been at variance and that is the explanation of the interview. D. was simply furious.

Lloyd George's anger was understandable. For months he had endured a campaign of denigration waged against him by *The Times*; only two weeks earlier Steed had referred to him in print as the most distrusted statesman in Europe, without straightforwardness or honour. And this was the newspaper editor with whom the King's private secretary had apparently chosen to gossip about his master's relationship with the Prime Minister. A few hours after their painful confrontation at Downing Street, Stamfordham wrote to assure the Prime Minister that his only motive in seeing Steed before his departure for New York had been to enlist his support for the Government in giving practical effect to the King's Belfast speech. It is doubtful whether Lloyd George was mollified or Stamfordham aware of his imprudence. Their mutual regard, never more than tepid, grew positively glacial for the rest of their lives.

That quarrel, however, cast no shadow over the King's support of Lloyd George throughout the resumed negotiations with de Valera. In these the King played more than a passive role. Often hot-tempered over small interruptions to his daily routine, he could demonstrate an enviable restraint in affairs of State. When de Valera seemed by the end of August to be deliberately obstructing progress, some of Lloyd George's colleagues pressed the Prime Minister to impose a time limit on the Irish leader. The draft reply to de Valera which the Prime Minister submitted for the King's approval was not quite an ultimatum; but its aggressive tone did not satisfy the King. By then both he and Lloyd George were on holiday in the Highlands of Scotland. They met at Moy Hall, Inverness, where the King was staying with the Mackintosh, head of an ancient Scottish family. The King urged the Prime Minister to remove all threats and contentious phrases from the draft. The amended letter, endorsed by the Cabinet at an emergency meeting in Inverness, proved acceptable to de Valera, who agreed to resume the suspended talks. That was the King's last contribution to the Anglo-Irish discussions, except to warn the Prime Minister against becoming enmeshed in haggles over terminology. On 6 December he had the joyful task of congratulating his ministers on having signed an agreement establishing the Irish Free State as a Dominion within the Commonwealth. 'It is mostly due to the P.M.'s patience and conciliatory spirit,' the King wrote in his diary, 'and is a great feather in his cap. I trust that now after seven centuries there may be peace in Ireland.'

His hope proved illusory. The King did not live to see the final severance of every tie that bound the Irish Free State to the Commonwealth. But throughout the remaining years of his reign he was an anguished yet impotent witness to broken promises and crude stratagems, to civil war and sectarian violence and bloodshed. 'What fools we were not to have accepted Gladstone's Home Rule Bill,' he told Ramsay MacDonald in 1930. 'The Empire now would not have had the Irish Free State giving us so much trouble and pulling us to pieces.'

Like so many of his subjects, the King felt the financial pinch of the postwar world. His Civil List, or official income, was fixed by Act of Parliament in 1910 'to make provision for the honour and dignity of the Royal Family'. It brought him £470,000 a year, of which £110,000 was for his personal use, the rest to maintain the functions of monarchy. He was also entitled to an annual sum from the revenues of the Duchy of Lancaster, which owned considerable property; in the first full year of his reign, 1911, this amounted to £64,000, but by 1921 it had fallen to £44,000. The Queen continued to receive an annuity of £10,000 originally voted 'for her sole and separate use' as Princess of Wales. The King's eldest son, the Prince of Wales, had no Civil List but instead received the substantial revenues of the Duchy of Cornwall, which could amount to £80,000 a year. His younger brothers were allowed £10,000 a year on coming of age and a further £15,000 on marriage. Princess Mary received £6,000.

Immediately after the accession, the Cabinet asked the Solicitor-General, Sir Rufus Isaacs, whether or not the King ought to be taxed. His opinion rested on the dictum of Lord Abinger: 'It never can be ... intended that His Majesty should take money out of one pocket to put it in another', and concluded that the King was thus exempt from taxation. The sole exception was a small sum levied on the sovereign's private real estate, such as houses and land, as enacted by a statute of George III. The King, therefore, was a rich man, at least during the first four years of his reign.

The suspension of State pageantry and entertainment during four years of war enabled certain economies to be made; and of course after 1915 there were no purchases of wines or spirits. The King did not pocket these savings, but in 1916 presented the Treasury with £100,000, to be used as the Government thought best. He also gave away £77,000 to charities.

With the coming of peace, however, there was little enough to spare. The monarchy was expected to shed some of its wartime austerity, yet the cost of living had doubled; the royal palaces needed new carpets and curtains, and four years of neglected maintenance had everywhere to be made good. The King had also assumed a heavy burden of philanthropy. He gave the Grand Duchess Xenia, sister of the murdered Tsar, a pension of £2,400, as well as the loan of Frogmore Cottage, and settled £10,000 a year on the Empress Marie, the Tsar's mother. Lesser sums from his own pocket went to supplement the meagre pensions of retired courtiers.

Queen Alexandra was a cause of particular anxiety to her son. In addition to a Civil List of £70,000, she enjoyed a life interest in the sum of £200,000 bequeathed to her by King Edward. That ought to have sufficed. But she was allowed no relief from death duties, supertax or income tax. When her affairs were discussed at a meeting of the Civil List Committee in 1910, Balfour said, with a feline want of sympathy: 'It would be interesting to know what are the revenues of the Court of Denmark.' By her late husband's wish, and with the entire approval of her son, she continued to live in Sandringham House with her unmarried daughter, Princess Victoria; and she once more made Marlborough House her London home. Since the King paid for much of the upkeep of Sandringham, even those two large establishments might have been within her means had she agreed to curb both her extravagance and her generosity. As it was, she lived amid a profusion of cut flowers, left no charitable appeal unanswered, and when urged to economize, took refuge in deafness. The King had no option but to make her a private allowance of £10,000 a year.

In 1920, however, after Stamfordham had pleaded her cause with Lloyd George, the Prime Minister instructed Sir Warren Fisher, Permanent Secretary to the Treasury, to examine her affairs. He discovered the illogicality by which Queen Victoria's surviving children paid no income tax, whereas Queen Alexandra continued to pay full income tax and supertax. 'Both', Fisher observed, 'cannot be right.' For once the Treasury behaved indulgently, not only remitting five-sevenths of Queen Alexandra's taxation, but making the concession retrospective to April 1919. Thus the King was in future relieved of that particular burden of £10,000 a year.

Yet there continued to be a growing deficit on the King's Civil List for salaries, pensions and household expenses. In 1919 it was £24,800; in 1920, £45,000; in 1921 an even larger figure was forecast, including a deficit of £19,000 on maintenance and repairs alone. There were two obvious remedies to meet this financial crisis: either Parliament must increase the annual Civil List, or the King must economize drastically. The first would be politically undesirable and certain to inflame republican sentiment. The second would involve the dismissal of both indoor and outdoor servants, and the abolition of such colourful occasions as State visits and the opening of Parliament, events which the King never ceased to dread, yet might be reluctant to see vanish for all time. Even more drastic measures were canvassed, such as the closing down of Windsor Castle and the sale of objects from the royal collections.

Then the Government remembered the valuable estates and capital of the Duchy of Lancaster, which already made an annual contribution to the sovereign's income. Could they not be raided on this single occasion to augment the Civil List and so tide over what all hoped was no more than a temporary embarrassment? A pedantic school of thought maintained that the King was not in fact Duke of Lancaster, since he could not claim the necessary descent from John of Gaunt. Hobhouse, when Chancellor of the Duchy of Lancaster, had tactlessly felt obliged to point this out to the King, adding that Queen Victoria, when travelling abroad incognito, was careful to call herself Countess of Lancaster. 'I got a very cold bow indeed,' Hobhouse recorded of his next encounter with the King. Whatever the merit of those genealogical niceties, there was no doubt that the sovereign had long enjoyed the revenues of the Duchy by hereditary right and ordinance. It was but a step for the Government in 1921 to introduce the Duchy of Lancaster (Appreciation of Capital Moneys) Bill, authorizing the transfer of £100,000 from Duchy funds to supplement the revenue payment for that year. By August, the King's balance sheet was looking much healthier.

Certain economies were nevertheless necessary. In July 1922, it was announced that twenty-two servants in the Royal Mews would have to be retired from 31 October. It was done as handsomely as possible. By the King's own command, the order ran, 'a specially generous pension scale has been drawn up in view of the enforced nature of these retirements, and in the case of men who are ineligible for pension owing to not having done ten years' service, a gratuity of one month's pay will be given for each completed year of service'. All twenty-two received sums in excess of the pensions they would have earned if they had completed their service, and any who in the meantime found other employment received their full pay and allowances until the end of October. Such liberal redundancy payments were less common in 1922 than two generations later.

In seeking further economies, the King could always depend on his wife's eye for domestic detail, a legacy of her straitened youth. She was open-handed with imaginative little presents: an agate snuff-bottle for an ambassador or a piece of Chinese jade for a colonial governor who had just lost his own collection by fire. But her enemy was waste. She did not hesitate to descend on the Prince of Wales's apartments, examine the pattern he had chosen for his new curtains, substitute a cheaper yet equally serviceable material, and even wield a tape measure to prove that he had ordered six yards too much. Visiting Lady Curzon in the country, the Queen was distressed when her car ran over a lamb which had strayed on to the road. 'Still,' she told her hostess in a consoling yet practical way, 'you will be able to eat it.' And a visiting preacher who lunched at Sandringham was surprised to be given half a pear from the Queen's plate.

In the closing months of his reign, King George V told Ramsay MacDonald how well he understood the Prime Minister's reluctance to accept a title on retirement. And he went on to say that if he himself were one of the new rich, the last thing he would do would be to run after a peerage. It was not that the King had lost faith in a hierarchical society; but that twenty-five years as the supposed Fountain of Honour had left him disillusioned by the wiles and extortion practised in his name.

The sale of honours to replenish party funds or their bestowal in return for political support is as old as parliamentary government itself. Stanley Baldwin used to recall with delight an eighteenth-century document at Welbeck, home of the Dukes of Portland: a list of persons who had to be squared by the Prime Minister. One was to be given an Irish peerage, someone else a bishopric for his brother, a third a sinecure in the public service, and a fourth merely the gratification of a ducal handshake. Later incumbents of Downing Street have expressed a distaste for such tariffs.

Lord Salisbury, badgered for peerages and places when forming his first administration in 1885, declared: 'The experience has been a revelation to me of the baser side of human nature.' And Asquith, compiling the Coronation Honours List of 1911, told Balfour that it was 'a task, as you well know, as uncongenial and even hateful, as can fall to man'. Yet even the most high-minded of Prime Ministers came to realize that patronage is power. Like the Empress Maria Theresa, when invited to share in the Partition of Poland, they wept but they took.

From the moment of his accession, the King tried to keep a restraining hand on both the size and content of Honours Lists. By ancient custom the sovereign could in theory ennoble or otherwise reward a subject without ministerial advice. In 1912, when Sir Edward Grey was appointed a Knight of the Garter, Knollys insisted that Asquith's secretary should delete from the official announcement a phrase that the King had *approved* the award. 'He is supposed to be the Fountain of Honour,' Knollys reminded Downing Street. The King was correspondingly pleased whenever the recipient of an honour wrote to thank him for it, as if the initiative had been his and not his Government's. Soon after Sir James Craig, the first Prime Minister of Northern Ireland, had been gazetted as Viscount Craigavon, Stamfordham replied to his letter of gratitude: 'I know it will be appreciated by His Majesty, as *nowadays* such expressions of thanks to the Sovereign are the exception rather than the rule.'

In practice there was no difference between the bestowal of an honour and any other act of government: ministers proposed and the sovereign gave his formal consent. It was, however, a field in which the King exercised his prerogative to the very limit. He held that an honour conferred in his name and often by his hand was too invested with the person of the sovereign to be left to an administrative abstraction known as the Crown. His scrutiny of each proposed Honours List was therefore painstaking and critical. Even Asquith's submissions, more reputable than those of Lloyd George, were sometimes resisted. The King refused to elevate a proconsul from earl to marquess 'in view of his incompetency and of his being the laughing stock of everybody who has to do with him'; to make a baronet of a Liberal whose 'only apparent claim is that he is the brother of the Postmaster General'; to bestow a Privy Counsellorship on a noted radical MP; or to reward a member of the College of Arms whom the King, Knollys explained, 'abominates'. When Asquith stood firm, the King was obliged to give way; a dubious honour was not worth a constitutional crisis. Only the would-be marquess had to wait for his promotion.

Scattered through Asquith's peacetime lists are names with little to recommend them for a high honour except money. Some had doubtless subscribed to Liberal Party funds, but they were neither so many nor so unknown as to evoke public comment. With the war, however, there arose a breed of new men: industrialists and financiers whose services, as Curzon delicately put it, had 'not been wholly untinged by the expectation of social preferment to come'. Some of these were accommodated by Asquith's Liberal administration and by the Coalition over which he presided in 1915–16. But it was not until Lloyd George had superseded him as Prime Minister that their aspirations were wholly fulfilled – at a price. In a manner unsuspected by Milton, time had run back and fetched the age of gold.

Between 1917 and 1922 there were four aspects of the distribution of honours which increasingly disturbed the King. They were the failure of the Prime Minister to consult him before promising titles to certain political or financial supporters; the number of honours recommended by the Prime Minister; the character of the recipients; and the use of go-betweens to sell the royal prerogative in the market-place.

The most brazen example of Lloyd George's failure to consult the King was in putting forward Sir Max Aitken for a peerage in December 1916, only six months after he had received a baronetcy. Since Lord Beaverbrook (as he swiftly became) had already been told of his intended elevation, the King felt that he could not reject the Prime Minister's submission. But Stamfordham told Lloyd George how 'surprised and hurt' the King had been, and continued:

His Majesty commands me to say that he feels that the Sovereign's Prerogative in this respect should not be disregarded, and he trusts that in future no honours whatever will be offered by any Minister until his approval has been informally obtained. His Majesty further asks that this may be made clear to your Colleagues.

That reference to 'your Colleagues' is significant. Bonar Law, as the senior Conservative in the Coalition, was scarcely less nonchalant than Lloyd George in the matter of honours, particularly where some favour was owed to a subject of Canadian origin.

In April 1918, the King was again called upon to redeem a rash promise made by Lloyd George to another newspaper proprietor and member of the Government. On the resignation of Lord Rothermere as Secretary of State for Air, the Prime Minister asked that he should be promoted from baron to viscount. This time there was resistance. Stamfordham told Lloyd George:

The King hopes you will not raise the question of Lord Rothermere's promotion in the Peerage. The newly constituted Air Force, of which he was Minister, has only been in existence twenty-four days when he resigns. Rightly or wrongly, his administration has been sharply criticised and is to be discussed in both Houses of

Parliament. He has only just been made a Privy Councillor which, in itself, is a high distinction.

A year later, Bonar Law repeated the request with disarming candour:

I earnestly hope that this recommendation may be allowed to go through. I must point out to you that, while I fully realise the difficulties raised in your letter, the Prime Minister undertook, at the time of Lord Rothermore's resignation, that he would support this recommendation to the King, and the Prime Minister, I think, would personally be placed in a very unpleasant position if His Majesty could not see his way to accept the recommendation.

Although some criticisms may be passed upon the success, or otherwise, of his short administration at the Air Ministry, his intense loyalty and assistance to the Government during the later and critical days of the war, and also at the General Election, have considerably increased the obligations due to him.

Stamfordham replied:

His Majesty gives his approval, but with much reluctance. He cannot help thinking that it would have been better if the Prime Minister had not given an undertaking to Lord Rothermere at the time of his resignation that he would be recommended to the King for promotion. This is another case of a quasi promise, and what is worse, a quasi committal of His Majesty!

During the very first weeks of the reign, and again in 1911, the King had complained to Asquith of the size of Honours Lists. They grew no smaller with the years. Between Asquith's taking office in 1908 and his fall nearly nine years later, ninety peerages were created, almost the same number as Lloyd George secured during his subsequent premiership of only six years. This ever-rolling stream of nobility affected the King's sense of humour. Soon after the death of the first Viscount Astor in 1919, *The Times* printed a facetious message from H.A.L. Fisher, President of the Board of Education, to the dead peer's daughter-in-law, Nancy. It began: 'I hate your being a Viscountess.' The King was enraged. He told Stamfordham to write to the Prime Minister saying how willing he would be to reduce the number of peerages, 'more than one hundred new ones since 1910 and some created contrary to what would have been the King's personal wish'. A cowed Downing Street replied that Fisher's message had been a private joke, not intended for publication. By 1922, Stamfordham was writing with weary fatalism to Lord Salisbury:

The whole question of honours grows more and more disagreeable and distasteful to the King, whose one object is to reduce the numbers that are submitted to him twice a year but you will naturally be inclined to reply that His Majesty's efforts are not very successful.

Even if each of Lloyd George's innumerable nominees had been deserving of reward, the King would still have deplored such wholesale ennoble-
ment. But their virtues were well concealed. As early in Lloyd George's
premiership as March 1917, Salisbury and a band of like-minded Conservatives were preaching 'the supreme importance of keeping our public life
pure and free from reproach'. It was, they pleaded, one thing for a political
party to reward its supporters; quite another to confer honours in return
only for large contributions to party funds. When they expressed their
disquiet in the House of Lords later that year, Curzon defended the practice
with artful eloquence:

People are rather apt, supposing they see in the newspapers that an honour has
been conferred upon some person unknown to themselves to imagine that the
honour has been bought. To be unknown to the public is not necessarily to be
corrupt. . . .
    Just as the soldier gives his valour or courage or genius; just as the artist gives
his talents; just as the captain of industry gives his energy or enterprise; just as the
man of science gives his inventions to the service of the State, so the wealthy man
gives, and in my view is entirely justified in giving, his wealth, which is very often
his only asset, for the benefit of the country.

Curzon's case was not entirely fanciful. Lord Lansdowne, the former
Viceroy of India and Foreign Secretary, spoke of the difficulty of drawing
a line betwen legitimate and corrupt payments to party funds. Asquith too,
another man of the utmost honour, insisted that contributions to party
funds ought not in themselves to disqualify the donors from public recognition. Lloyd George went further. In private conversation with a Conservative fund gatherer some years after ceasing to be Prime Minister, he
commended the sale of honours as a wholesome element in British political
life:

You and I know perfectly well it is a far cleaner method of filling the Party chest
than the methods used in the United States or the Socialist Party. . . . Here a man
gives £40,000 to the Party and gets a baronetcy. If he comes to the Leader of the
Party and says I subscribe largely to the Party funds, you must do this or that, we
can tell him to go to the devil.

The King was prepared to tell any man to go to the devil, but saw no
need to ennoble him first. He was equally enraged by Lloyd George's
manipulation of the royal prerogative to secure the political support of the
Press. In four years, nearly fifty proprietors and editors had become Privy
Counsellors, peers, baronets and knights. Beaverbrook, Rothermere and
Northcliffe were soon followed to the Upper House by Sir Edward Russell,
editor of the *Liverpool Daily Post*, and Sir George Riddell, chief proprietor
of the *News of the World*. The King objected to both; one because he was

past his eighty-fifth year, the other because he had been what was then known as the guilty party in a divorce case. Lloyd George, however, believed that neither age nor dalliance should deprive a customer of his coronet, and the King was obliged to give his consent.

However excessive the fruits of journalism, they were dwarfed by the rewards which Lloyd George heaped on industry and finance: twenty-six peerages, 130 baronetcies, 481 knighthoods. Not all the recipients, of course, had subscribed to the funds of either of the two Coalition parties; and of those who had subscribed, some would have qualified for honours by more conventional public service or by giving their money to genuine charities. But any corrupt system must be judged by its excesses. The King repeatedly tried to restrain Lloyd George from debasing the Honours Lists with men of dubious qualifications or none. In 1921, for instance, he wrote to the Prime Minister about a Newcastle shipbuilder, 'a personally unattractive character', whose conviction for hoarding food during the war had proved no obstacle to his being made a baronet. But it was not until the summer of 1922 that King, Parliament and public opinion united in condemnation of tainted honours.

The list published on 3 June 1922 to mark the King's birthday contained the names of five new peers: Sir Robert Borwick, Sir Joseph Robinson, Sir William Vestey, Sir Samuel Waring and Sir Archibald Williamson. Of these five, only Borwick, a manufacturer of baking and custard powders, escaped public censure and derision when their elevation became known.

Vestey's citation spoke of the immense wartime service he had rendered by placing his company's cold storage depots at the disposal of the Government without charge. But during the parliamentary debates provoked by this Honours List, the Secretary of State for War conceded that the Union Cold Storage Company had indeed been paid for the use of its warehouses at Le Havre and Boulogne. It also emerged that Vestey, in evidence to the Royal Commission on Income Tax in 1919, had admitted moving his meat business to the Argentine Republic during the war in order to avoid British taxes. The manoeuvre was estimated to have cost the Treasury £3 million and to have made between 3,000 and 5,000 British workers unemployed.

Waring was accused in the Commons of having made a fortune out of wartime contracts for military equipment, yet to have abandoned all those shareholders who had lost their money by investing in an earlier company of his. As these charges were being uttered, the new peer shouted from the distinguished strangers' gallery: 'That is a false statement.'

Williamson, who took the title of Lord Forres, defended himself with equal vigour on the floor of the Upper House. He was alleged to have pursued his South American interests in such a way as to have infringed wartime regulations against trading with the enemy. The Foreign Trade Department of the Foreign Office had been in no doubt that his company was sailing close to the wind. In its archives were a large dossier and a twelve-page memorandum on the firm's activities prepared for the War Cabinet by Lord Robert Cecil, the Minister of Blockade. 'The matter was referred to the Director of Public Prosecutions', Curzon's private secretary reported, 'and though they were not actually prosecuted, their licences were withdrawn for a time.' Three days later he wrote again to the Foreign Secretary: 'The firm's record in the war was putrid and they were told so by Sir E. Pollock, the Controller of the F.T.D. The record of the conversation exists together with the intercepted letters of the firm containing advice on Trading with the Enemy while keeping within the law, and a long series of F.T.D. minutes of a scathing character.' The writer, the future Lord Vansittart, could never resist a joke. 'O tempora o Forres', he added.

Lord Forres may perhaps be given the benefit of the doubt. Sir Joseph Robinson neither deserved nor indeed sought such indulgence. The citation for his peerage described him as chairman of the Robinson South African Banking Company. That bank, as it happened, had ceased to exist seventeen years earlier. The company with which his name had been more closely associated was Randfontein Estates. As its chairman, he had bought mining freeholds in his own name, then sold them to the company at a hugely higher price without informing the shareholders. The deception led to protracted litigation in the South African courts, which eventually ordered him to pay £500,000 compensation. As recently as November 1921, Robinson's appeal to the Judicial Committee of the Privy Council had been dismissed. There could be no excuse for his name to appear in an Honours List only seven months later.

Lloyd George was determined to ride the storm raised by the Vestey, Waring and Forres peerages. Robinson's record, however, was too black to defend; he must be persuaded to refuse the honour which had been announced but not yet officially gazetted. But when the emissary from Downing Street arrived at Robinson's suite in the Savoy Hotel, the deaf old swindler misunderstood his visitor's mission. 'How much more?' he is said to have asked, reaching wearily for his chequebook. At length he agreed to write the Prime Minister a letter which could be read out in the House of Lords. It was both poignant and dignified. He declared that he had not sought a peerage, that at eighty-two he had no desire for such things and that he therefore begged His Majesty's permission to decline it.

The King was not prepared to leave it at that. Four days later he wrote sternly to Lloyd George of his 'profound concern at the very disagreeable situation which has arisen on the question of Honours':

You will remember that both in conversation and in written communications I have deprecated the ever increasing number of those submitted for the half yearly Honours Gazette: and in recent years there have been instances in which honours have been bestowed where subsequent information has betrayed a lack of care in the enquiries made as to the fitness of the persons selected for recognition.

The case of Sir J.B. Robinson and all that it has evoked in the Debates of the House of Lords and in the newspaper reports of interviews given by him to Press representatives, must be regarded as little less than an insult to the Crown and to the House of Lords and may, I fear, work injury to the Prerogative in the public mind at home and even more in South Africa.

I fully recognise that the inordinate demands upon your time make it impossible for you, in spite of your marvellous capacity for work, personally to investigate the claims and qualifications of those persons whose names you submit for my approval for honours and rewards.

But I do appeal most strongly for the establishment of some efficient and trustworthy procedure in order to protect the Crown and the Government from the possibility of similar painful if not humiliating incidents, the recurrence of which must inevitably constitute an evil, dangerous to the social and political well being of the State.

Bowing to an outraged King, Parliament and public, Lloyd George appointed a Royal Commission 'to advise on the procedure to be adopted in future to assist the Prime Minister in making recommendations ... of names of persons deserving special honour'. Under the chairmanship of Lord Dunedin, a senior judge, it made two recommendations. The first was that a committee of three Privy Counsellors, none of them members of the Government, should in future scrutinize the records of all candidates for honours before their names were submitted to the sovereign; the second was that an Act of Parliament be passed imposing penalties both on those who promised to secure honours in return for payment and on those who promised payment in return for honours.

One member of the Royal Commission remained unsatisfied. Arthur Henderson, the Labour MP, belonging to a party which had never had an Honours List at its disposal, regretted that his colleagues had declined to inquire into previous transactions and to expose the names of both touts and customers in that unsavoury trade. He also urged that never again should an honour be conferred for political services alone. Henderson, who had served as minister without portfolio in the War Cabinet, was to become Home Secretary in the first Labour Government and Foreign Secretary in the second. He maintained his self-denying ordinance to the end, dying in 1935 as plain Arthur Henderson. Ten years later his son, as staunch a Labour man as himself, consented to become one of almost a hundred peers created by Clement Attlee between 1945 and 1951.

Henderson's disdain for political honours was needlessly austere. The mere existence of the Political Honours Scrutiny Committee proposed by the Dunedin Commission ensures that corrupt or otherwise unsuitable candidates do not reach even the Prime Minister's preliminary list, much less that submitted to the sovereign. Yet the system is not infallible, and a negligent or irresolute trio of Privy Counsellors has occasionally failed to dissuade a Prime Minister from recklessly repaying friendship with honour.

It is more difficult to measure the effectiveness of the Honours (Prevention of Abuses) Act, another recommendation of the Dunedin Commission. Since it reached the Statute Book in 1925, it has ensnared only one purveyor of honours and not a single paying customer. Others, however, may have been deterred by its penalties. Yet in March 1933, Baldwin told a friend: 'I've got a scoundrel coming to see me who says he was promised a K.C.V.O. in return for £10,000 to a hospital. He is a member of my Party so I cannot refuse to see him. I shall tell him he is liable to be prosecuted for trafficking in Honours.'

That anyone could hope to buy his way into the Royal Victorian Order, bestowed personally by the sovereign without ministerial advice, reveals both the gullibility of the ambitious and the extent to which touting continued even after the fall of Lloyd George. It was a familiar gambit of the honours broker to suggest that a donation to a hospital or other institution under royal patronage was a sure passport to a Buckingham Palace investiture. What remains surprising is that Baldwin's visitor was brazen enough to demand his illicit reward only a month after Mr J. Maundy Gregory had become the sole and much-publicized victim of the 1925 Honours (Prevention of Abuses) Act.

Gregory, the son of a clergyman, was the most plausible and, at first, successful of the honours touts. Under guise of giving voluntary help to charitable organizations such as the Order of St John of Jerusalem, he insinuated himself into their counsels, then exploited the spurious repute which the connection brought him. He set up offices near the Houses of Parliament that to the uninitiated could pass for a government department of exceptional importance. He bought the Ambassador Club, where he would ostentatiously entertain Lord Birkenhead and the exiled King George II of the Hellenes. He even maintained a link with Buckingham Palace through his cultivation of Sir John Hanbury-Williams, Marshal of the Diplomatic Corps and thus a senior member of the royal household.

Baldwin, Prime Minister in 1923-24 and again in 1924-29, insisted that any dabbling in honours necessary to raise funds for the Conservative Party should be conducted more discreetly than in the years of the Lloyd George Coalition. For the Conservatives at that time had been no less active than their Liberal partners in the sale of honours, merely less successful in disposing of their wares and retaining the proceeds. One reform initiated by Baldwin was to stamp out the trade of the independent middleman such as Gregory. His friend J.C.C. (later Lord) Davidson, chairman of the Conservative Party from 1926 to 1930, evolved an ingenious method of smashing the racket. He persuaded Mr Albert Bennett, a rich Conservative MP and assistant treasurer of the party, to introduce himself to Gregory as a man well placed to supply honours. Once accepted by Gregory as a trusted agent, Bennett acquired the names of all his clients, which he then reported to Downing Street. This secret intelligence ensured that not a single name on Gregory's list should ever appear in an Honours List. Since Gregory's trade depended on delivering the titles for which his clients had paid, his business collapsed.

Although the King did not often plead for an honour to be conferred on an individual subject, he asked Baldwin on at least six occasions in 1926 and 1927 to make Bennett a baronet; possibly he repeated his request in subsequent years. The correspondence between Buckingham Palace and Downing Street on the subject is cryptic. 'You are aware', Stamfordham wrote to Baldwin's private secretary, 'of the circumstances in which the King is interested in Mr Bennett.' It is tempting to assume that the King knew and approved of his role as a spy and wished him to be rewarded for his enterprise. There is no evidence, however, to support such a conjecture. It seems more likely that Bennett, a noted philanthropist, had made a handsome contribution to a cause near to the King's heart. The King eventually had his way, and in Baldwin's resignation honours of 1929, Bennett emerged as Sir Albert.

Gregory's arrest in 1933 on a charge of having offered to obtain a knighthood for a retired naval officer in return for £10,000 reveals how desperate he had become in his efforts to raise money. Not only did he have little prospect of securing a knighthood for his supposed client; he had chosen quite the wrong sort of victim. Lieut.-Cdr. E.W. Billyard-Leake, DSO, an intimate friend of the Mountbattens and godfather to one of their daughters, needed no such social prop. He called in the police.

The impending trial alarmed Baldwin who, although still leader of the Conservative Party, had in 1931 agreed to serve as Lord President of the Council in Ramsay MacDonald's 'National' Government. For what if Gregory were to plead not guilty and reveal in the witness box his list of satisfied clients over the years? There would surely be Conservatives as well as Liberals among them. He must be silenced. And silenced he was. Davidson left this account of the operation:

Nobody knew to what extent Maundy Gregory would betray his past in his desperation and financial stringency. We accordingly organized someone to go and see him, who told him that he couldn't avoid a term of imprisonment, but that if he kept silent we could bring pressure to bear on the authorities to let him live in France after his sentence had been served.

When this occurred he was met at the prison gates by a friend of mine who drove him in a motor car to Dover, took him to France, ensconced him in previously arranged accommodation, gave him a sum of money and promised him a quarterly pension on condition that he never disclosed his identity or made any reference to the past. ... We kept him until the end.

It has long been surmised that Gregory's silence was paid for by those who had most to fear from his revelations. That is not quite accurate. Some months after Gregory's release from Wormwood Scrubs prison, Baldwin came to the Prime Minister with a cynical demand that would have astonished his contemporaries. He asked that Sir Julien Cahn, a sporting philanthropist who had been knighted five years earlier, should be made a baronet in return for paying off Maundy Gregory with £30,000. An agitated MacDonald recorded his conversation with Baldwin:

He said that Maundy Gregory's papers and Maundy Gregory's presence here would stir up such a filthy sewer as would poison public life; that many innocent persons had become indirectly involved; that all parties were involved (I corrected him at once and said: 'Not ours.' He smiled and said that unfortunately friends of mine were. I replied that if they were I knew nothing about it. Then I remembered that Clynes and Henderson were mentioned at an earlier stage); that people like Winston Churchill, Austen Chamberlain, Birkenhead were involved; that Gregory had been used by Ll.G. and Bonar Law; that the subscription lists for the rebuilding of St. George's Chapel, Windsor, were involved; and several other things. Gregory, as indeed I know, was a blackguard who netted innocent people. ... The dunghill had to be cleared away without delay and £30,000 was required to do it. So I *had* to give the honour.

MacDonald held out for six months, then succumbed to renewed pressure from the Conservative leader. 'Mr. B. involves me in a scandal', he complained in his diary on 19 May 1934, 'by forcing me to give an honour. because a man has paid £30,000 to get Tory headquarters and some Tories living and dead out of a mess.' In the following month Cahn became a baronet. Lloyd George was not the only Prime Minister of King George V to muddy the Fountain of Honour.

The sale of titles was humiliating for the King and fatal to Lloyd George. Yet it was but one facet of an honours system that seemed to permeate every sphere of national life. Correspondence between the palace and Downing Street, itself the distillation of wider consultations, was incessant. A Viceroy or Governor-General sacrificed whole weeks of his working year in balancing the claims of one candidate and another. Curzon wrote of 'the insatiable appetite of the British-speaking community all the world over for titles and precedence'; by the end of his life he himself had acquired a Privy Counsellorship, an Irish barony, a United Kingdom earldom and marquessate, the Order of the Garter, the Order of the Star of India, the Order of the Indian Empire and the Royal Victorian Chain.

Honours there had always been. Not until the reign of King George v, however, did they cease to be the almost exclusive preserve of the well-born and the well-established. The Orders of the Garter, of the Thistle and of St Patrick were confined to the sovereign's family, the landowning nobility, elder statesmen, an occasional hero of the battlefield or of the war at sea. The Bath was reserved for senior officers of the army and the Royal Navy, the higher ranks of the civil service, a handful of politicians and other public men; the St Michael and St George for British officials overseas, particularly in the diplomatic and colonial services; the Orders of the Star of India and of the Indian Empire for those engaged in the civilizing mission of the British Raj; the Royal Victorian Order for personal service to the sovereign.

Nor, until the present century, was it generally resented that the aristocrat should have a prior claim on the distribution of honours. When in 1886 Queen Victoria wished to bestow the Grand Cross of the Bath on Mr W.H. Smith, the Conservative minister, he humbly asked leave to decline. Having spent his early years in trade, managing the family business of newsagencies and bookstalls, he thought himself unworthy of 'a decoration which, until recently at all events, has only been given to men of his social standing for very distinguished services'. As late as 1908, Edward vii refused Asquith's submission that Edward Grey should have the Garter. He maintained that there was no precedent since Sir Robert Walpole for bestowing so exalted an honour on a commoner, and that even a peer should be denied the Order unless he were at least an earl. When the more realistic King George v permitted his Foreign Secretary to become a Knight of the Garter four years later, his leniency was much criticized in smart society.

While seeking to preserve the nobility of the Garter in its strictest sense, Edward vii enlarged the boundaries of other honours; he scattered his own in profusion and encouraged his subjects to accept foreign ones. A generation earlier, even campaign medals were thought somewhat ostentatious. A crusty old general, eyeing the three Crimea medals worn at a regimental dinner by that noted agriculturist Lord Stafford, observed: 'Byng has been lucky with his pigs.' But Edward vii expanded the Royal Victorian Order sixfold in the first three years of his reign; and Fritz Ponsonby, who during the seven years he served Queen Victoria did not receive a single foreign decoration, acquired eighteen of them in her son's reign. As the King's first Prime Minister, Lord Salisbury, remarked: 'Any vigorous attempt to restrict decorations would cause a demise of the Crown.'

Edward VII founded a new honour, too. His Secretary for War, St John Brodrick, told a friend:

The King is giving us much trouble with Orders. He showers decorations right and left. There is to be a new 'Order of Merit' – limited to 24, I got it reduced from 60. It is for savants and soldiers. Its chief objects are that it is worn round the neck, and puts Edward VII on a par with Frederick the Great, who invented a similar one!

From its inception in 1902, the Order of Merit, like the Royal Victorian Order, has remained in the personal gift of the sovereign. King Edward, however, did indicate his willingness to consider any names put forward by the Prime Minister. It was not until 1946 that the Garter and the Thistle similarly became the preserve of the sovereign, who makes appointments to both Orders without ministerial advice.

King George V's opportunity to extend the scope of the Honours List came with the war. Until 1914 there were few awards for gallantry. The Victoria Cross was given very sparingly to both officers and other ranks in recognition of the utmost heroism; the Distinguished Service Order rather more generously to officers of middle and senior rank. Junior officers now acquired their own rewards for courage, the Distinguished Service Cross for the navy and the Military Cross for the army; later came a Distinguished Flying Cross. Like the DSO, these new decorations were at first given indiscriminately to staff officers and fighting officers alike; this demoralizing practice was later curbed. A parallel set of medals for gallantry was instituted for those below commissioned rank.

Haig thought that the King was naive in his definition of physical courage, as when he expressed the opinion that the Victoria Cross should be given for carrying a wounded man out of action. The Field-Marshal replied that there were medical dangers in carelessly moving a wounded man; only to his diary did he confide that military police were posted during a battle to prevent more unwounded men than necessary from accompanying a wounded man back from the firing line. It was equally charitable of the King that he should abolish the procedure by which holders of the VC convicted of serious criminal offences forfeited the award.

Civilians also had their share of new honours. Even before the war, Esher had suggested a new order of chivalry for 'persons connected with the Territorial Forces, charitable work of all kinds, missionary work overseas, etc. etc., from whom service is practically demanded by the State, and who get no chance of recognition from their Sovereign'. After 1914, the need became imperative. Not until 1917 was the Order of the British Empire instituted, 'in recognition of the manifold services, voluntary and otherwise, that have been rendered both by British subjects and their Allies in connection with the war'. The intervening years had been spent in luxuriant discussion of its name, statutes and insignia.

The inaugural list of names reflected every type of war service at home and abroad, and no less the social revolution that had overtaken the nation during three years of war. From a royal Duke, the Governor of the Bank of England and a future Lord Chancellor, it made its stately, all-embracing descent to factory foremen, munitions workers and trade union officials.

Another radical change proclaimed by the newest order of chivalry was the admittance of women on an absolute equality with men. Before 1917 the honours system scarcely recognized female existence, much less female distinction. Women had occasionally received peerages, although denied a seat in the House of Lords; among them was the Duchess of Teck's friend, Angela Burdett-Coutts, singled out for her philanthropy. The Order of Merit was ostensibly as welcoming to women as to men, but by 1917 Florence Nightingale alone of her sex had penetrated its rank; she was not admitted until her eighty-eighth year, and even then with considerable reluctance on the part of King Edward. The first investiture of the new order, held at Buckingham Palace in September 1917, struck a less churlish note. Men and women mingled alphabetically to receive their insignia from the King. By the custom of the time it was a bold decision. Not until the following year did women of thirty or more qualify for the vote; women between the ages of twenty-one and twenty-nine had to wait until 1928 for their political emancipation.

Little more than a year after its institution, the Order of the British Empire was divided into two parts. A military division would in future be reserved for members of the armed forces; a civil division for every other form of national service. Founded to reward endurance in war, it would henceforth recognize achievement in peace.

As sovereign of the new order, the King wished to show that he esteemed it no less than the older, more patrician orders of chivalry. He therefore appointed the Prince of Wales to be its first Grand Master. His thoughtful gesture did not protect the Order of the British Empire from ribaldry and disparagement during its early years. It was at first distributed too lavishly and too indiscriminately; one list of awards covered sixty quarto pages of the *London Gazette*. By the end of 1919 there were 22,000 recipients of all grades; half a century later that number had quadrupled. George Robey, it was said, would shortly appear in the music hall wearing OBE trousers. In 1922, during a debate on honours in the House of Lords, the Duke of Devonshire read out a letter from a tout who had a knighthood for sale – 'not of the British Empire, no nonsense of that kind, but the real thing'.

Soldiers, British and Allied alike, disdained an award identified with

15 Dressed for Ascot races. The King retained the serene elegance of the Edwardian age to the end of his days and was pained by the slovenly standards of the post-war world. Not even Lord Birkenhead was spared a royal rebuke when the King noticed a newspaper photograph of the Lord Chancellor arriving at Downing Street in an old grey suit and slouch hat.

16 The King and his Prime Minister, Lloyd George; each interrupted his Scottish holiday in the summer of 1921 to discuss the progress of the Anglo-Irish Treaty. They met at Moy Hall, Inverness. Between them is the King's host, the Mackintosh of Mackintosh.

17 Stanley Baldwin and the Marquess Curzon of Kedleston on the steps of No. 10 Downing Street in January 1924. Only a few months before, the King had chosen Baldwin to be Prime Minister instead of the more experienced Curzon. So the two statesmen were not always on such affable terms. On an earlier occasion, Baldwin wrote: 'I met Curzon in Downing Street, from whom I got a very chilly nod and the sort of greeting a corpse would give to an undertaker.'

18 The King in the grouse butts. He shot with old-fashioned hammer guns, his left arm very straight, hands gloved. He was among the best dozen shots of his generation. Not everyone approved. A Liberal Minister wrote: 'It is a misfortune for a public personage to have any taste so strongly developed as the craze for shooting is in our beloved Ruler.'

19 At the helm of *Britannia*, 1924. Although shooting was the King's first love, he equally excelled at sailing. For forty years his yacht continued to win prizes at Cowes, and he refused all offers of a more modern boat. The Queen did not share his ecstasy afloat. 'The *Britannia* has just passed us,' she wrote one August, 'and I saw the King looking very wet and uncomfortable in oilskins – what a way to enjoy oneself.'

20 The Queen's Dolls' House at Windsor, designed by Sir Edwin Lutyens on a scale of one inch to the foot. There were crown jewels in the strong room, toys in the nursery, marmalade in the larder; a library of miniature books, too, each no bigger than a postage stamp, presented by contemporary authors. George Bernard Shaw alone refused to contribute, 'in a very rude manner,' it was noted.

non-combatant service. The French scornfully referred to it as l'Ordre Britannique Embusqué. One French heart, however, received it with gratitude: the Empress Eugénie, who had lived in England since her husband's defeat at Sedan in 1870. Almost fifty years later, on the eve of her ninety-third birthday, the King sent his two elder sons to invest her with the Grand Cross of the British Empire in recognition of her having organized and paid for an Allied military hospital.

Simultaneously with the Order of the British Empire, the King instituted the far smaller Order of the Companions of Honour. Of limited membership, it was devised to reward service of national importance, but carried neither title nor precedence. The first recipients were nearly all senior representatives of the munitions industry, agriculture, transport, nursing and the Press; the name of Smuts has alone survived in the public memory. Not until a decade later could the Order be spoken of as a comparable though lesser Order of Merit.

The new labyrinth of awards laid an additional burden on the already overworked secretaries of Buckingham Palace and Whitehall. The honours system had long encroached upon their working day; now it seemed to have acquired a life and purpose of its own, almost beyond ministerial control. The archives of the Lloyd George era reveal that great issues of war and peace and progress were forever jostled, even eclipsed, by the minutiae of stars and ribbons, by arcane precedents and obstructive practices.

One such problem was the recognition of Lloyd George's incalculable wartime services. The most imaginative was the laurel wreath handed to him by the King on his return from Versailles; but that did not alone suffice. He could not be tempted by a peerage and banishment to the House of Lords. A grant of £100,000, such as given to Haig and Beatty, would require controversial legislation; so too would any addition to a Prime Minister's retirement pension of £2,000 a year. Some proposed that Lloyd George might fittingly become the first Knight of St David; the King, however, had long ago rejected plans for a wholly Welsh order of chivalry. Stamfordham suggested the Garter, but Balfour was doubtful. It would be awkward for the Prime Minister to have to nominate himself for the Order; in any case, he wrote, 'if we once begin giving the Garter for merit, irrespective of rank, the troubles of future Prime Ministers in recommending for that honour will be greatly increased'.

Bonar Law thought that the Order of Merit would be the most suitable award, since it was given on the initiative of the sovereign and without ministerial advice. The proposal did not please the King. He replied that civilian members of the Order were required to be eminent in the arts, literature or science; and that indeed the statutes seemed to have been drawn up with the deliberate intention of excluding politicians. Although technically correct, the King was being disingenuous. He had conferred the OM on Haldane in 1915 not in recognition of his Hegelian studies but to solace an ill-used Lord Chancellor. And when in 1916 he had likewise honoured Balfour 'for services to philosophy and literature', the candid recipient warned Stamfordham that the OM ought to be reserved for those of outstanding distinction in their fields and not regarded as 'another reward open to Party Statesmen who combine literary or other interests with their political work'. Balfour's letter continued: 'I think you will admit it to be a most extraordinary coincidence that out of 13 gentlemen chosen purely for their eminence in Literature, Science or Art, no less than five should be Privy Councillors and ex-Cabinet Ministers!'

Ostensibly, all five statesmen had received the Order of Merit for their services to learning and the arts. Even had Bryce and George Otto Trevelyan not been politicians, one might still have been honoured for his *Holy Roman Empire* and the other for his *Life and Letters of Lord Macaulay*; it is far more doubtful whether the same exalted recognition would have been given to Balfour's *Defence of Philosophic Doubt*, Haldane's *Pathway to Reality* or Morley's *Life of Gladstone*. Since the statutes had already been strained thus far, they could surely be made to admit a civilian war leader, even one who had scarcely ever put pen to paper. After a strong plea to the King by Bonar Law, the Prime Minister became a member of the Order of Merit.

Within a few weeks, Lloyd George's friends were again busy on his behalf. Churchill, as Secretary for War, submitted to the King that the Prime Minister should have the Distinguished Service Order. The King dismissed the suggestion out of hand; the statutes precluded any civilian from receiving that award. Churchill then asked that Lloyd George should have the three war medals issued to all members of the armed forces with the requisite service. It was a persuasive letter:

As the Prime Minister must have made 30 or 40 journeys to France and was on several occasions in zones where shells were falling, and as all these journeys were made in strict performance of necessary duty of the highest possible consequence, Mr. Churchill considers that the grant of the War Medals in these circumstances will be in every respect appropriate.

The King held that such medals were never meant for civilians, but he felt obliged to yield when he learnt that Churchill, in his cavalier way, had already promised them to Lloyd George and that 'the Prime Minister would rather have them than an earldom'. The King did, however, insist on two conditions: that Asquith should also receive the three war medals, but that no other minister should unless, like Churchill, he had earned them in the field while out of office.

Not until Churchill had pleaded Lloyd George's cause did he have the grace to write another letter, asking the King to accept the war medals. The King, who nearly always emerged from these encounters more creditably than his ministers, replied that he was ready to acquiesce, 'though feeling that I have in no way earned these honourable distinctions'.

With almost the entire Honours List at his disposal (to use no more mercenary a phrase), Lloyd George might have been expected to leave the King in undisputed control of the Order of Merit; it was, after all, by royal favour that he himself could hang its blue and red ribbon round his neck. In any case, the King was proud to be the guardian of the Order and took immense care in maintaining its standards of excellence. Thus Stamfordham wrote of the author of *The Golden Bough*: 'You can imagine the difficulty in selecting the *right* people for the OM. For two years and more we have been endeavouring to get a consensus of opinion in Frazer's favour – and on the whole succeeded in doing so.' In 1921, on the suggestion of Balfour and after similarly thorough inquiries, the King proposed that Gilbert Murray, the classical scholar, should be admitted to the Order.

Before the appointment was gazetted, the King followed his usual practice of informing Llord George as a matter of courtesy. To his astonishment, the Prime Minister replied that Murray's name must be withdrawn. He alleged that during the war Murray had been a pacifist 'and almost proGerman', adding that 'it would cause much annoyance to the Unionist Party, who were already in a mood which required to be placated rather than irritated'. The King replied that politics did not enter into the matter and that the Prime Minister had no say in disposing of the Order of Merit. Lloyd George, however, insisted and the King abandoned his proposal rather than risk a constitutional conflict. Murray eventually received the OM from King George VI in 1941.

Two former Prime Ministers, Rosebery and Balfour, privately expressed their sense of outrage that 'the Sovereign's absolute discretion' had been challenged. But it was an isolated episode, and for the rest of the reign the King met with no resistance to his candidates.

The King nevertheless suffered other setbacks in trying to curb the proliferation and preserve the traditions of the orders and decorations awarded in his name. Here he found himself thwarted by successive British Governments anxious to use them as emollients of foreign policy.

Not even the Victoria Cross was exempt. In 1921 the United States spontaneously offered her Medal of Congress to the British Unknown Warrior, who had been buried in Westminster Abbey on 11 November 1920. Then came the burial of the American Unknown Warrior in Arlington Cemetery, Washington. How was the tribute to be reciprocated? Curzon wrote in some trepidation to Stamfordham: 'The Prime Minister thinks very strongly that we shall be forced to strain a point and that no decoration but the VC will suffice.' Stamfordham's long and unyielding reply declared that the King had declined to give the VC even to the British Unknown Warrior. For the statutes of the decoration stated 'that neither rank, nor long service, nor wounds, nor any other circumstance or condition whatsoever, save the merit of conspicuous bravery, shall be held to establish a sufficient claim to the honour'. The letter concluded on a note of *hauteur*:

Further, His Majesty considers that to compare the Victoria Cross, the highest military decoration in the world, as an equivalent to the Congress Medal, which has only now been struck and with no history behind it, is to lose sight of all proportion, even with a view of satisfying political or international susceptibilities.

But as so often when expediency met principle, Lloyd George had his way. On 11 November 1921, the American Unknown Warrior, having earlier been invested with the Victoria Cross by Beatty, was buried in state. Hankey, who attended the ceremony, reported unfavourably on it to the Prime Minister:

It was much too long, with a curious medley of prayers, hymns, long speeches, musical performances by a quartette from the New York Opera, absurd little speeches by Foreign Officers, laying decorations and repeated wreath laying. The finale was a curious function by an old Indian chief dressed up like a picture in one of Fenimore Cooper's books, but I could not see it very well because the lady in front of me had a head dress like the Indian chief's.

A year later, it is sad to relate, at the burial of Belgium's Unknown Warrior, that small nation in whose defence Britain had gone to war in 1914, fared less well than the United States. 'The Military Cross would be quite sufficient for the Belgians,' Stamfordham told the War Office.

There was another exchange of views between the palace and the Foreign Office on the suggested award of the Garter to the Shah of Persia. Both King and Foreign Secretary agreed that the Order should no longer be conferred upon non-Christian sovereigns, in spite of two previous Shahs and two Emperors of Japan having received it. But like his father and his grandmother before him, George V was eventually obliged to break the rule for political ends. In 1929, the Emperor Hirohito became the third of his line to wear the blue riband.

Perhaps the most bizarre of all correspondences about honours for foreigners preceded the King's State visit to Italy in 1923. Would Mussolini be satisfied with the GCMG or must he have the superior GCB? That *chevalier sans peur et sans reproche* emerged from the discussion as an honorary Knight Grand Cross of the Most Honourable Order of the Bath.

Although required to conform to every ministerial whim, the King made only modest demands. Harold Nicolson writes that 'in the masses of documents bearing on the bestowal of honours now stored in the Archives at Windsor . . . only one instance can be found of King George himself writing to ask that an honour be conferred'. That, as we shall see, is not quite true; but the single episode which he quotes is illuminating. In 1930 the King suggested that an inventor of flying boats, E.S. Saunders, who was personally known to him, should receive a knighthood. The Prime Minister's private secretary replied that there were other inventors who had prior claims, and that in any case Downing Street was 'snowed under' with applications. The King minuted on this nonchalant response: 'I only hope that the spade used will be a large one and the snow not too deep. As I so seldom ask for a knighthood, I really think that I might be treated with anyhow some consideration occasionally.'

This shamed Downing Street into a further letter, which Nicolson does not quote. It explained that Saunders, as chairman of a Conservative Association, could not fittingly be rewarded by a Labour Prime Minister, even for aeronautical services.

In fact the King made several such requests over the years, though always sparingly. None was more persistent than his plea for A.J. Bennett's baronetcy; none more emphatic than his demand on behalf of Frederic Kenyon, director of the British Museum. 'I am directed by the King', Knollys wrote to Asquith, 'to say that he must decline to consider the recommendations of the Prime Minister for Honours until the name of Mr. Kenyon is included among them.' Kenyon was made a KCB shortly afterwards.

Medicine and the stage were professions which the King liked to see well rewarded. He was successful in securing immediate knighthoods for Frederic William Hewitt, the anaesthetist, and for Maurice Abbot Anderson, physician and surgeon to the Princess Royal for more than twenty years, a versatile practitioner whose contributions to learned journals included 'Replacement of severed portions of the nose' and 'Foreign bodies in rectum'. But Milsom Rees, laryngologist both to the royal household and to Covent Garden, had to wait five years. The actor George Alexander was similarly knighted at the King's suggestion. Ten years later, Stamfordham consulted H.A.L. Fisher as to whether Gerald du Maurier or Charles Hawtrey was the more deserving; one was the King's choice, the other Lloyd George's. Both received the accolade in 1922. Ben Greet was another actor-manager to be knighted on the King's recommendation. By contrast, Prebendary Carlile, of the Church Army, and General William Booth, of the Salvation Army, each became a Companion of Honour at his behest.

The King could not, however, persuade Lloyd George to ennoble General Sir Charles Monro. Stamfordham wrote of the rebuff:

Had he continued to occupy the position of an Army Commander in France, which he vacated to go to India, he would have received a Peerage and a money grant.... The Prime Minister would not recommend the Peerage; but it is whispered that the opposition came from the Secretary of State for War. It seems to me very unfair.

Stamfordham's surmise was almost certainly correct. Churchill never forgave Monro for having presided over the withdrawal from Gallipoli, writing of him in his *World Crisis*: 'He came, he saw, he capitulated.'

It is Churchill, too, who discerns the fatal flaw in every Honours List. 'A medal glitters,' he told the House of Commons, 'but it also casts a shadow.' For the one hungry sheep that is fed, a hundred look up in vain. Thus it was throughout the reign of King George V. Both the sovereign and his ministers (in varying degree) tried to regulate the flow equitably, but the experience was dispiriting. Their postbags were heavy with the servilities of the aspirant and the reproaches of the frustrated; neither rank nor achievement precluded an appetite at once ravenous and without shame. The sale of titles was contemptible, but it was not alone in poisoning national life. Over the Fountain of Honour hung a perpetual miasma of envy and discontent.

Throughout 1922, Lloyd George had been riding for a fall; and in October he fell. He was in part the victim of events beyond his control: unrest and unemployment at home, enmity and aggression abroad. But his sentimental regard for Greece brought the British Empire to the brink of war with Turkey; and even his Irish settlement, a triumph of subtle and imaginative diplomacy, evoked the mistrust of stolid Conservative colleagues. The Prime Minister's prolonged absences from the Commons, the use of advisers divorced from the public service, the reckless sale of honours to replenish party funds – all strained the Coalition to the point of rupture. Bonar Law might have saved him from the worst of his follies, but in March 1921 he had been obliged by ill health to retire from the Government. On 19 October 1922, Conservative MPs, meeting at the Carlton Club, decided by 187 votes to 87 to withdraw from the Coalition and so regain their independence as a party. Lloyd George at once resigned.

To a sovereign who disliked change, the loss of even so wilful a Prime Minister as Lloyd George was unwelcome. 'I am sorry he is going,' the King wrote. Lloyd George was less generous. More than ten years later, he spoke of kings to his confidante and future wife, Frances Stevenson, claiming that with the possible exception of the King of Serbia there was not one of outstanding strength in Europe. The conversation continues:

I suggested our own, but D[avid] said: 'Quite frankly, he is not a man of strength. He is admirable and reliable, but has never interfered in any emergency, and would not be capable of doing so should any emergency arise.' . . . There were just two or three pillars one regarded as being bulwarks against trouble – Mussolini, & the King of the Belgians amongst them, (& incidentally he is not a Belgian, said D). D. regards Hitler as a very great man.

The King would not have been dismayed by his supposed inferiority to Mussolini and Hitler.

Lloyd George's resignation brought three new Prime Ministers to office within fifteen months, each successive change involving the King in a different constitutional problem. The first and least of the difficulties was to find a man who would carry on the Government until the ensuing general election had revealed the strength of each party. On Bonar Law's retirement in 1921, Austen Chamberlain had been elected to succeed him as leader of the Conservatives within the Coalition. But at the Carlton Club meeting, Chamberlain remained loyal to Lloyd George, thus consigning himself to the political wilderness in common with Balfour and Birkenhead. 'He always played the game,' Birkenhead said of him, 'and he always lost.' Chamberlain's self-sacrifice left Bonar Law as the obvious candidate for the vacant premiership. Yet when consulted by Stamfordham, he seemed unwilling to accept it. Although his health had mended enough for him to attend the Carlton Club meeting and to vote with reluctance against Lloyd George, he pleaded that he was no longer leader of the Conservatives. This was swiftly remedied, and he kissed hands as Prime Minister on 23 October. The general election in the following month gave 344 seats to a united Conservative party. Labour doubled its representation to 138. The Asquithian Liberals won 60 seats and the followers of Lloyd George only 57.

'I once confessed to him', wrote Austen Chamberlain of Bonar Law, 'that I had made many attempts to read Gibbon's *Decline and Fall*, but had never succeeded in persevering to the end. He was astonished, and declared at once that he found that great procession of ambitious men, realizing their ambitions only to be cheated of their hopes, the most fascinating of all studies.' It is a far cry from those sybaritic tyrants to the abstemious Glasgow merchant whose wildest extravagance was a game of chess. Yet nothing in Gibbon eclipses the tragedy of his own career. Prime Minister at last, he was struck down by cancer of the throat. His tenure of office lasted no more than 209 days.

Although unspectacular, the new premiership exactly suited the mood of a nation at first bewitched and inspired, later exhausted and disillusioned by Lloyd George's dynamic leadership. Bonar Law saw his task as returning the country to the traditional methods of government. 'I confess frankly', he told the Carlton Club meeting, 'that in the immediate crisis in front of us, I do personally attach more importance to keeping our party united than to winning the next election.' He similarly determined to revive the practice of Cabinet responsibility which had atrophied under Lloyd George's near-presidential regime; and to dissolve that circle of unofficial advisers known as the 'Garden Suburb' which had acted independently of, and sometimes in opposition to, the foreign policy pursued by Lord Curzon. This reversion to familiar ways pleased the King, who had long forgiven Bonar Law his misguided advice over Home Rule. Mutual respect never broadened into warmth, much less intimacy; but it was with genuine sorrow that on 20 May 1923 the King received his Prime Minister's resignation. He at once wrote to Bonar Law:

I wish to express my heartfelt appreciation and gratitude for the patriotism and self-sacrifice which you evinced last autumn in consenting to take up the very responsible position of Prime Minister at a time of exceptional difficulties. Your having done so was of the greatest personal assistance to me.

I earnestly trust that with absolute rest and freedom from worry your health may be completely restored.

That same Sunday, the King prepared to exercise the most important of his prerogatives: the appointment of a new Prime Minister. Half a century later in such circumstances, the sovereign would await the election of a new party leader, then entrust the victor with office. In 1923 King George was denied so smooth a procedure; the choice was his alone.

The forty-eight hours that he took to reach a decision are among the most melodramatic in British political history, well chronicled, too, yet retaining elements of mystery. The death sentence passed on Bonar Law by his doctors; the ferment of speculation about his successor; the contest between Curzon and Baldwin, between an experienced but imperious Foreign Secretary in the Lords and a callow but amiable Chancellor of the Exchequer in the Commons; the attempt by Bonar Law's secretary to mislead the King as to the late Prime Minister's preference; the conflicting advice of Balfour, who recommended Baldwin, and of Salisbury, who recommended Curzon; Baldwin's humble readiness to serve under Curzon; Curzon's confident wait in Somerset for the royal telegram that would summon him to London and its leisurely delivery by a policeman on a bicycle (not even the Foreign Secretary thought it necessary in 1923 to have a telephone in his country house); the rapturous journey to Paddington; the almost unanimous newspaper forecasts in Curzon's favour; the seeming certainty of the premiership when the King's private secretary arrived at Carlton House Terrace; the catastrophic news that, even as Stamfordham spoke words of consolation, the scarcely considered Baldwin was being asked to form a new Government: such was the tragi-comedy directed and played out by its royal protagonist.

'Bonar Law's resignation', the King wrote in his diary, 'places me in a very difficult position as it is not easy to make up my mind whether to send for Curzon or Baldwin.' The task was complicated by three extraneous factors. The first was that the King and Queen were committed to spending a week at the Royal Pavilion, Aldershot, an unpretentious though comfortable wooden bungalow with a fine garden and a thick belt of fir trees to screen it from the sights and sounds of the largest garrison in the United Kingdom. Although only thirty-seven miles from London, the King decided to remain amid his rhododendrons and his azaleas. So Stamfordham returned alone to Buckingham Palace, reporting the results of his investigations by telephone.

The second difficulty was that Bonar Law resigned on the Sunday of a Whitsuntide weekend, when almost every Conservative politician had disappeared to the country until the following Tuesday morning. Stamfordham therefore had to search far and wide for the two statesmen he most wanted to consult on the King's behalf. Salisbury, leader of the House of Lords, trundled up from Devon in the guard's van of a milk train, declining to abandon the frock coat and tall hat he thought proper for the transaction of State business. Balfour, the only surviving Conservative Prime Minister other than Bonar Law, was similarly summoned from Norfolk, although suffering from phlebitis.

Finally, the King was handicapped in seeking a new Prime Minister by Bonar Law's unwillingness to declare a preference for either Curzon or Baldwin. Desperately ill, with only five months to live, he could not make the journey to Aldershot to take leave of the King. Instead, on that Sunday morning, he sent his private secretary, Colonel Ronald Waterhouse, and his son-in-law, Sir Frederick Sykes, with a letter of resignation.

It was not the only document they carried. Stamfordham, who placed much trust in the political sagacity of Davidson, Bonar Law's parliamentary private secretary, had asked him by telephone on either the Saturday or the Sunday for his personal opinion on the vacant premiership. This Davidson embodied in a hastily dictated memorandum which Waterhouse promised to hand to Stamfordham.

It was a cogent and sustained argument designed to press Baldwin's case at the expense of his rival. Curzon's experience of high office, his grasp of international affairs, his industry and mental equipment: all were summarized in a few lines. Then Davidson elaborated on the contrast between Curzon's failure to inspire complete confidence in his colleagues, either in judgement or strength of purpose in a crisis, and Baldwin's honesty, simplicity and balance. 'Lord Curzon', he continued, 'is regarded in the

public eye as representing that section of privileged conservatism which has
its value, but which in this democratic age cannot be too assiduously
exploited.' Turning from personalities to practical politics, Davidson em-
phasized that five of the six Secretaries of State already sat in the Upper
House, and that for a Prime Minister also to direct Government policy
from the Lords would be 'most strongly resented, not only by the Conservative party as a whole, but by every shade of democratic opinion in the
country'.

Since Davidson's memorandum came down decisively in favour of Baldwin, and since Baldwin was the ultimate choice of the King, it has sometimes
been assumed that those few typewritten sheets sealed Curzon's fate. There
is another reason why undue importance has been attached to Davidson's
memorandum. Waterhouse, it seems, was not content to be a mere messen-
ger. Although Davidson had not shown him the memorandum before
sealing it or told him of its contents, Waterhouse informed Stamfordham
that it 'practically expressed the views of Bonar Law': words which the
meticulous Stamfordham inscribed on the original envelope. Historians
may thus be forgiven for surmising that Waterhouse's unfounded assertion
had after all enabled the King to elicit Bonar Law's preference for Baldwin;
and that this had weighed heavily with him in his choice of a new Prime
Minister.

Perhaps Waterhouse had spoken as he did from self-importance; or
perhaps, knowing Davidson's likely views on the succession, he had seized
an opportunity of using them to further the cause of his friend Baldwin. It
is unnecessary to speculate. In later years Davidson declared: 'Even if
Waterhouse did misrepresent my memorandum, this can have had no
influence upon Stamfordham.' The King's private secretary had asked for
the memorandum, knew from whom it came and whose mind it reflected.

With habitual caution, Stamfordham nevertheless invited Waterhouse to
a second meeting at which he questioned him closely about Bonar Law's
supposed opinion of the rival candidates. Once more Waterhouse claimed
that Bonar Law would have favoured the selection of Baldwin. There is,
however, independent evidence to show that Waterhouse possessed neither
the knowledge nor the authority to make such a statement. His bona fides
need detain us no longer, for the King had already made up his mind that
the new Prime Minister, irrespective of personal qualities, must be answer-
able to the House of Commons. At least twelve hours before his second
interview with Waterhouse, Stamfordham confided this conclusion to Geoffrey Dawson, who had recently succeeded Wickham Steed as editor of *The
Times*. Stamfordham's record of the conversation reads:

I told Dawson frankly that the King was so far convinced that his responsibility to
the country made it almost imperative that he should appoint a Prime Minister

from the House of Commons. For were he not to do so, and the experiment failed, the country would blame the King for an act which was entirely his own and which proved that the King was ignorant of, and out of touch with the public.

No man played a more decisive part than Balfour in clarifying the King's mind. During his two interviews with Stamfordham on 21 May, he dwelt on the problems that would face a Prime Minister who sat in the House of Lords. One was the unusually high proportion of Cabinet appointments already held by peers. Another was the resentment that would be felt by the House of Commons if this trend were extended to include the Prime Minister. A third was the hostility to be encountered from the Labour Party; for although Labour held a majority of Opposition seats in the Commons, they were virtually unrepresented in the Lords and thus would be unable to question or challenge a Prime Minister who sat there.

Winston Churchill later described in *Great Contemporaries* Balfour's return to Norfolk to resume his convalescence. 'And will dear George be chosen?' a friend asked him. 'No,' he replied, 'dear George will not.' The implication of this mischievous story is that Balfour had deliberately framed his arguments to exclude Curzon from the premiership. If so, he went to remarkable lengths to disguise his antipathy. Stamfordham's record of their discussion includes this passage:

Lord Balfour said he was speaking regardless of the individuals in question, for whereas, on one side his opinion of Lord Curzon is based upon an intimate life-long friendship, and the recognition of his exceptional qualifications; on the other, his knowledge of Mr. Baldwin is slight and, so far, his public career has been more or less uneventful and without any signs of special gifts or exceptional ability.

There will nevertheless always be those who prefer to interpret political history in terms of personal intrigue; who attribute Curzon's downfall not to the needs of the constitution but to his own flaws of temperament. Certainly he could be overbearing and inconsiderate towards his colleagues. Only a month earlier, Lord Winchester, a financier of doubtful reputation, had written to the Prime Minister about a loan to Turkey which he hoped to float before the conclusion of the peace treaty. Bonar Law correctly passed the letter to Curzon for his comments, only to receive a blistering rebuke for having even entered into correspondence with Winchester. 'When these persons go to No. 10 instead of here,' the Foreign Secretary wrote, 'they are really reproducing one of the least admirable features of the L.G. regime.' Mortally ill and deeply wounded by Curzon's insulting reply, Bonar Law could scarcely be expected to recommend him as his successor four weeks later.

It could be argued that the King, too, had every reason to dread Curzon's claim to the premiership. During his first visit to India in 1905 he had been shocked to hear of Curzon's unpardonable rudeness to the new Viceroy, Lord Minto. Since then Curzon had censoriously opposed the transfer of the Indian capital from Calcutta to Delhi and the building of the new city, bold and visionary acts to which the King-Emperor had personally dedicated himself. 'Lord Curzon will no doubt continue to be hostile,' he wrote sorrowfully to Queen Alexandra, 'but then it is impossible to please him and after all he is not everybody.'

There exists a minute of October 1915 in which Stamfordham reports to the King that a senior civil servant thinks Curzon would make a much better Prime Minister than Asquith. 'I know Your Majesty will not concur in this opinion,' he adds. Equally significant is the King's complaint two years later that Curzon would be a more effective minister if his speeches were not over the heads of the public. As post-war Foreign Secretary, Curzon did not spare even Stamfordham those elaborate reproaches with which he would denounce the failings of his Cabinet colleagues. There was, for instance, the occasion when the King, at the request of the French ambassador, agreed to receive Poincaré at Buckingham Palace. Curzon, who thought the former French President both devious and anglophobe, addressed a long remonstrance to Stamfordham, of which this is but a sample:

I cannot help thinking that the French Ambassador had no right to apply to The King in this matter except through the Secretary of State. And would it not have been more in accordance with precedent if, before The King decided to grant the audience, you had sent me a line to tell me what were the views of His Majesty?

Stamfordham, nettled by the tone rather than the content of Curzon's letter, was not to be browbeaten. He replied:

It never occurred to me that the question should be referred to you before replying to Saint-Aulaire's letter. In my recollection of more than 40 years, I can frankly say that such requests, made by the Ambassador direct to the Sovereign, have invariably been dealt with without reference to the Foreign Office.

Such exchanges could not fail to leave an impression on both the King and Stamfordham of a temperament unsuited to the highest office of all. Sir Walter Lawrence, Curzon's private secretary in India and later a friend of the King's, assured his old master that the King regarded him with admiration and respect, but also with a certain awe. That is not entirely true. With growing confidence, the King had come to regard his Foreign Secretary's foibles with a humorous eye. Confined to bed one day in 1923 by a painful back, Curzon asked to be excused an audience at Buckingham Palace that evening. The King replied that he would instead come round to

Carlton House Terrace, just as the German Emperor used to visit the British ambassador in his pyjamas. Curzon absolutely refused, preferring to keep his appointment at the palace. 'To tell the truth,' he wrote to his wife, 'I knew the King well enough to be sure that even though he came in his great good nature, he would make a fine story of it afterwards.'

Whether holding Curzon in awe or in affectionate derision, the King would never have allowed a clouded personal relationship to affect a momentous constitutional duty, or purported to confine the office of Prime Minister to the Commons in order to exclude an able but prickly peer. The alternative is to accept that the King and his senior ex-Prime Minister entered into a conspiracy on behalf of Baldwin: a man for whom neither had a good word to say except that he sat in the Commons rather than in the Lords. So far-fetched a theory also demands that this letter, sent by Stamfordham to Balfour two days after Curzon's rejection, was written only to deceive posterity:

It is a matter of satisfaction to the King that you, with your exceptional experience of a long Parliamentary career and of the office of Prime Minister, should have confirmed his opinion that, at all events in the present circumstances, the Prime Minister of this country should be in the House of Commons.

That, in short, was the King's honest opinion, shared naturally enough by Labour and the Liberals, but also by most Conservatives. The only dissenting voice of importance came from Lord Salisbury, who urged that Curzon's long record of public service should not be disregarded. Perhaps he was also moved by family loyalty, for his father had been the last Prime Minister to sit in the Upper House. But Balfour, old Lord Salisbury's nephew, put on record that even at the turn of the century the arrangement would have failed to work efficiently had he not, as leader of the Commons, kept his uncle in touch with the latest currents of opinion.

More recent critics of the King's decision have pointed out how nearly Lord Halifax was preferred to Winston Churchill on Neville Chamberlain's resignation in May 1940. They are refuted by Halifax himself, who at the time laid 'considerable emphasis on the difficult position of a Prime Minister unable to make contact with the centre of gravity in the House of Commons'. He also wrote: 'I should speedily become a more or less honorary Prime Minister, living in a kind of twilight just outside the things that really matter.'

If in 1923 the King had misgivings about rejecting Curzon, it was not because he doubted the constitutional wisdom of his decision but because he realized how deeply it would wound Curzon's pride. That was why he instructed Stamfordham to summon Curzon to London, to be told of his

fate before it became public knowledge. During the painful scene that
ensued at Carlton House Terrace, Curzon protested vigorously against the
principle implied in his exclusion, that no member of the House of Lords
could ever be Prime Minister; and he told Stamfordham that as part of his
protest he would retire from public life, making clear to the country his
reason for doing so. Later that afternoon Stamfordham reported the conversation to the King, who had driven up from Aldershot to receive Baldwin
at the palace and offer him the premiership. Two laconic entries in the
King's diary dispose of Curzon's threat to resign:

22 May 1923. He was much upset and disappointed as of course he wanted to be
P.M. himself and he says he will retire into private life and his career is at an end.
We shall see. I much regret having hurt his feelings.

23 May 1923. I hear that Curzon is going to remain at the F.O. which I am very
glad of. He has changed his mind since yesterday.

On 29 May, the King sent for Curzon to soothe his pride and explain his
rejection. 'The interview was quite pleasant,' the King wrote, 'and he was
very nice in spite of what took place last week.' The kindliness of the King's
character glows in every line of the record kept by Stamfordham:

Today the King saw Lord Curzon and expressed his feelings of admiration and
gratitude for the very generous and patriotic manner in which Lord Curzon had
accepted the decision come to by His Majesty to appoint Mr Baldwin as Prime
Minister, which the King more than realised must have been a terrible disappointment: and at the same time His Majesty wished to express his appreciation of the
admirable and chivalrous speeches which Lord Curzon had made at the first
Cabinet, when he welcomed Mr Baldwin as Prime Minister, and also at the
Meeting of the Conservative Party on Monday, 28th May.
    The King told him that he was sure the whole country shared His Majesty's
views and also admired the wholehearted manner in which he had given his support
to Mr Baldwin, to whom Lord Curzon's continuance in the Office of Foreign
Minister was of the utmost importance and support.
    His Majesty further dwelt upon the very deep regret which he had experienced
in coming to a decision which, while he believed it to be the right one, nevertheless
he knew would be hurting to Lord Curzon, whom he had known for some 35 years
and regarded as an old friend, while his personal acquaintance with Mr Baldwin
was that of having met and spoken to him on a few recent occasions.

Stamfordham's account of the conversation does omit one theme, which
the King repeated to Neville Chamberlain two days later:

CURZON: 'Am I to understand then, Sir, that you consider that no peer can ever
be Prime Minister?'
KING: 'No, I didn't say that. What I said was that there were circumstances in

which it was very undesirable that a peer should be Prime Minister and in my view this was such a case.'

CURZON: 'But then what about the Foreign Secretary. He is almost as important as the Prime Minister, particularly in these days. How is it I can be a peer and Foreign Secretary at the same time without your objecting?'

KING: 'Because the Prime Minister is responsible for everything you do.'

No professor of constitutional law and practice could have put it more neatly.

Curzon appreciated the King's sympathy, but continued to brood over his misfortune. Walter Lawrence fed his resentment by claiming that he had heard members of the royal household tell untrue and malicious stories about him, and that if only Curzon had enlisted his help, he could have dissuaded the King from sending for Baldwin: an absurd boast, yet not unwelcome to Curzon's ears. Curzon also came to believe that Salisbury and Derby had played an important part in denying him the premiership. That too was remote from the truth. Salisbury had been one of his few champions. And Derby, although he loathed Curzon, had not even been consulted; his only role was to record a muddled and inaccurate account of the episode which, printed in his biography by Randolph Churchill, has subsequently misled other students of history.

The King had preferred Baldwin to Curzon for one reason alone: that he sat in the House of Commons. The new Prime Minister's ability and judgement were to be taken on trust. He had been in the Cabinet for little more than two years and Chancellor of the Exchequer for only a few months. Even during that brief spell at the Treasury, he had annoyed the King. After negotiating a settlement of the American debt, Baldwin had publicly pronounced the average Senator and Congressman to be a 'hick from way back'. When the King remonstrated with the Prime Minister, Bonar Law replied: 'I am very sorry that His Majesty should have noticed Mr. Baldwin's remarks to the Press. They were intended of course for consumption at home and he fully realises the harm they may have done in America.'

That inept reply did not satisfy the King. 'I don't see how I could very well help noticing the remarks,' he commented, 'as I always read the papers. ... I fear the harm is done and the Congress will be very annoyed and no wonder.'

Baldwin nevertheless became Prime Minister a few weeks later, and might have remained so for the next four years but for one of the most spectacular miscalculations in British political history. After scarcely five months at No. 10, he asked the King for a dissolution of Parliament in order to fight a general election on tariff reform. Some believed that he wanted to forestall a similar appeal to the country by Lloyd George, others that he

wished to drive the free traders out of the Government to make room for
Austen Chamberlain and Birkenhead. Such manœuvres did not concern
the King, who brought a wider perspective to events. He wrote of his
attempts to dissuade Baldwin:

I then pointed out to him that I strongly deprecated a dissolution at this moment
as I had implicit confidence in him and in the Conservative Party now in power,
and I considered that as most countries in Europe, if not in the world, were in a
chaotic and indeed dangerous state, it would be a pity if this Country were to be
plunged into the turmoil of a General Election on a question of domestic policy
which will arouse all the old traditional bitterness of the hard fought battles
between Protection and Free Trade: also that it was quite possible that his majority
might be reduced, or that he might not get a majority at all.

I was therefore prepared to take the responsibility of advising him to change his
mind, and I was also prepared for him to tell his friends that I had done so.

He answered that he had gone too far now and that the Country expected a
dissolution; he would appeal to the Country at once, and he hoped to get the
General Election over by about the 6th December, and he was ready to stand or
fall by the result.

That result, announced on 8 December 1923, justified the King's warning. The Conservatives lost nearly ninety seats, and with them their overall
majority. Britain stood on the brink of her first Labour Government.
Curzon, who had strenuously opposed the Prime Minister's reckless electoral gamble, did not lay the blame on him alone. 'This', he wrote, 'is the
price that we all have to pay for the utter incompetence of Baldwin and for
the madness of his selection by the King.'

The King was unadventurous in his friendships. Landowners of ancient
lineage and impeccable deportment, old shipmates, trusted members of his
own household: these were the men with whom he shot and raced and
sailed and occasionally dined. He also enjoyed the company of Archbishop
Lang, Rudyard Kipling (alone among men of letters) and Lord Revelstoke,
the partner in Baring Brothers who looked after his private finances.

Only a very few of his father's intimates survived into the new reign,
sometimes more from royal charity than affection: Sister Agnes, Lord
Esher, Albert Mensdorff and the Marquis de Soveral. Among them was
Lord Farquhar, in writing to whom the King would begin, 'My dear
Horace,' and end, 'Your sincere old friend, G.R.I.' Courtly and genial, he
seemed to epitomize both the financial probity of the City of London and
the open-handed hospitality of the country gentleman. The truth, as it
eventually emerged, was more bizarre.

Horace Farquhar was born in 1844, the fifth son of a baronet descended from Sir Walter Farquhar, physician to the Prince Regent. The family was of modest means but well connected. One of Horace's cousins was married to Charles Grey, Queen Victoria's first private secretary; another to Evelyn Ashley, private secretary to Lord Palmerston and Mr Gladstone, and the grandfather of Edwina Mountbatten. Farquhar began his career as a clerk in a Government office, then (according to his contemporary, Lord Huntly), 'dark-haired and good-looking, with plenty of assurance and push, he became acquainted with the Forbeses and, leaving the service, wormed himself into the house of Sir Charles Forbes & Co., India merchants'.

In 1883 he joined the small but respected banking house of Sir Samuel Scott, Bart. & Co., a connection which brought him both a substantial fortune and a wife, the widow of Sir Edward Scott. He acquired a predominant place in the bank by persuading his friend the Earl of Fife to invest in his care the considerable proceeds of land sales in Morayshire and Banffshire. In 1894 Scott's merged with Parr's Bank, on the board of which Farquhar remained for the next twenty-one years.

He used his money astutely. 'Dined last night with Horace Farquhar,' Edward Hamilton, another of Mr Gladstone's private secretaries, wrote in 1883, 'the best dinner in London.' Judicious gifts to the Conservative Party brought him a baronetcy. It was followed in 1898 by a peerage, after he had spent only three years as MP for West Marylebone. The distinction came as no surprise to him; as he confessed to Hamilton, he had subscribed more than the 'accepted tariff'.

Lord Fife, meanwhile, had in 1889 married the eldest daughter of the Prince of Wales and was created a duke. He brought his friend into the intimacy of the royal circle. On the death of Queen Victoria, King Edward VII appointed Farquhar to be Master of the Household and in 1907 would have promoted him to be Lord Steward had not Campbell-Bannerman insisted that what was then a political office should be filled by a Liberal. Farquhar was consoled with a Privy Counsellorship and appointed to be an extra lord-in-waiting to the King. Attendance at Court did not preclude either his continuing on the board of Parr's Bank or even his more adventurous operations on the Stock Exchange. Lord Lincolnshire wrote in his diary in February 1907:

A Siberian gold-mining company has been formed by some Jew speculators. Francis Knollys, Lord Stanley, Lord Howe, Sir West Ridgeway and others accepted directorships, and the shares were rushed up to £16. They have gone down with a rattle, and Horace Farquhar is said to have netted £70,000. He is supposed to have secured all those names, and the papers are open-mouthed at this scandal. It is deplorable that the King's private secretary and the Queen's Lord Chamberlain should have been 'let in' and mixed up in an affair like this.

If the future King George V knew of the scandal, it did not affect his regard for Farquhar, with whom he had shot in Norfolk for the past twenty years. On ascending the throne in 1910 he reappointed him to be a lord-in-waiting, and on the day he was crowned, accepted from him a portrait of the late King. Farquhar well knew how to choose imaginative presents. Little Prince Henry proved as fortunate as his father in receiving 'a nice box of soldiers with tents, both red and white'. Not even the war could curb his opulence; Asquith wrote after dining with him in March 1915:

A regular banquet of many courses, of which I only partook of about two. . . .
H. F. told me that a necklace of pearls which he gave his wife 20 or 30 years ago, having paid about £7,000 for it, is now worth from £40,000 to £45,000. Isn't this a rather disgusting form of unearned increment? – for it only goes to the very rich. I was pleased – in such an environment – to get out of Bridge with a loss of only 15/-.

The Prime Minister nevertheless appointed him to be Lord Steward of the Household three months later, and in 1917 he became a viscount. Sacrifice he left to others. After he had managed to have his valet exempted from military service, a fellow courtier wrote of him: 'Farquhar says the man is necessary and indispensable to keep him alive – indeed a service of national benefit.'

So into the years of peace, which found Farquhar rather more splendidly housed than were most members of the royal family. In addition to No. 7 Grosvenor Square, he took a lease from the Crown on White Lodge, Richmond Park, Queen Mary's old home. His country seat was Castle Rising, near Sandringham, sub-let to him by the King, who had taken a lease on both the house and the shooting from the owners of the estate. 'In an experience of forty years and more,' Lord Sandhurst, the Lord Chamberlain, wrote of a London ball given by the Farquhars, 'I never saw a better or better class entertainment – all the pretty people and all looking their best.' At one such dance in Grosvenor Square, Lady Elizabeth Bowes-Lyon met Prince Albert, Duke of York, for the first time since a children's party in 1905. It marked the beginning of their courtship; three years later, Farquhar lent them White Lodge in which to spend their first months of married life. And still the honours came. In 1922 he received both the Grand Cross of the Bath and an earldom.

By now, however, his conduct at court was thought to be decidedly eccentric. Although his office of Lord Steward had in recent years become little more than a sinecure (its duties transferred to a permanent official, the Master of the Household), Farquhar insisted on meddling in palace matters for which he had no responsibility. His skirmishes with the Duke of Atholl, who in 1921 had succeeded Lord Sandhurst in the parallel office of Lord

Chamberlain, caused particular scandal. The exact boundaries between the two departments had in the early years of Queen Victoria's reign outraged her husband's reforming spirit; he discovered, for instance, that whereas it was the Lord Steward who laid the fire, only the Lord Chamberlain could light it. By the nineteen-twenties, such demarcation disputes had generally been resolved. The Lord Steward, through the Master of the Household, was responsible for the domestic routine of the royal palaces; the Lord Chamberlain was responsible for all official occasions such as courts, levées, garden parties, receptions, investitures and State visits. The Lord Chamberlain also supervised the structure of the palaces in co-operation with the Office of Works, and was the intermediary between the sovereign and both the House of Lords and the Diplomatic Corps.

One facet of their relationship had never been satisfactorily resolved: who took precedence on ceremonial occasions. By an Act of Parliament of Henry VIII, it seemed to be the Lord Steward; but a recent committee appointed by King George to report on the administration of his household recognized that the far heavier burden of duties borne by the Lord Chamberlain entitled him to prevail. So determined was Farquhar to maintain the ancient supremacy of his office that he took to turning up at Buckingham Palace and claiming precedence over the Lord Chamberlain, even at functions where his presence was neither commanded nor required. A week before the wedding of Princess Mary in 1922, the Duke of Atholl wrote that he feared Farquhar might literally push him out of the way at the ceremony, as he had done before. That master of pageantry Lord Curzon was asked by the King to investigate the conflicting claims of the Lord Steward and the Lord Chamberlain, but his long and eloquent report was indecisive. The King, always indulgent towards Farquhar, granted him personal precedence, a settlement in which Atholl generously acquiesced as long as Farquhar ceased to interfere. Both Stamfordham and Ponsonby, however, were enraged by Farquhar's unseemly self-importance and de-lighted to see the end of his tenure as Lord Steward on the fall of the Lloyd George Government in October 1922. At Stamfordham's insistence, it was made clear that the earldom for which Lloyd George had recommended Farquhar was for political services, not a recognition of his years at court.

Darker shadows were already falling across his reputation. Only a few weeks before Lloyd George's defeat at the general election, Lord Lincoln-shire wrote of his alleged sale of honours: 'Horace Farquhar, who has a bad reputation in the City, is said to be the prime mover in this dirty business. Astor, who was made a viscount, paid £40,000 a year to the party funds through Horace till the day of his death.' As Treasurer of the Conservative Party, Farquhar had handled large sums of money properly subscribed for political purposes. In the early days of 1923, however, it emerged that he had diverted to Lloyd George's funds donations intended for the Conservative Party. Throughout the six years of the Lloyd George Coalition and the suspension of party strife between the Lloyd George Liberals and the Conservatives, it was admittedly not always easy to say into which account such gifts should be paid. At the same time there was no fusion of the two funds, and Farquhar ought to have been able to account for every penny which had passed through his hands. This he was unable to do.

The new Prime Minister, Bonar Law, who had brought the precise mind of the Glasgow merchant into politics, was disturbed by such disorder. From a senior member of the party he heard another version of the transactions between Farquhar and the late Lord Astor: that Astor had given him £200,000 to do exactly what he liked with. Of this sum, Farquhar claimed to have given £40,000 to a charity in which the King was interested and to have divided the rest between Conservative Party funds and those of Lloyd George. It could only be surmised why Astor, who in 1917 had received a viscounty from Lloyd George a mere fifteen months after his barony, should have placed such exceptional confidence in Farquhar; or indeed why Farquhar himself should have received two steps in the peerage on Lloyd George's recommendation. What concerned Bonar Law was that the £40,000 supposedly destined for Conservative funds could not be traced. Nor was it the only instance of Farquhar's imperfect book-keeping. In March 1923, the Prime Minister dismissed him as Treasurer of the Conservative Party.

Farquhar defended himself publicly. 'His position', it was announced in *The Times*, 'has always been one of difficulty and delicacy, inasmuch as he personally collected large sums, much of which was subscribed, and was expressed to be subscribed, for Coalition purposes.' However incomplete that explanation, Farquhar's failure to account for the money entrusted to him by Astor and others was not necessarily discreditable. Ill health throughout the early nineteen-twenties had evidently impaired both his memory and his ability to transact business. Lincolnshire described him as 'semi-idiotic', Bonar Law as 'gaga'. The King gave him the benefit of every doubt. He and Queen Mary dined in Grosvenor Square in May and called on their old friend for the last time in August, two weeks before Farquhar's death in his eightieth year.

Farquhar's Will was long and grandiose, his bequests many and generous, as befitted an estate provisionally sworn at £400,000 in the currency of 1923. The King was left two Louis Quatorze castors, together with anything he cared to choose from the contents of Castle Rising; the Queen, a Louis Seize commode, together with the contents of White Lodge. For Queen Alexandra there was a *sang de boeuf* vase, and for Princess Victoria

two Dresden quails. The family of Farquhar's business partner, the Duke
of Fife, who had died in 1912, were remembered with especial bounty. The
Duke's widow, styled the Princess Royal since 1905, had been well provided
for by her rich husband, so was left only two or three *objets d'art*. Her two
children, both daughters, fared better. Princess Maud was to receive a
diamond necklace as well as £50,000, unless she had already married, when
the same sum would go to her husband. Princess Arthur of Connaught was
also to have a diamond necklace, together with the contents of No. 7
Grosvenor Square and the residue of Farquhar's property not otherwise
bequeathed.

Nor were friends of lesser rank forgotten. Forty-eight of them, their
names a roll-call of the aristocracy, were each to receive £200 with which
to buy a memento. Among them were Stamfordham and Wigram; but
Wigram was to have an additional £3,000. Farquhar was childless. There
were, however, bequests to his kinsmen and generous provision for his
servants.

Informed by Wigram of their joint good fortune, the King congratulated
his assistant private secretary on a timely windfall that would more than
cover the expenses of his wife's recent illness; but he doubted whether
Farquhar's estate would realize the reported total of £400,000. The King
was more discerning than he could possibly have imagined. The fortune
made by banking and on the Stock Exchange; the proceeds of his philanthropic enterprises on behalf of Lloyd George and the Conservative Party
(if indeed they had failed to reach their intended destinations); those lavishly
bequeathed riches, those splendidly furnished houses: all were engulfed by
huge and unsuspected debts. Rumour had it that Farquhar, always a patron
of the stage, had invested recklessly in the theatres of London and Paris at
a time of depressed conditions. Whether by speculation or extravagance,
the net value of his estate was nil. Not one of his legatees received so much
as a silver matchbox or a penny piece.

Even that was not the end of the matter. It emerged in the following year
that Farquhar's trusteeship of the Fife estates had been exercised as irre-
sponsibly as his guardianship of Conservative funds, and that £80,000 of
trust money had disappeared. The law, unsentimental in such matters,
required his co-trustee, the Princess Royal, to refund the sum. 'She is', as
Lincolnshire noted, 'open-mouthed in consequence.' On 18 July 1924, she
raised part of the imposition by selling some family portraits at Christie's.

Misfortune has since continued to cloud Farquhar's memory. It will be
remembered that he did not own Castle Rising, but originally took it on a
lease from a member of the Howard family. This lease was later acquired
by the King, who, wanting to retain only the shooting rights, sub-let the
house to Farquhar. When the Howards repossessed Castle Rising after his

death, they noticed that a fine picture by Crome which they had not troubled to remove on first letting the house, had been re-hung high up on its wall. It was therefore not until some years later that the picture was brought down to be cleaned. Expert examination revealed it to be a copy.

EIGHT

HOME LIFE

Marble halls — Family circle — Sports and pastimes

'THERE are arguments for not having a Court,' wrote Bagehot, 'and there are arguments for having a splendid Court; but there are no arguments for having a mean Court.' This the King accepted, however much he would have preferred to live quietly in the country with his family. Although wartime austerity could not be ended overnight, there was a symbolic unsealing of the cellar doors at Buckingham Palace on 11 November 1918. Within three or four years, a sustained fall in the cost of living, the supplementary income from the Duchy of Lancaster and certain household economies enabled the King to revive much of the pre-war pageantry, ceremonial and hospitality which his role demanded. He was not an impresario like his father; but he did have a sense of occasion. The result was more memorable than he cared to admit.

Sometimes it must have seemed as if the age of Marie Antoinette had dawned again; before the State visit of the King and Queen of the Belgians in 1921, a dancing master was summoned to rehearse the Dukes of Northumberland and Abercorn in a quadrille. Those feathers and trains which Wigram would have abolished as impediments to progress reappeared in profusion at evening courts. Ladies of more mature years enhanced their beauty with whole galaxies of diamonds; yet none outshone the Queen's massive treasure trove, carried as gracefully as her train, of embroidered gold and silver thread eight feet long. The King had been less well endowed by nature; but he too, his kindly dignity buttressed by the tailor's art, was worthy of all the grandeur that monarchy can command.

Such perfection of stagecraft was occasionally enlivened by bizarre accidents and even egalitarian defiance. The Lord Chamberlain was unable to announce the name of one young lady about to be presented; in a fit of nerves, she had chewed her namecard into illegibility. And a United States ambassador let it be known that he would not compromise his reputation for independence by wearing the prescribed black knee-breeches. The

Prince of Wales, more tolerant of the New World than was his father, offered to mediate. He suggested that the ambassador should emerge from his embassy wearing evening trousers over his knee-breeches; these he would remove in a changing-room at the Palace, thus meeting the demands of both republicanism and monarchy. The ambassador spurned the subterfuge. 'Papa will not be pleased,' the Queen observed, 'what a pity such a distinguished man should be so difficult.' A later American ambassador also turned up at an evening court in trousers, although he had worn knee-breeches when staying at Windsor. 'We are making discreet inquiries,' Wigram noted anxiously. But when a newly arrived envoy from Soviet Russia asked the Kremlin whether he should wear knee-breeches at Buckingham Palace, he received the reply: 'If necessary you will wear petticoats.'

Such attire would certainly have been discouraged at the King's levées, those assemblies which offered loyal subjects their traditional right of access to the sovereign. They were confined to men only. In the absence of feminine allurement, the King found consolation in the gradual reappearance of an Army clad in scarlet and gold after years of workmanlike khaki. It filled the King, Stamfordham wrote, 'with feelings of delight which I can hardly describe'. The spectacle also attracted the young Chicago-born Henry Channon, who in 1923 arranged to have himself presented at a levée. He wrote of it in his sprightly diary:

It is a gorgeous male sight a levée . . . much preening and red and plumes and pomp and tightly fitting tunics and splendid English faces. We were in the queue for over an hour. Freddie Anstruther was next to me dressed as Hereditary Grand Carver of Scotland. Suddenly I heard Lord Cromer call out 'Mr Channon to be presented'. I advanced a few paces with as much dignity as possible and, in front of me, on a dais surrounded by the Court and the Corps Diplomatique, was the King. He seemed to have something oriental about him, something almost of a Siamese potentate, and I bowed very low. He dropped his head, as if to grunt, and I backed two paces, and then turned and walked away.

That inscrutable mask, however, missed neither solecism nor absurdity. At a levée in the following year the King noted that two senior generals were wearing eight stars apiece on their breasts, mostly of foreign orders. Such displays of valour, he decreed, should in future be confined to a constellation of four.

Channon was also asked to a State ball at Buckingham Palace in honour of the King of Rumania and his wife Queen Marie, one of King George's earliest loves. The years had not been kind to her, and the diarist's pen proved even unkinder:

Dominick Browne and I went, twin little Lord Fauntleroys in dark blue velvet, steel buttons, swords and flat hats, but without lace jabots. The Foreign Office people and the courtiers were in white and green and gold. At about ten the royalties entered, and bowed to the Corps Diplomatique, whose bench is on the right of the throne. The Queen of Roumania looked ridiculous in a green sea-foam crepe-de-chine saut-de-lit spotted with goldfish she had painted on herself. Her double chins were kept in place by strands of pearls attached to an exotic headdress. She was every inch une reine . . . de comédie! The ball reminded me of an engraving of the Congress of Vienna, and was not much more animated.

Mr Asquith, whom the King treated with much consideration during his years out of office, left a less waspish account of royal hospitality:

We dined last night at the Palace, and, as I murmured to my neighbour, marvelled upon the problem of what principle of selection they assort their guests, e.g., Lord Lonsdale and Rudyard Kipling. I had quite a good talk with the former about hunting, coursing, boxing and other congenial topics. The King was in his usual form – dogmatic and boisterous, and very friendly: and relieved to be rid of Ll.G.

More appreciative than either Channon or Asquith was the Comte de Saint-Aulaire, who with his wife was asked to lunch alone with the King and Queen on being appointed French ambassador in 1921. His predecessor in London for the past twenty-three years, Paul Cambon, warned him that the food in Queen Victoria's day had been 'execrable'. Saint-Aulaire found that of her grandson to be 'excellent, with a Château Margaux of the best year gently warmed to perfection'. His account continues:

The service was at once imperial and bourgeois: imperial through the origin and national dress of the four servants, a Scot, an Indian, a Sudanese, a black South African, who symbolised the sway of Great Britain throughout the world; bourgeois by the little bell which the King rang to call them, for they vanished into another room after each of the two or three dishes which made up the menu. To reduce their presence to a minimum, the King himself dealt with the drink.

Saint-Aulaire, the victim of exceptional short-sight, was certainly mistaken about the cosmopolitan range of the footmen, although not about the minimum number required to minister to that *partie carrée*. Later in the reign, when the King and Queen took a short holiday by the sea in a house borrowed from the Duke of Devonshire, the King told Ponsonby that he had brought very few servants. At a private cinema show one evening, to which the servants were invited, Ponsonby counted forty-five.

For all its splendour, Buckingham Palace was not what the King meant by home. It was there that he laboured over his papers, received ministers, entertained the Queen of Rumania and the Comte de Saint-Aulaire and Mr Henry Channon. But his heart remained elsewhere: at Balmoral in the autumn, Sandringham in the winter.

Even Windsor inspired pride rather than affection. 'From the moment
you arrived at the door,' Princess Alice would recall, 'to be met by footmen
with powdered hair, the housekeeper in black silk and the Master of the
Household and others, you felt as you do on entering a venerable cathedral.'
But no cathedral has ever boasted a banqueting hall able to seat nearly two
hundred guests at a single long table; a Waterloo Chamber hung with the
portraits painted by Lawrence to mark the Allied victory of 1815 ('Alors
pour battre Napoléon,' General de Gaulle was to inquire a century and a
half later, 'il vous a fallu tous ces messieurs?'); a suite of drawing-rooms,
the red and the green and the white, each more magnificent than the last;
the masterpieces of Rembrandt and van Dyck, of Canaletto and Stubbs; a
library incomparably rich in the drawings of Leonardo and Holbein, the
miniatures of Hilliard and Oliver; the finest craftsmanship of furniture and
clocks, porcelain and silver, bronzes and bindings, weapons and scientific
instruments. 'The treasure of the Nibelung!' exclaimed the wife of a
German ambassador dining at Buckingham Palace. She had yet to visit
Windsor.

Such profusion might have overwhelmed a more learned man than the
King. But he took it all in his stride. 'Everything here is of the best,' he
would say, surveying his possessions. Dates and that sort of thing he would
leave to his wife, who had both an eye and a memory, or to his librarians,
learned fellows like Fortescue and Morshead. But there was one object
which he cherished: a silver-gilt statuette of Lady Godiva. The reason was
that the short-sighted Queen Olga of the Hellenes had once been heard to
murmur as she peered at it: 'Ah, dear Queen Victoria.' That came high in
the King's repertoire of stories.

The Queen brought both knowledge and the wiles of the predator to
enlarging the Windsor collections. One is reflected in the descriptive labels,
each in her own hand, attached to even the humblest of pieces; the other in
those innumerable acquisitions which she bought or begged. Not all the
anecdotes of her persistence are exaggerated. Visiting the homes of friends,
acquaintances and strangers, sometimes self-invited, she would stand in
front of a covetable object and pronounce in measured tones: 'I am caressing
it with my eyes.' If that evoked no impulsive gesture of generosity, the
Queen would resume her tour. But on taking her leave, she would pause on
the doorstep and ask: 'May I go back and say goodbye to that dear little
cabinet?' Should even that touching appeal fail to melt the granite heart of
her host, her letter of thanks might include a request to buy the piece. Few
could resist that final assault. Lord Lincolnshire demanded and received
£300 for his Derby biscuit group of the sons of George III. And when Lord
and Lady Lee were asked to sell a little portrait of Charles II, they replied
that they would be honoured if the Queen would accept it as a gift, 'with

our humble duty'. This she did without demur, sending in return an inscribed photograph framed, as she explained, in 'Indian brocade which I bought myself at Benares'.

Next to family iconography, the Queen was captivated by the diminutive, a taste shared by most of the crowned heads of Europe. But whereas they were content with those tiny carved animals and other bibelots produced by Fabergé, she alone could display at Windsor the most grandiose dolls' house in the world. A tribute that took more than three years to design, construct and adorn, it was built on a scale of one inch to the foot, exactly as Swift depicted Lilliput in *Gulliver's Travels*. The architect was Sir Edwin Lutyens, the gardener Miss Gertrude Jekyll, the librarian Princess Marie Louise. Their inspiration was supported by 500 donors, 250 craftsmen, 60 artists and 600 contributors to the library.

The leading artists of the day decorated walls and ceilings, painted pictures to be hung in the rooms or contributed to the portfolios of water-colours and engravings in the library. There was a façade in the style of Wren, 102 inches long; a garden with shrubs and flowers; a garage with a Rolls Royce and a Daimler; a cellar with the finest vintages of Europe. The safe contained an insurance policy on the house, the kitchen a set of gold frying pans, the King's wardrobe a shooting-stick and a Field-Marshal's sword. There were Crown jewels in the strong-room, toys in the nursery, marmalade in the larder. Lifts and lavatories were marvels of mechanical ingenuity. China and plate, golf clubs and shotguns, fountain pens and despatch boxes, a stamp collection in its album: nothing was forgotten. The donors of these miniature treasures included the bearers of many household names: Boot, Chivers, Chubb, Dunhill, Duveen, Gibbons, Gilbey, Purdey, Rowntree, Tuck, Wedgwood and Wilkinson. Lord Waring, whose peerage had attracted so much unfavourable comment, gave the furniture for the Queen's boudoir. Other loyal contributors included a lady with the delight-ful name of Miss Queenie Victoria Beer. The youngest was Nigel Nicolson, aged five, a son of the future royal biographer, who was persuaded to part with a miniature chest of drawers. Not even a royal commission could deter Lutyens from a characteristic joke. One pillow of the bed was embroidered with the initials MG, the other with GM. They meant, he explained, 'May George?' and 'George May.'

Under the persuasive direction of Princess Marie Louise, who wrote two thousand letters in her own hand, a whole library of works by contemporary authors was assembled, each volume no bigger than a large postage stamp. Max Beerbohm contributed a whimsical tale that owed something to *Alice in Wonderland*, Hilaire Belloc a parable on the corruption of political life, Conan Doyle a new adventure of Sherlock Holmes, M.R. James a ghost story called *The Haunted Dolls' House*. There were poems by Hardy and

Aldous Huxley, Kipling and Housman and Sassoon. Somerset Maugham offered a cynical short story, Haldane a monograph on humanism. Sir John Bland-Sutton, the gynaecological surgeon, submitted a treatise on dolls' surgery, including injuries to the eyes and repairs to the bellows. Asquith sent a sentence from one of his early speeches, but thought it 'a singularly fatuous exercise'. George Bernard Shaw alone refused to contribute, 'in a very rude manner', the Princess noted.

The Queen made only one demand on her benefactors. She asked Lutyens to ensure that she could open the dolls' house at will, without needing to summon servants. That was the measure of her secret delight. It was all the greatest nonsense and the greatest fun.

Her husband, too, had his private pleasure at Windsor: the company of his old tutor, Canon Dalton. Queen Victoria had appointed him to the Chapter of St George's Chapel in 1884 as a reward for his devoted service to her grandsons, Prince Eddy and Prince George. Forty years later, and well into his ninth decade, he was still there. 'His stooped, bony frame', the Prince of Wales later wrote, 'might have been quarried from the same old grey stone as the Castle itself.' Walking near Frogmore one day with a young friend, Dalton came on the grave of one of Queen Victoria's dogs. 'I used to feed that dog with buns,' he said, 'and now even his memorial is rotting away.' And he stretched out a hand to touch the bronze tail that was already broken from the body. That portrait of the gentle, nostalgic old Canon is incomplete. A clerical colleague wrote of him:

His dominating personality, fortified by the absolute independence he had enjoyed during his long period as King George v's tutor, had hindered Dalton from understanding the meaning or the necessity of corporate responsibility. When he returned to clerical life, at Windsor, it was an almost unbearable irritation to him even to *think* that there were other people who had an equal right with him to a voice in the Chapter. He approached every meeting determined to fight over the smallest details, only to prevent his colleagues, whom he despised, from having their way. This point of view in a strong man inevitably made his colleagues miserable. The damage to our Chapter life was no less than the damage to our personal life. His effervescent temperament made it impossible for Dalton to confine his expressed contempt to our meetings; he broadcast his opinions to people in the Castle.

A boisterous humour designed to conciliate young naval officers offended the decorum of cloister and castle. He inquired of one Canon, recently laid low by phlebitis, 'How are the fleabites?' Of another he said: 'If the King sends that man to represent him at my funeral, I shall jump out of my coffin and spoil the whole show.' Dalton became noted for his rumbustious reading of the lessons, in which he endowed the Almighty with a thundering bass and Isaiah with a piping falsetto. And when a herd of tourists tried to follow him into a side chapel, he boomed: 'You must not come in here. I am just about to commit suicide.'

Yet his intellect was as powerful as his voice, and the King entrusted to him the early religious education of his own sons. Nor was Dalton without ambition. The royal family, who were spared his more outrageous displays, tried to secure preferment for him. King Edward VII, prompted by his son, suggested that Dalton be made Dean of Westminster; but the Prime Minister, Lord Salisbury, appointed a more conventional candidate.

In 1917, when the Deanery of Windsor fell vacant, Dalton's hopes rose again; for although that office, in common with most other bishoprics and deaneries, lay in the gift of the Prime Minister, it had become the custom to allow the sovereign a decisive say. But by then, not even the King dared cause further discord by promoting his autocratic old tutor. The appointment went to Albert Baillie, a godson of Queen Victoria and nephew of her favourite prelate, Dean Stanley. On learning the news, it is said, Dalton gave the King one of the worst hours he had ever spent. Stamfordham warned the new Dean on his first day at Windsor: 'It is not too much to say that Dalton has made your predecessor an unhappy man for a quarter of a century.' Poor Baillie had to endure similar torment for only fourteen years: until Dalton's death in 1931, in his ninety-second year.

It was always with a sense of homecoming that the King stepped down from the royal train at Ballater station after an overnight journey, inspected a guard of honour drawn from a Scottish regiment and drove the remaining eight miles to Balmoral. 'Glad to be in this dear place again after six years,' he wrote in August 1919, 'and to see all our nice people again.' He liked their independence and directness of speech; a few months after his death, the minister at nearby Crathie church heralded the arrival of King Edward VIII and Mrs Simpson by preaching a sermon on Nero.

As the problems of Westminster and Whitehall receded, he relaxed into joviality. 'And what is your name?' he asked the tiny granddaughter of a shooting friend. 'I am Ann Peace Arabella Mackintosh of Mackintosh,' she replied. 'Ah,' the King said humbly, 'I'm just plain George.'

Protocol at Balmoral between the wars was less stiff than at Buckingham Palace but hardly informal. The King dined in a kilt and wore the Order of the Thistle. For a small party there were eight footmen and five pipers. Three courses were served for luncheon and six for dinner. The same well-regulated luxury pervaded a picnic on the banks of Loch Muick: a cortège of huge maroon Daimlers with gold-plated radiators wending their way along the narrow pitching tracks, baskets of delicious food unpacked and served by footmen, sometimes a chef in a tall white hat to fry freshly caught trout. The men wore heavy tweed knickerbocker suits, long woollen stockings, highly polished brogue shoes and hats; the women, in a not dissimilar uniform, were discouraged from wearing trousers even when riding hill ponies.

Apart from such interludes, sport dominated each day's programme. The King excelled with both rifle and shotgun, and knew it. He could not resist writing to a friend that he had shot the heaviest stag ever killed at Abergeldie – it weighed 21 stone 11 pounds – then added: 'Burn this rubbish when read.' His skill on the grouse moor was legendary. In 1921, Eric Linklater and some fellow students hoped to have a cheap holiday in the Highlands and to earn a little money by being taken on as beaters. One day their services were not required, and the King noticed them standing about. In a 'voice that was rough about the edges and genial in essence', he invited them to stay and watch him shoot. Here is Linklater's memorable description of the drive:

They came in great numbers and at prodigious speed, for the wind was with them and the slope of the hill determined their course, and from the edge of the coveys the King took them down with inerrable aim. We knew, by that time, something about good shooting, and every bird that fell to the King's gun was dead in the air before it dropped. When a large covey came, and another closely followed, there were two, three, four dead birds in the air before the first had fallen. It was shooting as the ordinary first-class shot may dream of shooting. It was the very summit of marksmanship, the nonpareil of shooting, and while we watched – and we knew what to look for – not a bird came fluttering down, but every one was a meteor falling or a plummet dropping straight. Two or three of our own guns, across the valley, were good; but the King who had treated us so gently was supernacular.

Although the Queen would never upset the King by saying so, shooting bored her. 'It was so stiff,' she remarked of one party, 'I would have turned cartwheels for sixpence.' The climate too – what Esher called 'cold, grey and unwinning' – disagreed with her. Above all she had nobody to share her interest in museums and galleries, art dealers and auction rooms. One autumn, to her delight, she heard that the most aesthetic of her godsons, Sir Michael Duff, was staying at a nearby house, and she invited him over to dine. But she had hardly begun to question him when the King growled down the table: 'There you go again, May: furniture, furniture, furniture.' After her husband's death, Queen Mary preferred to spend September at the Palace of Holyrood, in Edinburgh, visiting Scotland's ancient monuments and country houses.

To relieve the King of political worries during his holiday at Balmoral there was usually a Minister in Attendance. As his role was official rather than social, it had long been understood that the invitation did not include his wife. In 1925, however, Stanley Baldwin proposed that Mrs Baldwin should accompany him. The Master of the Household, Sir Derek Keppel, repulsed her with the utmost courtesy. 'Their Majesties', he wrote to the Prime Minister's private secretary, 'are looking forward to Mr. Baldwin's visit and I know you will make it quite clear that it is only want of space that makes it impossible to make an exception to the old-established rule which I have quoted.' For all his supposed rustic charm and wisdom, Baldwin was not an entirely welcome guest. When the Queen inquired about some confidential political matter, he refused to answer, although her husband had allowed her to see his red boxes ever since he was Prince of Wales. 'He treated me like an inquisitive little girl,' she complained of the Prime Minister.

Neville Chamberlain left a happier impression on Balmoral, combining a brisk despatch of business with a love of country life and field sports. As he himself once said: 'I know every flower; S.B. knows none. I know every tree; S.B. knows none. I shoot and fish; S.B. does neither. Yet he is known as the countryman; and I am known as the townsman.' One year, having been invited to shoot on the Thursday, he asked if he might take his lunch and fish the river on the Friday. The King thought it a mad idea, told him so and was proved right. Chamberlain described in a letter to his sister how he flogged every possible pool in vain along ten miles of the bank. The river, he wrote, was 'not much more than a dribble as clear as gin and with a bright sun that showed up every pebble on the bottom'. On just such a day, Baldwin would have shut himself up in a frowsty bedroom reading Izaak Walton's *Compleat Angler*.

There is a footnote to Chamberlain's association with Balmoral which strictly belongs to another reign. In the autumn of 1938, King George VI tried to persuade him to stay for an extra day's shooting, offering to fly him down to London in time for a Cabinet meeting. Chamberlain declined; he had never flown before, disliked the sound of it and hoped he would never have to do so. A fortnight later he flew to Berchtesgaden, the first of his three flights to see Hitler that culminated in the ill-fated Munich Agreement.

By the wish of her late husband, Queen Alexandra lived on at Sandringham, that huge house peopled only by ghosts of the Edwardian Age. In the silent world of the deaf she struggled bravely to rekindle the glow of happier days. Lord Lincolnshire wrote in the last year of her life: 'Her hearing gone and her eyesight far from good. But she retains her old grace and charm, and her wonderful smile. She never complains and keeps her slim pretty figure.'

She was not quite alone. There was her only unmarried daughter, Princess Victoria, who devotedly remained by her mother's side while her

heart yearned for romance. Lord Rosebery had earlier been thought a likely
husband after the death of his first wife, Hannah Rothschild, but the match
did not prosper. Most other available suitors were German princes, on none
of whom Queen Alexandra could have been expected to smile. Princess
Victoria was sometimes considered daring in her attachments. At Windsor
in 1908, she and the diplomatist Lord Granville danced all the evening after
dinner, the servants having rolled up the carpet. 'I thought it not quite
approved of,' a guest noted. One friend remained faithful: Admiral Fisher,
almost thirty years her senior. He wrote of her in early middle age: 'Princess
Victoria, who used to be scraggy, lanky and anaemic, has developed into an
opulent figure with a rosy, plump face! She looked very handsome and I
told her so, and her tall figure makes her most imposing now.' But prolonged
spinsterhood and loneliness soured her nature. Always contemptuous of
her sister-in-law's morganatic blood and jealous of her superior education,
the Princess took her revenge in a too demonstrative assault on her brother's
affection. The Queen suffered so much from those conspiratorial telephone
conversations during which Princess Victoria poured mischief into the
King's ear that she acquired a lifelong distaste for the instrument. The
Princess initiated unpleasant little quarrels, too, about the ownership of
pictures and other possessions. That was the price which the royal family
paid for her selfless care of Queen Alexandra.

Two courtiers idolized the old Queen: her lady-in-waiting, Miss Charlotte Knollys, sister of the King's former private secretary, and Sir Dighton
Probyn, who served the royal family for more than half a century. Probyn
had won the Victoria Cross in the Indian Mutiny of 1857, although few
ever saw the decoration; it lay concealed by the patriarchal beard which
flowed down to his navel. In contrast to Charlotte Knollys, whose devotion
to Queen Alexandra left her with scarcely any personality of her own,
Probyn was as distinctive in character as in appearance. He had a fine
command of invective, as when he denounced Mr Gladstone: 'I pray to
God that he may be shut up as a Lunatic at once, and thus save the Empire
from the Destruction which he is leading her to. If he is not mad, he is a
Traitor.' Yet his politics were not always those of the officers' mess. In his
ninety-second year he travelled up from Sandringham to vote for Churchill,
who was challenging the official Conservative candidate in a Westminster
by-election. He also claimed that Lloyd George had 'won the war for us,
which I doubt very much if Asquith would have done had he remained as
Prime Minister'.

Probyn's dedication to Queen Alexandra, whom he called 'The Blessed
Lady', was absolute. As her financial guardian he could do little to curb her
extravagance and impulsive generosity; so he relieved the burden by refusing to draw a penny of his own salary. Nor would he even contemplate

retirement. Like Queen Alexandra, he invariably referred not to 'the King' but to 'King George'. Both the King and Queen, however, held 'dear old Probyn' in esteem and followed his precarious health with concern. Once he came near to death after collapsing at court because nobody could open the tight collar of his uniform. Thereafter Queen Mary always carried a penknife in her reticule.

Thus it was that Queen Alexandra and her tiny entourage remained at Sandringham House throughout more than half her son's reign. With her death in the winter of 1925, the King and Queen decided to move out of York Cottage. 'Very sad that tonight is the last night that we sleep in this dear little house in which we have spent 33 very happy years,' the King wrote. The Queen too, who might have been expected to welcome her escape from poky rooms, commonplace furniture and a persistent smell of cooking, wrote how much she would hate leaving her 'very cosy and comfortable home'. But having once made the break, they came to love their more spacious surroundings. 'You would be surprised to see how comfortable the Queen has made this beastly house,' Lady Desborough told Arthur Balfour, 'my great-uncle's, as you will remember, and sold at a ramp price by Lord Palmerston.'

Except for some tapestries woven from Goya cartoons and given to King Edward by Alfonso XII of Spain, Sandringham had not a single good picture, piece of furniture or other work of art. But everything was solid, free from meretricious luxury and spotlessly kept. 'Well-equipped writing tables, comfortable beds, bright fires in the bedrooms,' one guest noted. Another was enchanted to be given a bathroom with the motto, 'cleanliness is next to godliness' round the wall, a bath decorated with roses and a row of three wash basins, each marked for its purpose: head and face, hands, teeth. The King liked to escort newly arrived guests to their rooms to see that all was in order. When Birkenhead came to stay, the King noticed that by an oversight the fire had not been lit; so he got down on his knees with a box of matches, blowing hard until there was a blaze. But his *bonhomie* could be alarming. When a nervous neighbour at dinner allowed one of her long hairpins to drop into the soup, the King sought to put her at her ease by asking: 'Did you come here expecting to eat winkles?'

The Sandringham routine required stamina, even of the women. In the shooting season they came down to breakfast in day clothes, changed into thick tweeds for lunch with the guns, put on elaborate Ascot dresses for tea and reappeared in full rig for dinner. Men wore trousers instead of knee-breeches with their evening coats; the King, a white flower in his buttonhole, also wore the star and riband of the Garter. Breakfast was the only informal meal, made hazardous by the presence of the King's parrot, Charlotte, whom he allowed to roam at will. Charles Cust alone dared to complain when she dug her beak into his boiled egg. If the bird made a mess, the King would slide a mustard pot over it so that the Queen should not know of Charlotte's misbehaviour. He found her a companionable friend. Cruising in the Mediterranean, he wrote to Wigram: 'Glad Charlotte is all right and that the housemaid is taking care of her.'

Shooting lunches were prepared with the skill given to a State banquet and dinner was more a ceremony than a meal. A visiting parson noted that ten liveried serving men were required to wait upon a party of eight: five in dark blue with gold buttons and medals, five in red. The food was rich and interminable. Noticing one night that his librarian had helped himself sparingly, the King roared down the table: 'Morshead is not having any cream. Don't be afraid of it. It's ours, you know.' He was proud of his glasshouses, too. When a friend asked in admiration where the nectarines came from, the King replied: 'My allotment garden.' Guests departing by train for London took with them a sumptuous lunch of many courses with wine, port, coffee and even cigarettes: all packed in a basket labelled 'His Majesty the King' which the railway staff would collect at Liverpool Street station and return to Norfolk.

Christmas at Sandringham was an occasion for the family and a very few necessary courtiers. The ritual began on Christmas Eve with the distribution of beef to the estate workers: a cold performance that took place in the large coachhouse and lasted nearly an hour. The joints of meat, equivalent to five bullocks, were laid out on tables decorated with holly and received by the tenants in white towels. On Christmas morning there was the walk across the park to Sandringham church followed by an exchange of presents in the ballroom. Each person had his own length of table on which his presents were laid out, separated by a line of pink tape. In 1926, Lady Wigram recorded, the Queen gave the King a picture by Munnings of the carriage procession at Ascot; the King gave the Queen a large lozenge-shaped brooch containing all the regimental badges of the Brigade of Guards. The Prince of Wales received a dozen corks for wine bottles, each decorated with the Prince of Wales's feathers in silver. Lady Wigram was given a Kashmir shawl, a rose bowl, an antique tea-caddy of tortoise-shell, a grey leather bag, an evening bag of gold tissue, two little enamel boxes and an ashtray.

At dinner there were bowls of Christmas roses and scarlet crackers. All wore paper hats, except the King: the Queen in a mitre, the Prince of Wales in a penguin's head, the young Duchess of York in a poke bonnet. After dinner the four princes and the Duchess sang music hall songs in a low tone. The King, at the far end of the room, could not hear the words and said· 'Listen to those children of mine – rather delightful with their Christmas carols.' Then the King played the gramophone, *La Traviata* and the *Song of the Volga Boatmen*. Suddenly there was a tune which the party thought vaguely familiar: after a few bars they realized it was the National Anthem, and sprang to their feet. The King was in fits of laughter at his joke: 'You were talking so hard that I wondered how long it would be before you all got up.'

The King enjoyed his role as squire of the Sandringham estate. By the standards of the time he paid his workers well, liked to call on them in their homes, discreetly relieved the distress caused by death or other family catastrophe. One of his favourite stories was of the boy whom he had helped with his mathematics homework one evening, but who had refused a second offer a few weeks later. 'Oh, I see you have progressed beyond me, is that it?' the King inquired. 'No, sir,' the boy replied, 'but you got it wrong last time.' He liked to know exactly how every department was running, particularly greenhouses and stud, both of which he would show off to visitors on Sunday afternoons. There was nothing solemn about such inspections. Once he noticed that his sister the Queen of Norway kept a special handkerchief for her little spaniel. Throughout the rest of the walk he kept calling back to her remarks like, 'Where are its galoshes?' and 'Don't forget its cough drops.' In more serious vein he was a pioneer of flax growing in Norfolk, and arranged for Lord Craigavon, the Prime Minister of Northern Ireland, to see his experiments.

Not least there was the shooting, in which the King found perpetual delight and relaxation. Much rivalry, not all of it friendly, existed between Sandringham and Lord Leicester's neighbouring estate of Holkham. Although Sandringham was only half its size, the King boasted, he killed three times as many partridges. It was not for want of trying on Leicester's part. When somebody told him that the churchyard at Holkham was disgracefully overgrown, he replied: 'Nonsense, best breeding ground for partridges in England.'

Each year rather more than 20,000 head of game were shot at Sandringham, with another 10,000 or so on leased estates. Most were reared pheasants: and here a question mark must hang over the regime of Mr F. W. Bland, the head keeper – a stocky, bearded Yorkshireman who in his bottle-green livery with gold buttons and a square hat served the estate for more than half a century – for visitors and courtiers alike would remark not only on the number of birds but on the ease with which they could be shot. 'One sees pheasants everywhere in the park and gardens,' wrote a parson, 'the place is literally crawling with them.' Dighton Probyn told Lord Lincolnshire: 'The King is having good sport. They call it sport!!! – shooting tame pheasants. It does puzzle me.' And the King's equerry and friend, Sir Bryan Godfrey-Faussett, noted in his diary: 'A great many pheasants but alas on the whole not of the lofty nature, in fact some of them very fluffy ones.' The coverts planted in King Edward's day were designed to ensure that birds flew neither high nor fast. Behind wide screens of clipped evergreens lurked guns and loaders, some of them scarcely more mobile than the pheasants for which they lay in ambush. King George, who could bring down the highest and fastest pheasant with ease, must sometimes have found this galling. But he was a traditionalist, and what had been good enough for his father was good enough for him. Not until the reign of King George VI did reared birds give way to wild and a skilful replanting of woods ensure that even the flat Norfolk landscape had its share of rocketing pheasants.

Unlike his father, the King rarely invited a guest lacking in skill; he liked to see his birds cleanly shot. One year Sir Samuel Hoare was asked for the first time to stay at Sandringham, as a Norfolk man rather than as a Cabinet Minister. Hoare and his wife were enjoying a winter holiday in Switzerland, found it difficult to book places on the train, so asked to be excused. Within two or three days, Lady Maud Hoare had fallen and broken her leg. The King would refer chaffingly to this misfortune as a judgement on their refusing the royal invitation. Nor were the Hoares ever asked to stay again.

'What's the use of a house if you are never in it?' Mr Pooter used to ask, and the King would have agreed with him. A conscientious host on State occasions and a generous one in the comparative privacy of Balmoral and Sandringham, he was a reluctant and restless guest. Only twice in the post-war years could he be persuaded to undertake State visits to fellow sovereigns: Belgium in 1922 and Italy in 1923. During the first, he and the Queen stayed at the palace of Laeken, where his father had proposed marriage to his mother sixty years before. 'Very comfortable rooms,' he wrote, 'but May lives at one end of the Palace and I at the other and the house is very large. It is not very convenient.' Queen Mary was no less wretched at being separated from her husband. But in the middle of the night she heard the sound of her bedroom door quietly opening. She switched on the light and there, peering round the screen, was what she described as 'his dear, sad little face'. He had found his way to her alone and in the dark. From time to time his ministers tried to persuade him to improve international relations by travelling abroad. The King would reply that his father had done so in the cause of peace, but what had been the result? The Great War. He put it more tersely when asked to pay a State visit to Holland: 'Amsterdam, Rotterdam and all the other dams! Damned if I'll do it.'

Even in London the King would whenever possible dine alone with the Queen and, until her marriage, Princess Mary. Occasionally there was an evening at the house of a friend or political grandee; but he insisted on an uncrowded table, dinner completed within the hour and an early night. A game of cards might follow. Channon recorded a conversation with his friend Lord Gage, one of the King's entourage:

George Gage took the King and Queen to dine with the Roxburghes tonight to play bridge. As he went out looking rather fat in his Court Dress, I said to him 'Take some money with you, as you might have to pay the King's debts.' He retorted 'I am going out with George V, not George IV.' But apparently at the end of the evening, the King did say 'Have you any money Gage?' and they could only raise £2 between them!

More daringly, Curzon engaged the comedian George Robey to entertain the King and Queen after dinner. And during a royal visit to Knowsley, Derby procured the services of Georges Carpentier and his sparring partner, who gave a display of boxing in the riding school. The French newspapers referred with delight to 'les deux Georges', but there were many in England who thought it an indelicate spectacle to lay before a sovereign and his consort.

Derby was one of the very few old friends with whom the King liked to stay in the country. He would also visit the Duke of Richmond for Goodwood races and the Duke of Devonshire for the grouse shooting at Bolton Abbey. 'Though it only lasts three days,' Crewe wrote of one such occasion, 'it seems to take almost as much arranging as the Durbar.' In spite of meticulous planning, it sometimes became necessary to hold an emergency meeting of the Privy Council in a country house. 'Bed at 2.15,' the King wrote at Bolton Abbey, 'very sleepy and rather grumpy.'

Since the King found no intellectual excitement in sightseeing, the Queen was obliged to curb her curiosity. He once wrote to her about an excursion of his mother's: 'Fancy going all the way to Scotland for only nine days and to Norway for three, what an expense and how impractical! Thank God you are not like that; it would drive me mad.' When Queen Mary did escape on her own, she proved as exacting a guest as her husband. Visiting Holker, one of the houses belonging to the Cavendish family, she brought nine servants with her: two dressers, one footman, one page, two chauffeurs, one lady-in-waiting, one maid to the lady-in-waiting and one detective. A list of requests preceded the Queen:

1 A chair to be placed outside the Queen's bedroom on which a footman or page could sit by turns all night. [The quaintly named page was a man aged fifty.]
2 Freshly-made barley water to be put in her bedroom every two hours during the day.
3 Ice in the bedroom at 11.30 p.m.
4 Six clean towels every day. [The Queen brought her own sheets and pillowcases.]

When the King and Queen did move from one house to another, it was with all the stately and well-upholstered progress of a mediaeval monarch. For short journeys there would be a Daimler motor car, its high roof allowing passengers to enter and disembark while wearing a tall hat or elaborate toque. For more distant expeditions there was the royal train, painted in a livery of carmine-lake and cream. Each coach had an imposing entrance with double doors and a vestibule; even the headstocks behind the buffers were in the shape of lions' heads, covered with gold leaf. By order of King Edward VII, the interior of the train was designed to resemble that of the royal yacht, with white enamel paint and polished brass. Queen Mary brought a softer, more feminine touch to the décor: satinwood furniture from Lord Waring's emporium, green upholstery and silver beds adorned with the royal cipher. Frosted glass engraved with the insignia of the orders of chivalry protected the occupants of bedroom and bathroom from outside scrutiny. Elaborate printed orders governed each journey, often involving dislocation to ordinary services. Between Ballater and London, no fewer than seventeen engines waited with steam up along the route in case the royal locomotive should break down. Nothing was left to chance, from the evening delivery of the King's parliamentary telegram to the slowing down of the train at 6.30 a.m. so that the Queen could take her bath in comfort.

When the Empress Frederick, the King's aunt, was staying with the Duke and Duchess of Connaught in the country, she had arranged to leave by the 11.30 train from Bagshot station, on her way to Russia. At 11.25 she was sitting on the lawn completing a portrait of the Duke's Indian servant. Summoned, she deposited paint-box, brushes and palette on a chair, got into the carriage and was off. 'How delightful,' a non-royal guest noted, 'always to have someone to tidy up after you.'

The King's way of life depended upon just such cohorts of retainers who, in the broadest sense, not only tidied up after him but also anticipated his every wish and movement. Their numbers were prodigious. Sir John Fortescue, who in 1926 gave way to Owen Morshead as librarian, described the domestic arrangements at Windsor:

The royal kitchen kept sixty souls busily employed. In the stewards' room – a room contemporaneous with the cloisters of Westminster Abbey and roofed with the like vaulting – there were two dinners of one hundred each for the upper servants. In the servants' hall – a fourteenth century building with columns and vaulting of that period – there were two dinners of two hundred each for the lower servants.

At Sandringham, Lady Desborough noted that the exiled Queen of Spain, in spite of a professed pauperdom, brought with her a lady, a gentleman and three maids. It was not a peculiarly royal phenomenon. When the King and Queen visited Knowsley, two hundred people – family, guests and servants – slept in the house; that was without counting the outdoor staff, which included thirty-seven keepers. During a cruise in the royal yacht, the Marquis de Soveral's valet was seasick; so Soveral went unshaven for a whole day.

The secret of the smooth perfection of royal households, an old courtier once explained to the Prince of Wales, was to employ the equivalent of a man and a half for every job. It was a calling that offered security, promotion and a convivial standard of living that came to be demanded as of right. 'The amount of food and drink consumed during the stay of Their Majesties with me was simply stupendous,' Hardinge wrote of the post-Durbar visit to Calcutta, 'but it was the 150 English servants whom it was difficult for my Controller to satisfy.' A newly joined steward at Buckingham Palace described the welcome he received from two senior colleagues:

The three of us sat down at a round table in the next room, beautifully laid with spotless white linen and gleaming cutlery, while a black-liveried servant, quite a youth, served us with an excellent meal of soup, roast veal and vegetables, a sweet and some Stilton cheese, accompanied by a good white wine.

It was a delightful introduction to a new job, and, warmed by the sherry and the white wine, I felt expansive and confident.

Servants of every rank, he wrote, did themselves well; there was no excess, but neither was there any skimping. 'The place was run as a gentleman's household, without too nice a regard to economy or finance. . . . Food and drink were plentiful and no one seemed to mind much exactly how much they cost.' Only one perquisite was forbidden. Staying at Windsor in 1927, Sir Samuel Hoare received this injunction:

The Master of the Household presents his compliments and begs to ask the Guests of the King and Queen to refrain from offering presents of money to the Servants of Their Majesties' Establishment.

The Servants do not expect presents of any kind and the Master of the Household would greatly appreciate assistance on the part of Their Majesties' Guests in maintaining the observance of this regulation.

That thoughtful gesture was designed not to deprive the footman of his tip but to spare the unmoneyed guest embarrassment.

Many of those in royal employment scarcely ever saw the King; those who did experienced sudden storms and fitful sunshine. 'That's right,' he roared at a nervous footman who dropped a loaded tea-tray, 'break up the bloody Palace.' But there is no record of the culprit's having been dismissed. Order, tidiness and punctuality were his watchwords. When a new house-maid 'put everything back wrong', the King was beside himself with rage until the housekeeper, Mrs Rawlings, promised to have all his rooms photographed so that no object would ever again be displaced. At Sandringham he forbade odd articles of clothing to be left in the front hall; and there was laughter one evening when, as the party broke up, he scavenged someone's fan and someone else's handkerchief. On a less light-hearted occasion, rummaging about the drawing-room, he came on a dusty pile of music. 'Is this *yours?*' an angry King demanded of an even angrier Queen.

The slightest carelessness or difference of opinion could provoke an explosion. 'Good God, you can't come like that, you are in the wrong clothes,' the King exclaimed when an equerry turned up in trousers to escort him to a private dinner party. The culprit was instantly sent off to change into knee-breeches and had to follow in a cab. After an argument about who should have keys to Windsor Castle, Ponsonby wrote: 'We had a rare rough and tumble, and the roof of the whole castle nearly cracked from the violent vibrations of the Monarch's voice.' And Wigram one day received back the envelope in which he had written to the King, with the reproach: 'Your letter arrived just like this. I don't think much of your sealing wax.'

That the most senior and trusted members of his entourage could be rebuked with the same severity as a clumsy domestic servant was a royal failing not confined to King George v. Crowned heads, even the most democratic of them, dwell on an eminence from which everyone else seems to be much of a muchness. Monarchs discern a difference of function between a Lord Chamberlain and a footman, but scarcely any of social rank; they may share the joys and sorrows of their subjects, yet are blind to those gradations of society which elsewhere excite pride or envy. High-born courtiers have sometimes found this uncomfortable. Queen Victoria's *Leaves from the Journal of Our Life in the Highlands* owed its widespread popularity to the warmth and simplicity with which she entered into the lives of the humble. Lady Augusta Stanley, however, the daughter of a Scottish earl and for years one of the Queen's most valued ladies-in-waiting, resented that royal lack of restraint. To write about servants as if they were gentlemen, she complained, gave the dangerous impression 'that all are on the same footing'. Lady Ponsonby, wife of the Queen's private secretary, put it more brutally. She wrote of 'the cold egotism which seems to chill you in all royalties. . . . You felt they were pretty near indifferent as to which maid of honour, lady-in-waiting or equerry did the work.'

Although kindly by nature, King George and Queen Mary shared the unconscious assumption that royalty are a caste apart. 'Chips' Channon wrote of the marriage in 1923 of Lord Worcester (later Duke of Beaufort) to Lady Mary Cambridge, the Queen's niece: 'After the ceremony all the Royal Family, the King, the two Queens, Princesses, Empress of Russia, etc., stood for ages in front of St Margaret's kissing one another. Royalties in public always behave as if they were enjoying complete privacy.'

Queen Mary also had the quaint habit of referring to members of the royal family as 'dear so-and-so', but to commoners as 'poor so-and-so'. Thus she would ask a young friend, 'How is your poor grandmother?': a woman, as it happened, endowed with enviable health and fortune.

The King and Queen could be as exacting as any mediaeval monarch in the demands they made on their household, not least in physical stamina. 'There were piles of letters which seldom seemed to dwindle,' wrote a lady-in-waiting, 'and it was rare for me to lay down my pen before 1 a.m. Often it was much later. I can even remember finishing letters at 8 a.m., having a bath and coming down to breakfast at 9 a.m. to start a new day.' Palace ceremonial through the ages has also required much standing about: 'rather a perpendicular evening', as one long-suffering victim called it. When Queen Victoria's physician fell down exhausted in a faint after dinner, all she said was: 'And a doctor, too!'

For the most part, the royal household endured long hours and quarter-deck squalls without either complaint or rancour. If on occasion courtly plumes were ruffled, Stamfordham would remind his colleagues: 'We are *all* servants here, although some are more important than others.' Yet it was the King himself who dispelled any lingering clouds. 'I fear I was somewhat irritable,' he would tell a private secretary or equerry, 'but you know it means nothing.' Behind that royal carapace lay the kindliest of hearts.

He took immense trouble about the allocation of grace and favour houses to those courtiers who had most need of them. He made discreet gifts of money to meet medical expenses and was swift to write letters of sympathy, such as this one to Wigram in 1918: 'I am so sorry that you are seedy, but hope a couple of days in bed will put you right again. Don't bother so far as I am concerned, I can get on perfectly well.... I thought you looked pretty bad this morning, you ought not to have come with us yesterday. Hoping to find you quite recovered on my return.'

There were surprise presents, too. On giving Godfrey-Faussett a pair of porpoise-skin shooting boots, the King made him try them on at once. 'This was awkward,' the equerry wrote, 'as I had a hole in my sock.' The King had the rare quality of being considerate to the wives of the household, who were so often neglected. Since he himself could not bear to be separated from the Queen, he tried to arrange for husbands to be accompanied by their wives when the Court moved from one residence to another. Before the war, protocol demanded that actresses should not be received publicly by the sovereign. So when in 1914 John Fortescue, the royal librarian, married a young actress, he arranged for her to remain in London while he was on duty with the King at Windsor. When the King and Queen heard of this, they asked that Fortescue should bring his wife down to Windsor for the weekend, and both came to call on her. Later the antique rule was abolished; Mrs Fortescue was formally presented at a garden party and asked with her husband to dine at the castle. Fortescue's successor, Morshead, also brought his young American bride to Windsor. 'The King was like the very nicest sort of grandfather to me,' she would recall.

He applied the same system of kicks and halfpence to all those officials who, although not members of his household, acted as links between Government and palace or represented him abroad. Nobody was left in doubt of his displeasure when plans went wrong, least of all on naval occasions. Approaching the flagship on one such inspection, he was much put out at seeing that the lower platform of her gangway was three feet higher than the gunwale of his barge. 'When I go for a drive in London,' he barked, 'they send my carriage on beforehand to see if the bloody wheels go round. I expect the same thing to be done when I inspect my Fleet.'

Public servants also had cause to remember his gifts of sympathy and understanding when they needed them most. On the retirement of Sir Arthur Nicolson, the father of his future biographer, as Permanent Under-Secretary of the Foreign Office, the King realized what a chasm of emptiness stretched before him. So on the pretence that Stamfordham was overworked, he invited Nicolson to come to the palace each morning when the King would go through the latest telegrams with him. It was an arrangement which lasted until Nicolson acquired more absorbing work in the City. The King was equally considerate to Sir Edward Grigg on his return from Kenya after a difficult term as Governor of the colony. He told him: 'I know what you are feeling. You have been away a long time, trying very hard to get things done. You have not succeeded as you hoped, but no one seems to realize that you have even tried, or that you have been having a hard time, or bothered to say thank you. Well, *I* say thank you.'

That thoughtfulness endured to the end. In the very last days of his life, the King had a letter written from Sandringham to the Foreign Secretary, suggesting that an overworked official, Robert Vansittart, should be allowed 'a good rest, of which the King understands he is much in need'.

Harold Laski once described the role of the sovereign's private secretary as 'a dignified slavery'. It is a phrase which with equal justice could be used of Queen Mary's domestic life. For more than forty years she was the indispensable guardian of her husband's comfort and peace of mind, a perpetual shield against irritation and anxiety. To those ends she sacrificed some of her own personality, conforming to his every whim without resentment or even question. Although self-imposed, her servitude was absolute.

It was revealed most obviously in the Queen's appearance. Wearing what was already outmoded during the State visit to Paris in 1914, she had still not abandoned her long, full skirts, her toques and parasols, a decade later. Soon after the war she made one or two timid excursions into fashion: a wide-brimmed hat in summer, a scarcely perceptible raising of a hem to show off her elegant ankles. But the King, as much a wardrobe tyrant as his father, frowned upon the changes. She relapsed into a style of timeless dignity. None could claim that it was unbecoming. Returning to London in 1924 after an absence of ten years, Mensdorff wrote: 'She looks so much more beautiful, with the white hair of an older woman yet a youthful freshness of complexion. She has put on no weight and is today more attractive than she has ever been.'

The Queen scorned the use of paint and disapproved of it in others. A young duchess who had been instructed to kiss her hand at a ball, in her ardour left a perfect print of a scarlet mouth on the back of the royal kid-glove. 'She gave me one withering look that said all,' wrote the culprit, 'and I slunk away in disgrace.' Apparel that on others might have seemed bizarre, on her served only to rebuke the restless art of the couturier. For luncheon it might be a very large fur collar dyed purple and a toque made entirely of artificial pansies; at a garden party she bore down upon Mr Channon 'like the Jungfrau, white and sparkling in the sun'; Lady Pamela Berry, dazzled by a nocturnal display of jewels that included five diamond necklaces, exclaimed: 'She has bagged all the best.'

As in matters of dress, so in planning family holidays the Queen deferred entirely to her husband's wishes. How she would have liked to tour the castles and museums of Europe, enriching her knowledge of history and works of art. Instead she uncomplainingly endured the yearly tedium of Balmoral. In 1925, it is true, the King grumblingly agreed to a Mediterranean cruise on the advice of his doctors. The Queen of course accompanied him; but so did Princess Victoria, whom she had invited in order to give her a week or two of relief from looking after Queen Alexandra at Sandringham. It proved an unhappy arrangement. The Queen's love of natural beauty and of ancient monuments served only to inflame the innate philistinism of her sister-in-law, who not only subjected her to a torrent of mindless mockery but also incited the King to join in the cruel sport. 'I am so glad to be back,' the poor Queen wrote on her return home.

Shy by nature and unwilling to be thought an intruder on affairs of State, the Queen evolved her own method of rescuing the King from apprehension or perplexity. She would ask Stamfordham or some other trusted member of the household to pass on her advice as if it were his own. The Queen, however, acted alone in protecting her husband from one hazard; she did not like him to be contradicted at any time, particularly at meals and especially by women. Any visitor infringing this taboo was discouraged with unexpected ferocity; the infrequency with which the Queen unleashed her Teck temper made its use all the more memorable. She was said to be the only person of whom fearless Nancy Astor stood in awe. Even the landscape had to keep its distance. As the Queen arrived one day to inspect the new gardens at Windsor, a low-hanging branch of an oak grazed her toque. She gazed severely at the offending limb but without comment.

The Queen was formidable in defence of what was due to the person of the sovereign and to the dignity, almost the divinity, of kingship. Yet she was not without a sense of humour, however suppressed it may have been during her husband's lifetime. Princess Alice said of her sister-in-law: 'In youth she was gay and amusing and would often be in fits of laughter. As Queen she was so sedate, so *posée*. But after the King's death she blossomed out once more and all her great worth was revealed.'

Queen Mary's humour sometimes found expression in those mildly unkind practical jokes which seem to afflict royal families the world over. She cared little for dogs, but when staying with her niece the Duchess of Beaufort at Badminton she did become fond enough of one animal to enact a ritual each night at the end of dinner; she would ceremoniously give it a dog biscuit. On the evening the local bishop came to dine, it was to him that she delegated the duty, handing him the biscuit with a few words of explanation. But the prelate, rather hard of hearing, thought that he was being offered the Badminton equivalent of a sheep's eye at a desert feast. Accepting the mark of favour with misgiving, he munched his way through it to the last crumb. Other families, amid shouts of laughter, would at once have explained the mistake. That night nobody stopped him and nobody laughed until after his departure. It is not an agreeable story.

Yet the Queen could also display a gentler, more whimsical humour that has worn well with the years. When a friend mentioned a certain notorious lady whose successive marriages had obliged her to change her name seven times, she replied: 'Well, I have had to change mine quite a lot: Princess May, Duchess of York, Duchess of Cornwall, Princess of Wales, Queen. But whereas mine have been by accident, hers have been by enterprise.'

Lord Mountbatten used often to speak of the poignant circumstances in which he heard of his father's death. Prince Louis of Battenberg had never wholly recovered from his enforced retirement as First Sea Lord in 1914, the victim of a German name and ancestry. But on 4 August 1921, the anniversary of the outbreak of war, he was promoted to Admiral of the Fleet in belated recognition of his services to the Royal Navy. In the following month his son, who was serving in HMS *Repulse*, sought his captain's permission to invite Prince Louis (by now created Marquess of Milford Haven) for a short North Sea cruise in the dreadnought. His spirits restored by these imaginative gestures, the old admiral was put ashore at Invergordon and seen off to London by train. Mountbatten then returned to his ship, but a day or two later went on leave to Dunrobin Castle to stay with the Duke and Duchess of Sutherland. Within twenty-four hours he heard that his father had died of a heart attack. He broke down and wept. The Prince of Wales, a fellow guest, came to comfort him. 'I envy you a father whom you could love,' he said. 'If my father had died, we should have felt nothing but relief.'

There is a Hanoverian flavour about the Prince's sympathy, recalling an age when monarchs and their heirs quarrelled rancorously behind masks of respect and affection. Yet those traditional estrangements, as much political as personal, offer no key to the tensions between King George V and his eldest son. The Prince of Wales, far from waiting in hungry expectation to inherit the throne, dreaded the prospect of kingship and its burdensome restraints. Like many others of his generation who had survived the war, he demanded some measure of freedom from the stiff conventions of his upbringing. That his father denied him. 'A virtuous king', wrote Logan Pearsall Smith, 'is a king who has shirked his proper function: to embody for his subjects an ideal of illustrious misbehaviour absolutely beyond their reach.' That teasing paradox is not without truth; it helps to explain, for instance, the popularity of King Edward VII. His son, however, preferred to follow the example of Queen Victoria, believing that the survival of the monarchy depended upon rigid standards of morality and manners: two facets of human behaviour to which he attached equal weight. Thus the differences between an apprehensive King and a wilful heir, at least in the immediate post-war years, were conflicts not of principle but of temperament: absurd squabbles over dress and deportment that neither man was prepared to discuss with goodwill or resolve with understanding.

The Prince was twenty-seven when he spoke those chilling words of condolence to Mountbatten, yet still subjected to a parental surveillance that challenged both pride and reason. What made it harder to bear was the universal adulation which greeted his public appearances, particularly during a succession of arduous tours that took him to most parts of the Empire and beyond. Although endowed with boyish good looks, an engaging informality and ready charm, he was handicapped by shyness and uncertain stamina. 'I have just come back from seeing off the Prince of Wales at Victoria,' Curzon wrote in 1920. 'Crowds of cheering people. In a little tight naval uniform which clung close to his figure he did not look above 15, quite a pathetic little person.' The Prince also had to overcome an aversion to foreigners: one of the few beliefs he was able to share with his father. He told his confidante, Lady Coke: 'The more I live abroad (and I don't live anywhere else nowadays!!) the more thankful I am that I was born an Englishman.' All those embarrassments he surmounted with triumphant panache. Lord Reading, who had recently returned from a diplomatic mission to Washington, wrote to Stamfordham:

The Prince has proved a better Ambassador than all of us rolled into one. He has caught the American spirit, so difficult to understand quickly, and has done more in America to make their people comprehend the strength of the democratic support to our monarchy than all books and articles and propaganda.

A more remarkable tribute came from M. Jusserand, the French ambassador in Washington, who reported to his Government: 'Son succès a été complet auprès des gens les plus divers; les Anglais n'ont jamais rien fait qui ait pu si utilement servir à effacer les anciennes animosités.'

Even the King, so sparing with praise of his children, wrote to the Prince after his visit to Canada:

I offer you my warmest congratulations on the splendid success of your tour, which is due in a great measure to your own personality and the wonderful way in which you have played up. It makes me very proud of you and makes me feel very happy that my son should be received with such marvellous enthusiasm of loyalty and affection.

The euphoria did not last. The Prince of Wales, who was required by both his father and his entourage to behave with the circumspection of a proconsul, found much of his overseas itinerary of paralysing boredom. 'He showed no sign of taking an interest in the country, its institutions or government,' the British ambassador in Tokyo reported to London. The Prince also 'made the mistake of not quite realizing that he was in a foreign country ... and he seemed to think that he could alter his programme just as he pleased and refuse to go on expeditions for which long and expensive preparations had been made.' But with an understanding rarely shown by the King, Sir Charles Eliot's letter continues: 'I began to sympathize with him and to feel how dull and monotonous everything appears on a royal tour. Princes must think that red carpets and flags are a kind of vegetation that grows everywhere like grass and trees.' The Prince was guilty of endearing indiscretions, too, as when he loudly declared at a reception that the Governors of Hong Kong and Singapore were 'fossilized clerks who ought to be kept in a cupboard in Whitehall'.

He also lapsed from decorum in trying to procure informal companionship at successive stops along the route. The Japanese alone were co-

operative. 'With their usual excess of precaution,' Eliot told the Foreign
Secretary, 'they subjected every female thing that could come near him to
a medical examination.... There was nearly a terrible scandal because two
missionary ladies who wished to present him with a Japanese Bible were
hurried off by the police on the ground that they had not been inspected
and disinfected.'

All such improprieties, whether at home or abroad, were either reported
directly to the King or reached him by an intelligence network said to
include Princess Victoria and Sister Agnes. At one moment they were
considered grave enough to warrant a meeting at Downing Street attended
by Lloyd George, Stamfordham, the Prince himself and senior members of
his staff. It was made memorable by the Prime Minister's rebuke: 'If you
are one day to be a constitutional King, you must first be a constitutional
Prince of Wales.'

King George v has passed into history as a heavy-handed father, not
because he tried to impress on his son the danger of a scandal-ridden
monarchy; such apprehension was justified. Where he acted unwisely was
in rebuking peccadilloes with a severity that should have been reserved for
grave misconduct.

At Sandringham one Christmas, the Prince of Wales explained to Lady
Wigram the meaning of the fashionable psychological term 'complex'. His
own, he confessed, was impatiently shouting instructions to his chauffeur;
if the wrong turning were taken, it drove him to a frenzy. As for his father,
the Prince continued, he had two complexes: a passion for punctuality and
a fussiness about clothes. Both the King's preoccupations bore heavily on
his sons, although no more so than on his courtiers and members of the
Government. Indeed, his acute sense of time left its mark on national life
between the wars. When the Cabinet produced a report on the observance
of 11 November as an annual day of remembrance, the King insisted that,
'as no two watches agree', there must be maroons to mark the beginning
and end of the two-minute silence. Within the royal family, the story is still
told of Prince Henry's homecoming after several months abroad. He arrived
at the palace just as his father had sat down to dine. 'Late as usual, Harry,'
was the King's greeting.

Fearing the certainty of a rebuke, the princes rarely risked a breach of
punctuality. But in the cut and colour of their clothes, particularly naval or
military uniform, lay many a hazard. Even the most successful overseas
tour would be punctuated by letters from the King such as this:

From various photographs of you which have appeared in the papers I see that you
wear turned-down collars in white uniform, with a collar and black tie. I wonder
whose idea that was, as anything more unsmart I never saw; I have worn tunics for
20 years in white, which was very smart.

As the Duke of York prepared to return home from a similarly arduous tour, his father issued minute instructions about his uniform: 'Frock coat and epaulettes, without medals and riband, only stars.' The King added a last injunction: 'We will not embrace at the station before so many people. When you kiss Mama take your hat off.' Only one thing was worse than the wrong sort of clothes for an Empire tour and that was no clothes at all. It infuriated the King to see newspaper pictures of the Prince of Wales and Mountbatten cooling off at sea: 'You and Dick in a swimming pool together is hardly dignified, though comfortable in a hot climate, you might as well be photographed naked, no doubt it would please the public.'

At home the princes would stiffen in apprehension before entering their father's presence. One morning at breakfast the King said to his eldest son: 'I hear you were not wearing gloves at the ball last night. Please see that this does not occur again.' Another day there was a storm because the Prince of Wales's hunting boots had pink tops. When he appeared for the first time in the new style of trousers with turn-ups, the King asked with heavy sarcasm: 'Is it raining in *here*?' At the age of thirty he was similarly reprimanded in front of guests at Sandringham for coming in to tea in shooting clothes, having been to see a sick dog; he at once left the table and ordered tea in his room. There was an altercation at Balmoral between the King and the Prince over the correct way to wear the skean-dhu in the stocking; Prince George remarked engagingly to the Minister in Attendance that he never knew what to do with the knives and forks and other odds and ends demanded by the kilt.

One of the Prince of Wales's first acts on becoming King in 1936 was to abolish the wearing of the frock coat at court. But after his abdication a year later, he seemed to find merit in the customs of his father's day. Winston Churchill, invited to dine with the Duke of Windsor in France, found him wearing full Highland dress. He wrote to his wife: 'When you think you could hardly get him to put on a short coat and black tie when he was Prince of Wales, one sees the change in the point of view.'

King George saw in his son's cavalier attitude to dress the symptom of a deeper malaise: an unwillingness to prepare for his eventual role. By the post-war decade, scarcely a shadow of divine right remained to sustain the monarchy; its survival depended on the aptitudes and self-discipline of the monarch. It was not necessary, in the King's view, to appease the forces of republicanism, but rather to invoke those sober, middle-class beliefs that instinctively repel revolution. Little in the Prince of Wales's life seemed to reflect such values: rather a world of night clubs and painted finger nails, of equivocal weekends and loose marriage ties. During one Empire tour he was contemptuous of a telegram from his father warning him not to go dancing in Holy Week – 'Holy Week with a capital H and a capital W,' the

Prince sneered – and had to be dissuaded from sending a violent reply. It was also reported to Buckingham Palace that the Prince smoked too much and was 'rather free with alcohol'; but the King enjoyed a cigarette and knew of old how rumour could multiply a glass of wine and a thimbleful of port.

The King blamed some of his son's shortcomings on a raffish circle of friends. He particularly mistrusted Captain Edward Metcalfe, popularly known as 'Fruity', an ebullient cavalryman attached to the Prince's entourage during his tour of India and subsequently an equerry on his personal staff. In November 1924, the King tried to persuade his son to part with Metcalfe, but found him 'very obstinate'. A few months later he gave orders that Metcalfe was to be posted to India on the staff of a new Commander-in-Chief; within two years, however, he had bounced back and was once more in the Prince's service. The Earl of Dudley, an intimate friend of the Prince of Wales from Oxford days, also felt the King's displeasure when Sir Samuel Hoare, Secretary of State for India, nominated him to be Governor of Madras. Although Dudley was an able man of business who had acquired some knowledge of Indian affairs during his years in the Commons, the King refused to approve the appointment.

One way in which Metcalfe made himself unwelcome at court was by encouraging the Prince of Wales to ride in steeplechases. The King had often remonstrated with his son for overtaxing his strength with bouts of violent exercise. Now he feared that the Prince, a courageous but unskilled horseman, was endangering the succession to the throne. He told Queen Alexandra in 1924:

Yesterday David had a fall riding in a point to point race near Aldershot and bruised and cut his face a little and got slight concussion, but it is nothing serious.... It is too bad that he should continue to ride in these steeple chases. I have asked him not to on many occasions, everyone thinks it is a great mistake, as he runs unnecessary risks.

The Prince's equestrianism displeased his father in other ways. 'Why doesn't my son ride like a gentleman?' the King asked Metcalfe on observing that the Prince used a snaffle. With a courtier's presence of mind, Metcalfe replied: 'Because he does not have Your Majesty's hands.' The Prince took an unkind revenge. Shooting with his father at Sandringham in the year of his tumble near Aldershot, and having missed several birds, he put down his gun and called out: 'I think this is an old woman's game.'

What most haunted the King and Queen was their eldest son's refusal to marry. Instead he remained in his small bachelor quarters in St James's Palace, solaced by a succession of married women. Only once was his name linked to that of an unmarried girl: Lady Rosemary Leveson-Gower, the

younger daughter of the Duke of Sutherland, but it was never a serious
romance and in 1919 she married the Prince's friend, Lord Dudley. The
first of those married women with whom he fell in love was Lady Coke, the
confidante of his unhappy years in the army. 'You have been too angelically
kind to me for words,' he told her in 1917, 'and have absolutely changed
my life.' A few weeks later a chance encounter with Mrs William Dudley
Ward, the wife of a Liberal MP, began a liaison that lasted for the next
sixteen years. During that long attachment, other women flitted in and out
his life: but none could match Freda Dudley Ward in sweetness of nature
or generosity of heart. Until the Prince fell in love with Mrs Simpson, she
was his wife in all but name.

Such domestic fidelity brought no satisfaction to the King. He wanted to
see the Prince married, installed in Marlborough House and raising the
next generation of the royal family. In private he would refer disparagingly
to his son's mistresses as 'the lacemaker's daughter' or 'the South American
whore', as if both vocations carried much the same sort of stigma. Yet he
did try to understand that strain of melancholy in his son's character which
not even Freda Dudley Ward's love could entirely exorcize. In 1930 he
agreed to the Prince's request to restore Fort Belvedere, near Windsor, as
a country retreat. 'What could you possibly want that queer old place for?'
the King inquired. 'Those damn week-ends, I suppose.' Then he smiled.
'Well, if you want it, you can have it.' As the Prince later wrote of his
toytown castle: 'Soon I came to love it as I loved no other material thing.'

From time to time the King would plead with his son to put his life in
order both for his own sake and for that of the monarchy. An account of
one such conversation, given by the King to a friend, begins with a
significant disclaimer. The King assured the Prince that he did not intend
to have a row with him, which suggests that their previous discussions had
been less than harmonious. He went on to say that although the Prince was
now at the zenith of his popularity, the public would one day learn of his
double life and recoil from it with the vigour of the nonconformist conscience. It was true, the King continued, that all young men sowed their
wild oats; but wasn't the Prince at thirty-eight rather beyond that age? He
felt sure that his son was not at heart happy, and never would be until he
had settled down. And had he considered how lost and lonely he would feel
as a bachelor King living on his own in Buckingham Palace?

The Prince replied that he resented the way in which scandalmongers
told tales to the King about his private life; and that he believed the nation
had grown more tolerant in judging moral issues. Above all, he confessed
that the thought of marrying a foreign princess was distasteful to him, yet
understood that the King would not wish him to marry a commoner. On
this point the King explained that times had changed and that he would be

prepared to consider a suitable, well-born English girl. It was, the Prince replied, the first time that this had ever been suggested to him. That note of surprise on the part of the Prince is disingenuous. After the Privy Council meeting in 1917 which established the House of Windsor and renounced German titles, the King wrote: 'I also informed the Council that May and I had decided some time ago that our children would be allowed to marry into British families. It was quite a historical occasion.'

Since then the King had given permission for Princess Mary to marry Viscount Lascelles and for the Duke of York to marry Lady Elizabeth Bowes-Lyon. Had the Prince of Wales produced a bride of similar background, there is no reason to believe that the King would have withheld his consent. The Prince failed to confide in his father not because those he loved were lacking in royal blood but because they were one and all married women; and the most seismic of his romances was yet to come.

As the scandalmongers feasted on the Prince's reputation, the King grieved both for a wayward child and a threatened monarchy. But few suspected the burden he bore. Like Stevenson's Weir of Hermiston, another father who had lost his son's friendship and even his son's toleration, 'on he went up the great, bare staircase of his duty'.

The relationship between the King and his younger sons was scarcely less astringent. He believed that happiness lay only in a settled family life; and until they married he was ever on his guard against unsuitable attachments and other, more trivial failings. So much censure leavened by so little praise undermined their confidence. It cannot have been by chance that every one of his children was in some degree afflicted by nervous strain.

Prince Albert suffered least from parental reproof. In him the King recognized many of his own virtues: industry, sobriety, domesticity, the simple Christian faith of a sailor, courage in surmounting ill health and a frustrating stammer. They shared the same absorbed interest in the countryside and shooting and clothes; they wrote in almost identical hands. Yet it was an unequal partnership marked by the deference of a son for his father and of a subject for his sovereign. The King acknowledged that imbalance in a letter of 1923 to his son, by now Duke of York: 'You have always been so sensible and easy to work with and you have always been ready to listen to any advice and to agree with my opinions about people and things, that I feel that we have always got on very well together (very different to dear David).'

Yet not even that most submissive of sons could avoid a niggling rebuke across thousands of miles. On the strength of a newspaper photograph taken during the Duke's tour of New Zealand, the King wrote accusing him of inattention when inspecting a guard of honour; the blame lay not with a prince accustomed to ceremonial for the past twenty years but with the distorting lens of the camera. That same year, Prince Henry, a dedicated cavalry officer of twenty-seven, found this letter awaiting him on his return from cancelled army manœuvres:

I can't quite understand how you got leave and therefore missed the ride home. I should have thought that you would have remained with your men and shown thereby that you wished to share their discomfort, at least I should have done so if I had been your age. But no doubt times have changed since my young days.

To shirk either duty or discomfort would have been wholly out of character in Prince Henry, whose only ambition during those years between the wars was to command his regiment free from the encumbrance of royal protocol.

An engaging charm protected Prince George, the youngest and most handsome of the King's surviving sons, from the consequences of occasional folly. When the storm clouds blew up at Buckingham Palace or Sandringham he could depend on the sympathy if not the intervention of his mother. Alone of her children he had the historical and aesthetic curiosity to discuss with her all those works of art which in other royal eyes seemed scarcely to exist. Emotionally as rigid as the buckram on which rested her *parure* of diamonds and Garter star, she would soften into affection at the thought of him. 'Be an angel,' she began unexpectedly in a note to her husband's equerry, 'and find out for me from the Admiralty whether any ship is likely to go to Malta before Xmas as I have two or three largish parcels for Prince George.'

If the conduct of the boys remained almost wholly the King's preserve, the upbringing and welfare of Princess Mary was conceded to her mother. As early as 1912, the Queen had conceived an imaginative marriage for her only daughter, then aged fifteen. She would be betrothed to Ernst August of Hanover, heir to the Duke of Brunswick. As the only descendant in the male line of King George III, he would reunite what Queen Mary called the 'old' royal family (to which she belonged through her mother) to her husband's dynasty of Saxe-Coburg-Gotha, soon to be renamed the House of Windsor. Although Ernst August's kingdom of Hanover had been annexed to Prussia in 1866, the young Prince was nevertheless an eligible suitor. 'He will have a great fortune,' the Queen told Mensdorff at Windsor in the summer of 1912, 'and could be in England a lot.' She added that she would prefer such a husband for her daughter to the heir to a small country like Greece, Rumania or Bulgaria. Her plan came to nothing. Less than a year later, Ernst August married the only daughter of the German Emperor.

The war put an end to such dynastic matchmaking, and it was not until almost a decade later that Princess Mary was married to a Yorkshire landowner fifteen years her senior: Viscount Lascelles, heir to the fifth Earl of Harewood. Even before succeeding to the family estates, he had inherited a fortune of several million pounds from his eccentric great-uncle, Lord Clanricarde. The King shared his son-in-law's interest in racing, the Queen his knowledge of pictures and furniture. 'Being my only daughter,' the King wrote, 'I confess that I dread the idea of losing her, but thank God she will live in England.' He offered the family a marquessate, but they preferred to remain earls; marquessates, they believed, died out more quickly. In 1932, however, he took much delight in creating his daughter Princess Royal. The Queen in particular enjoyed her regular visits to Harewood, from which she would sally out to visit other country houses and pillage the well-stocked antique shops of Harrogate.

With the departure of Princess Mary to the North of England, her parents longed increasingly for daughters-in-law whom they could welcome into the family circle. These hopes were only partly satisfied. The Prince of Wales did not marry in his father's lifetime; Prince George delayed until 1934 and Prince Henry until 1935. The Duke of York, however, always more dependable than his brothers, made a memorably successful choice. In January 1923 he was betrothed to Lady Elizabeth Bowes-Lyon, youngest daughter of the fourteenth Earl of Strathmore. The King, easily cast down by the world's trouble, wrote in reply to a letter of congratulation: 'I think the French are playing the very devil. State of Ireland awful. Begin to doubt whether Lausanne will succeed in producing peace. Baldwin's mission to Washington about debt will fail I fear. So things look black everywhere, this event is the only gleam of sunshine.'

Chips Channon, with his inspired talent for popping up at the centre of events, had a few days earlier found himself a fellow guest of Lady Elizabeth at Lord Gage's house in Sussex. He noted her reaction to an embarrassing rumour:

The evening papers have announced her engagement to the Prince of Wales. So we all bowed and bobbed and teased her, calling her 'Ma'am': I am not sure that she enjoyed it. It couldn't be true, but how delighted everyone would be! She certainly has something on her mind. . . . She is more gentle, lovely and exquisite than any woman alive, but this evening I thought her unhappy and distraite. I longed to tell her I would die for her, although I am not in love with her. Poor Gage is desperately fond of her – in vain, but he is far too heavy, too Tudor and squirearchal for so rare and patrician a creature as Elizabeth.

Then came the official news of her betrothal, not to the Prince of Wales but to the Duke of York. Channon's diary continues:

I was so startled and almost fell out of bed when I read the Court Circular. . . . We have all hoped, waited, so long for this romance to prosper, that we had begun to despair that she would ever accept him. He has been the most ardent of wooers, and was apparently at St. Paul's Walden on Sunday, when he at last proposed to her. He motored at once to Sandringham and the announcement is the result, the royalties allowing her no time to change her mind. He is the luckiest of men, and there's not a man in England today that doesn't envy him. The clubs are in gloom.

Another chronicler, Mr Asquith, was bidden to inspect the wedding presents a day or two before the marriage ceremony in Westminster Abbey. As always when describing royal occasions, he wrote with a sneer:

I went in my knee breeches and medals after dinner to Buckingham Palace, where the rooms big as they are were very nearly crowded. There were huge glass cases like you see in the Bond St. shops, filled with jewels and every kind of gilt and silver ware: not a thing did I see that I would have cared to have or give. The poor little bride, everyone says is full of charm and stood in a row with the King and Queen and the bridegroom, and was completely overshadowed.

It must have been the very last time that Lady Elizabeth Bowes-Lyon was overshadowed, whether as Duchess of York, Queen Consort or Queen Mother. The King adored her at sight. 'The better I know and the more I see of your dear little wife,' he wrote to Bertie from Balmoral soon after the marriage, 'the more charming I think she is and everyone fell in love with her here.' The family marvelled at the King's response when she appeared slightly late for a meal, and apologized. 'I think', he said, 'we must have sat down two minutes early today.' For her part, the young Duchess found him 'angelic'. She wrote of the King after his death:

I miss him dreadfully. Unlike his own children I was never afraid of him, and in all the twelve years of having me as a daughter-in-law he never spoke one unkind or abrupt word to me, and was always ready to listen and give advice on one's own silly little affairs. He was so kind and dependable. And when he was in the mood, he could be deliciously funny too!

The serenity and sweet temper which she brought to the royal house have endured unbroken for sixty years. Yet those qualities alone would not have protected her from the buffets of fortune in peace and war. Descended from Kings of Scotland, she could also boast one of those rumbustious family histories punctuated by brawls and battles, rebellion and imprisonment, a heritage of robust self-confidence that was to sustain not only her marriage but the monarchy itself.

The King liked a book with a plot, a tune he could hum and a picture that told a story. Such simple tastes evoke the disdain of the sophisticated, who

contrast the artistic munificence of a Charles I or a George IV with the
supposed philistinism of later sovereigns (although of the two paragons,
one lost both his throne and his head, the other every shred of kingly
virtue). Some of these discontented aesthetes reproach successive generations of the royal family with little whinnies of despair. Others, more
courtly, resort to that literary device known as meiosis or litotes: the expression of an opinion by denying the contrary. Thus one historian of the Victorian Age has written: 'It would be an exaggeration to say that authorship
enjoyed any special consideration at the Royal Court; the interest which
the Queen took in the literature of the day was not particularly extensive.'

And Sir Theodore Martin, hagiographer of the Prince Consort, wrote of
Queen Victoria's etchings: 'Of them it is enough to say that the drawing is
not remarkable, and that, as etchings, the difficulties of the art have not
been overcome.'

Such impeachments are sometimes just, sometimes not. Queen Victoria,
as it happened, read *Cornwallis on the Sacrament* and Guizot's *Révolution de
l'Angleterre* while her hair was being done; filled album after album with
charming water-colour sketches; and sang to Mendelssohn, the composer
wrote, with only a very occasional false note. King Edward VII, it is true,
was of too restless a temperament to settle down to a good book. In the
unfamiliar atmosphere of a literary dinner he once inquired about the
qualifications of a fellow guest. 'An authority on Lamb', he was told. The
King, who believed that there was a time and place for everything, exclaimed incredulously: 'An authority on *lamb*?' Yet it was he who established the Order of Merit to reward the most distinguished minds in the
kingdom; and his advice to an aspiring man of letters recognized both the
pursuit of learning and the realities of life: 'Stick to Shakespeare, Mr Lee,
there's money in Shakespeare.' Sidney Lee, however, thought he knew
better and produced a two-volume life of King Edward VII.

King George V's approach to literature was respectful without being
reverent. He had scarcely reigned one month when Asquith's private
secretary telephoned the palace on Thomas Hardy's seventieth birthday to
suggest that a telegram to 'old Hardy' might be appreciated. 'It shall be
done,' came the reply; and Mr Hardy, of Alnwick, who made the King's
fishing rods, was astonished to receive royal congratulations on attaining an
age he had not attained, on a day which was the anniversary of nothing.
Three years later, on the death of Alfred Austin, the King proposed that
the office of Poet Laureate be allowed to lapse; only when Asquith pressed
for the appointment of Robert Bridges did he change his mind.

In spite of these misadventures, the King was neither indifferent to the
repute of authors nor ignorant of their works. He took much care in
selecting candidates for the Order of Merit (including both Hardy and

Bridges) and would have bestowed it on Kipling, Shaw and Housman had not all three of them refused. From 1890 until the end of his life he kept a reading list which shows that on average he read one book a week. Since he had to spend some hours of each day perusing official documents of one sort or another, as well as *The Times*, that is a remarkable achievement for a man who devoted much of his leisure to country pursuits. He enjoyed new novels as they appeared: John Buchan, Gilbert Frankau, A. E. W. Mason, C. S. Forester, Ernest Hemingway; even, with many expressions of disapproval, an unexpurgated edition of *Lady Chatterley's Lover* imported into Balmoral by a lady-in-waiting of liberal views. He was also heard shouting with laughter over *Some People*, by Harold Nicolson.

Mostly the King read memoirs and biographies, his comments echoing the sentiments of an earlier Sailor King, William IV: 'I know no person so perfectly disagreeable and even dangerous as an author.' He displayed an angry contempt for those who abused the confidences of friends or the trust of an official position in return for money. Mrs Asquith's *Autobiography*, published in 1920, provoked a particular storm. 'The King, who kept me for nearly an hour,' Curzon wrote to his wife, 'let fly about Margot.... He severely condemns Asquith for not reading and Crewe for reading and passing her scandalous chatter.'

He was shocked, too, when Sir Almeric FitzRoy, soon after his retirement as Clerk of the Privy Council, published two thick volumes describing the author's private conversations with ministers and others over a quarter of a century. It was a temptation of the office. Queen Victoria had been similarly outraged by the memoirs of Charles Greville, Clerk of the Privy Council from 1821 to 1859; and his editor, Henry Reeve, was denied the knighthood that would otherwise have come to him as registrar of the Council's Judicial Committee.

The King regretted the spate of contentious memoirs and diaries of the post-war era in which warriors and others refought their battles. He denounced Colonel Charles à Court Repington, military correspondent of *The Times*, as 'a cad and a blackguard'; reprimanded Field-Marshal French for reviving 'angry disputes and personal wrangling'; declared himself 'disgusted' by Admiral Bacon's book on Jutland. He nevertheless may himself have hankered after the fame and more material rewards of authorship. When Haig told him that he had been offered £100,000 for his memoirs, the King replied: 'Yes, and I expect they would offer me a million.' He also said to Baldwin that he could, if he chose, relate 'the most extraordinary things' that had been told him by other ministers. 'I hope, Sir,' Baldwin replied, 'that you will not write autobiographical articles in the Press?' The King said: 'Not till I'm broke!'

Any breach of confidence which touched his own family was certain to incur disfavour. There was, for instance, the curious episode of Sir Frederick Ponsonby and the Empress Frederick. Soon after the accession of Edward VII in 1901, Ponsonby had accompanied him to Friedrichshof, where his sister the Empress lay dying of cancer. During the visit, the Empress sent for Ponsonby and asked him to take back to England with him the many letters which she had written to her mother Queen Victoria. These had been returned to her from Windsor after the Queen's death earlier that year; but as they contained political indiscretions, she now wanted them removed from the reach of her son, the Emperor William, before her approaching death. Ponsonby promised to meet her wishes and before travelling back to London with the King he quietly added the two large boxes of letters to his own baggage. What remains extraordinary is that he did not then deposit them in the Royal Archives at Windsor, but instead kept them in his own custody for the next twenty-six years. In 1927 Ponsonby decided to edit and publish a selection of the letters, although it was far from certain that he was legally entitled to the copyright. With some plausibility, however, he argued that if the Empress had not intended him to publish them, she would have taken the simpler course in 1901 of giving them to her brother, King Edward. Although King George V was doubtful about Ponsonby's plan, he did not forbid it. The book appeared in 1928, provoking controversy in both England and Germany, as well as a threat of legal action for breach of copyright from the exiled Kaiser. 'The King at first seemed interested in the book,' Ponsonby later wrote, 'but when his sister the Princess Victoria denounced it as one of the most dreadful books ever published, he joined in the general abuse of it.' So much unwelcome publicity cannot have increased the King's confidence in his high-handed Keeper of the Privy Purse.

As the guardian of his grandmother's reputation, the King erupted with rage at the flippancy of Lytton Strachey's *Queen Victoria*, which appeared in 1921. Yet when the final volumes of Monypenny and Buckle's life of Disraeli were submitted to him before publication, he proved the most reasonable of censors. His sole doubt concerned Disraeli's reference to Queen Victoria as 'The Faery'; and when Rosebery pleaded that Disraeli had meant no disrespect but was borrowing a romantic image from Spenser's *Faerie Queene*, the King gave way. The King had been right to suspect gentle mockery in Disraeli's use of the phrase, and his refusal to veto it was therefore all the more enlightened. He showed the same tolerance on being asked whether he minded a remark of Gladstone's that was to appear in Crewe's life of Rosebery: 'The Queen alone is enough to kill any man.' He himself could speak with as much authority as any on his grandmother's strength of will; had he not resisted it forty years earlier, he would now be reigning as King Albert I.

Of all the volumes which passed through the King's hands, none brought him more pleasure than his stamp albums. He claimed that they had saved his life during the war by providing complete relaxation from affairs of State. In peacetime he tried to spend three afternoons each week looking at his collection under the guidance of Sir Edward Bacon, the curator. The King enjoyed his company, and on learning that he suffered from a weak chest, bought him a fur-lined coat with astrakhan collar to keep out the cold during his journeys between Croydon and the Palace. Godfrey-Faussett, his naval equerry, also took up the pastime, and the two old shipmates would exchange philatelic gossip. The King wrote to him in 1921: 'Glad you got a lot of stamps so cheap at the auction, look out you don't get ruined. Did you see that last week a pair of 2-cents British Guiana on envelope in Paris fetched £5250 and one Hawaiian 2-cents used fetched £3894. Wonderful!!!'

The King personally approved all new designs for stamps in Great Britain and the Crown Colonies. Only once did he fail to have his way. It was when the Inland Revenue determined to bring the stamp-printing monopoly of De La Rue to an end and divide it between De la Rue and Harrison. Although Harrison were hereditary printers to the sovereign, they lacked the experience of their rivals in producing stamps. 'Make me look like a stuffed monkey, don't they?' the King said of Harrison's first efforts, blurred and indelicate. The issue nevertheless went into circulation for a year before being replaced by a finer engraving.

It is due to the King's perceptive eye that the tradition of elegant, austere design continued throughout his reign and for a generation beyond (although briefly broken by an ornate issue to mark the British Empire Exhibition of 1924). Towards the end of his life he begged Sir Kenneth (later Lord) Clark, Surveyor of the King's Pictures, to discourage fancy issues of stamps, as if Great Britain were 'some ridiculous place like San Marino'. Clark, even then the guardian of civilized values, gladly gave his promise. Thirty years later, when he had become chairman of the postage stamp advisory committee, a new Postmaster General, Anthony Wedgwood Benn, informed Clark that he intended to make frequent issues of illustrative stamps. 'I told him', Clark wrote, 'that I could not agree with this and offered to resign, an offer that was most gladly accepted. Then I told him the story of King George V: he thought I must be a little mad.'

'The Prince Consort surprised me exceedingly by his intimate knowledge of what I may call *the conduct* of a picture,' Frith wrote after exhibiting his *Derby Day* at the Royal Academy in 1858:

He told me why I had done certain things and how, if a certain change had been made, my object would have been assisted. How the masses of light and shade might still be more evenly balanced, and how some parts of the picture might receive still more completion. I put many of the Prince's suggestions to the proof after the close of the Exhibition, and I improved my picture in every instance.

King George V did not inherit his grandfather's analytic eye, although Frith's *Ramsgate Sands*, exhibited four years earlier than *Derby Day* and bought by Queen Victoria, was one of his favourite pictures. He hung it in the private apartments at Buckingham Palace, together with the work of other trusted contemporaries such as Landseer and Winterhalter, Grant and Phillips; he was particularly attached to Meissonier's undemanding narrative piece, *The Brawl*. Over the years there has been well-bred comment that the man who inherited the finest private collections in the world should have surrounded himself with masters of lesser rank. But then it was he who had to live with them.

The King was nevertheless a proud and possessive trustee of his heritage. During a visit to the National Gallery, he bullied a hesitant Sir Kenneth Clark into becoming Surveyor of the King's Pictures. The reluctant courtier later described their conversation:

'Why won't you come and work for me?'
'Because I wouldn't have time to do the job properly.'
'What is there to do?'
'Well, Sir, the pictures need looking after.'
'There's nothing wrong with them.'
'And people write letters asking for information about them.'
'Don't answer 'em. *I want you to take the job.*'

What Clark had feared came to pass. At the Queen's behest he found himself immersed more in the family history of the House of Hanover than in the care and study of the splendid collections in his charge. It has sometimes been suggested that the Queen was on an altogether higher aesthetic plane than her husband. Her chosen fields of interest were royal iconography, particularly that of the descendants of King George III and Queen Charlotte; furniture; and the miniature, from the dolls' house to the trinkets of Fabergé. She was a dedicated researcher, annotator and labeller; but in all her life she never bought a really good or important picture, never patronized the most imaginative artists of her day. Even in scholarship she lacked humility. When told that the little group of Frederick, Prince of Wales, playing the cello to his sisters was by Philippe Mercier, she replied imperiously: 'We prefer the picture to remain as by Nollekens.'

It was always a memorable day when the King visited an exhibition. At the opening of the Tate Gallery extension, he stood before the French Impressionists and called out to the Queen: 'Here's something to make you laugh, May.' In the National Gallery he shook his stick at a Cézanne, and in another room confided to the director: 'I tell you what, Turner was *mad*. My grandmother always said so.' The Royal Academy's cautious experiments provoked him to write: 'I never saw a worse lot of pictures. Modern art is becoming awful I think.' And when required to sign Augustus John's diploma as a Royal Academician, he exclaimed: 'What, that fellow! I've a damned good mind not to sign it.' Even the sight of a classroom of schoolgirls painting a flower arrangement aroused his suspicion. 'Isn't that useless?' he asked the Education Minister. 'It trains the powers of observation,' H. A. L. Fisher replied. 'Perhaps,' the King conceded. It was, after all, the sort of argument used to justify stamp collecting: that and an interest in geography.

The King's instinctive dislike of modern painting was reinforced by the treatment he received at the hands of leading artists. Charles Sims, chosen to paint an official portrait, gave his sovereign the elegant stance of another century. The King complained that its turned-out toes made him look like a ballet dancer and ordered it to be destroyed; the canvas was burned on the premises of the Royal Academy. Oswald Birley's portrait, the hands of which similarly failed to please, suffered a gentler fate; it was merely hung behind a door. He was well content, however, with John Lavery's conversation piece of the King and Queen and two of their children, now in the National Portrait Gallery. When viewing the work in the artist's studio, the King said he would like to have a hand in it, and was allowed to add a touch of blue to the Garter ribbon; the Queen followed suit. It pleased Lavery to recall that Velázquez, when painting Philip IV of Spain, had permitted the King to add the red cross of a Knight of Calatrava to his portrait.

Many a work was written off in royal eyes because the artist had failed to show a concern for the correct display of military accoutrements and decorations. At St Paul's Cathedral in 1931, the King observed to Dean Inge that the sculptor of the Kitchener memorial bust had put his Garter star too near the middle of his chest. Yet the King himself did not always despise artistic licence. After Norman Wilkinson had painted a picture of the royal yacht *Britannia* in the Solent, he agreed that it was accurate in every detail but asked whether the artist would move the buoy a little nearer the vessel, so that *Britannia* would appear to be making a tighter and more seamanlike turn. Wilkinson agreed.

The King also brought his practical mind to bear on a wider problem. In 1921 Stamfordham wrote on his behalf to the Chancellor of the Exchequer:

The King asks if, when you are considering possible new forms of taxation, it has occurred to you that a tax might be put upon works of art which leave this country? It would have the double effect of bringing money, though perhaps only a small amount into the Revenue, and prevent a process, which if persisted in, will gradually result in denuding these Islands of some of their most priceless artistic possessions.

The vast purchasing power of the United States had already lured many privately-owned treasures across the Atlantic, and it was perceptive of the King to suggest how sales might be discouraged. Ultimately, however, the method adopted by successive British Governments depended on licensing rather than deterrent taxation.

'Went to Covent Garden and saw Fidelio,' the King wrote in his diary, 'and d—d dull it was.' That same year he heard *The Merry Widow* four times. *In a Monastery Garden*, *Rose Marie*, *Tea for Two*, *No, No, Nanette*: these were the melodies that brought him most pleasure, although the lighter classical repertoire was not excluded. 'He is quite wonderful,' the King said of the violinist Kubelik after a recital at Sandringham in his father's day, 'but I wish he didn't have long hair.' A typical evening's programme on the gramophone was Caruso singing Handel's 'Largo', followed by the 'Hallelujah Chorus' and ending with a record of the Aldershot Military Tattoo.

The King deplored most musical innovations, from American jazz to the operas of Richard Strauss. During the interlude that occurs in the ceremony of changing the guard at Buckingham Palace, the band of the Grenadier Guards, after months of practice, one morning played extracts from *Elektra*. But the King preferred Johann Strauss. He sent out a message to the bandmaster: 'His Majesty does not know what the band has just played, but it is *never* to be played again.' It was nevertheless at the King's personal request that Delius was made a Companion of Honour in 1929.

Another well-worn record to be played after dinner was entitled 'The Departure of the Troopship', a sentimental yet stirring piece. It ended with the National Anthem, at which everybody in the drawing-room, including the King and Queen, rose to their feet. It was among their favourite tunes, and George Plank, invited to decorate the ceiling of the King's bedroom in the Queen's dolls' house, did no wrong in painting a pergola of roses in which the flowers reflected the musical notation of 'God Save the King'. Some renderings displeased him. 'I do wish that musicians would not play it so quickly,' he complained to Sir Landon Ronald at the Albert Hall. 'They hurry it through as though they wanted to get it over, and to me it means a great deal and I look upon it almost as a hymn.' Ronald explained that King Edward had always urged him to 'hurry it up'.

The King's patronage of the stage evaded the higher drama. 'Saw King

Lear', he wrote as a young man, 'but did not care about it.' And it was only at the age of seventy-seven that Queen Mary, with her superior education, watched a performance of *Hamlet* for the first time. Curiosity drew them both to *The Miracle*, in which the Duke of Rutland's daughter achieved a *tour de force* in her silent role. But Lady Diana Cooper's laurels wilted when the King summoned her to the royal box and said: 'Of course, you've got no words to learn or say, and that's half the battle.' As in previous reigns, an entire theatrical company was sometimes invited to Balmoral. The King enjoyed the actors' green-room repartee every bit as much as the comedies they presented. 'Is it true that you once had to dress in a pigsty?' he asked a member of a small travelling company. 'Yes, Sir,' was the reply, 'but I think they were pedigree pigs.'

The cinema became a relaxation, almost an addiction of his later years. He enjoyed such popular films as *The Scarlet Pimpernel*, but for his wife's sake forbade anything immodest or suggestive (at a stage performance of *No, No, Nanette*', the Queen was seen to avert her head when the chorus appeared in the far from exiguous bathing costumes of 1925). The King imposed a more surprising prohibition; he did not want to be shown descriptive documentaries about his Empire, of which, he said, he 'heard and saw quite enough in other ways'. Anything about ships touched his heart; but again there were exceptions. He personally rebuked the Head Master of Eton for having allowed *The Battleship Potemkin* to be shown there. Claude Elliott pleaded that it was good for the boys to see new film techniques, even if they did come from Soviet Russia. 'Nonsense,' the King replied, 'it is certainly not good for the boys to witness mutinies, especially naval mutinies.'

Some of the King's subjects were doubtless disappointed by their sovereign's near-indifference to the fine arts; many more were heartened by his patronage of sport. When Lord Brabourne, the Governor of Bombay, bought a racehorse to run at local meetings, Wigram told him: 'The King feels sure that a Governor who takes part in the joys of life will be much more at home with the people in the Province.' The racecourse was one of the few public places where the King was seen to laugh: perhaps the first indication that he was his father's son.

On the subject of horseracing, it was a family divided. King Edward, three times winner of the Derby, had no cause to discourage his children. Queen Victoria, by contrast, sent her grandson this doleful warning on his twentieth birthday: 'As for betting or anything of that kind, no end of young and older men have been ruined, parents' hearts broken and great names and Titles dragged in the dirt.' Sure enough, there was the scandal of Prince Francis of Teck, whose gambling debt of £10,000 on a single race at The Curragh his brother-in-law reluctantly helped to settle. On the death of King Edward, many feared that the new sovereign would either disperse or reduce the royal stable. He did neither, prompted as much by economics as by sentiment. His father had established himself as one of the most successful owner-breeders of his generation. Over the years he won £146,128 in stakes, received £269,495 in fees from stallions and another £77,000 from sales: a total of almost half a million in the days when each was worth a golden sovereign.

Although considered by the royal trainer, Richard Marsh, to be a better and more informed judge of a horse than his father, King George was a consistently unlucky owner. He won a classic race only at his twenty-fourth attempt, when in 1928 his bay filly Scuttle took the One Thousand Guineas; yet he was never heard to blame either trainer or jockey for the poor performance of a horse. He endured a distressing episode at the Derby of 1913. As the field swept round Tattenham Corner, a brave but misguided suffragette sacrificed her life in deliberately bringing down the King's colt, called Anmer after a village on the Sandringham estate. To add to his vexation, on the following morning he received this note from an equerry: 'Inquiries are being made as to whether Your Majesty is going to wear a tall hat at Epsom today.' The King wrote angrily at the bottom of the sheet: 'Who are the damned fools? A tall hat is *always* worn at this meeting at Epsom.'

Denied the greater prizes of racing, the King nevertheless enjoyed its camaraderie. He followed his father's custom of giving a Derby Day dinner at Buckingham Palace to members of the Jockey Club. Another annual event was the house party at Windsor Castle for Ascot races; whenever he had a winner, each woman guest at dinner received a brooch bearing his racing colours of purple, scarlet and gold. There were few such favours for the irreverent Nancy Astor. 'You are really becoming too grand for words,' she told the Duke of Roxburghe at Ascot one year, 'never leaving the royal stand. You might just as well be the court dentist.' To the King's subsequent delight, Roxburghe retorted: 'If ever I do have to pull out the King's teeth, I shall certainly come to you for the gas.'

The King also enjoyed his visits to the Duke of Richmond for Goodwood races and sometimes to Lord Derby for the Grand National. The Duke, an abstemious but liberal host, used to celebrate the departure of his royal guests by dining off plain boiled beef and carrots. One year his son persuaded the family butler, Mr Marshall, to wear a pedometer throughout a single day in race week. It registered nineteen and a half miles. The King's visits to both Knowsley and Goodwood in 1924 were complicated by the intrusion of State business. At each he was required to hold a Privy Council before racing began; in March to authorize emergency powers in the event of an expected transport strike, and in July to confirm an adjustment to the boundary between Northern Ireland and the Irish Free State. At Goodwood a year later, when an impending coal strike demanded yet another sudden meeting of the Privy Council, the King suggested that it could again be held in his host's drawing-room. But the priggish Home Secretary, Sir William Joynson-Hicks, thought that the country might be shocked by such supposed frivolity. The King thus felt obliged to cut short his racing and return to London. 'Just like my luck,' he wrote in his diary. By the end of his reign he had grown bolder. When Baldwin became Prime Minister for the third time, the King told him that he hoped the Cabinet reconstruction would be complete before the First July meeting at Newmarket.

As a gambler, however, his confidence seemed to wane with the years. 'Laid £300 on Lemberg to win,' he wrote of the Goodwood meeting in 1909. 'It came off.' The following year, in a handicap at Epsom, he risked £100 each way on his father's Derby winner, Minoru, and lost the lot. Yet in 1924 he put no more than £1 on Master Robert, who won the Grand National at 25 to 1. It must have been a larger bet which led him to record the defeat of Scuttle in the Oaks of 1928: 'We returned home wiser but certainly poorer.' In common with most desultory punters, the King is unlikely to have shown a profit from season to season; but he clung to the comforting illusion that his winnings were copious enough to subsidize his stamp collection.

The King's patronage of sport did not end with the settlement of a bookmaker's account. He was a sportsman in the now outmoded sense: a contestant, not merely an unathletic but bellicose spectator. At both yachting and shooting he could outshine almost any man in his kingdom. Neither pursuit lent itself to popular appeal; yet his reported skill evoked interest and admiration even among the millions of his subjects who had never harnessed wind to sail or seen one high pheasant after another despatched with effortless grace. Shooting remained his first love; but before the grouse lured him north, between Goodwood and Balmoral, he would spend an ecstatic week at Cowes.

'The *Britannia* has just passed us,' the Queen wrote during one such August, 'and I saw the King looking very wet and uncomfortable in oilskins – what a way to enjoy oneself.' Built in 1892 for the Prince of Wales, later King Edward, the cutter *Britannia* won 122 first prizes out of 289 starts during her first five years of racing. The Prince then put her on the market, disgusted by the bullying behaviour of the Kaiser, who looked on Cowes week as an opportunity to humiliate his uncle. 'The regatta used to be a pleasant relaxation for me,' the Prince complained. 'Since the Kaiser takes command, it is a vexation.' The yacht passed through various hands. One owner was John Lawson Johnston, the manufacturer of Bovril. Another was the financier E. T. Hooley, reputed to have abandoned his purchase on discovering that she had no funnel. (In his long climb to respectability, Hooley had earlier bought Anmer Hall, but was persuaded to re-sell it to the Prince of Wales; he also gave a service of gold communion plate to St Paul's Cathedral to mark the Queen's Diamond Jubilee.) Eventually bought back by King Edward in 1902, *Britannia* was used as a pleasure boat for the next eleven years.

In 1913, King George had her re-rigged as a racing cruiser; but it was not until after the war that she embarked on her second racing career, no less glorious than her first. 'I am indeed proud in owning such a good yacht 39 years old,' he wrote in August 1932. Two years later he noted that *Britannia* had since 1893 sailed in 569 races, winning 231 first prizes and 124 others. Sometimes he would take the helm himself: a distinctive figure in an old white flannel suit and sailor's hat without a peak. More often he would relinquish it to the superior skills of his racing master, Sir Philip Hunloke. The King liked to win races but was a good loser, too. Apparently immune to the seasickness which afflicted him in larger vessels, he enjoyed the chaff and nautical gossip, the discomfiture of inferior boats and their crews, the utter release from affairs of State. He was every inch the image of a Sailor King. Except on the calmest of days, the Queen never ventured on board, but would drive round the Isle of Wight inspecting churches, country houses and antique shops.

At the approach of the King's Silver Jubilee of 1935, the yachtsmen of England asked whether they could present him with a new boat. The King refused. 'As long as I live,' he replied, 'I will never own any other yacht than *Britannia*.' Within a year he was dead. Early on the morning of 10 July 1936, *Britannia* was towed into deep water south of the Isle of Wight and sunk.

NINE

POLITICAL PRESSURES

Labour Government — Age of Baldwin —
Indian summer — At death's door —
MacDonald carries on

In November 1923, less than six months after becoming Prime Minister, Baldwin changed the pattern of British politics. Against the advice of the King, he pushed his party into a general election and miscalculated the mood of the country. The result, declared on 8 December, left the Conservatives with only 258 seats, Labour with 191 and the Liberals with 158. No party possessed an absolute majority yet each was capable of forming a Government with the support or acquiescence of one of the remaining two. Since there was no common ground between the Conservatives and Labour, whichever of those two parties won the support of the Liberals would command a parliamentary majority.

'The Prime Minister came to see me,' the King wrote in his diary on 10 December, 'and I asked him not to resign but to meet Parliament and see what happens.' On the following day, after a Cabinet meeting, Baldwin agreed to remain in office until the new House of Commons assembled in January. The King's preference for such a course did not imply any personal confidence in Baldwin, but was wholly constitutional. As Stamfordham put it: 'The Sovereign ought not to accept the verdict of the Polls, except as expressed by the representatives of the electorate across the floor of the House of Commons.' Although a somewhat narrow and disputable doctrine in a democratic age, it did have a practical advantage: it allowed the business of government to continue while the leaders of the three parties manœuvred for office.

Baldwin had his own reasons for agreeing with the King. His first instinct on 8 December had been to resign in shame and despair at having led his party into defeat. But he was swiftly convinced by the majority of his colleagues that it lay in the Conservative interest for him to remain leader of the party and, at least temporarily, Prime Minister. He would thus thwart that minority of Tories who were determined both to rid themselves of a disastrous leader and to ensure that Labour should at all costs be denied office. These die-hards proposed to outvote Labour in the new Parliament by forming a coalition of Conservatives and Liberals led by somebody – anybody in fact – other than Baldwin. Their candidates included Balfour, Derby, Austen Chamberlain, Neville Chamberlain, Asquith, Grey, even Reginald McKenna, a wartime Chancellor of the Exchequer who had lost his parliamentary seat in 1918. But as long as Baldwin remained the Conservative leader, there could be no such coalition or alliance. When, on 10 December, the King suggested that he might consider 'a working arrangement' with the Liberals, Baldwin replied that in 1922 he had killed the Lloyd George Coalition and would never join another. Nor did he think it either honourable or prudent for the two capitalist parties to unite artificially in order to outlaw Socialism. As his confidant, Davidson, wrote on 12 December: 'Any dishonest combination of that sort – which means the sacrificing of principles by both Liberal and Tory to deprive Labour of their constitutional rights – is the first step down the road to revolution.'

In any case, a Conservative–Liberal alliance to exclude Labour from office depended on Asquith's support; and this he declined to countenance, in spite of what he described as 'appeals, threats, prayers from all parts, and from all sorts and conditions of men, women and lunatics, to step in and save the country from the horrors of Socialism and Confiscation'. Disliking the Tories more than he disliked Labour, he declared that on the defeat of Baldwin's Government in the new Parliament, the King should ask Mac-Donald to form an administration which he and his fellow Liberals would keep in office as long as it avoided extremist policies. Asquith could also reflect with satisfaction that 'if a Labour Government is ever to be tried in this country, as it will be sooner or later, it could hardly be tried under safer conditions'.

After an initial hesitation in December that lasted no more than forty-eight hours, the King's sense of fair play had led him to the same conclusion. He told Davidson that 'a Socialist Government would have an opportunity of learning their administrative duties and responsibilities under favourable conditions and that it was essential that their rights under the Constitution should in no way be impaired'. Stamfordham, too, could look back with satisfaction on his conduct of negotiations with the party leaders. He wrote to a friend in mid-January:

Ever since the result of the General Election, I have taken for granted that, on Baldwin's defeat in the House of Commons, the King would send for Ramsay MacDonald; and I have deprecated any attempt to prevent his having the same facilities which would be accorded to any Minister entrusted by the Sovereign with the formation of a Government. I therefore entirely agree with what you say – as things are the sooner the Labour Party comes into power the better. Personally

I am not alarmed and, unless they are upset by their own extremists, it would not surprise me were they to remain in office for some time, during which they may do considerable good.

So it came to pass. The King opened the new Parliament on 15 January 1924. Six days later, at the end of the customary debate on the Address, Labour and Liberals united to defeat the Conservatives by seventy-two votes. Baldwin at once resigned as Prime Minister and MacDonald was summoned to the palace. The King wrote in his diary for 22 January 1924:

I held a Council, at which Mr Ramsay MacDonald was sworn in a member. I then asked him to form a Government, which he accepted to do. I had an hour's talk with him, he impressed me very much; he wishes to do the right thing. Today 23 years ago dear Grandmama died. I wonder what she would have thought of a Labour Government.

Members of the new Cabinet who celebrated over lunch the next day were burdened by no such solemnity. 'We were a jolly party,' wrote Beatrice Webb, wife of the President of the Board of Trade, 'all laughing at the joke of Labour in Office.'

MacDonald faced unusual difficulties in forming his Cabinet. Most newly-appointed Prime Ministers are embarrassed by a plethora of well-qualified supplicants; MacDonald could scarcely find enough party stalwarts with the ability or experience to fill even the major posts. For the second most important place in the Government, that of Foreign Secretary, he initially chose J. H. Thomas, a man of coarse speech and coarser wit who had demonstrated his administrative talents in directing a succession of railway strikes. But there was fierce hostility to the appointment within the Labour ranks; Thomas instead accepted the Colonial Office, where his instinctive patriotism and robust utterances were more appreciated.

In the absence of any more eligible candidate, MacDonald became his own Foreign Secretary. He was encouraged to assume this double burden by Arthur Ponsonby, the younger brother of Fritz, who after nine years in the Diplomatic Service had resigned to sit in the Commons as a Liberal; finding his colleagues inadequately radical, Ponsonby had then joined the Labour Party and in January 1924 was installed at the Prime Minister's elbow as Parliamentary Under-Secretary for Foreign Affairs. Philip Snowden, dour but competent, became Chancellor of the Exchequer; and the avuncular Arthur Henderson, who alone of his colleagues had sat in the Cabinets of Asquith and Lloyd George, Home Secretary. J.R. Clynes, the new Lord Privy Seal, wrote picturesquely of 'the strange turn in Fortune's wheel which had brought MacDonald the starveling clerk, Thomas the engine driver, Henderson the foundry labourer and Clynes the mill-hand, to this pinnacle beside the man whose forebears had been Kings for so many splendid generations. We were making history.'

MacDonald was obliged to recruit men of eccentric political pedigree to conduct government business in the House of Lords. Haldane, increasingly estranged from the Liberals since 1915, returned to the Woolsack as Lord Chancellor. Lord Parmoor, once a Conservative MP, had been ennobled by Asquith, joined the Labour Party after the war and now became Lord President of the Council. Another recent convert, Major-General Christopher Thomson, was appointed Secretary of State for Air. Lord Chelmsford, a former Viceroy of India without party ties, agreed to occupy the uncontentious office of First Lord of the Admiralty. Sir Sydney Olivier, who had retired from the public service in 1920, was like Thomson created a peer and appointed Secretary of State for India.

Having assembled these representatives of many political persuasions and all social classes, MacDonald was obliged to consult *Whitaker's Almanack* for a list of the minor posts yet to be filled. Some he could scarcely imagine would lie in his province: the Lord Chamberlain, the Lord Steward, the Master of the Horse and other grandees of the royal household. Yet for generations these court officials had been appointed by the Prime Minister of the day, remaining in office only as long as the current administration: a cumbersome and sometimes inefficient practice. During the Lloyd George Coalition, Stamfordham had suggested in vain that the office of Lord Chamberlain should become permanent and non-political. Such a course was now inescapable; Labour simply could not produce the men of aristocratic lineage and private means who traditionally occupied these great offices of State. The King therefore decreed that Lord Cromer, his Lord Chamberlain since the fall of the Lloyd George Coalition, should continue in office through all future changes of Government; that Lord Shaftesbury should similarly be reappointed Lord Steward; and that on the impending retirement of Lord Bath as Master of the Horse, Lord Granard should become his permanent successor. Three of the lords-in-waiting (a superior brand of equerry) were also to be appointed by the King without government advice, and relieved of their former political duties in the Upper House. But the Prime Minister of the day would continue to appoint the lesser court officials who acted as Whips in the Commons. These changes, made necessary by the first Labour Government, established precedents that all subsequent administrations have been content to follow.

A constitutional monarch may display no political preference, show no favour between one party and another. His role, according to Bagehot, resembles that of the Permanent Secretary to a government department;

he shares in the proceedings of successive administrations whatever their complexion. Since 1910, King George V had rarely broken the neutrality required of him, and then only in defence of what he conceived to be the national interest. Would this royal impartiality now survive the advent of a Labour Government?

At heart the King thought that nearly all change was for the worse, and if pressed to declare his private creed would doubtless have echoed the majestic declaration of an Eton Head Master: 'I have no politics but I vote Conservative for the good of the country.' Indeed, he had scarcely troubled to conceal his detestation of either Socialism or the Labour Party. In 1912 it prompted this letter from Buckingham Palace to Downing Street about Alfred Russel Wallace, the eminent naturalist whom King Edward had appointed to the Order of Merit four years earlier:

The King is rather scandalised that the possessor of the Order of Merit should avow himself to be a Socialist. I allude to Dr. Alfred Russel Wallace who in a letter which appears in today's Times on the occasion of a dinner to Mr. Hyndman glories in being a Socialist.

The King says he does not care whether a man is a Liberal, Radical or a Tory, but that he thinks the Order of Merit should not be given to Socialists.

It was no passing prejudice. In June 1923, little more than six months before the Labour Government took office, Neville Chamberlain told his sister of a recent conversation with the King. 'His language about the Labour Party', he wrote, 'was as violent as ever.' When in December 1923 the King urged Baldwin to remain in office until the new Parliament had met, Labour had no reason to believe that his motive was constitutional rather than obstructive. One veteran MP, George Lansbury, publicly reminded him of the fate of Charles I should he persist in thwarting the will of the people. Hysteria infected all political parties. 'The enthronement in office of a Socialist Government', Winston Churchill, still nominally a Liberal, wrote to *The Times*, 'will be a serious national misfortune such as has usually befallen great States only on the morrow of defeat in war.' Balfour, too, felt his foundations of belief crumble at the prospect of a socialist regime. 'It would be a national disaster if Labour came in now,' he told Birkenhead, 'even for a brief period.'

The King might have been expected to share their alarm. 'I fear he is apprehensive,' MacDonald wrote after kissing hands as Prime Minister. 'It would be a miracle were he not.' But from the moment Labour took office, the King seized every opportunity to demonstrate his trust both in public and in private; and when old friends presumed on their intimacy to commiserate with him on the affliction of a socialist Government, they were sharply snubbed for their pains.

All those ministers who left a record of Labour's first administration were unanimous in praising not only the King's propriety but also his warmth. 'If royalty had given the Labour Government the cold shoulder,' MacDonald wrote in his diary, 'we should have returned the call. It has not. It has been considerate, cordially correct, human and friendly. The King has never seen me as a Minister without making me feel that he was also seeing me as a friend.' Clynes saluted 'the genial, kindly, considerate personality of George v, a truly constitutional monarch who always put the will of the people nearest his heart'. And Thomas exclaimed: 'By God, he is a great 'uman creature.'

Relations between the intellectuals and their sovereign were more guarded. C.P. Trevelyan, the new Education Minister, resented the King's silence at his swearing-in, complaining that 'he went through the ceremony like an automaton'. Sidney Webb, a solemn sociologist not otherwise given to flights of fancy, claimed that after accepting his seals of office at the palace he had heard a noise like a first-class railway carriage. Haldane wrote patronizingly: 'I had a most friendly hour with the King yesterday and explained to him a good deal that he had not taken in.' The Lord Chancellor brought a lighter touch to a description of his colleagues:

Stories of the new Ministers are becoming the common talk of London dinner parties and about ninety per cent of them are apocryphal, but I believe it is true that Thomas introduced himself to the heads of departments of the Colonial Office with the statement, 'I'm here to see that there is no mucking about with the British Empire.' I hear that our new War Minister, Stephen Walsh, who is a very good fellow and a diehard trade-unionist, created an excellent impression on his generals by announcing that he stood for loyalty to the King. The Foreign Office is simply delighted at getting the courteous MacDonald in exchange for the autocratic Curzon, who has a way of treating his officials as if they were serfs. Altogether the departments have given the new Government a very friendly, even cordial reception.

Neither the King nor the country at large found cause for alarm in MacDonald's domestic policy. Holding office only by virtue of the Liberal vote in the Commons, Labour were obliged to pursue a mild and prudent course. Snowden's budget reduced the duties on tea, coffee, cocoa and sugar. There were increases in agricultural wages and unemployment benefits, promises of higher pensions and cheaper houses. On a personal level, correspondence between the palace and Downing Street reflected only trust and tranquillity: a welcome respite from Lloyd Georgian spite and Baldwinian sloth. In August 1924, after the Royal Yacht Squadron dinner at Cowes, Birkenhead brashly asked the King whether he liked MacDonald. The King replied that MacDonald always kept him better informed than had his previous Prime Ministers.

MacDonald could not, however, curb the radical wing of the party in its demand for a more extreme programme of socialism. Thus some left-wing MPs annoyed the King by voting against the provision of expenses for the Prince of Wales's tour of South Africa. Sidney Webb spoke for his Cabinet colleagues when he told his wife: 'We ought to use the King and Prince and it is all to their credit that they are zealous in seeking work.' As the opening of the British Empire Exhibition in April approached, the King also expressed 'grave concern at the almost weekly recurring strikes at Wembley where the agitators appear to come from outside'. But Thomas went down to appeal to the strikers in the name of the King, who opened the exhibition as arranged on St George's Day.

On only a single trivial matter was the Prime Minister unable to meet a royal request. The King wanted to find employment for his cousin, Prince Arthur of Connaught, and wondered whether he might be given the largely ceremonial office of Lord Lieutenant of London. The sitting incumbent, Lord Crewe, obligingly offered to resign, but MacDonald then feared that the Prince's appointment might arouse unnecessary hostility in the Labour Party. There was also a political complication: as Lord Lieutenant, Prince Arthur would have had to recommend new Justices of the Peace. So the King's suggestion was abandoned. Crewe retained his office for another twenty years and Prince Arthur devoted the rest of his life to raising two million pounds for the Middlesex Hospital.

During MacDonald's first audience as Prime Minister, the King tried to dissuade him from assuming the additional office of Foreign Secretary. Even Lord Salisbury, he was reminded, 'found it difficult to carry on the duties of both offices: indeed he did very little of the work of the Prime Minister, whereas nowadays the latter position in itself and its heavy responsibilities must be a serious tax upon anyone holding that office'. Curzon, the most industrious of Foreign Secretaries, endorsed the warning, certain that MacDonald must inevitably break down under the double burden.

The Prime Minister also suffered from an inability to delegate and an initial mistrust of civil servants; during his first days in office he attempted not only to read but even to open the quantities of letters that reached him by every post. Yet in foreign policy he scored an almost unbroken succession of triumphs. He renewed Britain's friendship with France and Italy, solved the tortuous problem of German reparations, secured a French withdrawal from the Ruhr, strengthened the machinery for international arbitration and disarmament. He also went far towards re-establishing commercial and diplomatic relations with Soviet Russia; but that bold success, for all the Prime Minister's idealism and persuasive skill, was ultimately to destroy his Government.

'I really am ashamed to trouble you with such trivialities as dress', Stamfordham wrote to MacDonald on 1 February 1924, 'when you are dealing with weighty matters of State.' It was a preoccupation which the King and his Court shared with the public at large. Curiosity about Labour policy seemed everywhere to be matched, even eclipsed, by a morbid interest in ministerial dress and deportment.

To the King, such things were part of the fabric of monarchy. He liked to see his ministers at levées and evening courts in the uniform traditional to such occasions: gold-encrusted coat, cocked hat and sword, with trousers by day and knee-breeches in the evening. Yet he wished to spare them both the expense that would fall on men of limited means and the embarrassment that some would feel on exposing themselves to egalitarian ridicule. He therefore agreed to be guided by Cabinet advice. Everybody tried to be helpful. The Lord Great Chamberlain suggested that the new ministers might wear the 'dignified and unobtrusive' plain black coat and knee-breeches of a parliamentary official, 'the dress of Dr. Johnson and perhaps John Milton'. In more practical vein yet with a certain detachment from such transactions, Stamfordham commended the virtues of 'Messrs. Moss Bros., which is I believe a well-known and dependable Firm'. From its premises in Covent Garden, ministers could obtain a complete suit of levée dress for £30 complete, compared with the £73 charged by a court tailor.

MacDonald took a relaxed view of these sartorial demands. 'Braids and uniforms', he wrote in his diary, 'are but part of an official pageantry and as my conscience is not on my back, a gold coat means nothing to me but a form of dress to be worn or rejected as a hat would be in relation to the rest of one's clothes.' Some of his colleagues, however, absolutely refused to don knee-breeches; and Thomas delighted the King by remarking: 'Of course poor Sidney Webb can't put 'em on. His wife wears 'em.'

The King readily agreed to the Cabinet's proposals. No minister would be compelled to attend court ceremonies; those who did attend would not be required to buy the more elaborate and expensive full-dress uniform of a Privy Counsellor; those who objected to uniform in principle could wear plain evening dress. Such was the outcome of a prolonged and many-sided correspondence. 'I held a levée at St. James,' the King wrote with satisfaction in his diary. 'The Prime Minister, Mr. Henderson and Mr. Thomas came in uniform, the other Ministers came in evening dress with tights.'

When a Labour incorruptible asked the Prime Minister why he had been to Buckingham Palace, MacDonald replied: 'Because its allurements are so great that I cannot trust *you* to go.' The King was as generous a host as at any time throughout the reign. Here is 'Chips' Channon on a State ball in May 1924:

There was no quadrille d'honneur, probably because it was feared that the Socialist Ministers and their wives would be too clumsy, and the American Ambassador was delighted. There was a pause after the music began, and no-one knew what to do. At last the Prince of Wales opened the ball with the Duchess of York and soon everyone was dancing. I saw Lord Cavan stopped by a court official as he had neglected to remove his sword.

Ramsay MacDonald was very distinguished in his Privy Councillor's full dress uniform ... green and white and gold ... and headed the second group, giving his arm to the Duchess of Buccleuch to whom, I hear, he made himself most affable. He has a fine profile, like a Roman coin, and looks like an engraving of himself. He was followed by Thomas, Minister of the Colonies, who, when asked by a white-wanded equerry if he would take in the Duchess of Atholl, replied in a very loud voice 'Rather', and left his house-keepery little wife to fend for herself.

It was perhaps on that evening that a minister's wife was said to have exclaimed: 'Me shoes is tight, me corset is tight, me 'usband is tight. Time to go 'ome.' To appease those often neglected wives, the King and Queen held a tea party at the palace which gave genuine pleasure. The rich and well-born Beatrice Webb was alone in refusing to be compromised. 'She fears the Court will wean Labour from the strait and narrow path and suspects Ramsay MacDonald of a partiality for duchesses,' Haldane noted. Yet the Lord Chancellor himself shared something of her prim austerity. After one palace banquet, served off gold plate, he wrote: 'The King kept us till a quarter to midnight – too late for people who had a mass of Cabinet papers to read.'

There were garden parties, too, at which several ministers turned up in ordinary suits instead of the customary morning coat and top hat; John Wheatley, the Minister of Health, wore a bowler and F. W. Jowett, First Commissioner of Works, a trilby. Jowett noted that the King was far less put out than MacDonald, and showed no trace of snobbishness either then or at other times. Some of the King's subjects were less tolerant. Lord Lee of Fareham wrote:

How the House of Commons end of the Terrace has gone off since the old days. Instead of the 'Garden party' effect to which we had been accustomed, there seemed to be mostly Labour members and their constituents having tea at long tables and it looked more like a School treat.

Equally distasteful were attempts to make a social spectacle of the new men. 'All the Yankee peeresses are mad to get Ramsey MacDonald and his daughter as novelties,' Lincolnshire observed. 'Miss MacDonald is said to be horrified at their low dresses and low demeanour.' The chatter never ceased. Lunching at the Athenaeum one day, John Buchan told Leo Amery that the Prime Minister was an illegitimate son of a former Lord Dalhousie and thus, as a half-uncle by marriage of Princess Patricia of Connaught, a kinsman of the King's.

It was scarcely as a member of his family that the King entertained MacDonald at each of his country houses; although not even royal blood could have ensured a warmer welcome for the Prime Minister. There was a memorable precedent for such visits. A generation earlier, the future King Edward VII had invited Henry Broadhurst, the Labour MP, to stay at Sandringham. An appreciative guest, Broadhurst wrote: 'On my arrival his Royal Highness personally conducted me to my rooms, made a careful inspection to see that all was right, stoked the fires, and then, after satisfying himself that all my wants were provided for, withdrew and left me for the night.'

Did Broadhurst then go supperless to bed? Nothing so inhospitable. It was simply that he had no evening clothes, so apparently would have looked and felt out of place in the dining-room with the rest of the party. 'In order to meet the difficulty,' he wrote, 'dinner was served to me in my own rooms each night.... I left Sandringham with a feeling of one who had spent a week-end with an old chum of his own rank in society.'

MacDonald had more reason to echo Broadhurst's gratitude. It is insensitive, as has long been the fashion, to pillory him as a social climber. He was a romantic, even a mystic, thrilling as much to the history of palace and castle as to the artless simplicity of his royal hosts. 'The kindly homeliness was that of a cottage,' he wrote of Windsor, 'and sat well in gilt halls. It was the natural blending of the two that was such a welcome experience.' He was touched, too, to find himself a rare guest at York Cottage, although its 'bourgeois want of dignity' offended his patrician instincts. As for Balmoral, it was for the son of Lossiemouth but a croft writ large. 'I found it cosy and homely and I enjoyed myself.' What a lot of fun the Webbs missed, self-impaled upon their rectitude.

MacDonald's efforts to improve Anglo-Russian relations alone cast a shadow across the King's regard. Since the murder of his Imperial cousins in 1918, the King had maintained an implacable loathing for the Soviet Government. Asquith wrote after dining at the palace in 1919: 'The King was rather excited over Russia, and talked a lot of man-in-the-bus nonsense about Bolshevics, etc. I told him I was sorry not to be able to agree with him and we parted on the best of terms.'

Two years later the King had misgivings about Lloyd George and the Genoa Conference. 'I suppose you will be meeting Lenin and Trotsky?' he asked. Lloyd George, at his most engaging, replied:

A little while ago I had to shake hands with Sami Bey, the representative of

Mustapha Kemal, a ruffian who was missing for the whole of one day, and finally traced to a sodomy house in the East End. . . . I must confess I do not think there is very much to choose between these persons whom I am forced to meet from time to time in Your Majesty's service.

This riposte drew roars of laughter. But in January 1924, MacDonald noted after his first audience that the King 'hoped I would do nothing to compel him to shake hands with the murderers of his relatives'. Labour's election manifesto, however, had promised an improvement in Anglo-Russian relations; and in spite of a plea from the King not to act hastily, MacDonald at once instructed the Foreign Office to recognize the Soviet Government. A few weeks later a Russian delegation arrived in London for talks with Arthur Ponsonby on the encouragement of trade and the payment of compensation for confiscated British property. As its leader, M. Rakovsky, held the diplomatic rank not of ambassador but only of *chargé d'affaires*, the King was spared the distasteful duty of receiving him. By August, the negotiations seemed to have foundered; Britain's terms were apparently too stiff. Then, almost overnight, the Commons learned that Ponsonby had reached agreement in detail on the two main topics, trade and compensation, and in principle on a third: the floating of a Russian loan on the London money market. Conservative die-hards were not alone in suspecting that the Government had succumbed to left-wing pressure.

On the very day that Arthur Ponsonby capitulated to Russia's terms, the Cabinet debated an equally sensitive issue. J. R. Campbell, acting editor of *The Workers' Weekly*, a Communist paper, had published an open letter inciting men of the fighting services to disobey when ordered to act against strikers. It had prompted the Attorney-General, Sir Patrick Hastings, a brilliant advocate but inexperienced politician, to institute proceedings against him for sedition. Such a prosecution was doubly unfortunate; it enraged large sections of the Labour and trade union movements; and it was unlikely to secure a conviction. On 6 August the Cabinet agreed with Hastings that the charges against Campbell should be dropped; it did so in defiance of the constitutional usage which precludes the executive from interfering with the course of justice.

That was a grave enough error, but worse was to follow. When the matter came before the Commons, MacDonald declared that he had never been consulted about the withdrawal of the prosecution or recommended such a course. On being told of this denial, the Secretary of the Cabinet, Maurice Hankey, exclaimed: 'That's a bloody lie.' Public opinion largely shared his view. And when in a subsequent debate the Prime Minister attempted to clarify his conduct, even Snowden had to admit that his performance was 'incoherent, evasive and prevaricating'.

Later generations may look more charitably on MacDonald. It now seems likely that throughout the Campbell case he was exhausted in mind and body, carrying the burden both of a Prime Minister's day-to-day business and a succession of gruelling diplomatic negotiations with the great powers of Europe. The King had warned him of this, but he had ignored the voice of experience.

It was not only in the confusion of the Campbell case that MacDonald's judgement failed. Honourable in money matters and fastidious in the distribution of honours, he allowed himself to blunder into a Lloyd Georgian practice. On a Prime Minister's salary of £5,000 a year he could not be called a poor man. But his tenure was precarious and the incumbent of No. 10 received no motor car or entertainment allowance; he even had to provide his own linen and china. His daughter Ishbel, who kept house for him, continued to buy the groceries from the Co-op; and to save the cost of coal fires, the family ate not in the private apartments but in the State rooms, which were heated at government expense.

When, therefore, an old friend, Alexander Grant, the biscuit manufacturer, offered to lend him a Daimler car and £40,000 in securities, MacDonald accepted with gratitude. The annual interest of £2,000 would be his, the capital sum remaining the property of Grant. There was nothing irregular about such a gift, or in keeping silent about it, at least by the standards of public life in the nineteen-twenties. There exists for instance among the papers of Winston Churchill a letter which he received when Secretary of State for War from Sir Abe Bailey. In it the South African financier confirms that he will make good the loss on any shares bought on his advice, the profit to remain Churchill's. Where MacDonald exposed himself to mockery and worse was in recommending his benefactor for a baronetcy in the next Honours List. Grant was not undeserving of reward; he had earlier given £100,000 towards the founding of the Scottish National Library. But MacDonald's inept timing caused both men much undeserved pain.

The Campbell case, meanwhile, for all its sinister implications and the Prime Minister's shuffling apologia, need not have brought down his Government. He had taken office on the understanding that he would resign only if defeated on a vital issue of policy or a vote of confidence. But this episode, he thought at first, was no more than a passing skirmish in the masquerade of party warfare. 'It is all one of those malicious newspaper stunts which are becoming so common nowadays,' he told the King. By the beginning of October, MacDonald realized that it had become a matter on which he must demand a vote of confidence. Both Opposition parties welcomed a pretext for humbling the Government. The Conservatives hoped for an election fought on the issue of Labour subservience to Communism; the Liberals, paradoxically, feared that the very moderation of the Labour ministers whom they had chivalrously put in power was eroding their own role as the natural alternative to Conservatism. The two parties united on 8 October to defeat the Government by 364 votes to 198.

On the following day the Prime Minister asked for a dissolution of Parliament. This the King conceded with reluctance, deploring that the country should be put to the expense and dislocation of a third general election within two years; nor, as he pointed out, would it necessarily result in a change of party strength in the Commons. Yet in practice there was no alternative; neither Baldwin nor Asquith was prepared to form a minority Government. That audience of 9 October was nevertheless cordial and at times almost affecting as sovereign and Prime Minister expressed their regard for each other. 'You have found me an ordinary man, haven't you?' was the King's parting remark.

The Government's supposed tenderness for Soviet Russia so dominated the election campaign that its respectable record on other issues went by default. Four days before the nation voted, the Zinoviev letter added to MacDonald's embarrassment. Purportedly written by Grigori Zinoviev, president of the Comintern, it instructed British Communists to enlist Labour supporters in working towards armed insurrection. A copy had been in the hands of the Foreign Office for the past two weeks while experts on Russia tried to decide whether it was genuine (a dispute that continues to this day). Sir Eyre Crowe, the Permanent Under-Secretary, then heard that the *Daily Mail* had obtained the text and intended to publish it; so he sent the Foreign Office copy to all newspapers, together with a protest addressed to Rakovsky at Soviet intrusion into British politics.

MacDonald, on a speech-making tour 200 miles from London, had been sent the letter some days earlier but was nevertheless unprepared for its publication. Always mistrustful of the Whitehall machine, he had not brought with him a Foreign Office secretary whom he could consult. A more astute politician might have turned the Zinoviev letter to advantage by denouncing Moscow's subversive tactics. As it was, he remained silent for two whole days before making an incoherent statement that served only to confirm Conservative fears. The Comintern and the Foreign Office, he felt, had between them cost him the election. When the King received Crowe's explanation, he minuted:

Under the circumstances Crowe was quite right to publish the letter, although it has certainly put the P.M. & his Party in a hole & their opponents will make great capital out of it. But it would have been much worse if the *Daily Mail* had published it and the F.O. had remained silent.

I suppose there is *no doubt* that Z's letter is genuine? I see the Communists say it is a forgery.

The publication of the Zinoviev letter and MacDonald's faltering touch are unlikely to have had a decisive effect on the result of the election. The mood of the country was reflected in a sweeping victory for the Conservatives of 413 seats, which gave them a comfortable majority over both their rivals. MacDonald resigned on 4 November 1924. He wrote:

King most friendly. Thanked me for what I had done.... Chaffed me about the Russian Treaty. Told him my successors would have to carry out the same policy. He hoped I was not to give up my car. Thought the attacks most unfair. That enabled me to refer to the Court dress attacks. He was annoyed and said it was an attack upon him. Hoped I would continue his friend as he would remain mine.

The King's own epitaph on his first Labour Prime Minister was characteristically laconic: 'I like him and have always found him quite straight.'

If the King felt relieved by a Conservative return to office, he betrayed no sign of it, but instead warned the new Government against either humiliating or provoking an embittered Labour Opposition. Baldwin disappointed him in some of his Cabinet appointments, particularly the choice of the solicitor Joynson-Hicks rather than the barrister Douglas Hogg (later created Lord Hailsham) for the Home Office, 'where in these times not only possible but probable difficulties in the internal government of the country necessitate an exceptionally able and strong administrator and one who has held a pre-eminent position at the Bar'. In the light of the general strike of 1926, that was a shrewd assessment. The King was also astonished by Baldwin's decision to make Churchill the new Chancellor of the Exchequer: an astute move that finally detached him from the Liberals and deprived Lloyd George of his most powerful ally should he try to resurrect the Coalition. Although the King was surprised by the appointment, his wartime mistrust of Churchill had abated and he had been impressed by the 'skill, patience and tact' he had brought to the Irish settlement. The new Chancellor, for his part, was scrupulously correct in his relations with the sovereign, although he could not suppress a whimsical humour when writing to his wife during a holiday in Deauville: 'Among other notorieties in the rooms I perceived the Shah of Persia also parting with his subjects' cash, handed to him packet by packet by his Prime Minister. Really we are well out of it with our own gracious Monarch!'

On one Cabinet post, the King and his Prime Minister were in complete accord: that the new Foreign Secretary should not be Lord Curzon but Austen Chamberlain. The arrogance and irritability which flawed Curzon's majestic intellect had left him as disliked in the Quai d'Orsay and the

Palazzo Chigi as· he was in the Foreign Office. Consoled with the lesser places of Lord President of the Council and Leader of the House of Lords, he at once embarked on a quarrel about minor court appointments. These, he wrote in outraged tones, the King 'had half begun to distribute without any knowledge that he must consult me in the matter. . . . Stamfordham was not either very reasonable or very agreeable about it.' Curzon died only four months later, after an operation that gave no cause for alarm. Hours before his death, there arrived at the palace a letter of graceful farewell from the King's 'faithful devoted friend and Minister'.

At least Joynson-Hicks, Churchill and Curzon were industrious. The Prime Minister was not. 'What can you do with a leader,' one angry colleague asked, 'who sits in the smoking room reading the *Strand Maga-zine?*' It was not his only sustenance. He would recline hour after hour on the front bench of the Commons perusing *Dod's Parliamentary Companion*, which helped him to become one of the most effective party managers of the century. He nevertheless preferred crosswords to Cabinet papers, and the King more than once expressed concern that Baldwin should spend the summer ruminating at some French spa while the red boxes piled up at No. 10. Even when the Prime Minister did remain at the helm, the King could not have found it reassuring to read of his appearance at the Eton and Harrow cricket match in a baggy old suit and soft hat.

Baldwin's lightness of touch, which could be mistaken for frivolity, also caused friction. His description of an all-night sitting of the Commons included this passage:

In the early hours of the morning the House bore many resemblances to St. James' Park at midday. Members were lying about the benches in recumbent position, some being overcome with sleep and completely oblivious to their surroundings, while others occasionally feigned an interest in the proceedings by making inter-ruptions from a sleepy and recumbent posture.

The King was shocked both by the loutish conduct of his faithful Commons and by the absence of any disapproving word from his Prime Minister. Stamfordham thereupon wrote a ponderous rebuke, of which a sample will suffice:

Members of Parliament now include ladies and such a state of things as you describe seems to His Majesty hardly decorous or worthy of the dignity and tradition of the Mother of Parliaments . . .

I am to state that you are quite at liberty to show what I have written to the Speaker.

That last sentence was ill-judged. Baldwin, although prepared to shrug off a royal rebuke on a matter for which he bore no responsibility, could not ignore a breach of constitutional practice. He reminded Stamfordham that 'one of the earliest historical objects of the House of Commons was to exclude the Crown from interfering in its proceedings' and quoted the dictum from Erskine May 'that all their proceedings may receive from His Majesty the most favourable construction'. He ended: 'The Prime Minister strongly deprecates the suggestion that he might approach the Speaker with your letter, and feels that it would be most unfortunate were any represen-tations to be made to him in this sense on behalf of His Majesty.'

The King, who at heart was no Charles i, grumblingly agreed to withdraw his censorious comments.

Baldwin's playful description of the all-night sitting was not the only parliamentary report to annoy his sovereign. On the eve of a visit to Australia and New Zealand by the Duke and Duchess of York, the Com-mons were asked to approve a supplementary estimate covering their expenses. The King had originally wished the young couple to travel with a small suite in an ordinary passenger ship. But when the Australian Government urged that their tour should be invested with pomp and stateliness, he agreed to their using HMS *Renown*; they were also to be supported by a large staff and to entertain the chief dignitaries at each port of call. That was not to the taste of the Labour Party.

Stamfordham acknowledged Baldwin's account of the debate in a letter of seven typewritten pages. 'His Majesty,' it began with deceptive mildness, 'read your report with the interest with which he always follows the graphic and often amusing accounts of the debates: but of that on February 17th you take a less serious and, I suppose, more "House of Commons" view than does the King.' He went on to quote from the speeches of nine Labour MPs, all of whom had cast doubt on the value of the tour: 'This pleasure trip ... joy ride ... starving the workers ... would not matter one iota to the country supposing they did not return ... begging for the Royal House ... mere figure-heads instead of the representatives of democratic Govern-ment, of art and of education ... sob stuff about Duchess leaving her child.' Then came Stamfordham's *coup de grâce*:

Though Parliament may discount these utterances as the irresponsible babble of the extremists of the Labour Party for the consumption of their constituents, His Majesty takes a graver view of these flippant, discourteous, if not insulting, allusions to his Family: and the King objects to the Royal Family being made a target to be shot at by Members of the Labour Opposition, unrebuked by their Leader and undefended by any Member of the Government.

So long as the Monarchy and the Empire exist, it is but natural that the Dominions should look for periodical visits from Members of the Royal Family: but for the reasons I have endeavoured to explain, the King has decided in future to refuse permission for any Member of the Royal Family to pay such official visits,

unless the expenses incurred are defrayed by the respective Dominions: and His
Majesty desires that this decision may be duly recorded.

Queen Elizabeth I could not have spoken more imperiously.

In October 1925, immediately after the Trades Union Congress had met in
what MacDonald called 'feverish uncertainty and widespread ill-will',
Henry Channon wrote in his diary:

Massereene confided to me something which I have long suspected but never heard
put into words, the feeling of disappointment and almost resentment that prevails
in a certain class of the King's lack of initiative. He is so uninspiring and does
nothing to stem the swelling Socialist tide. A man with more personality and charm
could achieve much, and become a rallying point. It is one of history's ironies to
supply thrones with weak kings in time of revolution.

Neither a twelfth viscount nor a young expatriate from Chicago realized
that George V saw himself as King not only of the well-born and the rich,
but also of the deprived and the poor. This he demonstrated again and
again throughout the industrial unrest that punctuated his reign. After a
five-week strike of coalminers in 1912 which forced the owners to accept
the principle of a minimum wage, he gave 1,000 guineas for the relief of
distress among strikers' families. In 1921 he warned the Cabinet that it
could not 'expect people to subsist upon the unemployment benefit of 15/-
for men and 12/- for women'. In January 1926, he asked the Government
to strengthen a paragraph in the Speech from the Throne on the difficulties
in the coal industry and to insert an appeal for unity. In April, a few days
before unrest in the coalfields at a proposed reduction of earnings precipitated the general strike, the King told Lord Durham at Newmarket races
that he was sorry for the miners. Durham, a considerable coal-owner,
replied that they were 'a damned lot of revolutionaries'. The King turned
on him furiously: 'Try living on their wages before you judge them.' He
also told one of his ministers, Leo Amery, that no coal-owner or investor
should be allowed to receive a dividend of more than ten per cent.

The King wanted to reign over a contented nation, and suffered intensely
when it was not so. 'I never seem to get any peace in this world,' he wrote
of an approaching strike. 'Feel very low and depressed.' When on 4 May
1926 the TUC declared a sympathetic strike with the miners, hoping to
paralyse transport and other essential services, the King was urged to
intervene as a mediator. But the precedents of the Parliament Bill and Irish
Home Rule were not encouraging. Stamfordham wisely replied that the
King would call a conference of reconciliation only on the advice of the
Prime Minister; and Baldwin remained silent. Nor was the Prince of Wales

allowed to undertake a fact-finding tour of the provinces and so risk being drawn into taking sides between the strikers and the Government.

Privately, however, the King showed compassion as well as caution. On 8 May, the *British Gazette*, an emergency newspaper published by the Government and edited by an exuberant Winston Churchill, declared that the armed forces should not be too squeamish in coming to the aid of the civil power. The King instructed Stamfordham to write to the Chief of the Imperial General Staff; he applied no stronger word than 'unfortunate' to the provocative announcement, but the War Office no doubt took his point.

The most decisive of the King's interventions in May 1926 was also in support of what he saw both as prudence and fair play. The Government had proposed a Bill making it illegal for a trade union to spend either its own funds or foreign contributions – presumably from Soviet Russia – on a strike 'intended to coerce or intimidate the Government or the community'. Until the measure could receive parliamentary approval, there was to be an Order in Council – instant legislation, as it were – forbidding banks to pay out such monies. Although a constitutional monarch may not in practice reject an Order laid before a meeting of the Privy Council, he is entitled to invoke his prerogative of persuasion; and this, on 9 May, he did most effectively. Stamfordham wrote of the encounter:

At the Council the King told both the Home Secretary and the Attorney General that he was not at all sure that the Government would be acting wisely in adopting either the measures authorised by the Order in Council or those to be obtained by the Bill to be introduced on the 11th. So far the situation was better and more peaceful than might have been expected. The spirit of the miners was not un-friendly, as shown by such instances as Saturday afternoon's Football Match at Plymouth between the police and the strikers: but any attempt to get hold of or control the Trades Union Funds might cause exasperation and provoke reprisals. If money were not forthcoming to buy food, there might be looting of shops, even of banks. The King laid stress also upon the inevitable uproar which the intro-duction of such a Bill would create in the House of Commons.

Stamfordham's memorandum continues:

In the afternoon of Monday, 10th May, private information reached the King that the Cabinet as a whole was by no means satisfied as to the proposed legislation: that there was a danger of the Prime Minister's being rushed by some of his hot-headed colleagues into legislation which might have disastrous effects, especially at the psychological moment when there is but little bitterness of feeling between the Government and the strikers.

After a further Cabinet meeting, the original Order forbidding the banks to pay out money to trade unions was watered down to one merely requiring details of such transactions to be supplied to the Government on demand.

Before even that innocuous measure could be implemented, the general strike had collapsed. The miners, however, refused to return to work for another six months. 'The Palace is like an ice house,' a courtier complained in November, 'only wood fires, no central heating is allowed, and the only coal fire is in the King's sitting room.' The King deserved his coal fire. By resisting the inflammatory legislation of his ministers, he helped to create an atmosphere of conciliation and an ultimate settlement largely free from bitterness.

It is this sympathetic and statesmanlike approach to industrial strife which dominates the chapter on the general strike in Harold Nicolson's life of the King. Yet the King could speak with two voices. However kindly his understanding of human anguish and frustration, however sharp his insight into the minds of his humbler subjects, he remained the prisoner of a naval upbringing. That early discipline had implanted in him a lifelong antipathy to disorder. 'Nice ladies, aren't they, breaking everybody's windows,' he wrote of the suffragettes, 'I hope they will be severely punished.' (Yet he did beg the Government to discontinue the 'shocking, if not almost cruel' practice of forcibly feeding those on hunger strike.) And the sovereign who had rebuked Churchill for referring to 'idlers and wastrels at both ends of the social scale' saw nothing incongruous in expressing 'disgust and shame' at the undergraduate rowdyism which traditionally followed the Oxford and Cambridge football match. (Here again, he was never quite consistent. Reading a newspaper account of one such university riot while breakfasting at Sandringham, he remarked across the table to an eminent proconsul: 'I see that your son was also my guest last night.')

There was thus an ambivalence in the King's approach to industrial unrest. Although not unsympathetic to the economic plight of strikers, he believed that no dispute ought to be furthered by violence, intimidation or any other breach of the law. With one hand he would offer financial relief from his own pocket; with the other he would demand exemplary measures to curb disorder. During the railway strike of 1911, he sent this telegram to the Home Secretary:

Accounts from Liverpool show that situation there more like Revolution than strike. Trust that the Government while inducing strike leaders and masters to come to terms will take proper steps to ensure protection of life and property. . . .

Strongly deprecate the half hearted employment of troops. They should not be called upon except as a last resource but if called upon, they should be given a free hand and the mob should be made to fear them.

Once the strike had been settled, the King asked the Prime Minister to devise legislation that would discourage both peaceful picketing and intimidation. Asquith replied:

As to 'picketing' the matter is being looked into in the light of recent events. My own belief is that the existing law (if enforced) is quite strong enough to deal with cases of intimidation. I am glad to see that there have been several successful prosecutions in the last few days. The difficulty is not so much in the law as in the impossibility often of procuring evidence.

Fifteen years later the King remained unsatisfied with the state of the law. On 5 May 1926 he was disturbed to read that the unloading of food in the docks was being prevented by pickets. He inquired of Baldwin: 'Would it not be possible to introduce emergency legislation to prevent the so-called peaceful picketing and so enable unloading to be carried out by non-Union labour; and at the same time relieve the police of the additional work imposed upon them in dealing with picket trouble?'

Downing Street replied that the King was in effect recommending an amendment to the Trades Disputes Act of 1906: an amendment which many Conservative MPs thought desirable but which would be 'highly controversial and so inopportune'. That same day, another letter was despatched from the palace:

The King is somewhat concerned to find from the official reports that the people who are ready and desirous of assisting the Government in the maintenance of law and order are suffering considerably from intimidation from the strikers and other evil disposed parties, with the result that transport, which is the mainspring of the Government arrangements, is threatened.

And he went on to urge that 'until Martial Law be proclaimed and the safety of the country passes into the hands of the Military . . . one Executive Officer should be responsible for all Police control'. In the same aggressive vein, he asked the Government whether union leaders who were threatening to call out more men, and so add one or two millions to the number of strikers, could not be arrested.

The King's readiness to suspend the rule of law is in abrupt contrast both to the restraint which he preached to his ministers at other times during the general strike and to the paternal benevolence which will always be associated with him. Within twenty-four hours, however, the strike was over and the King once more a constitutionalist. He wrote in his diary: 'Our old country can well be proud of itself, as during the last nine days there has been a strike in which 4 million people have been affected, not a shot has been fired and no one killed. It shows what a wonderful people we are.'

It was no State secret that the King disliked abroad. From the end of the war until his death seventeen years later, he spent scarcely more than eight weeks overseas; five of them on an enforced Mediterranean cruise after a bout of bronchitis, the rest on reluctant official visits to France, Belgium and Italy. Nor did the Queen ever undertake a foreign tour alone, even during the seventeen years of her widowhood.

'Dear, good boys but very exclusively English,' Queen Victoria wrote of her grandsons, 'and that is a great misfortune.' The naval cadet who on first seeing Spain wrote that 'one Englishman will do more in one day than ten natives', became the father who complained that one of his own sons had damaged a knee 'while playing French cricket whatever that is, I should think a very silly game'. The French duke who did not turn up for a tiger shoot specially arranged by the Viceroy of India evoked the scornful comment: 'These foreigners have not much idea of sport.' And Mensdorff, asked by the Prince of Wales in 1929 if he would suggest a visit to Austria and Hungary, recorded this conversation with the King:

'It would be very nice if the Prince could come some time to Vienna.'
'He has so much to visit in the Empire.'
'But it would be nice to see him in Vienna. Perhaps he might find a moment to come, as he has never been there.'
'Yes he might.'

Mensdorff knew that it would be useless to pursue the subject further.

No linguist himself, the King found both foreign languages and the misuse of his own a never-failing source of humour. 'Distant sounds of Latin loquacity, Teutonic thunder and Belgian bleating,' was how the Prime Minister's private secretary described an international conference, knowing that he would find an appreciative audience at Buckingham Palace. The King, who loved to hear his favourite stories repeated, would again and again ask Lord Louis Mountbatten to describe the visit of his sister, Crown Princess (later Queen) Louise of Sweden to Uppsala Cathedral. The Archbishop, determined to show off his knowledge of English, approached a chest of drawers in the sacristy with the startling announcement: 'I will now open these trousers and reveal some even more precious treasures to Your Royal Highness.'

A common language between the Old World and the New did nothing to dispel the King's insularity. 'The nearest I ever got to the United States,' he would say, 'was when I walked half-across Niagara, took off my hat and walked back again.' He gave no hint that he would have cared to continue further. Like so many of his generation, he saw the citizens of America through the distorting lens of caricature: brash, boastful and mercenary. Even a compliment could thus be unintentionally offensive, as when Haig wrote of General Pershing: 'I was much struck with his quiet gentlemanly bearing – so unusual for an American'; or when the King noted that a newly arrived ambassador, Robert Worth Bingham, was 'more British than the British'.

The King could never come to terms with the exaggeration and intrusiveness of the transatlantic Press. His first disagreeable experience of it was in 1890, when an Irish-American journalist published a totally untrue report of his stay in Montreal. He was alleged to have taken part in a street brawl, to have been arrested and hauled through the streets at the bottom of a police patrol wagon. This fabrication, reprinted throughout the world, brought alarmed telegrams of inquiry from both Queen Victoria and the future Edward VII. After the war the King was outraged by what he called the effrontery of American newspaper comment on his son's visit to New York. One headline read: 'Prince gets in with milkman.' The King observed: 'Fancy their saying that about you.' And in 1934 there emerged from a committee of the United States Senate an absurd but wounding lie that the King had been speculating in the sale of munitions. He was delighted, however, by this anti-Prohibition doggerel which his son had picked up in a Canadian border town:

> Four and twenty Yankees, feeling very dry,
> Went across the border to get a drink of rye.
> When the rye was opened, the Yanks began to sing,
> 'God bless America, but God save the King!'

When required to entertain individual Americans, the King readily put aside his prejudices. 'Mr. Franklin Roosevelt, Assistant Secretary to the U.S. Navy, a charming man, came to see me,' he wrote in 1918, 'and told me everything his Navy was doing to help in the war, which is most satisfactory.' In 1927 he received Charles Lindbergh, the first man to fly the Atlantic single-handed and non-stop. 'Now tell me,' he began, echoing the thought that must have crossed the minds of so many of his subjects, 'there is one thing I long to know. How did you *manage*?' The Queen, too, for all her shyness, could enchant American visitors. 'Perhaps we should still be one country,' she used to say, 'if my great-grandfather had not been so obstinate.'

The King believed that State visits between monarchs were expensive, irksome and futile; after 1923 he never again set foot officially on foreign soil, however hard his ministers pressed him. 'I failed to get His Majesty to smile at all upon the idea of a State visit to Madrid,' Stamfordham told Austen Chamberlain in 1926. 'The King's view is that State visits have ceased to be of any political importance.' But he remained a considerate and generous host. The young Crown Prince of Japan never forgot his reception at the Palace in 1921. An elaborate programme of entertainment included visits to Eton, Oxford, Cambridge, Sandhurst and Chequers; dinner with the Curzons at Carlton House Terrace and *Sybil* at Daley's Theatre, golf at Addington and a sitting to Augustus John. Half a century later, by now the Emperor Hirohito, he told the present writer with unconscious irony: 'King George treated me exactly like one of his own sons.'

Another survivor from the reign of George v who likes to recall the King's kindly tact is Count Dino Grandi. On arriving at Buckingham Palace in July 1932 to present his credentials as Italian ambassador, he found that he had left the vital document at his embassy in Grosvenor Square. As he was being shown into the King's presence, he just had time to explain the disaster to an official, who asked him to wait a moment and disappeared into the audience chamber. The official emerged smiling, to tell Grandi that His Majesty wished to apologize for delaying the audience for a few minutes. Meanwhile the ambassador's secretary had flown back to the embassy, retrieved the credentials and returned to the palace. Only then did the King send word that he was ready to receive Grandi. The ambassador made a good story of it; no doubt the King made a better.

'One of the things that comforted me when I gave up office,' Baldwin said at the end of his life, 'was that I should not have to meet French statesmen any more.' In this distaste for international affairs there is a superficial resemblance between the Prime Minister and his sovereign; yet any such comparison would be misleading. When Baldwin's colleagues began to discuss foreign policy in Cabinet, he would ostentatiously close his eyes. 'Wake me up', he said, 'when you have finished with that.' As Lord Halifax once observed, Baldwin was like an old fox that meets a smell he doesn't understand, and goes miles round to avoid it.

The King, by contrast, never shirked the duty of keeping himself well informed. In 1923 he even tried to add to his burden by asking that no important despatch should ever leave the Foreign Office without first being submitted to him; but the growing complexity of business and speed of communication made such Victorian customs impracticable, and he received an evasive answer. 'I have read your memorandum,' the King once said to Vansittart, 'not all of it, of course.' It was, that verbose official noted, 'an encouragement to brevity'; but also, perhaps, a reminder that the King did not care for an ornate and tortuous style that hid as much as it revealed. He liked gossip, however, and the Foreign Office would spice its solid fare with nuggets of human frailty extracted from the Secretary of State's correspondence: a brother sovereign who ill-treated his wife, an unfaithful consort, an oriental ruler addicted to unnatural vice. 'Horrible fellow,' was the King's usual annotation.

Few ambassadors or other officials whom the King received in audience failed to be impressed by the depth of his knowledge. Sir Miles Lampson (later Lord Killearn), who for seven years represented his country in Peking, wrote in his diary that the King knew far more of China than did any of his ministers, including the Foreign Secretary. Staying at Sandringham while on leave from his next post, Cairo, he noted their talk about Egypt: 'As usual H.M. knew all about it. Truly a wonderful man – and full of common sense and directness.' Even the omniscient Hankey, reporting on his tour of the Commonwealth, wrote: 'There was hardly a scrap of information, whether of a material or political kind, with which the King did not seem to be familiar.' But he left no lasting mark on events. He was consulted, he encouraged, he warned; policy, however, remained wholly in the hands of his ministers and their officials.

It has sometimes been claimed, notably in a work about Prince and Princess Louis of Battenberg authorized and inspired by their son, Lord Mountbatten, that there was a single exception to this: in 1922, when Prince Andrew of Greece, the father of Prince Philip, Duke of Edinburgh, was imprisoned by a Greek revolutionary Government and charged with treason. The disputed passage begins with an error and embraces several more:

The King was only too aware of the weak manner in which he had allowed Lloyd George to overrule his wish to help the Russian Imperial family to leave Russia. He was determined not to have what he regarded as the blood of another cousin on his hands. For the first and last time in his reign he exercised the royal prerogative.

The King telephoned the Admiralty and said that he wanted the Royal Navy to save his cousin, Prince Andrew of Greece, emphasizing that they must act at once to release him from prison.

The power of royalty, the despatch of a gunboat, could still influence events in foreign lands in 1922. The Admiralty, and Lord Curzon at the Foreign Office, acted swiftly. Commander Gerald Talbot, R.N., who had once been a naval attaché in Athens and knew more of the tortuous channels of Greek politics than most Greek politicians, was sent out from Switzerland where he was serving to begin negotiations with the Greek revolutionary leader, General Pangalos. The 6-inch-gunned cruiser, HMS *Calypso*, was sent to the Piraeus.

The papers now preserved in the Public Record Office tell a different story. They reveal that the King did not initiate the operation or even express encouragement except through the constitutional channel of the Foreign Office; that the responsibility for the secret mission undertaken by Talbot (who was no longer a serving officer) lay with certain Foreign Office officials, including, as it happened, Harold Nicolson; that the Greek revolutionaries allowed Prince Andrew to be smuggled out of prison only on condition that they did not appear to be submitting to British Naval pressure; and that HMS *Calypso*, far from 'steaming into Phaleron Bay,

cleared for action', was used only to transport the Prince to safety once
negotiations had been completed. The King did, however, show his appreciation of Talbot's courage and diplomatic skill by appointing him a Knight
Commander of the Royal Victorian Order.

When the present writer drew Lord Mountbatten's attention to the
official record of Prince Andrew's rescue, he generously admitted that he
had been misled by his 'rather defective memory' of events half a century
earlier; and that the King's role had been both passive and correct.

'George V, by the Grace of God, King of Great Britain, Ireland and the
British Dominions beyond the Seas, Defender of the Faith, Emperor of
India': each of those resounding styles and titles touched a chord in the
King's heart. Yet only once during his reign did he set foot in India, and
never in Australia or New Zealand, Canada or South Africa. When implored
to tour his Dominions, he would reply that he must do all or none, and that
the pressure of home business denied him long absences from London.
Instead he divided the role among his sons, whose youth and vigour were
more attuned to those bouncing democracies.

His own view of a dependent Empire had scarcely changed since he
sailed the world in a wooden man-of-war. In 1928 the Colonial Secretary
compared him to George III. 'The King more talkative not to say noisy
than usual,' Amery wrote after lunching at the palace. 'His main theme is
of course dislike of all the new developments in constitutional relations.'
Three years later, when the Statute of Westminster recognized the legislative autonomy of the Dominions, Wigram called it 'a pedantic document
drawn up by lawyers to satisfy the *amour propre* mainly of South Africa and
the Irish Free State'. That undoubtedly echoed his master's voice and
marked a cooling of the King's enthusiasm for his Dominions. For India,
however, he retained a paternal pride that transcended each successive
advance of the sub-continent towards self-government. He was the father
of his Indian people, all four hundred million of them.

The Prince of Berar once asked Somerset Maugham: 'Do you know the
difference between the Yacht Club in Bombay and the Bengal Club in
Calcutta? In one they don't allow either dogs or Indians; in the other they
don't mind dogs.' Since first visiting India as Prince of Wales, the King
had deplored the mindless colour bar which increasingly polarized European and Indian society. He gladly gave his patronage to the Willingdon
Club, named after the Governor of Bombay who founded it and opened it
to all races. Even in London he recognized the princely rank of men such
as the Maharaja of Bikanir, placing him on the Queen's right at a palace

luncheon in preference to a whole host of British grandees. As the King indignantly observed on that occasion, Bikanir and Sinha, the first Indians to be appointed to the Viceroy's Council, had been made honorary members of all the best clubs in London and yet neither would be admitted to a white man's club in India. He also reversed the decision of a court official who took it on himself to declare that Indians receiving honorary knighthoods were not entitled to the prefix 'Sir'.

Neither members of his family nor the official world were immune to racial prejudice. His black sheep of a brother-in-law, Prince Francis of Teck, had only a few years earlier excused himself from dining in the country with the Grand Duke Michael of Russia on learning that his hostess would be taken into dinner by an Indian prince. 'It isn't possible, I won't have it,' he exclaimed. 'Besides, it will make the Rajah uncomfortable.' Lady Diana Cooper had no such scruples in sitting next to the Aga Khan at the Ritz in 1919, but her presence affronted the Lord Great Chamberlain. 'The sight of natives entertaining smart society women', he wrote, 'is not pleasant.' In 1927, when Lord Lee of Fareham gave a garden party for 500 guests, his wife noted in her diary: 'One thing Arthur was firm about was that he would not have any *Indians* asked.' It was the same Lord Lee who, having presided over the Royal Commission on the Indian Civil Service, shamelessly pestered the Government until he received a GCSI, the most senior of all Indian knighthoods.

The King, by contrast, was always alert to protecting both the dignity and the interests of his princely Indian subjects. He resented the refusal of successive British Governments to allow artillery to the troops of the Indian Native States, writing in 1923: 'The King cannot help feeling that we do not sufficiently trust the Ruling Princes, whose existence and security is so closely bound up with that of the British Empire, both in time of war and of internal troubles, when they have never failed to come forward with offers of personal service, their troops and money.' It was less a matter of armament than of prestige, but the Cabinets neither of Baldwin nor of MacDonald would go further than to authorize machine-guns.

If the King did have a fault in his concern for the Indian princes, it was not that he paid them too little regard but too much: and sometimes of that excessively paternal kind which his own sons had long endured. Those rulers were after all illustrious men in their own States: one was even descended from the sun. The King-Emperor was not at all gratified to receive a telegram from the Raja of Pudukottai announcing his marriage in New South Wales to 'Miss Molly Fink, an Australian girl'. He was again put out to hear that another ruler, one of his pages at the Durbar of 1911, had subsequently become addicted 'to drink and low female company'; particularly deplorable, he found it, in an old boy of Wellington College.

Bikanir, appointed to the Imperial War Cabinet in London, was told that the King had spotted him in 'a bowler hat and a suit of dittos', and that in future he was to wear the puggaree. The Aga Khan was taken aside on a State occasion and ordered to see that the Maharaja of Rajpipla, who had omitted to give his trainer the customary present on winning the 1934 Derby with Windsor Lad, made good his lapse. Even the Aga Khan, the King thought, 'would do more good if he remained in India and kept in touch with his people instead of enjoying himself in Europe'.

Although by constitutional practice the appointment of Viceroy of India lay with the British Government, the King-Emperor had no hesitation in pressing his own candidates. He believed that neither previous knowledge of India nor political experience were essential qualifications for a Viceroy: 'Above all things he should be a great English gentleman: a man of character: a personality: a man of the world, of determination, fearless, independent, and who would never let down the British Raj.' On Chelmsford's retirement in 1921 the field included Churchill; Lytton, the Under-Secretary for India; Willingdon, successively Governor of Bombay and Madras; and Reading, the Lord Chief Justice. The King would have chosen Willingdon, but it was another ten years before he reached Delhi. The appointment went to Reading, whose supposed political sagacity, sharp forensic mind and liberal sympathies were considered protection enough against the wiles of Indian nationalism.

The King did have his way when Reading came home in 1926. He first proposed Field-Marshal Haig, but Baldwin preferred a civilian. It was then that the King suggested Edward Wood, the Minister of Agriculture, a foxhunting Yorkshire squire whose compassionate Christianity concealed a steely regard for law and order. Wood's name found much favour with the Cabinet. He went out to India as Lord Irwin, later succeeding to his father's title of Viscount Halifax.

In the autumn of 1930, the search for a successor to Irwin provoked a rare and extraordinary clash between the Prime Minister and the King's private secretary. MacDonald, who had taken office for the second time after Labour's victory in the general election of 1929, decided that the new Viceroy should be Lord Gorell. It was a perplexing choice. Gorell, the son of an ennobled lawyer, wrote contemplative poetry and detective fiction, was an authority on army education and had served briefly as Under-Secretary for Air in the Lloyd George Coalition. But at the age of forty-six he revealed no other aptitudes for a proconsular role. Gorell might nevertheless have gone to India had not MacDonald's intention come to the King's ear before he could express an opinion on it. Through Gorell's publisher, the news reached Lady Brassey who, assuming that the appointment had been confirmed, mentioned it in a letter to a member of the royal

household. The courtier in turn told Stamfordham who, ever protective
of the King's constitutional rights, complained to MacDonald that the
sovereign's prerogative of consultation seemed to have been ignored. The
Prime Minister wrote in his diary:

Saw Stamfordham at Palace reception in afternoon and had a very straight –
perhaps even angry – talk.... Made it clear to him that whilst I was P.M. I should
not tolerate a procedure which would entitle him to show the King officially and
communicate officially with me regarding personal letters on public affairs passing
between the Court entourage and their friends.

MacDonald was mollified by a graceful letter of apology from Stamfordham. But the episode did make the Prime Minister pause before formally
submitting Gorell's name for India. At his next audience, the King politely
confessed that he did not know Gorell, and wondered whether there were
other candidates to be considered. Baldwin, with less finesse, warned that
the Conservatives would never accept him. Irwin wrote from Delhi that the
rumoured appointment had 'filled Indian opinion with anxiety'. Such
concerted expressions of dismay put paid to Gorell's hopes. Who then was
to take his place?

There is evidence that the Prime Minister had in mind an even less
conventional statesman. This undated card from MacDonald was years
later found among the papers of J.H. Thomas: 'Absolutely secret to yourself. May I consider your name in connection with Viceroyalty? Hope you
will say yes. Details can be arranged.' The appointment of the former
railwayman might not have been unwelcome either to the King, who trusted
his judgement, or to the Opposition. A year earlier Beatrice Webb had
written of him with arid contempt: 'In spite of his bad language, his coarse
wit and his more than doubtful City transactions, no word of scandal or
disparagement appears in the capitalist Press. To the suburban Conservative, "Jimmy" seems the one redeeming personality in the Labour Government.' Certainly he would have made things hum in Delhi. On being asked
by the Prince of Wales about a recent visit to West Africa, during which his
children were laid low by dysentery and malaria, Thomas had replied:
'Gawd, it's a bugger of a country.' As Queen Mary said of him: 'He is such
a very straightforward man.'

MacDonald, with his patrician instincts, could not quite see Thomas in
a viceregal role. Instead he nominated Lord Willingdon, a former Liberal
MP who had not only governed two Indian provinces but had earlier
captained the cricket elevens of both Eton and Cambridge. 'Of course I
agreed,' the King wrote in his diary. 'I had proposed him to Lloyd George
nine years ago when he sent Reading.' Stamfordham, too, was delighted,
writing to Baldwin: 'The appointment of Willingdon averts what would

have been not a blunder but a disaster especially at this momentous time in
the history of India.'

Just how momentous emerges from the correspondence between the
King-Emperor and his Viceroys. Over the years those fortnightly letters
reflect India's progress from paternalism to partnership; from a benevolent
autocracy to a hesitant sharing of power; from Dominion status to independence, and so to membership of the Commonwealth, that ingenious and
civilized device by which Britain has exorcized the ghost of a no-longer
fashionable Empire. Only in retrospect does India's advance to self-government seem inevitable. At no moment in a Viceroy's life was any political
solution safe from racial and religious strife, any magnanimous gesture from
a questioning of motive. Each successive Viceroy found himself trapped in
a weary cycle of resentment and rebellion, of repression and reprieve.

The King made himself as well-informed as could any man across a
distance of five thousand miles. Either in his own hand or through his
private secretaries, he would punctiliously reply to the letters and telegrams
from Delhi. And the Viceroys, for their part, knowing how laborious the
King sometimes found his task, sugared their solid fare with sporting
gossip. The pursuit of birds and beasts under the British Raj was not so
much a recreation as a hieratic cult, and no Viceroy could be wholly effective
who neglected its skills.

Even as a boy, Irwin had overcome the handicap of an atrophied left arm
and taught himself to handle both rifle and shotgun. He delighted in telling
the King of a line of guns at Patiala one and a half miles long, with 500
infantry and 150 cavalry acting as beaters, his princely hosts directing the
shoot from the howdahs of twenty elephants; of the bags of sand grouse at
Bikanir so huge that he was glad to have taken the King's advice and padded
the butt of his guns with indiarubber and leather; or of breakfasting with
the Maharaja of Benares, who threw a rupee high in the air, then hit it with
a rifle shot – a trick he had performed before the King years earlier. Poor
Reading, who until he went out to India had wielded nothing more lethal
than a golf club or an affidavit, recorded his exploits on a note of apology.
At Bikanir, he told the King, he had fired 1,700 cartridges but added only
336 birds to a total bag of 6,988. Under the tutelage of the Maharaja Scindia
of Gwalior, however, the Viceroy was fortunate enough to shoot a tiger of
almost record length. Thus did the King vicariously re-live those idyllic
days which followed the Durbar ceremonial of 1911.

The Viceroys also illuminated their letters with pen sketches of those
Indian nationalists who presaged the end of British rule. In 1924 Reading
wrote that Pandit Nehru, educated at Harrow and Trinity College, Cambridge, now wore *Khaddar*, or homespun cloth, but 'of an extremely superior and finely woven kind'. The account continues:

It is said that in the old days before he joined Gandhi, when he lived in Allahabad as a celebrated and popular barrister, he not only kept open house and welcomed Europeans but was regarded, Sir, as the complete dandy, with more European suits of clothes and hats than I have ever myself possessed. As your Majesty is aware, all this is now changed, and he has become a leader of anti-Government agitation. The story goes – as is, alas! so often the case – that the change dates from a social slight by some British officers.

And here, in 1931, is Irwin on Gandhi:

I think that most people meeting him would be conscious, as I was conscious, of a very powerful personality, and this, independent of physical endowment, which indeed is unfavourable. Small, wizened, rather emaciated, no front teeth, it is a personality very poorly adorned with this world's trimmings. And yet you cannot help feeling the force of character behind the sharp little eyes and immensely active and acutely working mind.

The King regarded Indian nationalism as he did industrial unrest at home. He wanted a contented people and was prepared to accept a measured advance towards self-government. But he deprecated any challenge to law and order by the followers of Gandhi, any obstruction to the considered proposals of Whitehall and Delhi by a fractious assembly of princes. When Gandhi came to London in 1931 for the Round Table Conference on India, the King was reluctant to see him. 'What!' he exclaimed, 'Have this rebel fakir in the Palace after he has been behind all these attacks on my loyal officers?' But of course he relented; and although from time to time the King looked resentfully at Gandhi's bare knees, the two men found much to discuss. As Gandhi was taking his leave, the King uttered a stern warning. 'Remember, Mr Gandhi, I won't have any attacks on my Empire.' Sir Samuel Hoare, the Secretary of State for India, later recorded that Gandhi gave a grave and deferential reply: 'I must not be drawn into political argument in Your Majesty's Palace after receiving Your Majesty's hospitality.' And they parted on friendly terms.

That account was published by Hoare more than twenty years after Gandhi's audience with the King. But Wigram sent this more robust version to the new Viceroy, Willingdon, only a week or two after the encounter:

His Majesty, as is his custom, was very nice to [Mr. Gandhi], but ended up by impressing on him that this country would not stand a campaign of terrorism and having their friends shot down in India. His Majesty, warned Gandhi that he was to put a stop to this. ... Gandhi spluttered some excuse, but H.M. said he held him responsible.

The King spoke with the same severity when the Indian princes demonstrated their own brand of civil disobedience. On hearing that they had apparently rejected the federation proposed, among other constitutional advances, by the Government of India Bill, he told Hoare: 'I won't see them when they come to London. Why should they come to London at all and spend a lot of money? Tell them to stay in their States and look after their own subjects.'

Throughout even the worst of those political convulsions, the King-Emperor never doubted the permanence of his Indian Empire. The monument to his self-confidence stands on a ridge a few miles from the old city of Delhi: Viceroy's House, at once the Versailles and the Valhalla of the British Raj. 'Sloping gently upward', Robert Byron wrote soon after its completion in 1930, 'runs a gravel way of such infinite perspective as to suggest the intervention of a diminishing glass; at whose end, reared above the green tree-tops, glitters the seat of government, the seventh Delhi, four-square upon an eminence – dome, tower, dome, tower, dome, red, pink, cream and white, washed gold and flashing in the morning sun.'

From the moment the King proclaimed the new capital of India at the Durbar of 1911, he followed the construction of New Delhi with intense interest. His first instruction to the architect, Edwin Lutyens, was negative but aesthetically sound. 'I want', he said, referring to the Queen Victoria memorial outside Buckingham Palace, 'no —— Angel of Victory.' And for the next twenty years he was the most exacting of patrons. In 1916, when the Government thought it right to impose a measure of wartime economy on the plans, the architect wrote of an audience with the King:

The accommodation, thickness of walls and number of bathrooms were criticized; that there was no sitting room for the wife of the Viceroy attached to their bedroom suite. . . . His Majesty was very emphatic on the importance of using monoliths for the columns throughout the Palace. As to cost, it did not matter how long the Palace took to build so long as it was, when built, worthy of India and its purpose, and that if money was not forthcoming now, parts might for the time being be omitted and façades left unfinished.

The King was nevertheless impressed by Reading's warning that the more palatial the Viceroy's residence, the greater the expenditure, particularly on servants; and that it would be lamentable if this confined the Viceroyalty to rich men.

As it neared completion in 1928, Irwin's reference in a letter to 'Viceregal Lodge' drew a sharp inquiry from the King. Irwin apologized for that diminutive description, explaining that it was the name of his temporary perch. But he went on to argue that there was a case for calling even the new residence Viceregal Lodge: if the Viceroy's palace was designated a mere lodge, India could not fail to wonder what sort of house the King-Emperor himself occupied. When that suggestion found no favour, Irwin

21 Convalescing at Bognor, subsequently called Bognor Regis, in the spring of 1929. The King was fortunate to have survived a severe infection of the blood before the advent of either sulphonamide drugs or antibiotics. No fewer than eleven doctors and surgeons hovered at his bedside. But J. H. Thomas, the Labour Minister, said of his friend and Sovereign: 'It was his bloody guts that pulled him through.'

22 Canon Dalton, the King's boyhood tutor, in old age. Appointed to the Chapter of St George's Chapel, Windsor, soon after the cruise of the *Bacchante*, he remained there until his death nearly half a century later. Bombastic and quarrelsome, he was furious not to be appointed Dean of Windsor in 1917, and is said to have given his former pupil one of the worst hours of his life.

23 Sir Clive Wigram, who on Lord Stamfordham's death in 1931 served as private secretary to the King for the rest of the reign. 'He is always very genial,' Lord Reith wrote of him, 'but it seems to take a good deal to make him understand things.' That was a superficial judgment. It is true that Wigram was addicted to the use of sporting metaphor. But he handled constitutional crises such as the formation of the National Government of 1931 – 'my first Test Match,' he called it – with a sure touch.

24 The King at the microphone. For years he had resisted suggestions that he should broadcast an informal Christmas message. At last, in 1932, he reluctantly agreed. He proved a matchless exponent of the art, reaching out into the hearts of his people with paternal simplicity.

25 The Silver Jubilee celebrations of 1935. Inhabitants of the poorer streets of London on their way to cheer the King and Queen. Although the King deplored the fuss and expense, he was much moved by the love and loyalty which everywhere awaited him. At the thanksgiving service in St. Paul's Cathedral, Neville Chamberlain gazed across at the foreign ambassadors and thought: 'That'll show 'em.'

26 The King with his shooting pony, Jock. Even during the last days of his life, when no longer able to hold a gun, he rode the pony about the Sandringham estate, Queen Mary at his side. After his death, Jock, led by a groom, followed the coffin on the first stage of the funeral journey, from Sandringham House to the local railway station.

tried again with Viceroy's House. This time the King agreed, although amending it to The Viceroy's House. Kipling, who was staying at Balmoral, pleaded for the word 'palace'. He was told that there was only one palace: that of the King-Emperor.

For all that, the Viceroy's House, New Delhi, is indeed a palace, and Edwin Lutyens the last architect to receive so grandiose a commission. On the classical proportions of Europe he imposed those traditional Indian elements that make an ally of the fierce and effacing sun: deep shadows and contrasting colours and colonnades. Then he crowned the whole with a ponderous dome: a symbol of power yet a distraction from the daring simplicity of façade and cornice.

Lutyens never forgave his fellow architect, Herbert Baker, who had been entrusted with the Secretariat buildings, for having insisted that they should share the same ridge as the Viceroy's House and so deny it an unchallenged eminence. 'I have met my Bakerloo,' he declared. That defeat, however, was swallowed up in a greater. According to legend, every new city built at Delhi foretold the end of a dynasty. Twenty years after Irwin became the first to occupy the Viceroy's House, Mountbatten became the last.

Neither George V nor his ministers, not even the most radical of them, envisaged so swift an end to the British Raj. But one old friend of his may have done. Georges Clemenceau, the wartime leader of the French people, came out to India in 1920. He gazed on the half-built walls of New Delhi and exclaimed: 'What a splendid ruin it will make.'

On 21 November 1928, after a busy day at Buckingham Palace, the King felt too unwell to write his diary. Rather than break the habit of a lifetime, he dictated a brief entry to the Queen: 'I was taken ill this evening. Feverish cold they called it, and retired to bed.' Not until 27 April 1929 was he able to resume the diary in his own hand: five months during which he fought and vanquished the last enemy of all.

Lord Dawson of Penn, summoned to the palace by telephone, took immediate charge. 'I knew from the first time I looked at the King,' he later wrote, 'that we were in for a serious illness.' He had long prepared for just such an emergency. Aware that a pathologist might one day be required, he had three years earlier asked young Dr Lionel Whitby to carry out a complete set of tests on himself, including such unpleasant procedures as drawing blood from the veins; Dawson was thus able to judge whether Whitby had both the temperament and the technique to handle a sometimes irritable patient. When Whitby did enter the King's bedroom for the first time in the early hours of 22 November, limping from a war wound, he was received with courtesy. 'Have you lost your leg?' the King asked him. 'Well, it's very good of you to come and see me at this time of night.'

Whitby's tests revealed a streptococcal infection of the chest. Corroborative evidence came from Dr Graham Hodgson, the radiologist, who brought his apparatus into the palace garden on a lorry, paid out a cable through a window and took his plates as the King lay in bed: the first time X-rays had been made available to a patient outside the big hospitals. Although the photographs confirmed the clinical evidence that the lower two-thirds of the King's right lung were affected, they did not reveal a localized effusion which could be pinpointed and drained. Meanwhile bronchial spasms increased the King's pain and weakness. By 2 December the medical bulletin warned of 'a decline in the strength of the heart', and the Prince of Wales was summoned home from a safari in East Africa.

Since the King was no longer able to carry out his constitutional duties, a quorum of the Privy Council met next door to his bedroom to authorize the appointment of Counsellors of State. Balfour was too unwell to attend, his place as Lord President of the Council being taken by the Home Secretary, Joynson-Hicks. On the following day, however, he received a letter from Dawson that included both a description of the ceremony and a prognosis of the King's illness:

The bulletins have all along been very *genuine* and clear. But the crux is the *heart*, and while the lung trouble is practically over there remains a fight between whatever poison remains and the heart. Six hours sleep of last night means an increase of latent power. The fact of H.M.'s holding a Council and *signing his name* – and a good signature – is for me proof enough that he is better. It was sad tho' that the *President* was not there! Jix as his Representative was very much there and stood in the doorway between the bedroom and audience chamber at the further end of which the other P.C.s remained. H.M. after signing said 'he wished to see the P.C.s' but was told 'better not' – so that pleasure was postponed!

That confident, even jaunty tone was scarcely justified; the worst crisis in the King's illness had yet to come. But Dawson was determined not to sound a note of alarm. As he later wrote:

By the third or fourth day we had proved he had septicaemia, and just for public reasons were unable to say so. Not only is it an exceptionally big illness for any man to have and still more for a public person under modern conditions of Press and publicity, but this in itself presented a problem by itself occupying much time.

'The mischief in the lung', as Dawson called it, was overshadowed by a general infection of the blood. A decade later, sulphonamide drugs were available to combat the toxaemia; another five years, and penicillin was at hand to exert its near magic potency. But in the winter of 1928, a team of eminent specialists that eventually grew to eleven could do little more than watch the patient fight his own battle. The original abscess lay just behind the diaphragm; it thus eluded each new set of X-ray photographs, and even if detected could not have been drained without the strain of a surgical operation under anaesthesia.

Feverish and delirious, the King had by the afternoon of 12 December sunk into unconsciousness. Sister Black, the senior nurse, later wrote of that moment: 'The doctors had done everything that could be done. Human skill ended there.' Then Dawson came into the room. 'Will you give me a syringe?' he said suddenly. 'I think I will make one more try to find that fluid.' He explored the chest, and with that insight which resembles luck but is more usually the result of experience, detected the exact place within a few seconds. Plunging in the needle, Dawson at once drew off sixteen ounces of vicious matter. The King, still comatose, was operated on that evening by his surgeon, Hugh Rigby, for the removal of a rib and drainage of the abscess. His decline had been arrested.

If Dawson's crude but effective remedy today appears to belong to an earlier age of kingcraft, so too do the rumours which swept the capital. The Duke of York was amused to hear that the Prince of Wales was returning with all speed lest his younger brother should try to bag the throne in his absence. The French ambassador reported to his Government that the King was said to have died and the announcement of his demise postponed until his heir's return. Even the phlegmatic Baldwin gave his niece a melodramatic account of the Prince's arrival at his father's bedside: 'The old King, who had for nearly a week been practically unconscious, just opened half an eye, looked up at him and said: "Damn you, what the devil are you doing here?" And from that moment he turned the corner and began rapidly to get better. It was exactly like the scene in Henry IV when Prince Henry tries on the crown.'

The truth is less colourful. On hearing of his father's illness while travelling in Tanganyika, the Prince had indeed exclaimed to a friend: 'Imagine, I could be King of England tomorrow.' But it was without elation that he boarded HMS *Enterprise* at Dar-es-Salaam, covered the 4,700 miles to Brindisi in only eight days, rattled across Europe in Mussolini's own train and reached Buckingham Palace on the evening of 11 December. The King, although desperately weak, recognized his son. But there was no paternal explosion, merely a mumbled inquiry about the Prince's sport in East Africa. Nor did the King turn the corner that night. For the next twenty-four hours his strength continued to ebb away until Dawson's syringe brought him respite. With Rigby's successful operation that same evening, the microbic infection receded but exhaustion remained. Even two weeks later, Dawson could not be certain of recovery. 'Safety, and still more, convalescence', he wrote, 'are some distance away.'

Throughout her husband's ordeal, the Queen remained a pillar of strength. 'If only they were all like her,' Dawson said, 'how much easier it would be.' She was not only stoical of spirit but as practical as Florence Nightingale. When Dawson asked for moistened muslin to filter the air of the sickroom, the Queen knew just what was wanted and where to find it. She led Dawson along corridors and up back stairs to a small room at the top of the palace; made him climb on a chair and hand down a bundle from a cupboard; untied it to reveal some curtains of Queen Victoria's which years ago she had thriftily brought down from Balmoral and stowed away.

Dawson did not always have such an ally at hand. Margot Asquith, with one of her more inspired flights of fancy, used to say in old age: 'The King told me he would never have died if it had not been for that fool Dawson of Penn.' That venomous shaft, for all its absurdity, was typical of the social and professional jealousy to which Dawson was exposed. The story went the rounds that he had once treated a patient for jaundice for six weeks before realizing that the man was Chinese. And the surgeon Lord Moynihan, after an angry exchange about the medical care of one of the royal children, taunted his adversary with this jingle:

> Lord Dawson of Penn
> Has killed lots of men.
> So that's why we sing
> God save the King.

As the King lay at death's door in 1928, there was resentment among members of the medical profession that he had not brought into consultation that pioneer of thoracic surgery Arthur Tudor Edwards: it was even rumoured that doctors and students intended to demonstrate outside Dawson's house for the benefit of the Press.

The King was a bad patient, mistrustful of medical science, hating to be touched by hand or instrument and the victim of occasional melancholy; he later told MacDonald that he had asked his doctors whether he was to go mad like George III. But he was courageous, too. A visitor who found him in unusually high spirits, full of jokes and laughter, afterwards discovered he had just been told that further painful treatment was necessary; it was the King's way of demonstrating his fortitude. J.H. Thomas put it succinctly: 'It was his bloody guts that pulled him through.'

Refreshed by a daily egg beaten in brandy, the King slowly gained strength, and the thoughts of Dawson turned to convalescence. Four years earlier, after a severe attack of influenza and bronchitis, the King had been persuaded to join the royal yacht *Victoria and Albert* for a Mediterranean cruise. On that occasion his entourage had spared him most of the irritations of abroad. 'The King does not wish to see *any* French officials during his journey through France,' Stamfordham had warned the British ambassador in Paris. He was accompanied on that 1925 cruise by the Queen and his favourite sister, Princess Victoria; and each of the two escorting warships was commanded by an officer who shared the King's quarterdeck humour. Commander W.N.T. Beckett was said to breakfast off steaks and ale, sometimes garnished with a midshipman. Commander R.V. Holt had been the Boswell of the party:

The Queen says that she has never been anywhere without a programme before. They are frightfully excited about it and change their minds as often as they like. The Queen thinks Elba would be nice and Naples as she has never been there, but the King says the harbour is always full of dead dogs. So they think of anchoring in the bay somewhere. He also says Malta is a bloody place – he won't go there if he can help it.

Armed with volumes of his diary thirty and more years old, the King had hoped to recapture his days as a young naval officer. But there was a cold north-east wind, his cough persisted and the rest of the party went down with colds and temperatures. Stamfordham nevertheless suggested another convalescence abroad in 1929. 'I was told in rather strong language,' he wrote, 'that nothing of the sort would take place.' The problem was solved by Sir Arthur du Cros, who had earlier saved the King embarrassment by paying £64,000 for the return of the love letters written by King Edward to Lady Warwick. He now offered Craigweil, his house near Bognor, for as long as it might be required; it overlooked the Channel, thus enabling the invalid to breathe sea air without the inconvenience of putting to sea. When Asquith borrowed Craigweil as a summer retreat in 1916, a daughter-in-law wrote of it: 'Hideous house, but trees in the garden, splendid sea view; and comfortable Elsinore battlements to walk on.' Those amenities alone did not satisfy Dawson, who had the water supply tested and the drains examined, the carriage road levelled and a type of health-giving glass fitted to the windows of the King's room. On 9 February 1929, the new tenant was driven down from London by motor ambulance. He himself pulled up its window blinds so that he could once more enjoy the winter landscape and acknowledge the sympathetic waves of his people.

On only his fourth day at Bognor, the King was allowed to resume smoking; such was the gulf which separates medical opinion half a century ago from that of our own day. In retrospect, smoking may be seen as the scourge of the dynasty. Four successive sovereigns, all heavy smokers, died of ailments either caused or aggravated by the habit. The pattern was set by Edward VII, who by the time he sat down to breakfast had already enjoyed two cigarettes and a cigar. George V, when scarcely more than a boy, was supplied with cigarettes by his former tutor Dalton, and the habit became lifelong. He in turn put no restraint on his sons; Queen Mary's present to Prince Albert on his eighteenth birthday was a cigarette case. In the short term, however, those coveted cigarettes brought comfort and cheer to a weary patient and hastened his immediate recovery.

Old friends came down to visit the King, among them Archbishop Lang, recently translated from York to Canterbury on the retirement of Archbishop Randall Davidson. On Easter Day the King received from Lang his first Communion since falling ill. He also delighted in the company of his granddaughter, Princess Elizabeth, who was not quite three.

On a day when his spirits were low, the King complained that he would never have the strength to shoot again. He was persuaded to send for his gunsmith, who suggested that he might care to practise handling a gun to get his muscles working again. After so many years of gun discipline, the King did not like to have even an unloaded weapon inside the house. Purdey's therefore designed and made for him a replica of a real gun, of exactly the same measurements and weight, with the royal cipher in gold on the butt. Instead of a firing mechanism, however, an electric battery and bulb caused a bright flash of light to emerge from the barrel when the King pressed the trigger. Thus he could not only accustom himself once more to the feel of a gun, but also test his marksmanship with the help of a light-sensitive target. To spare him effort when he resumed shooting later that year, Purdey made him a set of 20-bore guns to replace the 12-bore which he had used all his life. 'I did not distinguish myself,' the King wrote on 21 October 1929, when shooting for the first time since his illness. So, he returned the 20-bore guns and Purdey made him a pair of light 12-bore, each weighing a shade under 6 lb. instead of the usual 6½ lb. Thereafter he began to shoot once more with his old brilliance.

From Bognor, the King also followed the ill-fortune of his racehorses. When his Glastonbury was just beaten by Rosebery's Midlothian (which had been entered for the race by mistake) he could not resist sending the successful owner a telegram: 'Confound Midlothian.' He received the reply: 'Lord Rosebery sends his humble duty and thanks His Majesty for his gracious congratulations.' The King acknowledged that Rosebery had scored a double victory.

After three months by the sea, the King was told that he could return home to complete his convalescence. Bognor, however, will always be associated with his recovery. It has been alleged that when he lay gravely ill seven years later, one of his doctors sought to soothe a restless patient with a whispered, 'Cheer up, Your Majesty, you will soon be at Bognor again.' To this the King is said to have replied, 'Bugger Bognor', and instantly expired. The tale carries a certain plausibility. The King was always emphatic in his language, not least when being fussed by his medical advisers. Sir Frederic Willans, for instance, his physician at Sandringham, has recalled how during that last illness the King would wave away his medicine with the words: 'Willans, I'm not having any more of your blasted muck.' But would that whimsical alliteration have been attached to his memory had he convalesced at Ramsgate or Cleethorpes, Scarborough or Torquay?

There is, however, a happier variant of the legend which rests on the authority of Sir Owen Morshead, the King's librarian. As the time of the King's departure from Bognor drew near, a deputation of leading citizens came to Craigweil to ask that their salubrious town should henceforth be known as Bognor Regis. They were received by Stamfordham, who, having heard their petition, invited them to wait while he consulted the King in another room. The sovereign responded with the celebrated obscenity, which Stamfordham deftly translated for the benefit of the delegation. His Majesty, they were told, would be graciously pleased to grant their request.

While the King was still at Bognor, the French ambassador in London reported to his Government that rooms had been reserved for the royal invalid at Professor Krödel's sanatorium in Bad Nauheim. M. Fleuriau was again misinformed. When the King left Craigweil on 15 May it was not for Germany but for Windsor. His progress, however, was disappointing. He had strength only for the shortest of walks and drives. The reason soon became apparent. An abscess caused by residual fragments of bone had formed at the site of the previous operation. On 31 May the abscess burst, bringing some relief from pain. It was nevertheless with a temperature of 102 °F that the King had to conduct a change of Government. The defeated Baldwin was received at Windsor on 4 June; MacDonald, his successor, on the following day. The new Prime Minister wrote in his diary:

Went to Windsor. King in Chinese dressing gown with pink edges and ground of yellow with patterns blue and green. Face seemed longer and brow longer, eyes rather staring and easily excited. Spoke at times rather loudly. Sat on sofa with table (small) and pad of paper and pencil in front of him. Obviously had been very ill. Not always discreet in talk and thundered against two in particular who were to be Ministers. Forgot to ask me to form Government but I had kissed hands. Most cordial personally.

The timetable of the change of Government unfortunately disposes of an agreeable legend: that the bursting of the King's abscess was the result of his laughing at one of J.H. Thomas's rude jokes. But the new Lord Privy Seal was not received at Windsor until 8 June, more than a week later.

On that same day, Lord Dawson of Penn was sworn of the Privy Council: an exceptional honour for a doctor, given at the King's insistence and against the wishes of the outgoing Prime Minister. It was not only a gesture from a grateful patient but also an act of reparation. Ten years earlier, when Lloyd George recommended Sir Bertrand Dawson for a peerage, the King had resisted the proposal. He thought that more senior doctors might feel that they had been passed over; and that if war service was to count, surgeons had a higher claim. Lloyd George, however, had persisted. He pacified the King by conceding that the honour should be regarded not so much as a reward for past service as a measure to strengthen the composition of the House of Lords. This the King accepted, and in 1920 Dawson received his peerage as an authority on public health.

It was unfortunate for Dawson that the bestowal of his Privy Counsellorship (as well as lesser honours for the other doctors and surgeons) should coincide with a continued discharge from the King's wound. In order not to cause public alarm, the King agreed to return to Buckingham Palace on 1 July and from there drive in state to Westminster Abbey six days later. He received a memorable welcome, but did not fail to remind his doctors of their shortcomings. 'Fancy a Thanksgiving Service', he told them, 'with an open wound in your back!' On 15 July another operation was performed for direct drainage of the residual abscess. This time it was completely successful. Next morning the King asked for tea and toast and an egg for breakfast: the beginning of an uninterrupted convalescence. Although the wound did not finally heal until 25 September, even then leaving the skin thin and sore, he was able to travel to Sandringham on 24 August.

With some justice he continued to make a butt of his doctors. He was overheard telling the new First Commissioner of Works, with appropriate gestures: 'They called it a minor operation, Mr. Lansbury, and they opened me from *here* to *here*.' But he had not lost his sense of humour. When congratulated on regaining his health, he replied: 'Yes, I'm pretty well again,' hastily adding, 'but not well enough to walk with the Queen round the British Industries Fair.' The organizers of the fair no doubt received the news with relief. A year or two earlier, looking at some new plastics made by De La Rue, he explained to the Queen: 'All made of milk.' 'Aren't they?' he barked at the chairman of the company. 'Yes, Sir,' the chairman replied untruthfully.

It was Albert Mensdorff who on 19 November 1929 recorded the King's complete recovery, almost exactly a year since the onset of his illness: 'He was in a good mood and cursed as in earlier days.'

'Of course, I know you won't believe me,' the King told the Revd Cyril Alington, Head Master of Eton, 'but throughout my illness I felt buoyed up by the prayers of my people.' Alington, who had been in Holy Orders for nearly thirty years, hastened to assure the Head of the Church of England that he too accepted Christian doctrine. But the King remained sceptical of his audience. 'I know you won't believe me,' he insisted.

In his grandmother's reign, a Fellow of the Royal Society had purported to subject the efficacy of prayer to scientific inquiry. Francis Galton wrote a paper for the *Fortnightly Review* in which he calculated the mean age attained by male members of various social classes over a period of eighty-five years. He demonstrated that in spite of sustained supplication for the long life of the royal family, English sovereigns were the shortest-lived of any category. Their average age at death was 64.04, compared with 67.31 for the aristocracy and 70.22 for the gentry; even those engaged in the fine arts, a supposedly profligate lot, lived to be 65.96. King George V confounded Galton's ponderous irreverence. Surviving the perils of December 1928, he lived on until 1936. In that year, the average age of death was 55.2; and the life expectancy of his contemporaries scarcely more than 40, or 47 if they survived their first year. The King died at almost 70.6. He had had every reason to put his trust in the efficacy of prayer.

His was a simple faith based on the Bible. The habit which he acquired in *Bacchante* of reading a chapter each night lasted to the end of his life: except, he would add scrupulously, during serious illness. Its mysteries, however, did not always accord with his own experience. 'A wonderful book,' he used to say, 'but there are some very queer things in it.' During his visit to the Holy Land as a midshipman he expressed a characteristic doubt: 'All the places are only *said* to be the places.' Nearly half a century later he enjoyed teasing the clergy about such enigmas. A visiting preacher wrote from Sandringham: 'The King was talking at the end of dinner over our port and cigars, raising absurd questions about the Flood and the Ark and Cain and Abel.'

Each Sunday, in England and Scotland alike, he worshipped according to the rites of the Established Church, in spite of the doctrinal gulf which separated his two kingdoms. At Sandringham, the vicar's warden was the head gardener; the parishioners' warden was the King. 'But I bargained that I should not be expected to take the bag round,' he said, 'I drew the line at that.'

Like all sailors, he enjoyed singing hymns. His favourites were 'Abide with me' and 'The day Thou gavest, Lord, is ended'. One Sunday, when on board the *Victoria and Albert*, he could not find them in their usual place; a new hymn book had been introduced. A broadside awaited the captain at the end of the service. 'I'll have all the bloody books burned,' the King told him, 'I'm not Defender of the Faith for nothing.' It was the most startling scene in the royal yacht since King Edward VII, attending morning service during convalescence from a celebrated operation, was exhorted to sing: '*Peace, perfect peace* – in the appendix'.

Visiting clergy were entertained sumptuously, though without their wives. Here is a passage from Dean Inge's diary:

To Windsor to preach before the King and Queen. I was met by a royal carriage drawn by two white horses, and by an enormous omnibus to carry my handbag. Two magnificent gentlemen escorted me to my apartments. The sitting-room contained portraits of Gladstone, Disraeli, Melbourne and other statesmen. In the evening a 'page', a splendid elderly personage, came to fetch me to the Red Drawing Room.

But sermons were required to be modest in length and simple in content. As Stamfordham warned: 'Preach for about fourteen minutes. If you preach for less, the King may say you are too lazy to prepare a sermon; if you preach for more than fourteen minutes, the King may say that the man did not know when to stop.' On a visit to Sandringham, Canon Woods followed his usual custom, he wrote, of preaching at the gamekeepers and kitchen-maids, and was warmly congratulated by both the King and the Queen.

Not every preacher came through the ordeal with credit. There was an early brush with Cosmo Lang. Against the King's known wishes, he took as his theme Christian missions overseas: an endeavour which the King thought both intrusive and futile. At lunch afterwards they had a set-to. Lang told the King that being a Christian carried with it a belief in the world-wide mission of Christianity. 'Then you tell me that with my views I can't be a Christian?' the King asked. Lang replied that he could only state the premises; it was for the King to draw the conclusions. 'Well, I call that damned cheek,' said the King. Later they became friends.

On liturgical matters he was a middle-of-the-road Anglican. He liked tradition and was proud to be the first English sovereign since James II to perform the rites of Maundy Thursday in Westminster Abbey. But at his Silver Jubilee service in St Paul's it was with reluctance that he allowed Lang to wear a mitre. After dining at Sandringham, a preacher wrote: 'The King talked about the iniquities of Communists, the plight of farmers and the shortcomings of Anglo-Catholics. Said to me point blank, "Are you an Anglo-Catholic?" I reassured him about that – told him I was more like a Quaker.'

Both the King and Queen, however, favoured the Revised Prayer Book which failed to gain parliamentary approval in 1927 and again in 1928, and regretted that the Commons had been stampeded by a cry of 'No Popery'.

Although a tenacious Anglican, the King showed a seemly and indeed courageous regard for the feelings of his Roman Catholic subjects. He found on ascending the throne that the 1689 Bill of Rights required a new sovereign, when addressing Parliament for the first time, to declare that 'the invocation or adoration of the Virgin Mary, or any other saint, and the sacrifice of the Mass, as they are now used in the Church of Rome, are superstitious and idolatrous'. Unless this offensive formula were modified, the King told Asquith, he would refuse to open Parliament. Asquith readily complied, introducing a Bill which required the sovereign merely to declare: 'I am a faithful Protestant, and that I will, according to the true intent of the enactments which secure the Protestant succession to the Throne of my Realm, uphold and maintain the said enactments to the best of my power according to law.'

The King's ministers did not always show the same delicacy in their attitude to Roman Catholicism. At a palace banquet given for delegates to the Imperial Conference of 1926, William Cosgrave, from the Irish Free State, wore a Papal order. It was spotted by the Home Secretary, Joynson-Hicks, an assiduous upholder of the Protestant faith, who complained to Lord Granard at this 'desecration of the Palace and introduction of a custom unknown since the Reformation'. But as Stamfordham gleefully noted, Joynson-Hicks had chosen to lay his grievance before the wrong court official. Granard, too, was a Roman Catholic.

Even the King, however, was put out on hearing of the toast given at a Roman Catholic banquet in Liverpool: 'His Holiness the Pope and His Majesty the King.' MacDonald stoked the fires by writing to Wigram: 'The Liverpool toast was treason, and I do not care who knows that that is my opinion. ... It embodied two faults of a first class order – first of all, the priority of the Pope to the King and, secondly, the coupling of them together.'

A few days later the Prime Minister sent off a second letter to say that where he wrote 'treason', he should have said 'sedition'; like Warden Spooner, who at the end of a sermon announced: 'Wherever I said Aristotle, I meant St Paul.' The controversy was eventually settled by the Pope's agreement that he would not be mentioned in toasts after a banquet, but only in a prayer or grace at the beginning.

In approving ecclesiastical appointments made by the Prime Minister of the day, the King showed an unexpected tolerance. 'I like Hensley Henson,' he said of that newly nominated, stimulating but supposedly heretical bishop, 'he is a very nice fellow.' And he personally recommended the future Archbishop William Temple for a vacant canonry of Westminster Abbey, 'in spite of a certain restlessness and love of change'. But sometimes he took a rigidly hierarchical view of the Church of England, as if it were simply the Royal Navy at prayer. Thus he refused to allow E. H. Fellowes, a minor canon of St George's, Windsor, to be promoted to the chapter, even though he was the leading scholar of sixteenth- and seventeenth-century music; it would, the King thought, be too great an elevation from the lower deck.

No couple more epitomized the virtues of a Christian marriage than King George and Queen Mary. 'Mind you give me a good big V,' he told the sculptor responsible for designing the first coinage of the new reign. 'I don't want to be mistaken for any of the other Georges.' Both he and his consort could nevertheless show compassion to those who had stumbled. When the parents of a young Mecklenburg-Strelitz discovered that she was about to have a baby by a footman and banished her to the south of France, it was her cousin Queen Mary (then Duchess of York) who went to comfort her and daily drove out in her company. The King was similarly indulgent whenever such lapses were reported to him from the royal estates. Those private attitudes, however, did not affect the rigid convention of official life: that no divorced or even separated husband or wife could be received at court.

The ninth Duke of Marlborough was almost alone in obtaining a limited dispensation from the rule. Although, as a Knight of the Garter, he was summoned to the annual chapter of the Order at Windsor, his name had for some years been deliberately omitted from the list of those invited to lunch with the King after the ceremony; for since 1907 he had been living apart from his American wife, Consuelo Vanderbilt. In 1911, Winston Churchill wrote to the King on behalf of his cousin, asking whether a chapter of the Garter need be recognized as a regular court occasion and pleading with the sovereign not to inflict a further snub on the Duke. The King instantly conceded that the Duke should lunch at the castle after the next chapter; but Knollys added that it was not to be taken as abrogating the general rule which excluded separated wives and husbands from court.

The barrier against divorced persons was even more vigorously defended. A Scottish nobleman who argued that his divorce had been purged by subsequent remarriage in a church received no satisfaction. 'That may well get you into the Kingdom of Heaven,' he was told, 'but it will no admit you to the Palace of Holyroodhouse.' Divorce was also a bar to entertainment by His Majesty's representatives abroad; so too was flagrant immorality. When a former Cabinet Minister embroiled in a homosexual scandal was about to visit Australia, the Governor-General and all State Governors were warned by Buckingham Palace not to offer him hospitality. The King regretted the need for such precautions. 'I always thought', he said, 'people like that shot themselves.'

In maintaining the sacredness of the marriage bond, the King allowed few lapses to go by default. He tried to deny a peer of ancient lineage his traditional claim to carry the Cap of Maintenance at the opening of Parliament because of his amorous escapades. 'As H.M. sits on the throne by hereditary right,' a member of the royal household observed, 'he must be careful not to challenge the rights of others.' The King also regretted the recall of a much-respected foreign envoy from London: 'He has been kicked out by some dirty intrigue. They want to send me a man who has three

wives alive, but we shall refuse him. I will not have a man with three wives.'
Nor did he.

In spite of the high moral tone and blameless lives of the King and
Queen, there were apparently some who discerned room for improvement.
They included a lady-in-waiting who one day presented the Queen with a
religious tract. It was returned with the majestic rebuke: 'You are neither
old enough nor good enough to give me this.' Queen Mary was a Christian
but she was also a Queen.

Had some bold prophet told the King that he was one day to preside over
a change of Government wearing a Chinese dressing-gown, he would
scarcely have believed his ears. But immediately after the general election
of 1929, the reopening of a surgical wound obliged him to receive both
Baldwin and MacDonald in his bedroom at Windsor. That was indeed a
revolution. So too was the instant transfer of power from Conservative to
Labour. After the general election of 1923, the King had asked the defeated
Prime Minister, Baldwin, to defer his resignation until the new Parliament
could meet. Disputable even in 1923, that narrow constitutional doctrine
had become outmoded by 1929. Labour now commanded 287 seats, compared with 261 Conservative and 59 Liberal: an effective though not overall
majority. There was nothing to recommend preserving the old Government
until it had been formally defeated at Westminster. As Stamfordham wrote:
'We must recognise that Democracy is no longer a meaningless sort of
shibboleth; with the enormous increase of voters by the women's franchise
it is the actual voice, for better or worse, the political voice of the State.'

Baldwin agreed. If he were to hang on, he told Stamfordham, the nation
would say: 'Here is this man clinging to office, he won't take his defeat, he
is trying to prevent the Labour Party from enjoying their victory.' So he at
once resigned, and the King sent for MacDonald.

At that audience of 5 June 1929, he chaffed his new Prime Minister on
leading a *Labour* Government, and wondered how many Cabinet Ministers
had qualified for that description by manual work. Behind his badinage lay
regard and affection. Even after the defeat of the first Labour Government
in 1924, the King had followed MacDonald's fortunes with friendly interest.
He was disturbed in 1928 to hear of the former Prime Minister's financial
difficulties and his struggle to supplement a meagre parliamentary salary of
£400 by journalism. So the King wrote to Baldwin, the then incumbent of
No. 10, suggesting that there should be adequate provision for a Prime
Minister both in office and on retirement. He proposed that the existing

salary of £5,000 ought to be doubled and paid free of tax; and that on completing three years' service, not necessarily consecutive, a Prime Minister should qualify for a retirement pension of £5,000. It was not until 1937 that Baldwin, in his last months of all as Prime Minister, was able to effect an increase in salary for his successors. By then, however, both the King and MacDonald were in their graves.

The Labour Cabinet of 1929 contained several familiar faces and few that were alarming. Although the King suggested Thomas for the Foreign Office, the post ultimately went to Henderson. Thomas instead became Lord Privy Seal, with responsibility for reducing unemployment. Snowden was once more Chancellor of the Exchequer. Clynes went to the Home Office and Webb, ennobled as Lord Passfield, to the Dominions Office. The Secretary for India was Wedgwood Benn, a man of both volatile temper and charm, who had deserted the Liberal Party two years earlier. The new Lord Chancellor was also a recent convert to Labour. In place of Haldane, who had died in 1928, the Prime Minister chose Lord Justice Sankey, author of a report which ten years earlier had urged the nationalization of the coal industry; more at ease with domestic than foreign policy, he acquired the habit of bringing a small atlas to the Cabinet table.

By 8 June, the King was fit enough to don a frock coat although not to leave Windsor for London. The new ministers therefore came down by train to be sworn in. They were met at the railway station by a row of open carriages from the royal mews. But there were not quite enough to go round, so the tail of the procession was brought up by a respectable one-horse brougham containing Sir Oswald Mosley, Chancellor of the Duchy of Lancaster, alone and bolt upright. On arrival at the castle, MacDonald was seen to hide a half-smoked cigar in a flower pot at the entrance. During the ceremony, the King broke the customary silence by telling the Minister of Labour, Miss Margaret Bondfield, how pleased he was to receive the first woman Privy Counsellor. 'His smile as he spoke,' she noted, 'was cordial and sincere.' Before returning to London, the ministers were offered a buffet luncheon. As the Chancellor of the Exchequer boarded the train, he told the stationmaster of his pleasure at being cheered in the Royal Borough. The stationmaster replied that the cheers came not from the people of Windsor but from a Midlands crowd recently arrived by excursion train. Snowden's long martyrdom had begun.

As in 1924, Labour was more successful abroad than at home. MacDonald, who continued to conduct much of his country's foreign policy, became the first British Prime Minister to visit a United States President in Washington: a conciliatory journey that led to agreement on naval parity. Snowden also did well in securing certain advantages in the payment of German reparations. As always, the King was generous with his praise and encouragement. It was, however, with increasing dismay that he watched Henderson's efforts to improve Britain's relations with Soviet Russia: a process begun by MacDonald in 1924 but interrupted by Austen Chamberlain in 1927.

Year after year, the King would simmer over the secret reports on Communist influence in Britain prepared by Scotland Yard, then tax his Government with indifference. Once he wrote to Balfour as Chancellor of Cambridge University to ask why Maurice Dobb, the well-known Marxist economist named in an intelligence report, was allowed to indoctrinate undergraduates. Balfour's inquiries led him to deny that Dobb's influence on Cambridge was anything more than academic. The King did his best to dispel the misguided idealism with which Labour welcomed every aspect of the Soviet system. He reminded the Foreign Secretary, a pious nonconformist, of the anti-Christian propaganda disseminated from Moscow, but could make no impression on him. 'Henderson is a damned ass and very conceited,' he confided to Mensdorff.

In the autumn of 1929, the King came into sharper conflict with his Government, who were determined to restore full diplomatic relations with Russia. This would oblige him to receive, shake hands with and entertain a fully accredited ambassador: the representative of a regime that had never disowned the heartless murder of the Tsar and his family. In 1924 he had been spared that disagreeable duty; Rakovsky, bearing the lesser rank of *chargé d'affaires*, was not required to be received by the sovereign. Five years later, the King begged both MacDonald and Henderson to confine Anglo-Russian representation to the same modest level. The two ministers expressed sympathy 'in what must naturally be a painful situation', but refused his request. The King therefore resorted to deception. When the new Russian ambassador, M. Sokolnikov, came to present his credentials on 20 December 1929, the King pleaded illness and asked the Prince of Wales to take his place. He could not, however, continue indefinitely to keep Sokolnikov at arm's length. On 27 March 1930 he shook hands with him after a levée; a few weeks later the Queen received the ambassador and his wife at Buckingham Palace. Even these sparse courtesies rankled. In 1933, after a garden party at Windsor, the King turned furiously on the Prime Minister for having manoeuvred him into shaking hands with Litvinov, the Russian Commissar for Foreign Affairs.

The Government had to be more circumspect in its domestic policy. Too confident a display of radicalism, and a mere fifty-nine Liberal MPs could combine with the Conservatives to obstruct or even unseat an administration commanding 287. Among the casualties of that alliance was Labour's attempt to reverse the Trades Disputes Act of 1927, which declared illegal any repetition of a general strike and imposed other restrictions on the trade union movement. 'Peaceful picketing' had long been a *bête noire* of the King's. But he recognized that 'the Labour Government is doing and will do much that is good and useful'. What threatened the programme of the Labour Government, and ultimately its survival, was neither parliamentary opposition nor royal discouragement; it was the menace of a financial and economic catastrophe beyond its control.

One of the first victims of the international crisis was the Credit Anstalt, Austria's biggest bank. It prompted this warning from the King's private secretary on 11 July 1931:

We are sitting on the top of a volcano, and the curious thing is that the Press and the City have not really understood the critical situation. The Governor of the Bank of England is very pessimistic and depressed. If a crash comes in Germany ... a Minority Government will hardly be able to deal with the situation, and it is quite possible that Your Majesty might be asked to approve of a National Government.

That sombre forecast reached a King already cast down by renewed ill health and sorrow. Since the beginning of the year he had mourned his eldest sister, the Princess Royal; his lifelong friend and equerry, Charles Cust; his selfless private secretary, Lord Stamfordham; his little dog, Snip. Dalton, whose failing powers he noted in June, was to die a month later. The King grieved, too, at the enforced exile of his cousins the King and Queen of Spain, a family misfortune but no less a tolling of the bell for monarchy itself.

Stamfordham's loss weighed with him most. He died aged eighty-one, still without thought of retirement: the devoted counsellor who for more than thirty years had guided his master through the shoals of statecraft. A constitutional monarch may not pause for grief. On the very day of Stamfordham's death, he chose Sir Clive Wigram to be his new private secretary. Twenty-four years younger than Stamfordham, Wigram had served a long and rigorous apprenticeship. Royal private secretaries are noted for their unwillingness to delegate, and Stamfordham was no exception. But in reply to a letter of congratulation on his promotion, Wigram was able to write: 'My dear old Chief always confided in me and was constantly saying, "When I am gone, don't forget this."'

Sir John (later Lord) Reith, of the BBC, echoed a widely held view when he said of Wigram: 'He is always very genial, but it seems to take a good deal to make him understand things.' Wigram, it is true, was never the intellectual equal of Stamfordham; but their contrasting styles seemed to widen the gap. Stamfordham was by temperament attuned to the council chamber, Wigram to the playing fields; one was punctilious, even peppery, the other approachable and of a ready humour. Stamfordham's letters were cast in a formal language that lent itself more to rebuke than to encouragement; Wigram could scarcely write half a dozen lines without a sporting metaphor that diminished their gravity. 'The Government', he wrote in June 1931, 'look fairly firm in the saddle at the moment, and without doubt Lloyd George and his team are proving sound half-backs to the Labour forwards.' But the letter he sent to the King a few days later, warning him of the approaching economic storm and the possible need for an all-party Government, lacked neither cogency nor prescience. And in the troubled weeks ahead, during what he was to call 'my first Test Match', Wigram showed a firmness worthy of Stamfordham himself.

It is doubtful whether any Government could have surmounted the world slump in trade and the financial crisis of 1931; but MacDonald's was memorably inept. The Prime Minister allocated no fewer than three of his Cabinet colleagues to stem unemployment, which throughout 1930 rose from 1.5 to 2.75 million. Thomas and Lansbury, however, lacked both imagination and thrust; and Mosley, who did produce a Keynesian scheme of public works, resigned after the Cabinet had rejected it as impracticable.

The misery which unemployment inflicts on human lives cannot be measured; but its impact on the Exchequer was all too calculable. The mounting cost to the nation of State benefits pointed, if not to bankruptcy, at least to a dangerously unbalanced budget. Conclaves of economists argued this way and that. But it was not until March 1931 that the Government appointed an independent committee to recommend how national expenditure could best be reduced. Its chairman was Sir George (later Lord) May, who had spent nearly half a century in the Prudential Assurance Company, broken only by a wartime interlude administering soldiers' canteens. After four and a half months of deliberation, the committee presented its report. It offered neither tea nor sympathy. To meet an estimated budget deficit for 1932 of £120 million, a majority of the committee recommended cuts in Government expenditure of £97 million: £67 million to be saved from a reduction in unemployment benefits and the remaining £30 million to be found out of taxation. Brooding on this severe prospect, MacDonald and his colleagues departed for their summer holidays.

They were soon summoned back to London. The May Committee's indictment of an unbalanced budget had further undermined confidence in Britain's financial stability and accelerated a run on the pound. On 12 August, a Cabinet Committee met to act on May's recommendations. It consisted of MacDonald, Snowden, Thomas, Henderson and William Graham, President of the Board of Trade. The Chancellor revealed to his shocked colleagues that May had underestimated the budget deficit for

1932; it would not be £120 million but £170 million. This unexpected blow left the Big Five (as the Cabinet Committee came to be called) with scarcely any room for manœuvre. Only by raising loans in New York and Paris could the Bank of England prop up the pound; but foreign bankers were unwilling to risk their money unless the British Government balanced its budget. There would thus have to be drastic cuts in public expenditure, particularly in the soaring cost of unemployment benefits.

By 19 August, the Big Five had reluctantly agreed to economies of £79 million, of which nearly £50 million was to be met by cuts in unemployment benefits; the remainder of the budget would be balanced by additional taxation. In proposing such unpalatable measures, albeit with reluctance, the Big Five were showing both realism and courage. For among the rank and file of the Labour movement, no issue was more emotive than the relief of unemployment. 'It was a bitter day,' wrote MacDonald, 'and grievous is our just complaint against Providence.'

On Wednesday, 19 August, from 11 in the morning until 10.30 at night, the Cabinet debated the report of the Big Five. There was a majority in favour of its recommendations, although many were unhappy about the scale of cuts in unemployment benefits. A minority rejected any reduction whatsoever in the dole, and instead pleaded for a tariff revenue. In spite of its indecision, the Cabinet did not reject the report, but hoped to reach an agreed solution during the next forty-eight hours.

Thursday, 20 August, brought a setback. The Conservative and Liberal leaders told the Prime Minister that they could not countenance new taxation of the order of £100 million, and that only further substantial cuts in expenditure, particularly in unemployment benefits, could restore public confidence. But even as the country's gold and currency reserves continued to drain away, worse was to come. The general council of the Trades Union Congress, led by Walter Citrine and Ernest Bevin, warned MacDonald that there must be no tampering with the social services, least of all with the dole. Thus was the Prime Minister ground between the millstones of rigid retrenchment and obstructive idealism.

The Big Five sat late that night, but failed to agree. 'We're done,' Thomas exclaimed in disgust as he left the Cabinet room. 'Bloody cowards!' For by then two of the Big Five had defected. Henderson and Graham, in deference to the TUC, would no longer support any but the most exiguous cuts in unemployment benefits. MacDonald was tempted to bring his frustrated administration to an end there and then. But by the following morning, Friday, 21 August, he had recovered some of his resilience and determined to make one last appeal to the divided Cabinet. It was in vain. Forty-eight hours earlier, the Cabinet had agreed in principle to the Big Five's recommended savings of £79 million, of which nearly £50 million was to come from cuts in unemployment benefits. These were now reduced to £56 million, of which only £22 million was to be cut from unemployment benefits. The revised figures were unlikely to satisfy the Opposition, much less the foreign bankers on whom Britain depended for her rescue from imminent bankruptcy. But the intransigent majority of Cabinet members would not be moved by threats. Rather than compromise on welfare payments, they were prepared to resign and leave social butchery to the Tories.

Throughout these painful exchanges, the King had remained at Sandringham; it was not for the sovereign to intervene between one faction of the Cabinet and another. But before leaving by train for his annual Scottish holiday on that Friday evening, he inquired whether the Prime Minister wished him to change his plans. MacDonald thought that it would further alarm the public if he cancelled his journey. That was an unwise decision; for already the leaders of the Opposition parties had told him that the Cabinet's latest financial proposals were 'wholly unsatisfactory', and had suggested that he should consult the King. Hardly had the King reached Balmoral on the Saturday morning when the Prime Minister sent a message that it might after all be necessary for him to return to London. 'I at once spoke to His Majesty,' Wigram later wrote, 'who quite rightly said that there was no use shilly-shallying on an occasion like this, and he would proceed south that night.' The King afterwards explained his sudden decision in a letter to the Archbishop of Canterbury: 'When I realized how serious the situation both political and financial had become, I felt that it was necessary for me to be in close touch with my Prime Minister and of course he couldn't come here.'

It proved to be one of the most important interventions of his reign. Within two hours of arriving back at Buckingham Palace on Sunday morning, the King received MacDonald. 'The Cabinet is divided,' he noted in his diary, 'and he fears he will have to resign.' The only gleam of hope the Prime Minister could offer was that the Cabinet had on the previous day agreed to ask the Bank of England whether an increase of cuts from £56 million to £76 million, including a ten per cent cut in unemployment benefits, would be enough to ensure an American loan. The Bank of England had at once consulted the New York banking house of J.P. Morgan, and an answer was expected that Sunday evening. But it was not an offer by the Cabinet, merely an inquiry. Even if New York agreed to a loan in return for promised cuts in expenditure of £76 million, the Cabinet remained free to reject such a solution.

MacDonald's lack of trust in that slippery manœuvre emerges from his conversation at the palace on Sunday morning. He wrote in his diary:

King most friendly and expressed thanks and confidence. I then reported situation and at end I told him that after tonight I might be of no further use and should resign with the whole Cabinet. He asked if I would advise him to send for Henderson. I said 'No', which he said relieved him. I advised him in the meantime to send for the leaders of the other two parties and have them report position from their points of view. He said he would and would advise them strongly to support me. I explained my hopeless parliamentary position if there were any number of resignations. He said that he believed I was the only person who could carry the country through . . . He again expressed thanks and sorrow.

The King, acting upon his Prime Minister's advice, next summoned the leaders of the Opposition parties to the palace. Lloyd George had in 1926 succeeded Asquith as leader of a reunited Liberal Party. Throughout the crisis of 1931, however, he was confined to bed after an operation. His place was taken by Sir Herbert Samuel, Postmaster General during the first years of the King's reign. He told the King that he would prefer MacDonald to remain in office in order to carry out the necessary programme of economies; but that if he failed to carry enough of his colleagues with him, then the best alternative would be for MacDonald to head a National Government containing members of all three parties. Later that afternoon, Baldwin gave similar advice on behalf of the Conservatives and agreed that if necessary he would serve under MacDonald.

Both in his contemporary record of those conversations and in a separate note a month later, Wigram wrote that it was Samuel's clarity of exposition which had convinced the King of the need for a National Government. That is also the view taken by Nicolson in his biography of the King. Certainly the Liberal leader, a spare-time philosopher, put the case with conviction. As he himself later recalled: 'The King listened attentively. He was quite a good listener sometimes.' But the Prime Minister's account of his own conversation at the palace earlier that morning reveals that the King had already determined to try for a National Government headed by MacDonald. What else could the King have meant when he told MacDonald that he was 'the only person who could carry the country through' and that he, the King, would strongly advise the leaders of the other parties to support him? Even as early in the ministerial crisis as that Sunday morning, the King needed no prompting on what his course should be.

That evening, while the Prime Minister waited at No. 10 for a telegram from the New York bankers in reply to the Cabinet's inquiry, the King had a single guest to dine. He was Mr (later Sir) Edward Peacock, one of the two directors of the Bank of England in day-to-day touch with the Prime Minister about the deterioration in Britain's gold and currency reserves. Left-wing partisans were later to refer to the establishment of the National Government on the following day as a 'bankers' ramp': and here, it seems, is evidence of just such a conspiracy. The truth is more prosaic. Peacock was indeed a director of the Bank of England; but he was also the partner in Baring's who two years earlier had succeeded the late Lord Revelstoke as adviser on the King's private finances. It was in that personal role that he had been summoned to dine at short notice. Peacock afterwards recalled that the political crisis had not been mentioned during dinner; instead, he and his sovereign, like two farmers at a cattle sale, had discussed fluctuations in the price of wheat and barley over the past ten years.

At about nine o'clock on Sunday evening, the reply of the New York bankers reached Downing Street. It offered only a short-term credit, and that hedged about with oppressive conditions. In plain language it meant that there could be no public loan unless the British Government was prepared to commit itself to severe retrenchment, including a cut of ten per cent in unemployment benefits. After the Prime Minister had appealed to his colleagues to weigh the proposed reduction in the dole against the sacrifices to be made by the country as a whole, each was invited to give his opinion. Eleven ministers supported the cuts; nine, including Henderson and Graham, Clynes and Lansbury, rejected them. No Government could continue on so wafer-thin a majority. MacDonald declared that he would at once see the King and advise him to hold a conference on the following morning attended by Baldwin, Samuel and himself. On his way out he said: 'I'm off to the Palace to throw in my hand.' Twenty-four hours later he was still Prime Minister – but of a National Government.

There can be no doubt that MacDonald truly intended to resign. For the past two days he had been saying so to all who would listen. He telephoned his son Malcolm with the message on both Saturday and Sunday. At Buckingham Palace on Sunday morning he declared that he had no other course, and afterwards wrote in his diary: 'I commit political suicide to save the crisis.' He repeated that there was no alternative when again received by the King late that night. And on returning to Downing Street for talks with the Opposition leaders, he spoke of his death warrant. Were he to join a Government of Conservatives and Liberals, he continued, he would be a ridiculous figure, unable to command support and bringing odium on them as well as on himself. Whatever else persuaded MacDonald to head a National Government, it was not premeditated ambition.

Yet that audience with the King on Sunday night did produce an improvement in spirits if not a change of mind. Peacock, who had not yet left the palace after dining with the King, noticed that the Prime Minister had gone into the King's room like a shattered man – 'scared and unbalanced' was Wigram's phrase – and emerged with head erect and confidence restored. For the second time that day, his sovereign had assured him that he was the only man to lead the country through the crisis and had asked him to reconsider his resignation. The King added that he knew MacDonald could depend on Conservative and Liberal support, and he agreed to preside over a meeting of the three party leaders on the following day. Until then MacDonald must withhold his resignation.

Next morning at 10 o'clock, when MacDonald, Baldwin and Samuel assembled in the Indian Room of the palace, the Prime Minister repeated his by now familiar litany; indeed, he had the resignation of the entire Cabinet in his pocket. For the third time in twenty-four hours, the King replied that it was out of the question. He told MacDonald that by remaining at his post with such colleagues as were still faithful to him, his position and reputation would be much more enhanced than if he succumbed; the Prime Minister must come to some arrangement with Baldwin and Samuel to form a National Emergency Government which would restore British credit and the confidence of foreigners. And in his best quarterdeck manner, the King impressed on the three party leaders that before they left the palace there should be a communiqué to end speculation at home and abroad. Then he withdrew to his own rooms to let them get on with it.

Rather more than an hour later, the party leaders sent a message asking the King to return. They had drawn up a memorandum agreeing to a National Government led by MacDonald; it would dedicate itself to economies of £70 million, including a cut of ten per cent in the dole. Although supported by both the Conservatives and the Liberals, the new ministry would not be a Coalition but a 'co-operation of individuals', to last only as long as the emergency. It was to be followed by a general election which the three parties would fight on their individual platforms. The King was pleased by his stage management. Wigram's note on the meeting with the three statesmen concludes:

His Majesty congratulated them on the solution of this difficult problem, and pointed out that while France and other countries existed for weeks without a Government, in this country our constitution is so generous that leaders of Parties, after fighting one another for months in the House of Commons, were ready to meet together under the roof of the Sovereign and sink their own differences for a common good and arrange as they had done this morning for a National Government to meet one of the gravest crises that the British Empire had yet been asked to face.

With that comforting little homily, the King sent them on their way.

At 12 noon MacDonald returned to Downing Street, where the Cabinet awaited him. Still hopelessly divided, they expected to hear that he had tendered their collective resignations to the King. Had he not left them the night before, exclaiming: 'I am off to the Palace to throw in my hand'? Instead he announced that he was to lead a National Government. 'Consternation when I reported,' he wrote in his diary. That morning there had been a renewed run on the Bank, and he asked his colleagues to share with him the burdens both of office and self-sacrifice. Only three agreed to do so: Snowden, Thomas and Sankey. But that token Labour force was enough to justify the formation of a National Government in name as well as in purpose.

'Looking worn and weary', as Wigram described him, MacDonald went back to the palace at four o'clock that afternoon. At last he was allowed to resign as Prime Minister of the Labour Government, but only in order to kiss hands as Prime Minister of a National administration. When its members received their seals of office two days later, MacDonald's mournful countenance was accentuated by his frock coat and black tie. 'You look as if you were attending your own funeral,' the King chaffed him. 'Put on a white tie and try to think it is your wedding.' The Prime Minister was not to be comforted. 'This is a lonely job,' he wrote.

Without the King's initiative there would have been no National Government. Three times in twenty-four hours MacDonald tried to resign and three times the King dissuaded him. Then he gave way and agreed to remain Prime Minister, an eminence for which he professed no enthusiasm. The motives of public men are rarely as base or as quixotic as their enemies would have us believe; and no portrait of MacDonald is complete which depicts him as the ambitious, fawning courtier of Labour mythology or the martyred patriot of his own invention. He did not become less willing to relinquish office during those forty-eight hours of crisis; but he did become less willing to relinquish office at the behest of Arthur Henderson. As one of the Big Five, Henderson had at first accepted the need for cutting the dole in order to save the credit of his country; then he changed his mind under pressure from the trade unions and carried half the Cabinet with him. 'They chose the easy path of irresponsibility and leave the burdens to others,' MacDonald wrote as his divided ministry broke up. And on the following day he told Margaret Bondfield: 'Until there is some new spirit in the Labour Movement, a Labour Government will run away from two things:- (1) [At] the orders of the T.U.C. and (2) An awkward crisis.'

There is nothing like hatred and contempt of one man's conduct for driving another along a contrary course; to that extent Henderson provoked MacDonald into forming the National Government. It was the King, however, who appealed to the Prime Minister's patriotism and sense of duty, who flattered him on the influence of his statesmanship at home and abroad, who stiffened him to break with nearly half a century of his radical past. The King did so, moreover, with both determination and pride. 'If I had failed,' he told Archbishop Lang at the beginning of September, 'there would have been a national disaster in a few hours, as a general election was out of the question.' It was a remarkable performance by a man ageing beyond his years who had recently been depressed by ill health and bereavement. The financial and political crisis of August 1931 seems to have renewed his physical stamina as much as his self-confidence. On 24 August, the day when he presided so decisively over the conference with the three party leaders and later commissioned MacDonald to form a National Government, he also walked in the garden of Buckingham Palace; entertained King George of the Hellenes to luncheon, his aunt Princess Louise to tea and Lord Cromer to dinner; visited his son Prince Henry, who was recovering in hospital from an operation for appendicitis; worked on his boxes; and looked at his stamp collection. As Wigram put it: 'Our Captain played one of his best innings with a very straight bat. He stopped the rot and saved his side. He was not-out at the end and had hardly turned a hair, or shown any signs of fatigue.'

The Labour Party, however, felt that it had been betrayed as much by the King as by MacDonald. Harold Laski epitomizes this long-lasting hostility:

It is notable that, in the formation of the National Government, no attempt was made by the King to elicit the views of the great bulk of the Labour Party who transferred their allegiance from Mr. MacDonald to Mr. Arthur Henderson. It appears certain that the impetus to the peculiar form of the new administration came wholly from the King. Mr. MacDonald was as much the personal choice of George v as Lord Bute was the personal choice of George iii. He is the sole modern Prime Minister who has been unencumbered by party support in his period of office; he provided only a name, while Mr. Baldwin supplied both the legions and the power that goes with the legions. We need not doubt that the King acted as he did wholly from a conception of patriotic obligation. But since it is known that a Baldwin Premiership was confidently expected at least as late as the night before the break-up of the Labour Government, it is not, I think, unreasonable to term Mr. Ramsay MacDonald's emergence as Prime Minister of the National Government a Palace Revolution.

That the King personally strove to establish a National Government is undeniable. But Laski's accusation that he acted unconstitutionally is entirely misplaced. As long as the sovereign accepts the formal advice of his Prime Minister, he can incur no personal reproach; and throughout the crisis of 1931, King George v never deviated from that course. Only in deciding to return to London from Balmoral at its very outset did the King fail to seek the approval of the Prime Minister; and that journey, although it had political consequences, cannot itself be called unconstitutional.

It is true that on three separate occasions – on Sunday morning, on Sunday night and on Monday morning – the King persuaded his Prime Minister not to resign. But persuasion is not unconstitutional; indeed, it is a royal prerogative. Had MacDonald persisted in his wish to resign, the King could not have prevented him. It was on the advice of the Prime Minister, moreover, that the King consulted Samuel and Baldwin on the

Sunday morning and summoned them to a conference with MacDonald at the palace twenty-four hours later; it was on the advice of the Prime Minister that the King then accepted their joint plan for a National Government.

Laski writes that the King should have elicited the views of those members of the Labour Party who transferred their allegiance from MacDonald to Henderson. But that would have been constitutionally correct only if the Prime Minister had advised the King to do so; or if the Prime Minister had resigned, thus obliging the King to seek a successor capable of forming a new Government. In 1923, for instance, when Bonar Law resigned, the King had quite properly canvassed the views of the Conservative Party before sending for Baldwin. In 1931, as long as MacDonald remained Prime Minister, the King had no such freedom of consultation.

Throughout the crisis, the King acted constitutionally. But did he also act wisely? Speed was essential. Almost hour by hour, the country's gold and currency reserves were draining away as foreign investors lost confidence. The King was thus denied the conventional course of action: to accept the Prime Minister's resignation and so set in motion the machinery for a general election. There was no time to seek the opinion of the electorate through the ballot box. Within constitutional limits, the King had to use his own discretion in finding an emergency Government stable enough both to encourage Britain's creditors and to command a parliamentary majority that could pass the necessary measures of retrenchment.

The choice was limited. One course was to accept MacDonald's resignation and send for the next senior member of his party. But Henderson, the leader of those Labour ministers opposed to drastic economies, would neither inspire confidence abroad nor retain a parliamentary majority over the combined Conservative and Liberal Parties. A more practical alternative was for the King to accept MacDonald's resignation and send for Baldwin, as leader of the next largest party in the Commons. With Liberal support, Baldwin could certainly have formed an administration strong enough to carry out a programme of retrenchment. But the King decided to go one better. He induced MacDonald to lead the new ministry and so proclaim to the world that Britain spoke with a united and resolute voice in her determination to remain solvent.

To demonstrate that he too would share the financial sacrifices of his people, the King voluntarily reduced his annual Civil List by £50,000 for as long as the emergency lasted. The Prince of Wales similarly gave up £10,000 a year from the revenues of the Duchy of Cornwall.

The National Government which faced Parliament for the first time on 8 September 1931 was rich in political experience. MacDonald restricted his

Cabinet to ten, half the usual number, so that it could act with speed and decisiveness. It contained four Labour members, four Conservatives and two Liberals. MacDonald, Snowden and Sankey retained their former offices, and J. H. Thomas became Secretary of State for both the Colonies and the Dominions. The Conservatives were Baldwin, Lord President of the Council; Neville Chamberlain, Minister of Health; Sir Samuel Hoare, Secretary of State for India; and Sir Philip Cunliffe-Lister, President of the Board of Trade. Lloyd George was still convalescent; in any case, his sympathies were more with Henderson than with MacDonald. But the Liberal Party was well rewarded; Samuel returned to the Home Office after an interval of sixteen years and Reading took the Foreign Office. The strength of the Government was not confined to the Cabinet. Among those prepared to fill lesser places were Austen Chamberlain, First Lord of the Admiralty, and Lord Crewe, Secretary for War; each had been promoted to the front bench in the reign of Queen Victoria and had subsequently held all but the very highest offices of State.

Such a display of talent was impressive enough to stop the run on the pound. The Government then redeemed its promise to introduce a National Economy Bill; by increasing taxation and making cuts of £70 million in State salaries and unemployment benefits, it ensured a balanced budget. Some senior judges, invoking the principle of judicial independence, pleaded for their salaries of £5,000 to be exempted; the man on the dole, who saw his weekly income reduced from 17s to 15s 3d, was denied so high-minded an appeal. The least docile victims of retrenchment were the naval ratings of the Atlantic Fleet. On hearing of proposed cuts in pay that in some instances were to be as much as one quarter, they organized a sit-down strike. The so-called Invergordon Mutiny could have been avoided had senior officers displayed qualities of leadership, imagination and administrative ability. The King, outraged by so shameful an episode, considered that all the Sea Lords should have resigned; only one of them in fact was relieved of his command. The discontent at Invergordon was prevented from spreading by a belated announcement that no sailor's pay would be cut by more than ten per cent, but the damage was irreparable.

The naval mutiny not only cast a shadow over the nation's pride; it also destroyed the fragile world confidence in Britain's future so recently restored by the National Government. On Wednesday, 16 September, withdrawals of gold from the Bank of England were £5 million; on Thursday, £10 million; on Friday, £18 million; on Saturday, a half day, £10 million. Within a fortnight the vaults would be empty. On Monday, 21 September, the Government therefore brought in a Bill to suspend the Gold Standard Act of 1925; one of the most controversial measures of Churchill's years at the Treasury, it required the Bank of England to sell gold at a fixed price.

The National Government had been formed precisely in order to avoid that most feared and supposedly inflationary of all economic remedies; now, within a month of taking office, it had succumbed.

As it turned out, the abandonment of the gold standard was far less harmful than had been feared. Banknotes did not turn into confetti overnight; and the devaluation of the pound sterling stimulated Britain's exports. It also proved to be a convenient pretext for appealing to the country. The National Economy Bill had been fiercely opposed by Henderson and his cohorts, passing the Commons by 309 votes to 249: an uncomfortably small majority for a measure designed to display national solidarity. By calling a general election, the Conservative element of the Government hoped to increase its strength at the expense of a divided Labour Party and to rule Britain in all but name. The Conservative slogan 'Safety First' had failed to win the general election of 1929; but throughout the turmoil of recent weeks it had acquired a new and potent appeal.

Two obstacles to this opportunist course had still to be overcome. On taking office as an emergency administration, the National Government had specifically promised that it would not fight a general election as a Coalition. This pledge it now broke by claiming that the abandonment of the gold standard had increased the need for a show of national unity. But if the election was to be fought on a manifesto common to all three parties, how could it reconcile a Conservative commitment to tariff reform with the free trade shibboleth of both Labour and Liberal?

The King, who after the swearing-in of the National Government on 26 August had resumed his holiday at Balmoral, returned to London on 29 September. At once he found himself embroiled in another Cabinet crisis. He wrote to the Duke of York: 'I am having a strenuous time with all the people I have to see, but I mean to do everything and anything in my power to prevent the old ship running on the rocks.'

Sir Herbert Samuel had much impressed the King by his clarity of mind during the formation of the National Government. Now he showed an awkward adherence to free trade principles that irritated his sovereign. The King wrote in his diary: 'He was quite impossible, most obstinate and said he would not look at tariffs and that there was a deadlock as regards Conservatives and Liberals in the Government. God Knows what can be done. ... Am much worried by political situation and I can't see a way out.'

At an audience on 3 October, MacDonald told the King that the Cabinet had spent day after day wrangling over the terms of a formula on which to appeal to the country, but had failed to reach a conclusion. There then ensued an all-too-familiar conversation. The Prime Minister said that he had failed and had better resign. The King replied that he would refuse to accept MacDonald's resignation, for he was the only person who could tackle the chaotic state of affairs. But at heart the King was as depressed as his Prime Minister. He even considered asking General Smuts, who happened to be in London, for his advice on reconstructing the Government. At last the Cabinet broke the deadlock. The National Government would ask the country for 'a doctor's mandate': the freedom to employ any remedy, even tariffs. But that contentious word was scarcely to be uttered, or at worst enveloped in the nebulous language of political deception. Relieved to hear that his ministers had come to some conclusion, any conclusion, the King gladly accepted their disingenuous formula. He granted an immediate dissolution of Parliament, to be followed by a general election on 27 October 1931.

For the next three weeks the King laid aside impartiality. 'Of course you are going to vote?' he asked Hankey after a meeting of the Privy Council. Hankey explained that as Secretary to the Cabinet and Clerk of the Council he was required to be detached from party politics, so had not done so since the war. The King said: 'This time it is different. I want the National Government to get every vote possible.' It was, he added, 'a command'.

The King wrote in his diary for 27 October: 'May and I dined alone. We listened to the returns of the election on the wireless, which made us happy as the National Government have won seats everywhere.'

It was the most sweeping victory in electoral history. The followers of Henderson lost more than 200 seats. Except for Lansbury, every single member of the former Labour Government who had opposed MacDonald was unseated. The National Government emerged with 558 seats, an emasculated Opposition with a mere fifty-six.

'Please God shall now have a little peace and less worries,' the King wrote next day. He celebrated by taking his family to Noël Coward's *Cavalcade* at Drury Lane. In a spontaneous demonstration of patriotism, the audience rose at the end of the performance to sing the National Anthem. A few days later he told Mensdorff:

The result of the elections is marvellous and it shows that this old country is absolutely sound. I know my countrymen well enough to feel that if they are only told the truth, however disagreeable it may be, that they will show their common sense and do the right thing at the right time. I feel that we have set a good example to other countries and hope that it will steady them a bit.

The election could be interpreted as a triumph for MacDonald; but it also marked the beginning of a protracted humiliation. Scorned by almost the entire Labour Party for his defection, he was increasingly ignored and sometimes derided by the Conservatives on whom he was obliged to depend for his political survival. Wigram recorded the reconstruction of the Government in the first days of November: 'The King saw Mr Baldwin, who told His Majesty that the Prime Minister was inclined to be wobbly and unable to make up his mind over the new Cabinet and had not advanced very far in its composition. Every new comer was inclined to sway him.'

Next day MacDonald gave the King a more convincing version: 'He told His Majesty that he found it a very difficult task forming his Cabinet – no sooner had he made a list than Baldwin came in and said that it would not do, as the Conservatives must have such and such key positions.'

The King enjoyed Cabinet-making. To ease the Prime Minister's task, he suggested that 'the Old Gang should be cleared out'. Sir Austen Chamberlain, Lord Crewe, Lord Reading, Lord Peel and Lord Amulree duly retired. Amulree, an elderly industrial arbitrator, had for the past two years been Secretary of State for Air. The King wanted him replaced by someone 'more active and able to fly'. MacDonald was only too willing to oblige. He chose Lord Londonderry, the husband of his most intimate friend and confidante. Other offices were less easily filled. The Conservatives asked that Sir Philip Cunliffe-Lister (later Lord Swinton) should become Foreign Secretary. Energetic and able, he was too abrasive a party politician to endear himself to the Prime Minister. MacDonald told the King that he would just as soon welcome back Henderson. The King wondered whether there might not be a place for Sir John Simon, whose services during the Mylius case he continued to remember with gratitude. In the end it was Simon who went to the Foreign Office, while Cunliffe-Lister took the Colonial Office.

Snowden's wish for a less arduous life in the Upper House as Lord Privy Seal led to a tussle over the Chancellorship of the Exchequer. The King thought that Baldwin might care to replace him at the Treasury; but Baldwin preferred to remain Lord President, without a busy department. 'He intimated', Wigram noted, 'that there would be plenty for him to do, as the Prime Minister knew nothing of the Conservatives, many of them young, impetuous and ambitious men.' Margot Asquith weighed in with an unsolicited telegram to Wigram: 'Implore you to influence H.M. against Neville Chamberlain going 11 Downing Street effect disastrous on all Liberals.' The Prime Minister agreed with her. So fervent an advocate of tariffs, he told the King, would cause a flutter among his free trade colleagues. But the Conservatives demanded their share of senior posts, and Chamberlain took the Treasury. Thus in spite of its huge parliamentary majority, the Government lacked harmony. During the reconstruction of the Cabinet, the King warned MacDonald that he ought to seek assurances from the two leading free traders, Snowden and Samuel, that they would not subsequently resign on the tariff issue and so break up the administration. The Prime Minister replied that he dare not risk losing the support of Samuel and his thirty-five Liberal followers at the very beginning of the new ministry; he preferred to postpone the conflict in the hope that some of those Liberals would eventually desert Samuel.

Within a few weeks, Chamberlain's proposal to levy a duty of ten per cent on all imported goods other than those from the Dominions split the Cabinet, as the King had predicted. But Snowden and Samuel, on the very brink of resignation, agreed to remain under a formula devised by the forensic brain of Lord Hailsham, the Secretary of State for War. It suspended the principle of collective Cabinet responsibility in favour of an 'agreement to differ' between the two factions. Although welcomed by the King as a means of staving off an immediate crisis at a time of exceptional difficulty, that flouting of constitutional tradition could not be expected to last; it was a mere papering over of the cracks. In September 1932, after the Ottawa Economic Conference had evolved a scheme of preferential tariffs for the Dominions, Snowden, Samuel and some other Liberals resigned their offices. Thereafter the so-called National Government acquired an almost wholly Conservative complexion.

'Your Majesty will find', MacDonald told the King, 'that a Prime Minister who does not belong to the Party in power will become more and more an anomaly, and, as policy develops, his position will become more and more degrading.' That was not his only humiliation. Long before the formation of the National Government, Beatrice Webb's cruelly doctrinaire mind had discerned flaws both of character and political belief in the Labour leader. She wrote in 1925: 'He is an egotist, a poseur and snob, and worst of all he does not believe in the creed we have always preached – he is not a Socialist and has not been one for twenty years: he is a mild radical with individual-istic leanings and aristocratic tastes.' She later stuck this paragraph from *The Times* in her diary:

The Prime Minister left Dunrobin Castle yesterday, after his visit to the Duke and Duchess of Sutherland, for Loch Choire, near Lairg, where he will be the guest of the Marquess and Marchioness of Londonderry. It is understood that he will return to Lossiemouth today and will go to Balmoral tomorrow.

MacDonald's romantic attachment to ancient names and great houses obsessed the Labour movement almost more than did his political defection.

The King was blind to such prejudice; he saw in his Prime Minister only the patriot and the friend. He counselled MacDonald not to overtax his strength, visited him in a nursing home after an operation on his eyes, took him to a race meeting for the first time in his life. He suggested that MacDonald might like to succeed the wayward Lord Beauchamp as Lord Warden of the Cinque Ports, with the use of Walmer Castle as a seaside retreat; he even offered to help with the cost of its upkeep. But MacDonald thought it too big a house for him; in any case, his heart was in the Highlands. Discussing books one day, the King told him that he was reading a life of Al Capone, the Chicago gangster. MacDonald absent-mindedly replied that the circulation of those criminal romances was deplorable and that he never read them. They both laughed at that.

Neither the King nor his Prime Minister found much amusement in another best seller of the nineteen-thirties: the *War Memoirs* of Lloyd George. The King deplored the publication of all contentious books that refought the political battles of the war. On hearing that Lloyd George was at work on his apologia, he asked Hankey to dissuade him. The message was not well received. 'He can go to hell,' Lloyd George replied. 'I owe him nothing. He owes his throne to me.' The wartime Prime Minister nevertheless submitted to the palace the draft of his chapter on the King. It was returned with but a single correction. Lloyd George had written: 'He picked out one worker at Sheffield whom he recognized as having served with him on HMS *Bacchante*.' The King, in pencil, had changed the word 'on' to 'in'. The author was delighted, saying it was just the difference between the sailor and the land man.

Good humour vanished, however, when the King, having also read the chapter on labour unrest, sent Wigram to plead that disparaging references to the wartime activities of MacDonald and Snowden should be deleted. Wigram did not attempt to justify their conduct in obstructing the war effort; he merely told Lloyd George that he could surely afford to be magnanimous towards men who later held high office. Lloyd George's characteristic response was to strengthen his case against the two Labour leaders. His secretary noted in her diary:

He says that he has not refrained in his book from attacking certain people e.g. Asquith and Kitchener, who were doing their very best according to their own lights to *help* during the war. He is therefore not going to spare one who, like Ramsay, did his best to thwart and hinder every effort to prosecute the war vigorously.

When eventually the fourth volume of the *War Memoirs* appeared, it reproduced MacDonald's manifesto of June 1917, promising 'to do for this country what the Russian Revolution has accomplished in Russia'; and much else in similar vein. It is doubtful whether MacDonald ever knew of the King's efforts to protect him from those disobliging ghosts of his radical past.

TEN

LAST YEARS

Menace of the dictators — Sunshine and clouds —
At the microphone — Silver Jubilee —
Demise of the Crown — Requiem

THE reign drew to its end in gathering cloud and fitful sunshine. The rise of the dictators seemed to threaten not only peace but civilization itself. 'The bomber', Mr Baldwin assured the Commons in 1932, 'will always get through.' Widespread unemployment, particularly in Wales and North-East England, touched the conscience of the nation without evoking a remedy. Yet it was against these darkening horizons that the monarchy displayed a new-found strength and the gruff old King submitted to deification.

Few suspected how pacifist a heart beat beneath the King's gold-encrusted uniforms as he led his Fleet to sea or watched the Brigade of Guards troop the colour on his birthday. 'A damnable war and a still more damnable peace,' became his constant refrain. He believed armaments to be as much the cause as the instrument of war. Lord D'Abernon, the British ambassador in Berlin, noted after an audience in 1921 that the King was 'a strong advocate of the total scrapping of all capital ships and submarines, and also of aeroplanes and gas warfare'. After sitting next to him at the Navy and Army rugby match in 1923, the First Lord of the Admiralty wrote: 'The King had a good deal to say about airships which he has a prejudice against, as indeed against all modern weapons, submarines, aeroplanes, poison gas and all the rest of it.' In 1925 he annoyed his old friend Admiral Beatty by pressing for the abolition of capital ships. In 1929 he urged MacDonald to put an end to submarines. In 1932 he told Simon of his dread of torpedoes and aerial bombs.

The King had an ingrained mistrust of flying, whether civil or military. Although allowed the courtesy of wearing a pilot's wings on the tunic of his Royal Air Force uniform, he never flew, even as a passenger. The motor car was good enough for him, as long as its speed did not exceed thirty miles an hour. As Secretary of State for Air, Hoare wrote that the King was 'strongly prejudiced against flying, the Air Ministry and the Air Force'. He sometimes persuaded the King and Queen to attend the annual RAF displays at Hendon; but they hated the noise and were always afraid that there would be an accident. The King did allow his sons to have flying lessons, and in 1919 Prince Albert became a qualified pilot. He was never happy, however, at the risks involved. The only lasting mark which he left on the RAF was at its formation in 1918, when Trenchard suggested that the equivalent rank to Admiral of the Fleet and Field-Marshal should be Marshal of the Air. The King thought that such a designation might poach on the preserves of the Almighty, and changed it to Marshal of the Royal Air Force.

Bruised by the experience of the Great War, the King looked on Europe with an anxiety that turned to despair. There was a moment of hope in 1925, when Germany was welcomed back into the concert of Europe. 'This morning the Locarno Pact was signed at the Foreign Office,' he wrote in his diary. 'I pray this may mean peace for many years. Why not for ever?' But with the growing menace of Mussolini and Hitler, his morale sagged. 'I am an old man,' he told Hoare, when not yet seventy. 'I have been through one world war. How can I go through another? If I am to go on, you must keep us out of one.' He had no illusions about the greed and ambitions of the Italian dictator. As early as 1923 he had replied to a memorandum from the Foreign Secretary: 'Mussolini seems to be anything but a friend of England, and certainly cannot be trusted.' And a few months later: 'Mussolini very much resembles a *mad dog* which must bite somebody, he is a dangerous man.' But by 1935, the year in which Mussolini sent his armies into Abyssinia, the King was not prepared to confront him. When Lloyd George spoke to the King about Mussolini in May of that year, he flared up and vehemently replied: 'I will not have another war. *I will not.* The last one was none of my doing and if there is another one and we are threatened with being brought into it, I will go to Trafalgar Square and wave a red flag myself sooner than allow this country to be brought in.'

It was a view shared by many of his subjects. Standing up to the dictators was less practicable than some chroniclers of those years have been willing to concede. There was the need not to strain the country's limited means of defence by simultaneously antagonizing Italy, Germany and Japan; the paralysing effect of Britain's vulnerability to air attack and the exaggerated reports of German military strength; the unwelcome prospect of rearming a Britain that had so recently escaped bankruptcy. What tarnishes the memory of the so-called appeasers is not that they were deterred from robustness by the strategic and economic realities of a defence policy; it is the sycophancy with which they embraced an evil regime, the callous indifference with which they witnessed the creeping enslavement of Europe.

The King did not live long enough to be put to the test; he died six weeks before Hitler's reoccupation of the Rhineland, and one can only speculate on whether he would have abandoned his pacifist sentiments in the face of continuing German aggression. But throughout the rise of the Nazis he expressed distaste for the men and their methods. As early as 1932 he forbade the Prince of Wales to attend the wedding of the Crown Prince of Sweden to Princess Sibylla of Saxe-Coburg because her father, the English-born and Eton-educated Duke of Saxe-Coburg, had become Hitler's henchman. The King spoke contemptuously of 'those horrid fellows Göring and Goebbels'. He deplored the Nazi practice of Jew-baiting and the blood-baths by which the National Socialist Party consolidated its power. And in an attempt at personal diplomacy, he warned the German ambassador that his country's needless and provocative scale of rearmament was driving Europe towards war.

Sir John Simon, the Foreign Secretary, regarded the Nazis with more indulgence. After visiting Germany in March 1935 he wrote to the King:

Though Herr Hitler's personal appearance is not striking, his photographs do not do justice to the charm of his bearing, which grows very much upon the visitor...

But the main impression which Sir John derived was that he regards himself as destined to be his country's deliverer from dishonour, and he is undoubtedly moved by the inspiring feeling that he is engaged in the moral rehabilitation of Germany. If Joan of Arc had been born in Austria, and worn a moustache, she might have conveyed much the same impression.

Sir Eric Phipps, the British ambassador to Germany from 1933 to 1937, also corresponded with the King. That was fortunate, for he painted a very different portrait of home life with Adolf Hitler:

It was strange to watch him ... undistinguished and almost clown-like, and to think of him leading this great people with, after all, great traditions ...

Fanatical atheism is a cardinal point in the Nazi creed. The methods the Nazis pursue may be in future more subtle than brutal, but their ultimate aim will always be the destruction of the Christian religion, after years perhaps of undermining it.

Wigram was instructed to congratulate Phipps on a 'despatch full of common sense'. He went on to say: 'The King feels that we must not be blinded by the apparent sweet reasonableness of the Germans, but be wary and not taken unawares.' A few weeks later, however, MacDonald found the King much upset by the latest Secret Service reports on German rearmament which Vansittart had just shown him. 'Rarely known him so gloomy,' the Prime Minister noted.

The pattern of the King's attitude to the dictators during the last year of his life is not wholly consistent. He showed a civilized repugnance for the aggressive creed of the dictators, resenting both their pretensions and their cruelty. Yet he continued to be haunted by memories of what he never ceased to call 'that horrible and unnecessary war': an experience so searing that, as he told Hoare, he would abdicate rather than go through it again. He wished to deter but not to provoke; he was a pacifist, but he was also a constitutional monarch and above all a patriot. Hoare, who succeeded Simon as Foreign Secretary in June 1935, was often summoned to the palace throughout the rest of that year. Not a man given to hyperbole, he later wrote: 'I believe that it was the anxieties of Abyssinia, coming as they did on the top of the Silver Jubilee celebrations, that killed the King.'

On the twentieth anniversary of his accession, the King tried to put into writing how much he owed to his wife: 'I can never sufficiently express my deep gratitude to you, darling May, for the way you have helped and stood by me in these difficult times.' Then, characteristically, he added: 'This is not sentimental rubbish, but what I really feel.' During his last sunset years, he looked increasingly to her for comfort and reassurance, and she never failed him.

He found delight, too, in his York grandchildren. Here a visitor to Sandringham in 1928 describes the future Queen Elizabeth II, then aged one year and nine months:

She perched on a little chair between the King and me, and the King gave her biscuits to eat and to feed his little dog with, the King chortling with little jokes with her – she just struggling with a few words, 'Grandpa' and 'Granny' and to everyone's amusement has just achieved addressing the very grand-looking Countess of Airlie as 'Airlie'. After a game of bricks on the floor with the young equerry Lord Claud Hamilton, she was fetched by her nurse, and made a perfectly sweet little curtsey to the King and Queen and then to the company as she departed.

Later that year she accompanied her grandparents to Balmoral, where Winston Churchill was a fellow guest. 'There is no one here at all', he wrote to his wife, 'except the family, the household and Princess Elizabeth – aged 2. The latter is a character. She has an air of authority and reflectiveness astonishing in an infant.' Even in the nursery she was no stranger to royal duties. Sir Owen Morshead liked to recall a morning at Windsor Castle, when the officer commanding the guard strode across to where a pram stood, containing Princess Elizabeth: 'Permission to march off, please, Ma'am.' There was an inclination of a small bonneted head and a wave of a tiny paw.

The marriage of two more of his sons also cheered the King's last years.

On 29 November 1934, Prince George wed Princess Marina of Greece in Westminster Abbey. 'She has not a cent,' the King cheerfully told Mac-Donald. But she had other qualities: grace and beauty and intelligence, a practical interest in the arts and a sense of style that was to inspire a generation of couturiers. 'The King was a perfect angel to her when she arrived in England as a shy bride,' the Princess's mother later told Harold Nicolson. Wigram noted with some surprise that he was even prepared to subordinate his otherwise immutable shooting plans to the wedding pro-gramme. It was a marriage of fairy-tale happiness, tragically cut short only eight years later when the Duke of Kent (as he had been created in 1934) died in a wartime air crash while serving in the RAF.

In August 1935, the King was pleased to hear that his third son, Prince Henry, Duke of Gloucester, wished to marry Lady Alice Montagu-Douglas-Scott, a daughter of the Duke of Buccleuch. Her quiet charm, determined character, sense of duty and love of country life made her the perfect wife for that conscientious but unwilling Prince of the Blood Royal. The Queen displayed her usual good sense and prudence. 'Don't buy a lot of jewellery in a hurry,' she wrote to her son, 'because Cousin Frederica of Hanover left you some nice diamond things which can be converted and I have various ornaments which I have long ago selected for your wife from my collection.' The death of the bride's father in October caused the ceremony on 6 November to be held in the privacy of the chapel at Buckingham Palace instead of in Westminster Abbey. But all wore their wedding clothes. Norman Hartnell had designed long Kate Greenaway frocks for the bridesmaids, including Princess Elizabeth and Princess Mar-garet Rose. The King ordered Hartnell to shorten them. 'I want to see their pretty little knees,' he explained. On the night of the wedding the King wrote in his dairy: 'Now all the children are married except David.'

The King's eldest son, who had reached the age of forty in June 1934, showed no readiness either to marry or prepare himself for the restraints of a constitutional monarch. As early as 1925, Channon wrote in his diary: 'The Prince of Wales one feels would not raise his finger to save his future sceptre. In fact many of his intimate friends think he would be only too happy to renounce it.' For the rest of his father's reign he continued to enchant an Empire with boyish charm, only occasionally marred by bore-dom and melancholy; at home he showed a genuine though intermittent concern for the unemployed. But neither his political judgement nor his private life inspired confidence among those who knew him best.

Mensdorff, who continued his visits to London year by year, left this account of a talk with the Prince in 1933:

Yesterday, at five o'clock, I was summoned to see the Prince of Wales. I am still under his charm. It is remarkable how he expressed his sympathies for the Nazis in Germany. 'Of course it is the only thing to do, we will have to come to it, as we are in great danger from the Communists here, too.' He naturally condemns the Peace Treaty. 'I hope and believe we shall never fight a war again, but if so we must be on the winning side, and that will be the German, not the French.' I was very surprised. I also asked him how he imagined that one got out of the National Socialist dictatorship. It was surely not a permanent condition ... He seemed not to have thought very much about all these questions. It is, however, interesting and significant that he shows so much sympathy for Germany and the Nazis.

The archives of the German Ministry of Foreign Affairs, captured by the Allies at the end of the second World War, reveal not only the Prince's tenderness for Nazi Germany but also the freedom with which he expressed his views. In January 1936, just before his father's last illness, he told the German ambassador in London that 'it was his firm intention to go to Berlin next summer for the Olympic Games'. The German ambassador in Washington was simultaneously sending his Government intelligence reports of the Prince's sympathy for Germany and detestation of French foreign policy. It included an even more astounding indiscretion: 'Nor did he hold his father's view that the King must blindly accept the Cabinet's decisions. On the contrary, he felt it to be his duty to intervene if the Cabinet were to plan a policy which in his view was detrimental to British interests.'

It was only a few months since the King had vainly rebuked his eldest son for expressing controversial opinions in public. The Prince, addressing a meeting of the British Legion, an ex-servicemen's organization, commended a visit by its members to Germany. This, the King pointed out, was contrary to Foreign Office policy; and he warned him of the danger of making political statements without first consulting the Government. The Prince took his father's reproof with ill grace. At Ascot races a few days later, he told the German ambassador that he was 'as convinced as ever' he had been right to speak his mind. He failed to see that his offence lay not in holding political beliefs but in allowing them to be known. Only two days later, the Prince again transgressed. He publicly criticized the pacifist London County Council for having forbidden school cadet corps to drill with even dummy rifles made of wood.

Such ill judgement on the verge of middle age could not fail to disturb the King. But it was in his son's private life that he found cause for a deeper sorrow. Since the beginning of 1934 the Prince of Wales had been infatuated by a divorced, remarried woman with two living husbands. The King learned of his son's attachment to Wallis Simpson with anger and despair. He thought her unsuitable as a friend, disreputable as a mistress, unthinkable as Queen of England. Only once did they meet, at a Buckingham Palace party a few days before the Duke of Kent's wedding. Mrs Simpson subsequently wrote of her reception by the King and Queen:

David led me over to where they were standing and introduced me. It was the briefest of encounters – a few words of perfunctory greeting, an exchange of meaningless pleasantries, and we moved away. But I was impressed with Their Majesties' great gift for making everyone they met, however casually, feel at ease in their presence.

The future Duchess of Windsor left no such fragrant memory on the King's mind. He complained furiously to Mensdorff that she had been smuggled into the palace against his will and without his knowledge. 'That woman in my own house!' he said. At least, he continued, Mrs Dudley Ward came of a much better class and had an established position. As for the Prince of Wales: 'He has not a single friend who is a gentleman. He does not see any decent society. And he is forty-one.' When Mensdorff pleaded that the Prince had many attractive qualities, including charm, the King replied: 'Yes, certainly. That is the pity. If he were a fool, we would not mind. I hardly ever see him and don't know what he is doing.'

Separated by more than years, both father and son shirked the issue during those last months of the reign. Discussion would in any case have resolved nothing, for neither spoke the language of the other. The Prince (as he himself put it) clung to 'a dream of being able to bring into my life what for so long had been lacking, without which my service to the State would seem an empty thing'. The King, for his part, believed that his son was prepared to betray the noblest of trusts: a heritage epitomized by the words which Shakespeare put into the mouth of Laertes:

> ... his will is not his own,
> For he himself is subject to his birth.
> He may not, as unvalued persons do,
> Carve for himself, for on his choice depends
> The safety and health of this whole state.

During his convalescence in 1929, the King had more than once confided to trusted members of his family that his eldest son would never succeed to the throne: a puzzling conjecture that at the time could be put down to low spirits. Six years later, he broadcast his fears more widely. A lady-in-waiting heard him say: 'I pray to God that my eldest son will never marry and have children, and that nothing will come between Bertie and Lilibet and the throne.' He told Baldwin: 'After I am dead, the boy will ruin himself in twelve months.' With such chilling valedictions did the old King take his leave.

Immediately after the wedding of the Duke and Duchess of Kent, the King wrote to MacDonald: 'The enthusiasm of the thousands who were expressing their love and affection for us and our children indeed gave me a lump in my throat and touched me enormously.' In the twenty-fifth year of his reign, he was discovering to his surprise that he had become the father of his people.

He never consciously sought popularity, least of all through the Press. He gazed unsmilingly into cameras and had no affable asides for reporters. Except for *The Times*, he scarcely recognized the existence of newspapers. When in 1926 the refusal of the *Daily Mail* printers to handle a hostile editorial precipitated the general strike, the Prime Minister's private secretary roused Wigram from his bed at Windsor. 'Don't be alarmed in the morning', he warned, 'when the *Daily Mail* fails to appear. Tell His Majesty, so that he does not go off at the deep end.' Wigram replied: 'We don't take the *Daily Mail* or the *Daily Express*.' The Queen, however, told the King what was in *The Daily Telegraph*, and Stamfordham took the *Manchester Guardian*. 'A very sound journal,' he wrote, 'though of course strongly Liberal.' But it was with *The Times* alone that both he and Wigram maintained confidential links. They supplied the paper with advance copies of the King's speeches and enlisted its help in making known his views.

A private line between the palace and Printing House Square had its uses during a constitutional crisis; but not even the most royalist of leading articles could touch the heart of the humbler subject. Stamfordham and Wigram, however, gradually came to see the untold potential of a new medium: sound broadcasting. And in the King they had a brilliant exponent of the art.

It was John Reith, general manager of the recently formed BBC, who in October 1923 first invited the King to deliver a Christmas or New Year message to his people. He received a discouraging reply. A few months later the BBC presented the King with a wireless set. In April 1924 his voice was heard on the air for the first time when he opened the British Empire Exhibition at Wembley. The broadcast aroused widespread interest and attracted an audience of ten million. The scorned *Daily Mail* arranged for massed crowds to hear it in Manchester, Leeds and Glasgow; a government inquiry at Cambridge suspended its sitting to listen, as did a magistrate's court at Gateshead. During the next eight years, the BBC continued to broadcast some of the King's speeches on ceremonial occasions. But even Stamfordham failed to lure him to the microphone for a more informal talk. Not until 1932, the year after Stamfordham's death, did Reith, Wigram and MacDonald persuade a still reluctant King.

'At 3.35', he wrote in his diary on Christmas Day, 'I broadcasted a short message of 251 words to the whole Empire from Francis' room.' The rest of the world heard him at 3.5 p.m. For the King was at Sandringham, where since the days of his father all clocks had been kept thirty minutes fast to extend the daylight hours. He spoke from a little room under the stairs, once the office of Knollys. Legend has it that the King used a gold microphone. It was in fact a standard one encased in Australian walnut. A thick cloth covered the table to deaden the sound of rustling paper, for the King's hands were known to tremble with nervousness. The text, of timeless simplicity, had been written by Kipling, and bore the hallmark of the master: 'I speak now from my home and from my heart to you all; to men and women so cut off by the snows, the desert, or the sea, that only voices out of the air can reach them.'

The King's delivery was worthy of his theme. 'Such an odd, hoarse voice,' A.C. Benson has written, 'as if roughened by weather.' In emphatic tones and the accent of an Edwardian country gentleman, it sufficed to carry his words to world-wide acclaim. With its very first delivery, the Christmas broadcast from Sandringham had become an institution.

Although moved by its reception, the King had no wish to repeat his triumph. It was an ordeal, he complained, which spoilt his Christmas. Some of his courtiers (but not Wigram) also thought that an annual broadcast would lose its impact through familiarity. The politicians, however, were encouraging. 'How interesting it would be,' MacDonald said to him, 'if we had a talkie of Queen Elizabeth.' The King was unimpressed. 'Damn Queen Elizabeth,' he replied. But when J. H. Thomas showed him a batch of appreciative letters from listeners throughout the Empire, he agreed to continue. The broadcasts of 1933, 1934 and 1935 never quite achieved the sublime appeal of 1932; perhaps the replacement of Kipling by Archbishop Lang as the principal draftsman exchanged magic for mere eloquence. Yet all who gathered year after year for the King's Christmas message awaited the voice of a friend.

The decision to proclaim the Silver Jubilee of George v came not from the King but from his ministers. If inspired by respect and affection, it also owed something to political opportunism. A display of patriotic enthusiasm would both encourage support for the Government at the approaching general election and warn the dictators not to provoke a proud and un-divided people. Although touched by the welcome which now greeted every public appearance, the King deplored the fuss and expense. He wrote to Mensdorff with mingled gratitude and apprehension:

In looking back during these last 25 years, I am indeed thankful for all that has been done for me. I have passed through some very difficult times, with a ghastly war which lasted over four years, thrown in. I do indeed appreciate all the love and affection which my people are expressing, from all over the world. The festivities will entail a lot of extra work, and I shall be pleased when they are all over, I hope I shall survive them. I remember so well both Queen Victoria's Jubilees and can't yet realise that I am having one now.

Nor could he ever quite accustom himself to being the focus of popular attention. Resting before the Jubilee at Compton Place, the Duke of Devonshire's house on the south coast, he remarked that the local parson seemed such a fine fellow: 'He filled his church to overflowing every Sunday we went to it.'

On 6 May 1935, twenty-five years to the day since succeeding to the throne, the King drove to St Paul's with his family for a service of thanksgiving. There was a first post, he noted, of 610 letters; a team of six greys to draw his carriage; a congregation of 4,406 in the cathedral; a temperature of 75 degrees. Only the crowds who lined the processional way and afterwards cheered him and the Queen on the palace balcony defeated his love of precision. He could do no more than describe them as 'the greatest number of people in the streets that I have ever seen in my life'. The only hitch was when twenty-six elderly prebendaries delayed the departure of the royal family from St Paul's by leaving the cathedral out of turn. 'A wonderful service,' the King told the Dean. 'The Queen and I are most grateful. Just one thing wrong with it – too many parsons getting in the way. I didn't know there were so many damn parsons in England. It was worse than a levée.'

Neville Chamberlain reflected the pride of millions of the King's subjects when he gazed across the cathedral at the foreign ambassadors and thought: 'This'll show 'em.' Broadcasting from Buckingham Palace that night, the King expressed the same sense of national unity in humbler words:

I can only say to you, my very very dear people, that the Queen and I thank you from the depths of our hearts for all the loyalty and – may I say so? – the love, with which this day and always you have surrounded us. I dedicate myself anew to your service for all the years that may still be given me.

Tuesday was free from formal engagements, but neither from tumultuous appearances on the palace balcony nor from correspondence. On that day alone, 1,077 letters arrived; the royal postbag continued to grow at the same rate for weeks on end. Wednesday was devoted to the Empire overseas. MacDonald wrote of the ceremony at St James's Palace:

Reception of Dominion Premiers the most touching and homely triumph of ceremony and loyal homage ever held. Ireland was out and the gap lay like a shadow of smallness over a ceremony of bigness and graciousness. The King's reply was a perfect expression of Sovereign affection and solicitude. When he came

to references and reminiscences personal to himself and the Queen his voice broke
and tears stood in her eyes. Everyone deeply moved. Here the Empire was a great
family, the gathering a family reunion, the King a paternal head. We all went away
feeling that we had taken part in something very much like a Holy Communion.

On Thursday it was the turn of the two Houses of Parliament to render
homage in Westminster Hall. By one of those ironies in which English
history abounds, Mr Speaker FitzRoy addressed the King while standing
only a few feet from the place where his own ancestor, Charles I, had been
tried for his life and found guilty.

A few weeks later, the King continued his Jubilee celebrations by review-
ing the Fleet at Spithead. A naval historian later wrote:

The assemblage of 160 warships looked impressive and included two aircraft
carriers; but to the knowledgeable it was painfully obvious that the proportion of
new ships present was small, and that few of the older ones (many of which were
of World War I vintage) had been fully modernised. In truth the shop window was
mainly filled with obsolescent goods.

Between those two events, with their echoes of past and future tragedy,
lay drives of undiluted joy through the decorated streets of London. It was
as if Father Christmas himself had arrived; the poorer the district, the more
ecstatic the welcome. The French painter Jacques Emile Blanche was told
during the Jubilee of a socialist newspaper which lost so many readers on
ceasing to publish news of the royal family that it was forced to resume its
coverage. This amused him hugely. 'Can anyone imagine *L'Humanité* or *Le
Populaire*', he wrote, 'reporting President Lebrun's receptions at Ram-
bouillet?' The resistance of the poor to republicanism confounded even so
plausible an exponent as H.G. Wells, who wrote in his novel, *The World of
William Clissold*:

I am puzzled by the readiness of liberal-minded English people to acquiesce in and
conform to the monarchy. The king is necessarily the head and centre of the old
army system, of the diplomatic tradition, of hieratic privileges, of a sort of false
England that veils the realities of English life. While he remains, the old army
system remains, Society remains, the militant tradition remains. They are all
bound up together, inseparably. The people cannot apprehend themselves in
relation to the world while, at every turn and crisis of the collective life, the national
king, the national uniforms, the national flags and bands, thrust blare and bunting
across the realities. For millions these shows are naturally accepted as the realities.

The earnest radical found it all most unfair and disheartening.

Throughout the apotheosis of that Jubilee summer, no man was more
amazed than the King himself. 'I didn't realize they felt like this,' he said.
It came as no surprise, however, to those who had served him. 'For
twenty-five years', Sir John Simon wrote, 'King George has done his task

under the tremendous shadow of his grandmother, and as the successor of his universally popular father. After suffering from this comparison for a quarter of a century, he has now suddenly realized that he holds as high a position in his people's hearts as Queen Victoria or King Edward ever did.' MacDonald, too, smiled upon his sovereign's new-found confidence and popularity. 'But with it all,' the Prime Minister noted, 'he retains the demeanour and status of a King.'

'Their Majesties have stood the course well,' Wigram wrote from Balmoral in August 1935. 'The pace was too hot for me and I had to come up here a month ago for a rest.' He was now Lord Wigram, having recently received a peerage in the King's Birthday Honours. But not even he had escaped those doubts and difficulties which so often mar the distribution of royal favour. The initiative for Wigram's barony had come, as is usual, from the Prime Minister. However kindly meant, it disconcerted the King. No member of his household was more deserving of reward than Wigram; but the King could not ennoble him alone without seeming to slight another senior courtier, Sir Frederick Ponsonby. And Ponsonby, in spite of his forty years of devoted service to three successive sovereigns, was too independent of mind and tongue to endear himself to the King. It was therefore decreed that neither Wigram nor Ponsonby should become a peer. On being told by the Prime Minister of the King's decision, Wigram replied:

Your generous recommendation is evidently embarrassing to His Majesty and of course I could never dream of placing His Majesty in a difficult position after all he has done for me. At the same time I am sure you will agree that it is bad luck to be dispossessed of a heritage through the vagaries of a colleague.

Impressed by the logic of Wigram's protest, MacDonald prevailed on the King to change his mind. Both Wigram and Ponsonby were accordingly gazetted peers in the same Honours List. It was as well that the King showed ultimate magnanimity to an old and faithful servant. For although Wigram lived for another twenty-five years to enjoy his reward, the newly created Lord Sysonby survived for only four months.

Securing a peerage for Wigram was one of MacDonald's last acts as Prime Minister. Ten days after the Jubilee, he told the King that his doctors would no longer allow him to carry so heavy a burden. The King had of course to consent to a change of premiership, but insisted that MacDonald should remain in the Cabinet as Lord President of the Council. He also offered him the Order of the Thistle, 'an honour which every good Scotsman coveted'. But MacDonald reluctantly declined the green riband on

learning that it would oblige him to adopt the prefix 'Sir'. MacDonald's
account of the audience continues: 'Said he feared I would not let him show
his esteem for myself personally and for the service I had given to him and
the country. His words were those of a close personal friend.'

On 7 June 1935 he resigned as Prime Minister and was succeeded by
Baldwin. MacDonald had held the office for seven years in all, and his
farewell audience with the King was both sorrowful and affectionate:

He said again looking sadly down to the floor with his right elbow on the arm of his
chair: 'I hoped you might have seen me through, but I now know it is impossible.
But I do not think it will be very long. I wonder how you have stood it – especially
the loss of your friends and their beastly behaviour.' Again: 'You have been the
Prime Minister I have liked best; you have so many qualities, you have kept up the
dignity of the office without using it to give you dignity.' 'You will see me as often
as you like and of course you will come this year to Balmoral and as you now have
nothing to do you will not merely stay a weekend'. And so. He made me doubly
and trebly sorry to lay down my office.

Later that day he returned to the palace for the exchange of seals. By
Baldwin's thoughtful design, his first duty was to utter the words: 'Malcolm
MacDonald, Esquire, to be sworn of the Privy Council.' The new Prime
Minister had promoted his predecessor's son to be Secretary of State for
the Colonies at the age of thirty-four: the first time that a father and son
had sat in the same Cabinet since Joseph and Austen Chamberlain did so
in the early years of the century. 'His coat fitted badly,' the proud parent
noted. It was as if the King himself had spoken.

Tired but elated, the King resumed the familiar pattern of his summer:
Cowes, Sandringham and Balmoral. For once, however, *Britannia* failed to
win a first prize, and he decided that she would not race again. At Sandringham, the Foreign Office telegrams spoilt his pleasure and prompted
him to summon the new Secretary of State, Samuel Hoare. 'We discussed
the Italian–Abyssinian question which is very serious,' he wrote, 'also silly
yachting trip David wants to make in Mediterranean.' The caprice of the
Prince, even under the shadow of war, continued to worry his father.

Balmoral, however, brought repose and the decorative addition of two
more daughters-in-law to the family circle. Though eternally faithful to the
Queen, he was as susceptible as any man to feminine charm. 'Nothing very
striking in the way of beauty,' he had concluded at the last evening court of
his reign. The King was no longer robust enough to stalk, but the deer, in
Churchill's phrase, were 'moved about for him'; and before he came south
for the last time, a loyal stag did its duty.

Returning to Sandringham for the pheasants, the King took part in his
last shoot on 14 November: a bag of nearly a thousand birds. It was also the
day of the general election; and although Baldwin lost seventy-nine seats,

the National Government still commanded a comfortable majority of 245. 'His side have batted well in this Test Match', Wigram noted, 'and there is no doubt that the skipper declared his innings closed at the right moment.' But Labour took its revenge on MacDonald, who in County Durham suffered a crushing defeat at the hands of Emanuel Shinwell. The King told him that he must nevertheless remain in the Government. 'He would be greatly grieved and unhappy were it otherwise,' MacDonald wrote after their talk on 19 November. 'Did not expect to live more than five years and, as I would likely live after him, his death would free me.' Himself exhausted both in body and mind, MacDonald obeyed his sovereign, was confirmed in office as Lord President of the Council, and wearily set about finding an amenable constituency.

Although in November 1935 the King was not more than seventy, few thought it likely that he could reign for another five years. It seemed to Baldwin during those autumn months that he was already 'packing up his luggage and getting ready to depart'. Mensdorff, too, a guest at Sandringham in mid-November, wrote: 'When the King is standing he reminds me of the Emperor Franz-Josef in his last years.' That was a melancholy comparison; the Austrian Emperor was eighty-six at the time of his death. There is evidence that the King himself was aware of his approaching end. When the Canadian Government inquired informally whether Lord Athlone, the Queen's brother, might agree to become the next Governor-General, the King demurred. Not having long to live, he explained, he wanted the Athlones to remain in England so that they could comfort his widow in her loneliness.

After the strain of the Jubilee, Dawson noted that the narrowing of the arteries to the King's brain caused him to fall asleep during the day, even at meals. Yet his nights brought only fitful repose; and Sister Black, who had remained with him since his serious illness of 1928-29, would often administer oxygen at about 3 a.m. to relieve restlessness. 'King very disturbed about the Italian situation,' MacDonald wrote on 27 November. 'Have never seen him in such a state of nerves: says he cannot sleep owing to it.'

On 3 December the death of his sister, Princess Victoria, plunged him into renewed misery. For once he could not face his public duties and cancelled the State opening of Parliament. But still the unbroken flow of red boxes demanded and received attention. Just before Christmas he had to preside over a change of Foreign Secretaries. Hoare, while passing through Paris on his way to a holiday in Switzerland, had devised an unworthy plan with Laval, the French Foreign Minister, by which Italy was to be appeased with 60,000 square miles of Abyssinian territory. It so outraged public opinion that the Cabinet was obliged to disown him, and

on 18 December he resigned. The King at once instructed Wigram to write
a generous letter of sympathy to the fallen minister. And when Hoare came
to the palace to deliver up his seals of office, the King tactfully turned the
conversation to their shared pastimes. 'Now you are free,' he said, 'you will
have more time for shooting. Go and shoot a lot of woodcock in Norfolk.'
The King then left to spend Christmas at Sandringham. But he could not
yet lay down his burden. On 23 December, Anthony Eden was summoned
to receive his seals of office as the new Foreign Secretary. Twenty-six years
later, Eden published an account of that audience, in which he quoted these
words of the King: 'I said to your predecessor: "You know what they're all
saying, no more coals to Newcastle, no more Hoares to Paris." The fellow
didn't even laugh.'

It may well be that in the course of their talk, the King repeated a *bon
mot* that was already going the rounds. But it is inconceivable that he should
have thrown so cruel a jest in Hoare's face at the nadir of his political
fortunes, then mocked him for his supposed lack of humour. Both the
King's letter of sympathy and Hoare's own published version of his farewell
audience throw further doubt on the accuracy of Eden's recollection. Kings
attract legends; but that is one from which his memory ought to be
preserved.

His Christmas broadcast, delivered in a voice that had grown weaker
during the past twelve months, once more reached out into the hearts of his
people. He spoke of their joys and sorrows, and his own; there was a special
word for the children and a last patriarchal blessing. The ordeal over, his
ebbing strength confined him to the simplest of pleasures. 'Saw my Kent
grandson in his bath,' he noted with satisfaction. He rode his fat little
shooting pony about the estate, planted a cedar tree in front of the house,
watched his wife arrange Queen Alexandra's collection of Fabergé which
had returned to Sandringham after the death of Princess Victoria. But he
had not lost his concern for the welfare of others. Having lent the Royal
Pavilion, Aldershot, to the recently married Gloucesters as their first home,
he took the trouble to write to his daughter-in-law, hoping that she was
finding it warm enough.

Alarmed by reports from Sister Black of the King's breathlessness,
Dawson invited himself over to Sandringham from Cambridge on 12
January. 'Found him feeling unwell,' he noted, 'no energy – felt life on top
of him and in conversation said so.' Dawson thought it unnecessary to
prolong his stay, but was prepared to return at short notice. On 15 January,
after a miserable day, the King went to bed early, and next morning decided
to stay in his room. The last entry he made in his diary, so punctiliously
kept since 1880, was on Friday, 17 January. There was an illegible reference
to snow and wind, and the words: 'Dawson arrived this evening. I saw him

and feel rotten.'

That day the Prince of Wales, summoned from a shooting party at Windsor, found his father sitting sleepily before a fire in his bedroom. There was a flicker of recognition before he relapsed into a twilight world. Realizing that the end could not be far off, Dawson did not recall the medical team which had pulled the King through his previous illness, but only Sir Maurice Cassidy, the heart specialist. On the same Friday evening, the first of six bulletins prepared the nation for the worst: 'The bronchial catarrh from which His Majesty the King is suffering is not severe, but there have appeared signs of cardiac weakness which must be regarded with some disquiet.' Throughout the next two days, the King drifted in and out of consciousness, his heart growing weaker. On Sunday the Prince of Wales left for London to consult the Prime Minister about arrangements for his succession. Shortly afterwards the Archbishop of Canterbury arrived at Sandringham. He had, as he later wrote, telephoned Wigram in the hope that 'if the anxiety grew, I might be allowed to come as, apart from the call of personal friendship, I felt the country would expect it'. The Queen, on being consulted, agreed. But the Prince of Wales, who returned to Sandringham on the following day, resented Lang's intrusion. He was later to describe him slipping in and out of his father's room, 'a noiseless spectre in black gaiters'.

Monday, 20 January 1936 was the last day of the King's life. That morning the Archbishop said some simple prayers with him, laid his hands on his sovereign's head and blessed him. Then, in a lucid moment, the King sent for his private secretary. Wigram found him with *The Times*, open at the imperial and foreign page. It was some paragraph which had caught his eye, Wigram thought, that prompted the celebrated inquiry, 'How is the Empire?' The King made a brave attempt to discuss business, then his mind faded. 'I feel very tired,' he said.

But King George V was not yet allowed to die in peace. As he could no longer perform his constitutional duties, a meeting of ministers in Downing Street had on the previous evening authorized the appointment of a Council of State to act on his behalf. That, however, could be effected only by a warrant signed by the sovereign himself in the presence of a quorum of Privy Counsellors. During his illness in 1928, the King had been alert enough to affix a bold signature to the necessary document. Now he was only fitfully conscious and had lost the use of his right arm. Dawson feared that the effort would put an intolerable strain on his patient: 'I was rather surprised at the decision of the Cabinet Ministers ... that a Privy Council should be held without delay. There was no urgent business ... but they seemed (to me unduly) nervous lest some public urgency might arise and did not want to await events.'

It was thus that on the morning of 20 January, three members of the
Privy Council came down to Sandringham by train. They were MacDonald,
the Lord President of the Council; Hailsham, the Lord Chancellor; and
Simon, the Home Secretary. Hankey, as Clerk of the Council, accompanied
them. Three more Privy Counsellors were already in the house: Dawson,
Wigram and Lang. Shortly before 12.15 they assembled in a sitting-room
which led to the King's bedroom; its only other occupant was Charlotte,
the tame parrot. Dawson went into the bedroom and could be heard
explaining the purpose of the meeting. Then the other Privy Counsellors
entered, forming an unobtrusive group in the doorway. The King was
propped up in an armchair, wearing a bright flowered dressing-gown. In
front of him was a portable bed-table on which rested the warrant he would
be required to sign. He received the visitors, Hankey noted, 'with a delightful smile of recognition'.

The Lord President read out the order paper, and the King was able to
say 'Approved' in a firm voice. Kneeling by the King's side, Dawson tried
to guide his pen, first in one hand, then in the other. And though the King
struggled to comply, he had not the strength. 'Gentlemen,' he said, 'I am
so sorry for keeping you waiting like this. I am unable to concentrate.' After
several minutes, he made two shaky marks which might be recognized as
G.R. Then, and only then, could the dying King lay down the burden of his
duty. And as the Privy Counsellors filed out, in tears, he dismissed them with
his familiar nod and smile. 'I was the last out,' MacDonald wrote, 'and I shall
never forget the look illuminated by attention . . . my final farewell to a gracious and kingly friend and a master whom I have served with all my heart.'

After lunching with the Queen at her express invitation, the Privy
Counsellors returned to London in the plane which had just brought the
Prince of Wales and the Duke of York back to Sandringham. For the rest
of that day the King slept gently on while the bulletins tolled the end of his
reign. At 5.30 in the afternoon it was announced that his strength was
diminishing. That evening, as the Queen and her children dined alone,
Dawson picked up a menu card in the household dining-room and on it
wrote a farewell of classic simplicity: 'The King's life is moving peacefully
towards its close.' The family gathered round the King's bed; and as his
earthly life slipped away, the Archbishop read the Twenty-Third Psalm
and the prayer that begins, 'Go forth, O Christian soul.' The final bulletin
was broadcast a few minutes after midnight: 'Death came peacefully to the
King at 11.55 p.m.'

Throughout her husband's last illness the Queen never faltered; she was practical, calm and kindly to the end. And as one King died, she paid homage to another. In a gesture both affectionate and historic, she took the hand of her eldest son and kissed it. 'Am brokenhearted,' she was later to write in her diary. But while duties remained there could be no pause for grief. She thanked the nurses and spoke words of comfort and gratitude to Dawson; both cast their thoughts over the vigilance, and sometimes the struggle, which they had shared for seven years.

King Edward VIII failed to display the same composure during his last hours as Prince of Wales. Because of the thirty-minute discrepancy between Sandringham time and Greenwich time, some mistake occurred which tried him beyond endurance. So he gave orders, even as his father lay dying, that every clock in the house was to be put back. 'I wonder', Archbishop Lang sighed, 'what other customs will be put back also.'

It was in fact the Queen who made the first change of the new reign. Dreading the fortnight of obsequies that followed the death of King Edward VII, she asked that her husband's body should not remain unburied for more than a week. Although that was instantly conceded, even the shortened ceremonial exposed her to a succession of rituals each less private than the last.

They began within twenty-four hours of the King's death when, in the late afternoon, his coffin was placed on a small bier and wheeled across the deserted park to Sandringham church. The King's piper led the way, playing a lament. The family and a courtier or two followed: scarcely a dozen mourners in all. A single torch guided them through the darkness as they braced themselves against the wind and the rain.

Having rested before the altar for thirty-six hours, guarded by game-keepers and gardeners, the coffin was taken by gun-carriage to Wolferton station, thence by train to London. It was just such a crisp sunny day as used to delight the King as he set off for the coverts. He was escorted on his last journey by a host of Norfolk neighbours, tenants and estate workers. His white shooting pony, Jock, was led by a groom. 'Just as we topped the last hill above the station,' King Edward VIII wrote, 'the stillness of the morning was broken by a wild familiar sound – the crow of a cock pheasant.'

From King's Cross to Westminster Hall, the procession remained of poignant simplicity: a gun-carriage followed by four brothers on foot. But to enhance the dead sovereign's progress through his capital, the Imperial Crown was secured to the lid of the coffin over the folds of the Royal Standard. As the cortège swung into New Palace Yard, the King saw a flash of light dance along the pavement. It was the jewelled Maltese cross that surmounts the crown, loosened by the jolting wheels and now lying in the gutter. 'A most terrible omen,' Harold Nicolson wrote in his diary on 23 January 1936.

Archbishop Lang was also apprehensive. Before leaving Sandringham he had discussed the arrival of the coffin in Westminster Hall:

The King had said to me that he did not wish any religious service to be held as – said he – he was anxious to spare the Queen. I insisted that, however short, there *must* be some service. Certainly the whole ceremony would have been, as it were, blank without it; and it was at the Queen's own wish that the one hymn – 'Praise my soul, the King of Heaven' – was to be sung.

The Archbishop had his way; and with that sense of theatre which he so often brought to his office, borrowed from Westminster Abbey a purple cope which had been worn at the funeral of Charles II.

During the four days that the coffin lay in state, nearly a million of George V's subjects filed slowly past, their footsteps deadened by a huge soft grey carpet. At midnight on 27 January, the King and his three brothers joined the officers of the Household Brigade guarding the catafalque. 'We stood there for twenty minutes in the dim candlelight and the great silence,' the King wrote. 'I felt close to my father and all that he had stood for.'

On the following day, King George V embarked on his last voyage of all. This time the gun-carriage bearing his coffin was manned by sailors. They drew him from Westminster to Paddington station; and when the train reached Windsor, through the precincts of the castle to St George's Chapel. He would have raged at arriving more than an hour late for his funeral service, though ultimately he was the cause of the delay. So vast were the crowds that scorned a raw winter morning to bid him farewell, they blocked the processional way.

Even on that sombre occasion, the chapel did not lack colour. Beneath rows of Garter banners, the heavy black crepe and veils demanded of women mourners were relieved by the glow of vestments and the trappings of those who had borne arms for their sovereign: plumes and ribbons, coats of scarlet and blue and gold. The ceremonial seemed to reflect the Court of an earlier King George and an order of precedence remote from the realities of power: titles and places, it might be supposed, that the reforming zeal of the Prince Consort had failed to sweep away almost a century before. 'What struck me', a public servant afterwards wrote on reading an account of the funeral in *The Times*, 'was the subordinate position of Cabinet ministers in the ceremony. One had to hunt through column after column to find out whether the Prime Minister had been present.' Baldwin, however, had his place. So did two former Prime Ministers, their antipathy unabated. Mac-Donald was shocked not only that Lloyd George had agreed to write about the funeral for the newspapers but that he made notes for it throughout the service.

Five foreign sovereigns supported their cousin in his grief: Christian of

Denmark, Haakon of Norway, Carol of Rumania, Boris of Bulgaria, Leo-
pold of the Belgians. Only Denmark and Norway were to last their regal
course; and all five were soon to endure occupation or emasculation of their
kingdoms by Nazi Germany. A similar fate awaited the representatives of
Italy and Austria: Umberto, Prince of Piedmont, and Prince Starhemberg.
Nor would fortune smile on three brave soldiers who had come to bury the
King: Pétain from France, Tukhachevsky from Russia, Mannerheim from
Finland. Spared that tragic roll-call, the England which George v be-
queathed to his son was indeed a demi-paradise.

As the triumphant litany of death unfolded, all marvelled at the dignity
and fortitude of the widowed Queen: but no less at the new King, who in
his forty-second year seemed still to have the promise of youth before him.
His father's coffin sank slowly to the vault below, and he sprinkled symbolic
earth from a silver bowl: a last salute at his own request. And so King
George v went to join his ancestors.

As the mourners emerged from St George's, they saw that the grass
surrounding the chapel was covered with wreaths. 'How often beauty is
sacrificed to size,' the Duchess of Bedford reflected, averting her eyes; for
the most magnificent of those tributes were as self-important as their
donors. But a friend of the late King lingered; and among the exotic thickets
she came on a wreath of humbler flowers, sent by a coster from the East
End of London. It portrayed a white pony with a purple saddle.

EPILOGUE

On the Death of King George V

Spirits of well-shot woodcock, partridge, snipe
Flutter and bear him up the Norfolk sky:
In that red house in a red mahogany book-case
The stamp collection waits with mounts long dry.
The big blue eyes are shut which saw wrong clothing
And favourite fields and coverts from a horse;
Old men in country houses hear clocks ticking
Over thick carpets with a deadened force;
Old men who never cheated, never doubted,
Communicated monthly, sit and stare
At a red suburb ruled by Mrs Simpson,
Where a young man lands hatless from the air.

JOHN BETJEMAN

ACKNOWLEDGEMENTS

Manuscript Sources

I am deeply grateful to Her Majesty the Queen for gracious permission to publish documents of which she owns the copyright. These include many extracts from the Royal Archives made by Sir Harold Nicolson when writing his biography of King George v but not included in his completed work. Among these transcripts, previously unpublished passages from the King's diaries and from the correspondence of his private secretaries have proved particularly valuable to the present writer. I am also indebted to Her Majesty for permission to reproduce pictures and photographs from the Royal Collections.

I should like to thank all others who have allowed me to reproduce letters and manuscripts of which they hold the copyright, or who have allowed me access to papers in their possession or care:

The Earl of Antrim (known as Viscount Dunluce), for the diary of Sir Schomberg McDonnell.

The Earl Baldwin of Bewdley, for letters written by his grandfather, the first Earl.

The Earl of Balfour, for private papers of his great-uncle, the first Earl, retained at Whittingehame and not deposited in the British Museum; and the Registrar of the National Register of Archives (Scotland) for arranging their temporary transfer so that I could examine them in Edinburgh.

Mr W. A. Bell, for the papers of his father-in-law, Geoffrey Dawson.

Mrs John Bennett, for the diary of her father, H. A. L. Fisher; and Dr Russell Bryant, for lending me transcripts from it.

The Earl of Bessborough, for certain family papers.

Sir John Betjeman, for allowing me to reproduce the earliest version of his poem *On the Death of King George V* as the epilogue to this book.

The University of Birmingham, for letters written by Neville Chamberlain and for extracts from his diary.

The Curators of the Bodleian Library, Oxford, for access to the papers of H. H. Asquith, Geoffrey Dawson, H. A. L. Fisher, the Marquess of Lincolnshire, J. S. Sandars and Viscount Simon.

The Hon. Mark Bonham Carter, for letters written by his grandfather, H. H. Asquith.

The Trustees of the British Museum for access to the papers of the first Earl of Balfour.

The Cambridge University Library for access to the papers of Earl Baldwin of Bewdley, the Marquess of Crewe, Lord Hardinge of Penshurst, Field-Marshal Jan Smuts and Viscount Templewood.

The Rt. Hon. Paul Channon and Mr Peter Coats for unpublished extracts from the diary of the late Sir Henry ('Chips') Channon.

The Master and Fellows of Churchill College, Cambridge, for access to an unpublished memoir by the Earl of Cavan and to the papers of Sir Bryan Godfrey-Faussett, Sir Hughe Knatchbull-Hugessen and Sir Eric Phipps; and for permission to publish letters written by the last of these.

Lady Silvia Combe, for allowing me to see letters written by H. R. H. the Prince of Wales, later King Edward VIII, to her mother Viscountess Coke, later Countess of Leicester.

The Viscount Esher, for unpublished extracts from the letters and diaries of his grandfather, the second Viscount.

The Duke of Fife, for an extract from the visitors' book of Mar Lodge, Aberdeenshire.

The French Government, for the use of its archives in the Ministry of Foreign Affairs; and in particular M. Jacques Perot, for his help in tracing despatches sent by successive French ambassadors in London to the Quai d'Orsay.

Mr David Godfrey-Faussett, for the papers of his grandfather Sir Bryan Godfrey-Faussett.

Mr John Gore, for his correspondence while writing *King George V: a Personal Memoir*.

Earl Haig, for unpublished extracts from the letters and diaries of his father, Field-Marshal Earl Haig.

The Hon. Julian Hardinge, for the papers of his great-grandfather, the first Lord Hardinge of Penshurst.

The Hertfordshire County Record Office, for the papers of Lady Desborough.

Princess Louis of Hesse and the Rhine for papers from the archives of the Grand Duke Ernst Ludwig of Hesse.

Mr C. R. V. Holt, for letters of his father, Vice-Admiral R. V. Holt.

The India Office Library, and in particular Dr R. J. Bingle, for access to the papers of successive Viceroys: Lord Curzon, Lord Chelmsford, Lord Reading and Lord Irwin; also for access to the papers of Lord Brabourne and of Field-Marshal Lord Birdwood; and for the use of letters covered by Crown Copyright.

The Lord Lever and Mr E. R. Wheeler, for information from the archives of the Duchy of Lancaster.

Brigadier A. W. A. Llewellen Palmer, for the papers of the Marquess of Lincolnshire.

The Clerk of the Records, House of Lords, for access to the papers of David Lloyd George and of Andrew Bonar Law.

The Librarian, House of Lords, for the diary of Sir Edmund Gosse.

The executrix of the late Malcolm MacDonald, for the papers of J. Ramsay MacDonald, now in the Public Record Office. In common with all who are allowed to use this archive, I am enjoined to state that MacDonald's diaries (to quote his own words) were 'meant as notes to guide and revive memory as regards happenings and must on no account be published as they are'. I should like to add, however, that, in my own experience, independent evidence generally confirms the accuracy of MacDonald's diaries.

The Master and Fellows of Magdalene College, Cambridge, for the diaries of A. C. Benson.

The Earl of Minto, for the Indian diary of his grandmother, wife of the fourth Earl.

The late Sir Owen Morshead, for certain of his papers.

The Trustees of the National Library of Scotland for access to the papers of the first Earl Haig, Lord Haldane and the fifth Earl of Rosebery; and for permission to quote from Lord Haldane's unpublished letters.

The National Railway Museum, York, for documents about the railway journeys of King George V.

Mr Nigel Nicolson, for allowing me to use the transcripts and notes made by his father, Sir Harold Nicolson, while writing his life of King George V; also for leave to quote from the diary of his grandfather, Sir Arthur Nicolson (Lord Carnock), now in the Public Record Office.

Mr Paul Paget, for the papers of Viscount Templewood.

The Public Record Office, for access to its Foreign Office archives, to the papers of J. Ramsay MacDonald and to the diary of Lord Carnock.

The Duke of Richmond and the Earl of March, for family papers at Goodwood.

The Earl of Rosebery, for letters written by his grandfather, the fifth Earl.

The Hon. Giles St. Aubyn, for allowing me to see transcripts of letters from the Knollys papers which he used in writing his life of King Edward VII.

The Marquess of Salisbury, for letters from the family archives at Hatfield.

The Viscount Scarsdale for the private correspondence of his uncle, the Marquess Curzon of Kedleston.

The Viscount Simon, for the letters and diaries of his father, the first Viscount.

Mrs Anne Symonds, for unpublished letters of H. H. Asquith to her mother, Hilda Harrisson.

Mr A. J. P. Taylor and the Beaverbrook Foundation, for the papers of David Lloyd George and of Andrew Bonar Law, now in the House of Lords Record Office.

Officials of the Haus-, Hof- and Staatsarchiv, Vienna, for the papers of Count Albert Mensdorff; and Dr Roy Bridge, of Leeds University, who lent me transcripts and translations of them.

Loelia, Duchess of Westminster, for letters of her father, Sir Frederick Ponsonby (Lord Sysonby).

The Lord Wigram, for the private papers and diaries of his father and mother.

The Most Revd Frank Woods, formerly Archbishop of Melbourne, and the Rt Revd Robin Woods, formerly Bishop of Worcester, for the letters and diaries of their father, Canon Edward Woods, later Bishop of Lichfield.

I have also drawn on the papers of the late Sir Ronald Waterhouse, private secretary to successive Prime Ministers, which are in my own possession.

Help and Advice

Her Majesty the Queen allowed me the rare privilege of visiting the private Royal Family Museum in Frogmore House, Windsor.

To Queen Elizabeth the Queen Mother I owe an enduring debt of gratitude for her kindness and encouragement. Again and again during our conversations about King George V, Her Majesty illuminated the stiff print of history with her personal recollections, and answered my many questions with patience. I must also thank the Queen Mother for allowing me to reproduce Sickert's portrait of King George V, now in her private collection, on the cover of this biography.

His Majesty the King of Norway, the late Princess Alice, Countess of Athlone, the Duchess of Beaufort and the late Earl Mountbatten of Burma were other members of King George's family who brought the past to life and submitted to my inquisition with the utmost good nature.

The Emperor Hirohito of Japan described to me the welcome he had received from the King during his visit to Britain in 1921 as Crown Prince.

The Queen's Librarian, Sir Robin Mackworth-Young, showed exceptional kindness and courtesy in placing his wisdom and experience at my disposal. Throughout my labours he drew my attention to little-known sources, saved me from blunders and helped me to trace elusive facts. I am also grateful to Sir Oliver Millar, Surveyor of the Queen's Pictures, to Mr Geoffrey de Bellaigue, Surveyor of the Queen's Works of Art, and to Miss Frances Dimond, guardian of the Queen's photographic collection, for allowing me to draw on their expert knowledge.

I should like to thank all those who have given me personal recollections of King George v or who have generously helped me in other ways: Lord Adeane; the Hon. Lady Aitken; the Hon. Richard Beaumont and Mr Harry Lawrence, of James Purdey and Sons, Ltd., the King's gunsmiths; Dr Alan Bell; Sir Isaiah Berlin; Lord and Lady Briggs; Mr and Mrs Michael Brock; Miss Meriel Brown; Mr Rohan Butler; Lord Clark; Viscount Coke; Professor David Dilks; the late Sir Michael Duff; Professor Leon Edel; Sir William Fellowes; the late Viscount Gage; Mr Martin Gilbert; the Earl of Gowrie; Count Dino Grandi; Mr John Grigg; the late Lady Hardinge of Penshurst; the late Mr Norman Hartnell; Lady Mary Harvey; Lady Home of the Hirsel; the late Lt. Col. H. R. S. Howard; Professor Michael Howard; the late Lady Islington; the late Sir Alan Lascelles; Mr James Lees-Milne; Earl Lloyd-George of Dwyfor; the London Library; the late Malcolm MacDonald; Miss Lorna MacEchern; Mr David Metcalfe; the late Sir Owen Morshead; Lady Morshead; Sir Claus Moser; Mrs Priscilla Napier; Dr David Newsome; Mr Richard Ollard; the late Lady Delia Peel; Sir John Plumb; Mr R. H. Reed; Eva, Countess of Rosebery; the late Capt. Stephen Roskill; Mr David Russell; Mr H. Wynder; Mr Kenneth Young.

I acknowledge with gratitude the skill of Mr Douglas Matthews in producing so admirable an index.

Finally, I must thank Miss Elizabeth Burke, of Weidenfeld and Nicolson, for the boundless encouragement, enthusiasm and efficiency she has displayed throughout the production of this book.

BIBLIOGRAPHY

I am grateful to the authors, publishers and copyright holders of the undermentioned books for permission, where necessary, to quote from them. Each individual mention is acknowledged in 'Source References'.

AGA KHAN, *Memoirs*, Cassell, 1954.

AIRLIE, MABELL COUNTESS OF, *Thatched with Gold*, Ed. Jennifer Ellis, Hutchinson, 1962.

ALBERT VICTOR, PRINCE, AND GEORGE, PRINCE, OF WALES, *The Cruise of H.M.S. Bacchante, 1879-1882*, Vols. I & II, Macmillan, 1886.

ALICE, H.R.H. PRINCESS, COUNTESS OF ATHLONE, *For My Grandchildren*, Evans Brothers, 1966.

ALTRINCHAM, LORD, *Kenya's Opportunity*, Faber, 1955.

ANDREWS, MARTIN, *Canon's Folly*, Michael Joseph, 1974.

ARTHUR, SIR GEORGE, *King George V*, Cape, 1929.

ARTHUR, SIR GEORGE, *A Septuagenarian's Scrap Book*, Thornton Butterworth, 1933.

ASQUITH, LADY CYNTHIA, *Diaries, 1915-1918*, Hutchinson, 1968.

ASQUITH, H. H., *H. H. Asquith: Letters to Venetia Stanley*, Ed. Michael and Eleanor Brock, O.U.P., 1982.

ASQUITH, MARGOT, *Autobiography*, Vol. II, Thornton Butterworth, 1922.

ATTLEE, C. R., *As It Happened*, Heinemann, 1954.

BAGEHOT, WALTER, *The English Constitution*, O.U.P. The World's Classics, 1929 edition.

BAHLMAN, DUDLEY (Ed.), *The Diary of Sir Edward Walter Hamilton, 1880-1885*, Vols I & II, O.U.P. 1972.

BAILEY, JOHN (Ed.), *The Diary of Lady Frederick Cavendish*, Murray, 1927.

BAILLIE, ALBERT, *My First Eighty Years*, Murray 1951.

BARNES, JOHN, AND NICHOLSON, DAVID, *The Leo Amery Diaries, Vol. I, 1896-1929*, Hutchinson, 1980.

BATTISCOMBE, GEORGINA, *Queen Alexandra*, Constable, 1969.

BEAVERBROOK, LORD, *Men and Power, 1917-1918*, Hutchinson, 1956.

BEHRMAN, S. N., *Conversation with Max*, Hamish Hamilton, 1960.

BELL, RT. REVD G. K. A., *Randall Davidson, Archbishop of Canterbury*, O.U.P., 1935.

BENNETT, GEOFFREY, *Charlie B: a Biography of Admiral Lord Beresford*, Peter Dawnay, 1968.

BENSON, A. C., AND WEAVER, SIR LAWRENCE (Eds.), *The Book of the Queen's Dolls' House*, Methuen, 1924.

BERTIE OF THAME, LORD, *Diary 1914-1918*, Vols I & II, Ed. Lady Algernon Gordon Lennox, Hodder & Stoughton, 1924.

BIRKENHEAD, 2ND EARL OF, *F. E.: The Life of F. E. Smith, First Earl of Birkenhead*, Eyre and Spottiswoode, 1959.

BIRKENHEAD, 2ND EARL OF, *Halifax*, Hamish Hamilton, 1965.

BLACK, CATHERINE, *King's Nurse, Beggar's Nurse*, Hurst & Blackett, not dated.

BLAKE, ROBERT (Ed.), *The Private Papers of Douglas Haig, 1914-1919*, Eyre and Spottiswoode, 1952.

BLAKE, ROBERT, *The Unknown Prime Minister: the Life and Times of Andrew Bonar Law*, Eyre and Spottiswoode, 1955.

BLAXLAND, GREGORY, *J. H. Thomas*, Muller, 1964.

BLUNT, WILFRID, *On Wings of Song*, Hamish Hamilton, 1974.

BOCCA, GEOFFREY, *The Uneasy Heads*, Weidenfeld & Nicolson, 1959.

BOLITHO, HECTOR, *My Restless Years*, Max Parrish, 1962.

BONDFIELD, MARGARET, *A Life's Work*, Hutchinson, 1949.

BONHAM CARTER, VIOLET, *Winston Churchill as I Knew Him*, Eyre & Spottiswoode, 1965.

BOYLE, ANDREW, *Trenchard*, Collins, 1962.

BOYLE, CLARA, *A Servant of the Empire*, Methuen, 1938.

BRIDGE, F. R., 'The British Declaration of War on Austria-Hungary in 1914', *Slavonic and East European Review*, Vol. XLVII, No. 109, January 1969.

BRIDGE, F. R., *Great Britain and Austria-Hungary, 1906-1914*, Weidenfeld & Nicolson, 1972.

BRIGGS, ASA, *The Birth of Broadcasting*, O.U.P., 1961.

BROADHURST, HENRY, *Henry Broadhurst, M.P.: the Story of his Life*, Hutchinson, 1901.

BROCKWAY, FENNER, *Socialism Over Sixty Years: the Life of Jowett of Bradford*, George Allen and Unwin, 1946.

BROWN, IVOR, *Balmoral*, Collins, 1955.

BRUCE LOCKHART, SIR ROBERT, *Diaries 1915-38*, Ed. Kenneth Young, Macmillan, 1973.

BRYANT, ARTHUR, *George V*, Peter Davies, 1936.

BURCHETT, GEORGE, *Memoirs of a Tattooist*, Oldbourne, 1958.

BURNHAM, LORD, *Peterborough Court*, Cassell, 1955.

BUTLER, ROHAN, AND BURY, J. P. T. (Eds.), *Documents on British Foreign Policy 1919-1939*, First series, Vol. XII, 1962, Vol. XIV, Pub. 1966, H.M.S.O.

BUXTON, AUBREY, *The King in his Country*, Longmans, Green, 1955.

BYRON, ROBERT, 'New Delhi', article in *Architectural Review*, January 1931.

CARRINGTON, CHARLES, *Rudyard Kipling*, Macmillan, 1955.

CAZALET-KEIR, THELMA, *From the Wings*, Bodley Head, 1967.

CECIL, LADY GWENDOLEN, *Life of Robert, Marquis of Salisbury*, Vol. III, Hodder and Stoughton, 1932.
CHALMERS, W. S., *David, Earl Beatty*, Hodder and Stoughton, 1951.
CHAMBERLAIN, AUSTEN, *Down the Years*, Cassell, 1935.
CHAMBERLAIN, AUSTEN, *Politics from Inside*, Cassell, 1936.
CHANDOS, LORD, *Memoirs*, Bodley Head, 1962.
CHARTERIS, BRIGADIER-GENERAL JOHN, *At G.H.Q.*, Cassell, 1931.
CHILSTON, VISCOUNT, *W. H. Smith*, Routledge, 1965.
CHURCHILL, RANDOLPH S., *Lord Derby: King of Lancashire*, Heinemann, 1959.
CHURCHILL, RANDOLPH S. (Ed.), *Winston S. Churchill*, Companion Volume II, Heinemann, 1969.
CHURCHILL, WINSTON S., *The World Crisis 1911-1914*, Thornton Butterworth, 1923.
CHURCHILL, WINSTON S., *Great Contemporaries*, Thornton Butterworth, 1937.
CLARK, ALAN (Ed.), *A Good Innings: the Private Papers of Viscount Lee of Fareham*, Murray, 1974.
CLARK, KENNETH, *Another Part of the Wood*, Murray, 1974.
CLIFFORD, HON. SIR BEDE, *Proconsul*, Evans Brothers, 1964.
CLYNES, J. R., *Memoirs 1924-1937*, Hutchinson, 1937.
COATS, PETER, *The Gardens of Buckingham Palace*, Michael Joseph, 1978.
COLSON, PERCY (Ed.), *Lord Goschen and his Friends*, Hutchinson, 1946.
COLVILLE, LADY CYNTHIA, *Crowded Life*, Evans Brothers, 1963.
COLVILLE, JOHN, *Footprints in Time*, Collins, 1976.
COOKE, A. B., AND VINCENT, J. R., *Lord Carlingford's Journal*, O.U.P., 1971.
COOPER, DIANA, *The Light of Common Day*, Hart-Davis, 1959.
COOPER, DUFF, *Old Men Forget*, Hart-Davis, 1953.
CORBITT, F. J., *Fit for a King*, Odhams, 1956.
CORY, WILLIAM, *Letter & Journals*, O.U.P. (Privately Printed), 1897.
CROSS, J. A., *Sir Samuel Hoare*, Cape, 1977.
CULLEN, TOM, *Maundy Gregory: Purveyor of Honours*, Bodley Head, 1974.
CUNNINGTON, C. WILLETT, *Looking over my Shoulder*, Faber, 1961.
CURZON OF KEDLESTON, MARCHIONESS, *Reminiscences*, Hutchinson, 1955.
CURZON OF KEDLESTON, MARQUESS, *Walmer Castle and its Lords Warden*, Macmillan, 1927.
CUST, SIR LIONEL, *King Edward VII and his Court*, Murray, 1930.
DAVID, EDWARD (Ed.), *Inside Asquith's Cabinet: from the Diaries of Charles Hobhouse*, Murray, 1977.
DEANE, ANTHONY C., *Time Remembered*, Faber, 1945.
DE LA BERE, SIR IVAN, *The Queen's Orders of Chivalry*, Spring Books, 1964.
DICTIONARY OF NATIONAL BIOGRAPHY, Supplementary Volumes, 1901-50, O.U.P.
DILKS, DAVID, *Curzon in India*, Vol. II, Hart-Davis, 1970.
DIXON, DOUGLAS, *The King's Sailing Master*, Harrap, 1948.

DOCUMENTS ON GERMAN FOREIGN POLICY 1918-1945, Series C, Vol. IV, H.M.S.O., 1962.

DONALDSON, FRANCES, *Edward VIII*, Weidenfeld & Nicolson, 1974.

DUGDALE, BLANCHE E.C., *Arthur James Balfour*, Vols I & II, Hutchinson, 1936.

DUGDALE, EDGAR T. S., *Maurice de Bunsen*, Murray, 1934.

EDEL, LEON, *Henry James: The Master, 1901-1916*, Hart-Davis, 1972.

EDEN, ANTHONY (EARL OF AVON), *Facing the Dictators*, Cassell, 1962.

EMDEN, PAUL H., *Behind the Throne*, Hodder & Stoughton, 1934.

EMILE BLANCHE, JACQUES, *Portraits of a Lifetime*, J. M. Dent, 1937.

ESHER, VISCOUNT (Ed.), *The Girlhood of Queen Victoria*, Vols I & II, Murray, 1912.

ESHER, VISCOUNT, *Journals and letters of Reginald, Viscount Esher*, Ed. M. V. Brett, Nicholson and Watson, Vols. I & II, 1934, Vols. III & IV, 1938.

EVANS, TREFOR E., *The Killearn Diaries, 1934-1946*, Sidgwick & Jackson, 1972.

FERGUSSON OF KILKERRAN, SIR JAMES *The Curragh Incident*, Faber, 1964.

FINGALL, ELIZABETH, COUNTESS OF, *Seventy Years Young*, Collins, 1937.

FISHER, H. A. L., *A History of Europe*, Arnold, 1941 edition.

FITZROY, SIR ALMERIC, *Memoirs*, Vols I & II, Hutchinson, not dated.

FLEMING, TOM, *Voices out of the Air: the Royal Christmas Broadcasts 1932-1981*, Heinemann, 1981.

FOOT, M. R. D., AND MATTHEW, H. C. G. (Eds), *The Gladstone Diaries*, Vol. III, O.U.P., 1975.

FORTESCUE, HON. SIR JOHN, *Author & Curator*, Blackwood, 1933.

FORTESCUE, JOHN, *The Royal Visit to India 1911-1912*, Macmillan, 1912.

FORTESCUE, WINIFRED, *"There's Rosemary ... There's Rue ..."*, Blackwood, 1939.

FRANKLAND, NOBLE, *Prince Henry, Duke of Gloucester*, Weidenfeld & Nicolson, 1980.

FRASER, PETER, *Lord Esher*, Hart-Davis MacGibbon, 1973.

FULFORD, ROGER, *The Prince Consort*, Macmillan, 1949.

FULFORD, ROGER (Ed.), *Your Dear Letter: Private Correspondence of Queen Victoria and the Crown Princess of Prussia, 1865-1871*, Evans, 1971.

FULFORD, ROGER (Ed.), *Darling Child: Private Correspondence of Queen Victoria and the Crown Princess of Prussia, 1871-1878*, Evans, 1976.

GALTON, FRANCIS, 'Statistical Inquiries into the Efficacy of Prayer', article in *Fortnightly Review*, Vol. LXVII, 1 Aug. 1872.

GERE, J. A., AND SPARROW, JOHN (Eds), *Geoffrey Madan's Notebooks*, O.U.P., 1981.

GILBERT, MARTIN, *Servant of India: Sir James Dunlop Smith*, Longmans, 1966.

GILBERT, MARTIN, *Sir Horace Rumbold*, Heinemann, 1973.

GILBERT, MARTIN, *Winston S. Churchill, Vol. IV (1916-1922), Vol. V (1922-1939)*, Heinemann, 1975 & 1976.

GILBERT, MARTIN (Ed.), *Winston S. Churchill*, Companion Volumes III (1972), IV (1977) and V (1979 and 1981), Heinemann, 1977.

GLADWYN, CYNTHIA, *Paris Embassy*, Collins, 1976.

GORE, JOHN, *Mary, Duchess of Bedford*, Murray (Printed for Private Circulation), 1938.

GORE, JOHN, *King George V: a Personal Memoir*, Murray, 1941.

GRAFFTEY-SMITH, LAURENCE, *Bright Levant*, Murray, 1970.

GRANTLEY, LORD, *Silver Spoon*, Hutchinson, 1954.

GWYNN, STEPHEN (Ed.), *Letters and Friendships of Sir Cecil Spring Rice*, Vols I & II, Constable, 1929.

HALIFAX, EARL OF, *Fulness of Days*, Collins, 1957.

HARDINGE, HELEN, DOWAGER LADY, *Loyal to Three Kings*, Kimber, 1967.

HARDINGE OF PENSHURST, LORD (1ST BARON), *My Indian Years, 1910-16*, Murray, 1948.

HARDINGE OF PENSHURST, LORD (3RD BARON), *An Incompleat Angler*, Michael Joseph, 1976.

HAREWOOD, EARL OF, *The Tongs and the Bones*, Weidenfeld & Nicolson, 1981.

HARRIS, JOHN (AND OTHERS), *Buckingham Palace*, Nelson, 1968.

HAYTER, SIR WILLIAM, *Spooner*, W. H. Allen, 1977.

HEARDER, H., AND LOYN, H. R., 'King George V, the General Strike, and the 1931 crisis', essay in *British Government and Administration: Studies presented to S. B. Chrimes*, University of Wales Press, 1974. .

HENDERSON, SIR NEVILE, *Water Under the Bridges*, Hodder & Stoughton, 1945.

HEUSTON, R. F. V., *Lives of the Lord Chancellors, 1885-1940*, O.U.P., 1964.

HIBBERT, CHRISTOPHER, *Edward VII*, Allen Lane, 1976.

HOUGH, RICHARD, *Louis and Victoria: the First Mountbattens*, Hutchinson, 1974.

HOUGH, RICHARD (Ed.), *Advice to a Grand-daughter: Letters from Queen Victoria to Princess Victoria of Hesse*, Heinemann, 1975.

HOUGH, RICHARD, *Mountbatten: Hero of Our Time*, Weidenfeld & Nicolson, 1980.

HOUSEMAN, LORNA, *The House that Thomas Built: the Story of De la Rue*, Chatto & Windus, 1968.

HUNTLY, MARQUIS OF, *Milestones*, Hutchinson, 1926.

HUSSEY, CHRISTOPHER, *The Life of Sir Edwin Lutyens*, Country Life, 1950.

HYDE, H. MONTGOMERY, *Lord Reading*, Heinemann, 1967.

HYDE, H. MONTGOMERY, *Baldwin*, Hart-Davis, 1973.

INGE, VERY REVD. W. R., *Diary of a Dean: St. Paul's, 1911-1934*, Hutchinson, 1950.

JAIPUR, MAHARANI OF, AND SANTHA RAMA RAU, *A Princess Remembers*, Weidenfeld & Nicolson, 1976.

JENKINS, ROY, *Mr Balfour's Poodle*, Heinemann, 1954.

JENKINS, ROY, *Asquith*, Collins, 1964.

JOLLIFFE, JOHN, *Raymond Asquith: Life and Letters*, Collins, 1980.

JONES, L. E., *An Edwardian Youth*, Macmillan, 1956.

JONES, THOMAS, *Lloyd George*, O.U.P., 1951.

JONES, THOMAS, *A Diary with Letters, 1931-1950*, O.U.P., 1954.

JONES, THOMAS, *Whitehall Diary, Vol. I 1916-25, Vol. II 1926-30*, O.U.P., 1969 & 1971.

KENNEDY, A. L., *'My Dear Duchess': Social and Political Letters to the Duchess of Manchester*, Murray, 1956.

KEPPEL, SONIA, *Edwardian Daughter*, Hamish Hamilton, 1958.

LANG, THEO, *My Darling Daisy*, Michael Joseph, 1966.

LASKI, HAROLD J., *Parliamentary Government in England*, Allen & Unwin, 1938.

LAVERY, JOHN, *The Life of a Painter*, Cassell, 1940.

LEE, ARTHUR GOULD, *The Empress Frederick Writes to Sophie*, Faber, 1955.

LEE, SIR SIDNEY, *King Edward VII*, Vols. I & II, Macmillan, 1925 & 1927.

LEES-MILNE, JAMES, *Harold Nicolson: a Biography, Vol. II 1930-1968*, Chatto & Windus, 1981.

LE MAY, G. H. L., *The Victorian Constitution*, Duckworth, 1979.

LINKLATER, ERIC, *A Year of Space*, Macmillan, 1953.

LLOYD GEORGE, DAVID, *War Memoirs*, Vols. I-VI, Nicholson and Watson, 1933-1936.

LLOYD GEORGE, DAVID, *The Truth about the Peace Treaties*, Vols I & II, Gollancz, 1938.

LOCKHART, J. G., *Cosmo Gordon Lang*, Hodder & Stoughton, 1949.

LONGFORD, ELIZABETH, *Victoria R. I.*, Weidenfeld & Nicolson, 1964.

LOWIS, GEOFFREY L., *Fabulous Admirals*, Putnam, 1957.

LUCAS, E. V. (Ed.), *The Book of the Queen's Dolls' House Library*, Methuen, 1924.

LUDWIG, EMIL, *Kaiser Wilhelm II*, Putnam, 1929.

LUTYENS, MARY (Ed.), *Lady Lytton's Court Diary*, Hart-Davis, 1961.

LUTYENS, MARY, *Edwin Lutyens*, Murray, 1980.

MACLEOD, IAIN, *Neville Chamberlain*, Frederick Muller, 1961.

MAGNUS, PHILIP, *King Edward the Seventh*, Murray, 1964.

MALLET, VICTOR (Ed.), *Life with Queen Victoria: Marie Mallet's letters from Court, 1887-1901*, Murray, 1968.

MARDER, ARTHUR J. (Ed.), *Fear God and Dread Nought: the Correspondence of Admiral of the Fleet Lord Fisher of Kilverstone, Vol. I 1854-1904, Vol. II 1904-1914, Vol. III 1914-1920*, Cape, 1952, 1956 & 1959.

MARIE, QUEEN OF ROUMANIA, *The Story of My Life*, 3 Vols., Cassell, 1934.

MARIE LOUISE, H.H. PRINCESS, *My Memories of Six Reigns*, Evans Brothers, 1956.

MARQUAND, DAVID, *Ramsay MacDonald*, Cape, 1977.

MARSH, RICHARD, *A Trainer to Two Kings*, Cassell, 1925.

MARTIN, SIR THEODORE, *Queen Victoria As I Knew Her*, Blackwood, 1908.

MASTERMAN, LUCY, *C. F. G. Masterman*, Nicholson and Watson, 1939.

MATTHEWS, VERY REVD W. R., *Memories & Meanings*, Hodder & Stoughton, 1969.

MAUGHAM, SOMERSET, *A Writer's Notebook*, Heinemann, 1949.

MEDLICOTT, W. N., DAKIN, DOUGLAS, AND LAMBERT, M. E., *Documents on British Foreign Policy 1919-1939*, Series 1A, Vol. VII, H.M.S.O., 1975.

MIDDLEMAS, KEITH, AND BARNES, JOHN, *Baldwin*, Weidenfeld & Nicolson, 1969.

MIDLETON, EARL OF, *Records and Reactions, 1856-1939*, Murray, 1939.

MILLAR, OLIVER, *The Queen's Pictures*, Weidenfeld & Nicolson and the BBC, 1977.

MINTO, MARY, COUNTESS OF, *India, Minto and Morley, 1905-1910*, Macmillan, 1934.

MONKSWELL, MARY, LADY, *A Victorian Diarist 1895-1909*, Murray, 1946.

MONYPENNY, W. F., AND BUCKLE, G. E., *The Life of Benjamin Disraeli, Earl of Beaconsfield*, 6 Vols., Murray, 1910-20.

MORGAN, KENNETH O., *Lloyd George Family Letters 1885-1936*, University of Wales Press and O.U.P., 1973.

MORRIS, A. J. A., *C. P. Trevelyan: Portrait of a Radical*, Blackstaff Press, 1977.

MORSHEAD, SIR OWEN, 'King George: a Broadcast to Children', *Listener*, 30 January 1936.

MOSLEY, NICHOLAS, *Julian Grenfell*, Weidenfeld & Nicolson, 1976.

MOSLEY, SIR OSWALD, *My Life*, Nelson, 1968.

MURRAY, ARTHUR C., *Master and Brother*, Murray, 1945.

MYLIUS, E. F., *The Morganatic Marriage of George V*, New York, Privately Printed, not dated.

NEWTON, LORD, *Lord Lansdowne*, Macmillan, 1929.

NICOLSON, HAROLD, *Lord Carnock*, Constable, 1930.

NICOLSON, HAROLD, *Comments 1944-1948*, Constable, 1948.

NICOLSON, HAROLD, *King George V: his Life and Reign*, Constable, 1952.

NICOLSON, HAROLD, *Diaries and Letters, Vol. I 1930-1939, Vol. II 1939-1945, Vol. III 1945-1962*, Collins, 1966, 1967 & 1968.

ORMATHWAITE, LORD, *When I Was at Court*, Hutchinson, 1937.

OWEN, FRANK, *Tempestuous Journey: Lloyd George, his Life and Times*, Hutchinson, 1954.

OXFORD AND ASQUITH, EARL OF, *H.H.A., Letters of the Earl of Oxford and Asquith to a Friend. First Series 1915-22, Second Series 1922-27*, Bles, 1933 & 1934.

PEARSON, HESKETH, *Gilbert and Sullivan*, Hamish Hamilton, 1935.

PEARSON, HESKETH, *Labby*, Hamish Hamilton, 1936.

PETRIE, SIR CHARLES, *The Life and Letters of the Rt. Hon. Sir Austen Chamberlain*, Vols. I & II, Cassell, 1939 & 1940.

POINCARÉ, RAYMOND, *Memoirs 1913-1914*, Translated and adapted by Sir George Arthur, Heinemann, 1928.

PONSONBY, ARTHUR, *Henry Ponsonby*, Macmillan, 1942.

PONSONBY, SIR CHARLES, *Ponsonby Remembers*, Alden Press, 1965.

PONSONBY, SIR FREDERICK, *Recollections of Three Reigns*, Eyre & Spottiswoode, 1951.

PONSONBY, MAGDALEN (Ed.), *Mary Ponsonby*, Murray, 1927.

POPE-HENNESSY, JAMES, *Lord Crewe: the Likeness of a Liberal,*.Constable, 1955.

POPE-HENNESSY, JAMES, *Queen Mary*, George Allen & Unwin, 1959.

PORTLAND, DUKE OF, *Men, Women and Things*, Faber, 1937.

POSTGATE, RAYMOND, *George Lansbury*, Longmans, Green, 1951.

REESE, M. M., *Master of the Horse*, Threshold Books, 1976.

Report from the Select Committee on the Civil List, H.M.S.O., 1971.

RHODES JAMES, ROBERT, *Memoirs of a Conservative: J.C.C. Davidson*, Weidenfeld & Nicolson, 1969.

RHODES JAMES, ROBERT, *Victor Cazalet*, Hamish Hamilton, 1976.

RIDDELL, LORD, *More Pages from My Diary, 1908-14*, Country Life, 1934.

ROBERTS, SIR SYDNEY, *Adventures with Authors*, C.U.P., 1966.

RONALD, SIR LANDON, *Myself and Others*, Sampson Low, not dated.

ROOSEVELT, ELLIOTT, AND BROUGH, JAMES, *The Roosevelts of Hyde Park*, W. H. Allen, 1974.

ROOSEVELT, THEODORE, *Letters*, Vol. VII, Harvard University Press, 1954.

ROPER, LANNING, *The Gardens in the Royal Park at Windsor*, Chatto & Windus, 1959.

ROSE, KENNETH, *Superior Person*, Weidenfeld & Nicolson, 1969.

ROSE, KENNETH, *The Later Cecils*, Weidenfeld & Nicolson, 1975.

ROSKILL, STEPHEN, *Hankey: Man of Secrets, Vol. I 1877-1918, Vol. II 1919-1931, Vol. III 1931-1963*, Collins, 1970, 1972 & 1974.

ROSKILL, STEPHEN, *Naval Policy Between the Wars, Vol. I 1919-1929, Vol. II 1930-1939*, Collins, 1968 & 1976.

ROSKILL, STEPHEN, *Earl Beatty: the Last Naval Hero*, Collins, 1980.

ROTHSCHILD, DOROTHY M., *The Rothschilds at Waddesdon Manor*, Collins, 1979.

ST AUBYN, GILES, *The Royal George*, Constable, 1963.

ST AUBYN, GILES, *Edward VII: Prince and King*, Collins, 1979.

SAINT-AULAIRE, COMTE DE, *Confession d'un Vieux Diplomate*, Flammarion, Paris, 1953.

SAMUEL, VISCOUNT, *Memoirs*, Cresset Press, 1945.

SANDARS, J. S. 'A Privy Councillor' in *Studies of Yesterday*, Philip Allan, 1928.

SANDHURST, VISCOUNT, *From Day to Day Vol. I, 1914-1915, Vol. II, 1916-1921*, Arnold, 1928 & 1929.

SITWELL, OSBERT, *Great Morning*, Macmillan, 1948.

SITWELL, OSBERT, *Queen Mary and Others*, Michael Joseph, 1974.

SMYTH, ETHEL, *What Happened Next*, Longmans, Green, 1940.

SOAMES, MARY, *Clementine Churchill*, Cassell, 1979.

SOMMER, DUDLEY, *Haldane of Cloan*, Allen & Unwin, 1960.

STEINER, ZARA, *The Foreign Office and Foreign Policy, 1898-1914*, C.U.P., 1969.

STEPHENSON, JOHN (Ed.), *A Royal Correspondence: Letters of King Edward VII and King George V to Admiral Sir Henry F. Stephenson*, Macmillan, 1938.

STEVENSON, FRANCES, *Lloyd George: a Diary*, Ed. A. J. P. Taylor, Hutchinson, 1971.

STUART, CHARLES (Ed.), *The Reith Diaries*, Collins, 1975.

SUMMERS, ANTHONY, AND MANGOLD, TOM, *The File on the Tsar*, Gollancz, 1976.

SYKES, CHRISTOPHER, *Nancy: the Life of Lady Astor*, Collins, 1972.

SYLVESTER, A. J., *Life with Lloyd George: the Diary of A.J. Sylvester 1931-45*, Ed. Colin Cross, Macmillan, 1975.

TEMPLEWOOD, VISCOUNT, *The Unbroken Thread*, Collins, 1949.

TEMPLEWOOD, VISCOUNT, *Nine Troubled Years*, Collins, 1954.

THE TIMES, THE HISTORY OF, Vol. IV, *The Times*, 1952.

THOMAS, J. H., *My Story*, Hutchinson, 1937.

TRZEBINSKI, ERROL, *Silence Will Speak: a Study in the Life of Denys Finch Hatton*, Heinemann, 1977.

VANSITTART, LORD, *The Mist Procession*, Hutchinson, 1958.

VICTORIA, QUEEN, *The Letters of Queen Victoria*. Third Series, 1886-1901. Edited by G. E. Buckle. Vols. I-III, Murray, 1930, 1931, 1932.

WALKER, KENNETH, *I Talk of Dreams*, Cape, 1946.

WARRENDER, LADY MAUD, *My First Sixty Years*, Cassell, 1933.

WATERHOUSE, NOURAH, *Private and Official*, Cape, 1942.

WATSON, ALFRED E. T., *King Edward as a Sportsman*, Longmans, Green, 1911.

WATSON, FRANCIS, *Dawson of Penn*, Chatto and Windus, 1950.

WEBB, BEATRICE, *Diaries, Vol. I, 1912-1924, Vol. II 1924-1932*, Ed. Margaret Cole, Longmans, Green, 1952 & 1956.

WELLS, H. G., *The World of William Clissold*, Benn, 1926.

WENTWORTH DAY, J., *King George V as a Sportsman*, Cassell, 1935.

WESTMINSTER, LOELIA DUCHESS OF, *Grace and Favour*, Weidenfeld & Nicolson, 1961.

WHEELER-BENNETT, JOHN W., *King George VI: His Life and Reign*, Macmillan, 1958.

WILKINSON, NORMAN, *A Brush with Life*, Seeley Service, 1969.

WILSON, SIR JOHN, *The Royal Philatelic Collection*, Dropmore Press, 1952.

WILSON, JOHN, *C.B.: a Life of Sir Henry Campbell-Bannerman*, Constable, 1973.

WINDSOR, H.R.H. THE DUKE OF, *A King's Story*, Cassell, 1951.

WINDSOR, H.R.H. THE DUKE OF, *A Family Album*, Cassell, 1960.

WINDSOR, DUCHESS OF, *The Heart Has Its Reasons*, Michael Joseph, 1956.

WRENCH, JOHN EVELYN, *Geoffrey Dawson and Our Times*, Hutchinson, 1955.

YOUNG, G. M., *Stanley Baldwin*, Hart-Davis, 1952.

YOUNG, KENNETH, *Arthur James Balfour*, G. Bell, 1963.

ZIEGLER, PHILIP, *King William IV*, Collins, 1971.

SOURCE REFERENCES

To avoid distracting the general reader, I have adopted a system of references that does not deface the text with innumerable figures or letters of the alphabet, yet allows each quotation or allusion to be traced swiftly to its source. All references have been grouped together here, each being prefaced by the number of the page, the number of the line and a catch phrase for easy recognition. The line number is that of the *last* line of the quotation or other statement in the main text.

BOOKS AND PERIODICALS

Each reference to a quotation or allusion consists of a catch-phrase for identification of the subject, the surname of the author, the title of the book or article (sometimes abbreviated for convenience), the volume number (where necessary) and the page. The full name of the author (or editor) of the book, the title, the publisher and the date of publication are listed alphabetically under the author's surname in 'Bibliography'.

When quoting with some frequency from the same book, I have omitted the title. Thus Harold Nicolson's *King George the Fifth* appears simply as Nicolson. In referring to other books by the same author, I give their titles. There are two less obvious abbreviations. *The Cruise of H.M.S. Bacchante*, supposedly written by Prince Albert Victor and Prince George but in fact by the Rev. John Dalton, appears as *Bacchante*. And the several Companion Volumes to the life of Winston S. Churchill by Randolph S. Churchill and Martin Gilbert appear simply as CV.

LETTERS, DIARIES AND OTHER MANUSCRIPTS

The reference to each letter consists of a catch-phrase to identify the topic, the name of the writer, the name of the recipient, the date, the archive where the letter is to be found (or if in print, the book) and sometimes its serial number. Quotations from memoranda and diaries follow a similar pattern, except that the diary of King George v appears simply as Diary.

The names of writers and recipients are referred to by the style they bore at the time: Prince George, Duke of York, Prince of Wales, King.

The following abbreviations have been used to indicate the manuscript collection or archive in which each quoted document is to be found:

A   Asquith Papers. Bodleian Library, Oxford.
B   Baldwin Papers. Cambridge University Library.
BM   Balfour Papers. British Museum.
BW   Balfour Papers. Private collection at Whittingehame.
C   Curzon Papers. India Office Library.
CK   Curzon Papers. Private collection at Kedleston.
E   Esher Papers. Churchill College, Cambridge.
GF   Godfrey-Faussett Papers. Churchill College, Cambridge.
H   Hardinge Papers. Cambridge University Library.
HG   Haig Papers. National Library of Scotland.
HL   Haldane Papers. National Library of Scotland.
IR   Irwin Papers. India Office Library.
L   Lincolnshire Papers. Bodleian Library, Oxford.
LG   Lloyd George Papers. Record Office, House of Lords.
M   Mensdorff Papers. State Archives, Vienna.
MD   MacDonald Papers. Public Record Office.
NC   Neville Chamberlain Papers. Birmingham University Library.
R   Rosebery Papers. National Library of Scotland.
RA   Royal Archives. Windsor.
RD   Reading Papers. India Office Library.
S   Salisbury Papers. Hatfield.
TM   Templewood Papers. Cambridge University Library.
W   Wigram Papers. Private collection.
WD   Woods Papers. Private collection.
WT   Waterhouse Papers. Private collection.

The names of other manuscript collections on which I have drawn are printed with each source reference.

PERSONAL REMINISCENCES

These, whether given to me by letter or in conversation, are acknowledged in the form: Lord Mountbatten to author, 9 June 1976.

SAILOR PRINCE

p. 1.   l.5   Safety delivered. Queen Victoria. Journal. 3 June 1865. Gore.
3.

p. 1. l.13 Called George. Prince of Wales to Queen Victoria. 11 June 1865. Nicolson. 4.

l.24 Girls to be Victoria. Queen Victoria to Prince of Wales. 13 June 1865. Nicolson. 4.

l.32 Interference. Queen Victoria to King Leopold. 11 March 1864. Battiscombe. 65.
Names we like. Prince of Wales to Queen Victoria. 16 July 1865. Nicolson. 4.

l.29 Fast people. Lady Frederick Cavendish. Diary. 20 Dec. 1872. Bailey. II. 146.

l.30 Fashionable society. Prince of Wales to Queen Victoria. 11 July 1880. Nicolson. 24.

l.40 Within your income. Pearson. *Labby*. 253.

p. 3. l.2 Beautiful women. Queen Mother to author. 6 May 1977.

l.23 Basta. Esher. 18 Nov. 1901. I. 318.

p. 4. l.7 No books. Cavendish. Diary. 20 Dec. 1872. Bailey. II. 146.

l.15 Lovely little face. Battiscombe. 143.

l.19 Prince George to Princess of Wales. 4 Jan 1888. RA.

l.22 Queen Victoria to Crown Princess. 16 June 1874. Fulford. *Darling Child*. 143.

l.27 Not a professor. Gosse. House of Lords Diary.

p. 5. l.14 Unfancied. Queen Victoria to Crown Princess. 17 March 1872. Battiscombe. 123.

l.26 Princely studies. Dalton to Queen Victoria. 31 Jan. 1874. Gore. 24.

l.30 Running deer. Gore. 20.

l.36 Merry and rosy. Queen Victoria to Crown Princess. 27 Jan. 1869. Fulford. *Your Dear Letter*. 222.

p. 6. l.2 Quarrels forbidden. Battiscombe. 122.

l.4 Dalton's record. 25 Nov. 1876. Nicolson. 8.

l.35 Somewhat deficient. Dalton to Queen Victoria. 11 Feb. 1877. Nicolson. 12–13.

p. 7. l.7 Nautical education. Queen Victoria to Dalton. 15 Feb. 1877. Nicolson. 14.

l.20 Health and happiness. Dalton to Queen Victoria. 14. Nov. 1877. Gore. 31.

l.38 Pocket money. King George v to Morshead. Jan. 1932. Nicolson. 15.

p. 8. l.3 Kisses. Prince George to Princes of Wales. 27 May 1879.

l.9 Birthday letter. Princess of Wales to Prince George. 2 June 1879. Gore. 36–37.

l.18 Mental powers. Dalton to Prince of Wales. 9 April 1879. RA.

p. 9.　l.12　Dalton in the wrong. A. Ponsonby. *Henry Ponsonby.* 19.

　　　　l.40　Rough seamen. Prince William to King George III. 24 Nov.
　　　　　　　1779. Ziegler. 32.

p. 10.　l.15　Naval officers. *Bacchante.* I. 618.

　　　　l.23　Protection. *Ibid.* I. 435–36.

　　　　l.32　Anniversary. Diary. 6 Aug. 1935. Nicolson. 517.

　　　　l.42　Gale damage. *Bacchante.* I. 442.

p. 11.　l.6　Black border. *Ibid.* I. 257–58.

　　　　l.19　Smashed to atoms. *Ibid.* I. 551.

　　　　l.24　John Scott. *Ibid.* II. 771.

　　　　l.38　Ideal shipmate. Memoir by Cdr. G. W. Hillyard, Gore. 47.

p. 12.　l.5　Midshipman's butter. *Bacchante.* I. 73.

　　　　l.7　Boiled rice. *Ibid.* II. 54.

　　　　l.15　Morning watch. *Ibid.* II. 551–52.

　　　　l.19　Pocket money. Bryant. *George V.* 25.

　　　　l.25　Knocked about. Pearson. *Gilbert and Sullivan.* 128.

　　　　l.29　Shark's head. *Bacchante.* II. 15.

　　　　l.35　Albatross. *Ibid.* I. 433.

p. 13.　l.4　Kangaroo. *Ibid.* II. 12.

　　　　l.10　Keyholes. Lord Henry Scott to John Gore. 18 Nov. 1938.
　　　　　　　Gore Papers.

　　　　l.18　Tattooed nose. Princess of Wales to Prince George. 30 Dec.
　　　　　　　1879. Nicolson. 23.

　　　　l.26　White skin. Dalton to Prince of Wales. 27 June 1880.
　　　　　　　Nicolson. 23.

　　　　l.31　Elaborate designs. *Bacchante.* II. 41, 46 and 99.

　　　　l.35　Certain improvements. Burchett. *Memoirs of a Tattooist.*
　　　　　　　100.

p. 14.　l.18　Open market. *Bacchante.* I. 346–357.

　　　　l.20　Ostridges. Diary. 2 March 1881. Nicolson. 26.

　　　　l.23　Pandemonium *Bacchante.* I. 104.

　　　　l.26　English skeletons. *Ibid.* I. 109.

　　　　l.28　Naval salutes. *Ibid.* II. 213.

　　　　l.33　Christian brothers. *Ibid.* II. 177.

　　　　l.39　Aristophanes. *Ibid.* II. 748.

p. 15.　l.19　Our greatest poet. Diary. 26 May 1906. RA.

　　　　l.21　Royal vocabulary. *Ibid.* 16 Nov. 1910.

　　　　l.25　Jungle leeches. Magnus. 137.

　　　　l.27　Tranby Croft. Prince of Wales to Prince George. 10 June
　　　　　　　1891. RA.

　　　　l.35　German and French. Queen Victoria to Prince of Wales.
　　　　　　　26 May 1880. Nicolson. 24.

p. 15. l.42 Sauerkraut. Princess of Wales to Prince George. 3 Oct. 1892. RA.

p. 16. l.4 Shooting and hunting. Prince George to Oliver Montagu. 28 Sept. 1892. Gore. 106.

l.9 Not fluent. Lady Wigram. Diary. 1926. W.

l.13 Atrocious. Clara Boyle. *A Servant of the Empire.* 209.

l.19 Facing difficulties. Dalton to Prince of Wales. 9 Jan. 1892. Nicolson. 30.

l.35 Owen Morshead to author (quoting Stamfordham) 23 Oct. 1976.

p. 17. l.6 Evening prayer. Princess of Wales to Prince George. 12 June 1883. Battiscombe. 164.

l.10 Holy Communion. Dalton to Prince George. ( ) Nov. 1883. Gore. 59.

l.11 Affectionate. *Ibid.* 11 July 1883. *Op.cit.* 58.

l.13 Cigarettes. Prince George to Dalton. 22 April 1884. *Op.cit.* 60.

l.28 Unassuming manner. Fisher to Queen Victoria. 8 Oct. 1885. Nicolson. 36.

l.39 Inclined to be lazy. Prince of Wales to Stephenson. 4 Jan. 1886. Stephenson. 64.

p. 18. l.3 Smoke too much. *Ibid.* 8 Sept. 1886. *Op.cit.* 85.

l.5 Coffee-housing. *Ibid.* 27 July 1886. *Op.cit.* 100.

l.9 Abusing me. Prince George to Stephenson. 23 June 1888. *Op.cit.* 134–35.

l.16 Unpopular in the Service. *Ibid.* 24 Sept. 1889. *Op.cit.* 155–56.

l.24 Torpedo boats. Gore. 90.

l.34 Lord Mountbatten to author. 9 June 1976.

p. 19. l.9 Boat in tow. Prince George to Stephenson. 15 June 1890. Stephenson. 173.

l.14 Sunday divisions. *Ibid.* 6 April 1891. Stephenson. 183.

l.18 Left undone. Lowis. *Fabulous Admirals.* 165.

l.35 Sweet little room. Prince George to Princess of Wales. 21 Oct. 1886. Nicolson. 38.

p. 20. l.2 Good son. Princess of Wales to Prince George. 10 May 1886. Battiscombe. 173.

l.5 A ripper. Lees-Milne. *Nicolson.* II. 230.

l.10 Darling Julie. Diary. 17 Feb. 1886. RA.

l.17 Cannot be. Battiscombe. 172.

l.25 Beloved chum. Queen Marie. *The Story of My Life.* I. 135.

l.36 Lot of rot. Prince George to Stephenson. 6 April 1891. Gore. 181.

p. 21.   l.24 Meaning of words. J.K. Stephen to Dalton. 31 Aug. 1883.
                 Magnus. 178.

         l.32 Copies to the papers. Sir Edward Hamilton. Diary. 14 Jan.
                 1885. Bahlman. II. 772.

         l.35 Forgotten thoughts. Hibbert. *Edward VII.* 183.

         l.42 Never there. Lady Geraldine Somerset. Diary. 19 Jan. 1885.
                 St. Aubyn. *Royal George.* 299.

p. 22.   l.3   Parade ground. *Ibid.* 5 Nov. 1885. *op. cit.* 299.

         l.12 Not a Duke. Queen Victoria to Empress Frederick. 3 June
                 1890. Pope-Hennessy. 194.

         l.24 Sensitive wife. Prince of Wales to Queen Victoria. 5 August
                 1891. Magnus 238.

p. 23.   l.5   Good of the country. Knollys to Ponsonby. 19 August 1891.
                 op. cit. 239.

         l.11 Both very happy. Princess May. Diary. 3 Dec. 1891. Pope-
                 Hennessy. 210.

         l.23 Hardly a break. A. Ponsonby. 113.

         l.25 Pope-Hennessy. 226.

                              MARRIAGE

p. 24.   l.13 Consolidated Fund. Lee. *King Edward VII.* 606.

         l.19 Prince and Duke. Queen Victoria to Prince George. 27 May
                 1892. Nicolson. 47.

         l.25 Duke of London. Gore. 104.

         l.27 Duke of York. Princess of Wales to Prince George. 28 June
                 1892. RA.

p. 25.   l.7   Albert rejected. F. Ponsonby. *Recollections.* 45.

         l.19 Hateful manœuvres. Diary. 27 July 1892. Nicolson. 47.

         l.25 German Orders. Prince of Wales to Prince George. 24 and
                 27 Aug. 1892. Magnus. 240.

         l.31 Not your fault. Princess of Wales to Prince George. 11 April
                 1890. Nicolson. 42.

         l.41 May's feelings. Queen Victoria to Prince George. 6 April
                 1892. RA.

p. 26.   l.8   Cousin Georgie. Prince George to Princess May. 29 March
                 1892. Pope-Hennessy. 235.

         l.18 Widow before wife. Prince of Wales to Queen Victoria. 14
                 Jan. 1892. Magnus. 239.

         l.32 Darling Georgie boy. Princess of Wales to Prince George. 29
                 April 1893. Nicolson. 50.

p. 26. l.35 Throw it away. Prince George to Princess May. 31 March 1893. Pope-Hennessy. 255.

p. 27. l.18 Talk business. *op. cit.* 262.

l.25 Indifferent. Lady Geraldine Somerset. Diary. 14 May 1893. *op. cit.* 263.

l.28 1,500 presents. Gore. 110.

p. 28. l.6 Great mistake. Lady Geraldine Somerset. Diary. 6 July 1893. Pope-Hennessy. 270.

l.13 Public tent. *Ibid.* 5 July 1893. St. Aubyn. 301.

l.20 First position. Empress Frederick to Princess Frederick-Charles of Hesse. 24 Feb. 1893. Pope-Hennessy. 259.

p. 29. l.3 Württemberg. Queen Victoria to Princess Mary. 30 Aug. 1892. *Op. cit.* 37

l.8 Jolly old maid. Lord Clarendon to Duchess of Manchester. 28 July 1859. Kennedy. *My Dear Duchess.* 64.

l.11 Vast undertaking. *Ibid.* 20 Sept. 1860. *Op. cit.* 116.

l.13 Finger in door. Magdalen Ponsonby. *Mary Ponsonby.* 5.

l.17 Fried potatoes. Pope-Hennessy. 54.

l.19 Plush pincushion. Mallet. *Life with Queen Victoria.* 30.

l.35 Dark skin. Queen Victoria to Crown Princess. 22 June 1867. Fulford. *Your Dear Letter.* 140.

l.36 Not handsome. *Ibid.* 4 April 1868. *Op. cit.* 183.

p. 30. l.4 Petite Anglaise. Princess Mary to Duchess of Cambridge. 1876. Pope-Hennessy. 82.

l.14 Stiff little courts. Queen Mary to Mensdorff. 26 Nov. 1931. M.

l.29 Wrong buttons. FitzRoy. *Memoirs.* I. 203.

l.39 Throne of Bulgaria. A. Ponsonby. 278.

p. 31. l.24 Mr Barker. Pope-Hennessy. 60.

l.39 Smell of garlic. Princess Mary to Prince Adolphus. 1 Dec. 1883. *Op. cit.* 122–23.

p. 32. l.14 Best clothes. *Op. cit.* 178.

l.34 Royal predicament. *Op. cit.* 186.

p. 33. l.5 Unlucky and sad. Queen Victoria to Empress Frederick. 3 July 1893. *Op. cit.* 272.

l.12 Glass cupboard. Empress Frederick to Princess Sophie. 1894. Gould Lee. 165.

l.27 In a hurry. Duchess of York to Duke of York. August 1894. Pope-Hennessy. 279.

p. 34. l.2 I adore you. Duke of York to Duchess of York. *Op. cit.* 280.

l.19 Württemberg hands. *Op. cit.* 105.

l.27 Own personality, Airlie. *Thatched with Gold.* 102.

p. 34.   l.30   Breaking the ice. Empress Frederick to Princess Frederick-
                   Charles of Hesse. 2 Feb. 1897. Pope-Hennessy. 258.

           l.36   Decidedly dull. Battiscombe. 199.

           l.39   Gives herself airs. Mallet. Diary. 9 Aug. 1898. 138.

p. 35.   l.2   Difficult position. Queen Victoria to Duchess of York. 9 Oct.
                   1897. Pope-Hennessy. 343.

           l.10   Cunnington. *Looking over my Shoulder.* 139.

           l.18   Queen displeased. Riddell. *More Pages.* 218

           l.23   Not speak English. Queen Victoria to Duchess of York.
                   6 Nov. 1893. Pope-Hennessy. 343-44.

           l.28   Should get ill. Duke of York to Duchess of York. 1894. *Op.
                   cit.* 309.

           l.30   Pining to shoot. Ellis to Knollys. St. Aubyn. *Edward VII.*
                   298.

p. 36.   l.2   Hired conjuror. Dorothy de Rothschild. 44-45.

           l.9   Month's absence. Duke of York to Salisbury. 18 April 1896.
                   S.

           l.24   Hates society. Somerset. Diary. 21 May 1894. St. Aubyn.
                   Royal George. 300.

           l.37   Dinner parties. Nicolson Papers.

           l.42   Queen was silent. Lytton. Diary. 22 Feb. 1896. Lutyens. 60.

p. 37.   1.3   Circular movement. Nicolson. *Diaries.* 21 March 1949. III.
                   167.

           l.13   Sacred name. Duke of York to Queen Victoria. 1 July 1894.
                   Nicolson. 54.

           l.18   Albert Victor. Queen Victoria to Prince George. 2 July 1894.
                   Ibid.

           l.32   Greville Memoirs. Gore. 127.

p. 38.   l.15   Xmas present. Prince Francis to Duchess of Teck. 21 Oct.
                   1896. Pope-Hennessy. 319.

           l.23   Errant emeralds. Princess Alice. *For My Grandchildren.* 129.

           l.33   No grievous length. Gore 126.

p. 39.   1.3   Well cared for. Empress Frederick to Princess Sophie. 1894.
                   Gould Lee. 165.

           l.8   Scandinavian sunsets. Disraeli to Lady Chesterfield. 15 Dec.
                   1873. Monypenny and Buckle. V. 297.

           l.29   No regret. Diary. 26 Aug. 1898. RA.

           l.32   Been at sea. A. Watson. *King Edward as a Sportsman.* 323.

           l.36   Put out an eye. Private information.

p. 40.   l.5   Glass case. Canon Woods. 1929. WD.

           l.8   Templewood. *Unbroken Thread.* 182.

           l.24   Very anxious. Diary. 16 Dec. 1899. RA.

p. 40. l.37 West Indies. Wilson. *Royal Philatelic Collection*. 6.

p. 41. l.11 Not quite right. A. Ponsonby. 87.

l.13 Colson. *Goschen*. 52.

l.22 Expenditure. Private information.

l.30 Pinching stamps. Wigram to Godfrey Thomas. 19 July 1920. W.

l.36 Saucepan. Grafftey-Smith. *Bright Levant*. 22.

l.41 Annual income. Lee. II. 27–28.

p. 42. l.2 Damned fool. Wilson. *Op. cit.* 41. It was an unused 2d 'Post Office' Mauritius stamp.

l.9 Unconquerable mind. Nicolson. *Comments 1944–1948*. 181–85.

l.16 Inalienable. Evidence of Lord Cobbold, Select Committee on the Civil List. 1971.

HEIR TO THE THRONE

p. 43. l.8 Benefit my country. Duke of York to Knollys. 19 April 1900. Knollys Papers.

l.13 Influence. Duke of York to Salisbury. 20 Oct. 1900. S.

l.18 Death of the Queen. Diary. 22 Jan. 1901. Nicolson. 60.

p. 44. 1.21 Imperial lies. Balfour to Edward VII. 6 Feb. 1901. *Op. cit.* 67–68.

l.42 Filial duty. Prince of Wales to Duke of York. 20 Aug. 1900. RA.

p. 45. l.4 Cry and comfort. Duke of York to Queen Alexandra. 21 March 1901. RA.

l.20 Pleasing the people. *Ibid*. 8 July 1901. Gore. 158.

l.34 Foreign competitors. Speech at Guildhall, London. 5 Dec. 1901. Nicolson 73–74.

p. 46. l.1 Commerce. King Edward VII to Duke of York. 11 April 1901. Magnus. 292.

l.9 Dear old England. Duke of York to Queen Alexandra. 3 Sept. 1901. RA.

l.20 Real estate. Esher to King George V. 22 Oct. 1911. III. 67.

l.23 Mistake. Wheeler-Bennett. 203.

l.35 Loving wife. Duke of York to Duchess of York. (   ) Pope-Hennessy. 368.

p. 47. l.2 Virtuous life. Hayter. *Spooner*. 108–109.

l.6 Home again. Bigge to Esher. 2 Aug. 1901. Esher. I. 303.

p. 48. l.3 Ponsonby's qualities. A. Ponsonby. 402–403.

p. 48.   l.20   Typewriters. Rosebery to H. Ponsonby. 24 Nov. 1893.
                    R 10202.

       l.23   First letter. Lord Adeane to author. 9 March 1979.

       l.32   Christmas correspondence. Prince of Wales to Bigge. 2 Jan.
                    1908. Gore 221.

       l.34   Own hand. Knollys to Hardinge. 15 Dec. 1910. H. 104.

       l.39   Time and trouble. Stamfordham to French. 15 July 1918.
                    RA.

       l.41   American typewriters. Houseman. *The House that Thomas
                    Built*. 164.

p. 49.   l.10   Statesman. Stamfordham to Irwin. 31 Aug. 1926. IR.

       l.11   Courtier. Stamfordham to Wigram. 7 Dec. 1912. W.

       l.24   Enormous help. Prince of Wales to Bigge. 1 Jan. 1902. Gore.
                    175.

       l.39   Soundest advice. *Ibid.* 25 Dec. 1907. *Op. cit.* 220–21.

p. 50.   l.8   The Cottage. Edward VII to Prince of Wales. 9 Dec. 1901.
                    RA.

       l.24   Spectacles. Esher. 21 June 1901. I. 300–01.

p. 51.   l.4   A dream. Pope-Hennessy. 380–81.

       l.7   Dirty house. *Op. cit.* 356.

       l.26   No letters. Esher. 16 Nov. 1907. II. 255.

       l.31   Subtly incorrect. Pope-Hennessy. 355.

       l.37   Usurper. Airlie. 108.

p. 52.   l.1   Dresses for India. Battiscombe. 259.

       l.9   Nobody can know. Queen Alexandra to Princess of Wales.
                    21 Jan. 1908. Pope-Hennessy. 328.

       l.34   Half pathos. Esher to George V. 20 May 1910. RA.

p. 53.   l.10   Fate of James II. FitzRoy. 9 Feb. 1908. I. 340.

       l.25   No shyness. Fisher to Lady Fisher. 2 Oct. 1903. Marder. I.
                    286.

       l.34   Intimate details. Windsor. *King's Story*. 44 and 76.

p. 54.   l.8   Pulls my beard. *Op. cit.* 38–39.

       l.11   Melting point. Wheeler-Bennett. 50.

       l.21   Child's mind. Airlie. 112.

       l.33   Family life. Windsor. *King's Story*. 6.

       l.39   Cowes. Windsor. *Family Album*. 64.

p. 55.   l.3   Sooner you begin. Wheeler-Bennett. 18.

       l.14   Rag doll. Lord Mountbatten to author. 9 June 1976.

       l.16   Guffaws. Lockhart. *Lang*. 253.

       l.19   Missing woodcock. Morshead. Memorial Broadcast. 1936.

       l.25   Tropical sun. Windsor. *King's Story*. 16.

       l.29   Wings cut off. April 1900. Imperial War Museum.

p. 55.   l.39   Sandwiches. Col. Henry Howard to author. 4 Oct. 1977.
p. 56.   l.4   Pheasants and hare. Lady Aitkin to author. 20 July 1977.
         l.27   Black eye. Wheeler-Bennett. 73.
         l.37   Bullingdon Club. Windsor. *Family Album.* 46–47.
p. 57.   l.3   Sometimes harsh. Nicolson. 365.
         l.22   Frightened of me. Churchill. *Derby.* 159.
p. 58.   l.6   Fathers and mothers. Windsor. *King's Story.* 192.
         l.15   Eton. Balfour to Princess of Wales. 17 Dec. 1904. BM 49686.
         l.16   Babies. Airlie. 113.
         l.20   Ill treatment. Windsor. 7. Wheeler-Bennett 17.
         l.29   Father and King. Pope-Hennessy. 391.
         l.39   Misguided. Princess of Wales to Esher. 5 March 1908. E 6/7.
p. 59.   l.7   Good judgment. Churchill. *Derby.* 157–58.
         l.13   Unprovoked. Wheeler-Bennett. 25.
         l.24   Mr Hansell. Windsor. *King's Story.* 56–57.
         l.34   The Navy. *Ibid.*
p. 60.   l.1   Bad boys. Queen Victoria to Dalton. 15 Feb. 1877. Nicolson.
              14.
         l.12   Bottom. Wheeler-Bennett. 47.
         l.26   William iv. Esher. 23 April 1908. E.
         l.40   Heartily sick. Queen to Prince Henry. 15 Nov. 1912.
              Imperial War Museum.
p. 61.   l.2   Same place. Wheeler-Bennett. 107.
         l.29   Curzon speech. 20 July 1904. Rose. *Superior Person.* 202.
p. 62.   l.14   Sail for Europe. Edward vii to Curzon. 28 Sept. 1905. C.
         l.20   Slippers. Minto. *India, Minto and Morley.* 11–12.
         l.22   Artillery. Gilbert. *Servant of India.* 29.
         l.34   Cleaned or overhauled. Lady Minto. Journal. 29 Dec. 1905.
         l.41   Unhinged. Edward vii to Prince of Wales. 26 Jan. 1906.
              RA.
p. 63.   l.3   Jumping hedges. Minto. 48.
         l.9   Misrepresented. Prince of Wales to Edward vii. 8 Jan. 1906.
              RA.
         l.11   Prejudice. Dighton Probyn to Birdwood. 16 March 1906.
              Birdwood Papers.
         l.22   Luggage. Lady Minto. Journal. 28–29 Dec. 1905.
         l.39   Dining room. Minto. 23–30.
p. 64.   l.7   Lady Halsbury. Lady Minto. Journal. 31 Dec. 1905.
         l.14   Railways and sport. Gilbert. *Servant of India.* 32.
         l.23   Not my words. Gore. 202.
         l.27   Extravagance. *Op. cit.* 198.
         l.36   Kinds of people. Fingall. *Seventy Years Young.* 302–03.

p. 65.   l.7   Conquered people. Queen Victoria to Salisbury. 27 May
                 1898. Rose. *Superior Person*. 327.

         l.13   Insults to Indians. Lee. I. 399.

         l.22   Inferiors. Prince of Wales. Notes on India. 1906. RA.

         l.39   Native officers. *Ibid*.

p. 66. l.10   Trust them. Prince of Wales to Esher. 12 April 1907.
                 E 10/30.

         l.24   Death with impunity. Curzon to Knollys. 14 Dec. 1902.
                 Rose. 344.

         l.32   Schoolchildren. Curzon to Alfred Lyttelton. 29 Aug. 1900.
                 Op. cit. 345.

         l.41   Monsters and tyrants. Prince of Wales. Notes on India.
                 1906. RA.

p. 67.   l.8   Lawrence's denial. Gore. 207.

         l.19   The *Times*. 18 May 1906.

         l.24   Years of India. Gilbert. *Servant of India*. 31–32.

         l.30   Vanish from sight. Princess of Wales's Diary. 19 March
                 1906. Pope-Hennessy. 399.

         l.31   Reading aloud. *Op. cit.* 399.

p. 68.   l.5   Princely language. Gilbert. *Op. cit.* 41.

         l.12   Renegade. Gore. 360.

         l.31   Terrible affair. Diary. 31 May 1906. RA.

p. 69.   l.5   Veterinary surgeon. Arthur Hardinge. *Diplomatist in Europe*.
                 218–219.

         l.13   Very modern day. Pope-Hennessy. 408.

         l.20   Marriage contract. Private information.

         l.30   Well as possible. Monkswell. *Victorian Diarist*. 109.

         l.38   Really clever. Esher. 9 May 1909. II. 387.

p. 70.   l.1   Frayed nerves. *Ibid*. 28 Sept. 1908. II. 346.

         l.5   Over-nervous. Hussey. *Lutyens*. 177.

         l.8   Doomed. Esher. 1 May 1908. II. 307.

         l.21   Charnel house. Rose. 7.

         l.33   Against it. Prince of Wales to Bigge. 15 Aug. 1905. RA.

         l.40   Resign. RA and BM 49686.

p. 71.   l.2   Brassey resigns. Curzon. *Walmer Castle*. 287.

         l.14   Instantly challenged. Dilks. *Curzon in India*. 249.

         l.26   Mischief. Esher. Journal. 23 April 1908 and 15 June
                 1914. E.

         l.29   Lloyd George. Hobhouse. Diary. 15 May 1910. David. 91.

         l.36   New arrangements. Marder. I. 272.

p. 72.   l.7   Disappointed. *Op. cit.* I. 366.

         l.14   Coal dust. Diary. 1 Aug. 1908. Gore. 225.

p. 72.   l.16   Finest steamer. Prince of Wales to Fisher. 5 Aug. 1908.
Marder. II. 187.

l.22   Boast. Fisher to F. Ponsonby. 4 May 1909. *Op. cit.* II. 248.

l.25   Dunghill. W. S. Churchill. *World Crisis.* I. 73.

p. 73.   l.4   Your only Love. Lang. *My Darling Daisy.* 26–27.

l.11   Cut at Ascot. St. Aubyn. *Edward VII.* 187–190.

l.19   Bacon's reports. Churchill. *Op. cit.* 76.

l.23   Nearly ruined. Beresford to Sturdee. 28 Oct. 1909. Bennett.
Charlie B. 307.

l.30   Selling me. Fisher to Esher. 7 July 1909. Marder. II. 255–
256.

EARLY REIGN

p. 74.   l.7   Heavy task. Diary. 6 May 1910. Nicolson 105.

p. 75.   l.4   King's last days. Lee. II. 710–18.

l.9   Royal Standard. Windsor. *King's Story.* 70.

l.14   The King lives. Lee. II. 8.

p. 76.   l.3   More ceremonious. Queen to Grand Duchess. 15 May 1910.
Pope-Hennessy. 421.

l.9   Suffused with tears. Morgan. *Lloyd George Family Letters.*
152.

l.12   Underclothes. Keppel. *Edwardian Daughter.* 53.

l.13   Black bow. Warrender. *My First Sixty Years.* 79.

l.15   Bradenham hams. *Ibid.*

l.18   Retired prematurely. Private information.

l.27   Mere show. Schomberg McDonnell. Diary. 6–20 May 1910.
Antrim Papers.

l.37   Violent change. *Ibid.*

l.39   Bills. Hobhouse. 30 Oct. 1910. David. 97.

p. 77.   l.1   Dog. FitzRoy. 20 June 1910. II. 414.

l.3   Unpacking. Riddell. 149.

l.13   Particular duty. Arthur. *King George V.* 210–12.

l.22   Hard on me. McDonnell. Diary. 19 May 1910. Antrim
Papers.

l.32   Inferior place. Mensdorff to Aehrenthal. 10 June 1910. M.
PA VIII/46.

l.36   Pichon's complaint. Grey to Althorp. 21 and 27 May 1910.
F.O. 800/99. PRO.

p. 78.   l.2   Coachman's colours. Theodore Roosevelt. *Letters.* VII. 412.

l.12   Received last. Ormathwaite. *When I was at Court.* 185.

l.24   Weight. Minto. 25–26.

p. 78.　l.25　Seven pounds. Visitors' Book. Mar Lodge.

　　　　l.27　Too tight. Diary. 22 Feb. 1930. RA.

　　　　l.37　Your fault. Wheeler-Bennett. 29.

p. 79.　l.4　Two coalminers. Lockhart. 217.

　　　　l.16　Rare occurrence. Lincolnshire. 14 Feb. 1912. L.

　　　　l.17　Shy nod. St. Aubyn. *Edward VII.* 298.

　　　　l.19　Exhausted. Asquith. 27 Feb. 1914. Jenkins. 269.

　　　　l.24　Looking glass. Gore. 391.

　　　　l.28　Versailles. Queen Mother to author. 21 July 1976.

　　　　l.39　Flannel suit. A. Clark. *Good Innings.* 98.

p. 80.　l.15　Homburg hat. Windsor. *Family Album.* 58–60.

　　　　l.31　No escape. Airlie. 128.

　　　　l.33　Long earrings. Queen Mother to author. 24 April 1979.

　　　　l.39　Next year's fashions. F. Ponsonby to Hardinge. 28 April
　　　　　　　1914. H.

p. 81.　l.4　Awake at five. Esher. 16 May 1910. III. 3.

　　　　l.6　Melancholy. Mensdorff to Aehrenthal. 17 March 1910. PA/
　　　　　　　VIII/144. M.

　　　　l.13　Prophecy. Esher. 28 July 1902. I. 345.

　　　　l.21　Decrepitude. Esher. *Girlhood of Queen Victoria.* II. 80–81.

　　　　l.35　Light Moselle. Minto. Diary. 18 March 1906.

p. 82.　l.2　Drinker King. Mensdorff to Aehrenthal. 2 Sept. 1910. PA
　　　　　　　VIII/146. M.

　　　　l.7　Steady hand. Private information.

　　　　l.16　Wife in Plymouth. Duke of York to Knollys. 25 April 1893.
　　　　　　　Knollys Papers.

p. 85.　l.21　Three children. Pope-Hennessy. 428.

　　　　l.28　Pay the bill. House of Commons. 28 June 1894.

　　　　l.32　No insouciance. Mensdorff to Aehrenthal. 17 March 1910.
　　　　　　　M.

p. 83.　l.8　Anglican Church. Mylius. 'Sanctified Bigamy'.

　　　　l.21　Prosecution. Hyde. *Reading.* 93–94.

　　　　l.25　Source of vexation. 18 Dec. 1910. CV. II.2.1219.

　　　　l.36　Sentence of the Court. 28 Dec. 1910. CV. II.2.1225.

p. 84.　l.7　Contempt. 24 Jan. 1911. CV. II.2.1234.

　　　　l.39　Falsity of the lie. John Simon. Diary. 3 Feb. 1911. Simon
　　　　　　　Papers.

p. 85.　l.1　Abominable libel. 1 Feb. 1911. CV. II.2.1236–37.

　　　　l.26　Remember his words. Isaacs to Stamfordham. 17 Nov. 1913.
　　　　　　　Hyde. 164.

　　　　l.31　Charming letter. Simon to King. 2 Jan. 1913. Knollys
　　　　　　　Papers.

p. 85.   l.39   The King's wife. 15 Feb. 1911. CV. II.2.1238.
p. 86.   l.7   Ball at Portsmouth. Mylins. *Morganatic Marriage.* 6.
       l.24   North America. *Ibid.* 7.
       l.33   Black Watch. Diary. June 1890. RA.
       l.41   Very pessimistic. Edel. *Henry James.* 87.
p. 87.   l.2   Cut out. *Ibid.* 296 and 565.
       l.12   Restaurant keeper. Private information.
       l.15   Respectable. To Lady Wigram. W.
       l.17   Luncheon. Lincolnshire. 20 Dec. 1912. L.
       l.20   A little far. Windsor. *King's Story.* 87.
       l.32   Palm without dust. Cory. *Letters and Journals.* 17 Nov. 1862.
           79.
p. 88.   l.25   Unofficial adviser. Midleton. *Records and Reactions.* 149.
       l.30   Nuisance. Lincolnshire. 11 Dec. 1905. L.
       l.32   Generally succeeds. Stamfordham to Bonham Carter. 27
           Oct. 1915. A.4.
       l.35   Snubbed by Grey. St. Aubyn. *Edward VII.* 376–77.
p. 89.   l.3   Kissed his hand. Esher. 5 March 1906. II. 149.
       l.7   Say the same. Esher. 7 Nov. 1913. E.
       l.22   Parlourmaids. Mensdorff. Diary. 18 March 1907. M.
       l.25   Horse and cow. Edward VII to Hardinge. 28 March 1909.
           Magnus. 409.
       l.26   Impotent. Vansittart. *Mist Procession.* 88.
p. 90.   l.4   Whipped hound. Hardinge to Goshen. 12 Oct. 1908. H.
       l.6   Damaged relations. Bridge. 145.
       l.13   Special place. Mensdorff to Aehrenthal. 2 Sept. 1910. M.
       l.14   Whispers. *Ibid.*, 17 March, 10 June and 2 Sept. 1910. M.
       l.28   Shocked courtiers. Esher. 21–24 Aug. 1910. III. 15–17.
       l.37   Well brought up. Mensdorff. Diary. 27 Aug. 1910. M.
p. 91.   l.7   Balmoral smell. Princess Alice. 77.
       l.9   Never warm. Mallet. 7.
       l.15   Really dangerous. Queen Victoria. *Letters.* 15 Sept. 1896.
           III. 75.
       l.19   Grumpy. Queen to Esher. 30 Sept. 1912. E. 6/7.
       l.23   Ugliest room. A. Ponsonby. 150.
       l.32   Scots accent. Lutyens. *Lytton.* 36.
       l.34   Prince of Wales to Duke of York. 13 Sept. 1894. RA.
       l.36   Swiss valet. F. Ponsonby. 150.
p. 92.   l.14   Ordinary people. Lloyd George to Margaret Lloyd George.
           8 Sept. 1910. Morgan. 153.
       l.22   Time to stop. *Ibid.* 10 Sept. 1910.
       l.26   Housemaid's knee. Owen. *Tempestuous Journey.* 195.

p. 92. l.35 Very well paid. Lloyd George to Margaret Lloyd George.
16 Sept. 1911. Morgan. 158–59.

p. 93. l.3 Country gentleman. Hobhouse. 25 Sept. 1910. David. 96.

l.13 Not a butcher. Churchill to Clementine Churchill. 20 Sept.
1913. CV. II.3.1780–81.

l.18 Victorian tartans. Churchill to Stamfordham. 20 Sept. 1927.
CV. V.I.1053.

l.30 Diamond circlet. Battiscombe. 274.

l.36 Royal Standard. Mensdorff to Aehrenthal. 10 June 1910. M.

p. 94. l.2 King George. Cynthia Colville. *Crowded Life.* 111.

l.8 Legacy. Hobhouse. 30 June 1910. David. 94.

l.13 Not *gemütlich*. Queen to Prince of Wales. 10 Dec. 1910. Pope-
Hennessy. 433.

l.27 Young bachelor. Essay to John Russell. Harris. *Buckingham
Palace.* 7.

l.34 Orchids. Airlie. 106.

l.41 King's misery. F. Ponsonby to Ria Ponsonby. 11 Dec. 1913.
Ponsonby Papers.

p. 95. l.4 Kensington Palace. Esher. *Girlhood of Queen Victoria.* I. 37.

l.7 Barometer. Windsor. *King's Story.* 6.

l.15 Measured mile. Haig. Diary. 11 Feb. 1918. Blake. 284–285.

l.17 Alarm clock. Windsor. *Op. cit.* 26.

l.25 To bed. Gore. 278.

l.37 Letters to George iv. Esher. 26 Jan. 1912. III. 117.

l.41 Saleroom. Sotheby's. 27 Oct. 1959. They were sold to the
Duke of Devonshire.

p. 96. l.3 Early nights. Esher. 16 April 1911. III. 48.

l.6 Commanding personality. Pope-Hennessy. *Crewe.* 81.

l.8 Bored and weary. Mensdorff. 31 Jan. 1914. M.

l.21 *Ballade tragique.* Behrman. *Conversation with Max.* 83.

l.32 Crabbing. Lincolnshire. 3 Nov. 1912. L.

l.36 Only one wife. Mensdorff to Aehrenthal. 2 Sept. 1910. M.

p. 97. l.14 Compromising letters. Lang. *My Darling Daisy. passim.*

l.31 Upper Norwood. Nicolson. 51.

l.39 Many a hint. Gould Lee. 164–65.

l.41 Curate and wife. Lockhart. *Lang.* 143.

p. 98. l.17 Doll's house. Airlie. 111.

l.25 Smell of cooking. Princess Alice to author. 21 Sept. 1976.

l.28 In the trees. Gore. 113.

l.37 Cust interferes. F. Ponsonby. 279.

p. 99. l.9 Obliged to receive. Carlingford. Journal. 12 March 1885.
Cooke and Vincent. 79.

p. 99. l.18 Perfection. Windsor. *Op. cit.* 183.

 l.36 Forty cartridges. 18 Dec. 1913. Gore. 230.

p. 100. l.2 Terrific slaughter. Lincolnshire. 4 Dec. 1912. L.

 l.5 Slow flight. Stamfordham to Wigram. 7 Dec. 1912. W.

 l.8 Filled with tears. Duchess of Beaufort to author.
   26 June 1976.

 l.9 £50,000 a year. Lincolnshire. 29 Nov. 1913. L.

 l.26 Finishes me off. Mensdorff. 10 Dec. 1911. M.

 l.38 Terrific scandal. Lincolnshire. 29 Nov. 1913. L.

 l.4 Never hesitated. Carington to Lincolnshire. 6 Dec. 1913. L.

p. 101. l.6 Everything fair. Masterman. 263.

 l.17 Just in time. Lincolnshire. 26 Feb. 1914. L.

 l.23 Don't encourage them. Private information.

 l.25 Terrible ordeal. King to Queen Alexandra. 6 Feb. 1911. RA.

 l.38 Confidence. Queen to Esher. 7 Feb. 1911. E6/7.

p. 102. l.3 Short one. Diary. 7 Feb. 1928. RA.

 l.4 Inordinate length. Roskill. *Hankey.* II. 132.

 l.16 Schoolgirl letter. Stamfordham to Lloyd George. 11 Feb.
   1920. L.G. F/29/4/4.

 l.19 Bothering. A. Ponsonby. 306.

 l.24 Pleasing pattern. Lord Mountbatten to author. 9 June 1976.

 l.27 Patent leather. Diary. 24 May 1913. RA.

 l.31 Peer's robes. Lincolnshire. 10 March 1913. L.

 l.34 Humble apology. *Ibid.* 7 Feb. 1922. L.

p. 103. l.10 English gentleman. Master of Elibank to Mrs Murray.
   22 June 1911. Murray. 81–82.

 l.17 Beloved Papa. Diary. 22 June 1911. Nicolson. 147.

 l.37 Legitimate pride. Murray. *Op. cit.* 81–82.

 l.41 Eighteen years. Diary. 22 June 1911. Nicolson. 147.

p. 104. l.4 Bath accepted. Pope-Hennessy. 438.

 l.11 F. Ponsonby to Mensdorff. 24 April 1911. M.

 l.21 Curzon. Murray. *Op. cit.* 81–82.

 l.27 Haul of debris. Grantley. *Silver Spoon.* 48.

 l.33 Coronation of 1838. Esher. *Girlhood of Queen Victoria.*
   28 June 1838. I. 361.

 l.41 Cabinet years. Hobhouse. 6 March 1913. David 133.

p. 105. l.1 Over 60 years. Diary. 10 March 1913. RA.

 l.4 Bad headache. Lincolnshire. 9 Dec. 1924. L.

 l.6 No such need. MacDonald. Diary. 19 Nov. 1935. MD.

CONSTITUTIONAL MONARCH

p. 106. l.2   Here always. Lady Desborough. Memoir of King George v.
                Desborough Papers.

l.4   Demanding attention. *Ibid.*

l.7   State papers. Woods. 1924. WD.

l.11   Breakfast. Sir Samuel Hoare. TM. RF. 1.

l.19   All prisoners. Bagehot. *English Constitution.* 283–84.

p. 107. l.2   Inaugurated reign. Churchill to King. 23 Oct. 1911. CV.
                II.2.1292–93.

l.11   New Year. Esher. *passim.*

l.14   Constant genuflexion. Laski. *Parlimentary Government in
        England.* 395.

l.27   John Burns. Masterman. 68.

l.29   Monarchy. Bagehot. 44.

p. 108. l.18   Three prerogatives. *Ibid.* 67.

l.30   Men of business. *Ibid.* 75.

l.39   House of Commons. Gladstone. Diaries. 13 July 1846. III.
        559.

p. 109. l.2   Increasing burden. Cecil. *Salisbury.* III. 180.

l.8   Minister's hand. Esher to Knollys. 28 Aug. 1905. II. 104–05.

l.15   Parliamentary gossip. 11 Jan. 1881. Queen Victoria. *Letters.*
        Second series. III. 181.

l.25   No elaboration. Balfour to Sandars. 27 Feb. 1904. BM.

l.27   Insultingly casual. Knollys to Esher. 29 Nov. 1907. II.265.

l.36   An idiot. Rhodes James. *Victor Cazalet.* 255.

l.41   All the talking. Clifford. *Proconsul.* 167.

p. 110. l.2   Fluid and voluble. Asquith to Churchill. 12 Sept. 1913. CV.
                II.3.1399.

l.6   Race of life. Lincolnshire. 29 Sept. 1911. L.

l.9   Lonely position. King to Rosebery. 4 June 1911. R 10123.

l.19   Oldest friend. King to Knollys. 17 March 1913. St. Aubyn.
        Edward VII. 435.

l.25   Prefer both. Knollys to Rosebery. 3 Feb. 1905. R 10040.

l.37   Through the Press. Knollys to Asquith. 9 Nov. 1911. A. 3.

p. 111. l.15   Social scale. Churchill to King. 10 Feb. 1911. CV. II.2.
                1037.

l.26   Social ladder. Knollys to Vaughan Nash (Asquith's private
        secretary). 11 Feb. 1911. *Ibid.*

l.37   Deeply regrets. Churchill to King. 13 Feb. 1911. *Ibid.* 1039.

p. 112. l.5   In the future. Knollys to Churchill. 14 Feb. 1911. *Ibid.*
                1040.

p. 112. l.19 Aristocracy. Queen Victoria to Prince of Wales. 7 Jan. 1868.
Magnus 73–74.

l.25 King's verdict. Edward VII to Prince of Wales. 19 March
1906. RA.

p. 113. l.17 This great nation. *The Times*. 16 Jan. 1906.

l.28 House of Commons. 26 June 1907.

l.30 Sow's ear. Edward VII to Prince of Wales. 26 Nov. 1906.
RA.

p. 114. l.15 Single–chamber rule. House of Lords. 24 Nov. 1909.

p. 115. l.23 Redmond. Diary. 18 May 1910. Nicolson. 131.

l.38 Agree to them. Knollys to Nash. 28 May 1910. A.2.

l.41 Submitted. *Ibid.* 4 June 1910. A.2.

l.10 Sensible people. *Ibid.* 18 June 1910. A.2.

l.33 No guarantees. Diary. 11 Nov. 1910. Nicolson. 133.

l.36 This Parliament. Bigge. Minute. 11 Nov. 1910. *Ibid.*

l.41 Next Parliament. Knollys to King. 14 Nov. 1910. *Op. cit.*
134.

p. 117. l.2 Conference. Asquith. Minute. 11 Nov. 1910. *Ibid.*

l.12 Present Parliament. Bigge to Nash. 15 Nov. 1910. *Ibid.*

l.34 Occasion should arise. Cabinet Minute. 15 Nov. 1910. *Op.
cit.* 136.

p. 118. l.2 Expected to grant. House of Commons. 21 Feb. 1910.

l.14 Carried into law. House of Commons. 14 April 1910.

l.22 Parliament Bill. Fraser. *Esher*. 217.

p. 119. l.2 Abusing the Government. A.C. Benson. Diary. 10 Nov.
1908. Magdalene College, Cambridge.

l.4 Official word. Esher. 23 April 1908. Hobhouse. 15 May 1910.

l.4 Vienna. Mensdorff to Aehrenthal. 2 Sept. 1910. M.

l.6 Liberal victory. Prince of Wales to Esher. 25 Dec. 1909.
E 6/5.

l.32 P.M. and Crewe. Knollys to King. 15 Nov. 1910. Nicolson.
137.

p. 120. l.6 Prime Minister. Elibank to Knollys. 14 Nov. 1910. Murray.
60–61.

l.14 Urge you strongly. Knollys to King. 15 Nov. 1910. Nicolson.
137.

l.24 Incautious words. Bigge. Memorandum. 15 Nov. 1910. *Ibid.*

l.37 Do what is right. Bigge to Elibank. 15 Nov. 1910. Murray.
61–62.

p. 121. l.7 Trust and pray. Diary. 16 Nov. 1910. Nicolson. 138.

l.23 Behaved disgracefully. Derby's diary. 20 August 1911.
Churchill. *Derby*. 126–27.

p. 122. l.4   Present crisis. Bigge. Memorandum. 18 Nov. 1910.

l.42   Own prompting. Undated note in Nicolson papers.

p. 123. l.10   Creation of Peers. Nicolson. 130.

l.21   Belated discovery. *Ibid.*

l.30   Royal Archives. GV K/2552/88. 9 Oct. 1910. Le May. *The Victorian Constitution.* 201.

p. 124. l.23   Responsible Ministers. Esher. 19 Nov. 1910. III. 34.

l.35   Conceal things. *Ibid.* 14 Oct. 1911. III. 65.

l.36   Childish. Bigge. Memorandum. 18 Nov. 1910. Nicolson. 138.

p. 125. l.3   Position of the King. Jenkins. *Mr Balfour's Poodle.* 124.

l.20   Ill treatment. Wigram. Memorandum. 9 Nov. 1931. RA.

l.21   Hoarse from talking. Esher. 4 Feb. 1911. E.

l.33   Reluctant to advise. Newton. *Lansdowne.* 410.

p. 126. l.14   That Body. Knollys to Asquith. 25 March 1911. A.2.

l.24   Plays at No. 10. *The Times.* 1 July 1911.

p. 127. l.2   Three persons. Jones. *Diary with Letters.* xvii.

l.8   Other people's wives. Magnus. *Kitchener.* 289.

l.11   Inviolably secret. Knollys to King. 15 Nov. 1910. RA.

l.15   Officially. Esher to King. 5 July 1911. III. 54.

l.25   Essentially theatrical. Young. *Balfour.* 310.

l.35   Two days' time. Asquith to King. 22 July 1911. Nicolson. 152-53.

p. 128. l.7   Intend to vote. Knollys to Asquith. 23 July 1911. *Ibid.*

l.40   J.B. Atlay. *D.N.B.* 1901-11.

p. 129. l.13   Baron de Forest. Derby. Diary. 20 August. 1911. Churchill. *Op. cit.* 127.

l.28   Hot-headed people. Pope-Hennessy. *Crewe.* 124.

p. 130. l.8   King's assent. House of Lords. 10 August 1911.

l.42   Bed at 12. Diary. 10 August 1911. RA.

p. 131. l.20   Footman's mistake. Godfrey-Faussett. Diary. 10 August 1911. GF.

l.35   Situation saved. Stamfordham to Curzon. 11 August 1911. C.

p. 132. l.5   Own idea. Diary. 11 Jan. 1911. RA.

l.13   Home-staying Ministers. Esher. 26 Nov. 1910. III. 37.

l.27   Queen not told. Hardinge. *Indian Years.* 45 and 49.

l.31   Think we ought. Hobhouse. 11 Nov. 1911. David. 107.

l.41   The Crown. Hardinge to Bigge. 4 April 1911. H. 104.

p. 133. l.25   Higher ranks. Lincolnshire. 18 Oct. 1911. L.

l.26   My woman Shaftesbury. Sir Michael Duff to author. 16 Sept. 1976.

p. 133. l.31 Court functions. Rosebery to King. 10 Sept. 1911. R 10123.

l.42 Queen's reading. Pope-Hennessy. 453.

p. 134. l.7 Governor-General. Hardinge. *Indian Years.* 45.

l.9 Crewe's modesty. Pope-Hennessy. *Crewe.* 103.

l.13 Rats killed. Hardinge to Stamfordham. 14 Sept. 1911. H.
104.

l.16 Good stout roof. Bigge to Hardinge. 24 Feb. 1911. *Ibid.*

l.20 Duchess of Devonshire. Godfrey-Faussett. Diary.
11 Dec. 1911. GF.

l.31 Eager faces. Clive Wigram to Herbert Wigram. 7 Dec. 1911.
W.

p. 135. l.14 No criticism. *The Times.* 13 Dec. 1911.

l.21 Quite tired. Diary. 12 Dec. 1911. Gore. 264-65.

l.30 Good faith. *Ibid.* 21 Oct. 1914. RA.

l.36 Neapl. King to Hardinge. 10 Feb. 1911. H. 104.

l.40 Almost destroyed. Pope-Hennessy. *Crewe.* 88.

l.42 No wallowing. Bigge to Hardinge. 24 Feb. 1911. H. 104.

p. 136. l.3 Suitable sport. Wentworth Day. *King George V as a
Sportsman.* 89.

l.6 Hard to beat. Diary. 16 Dec. 1911 *et seq.* RA.

l.8 No escape. Durham to Rosebery. 19 Dec. 1911. R 10123.

l.21 Neglected generally. Godfrey-Fausett. Diary. 2 Jan. 1912.
GF.

l.25 Getting rid of us. Hardinge. *Indian Years.* 61.

l.36 Indian Empire. Hardinge to King. 17 Dec. 1912. H. 105.

p. 137. l.2 Umbrella. Diary. 22 Feb. 1912. RA.

l.31 Very optimistic. Diary. 7 Feb. 1913. RA.

p. 138. l.31 Worst five minutes. Chamberlain. *Politics from Inside.*
486-87.

l.41 Behind the Throne. Esher to Balfour. 13 Sept. 1913. III.
135.

p. 139. l.1 Not opposed. Crewe to Asquith. (   ) Oct. 1913. A. 38.

l.3 Sleepless nights. Esher. 10 April 1914. III. 162.

l.15 Intolerable. Undated Memorandum. RA. K.2553(5) 98.

l.19 Hissed in the streets. Hobhouse. 17 Oct. 1913.

l.20 Damned impertinent. Curzon to Bonar Law. 10 Dec. 1913.
Blake. *Law.* 167.

l.27 Monitory. Stamfordham to Harcourt. 14 Nov. 1913. RA.

l.36 Seeking a way. Haldane to Mrs Haldane (   ) Dec. 1913.
Sommer. 285.

p. 140. l.3 Cut off his head. Gwynn. *Spring-Rice.* II. 188.

l.13 End of monarchy. Esher. 10 Sept. 1913. III. 126-131.

p. 140. l.28 Silver inkstand. Diary. 17 March 1913. RA.

l.35 Interview with Knollys. Diary. 13 Feb. 1913. RA.

p. 141. l.3 Public nature. Knollys to Asquith. 16 Feb. 1913. Copy in Crewe Papers. C. 58.

l.19 His own reward. Stamfordham to Knollys. 15 Nov. 1912. Knollys Papers.

l.23 The Crown. Asquith to Knollys. 19 July 1912. *Ibid.*

l.26 Mercy of God. Lincolnshire. 24 July 1911. L.

l.30 Clipped wings. Hobhouse. 8 August, 1913.

l.35 Studied coldness. Sandars to Balfour. 10 Aug. 1911. BM.

p. 142. l.7 With King's knowledge. Knollys to Balfour. 8 Sept. 1911. BM.

l.7 Second time. Esher. Memorandum. 10 Jan. 1911. III. 40–44.

l.25 Carrying the country. Balfour to Stamfordham. 1 Aug. 1911. Nicolson. 149.

l.38 Concrete problem. *Ibid.* 9 Aug. 1911.

p. 143. l.7 Calumnious charge. Knollys to Esher. 11 Aug. 1911. E 10/52.

l.10 Meet as strangers. Knollys to Balfour. 8 Sept. 1911. BM.

l.14 Him I will not. Churchill. *Derby.* 119.

l.19 Told of quarrell. Sandars to Derby. 3 Aug. 1911. *Op. cit.* 120.

l.31 Rosebery's help. King to Rosebery. 17 March 1913. R 10124.

p. 144. l.13 Grateful old friend. King to Knollys. 17 March 1913. St. Aubyn. *Edward VII.* 435.

l.21 Instructed soldiers. Asquith to Venetia Stanley. 15 Feb. 1915. 432.

l.36 Second eleven. Wigram to Duke of Connaught. 14 March 1932. RA.

l.40 Indeed lucky. King to Stamfordham. 25 April 1912. RA.

p. 145. l.4 Wigram's achievement. Stamfordham to Mrs Herbert Wigram. 29 Jan. 1912. W.

l.11 Aldershot. F. Ponsonby to Hardinge. 2 Aug. 1915. H.

l.20 It is absurd. Esher. 19 Aug. 1892. I. 60.

l.22 Miseries of etiquette. Mary Ponsonby. 19.

p. 146. l.3 The Munshi. F. Ponsonby. 13–15. Longford 535–37.

l.7 Husband's secrets. F. Ponsonby. 58.

l.11 Identical medals. A. Ponsonby. 391.

l.23 Offer withdrawn. F. Ponsonby. 283–85.

l.26 The Wash. *Ibid.* xi.

p. 146. 1.28 Best of them. Esher. 11 Oct. 1903. II. 26.

1.34 Unavoidable critic. F. Ponsonby. 279.

p. 147. 1.13 Kowtow to the King. F. Ponsonby to Ria Ponsonby. 4 April 1913. Ponsonby Papers.

1.42 His misgivings. Stamfordham. Minute of Asquith's audience. 11 Aug. 1913. RA.

p. 148. 1.12 Devolution. King's memorandum. 11 Aug. 1913. Nicolson. 223–24.

1.19 Royal Eye. Asquith to Churchill. 16 Sept. 1913. CV. II. 3. 1777.

1.22 Cordial and intimate. Churchill to Clementine Churchill. 20 Sept. 1913. *Ibid.* 1781.

1.23 Friendly and moderate. Churchill to Asquith. 21 Sept. 1913. A.38.

1.42 Contending factions. Asquith. Memorandum. 11 Sept. 1913. Jenkins. 543–45.

p. 149. 1.16 Chasm of principle. *Ibid.* 545–49.

p. 150. 1.3 Civilised world. King to Asquith. 22 Sept. 1913. Nicolson. 225–29.

1.8 Do their duty. Asquith to King. 1 Oct. 1913. A.38.

1.16 Danger to the State. Asquith to Bonar Law. 8 Oct. 1913. A. 38.

1.27 May yet be found. Stamfordham to Bonar Law. 20 Jan. 1914. Blake. *Bonar Law.* 168.

1.36 Few months earlier. Bonar Law to Stamfordham. 26 Jan. 1914. *Ibid.* 169.

1.38 Time and circumstance. Stamfordham to Bonar Law. 2 Feb. 1914. *Ibid.* 170.

p. 151. 1.8 Impossible to replace. Esher. 21 Jan. 1914. III. 155.

1.10 Tactful mediation. Minute of Asquith's audience with the King. 19 March 1914. Nicolson. 236–37.

1.14 See the King. Fitzroy. 16 Oct. 1913. II. 524.

1.15 Highest quarters. Asquith to V. Stanley. 27 Jan. 1914. 42–43.

1.18 Exposed. *Ibid.* 26 March 1914. 61.

1.26 The woman. Nicolson. *Diaries.* 29 July 1952. III. 226.

1.32 Mangold-worsels. Curzon to Law. 10 Dec. 1913. Blake. 167.

1.37 Absurd complaint. Speech at Bedford. 11 Oct. 1913.

p. 152. 1.2 What bird. Lord Winterton to author. 9 Nov. 1961.

1.11 Royal train. C. Colville. 49.

1.16 Make matters worse. Mensdorff. Diary. 8 May 1914. M.

1.19 Granards. Lincolnshire. 22 June 1914. L.

p. 152. l.22 In the crowd. C. Colville. 50.

l.29 Keep on bothering. King to Stamfordham. 2 Jan. 1914. Nicolson. 233.

l.35 You may provide. King to Asquith. 22 Jan. 1914. A.39.

l.39 Ulster Unionists. *Ibid.* 4 March 1914.

p. 153. l.6 Generous eye. Stamfordham to Law. 25 Feb. 1914. RA. King to Law. 7 March 1914. RA.

l.9 Stay of execution. House of Commons. 9 March 1914.

l.18 To the proof. 14 March 1914.

l.22 Be remembered. Minute of Asquith's audience with the King. 19 March 1914. RA.

l.29 Glorious history. King to Asquith. 21 March 1914. Fergusson. *The Curragh Incident.* 132–33.

l.37 Not the monarch. Minute of Asquith's audience with the King. 5 Feb. 1914. RA.

p. 154. l.25 Excused such duties. Fergusson. 55.

l.40 From the sovereign. *Ibid.* 115.

p. 155. l.9 Injudicious and improper. *Ibid.* 200.

l.16 Might never arise. Asquith to King. 24 March 1914. *Ibid.* 163.

p. 156. l.8 Evil influences. Stamfordham to Asquith. 24 March 1914. *Ibid.* 172.

l.12 The footmen. Eden. *Facing the Dictators.* 51–52.

l.20 Make me responsible. Lincolnshire. 5 March 1914. L.

l.24 Solution not found. King to Asquith. 7 April 1914. RA.

l.26 Hysterical letter. Asquith to V. Stanley. 7 April 1914. 63.

l.37 My house. King to Asquith. 18 July 1914. Nicolson. 242.

p. 157. l.3 Despotic acts. Queen Victoria to King Leopold. 11 June 1844. *Letters.* First series. II. 14.

l.11 Finding a solution. Stamfordham to Lowther. 18 July 1914. RA.

l.21 Such a suggestion. Asquith to V. Stanley. 22 July 1914. 109.

l.28 Necessity of Home Rule. *Ibid.* 24 July 1914. 122.

l.36 Republicanism. Morris. *C.P. Trevelyan.* 97.

l.38 To be a toad. *Ibid.* 98.

p. 158. l.2 Badly treated. King to Godfrey-Faussett. 28 July 1914. GF.

l.11 Racing. King to Duke of Richmond. 26 July 1914. Goodwood Papers.

l.13 Floored him. Esher. 12 June 1912. III. 95.

l.21 Impartial spirit. Nicolson. 178.

p. 159. l.2 Cheap herrings. Fisher to Arnold White. 22 Oct. 1910. Marder. II. 342.

p. 159. l.4   Highest naval rank. Asquith to McKenna. 26 Dec. 1910.
              Ibid. 348.

        l.8   Board of Admiralty. McKenna to Asquith. 7 Jan. 1911. A.
              24.

        l.15 Lord Crewe. Fisher to Jellicoe. 9 May 1911. Marder. II.
              369.

        l.25 Exact contrary. Fisher to Esher. 20 Oct. 1911. *Ibid.* II. 395.

        l.27 Royal Pimps. Fisher to Churchill. 2 Nov. 1911. CV II.2.
              1319.

p. 160. l.10 Filled up. Churchill to Clementine Churchill. 12 May 1912.
              CV II.3.1551.

        l.16 Naval Strategist. Prince Louis to Churchill. 1 July 1912.
              Ibid. 1584.

        l.21 No place. Churchill to King and King to Churchill. 27 Nov.
              1911. *Ibid.* 1345.

        l.23 Once more refused. Churchill to King. 28 Oct. 1912. King to
              Churchill. 29 Oct. 1912. *Ibid.* 1664.

        l.34 Its greatest men. Churchill to Stamfordham. 1 Nov. 1912.
              Ibid. 1665.

p. 161. l.8   Stir men's minds. Stamfordham to Churchill. 4 Nov. 1912.
              Ibid. 1666–67.

        l.17 This choice. Prince Louis to Churchill. 6 Nov. 1912. *Ibid.*
              1669.

        l.28 Rhyming with it. F. Ponsonby to Churchill. 3 August 1913.
              Ibid. 1760.

        l.40 Closely associated. Stamfordham to Curzon. 20 August 1913.
              Ibid. 1763.

p. 162. l.3   Live on land. Riddell. 78.

        l.5   Every important ship. Churchill. *World crisis.* I. 92.

        l.11 We could bombard. Bonham Carter. *Winston Churchill.* 262.

        l.27 Still alive. Ludwig. *Kaiser Wilhelm II.* 394.

        l.32 Questions of policy. Newton. *Lansdowne.* 293.

p. 163. l.2   John Bull. Mensdorff to Aehrenthal. 17 March. 1910. M.

        l.13 Abdominable German. Sitwell. *Queen Mary.* 22.

        l.30 Without a King. Hobhouse. 16 Oct. 1912. David 123.

        l.40 Top of the list. Bertie. Memorandum. 17 Feb. 1912. F.O.
              800/179. PRO.

p. 164. l.1   Too much of the French. Bertie to Grey. 21 Feb. 1912. *Ibid.*

        l.5   Liars. Knollys to Rosebery. 15 Feb. 1900. R 10040.

        l.13 Without enthusiasm. Mensdorff. 24 April 1914. M.

        l.19 Perfect lucidity. Poincaré. *Memoirs.* 129–30. Au *service de la
              France.* 1926–27.

p. 164. l.22   Vive la reine. Saint-Aulaire. *Confession d'un vieux diplomate.* 542.

l.25   Now talks French. F. Ponsonby to Hardinge. 28 April. 1914. H.

l.42   Won't we rejoice. Princess of Wales to Prince George. 17 Oct. 1888. RA.

p. 165. l.4   Not concern him. Prince George to Princess of Wales. 22 July 1890. RA.

l.13   Withered arm. Gore. 135.

l.18   Late King's coffin. McDonnell. Diary. 19 May 1910. Antrim Papers.

l.20   Noisy merriment. Mensdorff to Aehrenthal. 10 June 1910. M.

l.25   Khyber Rifles. Bigge to Hardinge. 17 Feb. 1911. H.

l.35   All our ships. Mensdorff to Aehrenthal. 2 Sept. 1910. M.

l.39   Cousin of the King. Mensdorff. Diary. 21 Nov. 1931. M.

p. 166. l.5   No objection. Nicolson. 185.

l.16   Calculations. Lady Wigram. Diary. 1926. W.

l.33   Glued to the keyhole. *Ibid.*

l.37   Dogmatic trash. Bell. *Davidson.* 240.

p. 167. l.8   Visit of this sort. Ponsonby to Hardinge. 3 June 1913. H.

l.25   Austrian Embassy. Mensdorff. 2 July 1914. M.

l.30   Murdered in Ireland. H.A.L. Fisher. *History of Europe.* 1116.

p. 168. l.31   Dear Bertie's life. Diary. 25 July to 4 Aug. 1914. *passim.* RA.

THE GREAT WAR

p. 169. l.18   Smile on duty. Gore. 148.

l.22   Glum and dyspeptic. Joliffe. *Raymond Asquith.* 284.

p. 170. l.2   Propaganda. Airlie. 146.

l.23   Balkan question. Mensdorff to Berchtold. 10 Aug. 1914. M.

l.35   George and Mary. Mensdorff. Diary. 14 Aug. 1914. M.

p. 171. l.3   Match to fire. Harewood to Mensdorff. 14 Aug. 1914. *Bridge.* 422.

l.13   After dinner. Hobhouse. 27 Jan. 1915. David. 219–20.

l.35   About three days. Hough. *Louis and Victoria.* 300.

l.38   Blue-eyed German. Asquith to V. Stanley. 27 Oct. 1914. 287.

l.41   Board of Admiralty. Prince Louis to Churchill. 28 Oct. 1914. CV III.1.226.

p. 172. l.3   In the country. Diary. 29 Oct. 1914. Nicolson. 251.

p. 172. l.13 Abusive letters. Sandhurst. *From Day to Day.* 26 Oct. 1916.

l.16 Only natural. Haldane to Curzon. 28 May 1915. C.

l.19 German professor. Esher. 8 Dec. 1907. E.

l.21 Sinuosities. Fisher to Mrs McKenna. 14 Dec. 1911. Marder II. 421.

l.25 His joke. Haldane to Mrs Haldane. 5 June 1912. HL. 5988.

l.35 Internment. Stamfordham to Bonham Carter. 4 Feb. 1915. A.4.

l.37 Criminal prisons. Nicolson. 255.

l.42 Wild beast. King to Prince Henry. 7 Oct. 1914. Frankland. 35.

p. 173. l.12 Like gentlemen. Nicolson. 272.

l.17 His own flag. Esher. 6 Feb. 1915. III. 215.

l.25 Orders of chivalry. Stamfordham to Bonham Carter. 6 June 1915. A.4.

l.31. Our sacred Church. Queen Alexandra to King. 12 May 1915. RA.

l.33 Stormed the Chapel. Mensdorff. 19 Oct. 1924. M.

l.39 Nice distinction. Asquith to V. Stanley. 24 Oct. 1915. 285.

p. 174. l.1 Little German friend. Stevenson. Diary. 25 Jan. 1915. 25.

l.5 Not an alien. Nicolson. 308.

l.8 Top to toe. Queen to Grand Duchess Augusta. 25 June 1911. Pope-Hennessy. 442.

l.22 Stamfordham's suggestion. Nicolson. 309.

l.30 Ridicule. Rosebery to Stamfordham. 24 May 1917. RA.

l.37 Changed his name. Bocca. *Uneasy Heads.* 170.

p. 175. l.9 A Peer. Ponsonby to Ria Ponsonby. 18 June 1917. Ponsonby Papers.

l.23 Asked for dukedom. *Ibid.*

l.28 Deplored the changes. Mensdorff. 19 Oct. 1924. M.

l.38 Until Monday. Haig. Diaries. 19 Dec. 1915. Blake. 119.

p. 176. l.3 Seat of War. *Ibid.* 17 April 1916. 140.

l.7 Sixty-one volunteers. Sandhurst. 11 Sept. 1915. 38.

l.11 And maid. Westminster. *Grace and Favour.* 69.

l.17 White waistcoats. Bertie. Diary. 27 Oct. 1915. I. 256.

l.25 Public expense. *Ibid.* 9 July 1915. I. 195.

l.31 Folies Bergères. Rhodes James. *Davidson.* 75.

l.35 Department. Roskill. *Hankey.* I. 250.

l.38 Hour of the day. Gore. 306.

p. 177. l.1 Navy blue. Carnock. Diary. 25 Sept. 1916. PRO 30/81/16.

l.11 Food control. Smuts to King. 18 Oct. 1917. Smuts Papers. 18.

l.16 Spartan regime. Sandars. *Studies of Yesterday.* 80-81.

p. 177. l.21 Gluttony. F. Ponsonby. 329.

l.23 Neither in profusion. Sandhurst. 26 May 1915. 216.

l.25 Napking ring. Marchioness Curzon. Reminiscences. 111.

l.28 Silver urn. Esher. 26 July 1915. III. 256.

l.33 Desert. W. Fortescue. 202.

l.35 A sweet. N. Chamberlain to Ida Chamberlain. 22 April 1917. NC 18/1/110.

l.37 Meat or wine. Sandhurst. II. 143.

l.40 Peaches and pears. Bertie. 4 Oct. 1917. II. 195.

p. 178. l.7 Like whitebait. C. Asquith. Diary. 6 March 1918. 418.

l.11 Depressing effect. Arthur. *King George V*. 323.

l.19 German submarines. 28 Feb. 1915. Lloyd George. *War Memoirs*. I. 325.

l.26 Rich and poor. Stamfordham to Lloyd George. 30 March 1915. LG C/5/6/12.

l.28 Great bore. King to Duke of Connaught. 9 April 1915. RA.

l.30 Not agreeable. King to Hardinge. 14 May 1915. H. 105.

l.37 Waterson Tuesday. Rosebery to King. 7 April 1915. RA.

l.40 Hiccough. Haig. Diary. 30.

p. 179. l.3 No one spoke. Lady Desborough to Patrick. Shaw-Stewart. N. Mosley. *Grenfell*. 244-45.

l.7 Barley water. Chalmers. *Beatty*. 319.

l.10 Ginger beer. Haig. 12 Aug. 1916. Blake. 160.

l.14 Liqueurs. Webb. Diaries. 23 July 1915. I. 42.

l.17 Non-alcoholic. Princess Alice to author. 21 Sept. 1976.

l.21 Champagne. Windsor. *Family Album*. 54.

l.26 Look foolish. A. Clark. 157.

l.28 Carted. Private information.

l.34 Statistics. Gore. 292.

p. 180. l.4 Such is war. Diary. 5 April 1917 and 10 Aug. 1916. RA.

l.6 Rather worn penny. Gere and Sparrow. *Madan*. 66.

l.10 An Englishman. King to Duke of Connaught. 20 Aug. 1916. RA.

l.15 Indian wounded. King to Hardinge. 26 Nov. 1914. H.

l.19 Now you are right. HAL Fisher. Diary. 12 Feb. 1918. Fisher Papers.

l.22 Napoleon's Marshals. Wigram. War Diary. 5 Dec. 1914. W.

l.32 Chicken. Chandos. *Memoirs* 57-58.

p. 181. l.7 Came over backwards. Charteris. *At G.H.Q.* 29 Oct. 1915. 120.

l.13 For any bombs. F. Ponsonby. 325.

p. 181. 1.15 Feel perturbed. Haig. Diaries. 28 Oct. and 1 Nov. 1915. HG
3155.103.

   1.18 Conceal the truth. Watson. *Dawson of Penn.* 139.

   1.29 Splendid night's sleep. Haig. Diaries. 29 Oct., 30 Oct.,
1 Nov. 1915. H. 3155. 103.

p. 182. 1.3 So much pain. King to Duke of Connaught. 29 Nov. 1915. RA.

   1.7 Sometimes pain. Watson. 139.

   1.11 Little stimulant. Nicolson. 262.

   1.14 Nightly telegram. Queen to Wigram. 16 Sept. 1917. W.

   1.16 First lady. Haig. Diaries. 5 July 1917. H.3155. 115.

   1.22 Agincourt. 8 July 1917. Pope-Henessy. 507.

   1.24 Very historical. Prince of Wales to Lady Coke. 7 July 1917.
Combe Papers.

   1.40 Things in general. Asquith to V. Stanley. 17 March 1915.

p. 183. 1.2 Shells. 4 August 1916. Morgan. 183.

   1.6 Race horses. Neville Chamberlain to Ida Chamberlain.
22 April 1917. N.C. 18/1/110.

   1.9 Word in edgeways. Esher. 19 Jan. 1915. III. 207.

   1.12 Single question. Princess Alice to author. 21 Sept. 1976.

   1.15 Get much in. Bruce Lockhart. 23 Oct. 1918. 47.

   1.21 Middle class. Longford. 567.

   1.25 Soldier's pay. Stamfordham to Bonham Carter. 11 Oct.
1914. A4.

   1.31 Food queues. Stamfordham to Davies. 11 Dec. 1917.
LG. F/29/1/50.

   1.35 Income tax. Roskill. *Hankey*. I. 529.

   1.39 By women. Stamfordham to Lloyd George. 9 May 1915.
LG. C/5/6/21.

p. 184. 1.8 Trivialities. Esher. 16 Feb. 1918. IV. 181.

   1.11 Out of favour. Lincolnshire. 18 Oct. 1911. L.

   1.17 Coal scuttle. Esher. *passim*. E.

   1.36 Hardly dignified. Stamfordham to Bonham Carter. 22 Sept.
1914. CV III.1.128.

p. 185. 1.1 Oversight. *Ibid*. 24 and 28 Sept. 1915. A4.

   1.6 Shake hands. Wigram to Lady Isobel Gathorne Hardy.
10 May 1917. W.

   1.11 Groom-in-waiting. FitzRoy. 22 Dec. 1917. II. 667.

   1.14 Duchess's funeral. Sandhurst. 17 March 1917. II. 152.

   1.24. Royal Artillery. Queen Victoria. *Letters*. Third series. III.
293 and 501.

   1.28 Canadian Minister. Standfordham to Asquith. 6 Oct. 1916.
A.4.

p. *186.* l.2   Deserved oblivion. F. Ponsonby to Rosebery. 26 Nov. 1914.
                  R 10124.

           l.13   Rarely plumbed before. F. Ponsonby to Curzon. 24 Feb.
                  1917. C.

           l.20   Military Cross. F. Ponsonby. 313.

           l.27   Brought in. Asquith to V. Stanley. 30 Oct. 1914. 297.

           l.34   At any price. *Ibid.* 28 Oct. 1914. 290.

p. *187.* l.1   Misgivings. Stamfordham. Memorandum. 30 Oct. 1914.
                  Nicolson. 252.

           .l.9   Prove groundless. King to Asquith. 29 Oct. 1914. *Ibid.*

           l.14   Kowtowing. Fisher to G. Lambert. 26 Oct. 1914. Marder
                  III. 29.

           l.20   Near him. *Ibid.* 8 Nov. 1914. *op. cit.* III. 67.

           l.26   I'll be sick. Fisher to Churchill. 3.30 a.m. 8 Dec. 1914. CV
                  III. 1. 229–30.

           l.38   Strategic idea. Fisher to King. 11 June 1915. Marder III.
                  259.

p. *188.* l.23   May drag out. Churchill to Fisher. 11 May 1915. *Ibid.* III.
                  219.

p. *189.* l.8   All the sea forces. Fisher to Asquith. 19 May 1915. *Ibid.* III.
                  241.

           l.14   Mental aberration. Nicolson. 263.

           l.19   Face of the enemy. Rhodes James. *Davidson.* 108.

           l.25   Victorious conclusion. King to Fisher. 12 June 1915.
                  Marder. III. 260.

           l.33   Kings will be cheap. Fisher to Scott. 20 Dec. 1916. *Ibid.* III.
                  405.

           l.35   Futile and Fertile. Fisher to Lambert. 30 Nov. 1917. *Ibid.*
                  III. 488.

           l.40   Real danger. King to Queen. 19 May 1915. CV III. 2.911.

           l.42   Become impossible. Diary. 22 May 1915. RA.

p. *190.* l.24   No less honour. Churchill to King. 19 Oct. 1933. CV
                  V.2.668.

           l.36   Stand the strain. King to Duke of Connaught. 20 Dec. 1915.
                  RA.

           l.12   East Africa. Stamfordham to Lord Buxton. 8 Dec. 1914. RA.

           l.16   Unfortunate enterprises. Stamfordham to Asquith. 21 July
                  1916. RA.

p. *192.* l.21   Buckingham Palace. Lady Haig to Sir George Arthur.
                  28 May 1934. HG. 3155.

p. 192. l.27 Doubts. Haig. Diaries. 11 Aug. 1914. 70.

       l.34 Schoolboys. *Ibid.* 14 July 1915. 98.

p. 193. l.2 Ought to be removed. *Ibid.* 24 Oct. 1915. 109.

       l.11 Without delay. Stamfordham to Asquith. 2 Dec. 1915. Nicolson. 268.

       l.21 Strictest confidence. King to Haig. 17 Dec. 1917. HG. 3155. 103.

       l.25 The enemy. Churchill to Clementine Churchill. 4 Dec. 1915. CV III.2.1311.

p. 194. l.3 No decision. Esher. 19 April 1916. IV. 19.

       l.11 The Empire. Haig. Diaries. 1 Nov. 1915. 111.

       l.13 Hiccoughs. Henry Wilson to Amery. 19 Aug. 1915. *Amery Diaries.* Barnes and Nicolson. 124.

       l.15 In the chair. Amery to Mrs Amery. 21 July 1915. *Ibid.* 123.

       l.21 At the Front. Raymond Asquith to Katharine Asquith. 22 Aug. 1916. Joliffe. 287.

       l.24 Recuperative days. Jenkins. 346.

       l.35 Discuss the situation. Haig to Lady Haig. 8 Sept. 1916. Blake. 164.

p. 195. l.18 Great beyond. St. George's Church. Eastergate. Sussex.

       l.24 Indecent. Asquith to Stamfordham. 8 June 1916. Owen. 316.

       l.35 Hardly listen. Roskill, *Hankey.* 10 June 1916. I. 283.

       l.39 As his deputy. Stamfordham to King. 17 June 1916. Owen. 318.

p. 196. l.7 Unfruitful offensive. Montagu to Asquith. 20 June 1916. *Ibid.* 319.

       l.17 Downing Street. Margot Asquith. *Autobiography.* II. 245.

       l.24 Impenetrable barrier. Jones. *Lloyd George.* 75.

       l.28 In the world. Roskill. *Hankey.* 1 Nov. 1916. I. 312.

       l.38 Fullest confidence. Diary. 4 Dec. 1916. RA.

p. 197. l.24 Cannot go on. Asquith to Lloyd George. 4 Dec. 1916. Jenkins. 446.

       l.34 At this hour. Lloyd George to Asquith. 5 Dec. 1916. *Ibid.* 452.

       l.36 Blackmailer. Roskill. *Hankey.* I. 327.

       l.42 The Germans. Diary. 5 Dec. 1916. Nicolson. 288.

p. 198. l.34 Form a Government. Stamfordham. Memorandum. 6 Dec. 1914. Nicolson. 290–91.

       l.39 Conduct of the war. *Ibid.* 292.

p. 199. l.10 House of Commons. 28 March 1945.

       l.18 Frozen world. Esher. 21 April 1917. IV. 107.

p. 199. l.23 Your Majesty. Lloyd George to King. 13 Dec. 1916.
LG F/29/1/1.

l.36 Feather pillow. Haig to Lady Haig. 14 Jan. 1918. Blake.
279.

p. 200. l.11 Perfect English. RA. K.1048. A1.

l.23 Own hand. MacDonald. Diary. 29 Sept. 1931. PRO.

l.24 Waste time. Roskill. *Hankey*. I. 340–41.

l.31 His very existence. Stamfordham to Balfour. 6 April 1917.
RA.

p. 201. l.2 Ruler without brains. Stevenson. Diary. 25 Jan. 1915. 25.

p. 202. l.2 Extend his role. Roskill. *Hankey*. I. 328.

l.33 At this juncture. Haig to King. 28 Feb. 1917. Blake. 203–05.

l.38 Protect your interests. Stamfordham to Haig. 5 March 1917.
Ibid. 205–06.

p. 203. l.8 See him tomorrow. Haig. Diary. 11 March 1917. *Ibid.*
208–09.

l.22 On his side. Cromer. Memorandum on Prime Minister's
audience. 12 March 1917. RA.

p. 204. l.3 Can be provided. Haig to Robertson. 8 Oct. 1917. Blake.
258.

l.34 Robertson's post. Beaverbrook. *Men and Power.* 197–98.

p. 205. l.9 No forecast. Amery. Diary. 12 Nov. 1917. 179.

l.21 Droll frivolity. Lloyd George. *War Memoirs*. V. 2818.

l.27 A Whipping. H.A.L. Fisher. Diary. 28 Dec. 1918. Fisher
Papers.

p. 206. l.10 Generally wrong. Stamfordham. Memorandum. 13 Feb.
1918. Beaverbrook. 409.

l.29 Ceased to be CIGS. *Ibid.* 16 Feb. 1918. *Op. cit.* 412–13.

l.34 In deep water. Diary. 13 Feb. 1918. RA.

p. 207. l.6 Special recognition. Blake. *Law*. 347.

l.13 His Ministers. Stamfordham to F. Guest. 8 Feb. 1918.
Owen. 464.

l.14 Administering the Duchy. Lloyd George to Stamfordham.
9 Feb. 1918. *Ibid.*

l.20 Without redress. J.T. Davies to Lloyd George. 28 May
1918. LG F/29/2/32.

l.41 Encouraging mutiny. Roskill. *Hankey*. 15 April 1918. I. 519.

p. 208. l.11 Ambassador in Paris. Vansittart. *Mist Procession*. 54.

l.18 Damp woman. Gladwyn. *Paris Embassy*. 164 and 177.

l.24 No earldom. Stamfordham to Lloyd George. 11 July 1918.
LG F/29/2/39.

l.34 Tsar at Balmoral. Lutyens. *Lady Lytton's Court Diary*. 73.

p. 209. l.3   On every subject. Duke of York to Queen Victoria. 28 Nov.
1894. Nicolson. 57.

l.6   Queen's servants. Lutyens. *Lytton*. 83.

l.17 Not against the Tsar. Diary. 13 March 1917. RA.

l.20 In despair. *Ibid*. 15 March 1917. RA.

l.25 End in anarchy. Lloyd George. *War Memoirs*. III. 1608.

l.30 In the past. King to Tsar. 19 March 1917. Nicolson. 299.

p. 210. l.2   For liberty. Lloyd George to Prince Lvov. 21 March 1917.
War Memoirs. III. 3616. (Lloyd George misdates it
24 March).

l.8   Founded on revolution. Stamfordham. Memorandum on
talk with Prime Minister. 22 March 1917. RA.

l.16 Stained with blood. Hough. *Mountbatten*. 40.

l.27 Reported to London. Buchanan to F.O. 19 March 1917. FO
371/2995. PRO.

l.29 Now a request. *Ibid*. 20 March 1917. FO 371/2998. PRO.

l.32 Place of residence. F.O. to Buchanan. *Ibid*.

l.39 During the war. Buchanan to F.O. 21 March 1917. Also
Meriel Buchanan. *Ambassador's Daughter*. 247. (Misdated
22 March 1917).

p. 211. l.13 Suitable dignity. Stamfordham. Minute of talk with Prime
Minister. 22 March 1917. RA.

l.34 Russian Government. Stamfordham to Balfour. 30 March
1917. Nicolson. 301.

l.42 H.M. Ministers. Balfour to Stamfordham. 2 April 1917.
Op. cit. 301.

p. 212. l.4   Fresh decision. Stamfordham to Balfour. 3 April 1917. RA.

l.13 Resentment. Stamfordham to Drummond. 5 April 1917. LG
F/3/2/17.

l.34 Imperial Majesties. Stamfordham to Balfour. 6 April 1917.
LG F/3/2/19.

p. 213. l.2   Government's proposal. *Ibid*. Letter no. 2.

l.10 Suitable residence. Balfour to Lloyd George. 6 April 1917.
Ibid.

l.24 Home in France. Stamfordham. Minute on talk with Prime
Minister and Foreign Secretary. 10 April 1917. RA.

l.33 That very afternoon. *Ibid*.

p. 214. l.2   Raised the question. F.O. to Buchanan. 13 April 1917. FO
800/205. PRO.

l.6   Ultimate fate. Buchanan. *Op. cit.* 154.

l.23 Serious embarrassment. Buchanan to F.O. 15 April 1917.
FO 800/205. PRO.

p. 215. l.24 Chaos in Russia. King to Knollys. 4 June 1917. Knollys
Papers.

l.30 Her promptings. Bertie to Hardinge. 22 April 1917. Lloyd
George. *Op. cit.* III. 1644.

p. 216. l.7 Emperor's death. Stamfordham to Balfour. 22 July 1918.
BM 49686.

l.13 Country and people. Diary. 25 July 1918. RA.

l.18 Poor innocent children. *Ibid.* 31 Aug. 1918. RA.

l.27 Come out alive. King to Knollys. 4 June 1917. Knollys
Papers.

l.39 Missing months. Summers and Mangold. *The File on The
Tsar.* 253–55.

p. 217. l.18 Brest-Litovsk. Stamfordham to Esher. 25 July 1918.
E. 21/10.

l.25 Of abuse. Esher to Stamfordham. 28 July 1918. Esher. IV.
208–09.

p. 218. l.2 Cabinet minutes. Sylvester. *Life with Lloyd George.* 9 April
1934. 106–07.

l.4 Jumpy and nervy. *Ibid.*

l.6 Scrapped chapter. *Op. cit.* 26 June 1934. 110.

l.11 Tsar's departure. Lloyd George. *War Memoirs.* III. 1644.

l.27 Taking you prisoner. Windsor. *King's Story.* 109.

l.38 Meals. *Ibid.* 114.

p. 219. l.5 Kept right away. Prince of Wales to Lady Coke. 18 March
1915. Combe Papers.

l.10 Burst of shrapnel. Windsor. 116.

l.13 Ypres. Prince of Wales to Lady Coke. 30 March 1916.

l.21 Suddenly grow up. Lord Edward Cecil to Lady Edward
Cecil. 9 May 1916. S.

l.27 Soft rotter. Prince of Wales to Lady Coke. 22 Aug. 1917.

l.36 Strength for battle. Lord Cavan. Unpublished Memoir.
Churchill College, Cambridge.

l.42 Military Cross. Prince of Wales to Lady Coke. 16 June 1916.

p. 220. l.7 Most depressing. *Ibid.* 14 March 1917.

l.10 Not for nobody. *Ibid.* 4 Sept. 1917.

l.22 Never a rest. Wheeler-Bennett. 79.

l.30 Latin verses. Frankland. 28.

l.32 Forefinger. Carnock. Diary. 29 Sept. 1916. PRO.

l.40 More of Eton. 23 April 1918. Frankland. 37.

p. 221. l.5 Fitzwilliam. Roberts. *Adventures with Authors.* 205.

l.13 Troubled spirit. Queen to Emily Alcock. 2 Feb. 1919. Pope-
Hennessy. 511.

p. 221. l.17 Break down. *Op. cit.* 505.

l.19 White beard. Curzon to Grace Curzon. 8 Aug. 1918. CK.

l.23 Football fields. Wigram to Cromer. 12 April 1918. W.

l.38 So red a road. *The Dynasts.* III. V.v.

p. 222. l.12 Seasoned. Stamfordham to Diaries. 28 April 1918. LG F/29/2/25.

l.22 Petrograd. Marquand. *Ramsay MacDonald.* 208.

l.29 Privy Council. Amery. Diary. 30 July 1918. 230.

l.37 Ideas of peace. Diary. 7 Oct. 1918. RA.

l.39 Wonderful day. *Ibid.* 11 Nov. 1918. Gore. 308.

p. 223. l.4 Bitter anxiety. Queen to Prince Henry. 24 Nov. 1918. Pope-Hennessy. 515.

l.13 No publication. Haig. Diary. 16 Nov. 1918. 344.

l.16 Hour of glory. Note in Wigram Papers.

l.32 No Derby. Airlie. 144.

RESTLESS DECADE

p. 224. l.5 Not good days. Oxford and Asquith. *Letters to a Friend.* 29 Oct. 1918. I. 30.

l.16 No other country. King to Mensdorff. 21 Oct. 1922. M.

l.26 Possibly revolution. Stamfordham to Lloyd George. 1 Sept. 1921. LG F/29/4/70.

p. 225. l.16 In their dust. Oxford and Asquith. 18 Nov. 1918. I. 84.

l.21 Newspapers. Neville Chamberlain to Hilda Chamberlain. 16 June 1923. NC 18/1/399.

l.28 Victorian period. Hyde. *Reading.* 403.

p. 226. l.3 Still obtain. Esher. *Girlhood of Queen Victoria.* 5 Oct. 1838. II. 41.

l.10 Don't quote me. Dixon. 248.

l.18 Dewsbury. A.C. Benson. MS Commonplace Book.

l.26 Mice. Clara Boyle. xix.

l.34 Better chronicled. Wigram to H.L. Verney. 19 April 1917. W.

l.41 Under a bushel. Wigram to Haig. 14 April 1917. W.

p. 227. l.15 Gospel of devolution. Wigram. Undated memorandum. W.

l.36 Live Monarchy. Wigram to Lang. 3 Jan. 1919. W.

p. 228. l.2 On a pedestal. Windsor. 136.

l.11 Red or blue. Private information.

l.14 Horses. C. Colville. 123.

l.17 Correct style. Godfrey-Faussett. Diary. 2 March 1925. GF.

l.20 KCVO. Private information.

p. 228. l.24 Visiting Queen. Lincolnshire. 12 May 1924. L.

l.27 Places at Court. Curzon memorandum. 7 March 1922. C.

l.30 Duchesses. Airlie. 158–59.

l.33 A trifle. Roskill. *Hankey.* 4 Dec. 1918. II. 28.

p. 229. l.11 Rivals. Laski. 392.

l.22 All its misery. Diary. 9 Nov. 1918. RA.

l.26 German gentleman. Elliott Roosevelt. *The Roosevelts.* 93.

l.33 Against her country. Wheeler-Bennett. 120–21.

l.35 Shaken hands. Diary. 14 Oct. 1920. RA.

l.38 My feelings. King to Grand Duke of Hesse. 16 May 1935. Hesse Archives. Darmstadt. D.24.

p. 230. l.3 Red-hot patriotism. Soames. *Clementine Churchill.* 161.

l.7 Necessary £7,000. Lincolnshire Papers.

l.13 Turned his back. Lincolnshire. Diary. 2 June 1919. L.

l.24 Explanation. Duff Cooper. *Old Men Forget.* 194–95.

l.33 Annual event. Mensdorff. Diary. *passim.* M.

l.40 By bus. Oxford and Asquith. 2 July 1923. II. 66.

p. 231. l.10 Half an hour. Roskill. *Hankey.* II. 99.

l.15 By river. Halifax. *Fulness of Days.* 84.

l.19 Grace and favour. Stamfordham to Curzon. 9 July 1919. C.

l.25 No condolence. Bruce Lockhart. 23 Nov. 1928. 74.

l.29 A present. *Ibid.* 30 Jan. 1936. 340.

l.35 Royal Archives. Pope-Hennessy. 289.

p. 232. l.7 Parliament Act. Stamfordham. Memorandum. 5 Nov. 1918. Nicolson. 328–29.

l.20 Not consulted. Stamfordham to E. Drummond. 18 Dec. 1918. BM. 49686.

l.22 Overruled. Roskill. *Hankey.* II. 36.

l.28 No gratitude. Lloyd George. *Peace Treaties.* I. 182.

l.29 Odious man. Lady Wigram. Diary. 13 April 1926. W.

p. 233. l.11 This forecast. Stamfordham to Lloyd George. 9 Jan. 1919. LG F/29/3/1.

l.19 His elevation. Heuston. *Lord Chancellors.* 381.

l.25 Laughter in court. *Ibid.* 382.

l.29 It never would. Owen Morshead. MS. on King George V.

l.35 Pretty little nest. Lincolnshire. 24 Aug. 1925. L.

p. 234. l.13 Rude letter. Birkenhead. *F.E.* 394–98.

l.28 H.M.'s pleasure. Stamfordham to Waterhouse. 12 Dec. 1926. Birkenhead to Stamfordham. 14 Dec. 1926. WT.

l.40 Unsuitable. Stamfordham to Lloyd George. 6 April 1922. LG F/29/4/99.

l.43 Political parasite. Roskill. *Hankey.* 10 Dec. 1916. I. 329.

p. 235. l.1   Baronetcies. Jones. Diary. 11 July 1922. I. 203.

      l.5   Cut off. Stamfordham to Diaries. 16 Sept. 1920.
            LG F/29/4/27.

      l.8   Additional duty. *Ibid.*

      l.17 Single reply. Rhodes James. *Davidson.* 107.

      l.32 Delayed me. Probyn to Birdwood. 16 March 1906. Birdwood
            Papers.

      l.39 Not on the line. Gore. 436.

      l.41 Noted it. Sandhurst. 19 March 1916. II. 34.

p. 236. l.4   No reply. Webb. Diaries. 147.

      l.8   Butler's pantry. Attlee. *As It Happened.* 159.

      l.19 Walk a mile. Wrench. *Geoffrey Dawson.* 22 and 320.

      l.20 Little hurt. Stevenson. Diary. 11 June 1921. 221.

      l.23 Entered their room. Rhodes James. *Davidson.* 67.

      l.25 Waiting room. Waterhouse. *Private and Official.* 202.

      l.26 Peppery. Lady Wigram. Diary W.

      l.31 In another man. Roskill. *Hankey.* 23 Nov. 1918. II. 23.

p. 237. l.4   Since Pitt. King to Stamfordham. 19 March 1921.
            Beaverbrook. 337–38.

      l.8   Regiment reprieved. Stamfordham to Diaries. 28 May 1920.
            LG F/29/4/11.

      l.16 Lend me him. Sylvester. 11 Feb. 1937. 171.

      l.23 Peacemaker. Stevenson. Diary. 29 June 1919. 187.

p. 238. l.9   Old coward. Lloyd George to Margaret Lloyd George.
            2 Sept. 1920. Morgan. 192.

      l.15 Return to Ireland. Rhodes James. *Davidson.* 98.

      l.20 Yelling match. F. Ponsonby to Ria Ponsonby. 20 Oct. 1920.
            Ponsonby Papers.

      l.39 Private secretaries. Lord Altrincham to Nicolson. 19 Dec.
            1950. Nicolson Papers.

p. 239. l.22 Justice and respect. Nicolson. 353–54.

      l.24 Cheering. Diary. 22 June 1921. Nicolson. 351.

      l.31 Sentimental people. Stamfordham. Memorandum. 25 June
            1921. Nicolson 354. (Misdated 24 July).

      l.39 Popular appeal. *Ibid.* RA.

p. 240. l.28 August 1914. *History of The Times.* IV.2.608–09.

      l.38 Said it at all. *Ibid.* 611.

p. 241. l.2   Westminster. House of Commons. 29 July 1921.

      l.9   Liberty to print. *History of The Times.* IV.2.609.

      l.14 Attacks on my Empire. Templewood. *Nine Troubled Years.*
            59–60.

      l.28 Simply furious. Stevenson. Diary. 29 July 1921. 232–33.

p. 241. l.32 Honour. *The Times.* 13 July 1921.

l.38 Belfast speech. Stamfordham to Grigg. 29 July 1921. L.G. F/29/4/63.

p. 242. l.14 From the draft. A. Hardinge. Memorandum. 7 Sept. 1921. Nicolson. 359.

l.18 Terminology. King to Lloyd George. 18 Sept. 1921. *Op. cit.* 360.

l.23 Peace in Ireland. Diary. 6 Dec. 1921. *Op. cit.* 361.

l.31 To pieces. MacDonald. Diary. 6 July 1930. MD.

l.39 Fallen revenue. Duchy of Lancaster to author. 27 Oct. 1977.

p. 243. l.12 No taxation. Solicitor-General. Memorandum. 12 June 1910. A.23.

l.18 Benefactions. F. Ponsonby to Asquith. 10 and 31 March 1916. A.4.

l.26 Tsar's mother. F. Ponsonby. 337.

l.28 Miss Phipps. Mallet. 3.

l.35 Court of Denmark. Hobhouse. 30 June 1910. 94.

p. 244. l.1 Deafness. Battiscombe. 293.

l.8 Cannot be right. Stamfordham to Lloyd George. 26 May 1920. LG F/29/4/10.

l.10 Retrospective. Arthur Davidson to Lloyd George. *Ibid.*

l.15 Deficit on repairs. Austen Chamberlain. House of Commons. 10 Aug. 1921.

l.35 Very cold bow. Hobhouse. 20 July 1913. 144.

p. 245. l.10 End of October. Reese. *Master of the Horse.* 304.

l.20 Six yards too much. Andrews. *Canon's Folly.* 153–54.

l.23 Able to eat it. Marchioness Curzon. 160.

l.24 Half a pear. Woods. 1929. WD.

l.28 A peerage. MacDonald. Diary. 16 May 1935. Marquand. 776.

l.38 Ducal handshake. Jones. *Diary with Letters.* 207.

l.2 Human nature. Cecil. *Salisbury.* III. 142–43.

p. 246. l.4 Hateful task. Asquith to Balfour. 7 June 1913. A.13.

l.15 Fountain of Honour. Knollys to Nash. 16 Feb. 1912. A.3.

l.21 The rule. Stamfordham to Craigavon. 27 Jan. 1927. RA.

l.32 Laughing stock. Knollys to Nash. 25 March 1911. A.2.

l.34 Postmaster General. Knollys to Bonham Carter. 7 June 1912. A.3.

l.35 Radical M.P. Knollys to Master of Elibank. 12 June 1912. Knollys Papers.

l.36 Abominates. Knollys to Nash. 13 June 1911. A.2.

p. 247. l.3   Social preferment. Curzon. Memorandum on Proposed
Order of the British Empire. 1 April 1917. C.

l.25   Your colleagues. Stamfordham to Lloyd George. 14 Dec.
1916. LG F/29/1/2.

p. 248. l.2   High distinction. *Ibid.* 25 April 1918. LG F/29/2/23.

l.13   Obligations due. Bonar Law to Stamfordham. 17 April 1919.
Beaverbrook. 241-42.

l.19   His Majesty. Stamfordham to Bonar Law. 17 April 1919.
Ibid.

l.34   Publication. Stamfordham to Davies. 10 Nov. 1919. Davies
to Stamfordham. 11 Nov. 1919. LG F/29/3/35-36.

l.39   Not successful. Stamfordham to Salisbury. 15 June 1922. S.

p. 249. l.6   Free from reproach. Salisbury to Lloyd George. 25 March
1917. S.

l.19   Benefit of the country. House of Lords. 7 August 1917.

l.22   Party funds. House of Lords. 29 June 1922.

l.25   Public recognition. House of Commons. 17 July 1922.

l.33   Go to the Devil. Rhodes James. *Davidson.* 279.

p. 250. l.1   Eighty-fifth year. Stamfordham to F. Guest. 25 April 1919.
LG F/21/3/17.

l.2   Divorce case. Beaverbrook. 245-46.

l.16   A baronet. Stamfordham to Davies. 17 July 1921. LG
F/29/4/34.

l.30   Boulogne. House of Commons. 17 July 1922.

l.34   Unemployed. Lord Strachie. House of Lords. 29 June
1922.

l.38   Earlier company. Ronald McNeill. House of Commons.
17 July 1922.

p. 251. l.8   Withdrawn for a time. Vansittart to Curzon. 19 July 1922. C.

l.15   O Forres. *Ibid.* 22 July 1922. C.

l.27   Dismissed. Lord Harris. House of Lords. 22 June 1922.

l.35   Chequebook. Earl of Swinton to author. 8 June 1951.

l.39   Decline it. House of Lords. 29 June 1922.

p. 252. l.19   The State. King to Lloyd George. 3 July 1922. LG
F/29/4/103.

l.30   In return for Honours. Report. Royal Commission on
Honours. Cmd. 1789. 1922.

l.36   Political services alone. *Ibid.*

p. 253. l.15   Trafficking. Baldwin to Jones. 4 March 1933. Jones. *Diary
with Letters.* 101.

l.36   Royal household. Tom Cullen. *Maundy Gregory. Passim.*

p. 254. l.11   Business collapsed. Rhodes James. *Davidson.* 280.

p. 254. l.18   Interested in Mr Bennett. Stamfordham to Waterhouse.
                 17 Dec. 1926. WT.
p. 255. l.7   Until the end. Rhodes James. *Op. cit.* 288.
          l.27   Give the honour. McDonald. Diary. 13 Dec. 1933.
                 Marquand. 746.
          l.32   Out of a mess. *Ibid.* 19 May 1934. 747.
p. 256. l.3   Precedence. Curzon. Memorandum. 1 April 1917. *Op. cit.* C.
          l.26   Distinguished services. Children. *W.H. Smith.* 205.
          l.32   Smart society. Esher. 22 July 1908 and 17 Feb. 1912. E.
          l.42   Her son's reign. F. Ponsonby. 273.
p. 257. l.2   Demise of the Crown. Brodrick to Curzon. 23 Oct. 1903. C.
          l.9   Similar one. *Ibid.* 29 April 1902.
          l.33   Firing line. Haig. 4 Dec. 1914. 79.
          l.40   Their Sovereign. Esher to Stamfordham. 27 Feb. 1914. III.
                 158.
p. 258. l.18   King Edward. Wilson. *C-B.* 579.
          l.37   Quadrupled. De la Bere. *Queen's Orders of Chivalry.* 158.
          l.38   OBE trousers. Walker. *I Talk of Dreams.* 205.
          l.41   The real thing. House of Lords. 17 July 1922.
p. 259. l.31   Welsh Order. Esher to Knollys. 14 April 1911. Knollys
                 Papers.
          l.36   Greatly increased. Blake. *Law.* 410.
          l.42   No politicians. Stamfordham to Law. 4 Aug. 1919. Bonar
                 Law Papers. 98/1/2.
p. 260. l.11   Ex-Cabinet Ministers. Balfour to Stamfordham. 1 June
                 1916. BW. 10.
          l.22   Order of Merit. King to Lloyd George. 5 Aug. 1919. LG F/
                 29/3/26.
          l.34   Appropriate. Churchill to King. 16 Oct. 1919. CV
                 IV.907.
          l.42   Out of office. Stamfordham. Memorandum. 16 Dec. 1919.
                 RA.
p. 261. l.2   War medals. Churchill to King. 19 Nov. 1919. RA.
          l.5   Distinctions. King to Churchill. 25 Nov. 1919. RA.
          l.15   Frazer's OM Stamfordham to Dawson. 1 Jan. 1925. Dawson
                 Papers.
          l.27   Conflict. Stamfordham. Memorandum. 5 Nov. 1921. RA.
          l.30   Absolute discretion. Rosebery to Stamfordham. 14 Nov.
                 1921. RA.
p. 262. l.2   Only the VC Curzon to Stamfordham. 9 Oct. 1921. C.
          l.12   Susceptibilities. Stamfordham to Curzon. 10 Oct. 1921. C.
          l.23   Indian chief's. Hankey to Lloyd George. 11 Nov. 1921. C.

p. 262. l.27 War Office. Stamfordham to Derby. 31 Oct. 1922. *Derby* 487.

l.32 Received it. Stamfordham to Curzon. 21 Oct. 1919. Curzon to Stamfordham. 4 Nov. 1919. C.

l.38 Superior GCB. Ponsonby to Curzon. 13 March 1923.

p. 263. l.4 Honour be conferred. Nicolson. 514.

l.13 Some consideration. 28 Nov. 1930. *Ibid.* 515.

l.17 Aeronautical services. Duff to Stamfordham. 6 Dec. 1930. RA.

l.24 Mr Kenyon. Knollys to Bonham Carter. 31 May 1912. A.3.

l.29 Abbot Anderson. Knollys to Asquith. 27 Feb. 1912. A.3.

l.33 Milsom Rees. Knollys to Nash. 13 April 1911. A.2. Stamfordham to Bonham Carter. 22 Dec. 1914. A.4.

l.34 Alexander. Knollys to Nash. 13 April 1911. A.2.

l.37 Du Maurier and Hawtrey. H.A.L. Fisher. Diary. 27 May 1921. Fisher Papers.

l.38 Ben Greet. Vansittart to Stamfordham. 17 April 1929. B. 178/295.

l.40 Salvation Army. Stamfordham to Baldwin. 2 Dec. 1925. WT.

p. 264. l.5 Very unfair. Stamfordham to Chelmsford. 13 Dec. 1920. Chelmsford Papers.

l.8 Capitulated. Churchill. *World Crisis.* 908.

l.11 Casts a shadow. House of Commons. 27 March 1941.

l.38 I am sorry. Diary. 23 Oct. 1922. Nicolson. 371.

p. 265. l.6 Very great man. Stevenson. Diary. 18 Feb. 1934. 253–54.

l.18 Always lost. Beaverbrook. *Men and Power.* xiii.

l.33 Of all studies. Chamberlain. *Down the Years.* 225.

p. 266. l.2 Next election. Blake. *Law.* 457.

l.17 Completely restored. King to Law. 20 May 1923. RA.

p. 267. l.5 Curzon or Baldwin. Diary. 20 May 1923. RA.

p. 268. l.8 Democratic opinion. Rhodes James. *Davidson.* 155.

l.17 Original envelope. Blake. *Law.* 520.

l.27 No influence. Rhodes James. *Davidson.* 164.

l.31 Rival candidates. Stamfordham. Memorandum. 22 May 1923. RA.

p. 269. l.3 With the public. *Ibid.* 21 May 1923. RA.

l.13 Who sat there. Balfour. Memorandum. 22 May 1923. BW.1.

l.16 George will not. Churchill. *Great Contemporaries.* 287.

l.25 Exceptional ability. Stamfordham. Memorandum. 22 May 1923. RA.

l.37 L.G. regime. Curzon to Law. 25 April 1923. Blake. *Law.* 510–11.

p. 270. l.8   Not everybody. King to Queen Alexandra. 15 Jan. 1912. RA.

l.12 This opinion. Stamfordham. Minute. 11 Oct. 1915. RA.

l.14 Over the heads. Newton. *Retrospection.* 242.

l.25 His Majesty. Curzon to Stamfordham. 3 Oct. 1921. C.

l.31 Foreign Office. Stamfordham to Curzon. 4 Oct. 1921. C.

l.36 Certain awe. Curzon to Grace Curzon. 13 Nov. 1923. CK.

p. 271. l.5   Fine story. *Ibid.* 2 Dec. 1923.

l.19 House of Commons. Stamfordham to Balfour. 25 May 1923. BW.1.

l.23 Disregarded. Rose. *Later Cecils.* 92.

l.28 Currents of opinion. Blanche Dudgale. *Balfour.* II. 346 and 360.

l.34 Centre of gravity. Birkenhead. *Halifax.* 454.

l.36 Really matter. *Ibid.* 455.

p. 272. l.6   To the country. Stamfordham. Memorandum. 22 May 1923. RA.

l.14 Since yesterday. Diary. 22 and 23 May 1923. RA.

l.17 Last week. *Ibid.* 29 May 1923.

l.35 Recent occasions. Stamfordham. Memorandum. 29 May 1923. RA.

p. 273. l.6   Everything you do. Chamberlain. Diary. 1 June 1923. NC. 2/21.

l.13 Dissuaded the King. Curzon to Grace Curzon. 13 Nov. 1923. CK.

l.15 Premiership. *Ibid.* 18 Nov. 1923.

l.20 Students of history. 29 May 1923. *Derby.* 503–04.

l.32 In America. Stamfordham to Law. 29 January 1923. RA.

l.36 No wonder. Hyde. *Baldwin.* 131.

p. 274. l.18 By the result. The King. Memorandum. 12 Nov. 1923. Nicolson. 380.

l.26 Madness. Curzon to Grace Curzon. 1 Jan. 1924. CK.

p. 275. l.10 India merchants. Huntly. *Milestones.* 168.

l.20 Best dinner. Hamilton. Diary. 21 March 1883. Bahlman. 412.

l.24 Accepted tariff. J.L. Lant. 'Lord Salisbury and the Honours Scramble.' *The Times.* 5 Dec. 1977.

l.42 Mixed up. Lincolnshire. 3 Feb. 1907. L.

p. 276. l.5   Portrait. King to Farquhar. 23 June 1911. W.

l.7   Red and white. Frankland. 9.

l.14 Loss at bridge. Asquith to V. Stanley. 16 March 1915. 484.

l.20 National benefit. Sandhurst. II. 32.

l.30 Looking their best. *Ibid.* April 1920. II. 334.

p. 276. l.32 Courtship. Wheeler-Bennett. 148.
p. 277. l.24 Literally push him. Atholl to Curzon. 14 Feb. 1922. C.
        l.27 Indecisive. Curzon. Memorandum. 7 March 1922. C.
        l.34 Years at Court. Stamfordham to Curzon. 10 Nov. 1922. C.
        l.40 £40,000 a year. Lincolnshire. 30 Aug. 1922. L.
p. 278. l.22 Imperfect book-keeping. Blake. *Law.* 497.
        l.28 Coalition purposes. *The Times.* 17 March 1923.
        l.30 Semi-idiotic. Lincolnshire. 24 Nov. 1922. L.
        l.33 Gaga. Law to Lord Edmund Talbot. 24 Jan. 1923. Blake.
              Op. cit. 497.
p. 279. l.16 His servants. *The Times.* 12 Sept. 1923.
        l.20 King's doubts. King to Wigram. 9 Sept. 1923. W.
        l.28 Depressed conditions. Huntly. *Milestones.* 169.
        l.36 Open-mouthed. Lincolnshire. 18 July and 19 Oct. 1924. L.
p. 280. l.5 A copy. Col. Henry Howard to author. 4 Oct. 1977.

HOME LIFE

p. 281. l.3 Mean Court. Bagehot. 46.
        l.6 Cellar doors. Sandhurst. II. 280.
        l.16 Quadrille. *Ibid.* II. 377.
        l.27 Illegibility. Portland. *Men, Women and Things.* 107–08.
p. 282. l.7 So difficult. Windsor. *King's Story.* 234.
        l.10 Discreet inquiries. Wigram to Bessborough. 24 May 1934.
              Bessborough Papers.
        l.12 Sir Isaiah Berlin to author. 7 Dec. 1980.
        l.19 Can hardly describe. Wheeler-Bennett. 244.
        l.30 Walked away. Channon. Diary. 4 June 1923. Coats Papers.
        l.35 Constellation of four. De la Bere. 200–01.
p.283. l.7 More animated. Channon. Diary. 14 May 1924. Coats
              Papers.
        l.15 Evidently relieved. Asquith to Hilda Harrisson. 7 March
              1923. Symonds Papers.
        l.28 With the drink. Saint-Aulaire. *Confession d'un vieux
              diplomate.* 542–43.
        l.35 Forty-five servants. F. Ponsonby. 356.
p. 284. l.4 Venerable cathedral. Princess Alice. 261.
        l.9 De Gaulle. Private information.
        l.16 Niebelung. Princess Marie Louise. 48–49.
        l.20 Possessions. Lord Clark to author. 12 June 1976.
        l.25 Queen Victoria. Eva Countess of Rosebery to author. 21
              Nov. 1975.

p. 284. l.34 Caressing it. Lord Clark to author. 12 June. 1976.
  l.37 Dear little cabinet. Lady Islington to author.
  l.40 Sons of George III. Lincolnshire. 24 Feb. 1924. L.
p. 285. l.3 Benares. A. Clark. 171.
  l.32 Chest of drawers. A.C. Benson. *The Book of the Queen's Dolls' House. Passim.*
  l.35 George May. Luytens. *Edwin Lutyens.* 183.
p. 286. l.6 Bellows. E.V. Lucas. *The Book of the Queen's Dolls' House Library. Passim.*
  l.8 Fatuous exercise. Asquith to Hilda Harrisson. 4 Sept. 1922. Symonds Papers.
  l.7 Rude manner. Princess Marie Louise. 201.
  l.10 Summon servants. Hussey. *Lutyens.* 451.
  l.18 Old grey stone. Windsor. *King's Story.* 35.
  l.22 Bronze tail. Bolitho. *My Restless Years.* 101.
  l.35 People in the Castle. Baillie. *My First Eighty Years.* 176.
p. 287. l.8 Conventional candidate. A.C. Benson. Conversation with Randall Davidson. Diary. April 1903. Magdalene College.
  l.19 Unhappy man. Baillie. 173.
  l.25 Nice people again. Diary. 19 Aug. 1919. Nicolson. 338.
  l.29 Sermon on Nero. Helen Hardinge. *Loyal to Three Kings.* 112.
  l.33 Just plain George. Lorna MacEchern to author. 4 Sept. 1981.
  l.38 Six for dinner. Samuel Hoare. TM. RF.1.
  l.41 Pitching tracks. Hardinge of Penhurst. *An Incompleat Angler.* 12.
p. 288. l.1 Trout. Westminster. *Grace and Favour.* 102.
  l.9 This rubbish. King to Godfrey-Faussett. 31 Aug. 1910. GF.
  l.26 Supernacular. Linklater. *A Year of Space.* 254-55.
  l.29 Sixpence. Sir Lawrence Jones to author. 8 July 1957.
  l.35 Furniture. Sir Michael Duff to author. 16 Sept. 1976.
p. 289. l.7 Old-established rule. Keppel to Waterhouse. 20 Sept. 1928. WT.
  l.12 Prime Minster. Airlie. 108-09.
  l.17 Townsman. Cazalet-Keir. *From the Wings.* 95.
  l.23 Every pebble. Chamberlain to Ida Chamberlain. 3 Sept. 1933. NC 18/1/1840.
  l.33 Munich Agreement. Lady Wigram. 'Handshakes'. W.
  l.39 Slim pretty figure, Lincolnshire. 20 Oct. 1924. L.
p. 290. l.3 Not prosper. Hibbert. *Edward VII.* 180.
  l.8 Rolled-up carpet. Cust. *King Edward VII.* 234.

p. 290. l.13 Most imposing. Fisher to Cecil Fisher. 27 June 1912.
Marder. II. 470.

l.19 Telephone. Princess Alice to author. 21 Sept. 1976.

l.20 Possessions. Lady Wigram. Diary. 12 April 1926. W.

l.33 Traitor. Probyn to H. Ponsonby. 3 Feb. 1886. A. Ponsonby.
355.

l.36 By-election. Knollys to Churchill. 20 March 1924. CV
V.1.129.

l.38 Prime Minister. Probyn to Birdwood. 15 Nov. 1922.
Birdwood Papers.

l.42 His own salary. *Ibid.* 11 Jan. 1922.

p. 291. l.2 King George. *Ibid.* 10 Dec. 1914.

l.6 Reticule. Eva Countess of Rosebery to author. 24 Nov. 1974.

l.11 Happy years. Diary. 28 March 1926. RA.

l.15 Comfortable home. Queen to Esher. 7 Dec. 1925. E 6/1.

l.19 Lord Palmerston. Lady Desborough to Balfour. 21 Nov.
(   ) BW. 26.

l.24 Bright fires. Woods. 1929. WD.

l.28 Hands and teeth. Sir Owen Morshead to author. 23 Oct.
1976.

l.31 Blowing hard. Countess Birkenhead to author. 25 Nov. 1976.

l.74 Winkles. Dowager Lady Hardinge to author.

p. 292. l.1 Boiled egg. C. Colville. 120.

l.3 Misbehaviour. Duchess of Beaufort to author. 26 June 1976.

l.5 Taking care of her. King to Wigram. 31 March 1925. W.

l.9 Five in red. Woods. 1929. WD.

l.12 It's our own. Sir Owen Morshead to author. 23 Oct. 1976.

l.14 Allotment garden. Dixon. 156.

p. 293. l.5 All got up. Lady Wigram. Diary. Christmas 1926. W.

l.13 Last time. Black. *King's Nurse, Beggar's Nurse.* 160–61.

l.19 Cough drops. Woods. 1924. WD.

l.26 Three times as many. Samuel Hoare. TM. RF.1.

l.29 Breeding ground. Col. Henry Howard to author. 4 Oct.
1977.

l.38 Crawling with them. Woods. 1929. WD.

l.40 Puzzle me. Lincolnshire. 8 Jan. 1923. L.

p. 294. l.1 Fluffy ones. Godfrey-Faussett. 3 Jan. 1913. GF.

l.4 Ambush. Buxton. King in his Country. 2.

l.19 Hoares. Samuel Hoare. TM. RF.1.

l.29 Not convenient. Diary. 8 May 1922. RA.

l.34 In the dark. Told by the Queen to Harold Nicolson, who
told James Lees-Milne. Nicolson. II. 233.

p. 294. l.37 The Great War. A. Chamberlain to Horace Rumbold.
                22 April 1926. Gilbert. *Rumbold.* 311.

          l.39 The other dams. David Russell, son of Sir Odo Russell, to
                author.

p. 295. l.10 Only £2. Channon Diary. 28 Feb. 1927. Coats Papers.

          l.17 Indelicate spectacle. Churchill. *Derby.* 394.

          l.22 The Durbar. Pope-Hennessy. *Crewe.* 141.

          l.25 Rather grumpy. Diary. 17 Aug. 1921. RA.

          l.30 Drive me mad. Battiscombe. 269.

          l.42 Pillowcases. Diana Cooper. *Light of Common Day.* 127.

p. 296. l.21 Queen's bath. Printed orders for journey from Ballater to
                London (Euston), 28–29 Sept. 1933.

          l.28 Tidy up. Ethel Smyth. *What Happened Next.* 11.

          l.38 Lower servants. John Fortescue. *Author and Curator.* 97–98.

p. 297. l.1   Three maids. Desborough Papers. 1935.

          l.4   Knowsley. Hobhouse. 15 July 1913. 143. Also Newton.
                Retrospection. 199.

          l.9   Man and a half. Windsor. *King's Story.* 184.

          l.14 Difficult to satisfy. Hardinge. *My Indian Years.* 57.

          l.26 How much they cost. Corbitt. *Fit for a King.* 15 and 78.

          l.33 No tipping. Samuel Hoare. 12 April 1927. TM. RF.11.

p. 298. l.2   Displaced. Gore. 415.

          l.7   Even angrier Queen. Private information.

          l.12 In a cab. Godfrey-Faussett. 2 March 1911. GF.

          l.15 Monarch's voice. F. Ponsonby to Esher. 2 April 1928.
                E 5/62.

          l.18 Sealing wax. King to Wigram. 23 Jan. 1925. W.

          l.34 Same footing. Longford. *Victoria R.I.* 375.

          l.37 Near indifferent. Magdalen Ponsonby. *Mary Ponsonby.* 5–6.

p. 299. l.2   Complete privacy. Channon. Diary. 14 June 1923. Coats
                Papers.

          l.6   Health and fortune. Giles St. Aubyn to author.

          l.12 A new day. C. Colville. 123.

          l.14 Perpendicular. Cust. 202.

          l.16 And a doctor. A. Ponsonby. 60.

          l.20 All servants. Lord Adeane to author. 3 Oct. 1974.

          l.23 Means nothing. Godfrey-Faussett. 6 Aug. 1908. GF.

          l.32 On my return. King to Wigram. 21 July 1918. W.

          l.35 In my sock. Godfrey-Faussett. 3 Aug. 1910. GF.

p. 300. l.5   At the castle. W. Fortescue. *There's Rosemary.* 183.

          l.8   Grandfather. Lady Morshead to author. 23 Oct. 1976.

          l.17 Inspect my Fleet. Lowis. *Fabulous Admirals.* 167–68.

p. 300. 1.26 In the City. Nicolson. *Lord Carnock.* 431.

1.31 Thank you. Altrincham. *Kenya's Opportunity.* 92.

1.35 Much in need. A. Hardinge to Eden. 9 Jan. 1936. RA.

1.37 Dignified slavery. *Fortnightly Review.* December 1942.

p. 301. 1.15 More attractive. Mensdorff. 19 Oct. 1924. M.

1.20 In disgrace. Westminster. *Grace and Favour.* 104.

1.23 Pansies. Diana Cooper. *Light of Common Day.* 127.

1.24 White and sparkling. Channon. Diaries. 22 June 1937.

1.26 All the best. *Ibid.* 16 Nov. 1938.

1.39 Glad to be back. 20 March 1925. Pope-Hennessy. 537.

p. 302. 1.11 Without comment. Lanning Roper. *Gardens at Windsor.* 33.

1.18 Her great worth. Princess Alice to author. 21 Sept. 1976.

1.31 His departure. Duchess of Beaufort to author. 26 June 1976.

1.33 By enterprise. Eva Countess of Rosebery to author. 24 Nov. 1974.

p. 303. 1.13 Nothing but relief. Lord Mountbatten to author. 9 June 1976. There is another version of the story in Hough's *Mountbatten,* p. 52.

p. 304. 1.2 Pathetic little person. Curzon to Grace Curzon. 16 March 1920. CK.

1.6 An Englishman. Prince of Wales to Lady Coke. 7 Jan. 1918. Combe Papers.

1.12 Propaganda. Reading to Stamfordham. 25 Nov. 1919. Hyde. *Reading.* 315.

1.16 Animosités. Jusserand to Pichon. 24 Nov. 1919. Quai d'Orsay Archives. 2.274.3.

1.23 Loyalty and affection. King to Prince of Wales. 12 Oct. 1919. *King's Story.* 144.

p. 305. 1.6 Visit to Japan. Sir Charles Eliot to Curzon. 1 and 23 May 1922. C.

1.14 Constitutional Prince. Lord Altrincham to author. 1 April 1954.

1.25 Clothes. Lady Wigram. Diary. 1926. W.

1.31 Two-minute silence. Stamfordham to Curzon. 17 Oct. 1923. C.

1.34 Late as usual. Queen Mother to author. 21 July 1976.

1.42 Very smart. Windsor. *Family Album.* 84.

p. 306. 1.5 Hat off. Wheeler-Bennett. 231-32.

1.10 Please the public. *Family Album.* 84.

1.12 Father's presence. Duchess of Beaufort to author. 26 July 1976.

1.14 Occur again. *Family Album.* 93.

p. 306. l.15 Pink tops. Queen Mother to author. 6 May 1977.

        l.17 Raining. Windsor. *King's Story*. 81.

        l.20 Ordered Tea. *Family Album*. 42.

        l.24 The kilt. Samuel Hoare. TM. RF.1.

        l.31 Point of view. Churchill to Clementine Churchill. 18 Jan. 1939. CV V. 1437.

p. 307. l.1 Violent reply. Eliot to Curzon. 22 April 1922. C.

        l.3 Free with alcohol. Mensdorff. 3 Nov. 1927. M.

        l.11 Very obstinate. Diary. 6 Nov. 1924. RA.

        l.13 Posted to India. King to Wigram. 31 March 1925. W.

        l.19 King refuses. Samuel Hoare. TM. RF.1.

        l.30 Unnecessary risks. King to Queen Alexandra. 16 March 1924. RA.

        l.34 Your majesty's hands. David Metcalfe to author. 17 Oct. 1980.

        l.37 Old woman's game. Woods. 1924. WD.

p. 308. l.6 Changed my life. Prince of Wales to Lady Coke. 27 May 1917. Combe Papers.

        l.16 Stigma. Private information.

        l.23 Material thing. *King's Story*. 235–37.

p. 309. l.2 Suggested to him. Private information.

        l.7 Historical occasion. Diary. 17 July 1917. RA.

        l.38 Dear David. Wheeler-Bennett. 154.

p. 310. l.3 Camera. *Ibid*. 220.

        l.9 My young days. Sept. 1927. Imperial War Museum.

        l.25 Prince George. Queen to Godfrey-Fausett. 30 Nov. 1921. GF.

        l.39 Bulgaria. Mensdorff. 21 June 1912. M.

p. 311. l.8 Live in England. King to Mensdorff. 17 Dec. 1921. M.

        l.10 More quickly. Harewood. *The Tongs and the Bones*. 2.

        l.26 Gelam of sunshine. King to Wigram. 16 Jan. 1923. W.

p. 312. l.5 Clubs in gloom. Channon. Diary. 5 and 16 Jan. 1923. Coats Papers.

        l.15 Completely overshadowed. Asquith to Hilda Harrisson. 24 April 1923. Symonds Papers.

        l.21 Fell in love. Wheeler-Bennett. 151.

        l.23 Two minutes early. *Ibid*.

        l.24 Angelic. Queen Mother to author. 6 May 1977.

        l.29 Funny too. Duchess of York to Dawson of Penn. 9 March 1936. Watson. 285.

p. 313. l.11 Not extensive. Emden. *Behind the Throne*. 120.

        l.15 Overcome. Martin. *Queen Victoria as I knew Her*. 48.

p. 313 1.18 Hair being done. Esher. *Girlhood of Queen Victoria. passim.*
        l.20 Mendelssohn. Blunt. *On Wings of Song.* 229.
        l.25 Authority on lamb. Hibbert. *Edward VII.* 175.
        l.37 Hardy's birthday. L.E. Jones. *An Edwardian Youth.* 113.
        l.40 Change his mind. Stamfordham to Bonham Carter. 5 June
            1913. Stamfordham to Asquith. 11 July 1913. A.3.
p. 314. l.8 Hemingway. Gore. 447–50.
        l.10 Lady Chatterley. J. Colville. *Footprints in Time.* 41.
        l.11 Some people. Nicolson to author. 23 August 1957.
        l.14 An author. Ziegler. *King William IV.* 73.
        l.20 Chatter. Curzon to Grace Curzon. 9 Nov. 1920. CK.
        l.32 Blackguard. *Ibid.*
        l.33 Wrangling. Nicolson. 343.
        l.34 Jutland. King to Godfrey-Faussett. 12 Jan. 1925. GF.
        l.37 A million. Woods. 1929. WD.
        l.41 I'm broke. Baldwin to Davidson. 1921. Middlemas. 85.
p. 315. l.25 General abuse. F. Ponsonby. *Recollections.* 110–13.
        l.30 Queen Victoria. Stevenson. Diary. 11 April 1921.
        l.35 King gave way. Buckle to Rosebery. 25 April 1918. R 10126.
        l.39 Kill any man. Wigram to Crewe. 14 July 1931. R. 10196.
p. 316. 1.4 Affairs of State. Morshead. Memorail broadcast. 1936.
        l.8 The Palace. Sir John Wilson. *The Royal Philatelic Collection.*
            59.
        l.13 Wonderful. King to Godfrey-Fausett. 26 June 1921. GF.
        l.22 Engraving. Houseman. 146.
        l.36 A little mad. K. Clark. *Another Part of the Wood.* 238.
p. 317. l.3 Every instance. Fulford. *Prince Consort.* 207.
        l.24 Take the job. K. Clark. *op. cit.* 237.
        l.34 Artists of her day. Millar. *The Queen's Pictures.* 208.
        l.37 Nollekens. *Ibid.* 233.
        l.41 Make you laugh. Lord Gage to author. 28 July 1976.
p. 318. l.2 National Gallery. Lord Clark to author. 12 June 1976.
        l.4 Becoming awful. Diary. 17 May 1931. RA.
        l.6 Not to sign it. A. Clark. *Good Innings.* 280.
        l.9 King conceded. H.A.L. Fisher, Diary. 5 March 1918.
        l.17 Royal Academy. K. Clark. *op. cit.* 51–52.
        l.19 Behind a door. Windsor. *Family Album.* 6.
        l.26 Calatrava. Lavery. *The Life of a Painter.* 158.
        l.31 Middle of chest. Inge. Diary. 12 Dec. 1931. 169.
        l.36 More seamanlike. Wilkinson. *A Brush with Life.* 32–33.
p. 319. l.4 Possessions. Stamfordham to Horne. 25 Nov. 1921. RA.
        l.11 Fidelio. Diary. 6 Feb. 1907. RA.

p. 319 l.16 Long hair. Gore. 183.

l.19 Military Tattoo. Woods. 1928. WD.

l.26 Never played again. Sitwell. *Great Morning*. 198.

l.28 Delius. Clynes. *Memoirs*. 47.

l.32 To their feet. Lord Clark to author. 12 June 1976.

l.35 God Save the King. Benson. 27.

l.40 Hurry it up. Ronald. *Myself and Others*. 126.

p. 320. l.2 King Lear. Gore. 109.

l.4 Hamlet. Pope-Hennessy. 143.

l.8 Half the Castle. Cooper. *Light of Common Day*.

l.13 Pedigree pigs. Ivor Brown. *Balmoral*. 196.

l.21 No documentaries. A. Clark. 322.

l.27 Naval mutinies. Harold Nicolson to author. 16 Feb. 1961.

l.33 The Province. Wigram to Brabourne. 30 Oct. 1934.
Brabourne Papers.

l.41 In the dirt. Queen Victoria to Prince George. 2 June 1885.
Nicolson. 35.

p. 321. l.9 Golden sovereign. A.E.T. Watson. *King Edward*. 223-24.

l.12 Informed judge. Marsh. *Trainer to Two Kings*. 286.

l.23 Epsom. Godfrey-Faussett to King. 5 June 1913, GF.

l.29 Racing colours. Gore. 383.

l.34 For the gas. Lady Wigram. Diary. 16 June 1926. W.

l.40 Goodwood. Duke of Richmond to author. 21 March 1980.

p.322. l.9 Just my luck. Diary. 30 July 1925. RA.

l.12 Newmarket. Wigram. Memorandum. 20 May 1935. RA.

l.15 It came off. Gore. 228.

l.18 Grand National. *Derby*. 569.

l.20 Certainly poorer. Diary. 8 June 1928. RA.

l.36 Enjoyment. Queen to Esher. 6 Aug. 1925. E 6/1.

l.42 Vexation. Dixon. 167-68.

p. 323. l.12 Indeed proud. Diary. 5 Aug. 1932. RA.

l.14 Prizes. *Ibid*. 2 Aug. 1934. RA.

l.27 Britannia. Wentworth-Day. 191.

POLITICAL PRESSURES

p. 324. l.13 See what happens. Diary. 10 Dec. 1923. RA.

l.15 January. *Ibid*. 11 Dec. 1923. RA.

l.19 Commons. Stamfordham to G.E. Buckle. 10 Dec. 1923. RA.
(Nicolson implies that it was the King who used this
argument to persuade Baldwin to remain in office. The

p. 324.　　　argument was in fact that of Stamfordham, and Baldwin needed no such persuasion).

p. 325. l.11　Join another. Stamfordham. Memorandum. 10 Dec. 1923. RA.

l.16　Road to revolution. Rhodes James. *Davidson.* 189.

l.21　Confiscation. Jenkins. *Asquith.* 500.

l.34　Impaired. Rhodes James. *op. cit.* 191.

p. 326. l.3　Considerable good. Stamfordham to Lord Gladstone. 16 Jan. 1924. RA.

l.13　Labour Government. Diary. 22 Jan. 1924. RA.

l.17　In Office. Webb. Diaries. II. 2.

p. 327. l.2　Making history. Clynes. 343.

l.16　Minor posts. *Ibid.* 21.

l.23　Non-political. Stamfordham to Curzon. 6 Nov. 1921. C.

p. 328. l.2　Complexion. Bagehot. 68.

l.19　Order of Merit. Knollys to Bonham Carter. 8 March 1912. A. 3.

l.23　Violent as ever. Chamberlain to Hilda Chamberlain. 16 June 1923. NC 18/1/399.

l.31　Defeat in war. *The Times.* 18 Jan. 1924.

l.34　Brief period. Balfour to Birkenhead. 11 Dec. 1923. BW. 1.

l.37　Miracle. MacDonald. Diary. 22 Jan. 1924. MD.

p. 329. l.7　As a friend. *Ibid.* 12 May 1924.

l.9　His heart. Clynes. 120.

l.10　Thomas. Chamberlain to Hilda Chamberlain. 10 Sept. 1933. NC.

l.14　Automaton. Webb (19) Jan. 1924. II. 2.

l.16　First class. Mosley. *My Life.* 216.

l.30　Cordial reception. Haldane to Mrs Haldane. 28 Feb. 1924. HL. 6007.

l.42　Prime Ministers. Wigram. Memorandum. 6 Aug. 1924. RA.

p. 330. l.6　Seeking work. Webb to Beatrice Webb. 19 Feb. 1924.

l.9　From outside. Stamfordham to MacDonald. 2 April 1924. MD. 30/69/1/197.

l.20　Abandoned. Stamfordham to Crewe. 11 and 24 May 1924. Crewe Papers. C. 58.

l.28　Serious tax. Stamfordham. Memorandum. 22 Jan. 1924. Nicolson. 385.

l.31　Double burden. Curzon to Grace Curzon. 6 Jan. 1924. CK.

l.35　Every post. Marquand. *MacDonald.* 307.

p. 331. l.3　Matters of State. Stamfordham to MacDonald. 1 Feb. 1924. MD 30/69/1/197.

p. 331.   l.17   John Milton. Lincolnshire to Stamfordham. 5 Jan. 1924. L. 4.

        l.21   Court tailor. Nicolson. 392.

        l.26   One's clothes. MacDonald. Diary. Marquand. 314.

        l.28   Webb's wife. Bruce Lockhart. 204.

        l.37   Tights. Diary. 11 March 1924. RA.

        l.40   Cannot trust you. MacDonald. Diary. 12 May 1924. MD.

p. 332.   l.13   Fend for herself. Channon. Diary. 14 May 1924. Coats Papers.

        l.16   Time to go. Lincolnshire. 18 Feb. 1924. L.

        l.17   Tea party. Malcolm MacDonald to author. 2 Feb. 1977.

        l.20   Duchesses. Sommer. *Haldane.* 400.

        l.24   Papers to read. Haldane to Mrs Haldane. 14 March 1924. HL. 6007.

        l.30   No snobbishness. Brockway. *Socialism over Sixty Years.* 208–09.

        l.35   School treat. A. Clark. 254.

        l.39   Low demeanour. Lincolnshire. 25 Feb. 1924. L.

        l.42   Kinsman. Amery. Diaries. 19 Feb. 1924. 371.

p. 333.   l.16   Rank in society. Broadhurst. 150–53.

        l.22   Welcome experience. Macdonald. 12 May 1924. MD.

        l.24   Want of dignity. *Ibid.* 19 Sept. 1929.

        l.26   Enjoyed myself. *Ibid.* 21 Sept. 1924, referring to visit that began on 30 August.

        l.34   Best of terms. Asquith to Hilda Harrisson. 10 Nov. 1919. Symonds Papers.

p. 334.   l.3   Your Majesty's service. Stevenson. Diary. 3 Feb. 1922. 241.

        l.6   His relatives. MacDonald. 22 Jan. 1924. MD.

        l.29   Conviction. Roskill. *Hankey.* II. 376.

        l.37   Bloody lie. *Ibid.*

        l.40   Prevaricating. *Ibid.* 377.

p. 335.   l.16   Government expense. Marquand. 307.

        l.20   Grant. *Ibid.* 360.

        l.26   Churchill's. Sir Abe Bailey to Churchill. 26 Nov. 1920. CV IV.2.1256.

        l.38   Newspaper stunts. MacDonald to King. 22 Aug. 1924. Nicolson. 399.

p. 336.   l.14   Parting remark. MacDonald. 9 Oct. 1924. MD.

        l.23   Dispute continues. *Times Higher Education Supplement.* 14 Oct. 1977 and subsequent correspondence in *The Times.*

        l.42   Forgery. Minute. 26 Oct. 1924. Nicolson. 402.

p. 337.   l.11   Continue friends. MacDonald. 4 Nov. 1924. MD.

p. 337. l.13 Quite straight. Nicolson. 403.

l.16 No provocation. Stamfordham. Memorandum. 4 Nov. 1924. Nicolson. 403.

l.22 At the Bar. Stamfordham to Baldwin. 6 Nov. 1924. B. 178/55.

l.29 Irish settlement. Stamfordham to Churchill. 1 April 1922. CV IV. 1845.

l.35 Gracious Monarch. *Ibid.* 1952.

l.38 Chamberlain. Stamfordham to Baldwin. 31 Oct. 1924. B. 178/52-54.

p. 338. l.6 Not agreeable. Curzon to Grace Curzon. 7 and 11 Nov. 1924. CK.

l.13 Strand Magazine. G.M. Young. *Baldwin.* 72.

l.19 King's concern. Stamfordham to Curzon. 5 Sept. 1923. C. Amery. Diary. 10 Oct. 1925. Wigram to Waterhouse. 26 Aug. 1926. WT.

l.29 Recumbent. Baldwin to King. 2July 1925. RA.

l.38 Speaker. Stamfordham to Baldwin. 3 July 1925, RA.

p. 339. l.8 His Majesty. Baldwin to Stamfordham. 10 July 1925. RA.

l.10 Comments. Stamfordham to Waterhouse. 15 July 1925. WT.

p. 340. l.2 Duly recorded. Stamfordham to Baldwin. 21 Feb. 1927. RA.

l.12 Revolution. Channon. Diary. 2 Oct. 1925. Coats Papers.

l.21 For women. Stamfordham to Hankey. 22 Sept. 1921. Nicolson. 342.

l.23 Appeal for unity. Jones. II. 5.

l.28 Judge them. Airlie. 178.

l.30 Ten per cent. Amery. 12 March 1926. 446.

l.33 Depressed. Diary. 29 July 1925. Nicolson. 415.

p. 341. l.2 Government. Stamfordham. Memorandum. 11 May 1926. RA.

l.9 Took his point. Stamfordham to Milne. 10 May 1926. Nicolson. 418.

l.42 On demand. Stamfordham. Memorandum. 11 May 1926. Nicolson. 419 and Hearder.

p. 342. l.5 Sitting room. Lincolnshire. 4 Nov. 1926. L.

l.16 Punished. King to Queen Alexandra. 2 March 1912. RA.

l.18 Hunger strike. Stamfordham to McKenna. 27 March 1913. Nicolson. 212.

l.22 Football match. Stamfordham to Balfour (Chancellor of Cambridge University) 15 Dec. 1927. BW. 21.

l.25 Also my guest. Earl of Gowrie to author. 7 June 1979.

p. 342. l.38 Made to fear. King to Churchill. 16 Aug. 1911.
CV II.2.1274.

p. 343. l.5 Procuring evidence. Asquith to Knollys. 8 Sept. 1911. A. 3.

l.12 Picket trouble. Stamfordham to Waterhouse. 5 May 1926.
Hearder. 238.

l.16 Inopportune. Waterhouse to Stamfordham. 7 May 1926.
Ibid. 239.

l.25 Police control. Stamfordham to Waterhouse. 7 May 1926.
Ibid. 239

l.28 Arrested. King's minute on War Office report. 11 May 1926.
Ibid. 240.

l.36 Elected to govern. King to Baldwin. 12 May 1926. B 177/5.

l.40 Wonderful people. Diary. 12 May 1926. Nicolson. 420.

p. 344. l.8 Great misfortune. Battiscombe. 185.

l.10 Ten natives. *Bacchante.* I. 226.

l.12 Silly game. Frankland. 29.

l.14 Idea of sport. King to Hardinge. 20 March 1914. H. 105.

l.21 He might. Mensdorff. 24 Nov. 1929. M.

l.27 Buckingham Palace. Duff to Wigram. 13 Aug. 1924. MD.
30/69/1/197.

l.34 Royal Highness. Lord Mountbatten to author. 9 June
1976.

l.38 Back again. Lady Morshead to author. 23 Oct. 1976.

p. 345. l.4 The British. Wigram. Memorandum. 26 April 1934. RA.

l.15 Milkman. Windsor. *King's Story.* 201.

l.17 Munitions. Templewood. *Nine Troubled Years.* 265.

l.23 Anti-Prohibition. Windsor. *op. cit.* 151.

l.28 Satisfactory. Diary. 29 July 1918. RA.

l.31 Manage. John Duncan Miller. *Times Literary Supplement.* 12
Nov. 1976.

l.34 Obstinate. Sitwell. *Queen Mary.* 58.

l.40 Importance. Stamfordham to Chamberlain. 11 July 1926.
Nicolson. 413.

p. 346. l.7 His own sons. Emperor of Japan to author. 13 Aug. 1971.

l.18 Credentials. Grandi to author. 6 Sept. 1976.

l.22 French statesmen. Jones. *Diary with Letters.* 538.

l.26 Wake me up. G.M. Young. 63.

l.28 Avoid it. Charles Ponsonby. 63.

l.34 Evasive answer. Stamfordham to Vansittart. 21 Aug. 1923.
Vansittart to Stamfordham. 31 Aug. 1923. C.

l.36 Brevity. Vansittart. 63.

l.42 Annotation. Curzon and Mensdorff Papers. *passim.*

p. 347. l.8   Directness. Killearn. *Diaries.* 21 Jan. 1936 and 1 Feb. 1934.

       l.11   Familiar. Roskill. *Hankey.* III. 141.

       l.33   Piraeus. Hough. *Louis and Victoria.* 348.

p. 348. l.2   Completed. F.O. Papers. 7585–88. PRO. Also Medricott. *Documents, passim.*

       l.7   Defective memory. Lord Mountbatten to author. 6 Sept. 1977.

       l.22   Relations. Amery. 16 Feb. 1928. 536.

       l.27   Irish Free State. Bessborough Papers.

       l.35   Don't mind dogs. Maugham. *A Writer's Notebook.* 268.

p. 349. l.5   Club in India. Stamfordham to Chelmsford. 4 April 1917. Chelmsford Papers.

       l.7   Sir. Chelmsford to Stamfordham. 30 Aug. 1916. Stamfordham to Chelmsford. 28 Sept. and 9 Nov. 1916. Chelmsford Papers.

       l.13   Umcomfortable. Warrender. 73.

       l.17   Not pleasant. Lincolnshire. 15 Oct. 1919. L.

       l.19   No Indians. A. Clark. 286.

       l.22   Knighthoods. *Ibid.* 253 and 258. Also Waterhouse Papers.

       l.30   Troops and money. Memorandum for Secretary of State for India. 22 Feb. 1923. B. 178/2–6.

       l.39   Australian girl. King to Hardinge. 11 Aug. 1915. H. 105.

       l.42   Wellington College. Stamfordham to Chelmsford. 1 Aug. 1917. Chelmsford Papers.

p. 350. l.6   Derby winner. Aga Khan. *Memoirs.* 82.

       l.8   In Europe. Stamfordham to Curzon. 17 Nov. 1921. C.

       l.15   British Raj. Stamfordham to Baldwin. 11 Oct. 1925. S. 178/108–11.

       l.19   Willingdon. Diary. 15 Dec. 1930. RA.

p. 351. l.9   Their friends. MacDonald. 29 Oct. 1930.

       l.11   Apology. Stamfordham to MacDonald. 1 Nov. 1930. RA.

       l.14   Other candidates. MacDonald. 26 Nov. 1930. MD.

       l.15   Baldwin warns. *Ibid.* 3 Dec. 1930.

       l.23   Arranged. Blaxland. *J. H. Thomas.* 243.

       l.30   Redeeming. Webb. *Diaries.* 28 July 1929. II. 212–13.

       l.33   Gawd. Blaxland. 214.

       l.34   Straightforward. *Ibid.* 267.

       l.40   Proposed him. Diary. 15 Dec. 1920. RA.

p. 352. l.2   India. Stamfordham to Baldwin. 22 Dec. 1930. S. 178/301–02.

       l.30   Beaters and bags. Irwin to King. 20 Jan. 1927 and 19 March 1928. IR.

p. 352. l.36 Birds and tigers. Reading to King. 2 May 1923 and
                12 March 1925. RD.

p. 353. l.7   British officers. *Ibid.* 10 Sept. 1924. RD.

l.14   Working mind. Irwin to King. 13 March 1931. IR.

l.30   Hospitality. Templewood. *Nine Troubled Years.* 59–60.

l.39   Responsible. Wigram to Willingdon. 2 Dec. 1931. Nicolson.
                509.

p. 354. l.5   Own subjects. Templewood Papers. RF. 1.

l.16   Morning sun. Robert Byron. *Architectural Review.* January
                1931.

l.21   Angel of Victory. Hussey. *Luytens.* 247.

l.31   Unfinished. *Ibid.* 363–64.

l.35   Rich men. Reading to King. 16 March 1922 and 13 March
                1924. RD.

p. 355. l.4   Only one palace. Irwin Papers. *passim.* 1928. IR.

l.28   Retired to bed. Diary. 21 Nov. 1928. RA.

l.33   Serious illness. Watson. *Dawson of Penn.* (from which most
                of the medical details of this chapter are taken).

p. 356. l.29 Postponed. Dawson to Balfour. 4 Dec. 1928. BW. 24.

p. 357. l.8   Human skill. Catherine Black. 153.

l.20   In his absence. Duke of York to Prince of Wales. 6 Dec.
                1928. *King's Story.* 223.

l.22   Heir's return. Fleuriau to Briand. 11 Dec. 1928. Quai
                d'Orsay Archives. 2.248.3.

l.28   Tries on the Crown., Donaldson. *Edward VIII.* 137–38.

l.31   King of England. Trzebinski. *Silence Will Speak.* 268.

l.36   Prince's sport. *King's Story.* 224.

p. 358. l.13 That fool. Mark Bonham Carter to author. 23 Oct. 1978.

l.21   Lord Moynihan. Private information.

l.23   Tudor Edwards. Private information.

l.34   Bloody guts. Thomas to Lady Wigram. W.

p. 359. l.2   In Paris. Stamfordham to Crewe. 1 March 1925. Crewe
                Papers. C. 58.

l.13   Malta. Commander R.V. Holt to Mrs Holt. 22 March 1925.
                Holt Papers.

l.20   Strong language. Stamfordham to Lord Athlone. 9 July
                1929. Nicolson. 433.

l.28   Battlements. Cynthia Asquith. 13 Aug. 1916. 204.

l.41   Cigar. Hibbert. 223.

p. 360. l.1   Cigarette case. Wheeler-Bennett. 70.

l.20   Target. Harry Lawrence to author. 9 Feb. 1977.

l.23   Distinguish myself. Diary. 21 Oct. 1929. RA.

p. 360. l.33   Double victory. C. Colville. 49.

p. 361. l.2   Blasted muck. Gore. 439.

l.13   Their request. Sir Robin Mackworth-Young to author. 10 Sept. 1982.

l.16   Bad Nauheim. Fleuriau to Briand. 28 March 1929. Quai d'Orsay Archives. 2.274.3

l.19   Only short drives. Lady Desborough to Lady Salmon. 22 May 1929. Desborough Papers.

l.32   Personally. MacDonald. 5 June 1929. MD.

p. 362. l.2   Higher claim. Stamfordham to Edmund Talbot. 30 May 1919. LG F/21/3/25.

l.14   Open wound. Gore. 395.

l.24   Here to here. Postgate. *Lansbury.* 252.

l.27   Industries Fair. Gore. 359.

l.31   Untruthfully. Houseman. 164.

l.34   Earlier days. Mensdorff. 19 Nov. 1929. M.

l.41   Won't believe me. Lady Home to author. 7 July 1976.

p. 363. l.9   Age at death. *Fortnightly Review.* 1 Aug. 1872.

l.13   First year. Sir Claus Moser to author. 4 Aug. 1977.

l.17   Serious illness. Morshead. Memorial Broadcast. 1936.

l.19   Queer things. Matthews. *Memories and Meanings.* 192.

l.25   Cain and Abel. Woods. 1928. WD.

l.31   Take the bag. Deane. *Time Remembered.* 208.

l.37   Defender of the Faith. Duchess of Beaufort to author. 26 June 1976.

l.40   Appendix. Private information.

p. 364. l.6   Drawing Room. Inge. 10 June 1911. 11.

l.11   When to stop. Andrews. *Canon's Folly.* 129.

l.13   Congratulated. Woods. 1924 and 1929. WD.

l.22   Damned cheek. Lockhart. *Lang.* 144.

l.27   Mitre. *Ibid.* 418.

l.31   Quaker. Woods. 1933. WD.

l.34   No Popery. *Ibid.* 1928.

p. 365. l.5   According to Law. Nicolson. 162–63.

l.14   Granard. Stamfordham to Irwin. IR.

l.21   Together. MacDonald to Wigram. 18 June 1934. MD.

l.31   Nice fellow. Inge. 18 Jan. 1918. 43.

l.33   Love of change. Stamfordham to Lloyd George. 12 March 1919. LG F/29/3/15.

l.39   Lower deck. Richard Ollard to author. 7 Oct. 1981.

p. 366. l.6   In her company. Pope-Hennessy. 340–42.

l.7   Royal estates. Private information.

p. 366. l.23 Excluded from court. Churchill to King. 21 May 1911.
Knollys to Churchill. 22 May 1911. CV II.2.1082–83.

l.32 No hospitality. Private information.

l.40 Rights of others. Lincolnshire. 10 Feb. 1920. L.

p. 367. l.1 Three wives. Mensdorff. 31 Oct. 1935. M.

l.7 Rebuke. Lady Delia Peel to author. 11 Dec. 1977.

l.25 Voice of the State. Stamfordham to Sandars. 3 June 1929.
Sandars Papers. C.770.

l.28 Their victory. Stamfordham. Memorandum. 2 June 1929.
RA.

l.32 Manual work. *Ibid.* 5 June 1929. RA.

p. 368. l.2 Retirement pension. Stamfordham to Baldwin. 23 June
1928. RA.

l.8 Suggested Thomas. Stamfordham. Memorandum. 5 June
1929. RA.

l.18 Cabinet table. Heuston. 527.

l.26 Flower pot. Lady Wigram. 'Handshakes'. W.

l.30 Sincere. Bondfield. *A Life's Work.* 277–78.

l.35 Excursion train. Lady Wigram. 'Handshakes'. W.

p. 369. l.7 Indifference. Stamfordham to Waterhouse. 24 Feb. 1925.
WT.

l.11 Academic. Stamfordham to Balfour. 2 Sept. 1925. Balfour to
Stamfordham. 10 Sept. 1925. BW.21.

l.16 Very conceited. Mensdorff. 19 Nov. 1929. M.

l.25 Modest level. MacDonald. 19 Sept. 1929. MD.

l.27 Refused. Nicolson. 441.

l.36 Russians. MacDonald. 5 Nov. 1929 and 18 June 1933. MD.

p. 370. l.4 Good and useful. Mensdorff. 21 Nov. 1929. M.

l.16 National Government. Wigram to King. 11 July 1931.
Nicolson. 449.

l.29 Chose Wigram. Diary. 31 March 1931. RA.

l.35 Don't forget. Wigram to John Simon. 19 April 1931. Simon
Papers.

l.38 Understand things. Reith. Diary. 17 Nov. 1932. 182.

p. 371. l.7 Labour forwards. Wigram to Bessborough. 1 June 1931. W.

l.11 Test Match. Wigram to Lang. 27 Aug. 1931. W.

p. 372. l.15 Providence. MacDonald. 17 Aug. 1931. Marquand. 615.

l.34 Bloody cowards. Duff to Wigram. 21 Aug. 1931. RA.

l.38 There and then. *Ibid.*

p. 373. l.1 Unemployment benefits. Marquand. 626.

l.16 Consult the King. MacDonald. 22 Aug. 1931 (referring to
21 Aug.) MD.

p. 373. l.21 Proceed south. Wigram. Memorandum. 22–24 Aug. 1931. RA.

      l.25 Come here. King to Lang. 2 Sept. 1931. Gore. 409.

      l.29 Have to resign. Diary. 23 Aug. 1931.

p. 374. l.6 Thanks and sorrow. MacDonald. 23 Aug. 1931. MD.

      l.22 Biography. Nicolson. 461.

      l.25 Good listener. Samuel to Nicolson. 24 Feb. 1949. Nicolson Papers.

      l.31 Support him. MacDonald. 23 Aug. 1931. MD.

p. 375. l.6 Ten years. Peacock to Nicolson. 17 Feb. 1949. Nicolson Papers.

      l.20 My hand. Nicolson. 464.

      l.24 Saturday and Sunday. Malcolm MacDonald to author. 2 Feb. 1977.

      l.27 Save the crisis. MacDonald. 23 Aug. 1931. MD.

      l.28 Late that night. Wigram. Memorandum. 22–24 Aug. 1931. RA.

      l.32 As on himself. Macleod. *Chamberlain.* 151.

      l.38 Sacred and unbalanced. Wigram. Memorandum. 22–24 Aug. 1931. RA.

      l.39 Confidence restored. Peacock to Nicolson. 17 Feb. 1949. Nicolson Papers.

p. 376. l.2 Withhold resignation. Wigram. *Op. cit.*

      l.33 Asked to face. *Ibid.*

      l.41 Consternation. MacDonald. Diary. 24 Aug. 1931. MD.

p. 377. l.12 Your wedding. Templewood. *Nine Troubled Years.* 22.

      l.13 Lonely job. MacDonald. 24 May 1931. MD.

      l.28 Leave the burdens. *Ibid.*

      l.31 Awkward crisis. MacDonald to Bondfield. 25 Aug. 1931. Marquand. 644–45.

      l.41 Out of the question. King to Lang. 2 Sept. 1931. Gore. 409.

p. 378. l.9 Stamp collection. Diary. 24 Aug. 1931. RA.

      l.12 Signs of fatigue. Wigram to Lang. 27 Aug. 1931. Gore. 409.

      l.29 Palace Revolution. Laski. 403.

p. 379. l.39 Duchy of Cornwall. F. Ponsonby to MacDonald. 5 Sept. 1931. Halsey to MacDonald. 7 Sept. 1931.

p. 380. l.22 To be exempted. Heuston. 513–19.

      l.30 Should have resigned. Roskill. *Hankey.* II. 557.

p. 381. l.29 Running on the rocks. King to Duke of York. 30 Sept. 1931. RA.

      l.36 See a way out. Diary. 2 Oct. 1931. Nicolson. 492–93.

p. 382. l.1   Chaotic state. Wigram. Memorandum. 3 Oct. 1931. *Ibid.*
                  493.
          l.3   General Smuts. *Ibid.* 6 Oct. 1931. RA.
          l.17 A command. Roskill. *Hankey.* II. 569.
          l.20 Seats everywhere. Diary. 27 Oct. 1931. RA.
          l.27 Less worries. Diary. 28 Oct. 1931. RA.
          l.35 Steady them. King to Mensdorff. 3 Nov. 1931. M.
p. 383. l.3   Sway him. Wigram. Memorandum. 2 Nov. 1931. Nicolson.
                  494.
          l.7   Key positions. *Ibid.* 3 Nov. 1931. RA.
          l.9   Old gang. *Ibid.* 2 Nov. 1931. RA.
          l.13 Able to fly. *Ibid.* 29 Oct. 1931. RA.
          l.19 Henderson. *Ibid.* 3 Nov. 1931. RA.
          l.21 Simon. *Ibid.*
          l.30 Ambitious men. *Ibid.* 29 Oct. 1931. RA.
          l.33 All Liberals. Lady Oxford to Wigram. 3 Nov. 1931. RA.
p. 384. l.2   Desert Samuel. Wigram. Memorandum. 3 Nov. 1931. RA.
          l.10 Welcomed. King to MacDonald. 23 Jan. 1932. Nicolson.
                  497.
          l.20 Degrading. MacDonald to King. 11 Sept. 1932. *Ibid.* 498.
          l.26 Aristocratic tastes. Webb. 22 June 1925. II. 65.
          l.31 To Balmoral. *The Times.* 5 Sept. 1930.
          l.36 Operation. Diary. 11 Feb. 1932. RA.
          l.37 Race meeting. *Ibid.* 12 May 1934. RA.
p. 385. l.2   Highlands. MacDonalds. 2 April 1932. MD.
          l.5   Criminal romances. *Ibid.* 17 Feb. 1931.
          l.12 Owes his throne. Sylvester. *Life with Lloyd George.* 93–94.
          l.18 Land man. *Ibid.* 94.
          l.24 High office. *Ibid.* 107–08. 25 April 1934.
          l.31 Prosecute the war. Stevenson. 24 April 1934. 269.
          l.34 Russia. Lloyd George. *War Memoirs.* IV. 1497.

LAST YEARS

p. 386. l.4   The bomber. House of Commons. 10 Nov. 1932.
          l.12 Damnable peace. Mensdorff. 18 Nov. 1932. M.
          l.16 Gas warfare. 3 Dec. 1921. *Documents on British Foreign
                  Policy.* 1st series. XIV. 545.
          l.20 Rest of it. Amery. 3 March 1923. 323.
          l.21 Capital ships. Roskill. *Naval Policy.* I. 443–44.
          l.22 Submarine. Stamfordham to MacDonald. 10 July 1929. *Ibid.*
                  II. 39.

p. 386. l.23 Aeriel bombs. Wigram to Simon. 14 Nov. 1932. RA.

p. 387. l.1 30 m.p.h. Henderson. *Water Under the Bridges*. 199.

l.7 Risks involved. Samuel Hoare. TM. RF.1.

l.11 Marshal of the RAF. Boyle. *Trenchard*. 338.

l.16 For ever. Diary. 1 Dec. 1925. RA.

l.20 Out of one. Templewood. *Nine Troubled Years*. 159.

l.23 Cannot be trusted. Stamfordham to Curzon. 5 June 1923. C.

l.25 Dangerous man. King to Wigram. 9 Sept. 1923. W.

l.31 Brought in. Stevenson. 10 May 1935. 309.

p. 388. l.9 Hitler's henchman. Mensdorff. 22 Nov. 1932. M.

l.10 Goebbels. *Ibid*. 31 Oct. 1935.

l.12 Jew-baiting. Wigram to Phipps. 12 June 1934. Phipps. II. 3/1/38.

l.12 Bloodbaths. Wigram to Brabourne. 9 July 1934. Brabourne Papers.

l.14 Towards war. Wigram. Memorandum on King's talk with German ambassador. 24 April 1934. Nicolson. 521–22.

l.23 Same impression. Simon to King. 27 March 1935. RA.

l.31 Christian religion. Phipps to King. 2 Jan. 1935. Phipps Papers. II.3/1/77.

l.36 Taken unawares. Wigram to Phipps. 16 Jan. 1935. *Ibid*. II.3/1/86–87.

l.39 So gloomy. MacDonald. 19 Feb. 1935. MD.

p. 389. l.4 Unnecessary war. King to Grand Duke of Hesse. 16 May 1935. Hesse Archives. D.24 37/1.

l.5 Abdicate. TM. RF. I.

l.11 Killed the King. *Ibid*.

l.18 I really feel. Pope-Hennessy. 548.

l.30 Departed. Woods. 1928. WD.

l.35 In an infant. Churchill to Clementine Churchill. 25 Sept. 1928. CV V.1.1349.

l.40 Tiny paw. Sir Owen Morshead to author. 23 Oct. 1976.

p. 390. l.3 Not a cent. MacDonald. 5 Oct. 1934. MD.

l.7 Shy bride. Lees-Milne. *Nicolson*. II. 257.

l.9 Programme. Wigram to Brabourne. 2 Nov. 1934. Brabourne Papers.

l.21 My collection. Queen to Duke of Gloucester. 19 Aug. 1935. Frankland. 123.

l.27 Pretty little knees. Norman Hartnell to author. 17 March 1977.

l.28 Except David. Diary. 6 Nov. 1935. Gore. 435.

p. 390. l.35 Renounce it. Channon. Diary. 2 Oct. 1925. Coats Papers.

p. 391. l.10 The Nazis. Mensdorff. 1 No. 1933. M.

l.16 Olympic Games. Hoesch to Foreign Minister. 21 Jan. 1936. *Documents on German Foreign Policy.* C.IV.1024.

l.23 British interests. Luther to Foreign Minister. 21 Jan. 1936. *Ibid.* 1017.

l.29 The Government. *King's Story.* 252.

l.32 Speak his mind. Hoesch to Foreign Minister. 20 June 1935. *Documents. Op. cit.* 330–31.

p. 392. l.8 In their presence. Duchess of Windsor. *The Heart Has its Reasons.* 205.

l.18 What he is doing. Mensdorff. 31 Oct. 1935. M.

l.24 An empty thing. *King's Story.* 258.

l.31 This whole state. *Hamlet.* I.iii.17

l.35 Low spirits. Queen Mother to author. 24 April 1979.

l.38 The throne. Airlie. 197.

l.39 Twelve months. Middlemas. *Baldwin.* 976.

p. 393. l.4 Touched me. King to MacDonald. 4 Dec. 1934. MD. 30/69/1/6/2.

l.15 *Daily Express.* Jones. II. 33.

l.16 *Daily Telegraph.* Burnham. *Peterborough Court.* 144.

l.18 Strongly Liberal. Stamfordham to Irwin. 13 Sept. 1928. IR.

l.20 King's speeches. Stamfordham to Dawson. 22 Jan. 1930. Dawson Papers. 6.

l.21 His views. *Ibid.* 2 Dec. 1930. Box 14. Also Wrench. 309.

l.30 Discouraging reply. Fleming. *Voices from the Air.* 6.

l.37 Gateshead. Briggs. *The Birth of Broadcasting.* 290–91.

l.41 Still reluctant. Wigram to Bessborough. 23 Nov. 1932. W.

p. 394. l.1 Whole Empire. Diary. 25 Dec. 1932. RA.

l.8 Nervousness. Fleming. 7–9.

l.9 Simplicity. Carrington. *Kipling.* 495–96.

l.12 Reach them. Fleming II.

l.14 Weather. Benson. Diary. June 1910.

l.19 Spoilt Christmas. Gore. 422.

l.24 Queen Elizabeth. MacDonald. 6 June 1933. MD.

l.26 Agreed to continue. Thomas. *My Story.* 14–15.

l.28 Mere eloquence. Lang to Gore. 15 March 1940. Gore Papers.

p. 395. l.5 Having one now. King to Mensdorff. 29 April 1935. M.

l.10 Every Sunday. Gore. 429.

l.18 In my life. Diary. 6 May 1935. Gore. 430.

l.24 Damn parsons. Matthews. 193.

p. 395. l.27 Show 'em. Chamberlain to Hilda Chamberlain. 12 May
          1935. NC 18/1/915.
       l.32 Given me. Nicolson. 525.
       l.36 Postbag. Diary. 7 May 1935. RA.
p. 396. l.4   Holy Communion. MacDonald. Diary. 8 May 1935. MD.
       l.16 Obsolescent goods. Roskill. *Naval Policy*. II. 252.
       l.25 President Lebrun. Blanche. *Portraits of a Lifetime*. 177.
       l.36 The realities. H. G. Wells. *The World of William Clissold*.
          III. 314.
       l.39 Felt like this. Black. 170.
p. 397. l.4   King Edward. Simon. *Retrospect*. 206–07.
       l.7   Status of a King. MacDonald. Diary. 16 May 1935. MD.
       l.10 For a rest. Wigram to Knatchbull-Hugessen. 8 Aug. 1935.
          K.H. 2/2.
       l.25 A colleague. Wigram to MacDonald. 17 May 1935.
          MD. 30/69/1/627.
p. 398. l.3   Personal friend. MacDonald. Diary. 16 May 1935. MD.
       l.15 My office. *Ibid*. 7 June 1935. MD.
       l.23 Proud parent. *Ibid*.
       l.30 Mediterranean Diary. 19 Aug. 1935. RA.
       l.37 Beauty. *Ibid*. 23 June 1933. RA.
       l.39 Did its duty. Churchill to Clementine Churchill. 25 Sept.
          1928. CV. V.I.1349.
p. 399. l.3   Innings closed. Wigram to Phipps. 15 Nov. 1935. Phipps
          Papers. 4/1/24.
       l.9   Free me. MacDonald. Diary. 19 Nov. 1935. MD.
       l.16 Ready to depart. Jones. *Journal with Letters*. 164.
       l.18 Franz-Josef. Mensdorff. 15 Nov. 1935. M.
       l.25 Princess Alice to author. 21 Sept. 1976.
       l.30 Restlessness. Watson. 273.
       l.33 Cannot sleep. MacDonald. Diary. 27 Nov. 1935. M.
p. 400. l.2   Fallen minister. Wigram to Hoare. 19 Dec. 1935. RA.
       l.5   Norfolk. Templewood. *Nine Troubled Years*. 188.
       l.12 Didn't even laugh. Eden. *Facing the Dictators*. 317.
       l.14 Going the rounds. Bruce Lockhart. Diaries. 15 Dec. 1935.
          334.
       l.26 Kent grandson. Diary. 7 Jan. 1936.
       l.33 Warm enough. King to Duchess of Gloucester. 14 Jan. 1936.
          Frankland. 126.
       l.37 No energy. Watson. 275.
p. 401. l.1   Feel rotten. Diary. 17 Jan. 1936. RA.
       l.4   Twilight world. *King's Story*. 261–62.

p. 401. l.17 Expect it. Lockhart. *Lang.* 390.

l.20 Black gaiters. *King's Story.* 264.

l.27 The Empire. Wigram to Dawson. 31 Jan. 1936. Wrench 329.

l.28 Very tired. Wigram. Memorandum on the King's last days. RA.

l.42 Await events. Watson. 278.

p. 402. l.23 Nod and smile. Wigram. Memorandum; Watson. 278; Roskill 215–17; Lockhart. 391.

l.25 All my heart. MacDonald. Diary. 20 Jan. 1936. M.

p. 403. l.2 Kissed it. *King's Story.* 264.

l.6 Seven years. Watson. 279.

l.11 Clocks put back. Donaldson. 177–78.

l.12 Other customs. Lockhart. 392.

l.24 Wind and rain. Lady Desborough to Dawson. Watson. 281.

l.32 Cock pheasant. *King's Story.* 267.

l.41 Terrible omen. Nicolson. Diary. 23 Jan. 1936. I. 241.

p. 404. l.10 Charles II. Lockhart. 293.

l.16 Stood for. *King's Story.* 269.

l.36 Prime Minister. Jones. *Diary with Letters.* 168–69.

l.40 Lloyd George. MacDonald. Diary. 28 Jan. 1936. MD.

p. 405. l.18 Sacrificed to size. Gore. *Duchess of Bedford.* 443.

l.22 White pony. Jones. *Diary with Letters.* 168.

INDEX

Note: in the subheadings, King refers to George v, and Queen to Mary; others are named, e.g. Edward VII. Names and titles used are those most common and familiar within the period of the text, e.g. Wales, Prince of (not Edward VIII); Eden, Anthony (not Avon, Earl of).